The Library of
Daniel Garrison Brinton

John M. Weeks

With the assistance of Andree Suplee, Larissa M. Kopytoff,
and Kerry Moore

University of Pennsylvania Museum of
Archaeology and Anthropology

Library of Congress Cataloging-in-Publication Data

University of Pennsylvania. Museum of Archaeology and Anthropology.
  The library of Daniel Garrison Brinton / University of Pennsylvania
Museum of Archaeology and Anthropology ; John M. Weeks with the
assistance of Andree Suplee.
     p. cm.
Includes bibliographical references and index.
  ISBN 1-931707-46-4 (alk. paper)
  1. Brinton, Daniel Garrison, 1837-1899—Ethnolgical collections. 2.
Books—Private collections—Pennsylvania—Philadelphia. 3. University
of Pennsylvania. Museum of Archaeology and Anthropology.
Library—Ethnological collections. 4.
Libraries—Pennsylvania—Philadelphia x Special collections. I. Weeks,
John M. II. Suplee, Andree. III. Title.

  GN36.U62 P487 2002b
  018'.2--dc21

                2002152502

John M. Weeks is Museum Librarian at the University of Pennsylvania. His other
bibliographic publications include *Middle American Indians: A Guide to the Manuscript Collection at Tozzer Library, Harvard University* (Garland, 1985), *Maya Ethnohistory: A Guide to Spanish
Colonial Documents at Tozzer Library, Harvard University* (Vanderbilt University Publications
in Anthropology, 1987), *Mesoamerican Ethnohistory in United States Libraries: Reconstruction of
the William E. Gates Collection of Historical and Linguistic Manuscripts* (Labyrinthos, 1990), *Maya
Civilization* (Garland, 1992; Labyrinthos, 1997, 2002), and *Introduction to Library Research in Anthropology* (Westview Press, 1991, 1998). Since 1972 he has conducted excavations in Guatemala, Honduras, and the Dominican Republic.

Andree Suplee received a BA in Anthropology from the University of Pennsylvania;
Larissa M. Kopytoff received a BA in History from the University of Pennsylvania;
and Kerry Moore received a BA in Classics from the University of Wisconsin.

Contents

Illustrations vii

Preface and Acknowledgments. ix

Introduction. 1

    Daniel Garrison Brinton 3

    Karl Herman Berendt 7

    Library of the University of Pennsylvania Museum

        of Archaeology and Anthropology 14

    Organization of the Catalog 17

Appendix: Titles of Serials in the Brinton Library 19

Notes 31

References 33

Catalog. 37

Index 393

Illustrations

Daniel Garrison Brinton. 4

Karl Herman Berendt. 7

Map of Karl H. Berendt's journey across the Yucatan peninsula 9

Interior of the University of Pennsylvania Museum Library 15

Title page from *Notes on the Floridian Peninsula* 38

Title page from *American Hero-Myths*. 50

Francisco Belmar 65

Title page from *The Maya Chronicles*. 75

Lorenzo Boturini Benaducci 84

Charles Etienne Brasseur de Bourbourg 89

Daniel G. Brinton 97

Title page from *Aboriginal American Authors* 108

Désiré Charnay. 120

John W. Dawson 137

Title page from *Güegüence*. 149

Joaquín García Icazbalceta. 168

Title page from *The Annals of the Cakchiquels*. 173

Samuel F. Haven 189

Title page from *The Lenâpé and Their Legends*. 197

Title page from *Ancient Nahuatl Poetry* 210

Increase A. Lapham 221

Nicolás León 226

John Lubbock. 233

Clements R. Markham 241

Title page from *Essays of an Americanist* 256

Title page from *Races and Peoples* 268

Adolf E. Nordenskjöld 277

Miguel T. Palma 283

Antonio Peñafiel 287

Oscar Peschel 290

John W. Powell 299

Karl C. Rafn 305

H. Johannes Rink 314

Cecilio A. Robelo 317

Agustin de la Rosa 319

Léon Louis Lucien Prunol de Rosny 320

Bernardino de Sahagún 326

Title page from *Rig Veda Americanus* 337

Title page from *A Primer of Maya Hieroglyphics* 350

Title page from 362

Theodor Waitz 379

Daniel Wilson 385

Jeffries Wyman 389

Preface and Acknowledgments

The compilation of the catalog of the Daniel Garrison Brinton Library at the University of Pennsylvania Museum of Archaeology and Anthropology was begun in 1998 and completed in 2001. Much of the work was undertaken by student workers in the Museum Library as time from other tasks permitted. The contents of individual shelf list cards for the entire collection were entered into a single bibliographic database arranged by Dewey Decimal classification number. Larissa Kopytoff checked the existing holdings within the collection against the shelf list. The information presented in the shelf list, usually consisting only of author, short title, and date of publication, was corrected, expanded, or modified to provide more accurate and complete bibliographic information. The inventory was then rearranged from call number to name of author.

Kerry Moore and Andree Suplee inventoried the individual contents of more than 200 volumes of bound pamphlets and publishers' offprints. Many of these items possess only minimal bibliographic information,

usually only author, title, and pagination. Andree Suplee spent almost a year resolving inconsistencies between different editions, and correcting inaccuracies and omissions. The bibliographic information has been verified or expanded by examination of the original work or from standard reliable library catalogs, including the *National Union Catalog*, the published catalogs of the Peabody Museum of Archaeology and Ethnology at Harvard University, and electronic catalogs, such as WorldCat and RLIN. Unfortunately, there were many unique items not found in standard bibliographic sources and their listings remain incomplete. Throughout the inventorying of the Brinton Library Sara Rydell, then a student at Bryn Mawr College, and Carole Linderman identified volumes in need of preservation or special treatment, and prepared customized archival-quality boxes for these items.

I wish to express my special appreciation for the financial assistance so generously given by the University of Pennsylvania Libraries, Dr. Paul Mosher, Director, and The Brinton Association of America, Inc., Dr. Edward S. Brinton, President. This volume would never have been published without their timely support.

In addition to those responsible for the preparation of the inventory, we are also grateful to the following for their good will and support. Dr. Jeremy A. Sabloff, The Williams Director, University of Pennsylvania Museum of Archaeology and Anthropology, and Dr. Paul Mosher, Vice Provost and Director of the University of Pennsylvania Libraries, have consistently been solid supporters of the Museum Library and its collections. Dr. Mosher has created a climate in which bibliographic and other kinds of scholarship by professional librarians are encouraged. Ms. Patricia Renfro, Associate University Librarian at Columbia University, was supportive of the project from its inception. Dr. J. Dennis Hyde, Director of Collection Development for the University of Pennsylvania Libraries, arranged for a special funding allocation for preservation boxing, and has remained enthusiastic about the project throughout its duration. Dr. Michael Ryan, Head of Special Collections, and John Pollard, Special Collections, have repeatedly emphasized the importance of the Brinton Library and the need to improve its accessibility to scholars and students.

Several visitors to the Museum Library have reemphasized the importance of the Brinton Library to the history of Americanist anthropology. Some of these include L.

Buddy Gwin, Esq. (Mashantucket Pequot tribe), Dr. Sandra Noble (Foundation for the Advancement of Mesoamerican Studies, Inc.), Prof. Enrique Florescano (Universidad Nacional Autonoma de Mexico), and Dr. Laura Caso Barrera (Colegio de Mexico). Dr. George Stuart, National Geographic Society, generously donated a collection of correspondence from Phillip J. J. Valentini to Karl H. Berendt. Finally, for the last century Museum librarians Anne Fadil, Martha B. Thompson, Cynthia Griffin, and Jean Shaw Adelman, as well as Museum and University Library administrators have recognized the importance of the collection and have maintained its integrity as a distinct entity within the Museum Library.

This volume was edited and designed by University Museum Publications under the direction of Walda Metcalf. I am deeply grateful to Jennifer Quick, Senior Editor, for her work in editing the original manuscript and guiding its development to publication. It has been my good fortune to benefit from their editorial expertise and great sense of humor. Gregory Borgstede, a graduate student in the Department of Anthropology, skillfully created the map of Karl Berendt's explorations.

All inquiries concerning restrictions or use of the Brinton Library should be addressed to the Museum Librarian, University of Pennsylvania Museum of Archaeology and Anthropology, 3260 South Street, Philadelphia, Pennsylvania 19104-6324.

Introduction

The birth of American anthropology took place during the period between 1860 and 1890. The publication in 1859 of Charles Darwin's *On the Origin of Species by Means of Natural Selection, or the Preservation of Favored Races in the Struggle for Life* completely transformed the scientific thinking of the 19th century. Natural phenomena that had puzzled previous generations suddenly became explicable according to the natural laws of evolution. The formation of the solar system represented stages in the evolution of the universe. In geology, the relative placement and the contents of the earth's strata allowed the dating of these strata. In archaeology, the Stone, Bronze, and Iron Ages were identified, documented, and described as an evolutionary progression. Even in philology, evolutionism became the basis for linguistic theory and methodology in the study of historical linguistics.

The theories and findings of the many evolution-based sciences provided a new context for the study of humankind. With each new finding in geology, archaeology, and biology, the beginning of the universe receded ever more distantly into the past. Biblical chronology could no longer contain the time required for the slow transformations that took place in the history of the earth. Increasingly thinkers concluded that the universe had been operating under uniform laws of constant change throughout time. The natural laws of the universe, accepted so uncritically in the 18th century, retained their uniformity and stability, but the timeless world of their operation was exchanged for a dynamic one best comprehended through evolutionary hypotheses.

Such thinking had profound implications for the study of human societies and cultures during the last half of the 19th century. The theory and method of evolutionism, which made possible the rapid advances in the natural sciences, seemed to offer the same rewards to the social sciences as they emerged as intellectual and, later, academic disciplines. The history of humankind came to be seen as a series of steps in a developmental sequence. Societies and cultures were portrayed as the slow accumulation of custom and belief obeying laws both natural and evolutionary. If Darwin had demonstrated that human beings were the end product of a long evolutionary process, could not the institutions and customs of civilization have developed from savagery according to the same basic laws? French mathematician Auguste Comte, German socialist Karl Marx, and English social theoretician Herbert Spencer were among the many social philosophers who accepted this challenge.

Evolutionism thus became the framework for the new anthropology. In the hands of scholars such as Edward Tylor and John Lubbock in England and Lewis Henry Morgan in the United States, anthropology gained new authority for its analysis of human culture and societies. There was now a trend to utilize more and better authenticated data, but the basic assumptions remained unchanged: the uniformity of human mental characteristics over time and space allowed comparisons regardless of geography or history; there were universal similarities of developmental stages in the course of the evolution of specific cultures; and European standards represented the ideal of progress to measure the direction and degree of development. The classic expression of these assumptions as the basis for the dominant academic theory of the period can be seen in the introduction to *Primitive Culture* (1871) by Edward Tylor, the scholar usually considered to be the founder of modern anthropology. Tylor and

other anthropologists of the period transformed the 18th-century conceptual and logical relationships of a classificatory scheme embracing all existing and ancient peoples into the sequential relationship of a time series by analogy to the development of organic growth.

Anthropological research during the last quarter of the 19th century emphasized the systematic description of indigenous languages and cultures, their archaeological remains, and the classification of these data into formal typologies. Publication of well-documented classificatory and descriptive works increased at the expense of the more speculative, although the latter did not disappear entirely. At the same time there was a growing specialization of the American academic and professional worlds.

In 1879 the Bureau of American Ethnology was formed and, soon afterwards, new departments of anthropology in museums at the University of Pennsylvania and Harvard University were created. These institutions devoted their efforts to recording and collecting ethnographic information on and materials of vanishing peoples, especially the North American Indians. Although much of the research of these new professional anthropologists was framed according to the evolutionary assumptions of the late 19th century, their findings increasingly tended to question the evolutionary approach to their field. Thus, by the early decades of the 20th century the older evolutionary anthropology was being successfully challenged by the modern conception of cultural pluralism and relativism.

This was the scientific milieu within which Daniel G. Brinton pursued his investigations and within which he assembled his research library.

Daniel Garrison Brinton

Daniel Garrison Brinton was born in Thornbury, Chester County, Pennsylvania, on May 13, 1837.[1] Like many other late–19th century anthropologists, Brinton was an amateur whose independent means allowed him to pursue personal scholarly research. He received his B.A. degree in 1858 from Yale University, where he developed literary and bibliophilic interests. He prepared for a career as a physician at Jefferson Medical College in Philadelphia (1858–1860; M.D., 1861) and, after a year of study at Heidelberg and Paris, he began practicing medicine in West Chester, a community located west of Philadelphia.

In August 1862 Brinton entered the Union Army as acting assistant surgeon and the following year was commissioned as a surgeon in the United States Volunteers. As Surgeon-in-Chief of the Second Division, Eleventh Corps of the Army of the Potomac, he saw action at Chancellorsville, Gettysburg, Lookout Mountain, and Missionary Ridge. In August of 1865 he was breveted Lieutenant Colonel and discharged, and subsequently returned to his medical practice. Brinton served as assistant editor of the *Medical and Surgical Reporter* between 1867 and 1874, and as editor from 1874 to 1887. In 1887, at the age of fifty, he retired to devote himself to the study of anthropology.

Even as he embarked on a distinguished career as a physician, his interest in Native American anthropology competed with his medical practice. Ultimately it became the field that claimed his entire attention. He devoted years to researching the topic, and from the publication of his first book, *Notes on the Floridian Peninsula, Its Literary History, Indian Tribes and Antiquities* (1859), until his death in 1899, he published a series of writings that included twenty-three books and more than two hundred articles and essays. These works considered a wide range of subjects, including mythology and folklore, ethnography and linguistics of American Indians from South America to the Arctic, prehistory and physical anthropology of native North America, and indigenous American literature and writing systems, among others.

Brinton was one of the academic pioneers in American anthropology. He was appointed Professor of Ethnology and Archaeology at the Academy of Natural Sciences of Philadelphia in 1884, and in 1886, Professor of Archaeology and Linguistics at the University of Penn-

Daniel Garrison Brinton, by M. Dantzig (University of Pennsylvania Museum, Philadelphia, neg. S8-139854).

sylvania, the second American university to create a chair in anthropology. He was, with Albert Gallatin and Lewis Henry Morgan, one of the founders of the modern ethnological study of the American Indians. In the field of linguistics he showed ability in mastering and classifying Indian languages. Brinton strongly contested the theory of the Asiatic origin of American Indian civilizations, seeking to prove, on the basis of studies of morphological traits, that the American Indian languages constituted one of the great speech families of the world.

His *The American Race: A Linguistic Classification and Ethnographic Description of the Native Tribes of North and South America* (1891) was a seminal work.

But Brinton's most significant contributions were in the field of religion and mythology. He collected, translated, and annotated texts of indigenous mythology and folklore for his *Library of Aboriginal American Literature* series (1882–1890). Brinton himself edited most of the volumes in this series, including a publication of major importance, *The Maya*

Chronicles (1882). In addition to gathering source materials, Brinton carried thorough analyses and synthetic interpretations, beginning with *The Myths of the New World: A Treatise on the Symbolism and Mythology of the Red Race in America* (1868), and ending with his *Religions of Primitive People* (1897). The assumption of the psychic unity of mankind underlies all his work in the field of comparative religion and impelled him to argue for the spontaneous origin of religious parallelisms.

Brinton's investigations were based on archival or library research rather than on primary fieldwork. He assembled a personal library, monumental in scale, that reflects the background materials used in most of his research.

A few months before his death on October 27, 1899, Brinton formalized the bequest of his library to the University of Pennsylvania. The *American Anthropologist* (1898:598) reported that Brinton's library covered "the whole American field" and was gathered to facilitate "comparative study." Today the Daniel Garrison Brinton Library at the University of Pennsylvania Museum Library remains the only existing intact research library of a scholar prominent in the development of late 19th century American anthropology.

Brinton's research interests emphasized Mexico and Central America because these groups "achieved a higher grade of culture than those of the regions to the north" and because of "a much larger body of literature upon them." Brinton's extensive scholarly network allowed him to obtain most published works, especially many small and arcane essays, issued during the last quarter of the 19th century. The collection grew through personal acquisitions, as well as the purchase of parts of other collections, including those of French Mayanist Charles Etienne Brasseur de Bourbourg, Alphonse Pinart, the American bibliophile Henry C. Murphy, and the German physician Karl Hermann Berendt. Brinton also paid a scribe to copy certain manuscripts he was unable to purchase.

The Brinton Library today consists of over four thousand items. It occupies approximately 180 feet of shelf space. Other than an abbreviated shelf-list file maintained at the Museum Library, there is no single catalog yet available for the entire Brinton Library. A list of manuscripts assembled by Karl Hermann Berendt and acquired by Brinton was published posthumously (Brinton 1900; Weeks 1998).

The materials in the Daniel Garrison Brinton Library include monographs, pamphlets, and offprints from academic journals (there are one hundred sixty-two bound volumes of more than two thousand pamphlets or offprints of professional journal articles), as well as manuscripts and transcriptions of original manuscripts. The Brinton Library contains material pertaining to a variety of subdisciplines and subjects within late 19th century anthropology. Some of these include: the social issues and context of anthropology and archaeology; general archaeology and prehistory; cultural description and analysis, social organization and structure, ceremonial behavior, and material culture; the disciplinary professionalization of anthropology, professional societies, and education; ethnographic and archaeological fieldwork; folklore, mythology, and religion; linguistics and philology (linguistic philology is an area in which Brinton's holdings were exhaustive); museums and their development, operation, and collections; physical anthropology, medical anthropology, anthropometrics, craniology, race, and general human evolution; scientific societies and publishing; and bibliography.

In addition to conventional anthropological reports and studies, the collection includes accounts of exploration, early travel narratives, colonial histories, Indian captivity tales, missionary reports, and translations of the Bible and other religious tracts into the indigenous languages of North and Central America. Materials written in Spanish, French, Italian, and German are well represented. Periodicals include materials from leading antiquarian and anthropological organizations, as well as issues from local historical societies. In addition, publications from most of the major European learned societies are included. The Appendix gives a list of serial titles represented in Brinton's pamphlet collection.

The value of the collection as a whole lies primarily in the unity of subject matter, and secondarily in its enrichment from its original owner. Its scope reflects Brinton's intellectual depth and wide-ranging curiosity. He attempted to keep current in all areas of ethnography and linguistics. While he avoided extreme specialization, he also dealt with many subjects about which he knew comparatively little. At the end of his life the image of the ideal scholar was changing. It was becoming more highly respected to know a great deal about a small field. With the information explosion of the late 19th and early 20th centuries, the new professionalism and specialized disciplinary training made the intellectual style of Brinton seem increasingly alien and anachronistic.

In several areas Brinton was at a transition point in the history of American anthropology. Fieldwork was becoming a methodological standard for serious professional students of anthropology. Academic teaching of anthropology became important both for providing institutional support for the discipline and for training a new generation of practitioners. And the effort to achieve terminological consensus reflected the increasing need for professional identity and solidarity among anthropologists.

Karl Herman Berendt

The part of the Daniel Garrison Brinton Library perhaps most well-known to modern scholars consists of the hand-written transcriptions of rare linguistic material and other miscellaneous manuscripts sold to Brinton by Karl Herman Berendt.

Berendt was born in Danzig (Gdansk) on November 12, 1817, and studied at various German universities before receiving his medical degree at the University of Königsberg (Kalingrad) in 1842.[2] He began a medical practice in Breslau (Wroclaw) in 1843 and later served as *privat-docent* in surgery and obstetrics at the University of Breslau. In 1848 he was a member of the *Vor-Parlament* at Frankfurt-am-Main where his liberal political views resulted in his dismissal from the University and his removal to Graudenz (Grudziadz) and, in 1851, to the Americas. Berendt, like so many other Europeans at this time, probably saw in the free institutions of America a democratic model that suited his political philosophy. He proceeded from New York to Nicaragua, where he spent two years conducting a range of natural historical and anthropological investigations. Two years later he moved to Orizaba, Mexico, and then to Vera Cruz, where he remained from 1855 to 1862.

He soon abandoned the practice of medicine and devoted himself to natural science, linguistics, and ethnology. Much of his time was spent traveling throughout the southern Mexican states of Chiapas, Tabasco, and Yucatan, collecting natural history specimens for the Smithsonian Institution (Baird 1865). Part of 1864 was spent at the library of John Carter Brown in Providence, Rhode Island, transcribing two important Maya vocabularies compiled during the colonial period, Antonio Ciudad Real's 16th-century *Diccionario de Motul*, and the *Compendio de nombres en lengua cakchiquel* by the Franciscan Pantaleón de Guzmán.

A letter from John R. Bartlett, an agent for John Carter Brown, to E. G. Squier, dated December 26, 1864, Providence, Rhode Island, provides one of the few personal accounts of Berendt:

Karl Herman Berendt
(Brinton 1900).

There is a Dr. Berendt here who will go to N[ew] Y[or]k in a few days, to whom I will give a letter of introduction to you. He has lived in southern Mexico many years (10 I think), chiefly in Tabasco. He has also visited Yucatan, Chiapas, etc. His specialty is natural hist[ory], but he had paid much attention to the Ind[ia]n languages. He heard in Central Am[erica] of the Maya dic[tionary] which the abbe Brasseur brought here, and by making inquires in N[ew] Y[ork] of some of our Ethnological [Society] friends, soon traced it to Providence, which at once brought him here.

Seeing its importance, he determined to remain and transcribe the whole, and in two hours after his arrival he was at work in my office. It took him two months to accomplish the work; and having made some pleasant acquaintances here and free accepts Mr. Brown's library, he has continued here, boarding at the same house where I am.

I have never met with such a literary worker, nor one who reminds me to much of Humboldt and his…labor. He is well nosed in early American bibliography and has all old Spanish written at his tongue end. It was his intention to…a thorough exploration of Yucatan, as he understands Maya pretty well, while his profession as a medico would greatly aid him. However, he is not quite decided what course he will take. He met Brasseur and his works in N[ew] Y[ork], and can tell you all his plans.

On December 2, 1865, he left the United States on the bark *Pallas* for Belize City in the Crown Colony of British Honduras (Belize). With scientific instruments furnished by the Smithsonian Institution and with the financial support of several interested individuals and learned societies in Chicago and Philadelphia, Berendt planned to conduct geographical and anthropological studies within a transect extending from the Caribbean Sea, through Belize, the Petén region of northern Guatemala, the state of Chiapas in southwestern Mexico, to the Pacific Ocean (Berendt 1868).

While in Belize City he met with various Crown officials and obtained copies of several ancient manuscript maps of the Colony surveyed by the Crown engineer. He also made the acquaintance of Alexander Henderson, a Baptist missionary himself compiling a Yucatec Maya dictionary from the Bacalar region of western Belize. Copies of many of Henderson's rare tracts in the Maya language were acquired by Berendt and are now in the Brinton Library.

Berendt left Belize City on January 12, 1866, traveling by large dugout canoe on the Belize River, and after thirteen days reached San Pedro Buenavista, a few kilometers above the confluence of the Belize River with the Macal River. Specimens collected along the way included species of pine and oak, land and fresh water mollusks, and birds. Measurements of the river were made, and he collected names of settlements, mostly logging operations, existing along the river. Travel was difficult and when logging camps could not be reached, he camped in the forest using the leaves of the *corozo* palm for shelter and protection.

Berendt waited for about a month at San Pedro Buenavista for mules and muleteers to be sent from Guatemala. For smaller articles he used Maya carriers from local villages. He then traveled on

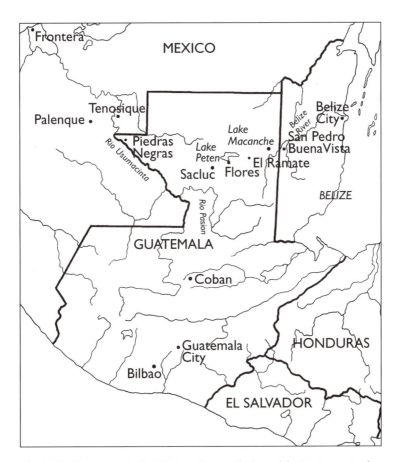

The 1865–1867 journey by Karl H. Berendt across the base of the Yucatan peninsula, southern Mexico.

the main road from the frontier settlements on the banks of the Belize River to the Petén region of northern Guatemala; he noted that rest stations where water, food, and palms for camp building were available stood at 20-kilometer intervals along the way. He departed the main trail at one of these stations for another road recently opened to Lake Macanché, and then proceeded to El Remate, an abandoned hamlet on the northern part of Lake Petén. Here Berendt was met by four canoes and then paddled for twelve hours along the northern shore of the lake, around Punta Nima, to Flores. Berendt noted the existence of several archaeological sites on the peninsula that separates the lake. He describes Flores at that time as consisting of "about 900 inhabitants, who live, crowded together, in miserable huts built of sticks covered with mud and roofed with palm leaves" (Berendt 1868). Berendt spent a month at Flores collecting specimens and examining archaeological ruins throughout the region.[3]

Because of the difficulty of canoe travel, Berendt relocated to Sacluc, a mahogany logging settlement in a large savanna 30 kilometers southwest of Flores, midway between Lake Petén and the Río Pasion. Sacluc was a rough place populated with migrant loggers from Tabasco, Campeche, and Yucatan, and runaway Blacks from the British West India regiments. From Sacluc, excursions were made along the Río Pasion and its tributaries and lagoons, where Berendt continued ethnographic and linguistic studies among the Lacandon Maya and, during occasional chance meetings, with Kekchí Maya from the Alta Verapaz region of Guatemala. While in Lacandon country he apparently adopted an orphaned Yucatec boy named José Sabino Uc.

By October of 1866, Berendt's movement further west was postponed by a Maya insurrection that resulted in the abandonment of settlements and cessation of all communications between Belize and the Petén region. Berendt waited for several months in Sacluc to reestablish communication with settlements located on the Gulf of Mexico and coastal Belize. Unable to locate mules or local bearers to transport his collections, he eventually left Sacluc in April 1867 for Tenosique on the Río Usumacinta and San Juan Bautista, the capital of Tabasco, on the banks of the Río Grijalva. Here Berendt revised and completed surveys of the Río Usumacinta and its tributaries, and followed its course some 25 kilometers upriver from Tenosique to the so-called large cataract. On his return he visited the famous Classic period Maya ruins at Palenque, and was able to complete a map of the region and collect vocabularies for several indigenous languages.

While in Tabasco unclear "private business rendered a visit to the United States of importance to [his] personal interests" (Berendt

1868). In December 1867, Berendt returned to Central America in order to bring back his collections being stored at Flores or Sacluc. The Peabody Museum of American Archaeology and Ethnology at Harvard University now subsidized Berendt's researches rather than the Smithsonian Institution (Wyman 1868:18; 1871:7). This trip appears to have been reasonably successful since, by 1873, the Museum had received eight crates containing approximately 200 antiquities, human remains, and other objects of archaeological or ethnographic value (Wyman 1871:7; 1872:26; 1873:6; 1874:23-24).

By 1869 Berendt had explored the ruins of Centla, located at the drainage of the Río Grijalva and Río Usumacinta on the Gulf of Mexico, where the *conquistador* Hernán Cortés defeated a large force of Maya Indians in 1519. He visited the United States several times between 1869 and 1876, the year of his last visit. By the late 1860s Berendt was experiencing financial difficulties and most of the monographs in his personal library, together with a collection formed by Augustin Fischer, chaplain to the Emperor Maximilian of Mexico, were sold at auction in London (*Bibliotheca Mejicana* 1869). Most of 1871 and 1872 was spent in New York, accompanied by his adopted son.

In 1874 Berendt settled at Cobán, the center of the German coffee plantations in the Verapaz region of northern Guatemala. He purchased land with coffee groves, acquired the first printing press in Cobán, and co-founded the local newspaper, *El Quetzal* (Frey 1938; Terga Citrón 1991:8). He visited Philadelphia during the summer of 1876 in order to examine the manuscripts in Central American indigenous languages at the American Philosophical Society. At this time he probably finalized arrangements with Daniel G. Brinton to purchase his valuable collection of manuscripts.

While in the United States Berendt was commissioned by Adolf Bastian, director of the Königliche Museen zu Berlin, to supervise the excavation, cutting-up, and transporting of prehispanic monuments from the site of Bilbao (Santa Lucia Cotzumalhuapa) on the Pacific coastal piedmont of Guatemala. Together with a German engineer from Koblenz named Albert Napp, he began working at the site in February of 1877. Despite many hardships, Berendt evidently kept meticulous records of the progress of the work from January 1877 to March 1878 in a diary to his wife, Anna (Parsons 1967-1969: 2:17-18). He imported special saws to remove the carved surfaces of the sculptures from their backs and heavy bases so they could be moved and shipped with less effort and weight. In a little over a year, although ridden with chronic kidney disease and suffering from hardships imposed by local living conditions, he performed a tremendous task, supervising the excavations, mapping, crating, and preparation for shipment of the monuments. It was fortunate that he expedited the work because he became ill and died on April 12, 1878, in Guatemala City.

Most of his reports were sent earlier to Bastian in Germany, who saw to their publication (Bastian 1882). The remainder of the diary and his field drawings and maps were preserved by his son who wrote about them to Bastian on April 12, 1878. Their present location is unknown (Parsons 1967–1969:2:17).

After a series of delays, some thirty major stone monuments and a number of minor pieces were placed aboard the German vessel *José Ginebra* in late 1880, arriving at the port of Stettin, Germany, in August of 1881. The monuments were finally put on exhibit by Bastian early in 1883.[4] As a result of the removal of these sculptures to Berlin, the Guatemalan government realized the intrinsic value of its prehispanic heritage. On November 15, 1893, President José Maria Reyna Barrios passed a decree prohibiting the unauthorized excavation of any Maya ruins, vandalism at archaeological sites, and the exportation of archaeological objects.

Although not a scholar of Brinton's stature, Berendt contributed many essays in English, German, and Spanish to such works as *American Historical Record, Annual Report of the Smithsonian Institution, Bulletin of the American Geographical Society, Petermanns Geographische Mittheilungen, Revista de Mérida, Zeitschrift für Ethnologie*, and the *Deutsch-Amerikanisches Conversations-Lexikon*. Unfortunately, few of Berendt's investigations resulted in publication, and many of his manuscripts and transcriptions were eventually deposited in the University Museum Library as part of the Brinton bequest. Some manuscripts were also acquired by the Bureau of American Ethnology and are now in the National Anthropological Archives in Washington, DC.

Berendt made his greatest contribution though his transcriptions of important manuscripts in indigenous languages. After Mexico, Guatemala, and Honduras gained national independence and the monastic orders were suppressed, vast amounts of documentation previously accumulated in municipal, departmental, and ecclesiastical libraries became the property of local governments and were transferred to official libraries and archives in national as well as regional capitals. Berendt spent a month in 1875 visiting various archives in Guatemala City, including the national archives of Guatemala, the archives of the Audiencia of Guatemala, various municipal archives, the library of the Universidad de San Carlos, and the library of the Sociedad Económica de Amigos de Guatemala.

In his essay "Collections of historical documents in Guatemala," Berendt (1877:421) expressed his appreciation of the scholarly value of early manuscripts for modern ethnohistorical research:

> it is safe to say that [archives and libraries in Guatemala City] contain many rare and unique documents whose study would considerably extend our knowledge of the history of this continent, particularly regarding the periods of the conquest and of the Spanish domination, and also of the condition of the country and people before the conquest. (1877:421)

Berendt suggested that inventories and transcript copies of selected documents in various archives would make the contents available to other scholars and, perhaps more importantly, preserve valuable sources of information threatened by poor preservation and conservation, sale, or theft.

Berendt's transcriptions were made available early to other contemporary scholars, as demonstrated by citations to the collection in the works of the prominent Swiss linguist Otto Stoll and others. In 1885 James Constantine Pilling published his monumental *Proof-Sheets of a Bibliography of the Indian Languages of North America* (1885) which identifies most of the Berendt manuscripts in Brinton's possession. In the early decades of the 20th century Charles P. Bowditch, a figure instrumental in the development of Mayanist studies at Harvard University's Peabody Museum of Archaeology and Ethnology, assembled his personal notes on the Berendt material at the University of Pennsylvania in his *Collection of Volumes in Berendt's Linguistic Collection* (Bowditch n.d.).

The Berendt Collection, now at the library of the University of Pennsylvania Museum, comprises 183 entries pertaining to more than 40 indigenous Mexican and Central American languages and covers the period from the middle 16th through the late 18th centuries. It includes 40 original manuscripts, 43 transcriptions of original manuscripts, 34 published monographs, 6 transcriptions, either complete or partial, of published monographs, and some 60 unpublished manuscript notes by Berendt. There are also numerous miscellaneous notes, correspondence, and other items of ephemera pasted or inserted in several volumes. Many of these languages are now moribund or extinct, making the collection one of the most important of its kind (Weeks 1998). Alfred Marston Tozzer (1914:147), a Mayanist at Harvard University and the Peabody Museum of Archaeology and Ethnology, offers the following evaluation of the Berendt collection: "Up to the time when Mr. [William E.] Gates[5] began his photographic reproductions every student of Maya linguistics was absolutely dependent upon his Berendt material."

Brinton's interests, broad and sweeping as they were, provided the rationale for his study of Native American linguistics and folklore. The use of historical material stimulated Brinton to collect books and manuscripts in preparation for his research. Brinton's library remained the most complete for Mesoamerican studies until the collecting activity of William E. Gates between 1911 and 1916 (Weeks 1990). Unlike Gates, Brinton's collecting spirit did not exceed his scholarly desire to assemble his sources for study, and, unlike Gates, he never considered his library an investment that could be converted to cash when necessary.

Daniel G. Brinton and Karl Hermann Berendt were remarkable men, each utterly unique in his own way and unusually interesting. It is pointless to argue whether the subject attracts curious personalities or visa versa. Both men did enjoy a common condition: the scholarly freedom both to choose the problems they wished to investigate and to determine the method of approaching those problems.

Brinton was the Philadelphia patrician. He resisted the evils of specialization and attempted to reduce elaborate factual data to satisfactory explanations. Good judgment, a disciplined mind, and a superior intellect guided him through an extremely productive scholarly career. Berendt, by contrast, was a loner, an expatriate by choice who led a singular lonely life devoted to the investigation of the indigenous languages and cultures of southern Mesoamerica. No domestic ties held him to one place. Of the enormous body of information he assembled, only a small portion was published during his lifetime. However, Berendt appreciated early the scholarly value of manuscripts in indigenous languages and provided the documentary foundation for future generations of Mesoamerican scholars.

It is interesting to note that Brinton's prolific writing on the indigenous cultures of southern Mesoamerica and Central America began shortly after his acquisition of the Berendt manuscripts. Brinton was keenly aware of his debt to the German fieldworker and dedicated *The Maya Chronicles* (1882) to Berendt: "To the memory of Carl Hermann Berendt, M.D., whose long and earnest devotion to the ethnology and linguistics of America has made this work possible, and whose untimely death has lost to American scholars results of far greater importance, this volume is dedicated."

Library of the University of Pennsylvania Museum of Archaeology and Anthropology

The Brinton Library was first housed in Furness Hall on the campus of the University of Pennsylvania until the opening in 1898 of the present Lombardy Renaissance-style University Museum building designed by architects

Interior of the University of Pennsylvania Museum Library, ca.1955, by Reuben Goldberg (University of Pennsylvania Museum, Philadelphia, neg. 61842).

Wilson Eyre, Jr., Walter Cope, Emlyn Stewardson, and Frank Miles Day. The collection was then relocated to the Elkins Library Room, where for more than 40 years the library shared the quarters with the Museum's numismatics collections, pieces of sculpture, and a few portraits. During that time the library collection developed rather unsystematically through curatorial donations of their own publications, exchange arrangements made with colleagues or institutions around the world, and gifts. Until 1942 there was one part-time librarian, and library use was restricted to Museum staff and a few scholars.

Cynthia Griffin was appointed as the first full-time Museum Librarian in 1942. At the time of her appointment the library contained approximately 16,000 volumes, and was mostly uncataloged. Circulation, limited to only within the Museum, was approximately 1,000 transactions annually. Miss Griffin reorganized the library, opened it to student use, planned for growing collections, and expanded exchange relationships throughout the world. The Museum Library soon entered a period of rapid and systematic growth. The holdings increased in size from 18,922 volumes by 1945, to more than 50,000 volumes in 1971 when she retired. Two full-time assistants were added to the staff, and circulation increased to over 14,000 items a year. The collection was completely cataloged, although stack growth over the years had reduced reading space to only two tables with seating limited to 16 patrons (Griffin 1955, 1958).

In 1971 the library moved to its present quarters, occupying 12,000 square feet on three levels in the new Academic Wing of the University Museum, designed by Mitchell/Giurgola Associates. Jean Shaw Adelman succeeded Griffin as Museum Librarian. Ms. Adelman continued to expand the resources and mission of the library as it became administratively part of the University of Pennsylvania Libraries.

As the Museum Library was integrated into the larger university library system, it never lost its unique character, and continues to serve specialists especially in the areas of its greatest strength: Mesoamerican indigenous cultures and Egyptology, both early and ongoing foci of research for the Museum. From its inception the library has benefited not only from generous gifts of books and funding, but also from the ability to exchange publications issued by the University Museum for foreign publications. John and Ada H. H. Lewis contributed generously to the building and furnishing of the library when the new wing of the Museum was built. The George Clapp Vaillant Fund, named for the former director of the University Museum (1941–1945), and other major bequests have made it possible for the library to continue to acquire special materials it would not otherwise be able to afford.

The scope of the library collection has always emphasized anthropology, including prehistoric, Classical, and Near Eastern and South Asian archaeology, cultural and social anthropology, biological and physical anthropology, and anthropological linguistics, as well as related fields such as museology. Special attention has always been given to the curricular and research requirements of the faculty in the Department of Anthropology and the curatorial staff of the University Museum.

The Museum Library presently possesses over 120,000 volumes, with an annual circulation of about 15,000 items, and maintains 550 active journal subscriptions as well as almost 300 exchange partners around the world. It has a seating capacity for 154 scholars and students, in addition to three seminar rooms and a photographic studio.

Because of the generous bequest of Daniel G. Brinton and the visionary efforts of its professional librarians, in little more than a century the Museum Library has developed from a few cabinets in Furness Hall on the campus of the University of Pennsylvania into one of the most important and comprehensive anthropology and archaeology libraries in the world.

Organization of the Catalog

From the time the Brinton Library was bequeathed to the University of Pennsylvania up until the present, the only guide to the collection in existence consisted of an extremely abbreviated card catalog shelf list kept in the Museum Library staff area. The collection appears to have been catalogued in the 1940s, and handwritten or typescript entries can be found throughout the remnants of the now obsolete card catalog. The reasons such a guide was not prepared much earlier, or even before the collection was bequeathed, are mostly circumstantial. It is hoped that the publication of this expanded inventory of the Brinton Library will contribute substantially to making the collection more usable for the study of the history of American anthropology during the period 1875 to 1900.

The material as a whole is extremely important for any historian who wishes to trace the development of modern American anthropology. These writings offer insights into the modern history of ideas of race and culture, and the institutional development and disciplinary coalescence of modern anthropology. Finally, this material is a convenient focus for historians interested in chronicling the intellectual shift from evolutionary to historical and functionalist modes of ethnological analysis.

The catalog of the Daniel Garrison Brinton Library contains some 4,500 entries covering over 400 years of literature and representing material in most West European languages, as well as several indigenous languages. Individual entries are arranged numerically and alphabetically according to a standardized format. Where known or imputed, the author is indicated. Where no author is entered, items are assumed to be anonymous and are arranged by title. Authorship is followed by title, series (if any), publisher, place of publication, date of publication, pagination, and Brinton Library classification number. Journal literature consists of title, followed by volume, number (if any), pagination, date of publication, and Brinton Library classification number. Basic bibliographic information is followed by brief notes, including biographical notes, contents of collected volumes, format statements, and so forth. Biographical notes are based on material presented in Field (1873), *Frank T. Siebert Library* (1999), Pilling (1885), and Winters (1991). Inevitably some entries are incomplete; such is the case with many of the offprints and pamphlets bound by Brinton. All incomplete entries have been searched in the *National Union Catalog*, published library catalogs, and electronic bibliographical databases.[6] In these cases technical perfection has been sacrificed in favor of comprehensive collection representation.

The index is arranged alphabetically and includes personal names and corporate names, geographic names, and the names of ethnic and linguistics groups, and archaeological sites, as well as general subject areas. The vocabulary used in construction of subjects terms is necessarily arbitrary and cannot serve the needs of all users equally well. They relate more to personal research interests than to areas with which I am less familiar. They should still prove adequate for providing access to most of the subjects included in the catalog.

Appendix

Titles of Serials in the Brinton Library

Aaborger for Nordisk old Kyndoghed og Historie udgivne af det Kongelige Nordiske Oldskrift-Selskab. Copenhagen.

Académé de Stanislas. Mémoires. Paris.

Académe Royale des Sciences et del Lettres de Danemark. Mémoires. Copenhagen.

Académie des Inscriptions et Belles Lettres. Comptes Rendus. Paris.

Académie Nationale des Sciences, Arts et Belles Lettres du Caen. Mémoires, Caen.

Academy of Natural Sciences of Philadelphia. Journal. Philadelphia.

Academy of Natural Sciences of Philadelphia. Proceedings. Philadelphia.

Academy of Sciences of St. Louis. Transactions. St. Louis.

Ägyptica. Leipzig.

Alienist and Neurologist. St. Louis.

Am Ur-Quell: Monatschrift für Völkskunde. Hamburg.

American Academy of Arts and Sciences. Memoirs. Boston.

American Academy of Arts and Sciences. Proceedings. Boston.

American Academy of Political and Social Sciences. Annals. Philadelphia.

American Anthropologist. Washington, DC.

American Antiquarian Society. Proceedings. Worcester, MA.

American Antiquarian. Cleveland.

American Architect. New York.

American Association for the Advancement of Science. Proceedings. Philadelphia.

American Ethnological Society. Bulletin. New York.

American Ethnological Society. Transactions. New York.

American Field. New York.

American Geographical Society. Bulletin. New York.

American Geographical Society. Journal. New York.

American Geologist. Minneapolis.

American Historical Association. Annual Report. Washington, DC.
American Historical Association. Papers. Washington, DC.
American Historical Magazine. New Haven, CT.
American Historical Record. Philadelphia.
American Historical Register. Philadelphia.
American Institute of Architects. Journal. Washington, DC.
American Institute of Mining Engineers. Transactions. Reno.
American Journal of Archaeology. Baltimore.
American Journal of Insanity. Utica, NY.
American Journal of Pharmacy. Philadelphia.
American Journal of Philology. Baltimore.
American Journal of Psychology. Ithaca.
American Journal of Science and Arts. New Haven, CT.
American Journal of Science. New Haven, CT.
American Journal of Sociology. Chicago.
American Magazine of Natural Science. Sac City, IA.
American Medical Association. Journal. Chicago.
American Monthly. New York.
American Museum of Natural History. Bulletin. New York.
American Naturalist. Salem, MA.
American Oriental Society. Proceedings. New Haven, CT.
American Philological Association. Proceedings of the Annual Session. Hartford, CT.
American Philological Association. Transactions. Hartford, CT.
American Philosophical Society. Proceedings. Philadelphia.
American Philosophical Society. Transactions. Philadelphia.
American Review. New York.
Anatomischen Gesellschaft. Verhandlungen. Strasbourg.
Anatomischer Anzeiger. Jena, Germany.
Annales de l'Alliance Scientifique. Paris.
Annales de Philosophie Chrétienne. St. Germaine.
Anthropological Institute of Great Britain and Ireland. Journal. London.
Anthropological Institute of New York. Journal. New York.
Anthropological Institute. Journal. London.
Anthropological Review. London.
Anthropological Society of Washington. Special Papers. Washington, DC.
Anthropological Society of Washington. Transactions. Washington, DC.
Anthropologie. Paris.
Anthropologische Gesellschaft in Wien. Mitteilungen. Wien.
Antiquarischen Gesellschaft. Mitteilungen. Leipzig.
Anzeiger für Schweizerische Altertumskunde. Zürich.
Archaeological Institute of America. Papers. Boston.
Archaeological Journal. London.

Archaeologist. Waterloo, IN.

Archiv für Anthropologie. Braunschweig.

Archiv für Naturgeschichte. Leipzig.

Virchow's Archiv für Pathologischen Anatomie und Physiologie und für
Klinische Medicin. Berlin.

Archiv für Religionswissenschaft. Stockholm.

Archivio per l'Antropologia e la Etnologia. Firenze.

Archivio per le Tradizioni Popolari. Palermo.

Asiatic Quarterly Review. London.

Asiatic Society of Bengal. Journal. Calcutta.

Association Française pour l'Avancement des Sciences. Paris.

At Home. St. Paul, MN.

Athenée Oriental. Paris.

Auk. Washington, DC.

Beiträge zur Anthropologie Braunschweigs. Braunschweig.

Beiträge zur Assyriologie und Semitische Sprachwissenschaft. Leipzig.

Berliner Anthropologischen Gesellschaft für Anthropologie, Ethnologie
und Urgeschichte. Verhandlungen. Berlin.

Biblical World. Chicago.

Bibliothèque Ethnographique. Paris.

Bibliothèque Linguistique Américaine. Paris.

Bihang till K. Svenska Vet. Akad. Handlingar. Stockholm.

Biological Laboratories of Columbia College. Zoological Studies. New
York.

Boston Herald. Boston.

Boston Society of Natural History. Anniversary Memoirs. Boston.

Boston Society of Natural History. Proceedings. Boston.

Botanical Gazette. Chicago.

Botanisches Centralblatt. Jena, Germany.

Brighton Herald. New York.

Bristol and Gloucester Archaeological Society. Transactions. Bristol.

Brooklyn Daily Eagle Almanac. Brooklyn.

Bucks County Historical Society. Contributions of American History.
Doylestown, PA.

Buffalo Medical Journal. Buffalo.

Buffalo Society of Natural Sciences. Bulletin. Buffalo.

Bulletin de Géographie Historique et Descriptive. Paris.

Bulletino di Paletnologia Italiano. Morelli.

Bulletins d'Anthropologie de Paris. Paris.

Bureau of Ethnology, Smithsonian Institution. Annual Report. Washington, DC.

Bureau of Ethnology, Smithsonian Institution. Bulletin. Washington, DC.

California Academy of Sciences. Memoirs. San Francisco.

Canadian Indian. Owen Sound, Ontario.

Canadian Institute. Annual Report. Toronto.

Canadian Institute. Proceedings. Toronto.

Canadian Institute. Transactions. Toronto.

Canadian Journal. Toronto.

Canadian Naturalist. Montreal.

Canadian Record of Science. Montreal.

Central Ohio Scientific Association of Urbana. Proceedings. Urbana, OH.

Central Ohio Scientific Association. Proceedings. Urbana, OH.

Centralblatt für Anthropologie, Ethnologie und Urgeschichte. Berlin.

Centralblatt für Bibliothekswesen. Leipzig.

Chicago Medical Recorder. Chicago.

Cincinnati Lancet Clinic. Cincinnati.

Cincinnati Society of Natural History. Journal. Cincinnati.

Columbia University. Biological Laboratories. Studies. New York.

Commission Locale Néerlandaise. Rapport. Amsterdam.

Congress of American Physicians and Surgeons. Transactions. New Haven, CT.

Connecticut Academy of Arts and Sciences. Transactions. New Haven, CT.

Correspondant. Paris.

Cosmos di Guido Cora. Torino.

Davenport Academy of Natural Sciences. Proceedings. Davenport, IA.

De Gids. Amsterdam.

Denison Quarterly. Granville, OH.

Dental Cosmos. Philadelphia.

Dental Review. Chicago.

Der Urquell. Leiden.

Deutsche Geologische Gesellschaft. Zeitschrift. Stuttgart.

Deutschen Anthropologischen Gesellschaft. Correspondenzblatt. Braunschweig.

Deutschen Gesellschaft für Anthropologie, Ethnologie und Urgeschichte. Correspondenzblatt. Braunschweig.

Deutschen Wissenschaftlichen Vereins zu Santiago. Verhandlungen. Santiago de Chile.

Deutschen Zeitschrift für Geschichtswissenschaft. Freiburg.

Direccion de Obras Publicas. Revista. Santiago de Chile.

École d'Anthropologie de Paris. Revue Mensuelle. Paris.

Englische Studien. Leipzig.

Essex Institute. Bulletin. Salem, MA.

Ethnographical Survey of the United Kingdom. Report. London.

Ethnological Journal. London.

Ethnological Society of London. Journal. London.

Ethnological Society of London. Transactions. London.

Ethnologisches Notizblatt. Berlin.

Études de Grammaire Comparée. Paris.

Field Columbian Museum. Anthropological Series. Chicago.

Folklore Journal. London.

Folk-Lore Society. Publications. London.

Forum. New York.

Frank Leslie's Illustrated Newspaper. New York.

Franklin Institute. Journal. Philadelphia.

Freien Deutschen Hochstistes zu Frankfurt am Main. Berichten. Frankfurt am Main.

Fünften Deutschen Geographentagews zu Hamburg. Verhandlungen. Hamburg.

Gazette Archéologique. Paris.

Geográfico Argentino. Boletín. Buenos Aires.

Geografisck Tidskrift. Copenhagen.

Geographical Club of Philadelphia. Bulletin. Philadelphia.

Geographisches Gesellschaft. Mitteilungen. Wien.

Geographisches Jahresberichte. Strasbourg.

Geological Society of America. Bulletin. New York.

Georgia Historical Society. Collections. Savannah.

Gesellschaft für Erdkunde zu Berlin. Zeitschrift. Berlin.

Globe Journal Geographique. Genéve.

Globus. Braunschweig.

Gloucester Journal. Gloucester, England.

Hahnemannian Monthly. Philadelphia.

Harper's New Monthly Magazine. New York.

Harper's Weekly. New York.

Hebraica. Chicago.

Historical Magazine. Morrisania, NY.

Historical Register. London.

Historical Society of New York. Proceedings. New York.

Homme. Paris.

Hoosier Mineralogist and Archaeologist. Indianapolis.

Illustrated Archaeologist. London.

Imperial University of Japan, College of Science. Memoirs. Tokyo.

Indianapolis Journal. Indianapolis.

Inlander. Dayton, OH.

Instituto Geográfico Argentino. Boletín. Buenos Aires.

Instituto Lombardo di Scienze e Lettere. Revista. Milan.

Instituto Paraguayo. Revista. Asunción.

International Congress of Americanists. Proceedings. Nancy, France.

International Congress of Anthropology. Memoirs. Paris.

International Congress of Orientalists. Proceedings. Paris.

International Congress of Prehistoric Archaeology and Anthropology. London.

International Congress of Prehistoric Archaeology, Anthropology, and Zoology. Proceedings. London.

International Dental Journal. Philadelphia.

International Folklore Congress. Transactions. London.

International Journal of Ethics. Chicago.

Internationalen Wissenschaftlichen Lepraconference zu Berlin. Mittheilungen und Verhandlungen. Berlin.

Internationales Archiv für Ethnographie. Leiden.

Iowa State Horticultural Society. Transactions. Des Moines.

Jahresberichte der Anatomie und Physiologie. Jena, Germany.

Journal Asiatique. Paris.

Journal do Commercio. Rio de Janeiro.

Journal of American Folklore. Washington, DC.

Journal of Anatomy and Physiology. London.

Journal of Biblical Literature. New York.

Journal of Comparative Neurology. New York.

Journal of Cutaneous and Genito-Urinary Diseases. New York.

Journal of Geology. Chicago.

Journal of Nervous and Mental Disease. New York.

Journal of Pharmacy. Philadelphia.

Journal of Philology. London.

Journal of Speculative Philosophy. St, Louis.

K. K. Naturhistorischen Hofmuseums. Annalen. Wien.

Kaiserlichen Akademie der Wissenschaften in Wien. Sitzungsberichte. Wien.

Kamloops Wawa. Kamloops Wawa, British Columbia.

Kansas City Review of Science. Kansas City.

Kentucky Geological Survey. Memoirs. Frankfort.

Kongeligt Nordiske Oldskrfift Selskab. Mémoires. Copenhagen.

Königlich Preussischen Akademie der Wissenschaften zu Berlin. Sitzungsberichte. Berlin.

Königlichen Akademie der Wissenschaften zu Berlin. Abhandlungen. Berlin.

Königlichen Museum für Völkerkunde. Veröffentlichungen. Berlin.

La Nacion. Buenos Aires.

Lippincott's Magazine of Popular Literature and Science. Philadelphia.

Literary and Historical Society of Quebec. Transactions. Quebec.

Literaturblatt für Germanische und Romanische Philologie. Leipzig.

Lyceum of Natural History of New York. Annals. New York.

Macalaster College. Contributions. St. Paul, MN.

Magazine of American History. New York.

Magazine of Western History. New York.

Maryland Academy of Sciences. Transactions. Baltimore.

Meddelelser om Gronland. Copenhagen.

Medical News. Philadelphia.

Medical Record. New York.

Mémoires des Antiquaires du Nord. Copenhagen.

Milwaukee Parkman Club. Publications. Milwaukee.

Minnesota Academy of Natural Sciences. Bulletin. St. Paul, MN.

Minnesota Historical Society. Collections. St. Paul, MN.

Modern Language Notes. Baltimore.

Monist. Chicago.

Monitore Zoologico Italiano. Firenze.

Moskauer Congresses für Anthropologie und Urgeschichte. Berichten. Moscow.

Musei di Zoologia ed Anatomia Comparata. Bollettino. Torino.

Museo de La Plata. Anales. La Plata, Argentina.

Museo de La Plata. Revista. Buenos Aires.

Museo Michoacano. Anales. Morelia, Mexico.

Muséon. Louvain, Belgium.

Museu Nacional do Rio de Janeiro. Archivos. Rio de Janiero.

Muséum d'Histoire Naturelle de Lyon. Bulletin. Lyon.

Museum des Missionshauses zu Basel. Katalog der Ethnographischen Sammlung. Basel.

Museum für Völkerkunde. Veröffentlichungen. Berlin.

Museum of American Archaeology. Annual Report. Philadelphia.

Museum. Philadelphia.

National Academy of Sciences. Memoirs. Washington, DC.

National Academy of Sciences. Memoirs. Washington, DC.

National Geographic Magazine. Washington, DC.

Natural Science Journal. New Bedford, MA.

Natural Science. London.

Nature's Realm. New York.

Naturfirschenden Gesellschaft. Vierteljahrsschrift. Zürich.

Naturforschenden Gesellschaft in Basel. Verhandlungen. Basel.

Naturwissenschaftliche Wöchenschrift. Berlin.

Nederlandsche Spectator. Te Arnhern.

New Englander. New Haven, CT.

New York Academy of Anthropology. Transactions. New York.

New York Academy of Science. Transactions. New York.

New York Medical Journal. New York.

New York Medical Record. New York.

New York State Agricultuiral Society. Annual Report. Albany.

Nord und Süd. Berlin.

Nordiska Museet. Meddelanden. Stockholm.
Nordiske Fortidsminder. Copenhagen.
Nu English Herald. Minneapolis.
Nueva Revista de Buenos Aires. Buenos Aires.
Nueva Revista de BuenosAires. Buenos Aires.
Numismatic and Antiquarian Society of Philadelphia. Proceedings.
    Philadelphia.
Occident. Philadelphia.
Ohio Scientific Association of Urbana. Proceedings. Urbana, OH.
Ohio State Archaeological and Historical Society. Annual Publications.
    Columbus.
Oriental Club of Philadelphia. Proceedings. Philadelphia.
Oriental Quarterly Review. London.
Rechtsgeleerd Magzijn. Leiden.
Pacific Science Monthly. San Buenaventura, CA.
Pädagog Zeitschrift. Basel.
Pedagogical Seminary. Worcester, MA.
Peabody Museum of American Archaeology and Ethnology. Annual Re-
    port. Cambridge, MA.
Peabody Museum of American Archaeology and Ethnology. Archaeologi-
    cal and Ethnological Papers. Cambridge, MA.
Peabody Museum of American Archaeology and Ethnology. Memoirs.
    Cambridge, MA.
Peabody Museum of American Archaeology and Ethnology. Reports.
    Cambridge, MA.
Pedagogical Seminary. Worcester, MA.
Pediatrics. New York.
Pennsylvania Library Club. Occasional Papers. Philadelphia.
Pennsylvania Magazine of History and Biography. Philadelphia.
Petermann's Mittheilungen. Gotha, Germany.
Petite Bibliothèque Americaine. Paris.
Pharmaceutical Journal and Transactions. London.
Philological Society. Transactions. London.
Philosophical Review. Ithaca.
Philosophical Society of Washington. Bulletin. Washington, DC.
Poet-Lore. Washington, DC.
Political Science Quarterly. New York.
Popular Science Monthly. New York.
Prähistorische Blätter. München.
Preussischen Jahrbucher. Sonderabruck. Berlin.
Psychological Review. Washington, DC.
Public Library of the City of Boston. Bulletin. Boston.
R. Accademie Medica di Roma. Bulletino. Rome.

Rechtsgeleerd Magazijn. Leiden.
Reliquary and Illustrated Archaeologist. London.
Revista de Buenos Aires. Buenos Aires.
Revista de Mérida. Mérida, Mexico.
Revista Natura ed Arte. Milan.
Revue Américaine. Paris.
Revue Celtique. Paris.
Revue d'Anthropologie. Paris.
Revue d'Ethnographie. Paris.
Revue de Geographie. Paris.
Revue de l'Histoire des Religions. Paris.
Revue de Linguistique et de Philologie Comparée. Paris.
Revue de Linguistique. Paris.
Revue des Deux Mondes. Paris.
Revue des Questions Historiques. Paris.
Revue des Questions Scientifiques. Louvain, Belgium.
Revue des Religions. Paris.
Revue des Sciences et de Leurs Applications aux Arts et à l'Industrie. Paris.
Revue des Traditions Populaires. Montévrain, France.
Revue Materiaux pour l'Histoire Primitive de l'Homme. Paris.
Revue Orientale et Américaine. Paris.
Revue Scientifique. Paris.
Revue Tunisienne. Tunis.
Rhode Island Historical Society. Publications. Providence.
Romania. Paris.
Royal Geographical Society. Journal. London.
Royal Geographical Society. Proceedings. London.
Royal Geographical Society. Supplementary Papers. London.
Royal Society of Canada. Transactions. Montreal.
Royal Society of Edinburgh. Proceedings. Edinburgh.
Royal Society. Proceedings. London.
San Francisco Bulletin. San Francisco.
Schweizerischen Archiv für Völkskunde. Zürich.
Schweizerischen Vierteljahrsschrift für Zahnheilkunde. Zürich.
Science. Washington, DC.
Sciences Biologiques. St. Pétersbourg.
Scientific Laboratories of Denison University. Bulletin. Granville, OH.
Scottish Geographical Journal. Edinburgh.
Scribner's Magazine. New York.
Shea's Library of American Linguistics. New York.
Smithsonian Institution. Contributions of American Ethnology. Washington, DC.
Smithsonian Institution. Contributions to Knowledge. Washington, DC.

Sociedad Científica Alzate de Mexico. Memorias. Mexico City.
Sociedad Científica Argentina. Anales. Rio de Janeiro.
Sociedad Económica de Amigos de Guatemala. Miscelanea. Guatemala.
Sociedad Económica. Memorias. Madrid.
Sociedad Geográfica de Lima. Boletín. Lima.
Sociedad Mexicana de Geografía y Estadistica. Boletín. Mexico City.
Sociedad Mexicana de Geografía. Boletín. Mexico City.
Società Asiatica Italiana. Giornale. Firenze.
Società Geografica Italiana. Bollettino. Rome.
Società Italiana di Scienze Naturali. Atti. Milan.
Società Romana di Antropologia. Atti. Lanciano.
Società Romana di Antropologia. Statuto. Rome.
Società Veneto-Trentina di Scienze Naturali. Atti. Padova.
Société Algerienne de Climatologique. Bulletin. Alger, Algeria.
Société Américaine de France. Annuaire. Paris.
Société Américaine de France. Archives. Paris.
Société d'Anthropologie de Lyon. Bulletin. Lyon.
Société d'Anthropologie de Paris. Bulletins. Paris.
Société d'Anthropologie de Paris. Mémoires. Paris.
Société d'Anthropologique de Paris. Journal. Paris.
Société d'Ethnographie. Actes. Paris.
Société d'Ethnographie. Annuaire. Paris.
Société d'Ethnographie. Bulletin. Paris.
Société d'Ethnographie. Compte rendus des seances. Paris.
Société d'Ethnographie. Mémoires. Paris.
Société d'Histoire, d'Archéologie et de Littérature de l'Arrondissement
    du Beanue. Mémoires. Paris.
Société Dauphinoise d'Ethnologie et d'Anthropologie. Bulletin. Grenoble.
Société de Geographie. Bulletin. Paris.
Société de l'Histoire de France. Bulletin. Paris.
Société de Linguistique. Bulletin. Paris.
Société de Statistique de Paris. Journal. Paris.
Société Imperiale des Amis des Sciences Naturelles, d'Anthropologie et
    d'Ethnographie de l'Université de Moscow. Moscow.
Société Nationale des Antiquaries de Paris. Mémoires. Paris.
Société Nationale des Sciences Naturelles et Mathematiques de Cher-
    bourg. Mémoires. Cherbourg.
Société Niçoise des Sciences Naturalles, Historiques et Geographiques.
    Bulletin. Nice.
Société Normande de Géographie. Bulletin. Rouen.
Société Philologique. Actes. Paris.
Société Philologique. Boletin. Paris.
Société Royal de Geographie d'Anvers. Bulletin. Anvers.

Société Scientifique de Bruxelles. Annales. Brussels.

Society for Psychical Research. Proceedings. London.

Society of Antiquaries of Scotland. Proceedings. Edinburgh.

Society of Biblical Archaeology. Proceedings. London.

Society of Friends. Yearly Meeting. Philadelphia.

St. Paul Pioneer Press. St. Paul, MN.

State Historical Society of Wisconsin. Proceedings. Madison.

Sunday School Times. Philadelphia.

T'oung Pao. Leiden.

Tacoma Academy of Science. Proceedings. Tacoma, WA.

Technology Quarterly. Boston.

Texas Academy of Science. Transactions. Austin.

Therapeutic Gazette. Detroit.

Timenri. Georgetown.

Travaux Relatifs à la Philologie et à l'Archeologie Egyptiennes et Assyriennes. Paris.

Über Land und Meer. Stuttgart.

United States Board on Geographical Names. Bulletin. Washington, DC.

United States Bureau of Indian Affairs. Report of the Commissioner of Indian Affairs. Washington, DC.

United States Geological and Geographical Survey. Bulletin. Washington, DC.

United States Geological and Geographical Survey. Miscellaneous Publication. Washington, DC.

United States National Museum, Smithsonian Institution. Annual Report.
Washington, DC.

United States National Museum, Smithsonian Institution. Proceedings.
Washington, DC.

Universalist Quarterly. Boston.

Universidad de Chile. Anales. Santiago de Chile.

Universita Toscane. Annali. Pisa.

University Medical Magazine. Philadelphia.

University of Chicago. Department of Anthropology. Bulletin. Chicago.

University of Pennsylvania, Botanical Laboratory. Contributions.
Philadelphia.

University of Pennsylvania, Free Museum of Science and Art. Proceedings. Philadelphia.

University of Pennsylvania, Museum of Science and Art. Bulletin.
Philadelphia.

Utica Morning Herald. Utica, NY.

Vereins für Erdkunde zu Leipzig. Mitteilungen. Leipzig.

Vereins für Völkskunde. Zeitschrift. Berlin.

Verhandlungen der Deutschen Odontolog. Berlin.

Vierteljahrsschrift für Wissenschaftliche Philosophie und Soziologie. Leipzig.

Virchow's Archiv für Pathologische Anatomie und Physiologie und für Klinische Medecin. Berlin.

Wagner Free Institute of Science. Transactions. Philadelphia.

Western Reserve and Northern Ohio Historical Society. Transactions. Cleveland.

Western Reserve University Bulletin. Cleveland.

Wiener Zeitschrift für Kunde des Morgenlandes. Wien.

Wisconsin Academy of Sciences, Arts and Letters. Transactions. Madison.

Wyoming Historical and Geographical Society. Proceedings. Wilkes-Barre, PA.

Yale Review. New Haven, CT.

Zeitschrift Anglia. Breslau, Poland.

Zeitschrift der Gesellschaft für Erdkunde. Berlin.

Zeitschrift für Ägyptische Sprache und Alterthumskunde. Leipzig.

Zeitschrift für Assyriologie. Leipzig.

Zeitschrift für Assyriologie und Verwandte Gebiete. Leipzig.

Zeitschrift für die Alttestamentliche Wissenschaft. Berlin.

Zeitschrift für die Kunde des Morgelandes. Leipzig.

Zeitschrift für Ethnologie. Braunschweig.

Zeitschrift für Insterburger Alterhumsvereins. Insterburg, Germany.

Zeitschrift für Socialwissenschaft. Berlin.

Zoological Society of London. Proceedings. London.

Zoologisch, Mineralogischen Vereines in Regensburg. Korrespondence-blatt. Regensburg, Germany.

Notes

1. Regna Darnell (1970, 1971, 1976, n.d.) has prepared the only book-length treatment of Brinton, first as an M.A. thesis at the University of Pennsylvania (1967) and later published as a monograph (1988). Following Brinton's death in 1899, a series of obituaries appeared in many significant anthropological journals, including American Anthropologist (1899), *Bulletin of the Free Museum of Science and Art* (1900), *Conservator* (Michael 1899; Traubel 1899), *Globus* (Boas 1899), *Journal of American Folklore* (Chamberlain 1899), *Freedom: A Journal of Anarchist Communism* (1899), and *Science* (McGee 1899). Other biographical treatments are found in the *Dictionary of American Biography* (Michelson 1929), *International Encyclopedia of the Social Sciences* (Wissler 1937), *International Directory of Anthropologists* (Ogburn 1991), and *Daniel Garrison Brinton Centenary* (1937). Excerpts from Brinton's diary of military service as Surgeon-in-Chief of the Second Division to the Eleventh Corps of the Army of the Potomac and witnessed fighting at Chancellorsville and Gettysburg has been published (Thompson 1965). After Brinton's death, Stewart Culin and Helen Abbott Michael, together with Mrs. Sarah M. Brinton, worked to organize memorial observances and establish a Brinton Chair of American Archaeology and Ethnology at the University of Pennsylvania. The effort to devise a memorial circular to raise funds to commission a portrait of Brinton was ultimately unsuccessful. In 1900 Stewart Culin edited the *Brinton Memorial Meeting* (1900), a memorial volume by twenty-six learned societies, with an address by Albert H. Smyth and a bibliography of Brinton's published works by Culin. More recent assessments of Brinton and his work can be found in Tooker (n.d.), Baker (2000), and Weeks (2000), among others. The personal papers of Brinton are dispersed among the archives of the University of Pennsylvania Museum of Archaeology and Anthropology, and the Brooklyn Museum. The Rare Books and Manuscripts Library, Van Pelt-Dietrich Library, University of Pennsylvania, has some Brinton manuscripts donated by his grandson, Dr. D. G. Brinton Thompson. These consist of lecture notes, maps, scrap books, and printed material by and about Brinton, as well as some correspondence notebooks.

2. Biographical information on Berendt is limited but includes Brinton's (1884, 1900) "Memoir of C. H.

Berendt," as well as a few notices in *Appleton's Cyclopedia of American Biography* (1901) and *Revista de Mérida* (Carrillo y Ancona 1869). Martínez Alomía (1906:245–249) and Carmack (1973:234) provide brief considerations. Correspondence between Berendt and Charles Rau from 1869 to 1876 is in the National Anthropological Archives, and a collection of postcard exchanges between Berendt and Phillipp J. J. Valentini is in the collection of the University of Pennsylvania Museum of Archaeology and Anthropology. There is a portrait of Karl Hermann Berendt with an Indian boy, presumably his son Sabino, in the National Anthropological Archives (Glenn 1996).

3. Some of these ruins probably included the Maya sites of Chochquitán, La Hondradez, Nakúm, Tayasal, Topoxté, Ucanal, Xultún, and Yaxhá.

4. In his monograph on the archaeological investigations at Bilbao, Parsons (1967–1969) illustrates twenty-nine of the monuments shipped by Berendt to Bastian at the Königliche Museen zu Berlin. These include Monuments 1–9, 13–15, 20, 26, 30–32, 40, 46, 47, 49, 64, 67, 69, 70, and 72–75. By 1892 plaster casts of thirteen of the monuments were prepared for an exhibit in Hamburg to celebrate the fourth centenary of the discovery of America. Several of the casts were exhibited in the Guatemalan pavilion at the Columbian Exposition in Chicago in 1893. These eventually became part of the collections at the American Museum of Natural History in New York.

Others were donated by the German government to Spain and shown at Madrid in 1892. Today they are in the Museo de América in Madrid.

5. William E. Gates gathered together the largest collection of Mesoamerican manuscripts ever assembled. He collected original manuscripts or photographic reproductions of most known linguistics documents on the languages of central and southern Mexico, and the Maya region. Gates made several duplicate sets and these were eventually sold and added to the collections at the Peabody Museum of Archaeology and Ethnology at Harvard University, the Latin American Library at Tulane University, the Ayer Collection at the Newberry Library, the Library of Congress, and the libraries at Princeton University and Brigham Young University (Weeks 1990).

6. Incomplete entries have been searched in the *Research Libraries Group Union Catalog* (RLIN), and the *OCLC Firstsearch Union Catalog* (WorldCat). Published library catalogs include: *Catalogues of the Peabody Museum of Archaeology and Ethnology, Harvard University* (Boston: G. K. Hall, 1963–1979; 84 v.); *Catalog of the Latin American Library of the Tulane University, New Orleans* (Boston: G. K. Hall, 1970–1978. 15 v.); *Catalógos de la Biblioteca Nacional de Antropología e Historia, México* (Boston: G. K. Hall, 1972. 10 v.); *Dictionary Catalog of the American Indian Collection, Huntington Free Library and Reading Room, New York* (Boston: G. K. Hall, 1977. 4 v.).

References

Baird, Spencer E. 1865. Report of the Assistant Secretary. *Annual Report of the Smithsonian Institution for 1864,* pp. 74–88. Washington, DC.

Baker, Lee D. 2000. Daniel G. Brinton's Success on the Road to Obscurity, 1890–99. *Cultural Anthropology* 15(3): 394–423.

Bastian, Adolf. 1882. *Steinsculpturen aus Guatemala.* Berlin: Weidmannsche Buchhandlung.

Berendt, Karl H. 1868. Report of Explorations in Central America. *Annual Report of the Smithsonian Institution for 1867*, pp. 421–426. Washington, DC.

Berendt, Karl H. 1877. Collections of Historical Documents in Guatemala. In *Annual Report of the Smithsonian Institution for 1876*, pp. 421–423. Washington, DC.

Bibliotheca Mejicana: Books and Manuscripts Almost Wholly Relating to the History and Literature of North and South America, Particularly Mexico; To be Sold by Auction, by Messrs. Puttick & Simpson, at Their House, 47, Leicester Square, London, on Tuesday, June 1st, 1869, and 7 Following Days. 1869. London: Puttick and Simpson.

Boas, Franz. 1899. Daniel G. Brinton [obituary]. *Globus* 76:165–166.

Bowditch, Charles P. n.d. Collection of Volumes in Berendt's Linguistic Collection. Manuscript, Tozzer Library, Harvard University. 93 leaves.

Brinton, Daniel G. 1859. *Notes on the Floridian Peninsula, Its Literary History, Indian Tribes and Antiquities.* Philadelphia: J. Sabin.

Brinton, Daniel G. 1868. *The Myths of the New World: A Treatise on the Symbolism and Mythology of the Red Race in America.* New York: Leypoldt and Holt.

Brinton, Daniel G. 1882. *The Maya Chronicles.* Philadelphia.

Brinton, Daniel G. 1884. Memoir of Dr. C. H. Berendt. *Proceedings of the American Antiquarian Society* 3:205–210.

Brinton, Daniel G. 1891. *The American Race: A Linguistic Classification and Ethnographic Description of the Native Tribes of North and South America.* New York: N.D.C. Hodges.

Brinton, Daniel G. 1897. *Religions of Primitive People.* New York: George P. Putnam.

Brinton, Daniel G. 1900. *Catalogue of the Berendt Linguistic Collection.* Philadelphia: Department of Archaeology and Paleontology, University of Pennsylvania.

Brinton, Daniel G., ed. 1882-1890. *Library of Aboriginal American Literature*. 8 vols. Philadelphia.

Carmack, Robert M. 1973. *Quichean Civilization: The Ethnohistoric, Ethnographic, and Archaeological Sources*. Berkeley: University of California Press.

Carrillo y Ancona, Cresencio. 1869. El doctor Berendt y la lingüística. *Revista de Mérida* 1:11-14.

Chamberlain, Alexander F. 1899. Daniel G. Brinton (obituary). *Journal of American Folk-Lore* 12:215-225.

Chamberlain, Alexander. 1899. In Memoriam: Daniel Garrison Brinton. *Journal of American Folk-Lore* 12:215-225.

Cooper, John M. 1917. *Analytical and Critical Bibliography of the Tribes of Tierra del Fuego and Adjacent Territory*. Bureau of American Ethnology, Bulletin 63. Washington, DC.

Culin, Stewart. 1900. Bibliography of Daniel G. Brinton, M.D. Philadelphia. 28 p. Based on an annotated bibliography covering publications up to 1892 prepared and printed by Dr. Brinton. Reprinted from American Philosophical Society Memorial Volume.

Culin, Stewart. 1900. *Brinton Memorial Meeting; Report of the Memorial Meeting Held January Sixteenth, Nineteen Hundred, Under the Auspices of the American Philosophical Society*. Philadelphia: American Philosophical Society.

Daniel G. Brinton. 1900. *The Conservator* (February): 189.

Daniel G. Brinton Is Dead. 1899. *Freedom: A Journal of Anarchist Communism* (November): 74.

Daniel Garrison Brinton Centenary, 1837-1937. 1937. Media, PA: Delaware County Institute of Science. 3 p.

Darnell, Regna D. 1967. *Daniel Garrison Brinton: An Intellectual Biography*. M.A. thesis, Department of Anthropology, University of Pennsylvania. 164 leaves.

Darnell, Regna D. 1970. The Emergence of Academic Anthropology at the University of Pennsylvania. *Journal of the History of the Behavioral Sciences* 6:80-92.

Darnell, Regna D. 1971. The Professionalization of American Archaeology. *Social Science Information* 10: 83-103.

Darnell, Regna D. 1976. Daniel Brinton and the Professionalization of American Anthropology. In *American Anthropology: The Early Years,* ed. John V. Murra, pp. 69-98. St. Paul, MN: American Ethnological Society .

Darnell, Regna D. 1988. *Daniel Garrison Brinton: The Fearless Critic of Philadelphia*. Philadelphia: Department of Anthropology, University of Pennsylvania.

Darnell, Regna D. n.d. Daniel Garrison Brinton. *American National Biography Online* (articles/14/14-00073-article.html).

Darwin, Charles. 1859. *On the Origin of Species; By Means of Natural Selection or the Preservation of Favored Races in the Struggle for Life*. London: J. Murray.

Dr. Daniel G. Brinton [obituary]. 1899. *American Anthropologist* 1:598.

Field, Thomas W. 1873. *An Essay Toward an Indian Bibliography; Being a Catalogue of Books, Relating to the History, Antiquities, Lan-*

guages, Customs, Religion, Wars, Literature, and Origin of the American Indians, in the Library of Thomas W. Field. New York: Scribner, Armstrong.

Frank T. Siebert Library of the North American Indian and the American Frontier. 1999. 2 vols. New York: Sotherby's.

Frey, Martin. 1938. Deutschtum in der Alta Verapaz; herausgegeben Analässlich des 50 jährigen Bestehens des Deutschen Vereins zu Coban, Guatemala, 1888-1938. Stuttgart: Deutschen Verlagsanstalt.

Glenn, James R. 1996. Guide to the National Anthropological Archives, Smithsonian Institution. Rev. ed. Washington, DC: National Anthropological Archives.

Griffin, Cynthia. 1955. The Museum Library. University Museum Bulletin 19(2): 23-27.

Griffin, Cynthia. 1958. University Museum Library. Bulletin of the Special Libraries Council of Philadelphia and Vicinity 24(3): 25, 28-29.

In memoriam: Daniel G. Brinton. 1900. Bulletin of the Free Museum of Science and Art 2(3):199-200.

Karl Hermann Berendt. 1901. In Appleton's Cyclopedia of American Biography, ed. James G. Wright, v. 7, p. 22. New York: D. Appleton.

Martínez Alomía, Gustavo. 1906. Historiadores de Yucatán; apuntes biográficos y bibliográficos de los historiadores de esta península desde su descubrimiento hasta fines del siglo XIX. Campeche.

McGee, W. J. 1899. Daniel G. Brinton. Science 10(242): 193-196.

Michael, Helen A. 1899. Daniel Garrison Brinton. The Conservator (September): 102-103.

Michelson, Truman. 1929. Brinton, Daniel Garrison. In Dictionary of American Biography, v. 3, pp. 50-51. New York.

Ogburn, Joyce. 1991. Brinton, Daniel G. In International Directory of Anthropologists, ed. Christopher Winters, pp. 82-83. New York: Garland.

Parsons, Lee A. 1967-1969. Bilbao, Guatemala: An Archaeological Study of the Pacific Coast Cotzumalhuapa Region. 2 vols. Milwaukee Public Museum, Publications in Anthropology, 11-12. Milwaukee.

Pilling, James C. 1885. Proof-Sheets of a Bibliography of the Indian Languages of North America. Washington, DC: Government Printing Office.

Smyth, Albert. 1900. Brinton Memorial Meeting. Philadelphia: American Philosophical Society. [Comprised of a collection of facsimile letters from individuals and organizations concerning the establishment of a Chair of American Archaeology and Ethnology in the University of Pennsylvania in honor of Dr. Daniel Garrison Brinton.]

Terga Cintron, Ricardo. 1991. Almas gemelas: un estudio de la inserción alemana en las Verapaces y la consecuente relación entre los Alemanes y los K'ekchies. Cobán, Guatemala: Imprenta y Tipografia El Norte.

Thompson, D. G. Brinton. 1965. From Chancellorsville to Gettysburg, a Doctor's Diary. Pennsylvania Mag-

azine of History and Biography 89:292-315.

Tooker, Elisabeth. n.d. Daniel Garrison Brinton's Place in the History of American Anthropology. Manuscript, Museum Library. 10 leaves.

Tozzer, Alfred M. 1921. *A Maya Grammar; With Bibliography and Appraisement of the Works Noted.* Papers of the Peabody Museum of American Archaeology and Ethnology, 9. Cambridge, MA.

Traubel, Horace L. 1899. Editorial on D. G. Brinton. *The Conservator* (November): 131-132.

Tylor, Edward B. 1871. *Primitive Culture: Researches into the Development of Mythology, Philosophy, Religion, Art, and Custom.* 2 vols. London: John Murray.

Weeks, John M. 1990. *Mesoamerican Ethnohistory in United States Libraries: Reconstruction of the William E. Gates Collection of Historical and Linguistic Manuscripts.* Culver City, CA: Labyrinthos.

Weeks, John M. 1998. Karl Hermann Berendt: colección de manuscritos lingüísticos de Centroamérica y Mesoamérica. *Mesoamérica* 36: 619-693. Antigua, Guatemala.

Weeks, John M. 2000. The Daniel Garrison Brinton Collection. In *The Penn Library Collections at 250: From Franklin to the Web*, pp. 165-181. Philadelphia: University of Pennsylvania Libraries.

Winters, Christopher, ed. 1991. *International Dictionary of Anthropologists.* New York: Garland.

Wissler, Clark. 1937. Daniel Garrison Brinton (1837-1899). In *Encyclopedia of the Social Sciences*, ed. Edwin R. Seligman, v. 3, pp. 4-5. New York: Macmillan.

Wyman, Jeffries. 1868. Report of the Curator. In *First Annual Report of the Trustees of the Peabody Museum of American Archaeology and Ethnology*, pp. 1-18. Cambridge, MA: Press of John Wilson and Sons.

Wyman, Jeffries. 1871. Report of the Curator. In *Fourth Annual Report of the Trustees of the Peabody Museum of American Archaeology and Ethnology*, pp. 1-24. Boston: Press of A.A. Kingman.

Wyman, Jeffries. 1872. Report of the Curator. In *Fifth Annual Report of the Trustees of the Peabody Museum of American Archaeology and Ethnology*, pp. 1-30. Boston: Press of A.A. Kingman.

Wyman, Jeffries. 1873. Report of the Curator. In *Sixth Annual Report of the Trustees of the Peabody Museum of American Archaeology and Ethnology*, pp. 1-23. Cambridge, MA: Salem Press.

Wyman, Jeffries. 1874. Report of the Curator. In *Seventh Annual Report of the Trustees of the Peabody Museum of American Archaeology and Ethnology*, pp. 1-37. Cambridge, MA: Salem Press.

Catalog

1. Abadiano, *Dionisio. Estudio arqueológico y jeroglífico del calendario ó gran libro astronómico histórico y cronológico de los antiguos indios.* Imprenta de la Secretaría de Fomento, México, 1889. 202 p. Br913.72 Ab14.

2. Abbott, Charles C. A Recent Find in the Trenton Gravels. *Proceedings of the Boston Society of Natural History* 22:96-14, 1882. Br572C An8141 v.20; Br572C An8141 v.41. Abbott, sponsored by Frederick Ward Putnam at Harvard, excavated in the Trenton Gravels of New Jersey and discovered tools made of argillite that appeared to date before the end of the Pleistocene Ice Age. It was later shown that the layers were much more recent.

3. Abbott, Charles C. Evidences of the Antiquity of Man in Eastern North America: Address. *Proceedings of the American Association for the Advancement of Science,* 1888. 25 p. Br572C An8141 v.41.

4. Abbott, Charles C. Flint Chips. *Annual Reports of the Trustees of the Peabody Museum of American Archaeology and Ethnology* 2(3): 506-520, 1880. Br913.07 H265.

5. Abbott, Charles C. Idols and Idol Worship of the Delaware Indians. *American Naturalist* 16(10): 799-802, 1882. Br572C An8141 v.13.

6. Abbott, Charles C. *Primitive Industry or, Illustrations of the Handiwork in Stone, Bone and Clay, of the Native Races of the Northern Atlantic Seaboard of America.* G. A. Bates, Salem, MA, 1881. 560 p. Br913.7 Ab27.

7. Abbott, Charles C. Recent Archaeological Explorations in the Valley of the Delaware. *Philology, Literature, and Archaeology* 2(1), 1892. 30 p. Br572C An8141 v.124.

8. Abbott, Charles C. Report on the Discovery of Supposed Paleolithic Implements from the Glacial Drift, in the Valley of the Delaware River, near Trenton, New Jersey. *Annual Reports of the Trustees of the Peabody Museum of American Archaeology and Ethnology* 2(1): 30-43, 1877. Br913.07 H265.

9. Abbott, Charles C. Second Report on the Paleolithic Implements from the Glacial Drift, in the Valley of the Delaware River, near Trenton, New Jersey. *Annual Reports of the Trustees of the Peabody Museum of American Archaeology and Ethnology* 2(2): 225-257, 1878. Br572C An8141 v.35; Br913.07 H265.

10. Abbott, Charles C. Stone Age in New Jersey. *Annual Report of the United States National Museum, Smithsonian Institution, Annual Report for 1875*, 246-380, 1877. Br572C An8141 v.112.

11. Abbott, Charles C. The Use of Copper by the Delaware Indians. *American Naturalist*

18:774-777, 1885. Br572C An8141 v.13.

12. Abbott, William L. Descriptive Catalog of the Abbott Collection of Ethnological Objects from Kilima-Njaro, East Africa; Collected and Presented to the United States National Museum. *Annual Report of the United States National Museum, Smithsonian Institution, for 1891*, pp. 1-50, 1892. Br572C An8141 v.86. Abbott received an M.D. degree from the University of Pennsylvania and, around 1880, began a career as a collector of natural history specimens from the Greater Antilles, East Africa, Kashmir, Turkestan, Malaya, and the East Indies. He donated more than 8,500 ethnological specimens to the Smithsonian Institution; additional materials from his collections are in the Peabody Museum of Archaeology and Ethnology at Harvard University, and in other museums. He also collected archaeological and physical anthropological specimens together with many anthropologically significantly photographs.

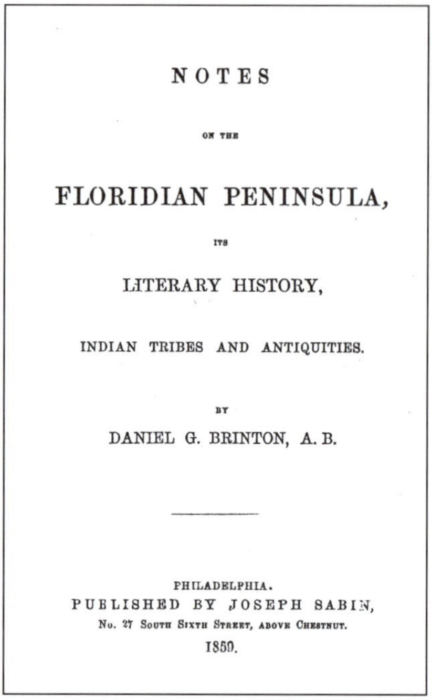

NOTES

ON THE

FLORIDIAN PENINSULA,

ITS

LITERARY HISTORY,

INDIAN TRIBES AND ANTIQUITIES.

BY

DANIEL G. BRINTON, A. B.

PHILADELPHIA.
PUBLISHED BY JOSEPH SABIN,
No. 27 South Sixth Street, above Chestnut.
1859.

Title page from Brinton's Notes on the Floridian Peninsula *(1859).*

13. Abel, Karl. Ägyptisch-Indoeuropäische Sprachverwandtschaft. *Berichten des Freien Deutschen Hochstistes zu Frankfurt am Main* 3:440-452, 1890. Br572C An8141 v.46; Br572C An8141 v.56.

14. Abel, Karl. Gegen Herrn Professor Erman zwei Ägyptologische Antikritiken. Leipzig, 1887. 32 p. Br572C An8141 v.56.

15. Abel, Karl. Gegensinn im Altägyptischen. *Verhandlungen der Berliner Anthropologischen Gesellschaft für Anthropologie, Ethnologie und Urgeschichte*, pp. 500-507, 1886. Br493.02 Ab32.

16. Abel, Karl. *L'affinité étymologique des langues Égyptienne et Indo-Européennes*. Imprimerie Nationale, Lisbonne, 1892. 29 p. Br572C An8141 v.116.

17. Abel, Karl. *Nachtrag zum Offenen Brief an Professor Dr. Gustav Meyer in sachen der Ägyptisch-Indogermanischen Sprachverwandtschaft*. Verlag von Wilhelm Friedrich, Leipzig, 1891. 26 p. Br572C An8141 v.46.

18. Abel, Karl. *Offener Brief Professor Dr. Gustav Meyer in sachen der Ägyptisch-Indogermanischen Sprachverwandtschaft*. Verlag von Wilhelm Friedrich, Leipzig, 1891. 35 p. Br572C An8141 v.46.

19. Abel, Karl. *Über wechselbeziehungen der Ägyptischen, Indoeuropaeischen und Semitischen Etymologie.* Verlag von Wilhelm Friedrich, Leipzig, 1888. 168 p. Br572C An8141 v.46.

20. Abel, Karl. Und Noah sprache. In *Mélanges Charles de Harlez; recueil de travaux d'érudition offert à Mgr. Charles Harlez à l'occasion du vingt-cinquième anniversaire de son professorat à l'Université de Louvain, 1871-1896.* E.J. Brill, Leiden, 1896. 4 p. Br572C An8141 v.146.

21. Abe-Lallemant, Robert C. *Riese durch nord Brasilien in Jahre 1859.* Brockhaus, Leipzig, 1860. Br918.1 Ab3.

22. Academy of Natural Sciences of Philadelphia. *Members and Correspondents of the Academy of Natural Sciences of Philadelphia.* Binder and Kelly, Philadelphia, 1893. 62 p. Br572C An8141 v.136.

23. Achelis, Thomas A. H. *Post under die vergleichende Rechtswissenschaft.* Verlagsanstalt und Druckerei, Hamburg, 1896. 39 p. Br572C An8141 v.146.

24. Achelis, Thomas. *Adolf Bastian.* Verlagsanstalt und Druckerei, Hamburg, 1891. 36 p. Br572C An8141 v.88.

25. Achelis, Thomas. Der Maui-Mythus. In *Bastian-Festschrift.* Verlag von Dietrich Reimer (Ernst Vohsen), Berlin, 1896. 17 p. Br572C An8141 v.146.

26. Achelis, Thomas. *Die Entwickelung der modernen Ethnologie.* E. S. Mittler und Sohn, Berlin, 1889. 149 p. Br572 Ac42.

27. Achelis, Thomas. Die Grundbegriffe in den Kosmogonien der alten Völker. *Archiv für Anthropologie* 22:273-288, 1893. Br572C An8141 v.145.

28. Achelis, Thomas. Die philosophische Bedeutung der Ethnologie. *Vierteljahrsschrift für Wissenschaftliche Philosophie und Soziologie* 17(3): 295-311, 1892. Br572C An8141 v.138.

29. Achelis, Thomas. Ethnologie und Ethik. *Zeitschrift für Ethnologie* 4:66-77, n.d. Br572C An8141 v.138.

30. Achelis, Thomas. Methode und Aufgabe der Ethnologie. *Zeitschrift der Gesellschaft für Erdkunde* 1-2, 1885. 14 p.; 12 p. Br572C An8141 v.138.

31. Achelis, Thomas. *Moderne Völkerkunde deren Entwicklung und Ausgaben.* Enke, Stuttgart, 1896. 487 p. Br572 Ac42.2.

32. Achelis, Thomas. Mythologie und Völkerkunde. *Nord und Süd* 81:356-372, 1877. Br572C An8141 v.153.

33. Acosta, Joaquín. *Compendio histórico del descubrimiento y colonización de la Nueva Granada en el siglo décimo sexto.* Imprenta de Beau, Paris, 1848. 460 p. Br986 Ac77.

34. Acosta, José A. *Oraciones devotas que comprenden los actos de fé, esperanza, caridad, afectos para un cristiano y una oración para pedir una buena muerte; en idioma yucateco, con inclusión del Santo Dios.* Imprenta a cargo de Mariano Guzman, Mérida de Yucatán, 1851. 10 p. Br498.21 Mac78. Spanish and Yucatec Maya arranged in parallel columns.

35. Acosta, José de. *Historia natvral y moral de las Indias; en qve se tratan las cosas notables del cielo, y elementos, metales, plantas, y animales dellas; y los ritos, y*

ceremonias, leyes, y gouierno, y guerras de los Indios. En la emprenta de Iayme Cendrat, Barcelona, 1591. 345 leaves. Br972.9 Ac7a. "Acosta, a native of Medina del Campo, entered the Society of Jesus at the age of fourteen, and in 1571 when thirty-one years old, became the deputy provincial of Peru. He died at Salamanca in 1600, having passed the greater part of the intervening years in America. His work has been justly esteemed" (Field 1873:2). This is one of the most celebrated early works on America, especially the state of South America in the early 17th century, and the early history of the Indians of Peru.

36. Acosta, José de. *Tercero catecismo y exposición de la doctrina christiana por sermones para que los curas, y otros ministros prediquen y enseñen à los Indios, y à las demàs personas; conforme a lo que se proveyò en el Santo Concilio Provincial de Lima el año pasado de 1583. Mandado reimprimir por el Concilio Provincial del año de 1773.* En la oficina de la calle de San Jacinto, Lima, 1773. 515 p. Br498.7 KT 272.

37. *Adaieli wacinaci okonomuntu ajiahu Genesis ibena bibici sabetu ajiahu Jesus Christ w'adaien okonomuntu apostleno onyisia okonomuntu ajiahu bajia.* W. M. Watts, London, 1856. 435 p. Br498.77 ArB 47.5. Collection of biblical selections translated into Arawak.

38. Adair, James. *The History of the American Indians; Particularly Those Nations Adjoining to the Mississippi, East and West Florida, Georgia, South and North Carolina, and Virginia; Containing an Account of Their Origin, Language, Manners, Religious and Civil Customs, Laws, Form of Government, Punishments, Conduct In War and Domestic Life, Their Habits, Diet, Agriculture, Manufactures, Diseases and Method of Cure, and Other Particulars, Sufficient to Render It A Complete Indian System; With Observations On Former Historians, the Conduct of Our Colony Governors, Superintendents, Missionaries, &c.; Also An Appendix, Containing A Description of the Floridas, and the Missisippi* [sic] *Lands, With Their Productions; the Benefits of Colonising Georgiana, and Civilizing the Indians; And the Way to Make All the Colonies More Valuable to the Mother Country.* Printed for Edward and Charles Dilly, in the Poultry, London, 1775. 464 p. Br970.1 Ad12. Adair (c. 1709–c. 1783), a Scotch-Irish immigrant, operated as a trader among most of the major tribes of the southeastern United States. During the 1740s and 1750s he lived among the Chickasaw. Although this volume is often ridiculed for his speculation on the Jewish origin of the American Indians, it contains much useful ethnographic information.

39. Adam, Lucien, and V. Henry, eds. *Arte y vocabulario de la lengua chiquita, con algunos textos traducidos y explicados, compuestos sobre manuscritos inéditos del XVIII siglo.* Bibliothèque Linguistique Américaine, 6. Maisonneuve, Paris, 1880. 136 p. Br497C Am3.

40. Adam, Lucien. *De l'incorporation dans quelques langues américaines.* Georges Jacob, Orleans, n.d. 28 p. Br572C An8141 v.47.

41. Adam, Lucien. Du genre dans les diverses langues. *Mémoires de l'Académé de Stanislas pour 1882.* Paris, 1883. 35 p. Br572C An8141 v.47.

42. Adam, Lucien. *Du parler des hommes et du parler des femmes. Mémoires de l'Académé de Stanislas pour 1877.* Paris, 1878. 32 p. Br572C An8141 v.52.

43. Adam, Lucien. *Esquisse d'une grammaire comparée des dialectes Cree et Chippeway.* Maisonnueve et Cie., Paris, 1876. 61 p. Br572C An8141 v.52.

44. Adam, Lucien. *Études sur six langues américaines; Dakota, Chibcha, Nahuatl, Kechua, Quiché, Maya.* Maisonneuve, Paris, 1878. 165 p. Br498 Ad14.

45. Adam, Lucien. *Grammaire de la langue Jâgare.* Maisonneuve Freres et Ch. Leclerc, Paris, 1885. 60 p. Br572C An8141 v.5. "An important treatise on Yahgan grammar…based on Dr. [R.] Garbe's work and on the translation of Rev. Thomas Bridges' Yahgan translation of the Gospel of St. Luke" (Cooper 1917:66).

46. Adam, Lucien. *La langue Chiapanèque; observations grammaticales, vocabulaire méthodique, textes inédits, textes rétablis.* A. Hölder, Vienne, 1887. 117 p. Br498.12 Cad15.

47. Adam, Lucien. *La Taensa a-t-il été forgé de toutes pièces.* Paris, 1885. 22 p. Br572C An8141 v.47. Bound with Daniel G. Brinton, The Taensa grammar and dictionary; a reply to M. Lucien Adam. *American Antiquarian* 7, 1885. 2 p.

48. Adam, Lucien. *La Taensah a pas été forgé de toutes pièces.* Paris, 1885. 4 p. Br572C An8141 v.47. Includes correspondence with F. Müller.

49. Adam, Lucien. *Langue Mosquito; grammaire, vocabulaire, textes.* Bibliothèque Linguistique Américaine, 14. Maisonneuve, Paris, 1891. 134 p. Br497C Am3.

50. Adam, Lucien. *Materiaux pour servir à l'établissement d'une grammaire comparée des dialectes de la famille Kariri.* Bibliothèque Linguistique Américaine, 20. Maisonneuve, Paris, 1897. 123 p. Br497C Am3.

51. Adam, Lucien. *Matériaux pour servir à l'établissement d'une grammaire comparée des dialectes de la famille Caribe.* Bibliothèque Linguistique Américaine, 17. Maisonneuve, Paris, 1893. 139 p. Br497C Am3.

52. Adam, Lucien. *Matériaux pour servir à l'établissement d'une grammaire comparée des dialectes de la famille Guaicuru (Abipone, Mocovi, Toba, Mbaya).* Bibliothèque Linguistique Américaine, 23. Maisonneuve, Paris, 1899. 168 p. Br497C Am3; Br498.97 Ad14.

53. Adam, Lucien. *Matériaux pour sevir à l'établissement d'une grammaire comparée des dialectes de la famille Tupí.* Bibliothèque Linguistique Américaine, 18. Maisonneuve, Paris, 1896. 136 p. Br497C Am3.

54. Adams, Herbert B., and Henry Wood. *Columbus and His Discovery of America.* Johns Hopkins Press, Baltimore, 1892. 88 p. Br572C An8141 v.118.

55. Adelung, Johann C. *Mithridates, oder, allgemeine Sprachenkunde mit der Vater unser als Sprachprobe; in bey nahe fünfhundert Sprachen und Mundarten; von Johann Christoph Adelung, Hofrafth und Ober-Bibliothekar zu Dresden; mit Benützung einiger Papieredesselben fortgesetzt, und aus zum Theil ganz neuen oder wenig bekannten Hülfsmitteln bearbeitet von Dr. Johann Severin Vater.* In der Vossischen Buchhandlung, Berlin, 1812–1816. 808 p. Br409 Ad3.1. English title: *Mithradetes, or General Linguistics, With the Lord's Prayer as Proof in Nearly 500 Languages and Dialects by Johann Christoph Adelung, Aulic Counsellor and*

Chief Librarian at Dresden; Continued With the Use of His Papers and Some Quite Unknown Sources by Dr. Johann Severin Vater. Includes grammatical analyses or vocabularies for most of the languages of the world. A large portion of the volume is devoted to the aboriginal languages of the Americas.

56. Adler, Cyrus, and Immanuel M. Casanowicz. Biblical antiquities; a description of the exhibit at the Cotton States International Exposition, Atlanta, 1895. *Annual Report of the United States National Museum, Smithsonian Institution, for 1896,* pp. 943-1023, 1898. Br210.93 Ad55.

57. Adler, Cyrus. Progress of Oriental science in America during 1888. *Annual Report of the United States National Museum, Smithsonian Institution, for 1888,* pp. 675-702, 1890. Br572C An8141 v.86.

58. Adler, Cyrus. Report on the Section of Oriental Antiquities in the United States National Museum, 1888. *Annual Report of the United States National Museum, Smithsonian Institution, for 1887-1888,* pt. 2, pp. 93-104, 1890. Br572C An8141 v.86.

59. Adler, Cyrus. Report on the Section of Oriental Antiquities in the United States National Museum, 1889. *Annual Report of the United States National Museum, Smithsonian Institution, for 1888-1889,* pp. 93-104, 1891. Br572C An8141 v.86.

60. Adler, Cyrus. Shofar; its use and origin. *Proceedings of the United States National Museum, Smithsonian Institution* 16:287-301, 1893. Br572C An8141 v.117.

61. Adler, George J. *Wilhelm von Humboldt's Linguistical Studies.* Wynkoop and Hallenbeck, New York, 1866. 47 p. Br572C An8141 v.54.

62. Aguilar, Francisco. Plática en lengua pocomchí, por Fr. Francisco Aguilar, cura de Tactic, Tamahú, 17 de diciembre de 1822. 24 p. Br498.21 Pag 94.3. Manuscript; the introduction, dated October 1875 and signed by Karl H. Berendt, states this is a transcription of a manuscript of 16 leaves in the parish archive of Cahabón, Alta Verapaz. The sermon is arranged Spanish and Pokomchí on opposite pages.

63. Aguilar, Francisco. Pláticas en pocomchí, 1818, 1822. 15, 40 leaves. Br498.21 Pag 94.2. Original manuscript obtained from the parochial archives of Cahabón in Vera Paz. The first sermon, "Plática para que los yndios no digan al ministro, Quando te bas?, año de 1822, en poconchí," is arranged Spanish and Pokomchí on opposite pages. The monogram of P. Aguilar appears on the top of the second leaf. The second sermon, "Sermón de Ntra. Sra. del Stmo. Rosario, año de 1818, [en] poconchí," is also arranged Spanish and Pokomchí on opposite pages.

64. Aguilar, Francisco. Sermones y pláticas en lengua castellana y pocomchí, 1818-1820. 30, 79, 97 leaves. Br498.21 Pag 94. Manuscript; Pokomchí and Spanish arranged in parallel columns.

65. Aguilera, Hippólito de. Doctrina christiana en pocomchí; escrita por Fr. Hippólito de Aguilera, Predicador, cura de este partido de el Pocomché, Santa María Tactic, 2, 14 p. Br498.21 Pag 94.4. Transcription of an original manuscript, dated 1741, in the parochial archives of Cobán, Alta Verapaz, Guatemala.

66. Albis, Manuel M. The Indians of Andaqui, New Granada; notes of a traveller, published by José María Vergara y Vergara, and Evaristo Delgado, Popayan, 1855. *Bulletin of the American Ethnological Society* 1:53-72, 1860-1861. Br572C An8141 v.84.

67. Albornoz, Juan de. *Arte de la lengua chiapaneca compuesto por el M. R. Padre Fray Juan de Albornoz; y Doctrina cristiana en la misma lengua escrita por el Padre Mtro. Fray Luis Barrientos*. E. Leroux, Paris; A. L. Bancroft, San Francisco, 1875. 72 p. Br498.12 CA1 12.

68. Albornoz, Juan de. Arte de la lengua chiapaneca, compuesta por el R. P. Fr. Juan de Albornoz, de la Orden de Predicadores; copiado de un manuscrito en poder del abate Brasseur. Mérida de Yucatán, 1870. 40 leaves. Br498.12 Cal 12a. Manuscript; explanations are given in Spanish, with examples in Chiapanec, and cover topics of grammar such as orthography, verb conjugations, tenses, participles, gerunds, nouns, and numbers. The manuscript is signed by Father Albornoz on October 8, 1691.

69. Aldana, Ramón. *La Cabeza y el corazon; drama original*. Edición de la Revista de Mérida, Mérida, 1869. 30 p. Br868.1 A12C.

70. Alejandre, Marcelo. *Cartilla huasteca con su gramática, diccionario, y varias reglas para aprender el idioma; contiene ademas varias noticias tradicionales, huastecas y de la conquista española, fórmulas sacramentales, etc.* Oficina Tipografica de la Secretaria de Fomento, México, 1890. 179 p. Br498.21 HA1 2.

71. Aleman, Lorenzo de. *Elementos de gramática castellana dispuestos para uso de la juventud; nueva edición por el Lic. D. J. E. de la Rocha*. Imprenta de la Paz, León de Nicaragua, 1858. 202 p. Br498.21 AC23.

72. Aleman, Lorenzo de. Grammaire élémentaire de la langue quichée. *Proceedings of the International Congress of Americanists (5 session, Copenhagen, 1883)*, 1884. 26 p. Br572C An8141 v.55.

73. Alencar, José Martiniano de. *Ubirajara lenda tupy*. Garnier, Rio de Janeiro, 1875. 207 p. Br869.1 Al26U.

74. Alexandre, Charles. *Le crane de Remagen, le Kertag les Chevaux de Rekhmara et le livre de Cheval, de M. Mégnin*. Asselin et Houzeau, Paris, 1896. Br572C An8141 v.157.

75. Alexandre, Charles. *Note sur une troisième phalange de Cheval provenant de la Grotte de la Salpétrière*. Asselin et Houzeau, Paris, 1898. Br572C An8141 v.157.

76. Alfaro, Anastasio. *Antigüedades de Costa Rica*. Tipografía Nacional, San José, 1894. 37 p. Br572C An8141 v.146; Br913.7286 A122.

77. Alfaro, Anastasio. *Informe presentado al Señor Secretario de Estado en el Despacho de Fomento*. Tipografía Nacional, San José, 1895. 24 p. Br572C An8141 v.145.

78. Alfaro, Anastasio. *Mamíferos de Costa Rica*. Tipografía Nacional, San José, 1897. 49 p. Br572C An8141 v.146.

79. Alger, Abby L. A collection of words and phrases taken from the Passamaquoddy tongue, 1885. 15 p. Br497.11 A A13; Br572C An8141 v.51.

80. Alger, Abby L. Grandfather Thunder. *Popular Science Monthly* 43:651–652, 1893. Br572C An8141 v.119.

81. Allen, Frederic D. *Remnants of Early Latin*. Ginn, Boston, 1889. 106 p. Br478 Al5.

82. Allen, G. A. Manners and customs of the Mohaves. *Annual Report of the United States National Museum, Smithsonian Institution, for 1890*, pp. 615–616, 1891. Br572C An8141 v.124.

83. Allen, Harrison. A study of Hawaiian skulls. *Transactions of the Wagner Free Institute of Science* 5:15-55, 1898. Br572C An8141 v.160.

84. Allen, Harrison. An analysis of the life-form in art. *Transactions of the American Philosophical Society* 15:279-350, 1861. Br572C An8141 v.93.

85. Allen, Harrison. Crania from the mounds of the St. John's River, Florida: a study made in connection with crania from other parts of North America. *Journal of the Academy of Natural Sciences of Philadelphia* 10(4):367-448, 1896. Br572C An8141 v.161.

86. Allen, Harrison. Demonstration of skulls showing the effects of cretinism on the shape of the nasal chamber. *New York Medical Journal,* 1895. 5 p. Br572C An8141 v.135.

87. Allen, Harrison. Morphology as a factor in the study of disease. *Transactions of the Congress of American Physicians and Surgeons,* 1894. 27 p. Br572C An8141 v.131.

88. Almeida Nogueira, Baptista C. de. *Apontamentos sobre a abaneeñga tambem chamado guaraní ou tupí ou lingua geral dos Brasis.* Rio de Janeiro, 1876-1880. Br498.75 Gal 64.

89. Alphabet on the Delaware stone found near Newark, Ohio. *The Occident,* pp. 526-529, 1868. Br572C An8141 v.38.

90. Alva, Bartolomé de. *Confessionario mayor, y menor en lengva mexicana; y platicas contra las supresticiones* [sic] *de idolatria, que el dia de oy an quedado a los naturales desta Nueua España, è instrución de los santos sacramentos &c...nvevamente compvesto por el bachiller don Bartholome de Alua, beneficiado del partido de Chiapa de Mota.* Impresso en Mexico, por Francisco Salbago...por Pedro de Quiñones, 1634. 51 leaves. Br498.22 AzAL 88. A pastoral aid for administering the sacrament of penance to natives; includes Nahuatl versions of common Catholic prayers.

91. Alvarado Tezozómoc, Fernando. *Crónica mexicana; precedida del Codice Ramírez, manuscrito del siglo XVI intitulado; Relación del orígen de los indios que hábitan esta Nueva Espana según sus historias.* Imprenta y litog. de I. Paz, México, 1878. 712 p. Br898.22 AzR143A.

92. Alvarado, Lucas. Vocabularios de las lenguas vizeita y caché, colectados por Dr. Lucas Alvarado, 1873. Br498.21. Manuscript; transcription by Karl H. Berendt of 291 glosses.

93. Alvarez, José S. *En el mar austrál; cróquis fueguinos.* Ivaldi y Checchi, Buenos Aires, 1898. 262 p. Br918.2 A122.

94. Amaro, Juan R. *Doctrina extractada de los catecismos mexicanos de los padres Paredes, Carochi y Castaño, autores muy selectos; traducia al castellano para mejor instrucción de los indios, en las oraciones y misterios principales de la doctrina cristiana, por el presbitero capellan don Juan Romualdo Amaro...va añadido en este catecismo, el preámbulo de la confesión para la mejor disposición de los indios en el santo sacramento de la penitencia...con un modo práctico de contar.* Imprenta de L. Abadiano y Valdes, México, 1840. 79 p. Br498.22 AzAm 14.

95. Ambrosetti, Juan B. *Antigüedades calchaquíes; datos arqueológicos sobre la provincia de Jujuy.* Coni Hermanos, Buenos Aires, 1902. 97 p. Br913.82 Am12.

96. Ambrosetti, Juan B. *Arqueología argentina; cuatro pictografías de la región calchaquí.* Coni Hermanos, Buenos Aires, 1903. 13 p. Br913.82 Am12.2.

97. Ameghino, Florentino. *La antigüedad del hombre en el Plata.* G. Masson, Paris; Igon Hermanos, Buenos Aires, 1880-1881. 2 v. Br573.3 Am34.

98. Ameghino, Florentino. *Noticias sobre antigüedades indias de la Banda oriental.* Imprenta de la Aspiración, Merced, 1877. 80 p. Br572C An8141 v.12; Br572C An8141 v.71.

99. *American Anthropologist.* v. 1 (1888)-v. 2 (1889), v. 7 (1894)-v. 9 (1896), v. 11 (1898). Br572.05 Am3.

100. American Antiquarian Society. *Officers of the American Antiquarian Society, From Its Incorporation in 1812 to January 1, 1881, With a List of Members.* Worcester, MA, 1879-1881. Br913.06 Am3.2.

101. American Antiquarian Society. *Publications of the American Antiquarian Society, Compiled by Nathaniel Paine.* Worcester, MA, 1892. 26 p. Br913.06 Am32.2.

102. American Antiquarian Society. *Roll of Membership of the American Antiquarian Society, With a List of Officers, 1897.* Worcester, MA, 1897, 18 p. Br913.06 Am3.

103. *American Antiquarian; A Quarterly Journal Devoted to Early American History, Ethnology, and Archaeology.* v. 1 (1887)-v. 21 (1899). Br913.05 Am32.2.

104. American Bible Society. *Specimen Verses From Versions in Different Languages and Dialects; in Which the Holy Scriptures Have Been Printed and Circulated by the American Bible Society and the British and Foreign Bible Society.* 2d ed. American Bible Society, New York, 1885. 64 p. Br214M Am36. The text of John III, 16, translated into Cree, Greenland Eskimo, Tinne, Maliseet, Mohawk, Choctaw, Seneca, Dakota, Ojibway, Muskokee, Cherokee, Delaware, Nez Perce, and Yucatec.

105. American Ethnological Society. *Bulletin of Proceedings*, 1863. 16 p. Br572C An8141 v.58.

106. American Ethnological Society. *Transactions.* v. 1 (1845)-v. 3 (1853). Br572.06 Am3.

107. American Folklore Society. Committee of the Philadelphia Chapter of the American Folklore Society. *Folklore: Hints for the Local Study of Folk-Lore in Philadelphia and Vicinity*, 1890. Br572C An8141 v.88.

108. American Folklore Society. *Officers, By-Laws, Branches, and Publications*, 1894. 16 p. Br572C An8141 v.134.

109. American Historical Association. *Bibliography of Papers and Reports of the American Historical Association*, 1897. Br973C Am35.2.

110. American Historical Association. *Officers, Act of Incorporation, Constitution*, 1894, 1897. Br906 Am3.1.

111. American Historical Association. *Programme of the Thirteenth Annual Meeting*, 1897. Br906 Am3.1a.

112. *American Journal of Sociology*, v. 1, 1851. Br305 Am353.

113. *American Magazine of Natural Science* 1(7-8), 1892-1893. Br572C An8141 v.129.

114. American Numismatic and Archaeological Society. *Articles of Incorporation and Constitution and By-Laws of the American Numismatic and Archaeological So-*

ciety. Society's Rooms, New York University Building, Washington Square, New York, 1884. 24 p. Br572C An8141 v.120.

115. American Oriental Society. *Proceedings of the American Oriental Society at Princeton, New Jersey, October 22d and 23d, 1890*, pp. xxxv–lxxviii. The American Oriental Society, 1890. Br572C An8141 v.5.

116. American Philological Association. *Proceedings of the Sixteenth Annual Session of the American Philological Association*. John Wilson and Son, University Press, Cambridge, MA, 1884. Br572C An8141 v.84.

117. American Philological Association. *Transactions*, v. 1 (1869)–v. 12 (1879). Br406 Am3.5.

118. American Philosophical Society. *Supplementary Report of the Committee Appointed to Consider an International Language; Read before the American Philosophical Society, December, 1888*. Philadelphia, 1888. 8 p. Br572C An8141 v.26.

119. Ames, John H., trans. Memoir of the Sioux or Nadouesis; introduction and notes by Edward D. Neill. *Macalester College Contributions* 1(10): 229–238, 1860. Br572C An8141 v.10. Copied from an original manuscript in Département de la Marine, Paris.

120. Ammon, Otto. Warum siegten die Japaner? *Naturwissenschaftliche Wöchenschrift* 10(11): 129–136, 1895. Br572.952 Am66.

121. Anales de Cuauhtitlan. *Anales de Cuauhtitlan; noticias historicas de Mexico y sus contornos, compilado por José Fernando Ramirez y traslado por los señores Faustino Galicia Chimalpopoca, Gumesindo Mendoza y Felipe Sánchez Solis; publicación de los Anales del Museo Nacional*. Escalante, México, 1885. 84 p. Br972 An14.

122. *Anales del Museo Michoacano*. v. 1 (1888)–v. 3 (1890). Guadalajara, México. Br913.72 M81.

123. Anchieta, José de. *Arte de grammatica da lingua mais usada na costa do Brasil*. B. G. Teubner, Lipsia, 1874. 82 p. Br498.75 Gan 26.

124. Anchieta, José de. *Grammatik der Brasilianischen Sprache, mit Zugrundelegung des Anchieta*. Druck von B. G. Teubner, Leipzig, 1874. 178 p. Br498.75 P 69. German-language translation of *Arte de grammática da lingua mais usada na costa do Brasil*.

125. Anchorena, José D. *Gramática quechua, o, del idioma del imperio de los Incas; compuesta por José Dionisio Anchorena*. Imprenta del Estado, Lima, 1874. 187 p. Br498.7 KAn 23.

126. Ancona, Eligio. *Historia de Yucatán desde la epoca mas remota hasta nuestros dias*. M. H. Argüelles, Mérida, 1878–1880. 4 v. Br972.6 An25.

127. Anderson, Edward L. *The Universality of Man's Appearance and Primitive Man*. David Douglas, Edinburgh, 1891. 28 p. Br572C An8141 v.8.

128. Anderson, J., and G. F. Black. Reports on local museums in Scotland. *Proceedings of the Society of Antiquaries of Scotland* 22:331–422, 1888. Br572C An8141 v.128.

129. Anderson, Rasmus B. *America Not Discovered by Columbus: An Historical Sketch of the Discovery of America by the Norsemen in the 10th Century; by Rasmus B. Anderson; With an Appendix on the Historical, Linguistic, Literary and Scientific Value of the Scandinavian Languages.* S. C. Grigg, Chicago; Trübner, London, 1877. 120 p. Br973.1 An2a.

130. Anderson, Robert E. *The Story of Extinct Civilizations of the East.* D. Appleton and Company, New York, 1897. 213 p. Br930 An22.

131. Anderson, Winslow. *A Description of the Desiccated Human Remains in the California State Mining Bureau.* California State Mining Bureau, Bulletin 1, 1888. Sacramento. 41 p. Br572C An8141 v.164.

132. Andrade, José Maria Tavares de. *Catalogue de la riche bibliothèque de D. José Maria Andrade. Livres manuscrits et imprimés; littérature française et espagnole; histoire de l'Afrique, de l'Asie et de l'Amérique; 7000 pièces et volumes ayant rapport au Mexique ou imprimés dans ce pays, dont la vente se fera lundi 18 janvier 1869 et jours suivants à Leipzig, dans la salle de ventes de MM. List et Francke.* List et Francke, Leipzig, 1869. 368 p. Br972B An2.

133. Andrée, Richard. Amerikanische Phallus-Darstellungen. *Verhandlungen der Berliner Anthropologischen Gesellschaft für Anthropologie, Ethnologie und Urgeschichte* 16:678-680, 1895. Br572C An8141 v.138.

134. Andrée, Richard. Besessene und Geisteskranke, ethnographisch Betrachtet. *Mitteilungen des Anthropologische Gesellschaft in Wien* 4:60-62, 1884. Br572C An8141 v.26.

135. Andrée, Richard. Braunschweigische Bauerntrachtbilder. *Beiträge zur Anthropologie Braunschweigs* 21:123-133, 1898. Br572C An8141 v.164.

136. Andrée, Richard. *Das Zeichnen bei den Naturvölkern.* Selstverlage des Verfassers, Wien, 1887. 9 p. Br572C An8141 v.97.

137. Andrée, Richard. Der Baum als Mitgift. *Mitteilungen des Anthropologische Gesellschaft in Wien* 4:62-63, 1884. Br572C An8141 v.26.

138. Andrée, Richard. Die Grenzen der niederdentschen Sprache. *Globus* 59(2-3), 1919. 19 p. Br572C An8141 v.46.

139. Andrée, Richard. Die Masken in der Völkerkunde. *Archiv für Anthropologie* 16:477-506, 1866. Braunschweig. Br572C An8141 v.97.

140. Andrée, Richard. *Die Metalle bei den Naturvölken; mit Berücksichtigung prähistorischer Verhältnisse.* Verlag von Veit, Leipzig, 1884. 166 p. Br572C An8141 v.89.

141. Andrée, Richard. Die Pleiaden im Mythus und in ihrer Beziehung zum Jahresbeginn und Landbau. *Globus* 64(22): 1-5, 1876. Br270.1 An26.

142. Andrée, Richard. Die prähistorischen Steingeräthe im Volksglauben. *Mitteilungen des Anthropologische Gesellschaft in Wien* 3:111-115, 1882. Br572C An8141 v.26.

143. Andrée, Richard. Die Steinzeit Afrika's. *Internationales Archiv für Ethnographie* 3:81-84, 1890. Br572C An8141 v.102.

144. Andrée, Richard. Ein Idol vom Amazonenstrom. *Mitteilungen der Anthropologischen Gesellschaft in Wien* 9:253-265, 1880. Br572C An8141 v.19.

145. Andrée, Richard. Ethnographische Karten. *Mitteilungen des Vereins für Erdkunde*

zu Leipzig, 1885, 1886. 66 p. Br572C An8141 v.31.

146. Andrée, Richard. *Ethnographische Parallelen und Vergleiche*. J. Maier, Stuttgart, 1878. 303 p. Br572 An26.

147. Andrée, Richard. *Ethnographische Parallelen und Vergleiche*. Veit und Comp., Leipzig, 1889. 273 p. Br572 An26a.

148. Andrée, Richard. Metallkunde. *Mitteilungen der Anthropologischen Gesellschaft in Wien* 14, 1885. 11 p. Br572C An8141 v.71.

149. Andrée, Richard. Swingel und Hase. *Verhandlungen der Berliner Anthropologischen Gesellschaft für Anthropologie, Ethnologie und Urgeschichte*, pp. 340-342, 1887. Br572C An8141 v.4.

150. Andrée, Richard. Teobert Maler und seine Erforschung der Ruinen Yukatans. *Globus* 68(16): 245-247, 1895. Br572C An8141 v.161.

151. Andrew, William. *Gravitation, and What It Is; No Ice Ages*. Dodgeville, MA, 1895. 15 p. Br521.12 An2.

152. Andrews, E. B. Report of explorations of mounds in southeastern Ohio. *Annual Reports of the Trustees of the Peabody Museum of American Archaeology and Ethnology* 2(1): 51-74, 1877. Br913.07 H265.

153. Andrews, E. B. Report on exploration of Ash Cave in Benton Township, Hocking County, Ohio. *Annual Reports of the Trustees of the Peabody Museum of American Archaeology and Ethnology* 2(1): 48-50, 1877. Br913.07 H265.

154. Anghiera, Pietro Martire d'. *De rebvs oceanicis et novo orbe, descades tres, Petri Martyris ab Angleria, mediolanensis*. Apud Geruinum Calenium & Haeredes Quentelios, Coloniae, 1574. 655 p. Br917.29 An44.

155. Angiulli, Andrea. *Rassegna critica di filosofia, scienze e lettere*. Tipo-litografia della Rassegna Critica di F. Colagrande, Napoli, 1890. 32 p. Br572C An8141 v.65.

156. Angrand, Léonce. Antiquités américaines. *Revue Générale de l'Architecture et des Travaux Publics* 24, 1866. 45 p. Br572C An8141 v.93.

157. Angrand, Léonce. *Inventaire des livres et documents relatifs à l'Amerique*. Bibliothèque Nationale, Paris, 1887. 75 p. Br572C An8141 v.40.

158. Anléo, Bartolome. Arte de lengua kiché, compuesto por N. M. R. Pe. Fr. Bartolomé Anléo, religioso menor de N. S. P. San Francisco; copia tomada de una copia en poder de Dr. E. G. Squier en Nueva York, sacada de una copia en la Biblioteca Imperial en Paris, la cual había sido tomada del original por Fr. Anto. Ramírez de Utrilla, el año de 1744. 136 p. Br498.21 KiAn64. Manuscript; note on pp. 132-133 gives "Este Arte de lengua quiché fué compuesto por N. M. R. P. Fr. Bartholomé de Anléo, cuyo original tubo N. M. R. P. Fr. Antonio Melian de Betancur. Pe. dos veses, ministro proal. de la Sta. Prova. y ministro exelentissimo en los idiomas de los naturales y su P. M. R. me lo donó a mi Fr. Antonio Ramírez de Utrilla, de cuyo original fué traslado este de mi mano, y le acabe en veinte y seis de agosto, en el pueblo de N. S. P. Sn. Franco. Panahachel. año de 1744."

159. *Annales de Domingo Francisco de San Anton Muñon Chimalpahin Quauhtlehuanitzin, sixième et septième relations (1258-1612)*. Bibliothèque Linguistique Américaine, 12. Maisonneuve, Paris, 1889. Br497C Am3.

160. Anthropological Institute of Great Britain and Ireland. *List of Members*. London, 1881. 19 p. Br572C An8141 v.26.

161. Anthropological pamphlets. v. 1–166. Br572C An8141.

162. Anthropological Society of Washington. *Abstract of Transactions of the Anthropological Society of Washington, D.C., With the Annual Address of the President, For the Year.* Washington, DC, 1881. 150 p. Br572.06 W274a.

163. Anthropological Society of Washington. *By-laws of the Anthropological Society of Washington, With a List of Its Officers and Members.* Herbert A. Gibbs, Washington, DC, 1894, 18 p. Br572C An8141 v.136.

164. Anthropological Society of Washington. *Transactions.* v. 1–3, 1879–1885. Washington, DC. 3 v. Br572.06 An85.

165. Anthropology; extracts from the anthropological notes for 1883. *American Naturalist* 18, 1885. Br572C An8141 v.8.

166. *Antiquitates Americanae sive scriptores septentrionales rerum ante-columbianarum in America; Samling af de i nordens okdskrifter indeboldte efterretninger om de gamle nordboers opdagelserieser til America fra det 10 de til det 14de arrhundrede editit Societas regia officinae antiquariorum septentrionalium.* Typis officnae Schulzianae, Hafniae, 1837. 479 p. Br973.1 R126.

167. Antiquities of Man in America; clippings from various newspapers, 1873–1897. 81 p. Br913.7 An88. Contents include: H. C. Mercer, "An ancient argillite quarry and Indian village site on the Delaware," 1897; "Ulster Indian antiquities: remarkable pictographic Indian gravestones and gorgets" (*Sunday Telegram*, November 12, 1898. Newburgh, NY); "New archaeology: beginning of things civilized was not in Egypt, but in America; What archaeologists know in substantiation; Major Beebe's work" (*Providence Journal*, October 22, 1893); "Brinton's The American Race" (*The Standard*, October 10, 14, 20, 1893. Buenos Aires); Gaetano Polari, "The new Etruscology" (Lugano, March 26, 1893); "Central American hieroglyphics" (*Frank Leslie's Illustrated Newspaper*, April 5, 1873. New York); Frederick Starr, "Sign language in print" (*Science*, May 26, 1893); C. Guay, "Etimologies interessantes: noms tires de la langue Micmac," n.d.; Francis B. Lee, "Indian place names in Cape May" (*Star*, n.d.); Gustav Brühl, "Ein Spazierritt durch das Land des Quetzal" (*Cincinnati Bolfsfreund*, August 2, 1888); William M. Beauchamp, "The Lord's Prayer in Onondaga" (The *Gospel Messenger*, January 18, 1880. Syracuse, NY); "Zur Jörderung der Bolfsfunde, insbeiondere in Sachsen" (*Dresden Journal*, March 11, 1896); Karl H. Berendt, "Zur Ethnologie von Nicaragua" (*Correspondenz-Blatt der Deutsche Gesellschaft für Anthropologie, Ethnologie und Urgeschichte*, June, 1875. Munchen); Felix von Luschan, "Die fünflichen Berunstaltungen des menschlischen Körpers" (*Frankfurter Zeitung*, March 13, 1897); T. Achelis, "Americanische Culturheröen" (*Beitung für Litteratur, Kunst und Wissenschaft; Beilage des Hamburgischen Correspondenten*, December 20, 1896); "The Thlinket Indians; Lieut. [Frederick] Schwatka's notes of a strange race," n.d.; "Novel religious rites; dancing, poker, and holidays of religious origin" (February 16, 1897. New Haven, CT); The Asamese race (*Dibrugarh*, February 8, 1896);

Charles A. Dilg, "Frozen-up Chicago; glimpses of this city's site in the glacial period; relics of those days" (*The Daily Inter-Ocean*, July 6, 1896); "Are we changing into Indians: Results of a scientific investigation in Pennsylvania made by the distinguished anthropologist, Prof. Frederrick Starr, of the University of Chicago "(*Star*, November 15, 1896. St. Louis); Frank H. Cushing, "Relics of an unknown race discovered: Frank Hamilton Cushing, the explorer, writes of a strange pre-historic people who built little cities of sea-shells on the islands along the coast of Florida" (*The Journal*, June 21, 1896); "Assamese v. Bengali" (*Times of Assam*, April 27, 1895).

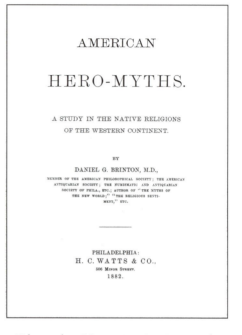

AMERICAN

HERO-MYTHS.

A STUDY IN THE NATIVE RELIGIONS
OF THE WESTERN CONTINENT.

BY

DANIEL G. BRINTON, M.D.,

MEMBER OF THE AMERICAN PHILOSOPHICAL SOCIETY; THE AMERICAN
ANTIQUARIAN SOCIETY; THE NUMISMATIC AND ANTIQUARIAN
SOCIETY OF PHILA., ETC.; AUTHOR OF "THE MYTHS OF
THE NEW WORLD," "THE RELIGIOUS SENTI-
MENT," ETC.

PHILADELPHIA:
H. C. WATTS & CO.,
506 MINOR STREET.
1882.

Title page from Brinton's American Hero-Myths *(1882).*

168. Antón, M. *Antropología de los pueblos de América anteriores al descubrimiento*. Establecimiento Tipográfico Sucesores de Rivadeneyra, Madrid, 1892. 47 p. Br572C An8141 v.113.

169. Anunciación, Juan de la. *Sermonario en lengua mexicana, donde se contiene (por el orden del Missal nveva Romano,) dos sermones en todas las dominicas y festiuidades principales de todo el ano; y otro en las fiestas de los sanctos, con sus vidas, y comunes; con vn cathecismo en lengua mexicana y española, con el calendario; compuesto por el reuerendo padre Fray Iuan de la Annunciacion*. Por Antonio Ricardo, Mexico, 1577. 267 leaves. Br498.22 AzJ87.

170. Apes, William. *A Son of the Forest; The Experience of William Apes, A Native of the Forest; Comprising a Notice of the Pequod Tribe of Indians*. New York, 1829. 216 p. Br970.1 Ap25.

171. Apes, William. *Indian Nullification of the Unconstitutional Laws of Massachusetts Relative to the Marshpee Tribe, Or, the Pretended Riot Explained, by William Apes, an Indian, and Preacher of the Gospel*. Press of Jonathan Howe, Boston, 1835. 168 p. Br970.5 Ap2. Apes, a Pequot Indian, argues that the descendents of the men who sold the son of King Philip, and more than two hundred of his subjects, into slavery still held the remnants of the tribe in slavery. The unscrupulous selectmen of any town in Massachusetts could pay the entire annual tax of a town by

seizing the proceeds of the labor of two or three Indians. Apes argues that if any active Native American whalemen, as many of the Gayhead and Nantucket harpooners were, should be entitled to a share of five or six hundred dollars, the selectmen could seize it to defray any expenses for indigent Indians.

172. Appun, Karl Ferdinand. *Unter den tropen Wanderungen durch Venezuela, am Orinoco, durch Britisch Guyana und am Amazonenstrome in den Jahren 1849-1868*. H. Costenoble, Jena, 1871. 2 v. Br918.7 Ap68.

173. *Apuntaciones para la estadística de la provincia de Yucatán que formaron, de orden superior en 20 de marzo de 1814, los señores Calzadilla, Echánove, Bolio y Zuaznávar*. Ediciones del Gobierno del Estado, Mérida, México, 1871. Br972.6 C139.

174. Ara, Domingo de. Extractos del "Arte de la lengua tzendal," por el R.P.Fr. Domingo de Ara, de la Orden de Santo Domingo. 8 p. Br498.21 TzAr 12. Manuscript; probably an extract of Fr. Domingo de Ara, "Bocabulario de lengua tzeldal según el orden de Copanbaztla," a manuscript of 150 leaves, arranged Tzeltal and Spanish. Opposite the title page reads, "De consensu superioris habet ad ejus ussum fray Alonso de Guzmán," and on the verso of leaf 128, the last of the vocabulary, "año de 1616 años se transladó este bocabulario." The following four leaves give the beginning of the arte of Ara with the title, "Ars tzeldaica facta a Ro. P. Fr. Dominico de Ara ordinis Praedicatorum." The original manuscript was replaced by a more recent copy in the library of the convent in Copanaguastla and eventually transferred to the Dominican monastery at Ciudad Real, where the last provincial of the order presented it, as well as other original manuscripts, to Brasseur de Bourbourg in 1859.

175. Ara, Domingo de. Vocabulario de la lengua española y tzeldal. n.d. Br498.21 TzV 853. Manuscript.

176. Archaeological Institute of America. American Series. *Papers*, 1-5, 1881-1892. Br913.06 Ar2.1.

177. Archaeological Institute of America. *Annual Report of the Executive Committee...Presented at the Annual Meeting of the Institute, for 1879-1880*. John Wilson and Son, Cambridge, MA, 1880. 26 p. Br572C An8141 v.35.

178. *Archiv für Ethnographie*. v. 1, 5, 7, n.d. Br572.05 In8.

179. *Archiv für Religionswissenschaft*. Stockholm. v. 1 (1898)–v. 2 (1899). Br205 Ar2.

180. *Are ua uuhil tioxilah evangelio rech canimahuau Jesu-Cristo, quereka San Marcos*. San Jose, Costa Rica, 1899. 88 p. Br498.21 KiB47.22. Translation of the Gospel of St. Mark into Quiché Maya.

181. Arellano, J. *Catálogo de las antigüedades de Costa Rica*. El Progresso Editorial, Madrid, 1892. 37 p. Br572C An8141 v.136.

182. Arenas, Pedro de. *Guide de la conversation en trois langues, français, espagnol, et mexicain, contenant un petit abrégé de la grammaire mexicaine, un vocabulaire des mots les plus usuels et des dialogues familiers; par Pedro de Arenas; revu et traduit en français par M. Charles Romey*. Maisonneuve et Cie., Paris, 1862. 72 p. Br498.22 AzAr 3.2.

183. Arenas, Pedro de. *Vocabulario manual de las lenguas castellana, y mexicana; en que se contienen las palabras, preguntas, y respuestas mas comunes, y ordinarias que se suelen ofrecer en el trato, y comunicación entre Españoles, é Indios; compuesto por Pedro de Arenas; reimpreso con lisencia y aprobacion*. En la oficina de Don Pedro de la Rosa en el Portal de las Flores, En la Puebla de Los Angeles [Mexico], año de 1793. 144 p. Br498.22 AzAr 3.

184. Arlach, H. de T. d'. *Souvenirs de l'Amerique Centrale*. Charpentier, Paris, 1850. 168 p. Br572C An8141 v.63.

185. Armand, M. *Des monuments symboliques de l'Algérie*. Bouchard-Huzard, Paris, 1868. 24 p. Br572C An8141 v.94.

186. Armand, M. Les musées d'ethnographie. *Revue des Traditions Populaires* 3(5): 241–246, 1888. Br572C An8141 v.49.

187. Armas, Juan I. de. *Les crânes dits déformés; mémoire 1o en espagnol à la Société Anthropologique de la Havane, 1885*. Société Anthropologique de la Havane, Havana, 1885. 16 p. Br572C An8141 v.40.

188. Arnaud, Charles. *Tshistekiigan tshe apatstats irnuts; 1891 kie 1892*. Kapishtikueniats Akuniguano: A. Coté, Québec, 1891. 25 p. Br497.12 MnAr6. Devotional literature in Montagnais.

189. Arroyo de la Cuesta, Felipe. *Extracto de la gramatica mutsum, ó de la lengua de los naturales de la misión de San Juan Bautista, compuesta por el Rev. Padre Felipe Arroyo de la Cuesta*. Shea's Library of American Linguistics, 4. Cramoisy Press, New York, 1861. 48 p. Br497C Sh3; Br497C Sh3a. The Mutsun occupied a valley in Alta California approximately 40 miles northwest of Monterrey, and were the most northerly tribe for whose language the Spaniards compiled a grammar. The San Juan Bautista Mission was established among the Mutsun in 1799.

190. Arroyo de le Cuesta, Felipe. *A Vocabulary or Phrase Book of the Mutsun Language of Alta California*. Shea's Library of American Linguistics, 8. Cramoisy Press, New York, 1862. 96 p. Br497C Sh3; Br497C Sh3a.

191. Arte breve en lengua tzoque, conforme se habla en Tecpatlán, precedido de la doctrina cristiana y catecismo en la misma lengua; copiado de un manuscrito en poder del Abate Brasseur. Mérida de Yucatán, 1870. 57 p. Br498.35 Zar 78. Manuscript; a grammar on the language of the Zoque Indians, preceded by a catechism translated into the same language. Originally part of a larger work which included a vocabulary, apparently copied from a manuscript by Fr. Luis González titled, "Arte breve en lengua tzoquem, conforme se habla en Tecpatlán. Se antepone un catecismo con doctrina cristiana en la misma lengua" (1652. 68 p.).

192. Arte de la lengua vulgar mexicana, qual se habla en Ezcuintla y otros pueblos de el reyno. n.d. 30 leaves. Br498.22 AzAr 78. Manuscript.

193. Arte de lengua cacchi para bien común; traslado de uno que tuvo el Pe. Pdor. Grl. Fray Joséph Ruiz, que de Dios gose. San Juan Chamelco, 1741. 41 p. Br498.21 Kar 78. Manuscript; the introduction by Karl H. Berendt describes the original manuscript as "en el archivo de la parroquia de Cobán se halla un libro manuscrito en quarto conteniendo en 192 fojas en numeraciones coherente varios escritos en

Pocomchí y Kekchí, copiados por Juan de Morales, nuestro fiscal del pueblo de San Juan de Chamelco."

194. Ashbee, Henry S. *A Bibliography of Tunisia, From the Earliest Times to the End of 1888; In Two Parts; Including Utica and Carthage, the Punic Wars, the Roman Occupation, the Arab Conquest, the Expeditions of Louis IX, and Charles V, and the French Protectorate*. Dulau and Company, London, 1889. 144 p. Br961.1B As3. The first part (p. 7–79) originally appeared in *Travels in Tunisia* by Alexander Graham and H. S. Ashbee, 1887; the second part contains books and articles formerly omitted and bringing it down to date.

195. Ashmead, Albert S. American pathological notes. *University Medical Magazine*, 1895. 3 p. Br572C An8141 v.138; Br617 As36. Albert Sidney Ashmead (1850–1911) practiced medicine until 1873 when he was appointed Foreign Medical Director of the Tokyo Fu Hospital in Japan. Ashmead returned to America in 1876 and practiced medicine in Kansas. He moved to New York in 1882 and began a study of leprosy. He helped form the 1897 International Leprosy Congress. He also pursued research in syphilis, insanity, pellagra, and Asiatic diseases, such as beriberi. In the 1890s, Ashmead became involved in a dispute with Rudolph Virchow over leprosy in pre-Columbian Peru.

196. Ashmead, Albert S. Autochthonous syphilis in Bolivia and Peru. *Journal of Cutaneous and Genito-Urinary Diseases*, October, 1895. 3 p. Br572C An8141 v.138.

197. Ashmead, Albert S. Descent and variation of the bacillus. *Mitteilungen und Verhandlungen des Internationalen Wissenschaftlichen Lepraconference zu Berlin*, 1898. 8 p. Br572.97 L524a.

198. Ashmead, Albert S. Migration of syphilis from East Asia into America by way of the Behring Sea. *Journal of the American Medical Association*, 1894. 8 p. Br572C An8141 v.136.

199. Ashmead, Albert S. Object of the Berlin Leprosy Conference, 1897. 4 p. Br572.97 L524a.

200. Ashmead, Albert S. Origin of syphilis in ancient America. *Journal of Cutaneous and Genito-Urinary Diseases*, 1895. 3 p. Br572C An8141 v.136.

201. Ashmead, Albert S. *Peculiarities of Colombian Leprosy*. American Medical Association Press, Chicago. 15 p. Br572C An8141 v.143.

202. Ashmead, Albert S. Photographs of two ancient Peruvian vases, with some particularities presented by them, and some observations about them. *Journal of Cutaneous and Genito-Urinary Diseases* 13, 1895. 2 p. Br572C An8141 v.138.

203. Ashmead, Albert S. *Pre-Columbian Leprosy*. American Medical Association, Chicago, 1896. 66 p. Br572C An8141 v.143.

204. Ashmead, Albert S. Pre-Columbian syphilis. *The Medical News* 59, 1891. 4 p. Br572C An8141 v.110.

205. Ashmead, Albert S. Prof. Bandelier's views on Huacos pottery deformations and pre-Columbian syphilis. *Journal of Cutaneous and Genito-Urinary Diseases*, February, 1896. 11 p. Br572C An8141 v.138; Br572.97 L524a.

206. Ashmead, Albert S. Racial degeneracy in America: goitre and dwarfing. *University*

Medical Magazine, January, 1896. 21 p. Br572C An8141 v.138.

207. Ashmead, Albert S. *Racial Immunity and Innoculation*. Moore and Company, New York, 1891. 8 p. Br572C An8141 v.9.

208. Ashmead, Albert S. Scarlet fever and the immunity of the Japanese. *New York Medical Record*, 1891. 1 p. Br572C An8141 v.9.

209. Ashmead, Albert S. Synopsis of a Chinese secret; manuscript on syphilis, reprinted in Japan, AD 1724, originally written by Chin-Shi-Sei, who lived under the dynasty of Ming (AD 1368-1744). *University Medical Magazine*, 1894. 5 p. Br572C An8141 v.136.

210. Ashmead, Albert S. Tuberculosis and leprosy in Japan: a study in ethnological pathology. *Journal of the American Medical Association*, 1891. 31 p. Br572C An8141 v.9.

211. Aubin, Joseph M. A. *Notice sur une collection d'antiquités mexicaines (peintures et manuscrits)*. Imprimerie Administrative de Paul Dupont, Paris, 1851. 27 p. Br572C An8141 v.128.

212. Aubin, Joseph M. A. *Notice sur une collection d'antiquités mexicaines; extrait d'un mémoire sur la peinture didactique et l'écriture figurative des anciens mexicains; mémoire sur la peinture et l'écriture figurative des anciens Mexicains*. Paris, 1851. 27 p. Br572C An8141 v.44; Br917.2 Au12.

213. Aubin, Joseph M. A., and E. T. Hamy. *Mémoires sur la peinture didactique et l'écriture figurative des anciens mexicaines; recherches historiques et archéologiques*. Imprimerie Nationale, Paris, 1885. 106 p. Br572C An8141 v.104.

214. Auburtin. Instructions ethnologiques pour le Mexique. *Bulletin de la Société d'Anthropologie de Paris* 3(2): 212-236, 1862. Br572C An8141 v.10.

215. Avila, Francisco de. *Arte de la lengua mexicana, y breves platicas de los mysterios de N. santa fee catholica, y otras para exortación de su obligación á los Indios; compuesto por Francisco de Avila, predicador, cura ministro por Su Magestad del pueblo de la Melpan, y lector del idioma mexicana, del Orden de los Menores de N. P. San Francisco; dedicado al M. R. P. F. Ioseph Pedrasa*. Ribera Calderõ, México, 1717. 13, 37 leaves. Br498.22 AzAv 5. The author was curé of Milpa-Alta, in the diocese of Mexico, and for twenty years taught the Mexican language in the convent of the Franciscan order, of which he was a member.

216. Avila, José, and Jorge Ponce. *Instrucción para el cultivo del añil en la republica*. Imprenta de la Paz, Guatemala, 1869. 34 p. Br572C An8141 v.69.

217. Ayeta, Francisco. *Vltimo recvrso de la provincia de San Joseph de Yucathan, destierro de tinieblas, en qve ha estado sepvltada sv inocencia, y confvndidos svs meritos; jvsticia desagraviada, y hasta aora no defendida, ni debidamente manifestada; pleyto con la clerecia de Yvcathan; sobre diferentes doctrinas, qve con violentos despojos, vnos con mano de jvsticia, y otros sin ella, se han vsvrpado a dicha provincia*. Madrid, 1694. 200, 123 leaves. Br972.6 Ay28.

218. Ayres, W. O. The ancient man of Calaveras. *American Naturalist* 16(11): 845-854, 1882. Br572C An8141 v.13.

219. Aznar Barbachano, Tomas. Indice alfabetico de las plantas…con sus nombres vulgares, sus nombres cientificos ó botanicos, y los de las familias a que pertenecen.

Br498.21 MAz 43. From *Secciones de botanica*, por Joaquin y Juan Dondé, pp. 229-236. Mérida, 1876.

220. Aznar, Barbachano, Tomas. *Nuevos elementos de gramatica de la lengua castellana*. Imprenta de la Soc. Tip., 1868. 255 p. Br468 Az.

221. Babbitt, E. H. *The American Dialect Society* [circular]. New York, 1895. 8 p. Br572C An8141 v.142.

222. Babbitt, Frances E. Vestiges of glacial man in Minnesota. *American Naturalist* 18(6): 594-605, 697-708, 1884. Br572C An8141 v.13.

223. Bache, R. M. Reaction time with reference to race. pp. 475-486, n.d. Br572C An8141 v.138.

224. Baegert, Jacob. An account of the aboriginal inhabitants of California peninsula, as given by Jacob Baegert, a German Jesuit missionary, who lived there seventeen years during the second half of the last century. *Annual Report of the United States National Museum, Smithsonian Institution, for 1863*, pp. 352-369, 1864. Br572C An8141 v.38; Br913.7 R19.3.

225. Bahnson, Kristian. Gravskikke hos Amerikaniske folk. *Aarboger for Nordisk old Kyndogbed og Historie, udgivne af det Kongelige Nordiske Oldskrift-Selskab*, pp. 125-218, 1882. Br572C An8141 v.34.

226. Baile del güegüence ó macho raton; comedia de los indios mangues en lengua nahuatl de Nicaragua. Masaya, 1874. 53 p. Br898.12 MG933. Manuscript; a Nahuatl-Spanish text in English translation with introduction and notes by Karl H. Berendt, including "Vocabulary of Nahuatl and provincial, unusual or antiquated Spanish words" (pp. 83-92).

227. Baissac, Charles. *Le Folk-lore de l'Ile-Maurice; texte créole et traduction française*. Maisonneuve et Ch. Leclerc, Paris, 1888. 466 p. Br398 B162. Study of Mauritius folklore.

228. Baker, George A. *The St. Joseph-Kankakee Portage; its location and use by Marquette, La Salle and the French voyageurs*. Northern Indiana Historical Society, South Bend, 1899. 48 p. Br977.2 B174.

229. Baker, Theodore. *Über die Musik der nordamerikanischen Wilden*. Druck von Breitkopf und Härtel, Leipzig, 1882. 82 p. Br572C An8141 v.65.

230. Baldwin, Christopher C. Early maps of Ohio and the West. *Western Reserve and Northern Ohio Historical Society*, 1875. 25 p. Br572C An8141 v.7.

231. Baldwin, Christopher C. Indian narrative of Judge Hugh Welch of Green Springs, Seneca and Sandusky Counties, Ohio. *Western Reserve and Northern Ohio Historical Society*, Tract 50, 2(50): 105-110, 1879. Br572C An8141 v.27.

232. Baldwin, Christopher C. Review: Man and the Glacial Period, by G. F. Wright. *American Anthropologist* 6:5-22, 1893. Br572C An8141 v.125.

233. Baldwin, John D. *Ancient America, In Notes on American Archæology*. S. Low, Son, and Marston, London, 1872. 299 p. Br913.7 B194. The most comprehensive volume on the archaeology and prehistory of America before the publication of Bancroft's *Native Races* (1875).

234. Baligny, W. Études azteques I. pp. 506-507, n.d. Br572C An8141 v.48.

235. Bamps, A. Compte-Rendu de l'Assemblée Génerale du Comité Central d'Organisation de la 3ᵉ Session du Congrès International des Américanistes. Bruxelles, 1879. 32 p. Br572C An8141 v.111.

236. Bamps, A. *L'exposition d'antiquités américaines ouverte à Madrid à l'occasion de la 4ᵉ Session du Congrès International des Americanistes.* Typographie Ve. Ch. Vanderauwera, Bruxelles, 1883. 82 p. Br572C An8141 v.111.

237. Bamps, A. La céramique américaine au point de vue des élements constitutifs de sa pâte et de sa fabrication. *Proceedings of the International Congress of Americanists (5 session, Copenhagen, 1883),* pp. 274-281, 1884. Br572C An8141 v.111.

238. Bamps, A. *La quatrième session du Congrès International des Américanistes et les Expositions de la Flore et des Antiquités Américaines, à Madrid.* Typographie Ve. Ch. Vanderauwera, Bruxelles, 1882. 226 p. Br572C An8141 v.111.

239. Bamps, A. *La science américaniste apropos du Congrès International de Madrid.* Typographie de Charles Peeters, Louvian, 1882. 24 p. Br572C An8141 v.111.

240. Bamps, A. Le calendrier aztèque. *Muséon* 5:487-500, 1886. 16 p. Br572C An8141 v.111.

241. Bamps, A. *Les antiquités équatoriennes du Musée Royal d'Antiquités de Bruxelles,* 1888. 64 p. Br572C An8141 v.111.

242. Bamps, A. Tomebamba; antique cité de l'empire des Incas. *Muséon,* 1887. 17 p. Br572C An8141 v.111.

243. Bancroft, Hubert H. *History of the Pacific States of North America.* A. L. Bancroft, San Francisco, 1882-1887. 3 v. Br972 B22. Includes v. 1-3, Central America, only.

244. Bancroft, Hubert H. Methods of literary work. *San Francisco Bulletin,* n.d. 5 p. Br572C An8141 v.58.

245. Bancroft, Hubert H. *The Early American Chroniclers.* San Francisco, 1883. 45 p. Br572C An8141 v.58.

246. Bancroft, Hubert Howe. *The Native Races of the Pacific States of North America.* Longmans, Green, and Company, London, 1875-1876. 5 v. Br572.979 B22b.

247. Bandelier, Adolph F. A. *A Visit to the Aboriginal Ruins in the Valley of the Rio Pecos.* Papers of the Archaeological Institute of America. American Series, 1. Boston, 1881. 135 p. Br913.06 Ar2.1. Bandelier's (1840-1914) research interests dealt primarily with ethnographic and documentary studies of Mexico, the American Southwest, and the Andes of Peru and Bolivia. He was the first American to do ethnohistorical research in a modern manner, to rely on oral tradition and written documentation.

248. Bandelier, Adolph F. A. *Final Report of Investigations Among the Indians of the Southwestern United States, Carried on Mainly in the Years from 1880 to 1885.* Papers of the Archaeological Institute of America. American Series, 3-4. J. Wilson and Son, Cambridge, MA, 1890-1892. 2 v. Br913.06 Ar2.1.

249. Bandelier, Adolph F. A. *Hemenway Southwestern Archæological Expedition; Contributions to the History of the Southwestern Portion of the United States.* Papers of the Archaeological Institute of America. American Series, 5. J. Wilson and Son, Cambridge, MA, 1890. 206 p. Br913.06 Ar2.1.

250. Bandelier, Adolph F. A. On the art of war and mode of warfare of the ancient Mex-

icans. *Annual Reports of the Trustees of the Peabody Museum of American Archaeology and Ethnology* 2(1): 95-161, 1877. Br572.972 B22; Br913.07 H265.

251. Bandelier, Adolph F. A. On the distribution and tenure of lands, and the customs with respect to inheritance, among the ancient Mexicans. *Annual Reports of the Trustees of the Peabody Museum of American Archaeology and Ethnology* 2(2): 385-448, 1878. Br913.07 H265.

252. Bandelier, Adolph F. A. On the social organization and mode of government of the ancient Mexicans. *Annual Reports of the Trustees of the Peabody Museum of American Archaeology and Ethnology* 2(3): 557-699, 1880. Br913.07 H265.

253. Bandelier, Adolph F. A. *Report of an Archæological tour in Mexico, in 1881.* Papers of the Archaeological Institute of America. American Series, 2. Cupples, Upham, and Company, Boston; N. Trübner and Company, London, 1885. 326 p. Br913.06 Ar2.1.

254. Bang, Willy. Beitrage zur Kunde der Asiatischen Sprachen. *T'oung Pao; archives pour servir à l'etude de l'histoire des langues, de la géographie et de l'ethnographie de Asie Orientale* 2(3), 1891. 23 p. Br572C An8141 v.46.

255. Bang, Willy. Bulletin critique. *T'oung Pao; archives pour servir à l'étude de l'histoire des langues, de la géographie et de l'ethnographie de Asie Orientale* 6(2), 1895. 4 p. Br572C An8141 v.138.

256. Bang, Willy. Ein Beitrag zur Würdigung der Pahlavi-Gathas. pp. 363-370, 1889. Br572C An8141 v.46.

257. Bang, Willy. *Études Ouraloaltaïques.* Imprimerie J.-B. Istas, Louvain, 1891. 15 p. Br572C An8141 v.46.

258. Bang, Willy. *Les langues Ouralo-Altaïques et l'importance de leur étude pour celle des langues Indo-Germaniques.* Mémoires Couronnes et autres mémoires publiés par l'Académie Royale de Belgique 49, 1893. 19 p. Br572C An8141 v.138.

259. Bang, Willy. Mélanges. *T'oung Pao; archives pour servir à l'étude de l'histoire des langues, de la géographie et de l'ethnographie de Asie Orientale* 6(2): 216-228, 1895. Br572C An8141 v.138.

260. Bang, Willy. Textes mandchous. *T'oung Pao; archives pour servir à l'étude de l'histoire des langues, de la géographie et de l'ethnographie de Asie Orientale,* n.d. 25 p. Br572C An8141 v.46.

261. Bang, Willy. Über das Verbum im Huzvares. *Giornale della Società Asiatica Italiana* 4: 218-224, 1890. Br572C An8141 v.46.

262. Bang, Willy. *Uralaltaische Forschungen.* Verlag von Wilhelm Friedrich, Leipzig, 1890. 44 p. Br572C An8141 v.46.

263. Bang, Willy. Zu den köktürkischen Inscriften. *T'oung Pao; archives pour servir à l'étude de l'histoire des langues, de la géographie et de l'ethnographie de Asie Orientale* 9, 1898. 25 p. Br572C An8141 v.163.

264. Bang, Willy. Zur Erklärung der altpersischen Keilschriften. In *Mélanges Charles de Harlez; recueil de travaux d'érudition offert à Mgr. Charles Harlez à l'occasion du vingt-cinquième anniversaire de son professorat à l'Université de Louvain, 1871-1896.* E. J. Brill, Leiden, 1896. 11 p. Br572C An8141 v.146.

265. Bang, Willy. Zur Erklärung der köktürkischen Inschriften. *Wiener Zeitschrift für Kunde des Morgenlandes* 12:34-54, 1898. Br572C An8141 v.164.

266. Bang, Willy. *Zur Vergleichenden Grammatik der Altaischen Sprachen.* Alfred Hölder, Wien, 1895. 12 p. Br572C An8141 v.138.

267. Baptista de la Concepción, Juan. *A Iesv Christo S.N. ofrece este Sermonario en lengua Mexicana; su indigno sieruo Fr. Ioan Baptista de la Orden del Seraphico Padre Sanct Francisco, della Prouincia del sancto Euangelio.* En casa de Diego López Daualos y a su costa, México, 1606. 22 p., 709 p. Br498.22 AzB 227.

268. Baptista de la Concepción, Juan. *Advertencias, para los confessores de los naturales; compvestas por el padre fray Ioan Baptista, de la Orden del Seraphico Padre Sanct Francisco, lector de theologia, y guardian del conuento de Sanctiago Tlatilulco; de la Prouincia del Sancto Euangelio.* En el conuento de Sanctiago Tlatilulco, por M. Ocharte, en Mexico, 1600-1601. 2 v. Br262.143 B227.

269. Baptista de la Concepción, Juan. *Huehuetlahtolli platica que hace el padre al hijo avisandole, o amonestandole que sea bueno.* Juan Pablos, Mexico, 1599. 95 p. Br498.22 AzB 227.2. Lacks title page, beginning of the introduction, and from leaf 87 to the end of the volume.

270. Baptista de la Concepción, Juan. *Memoria sobre la influencia del Catolicismo en la conquista y civilización de los pueblos del archipielago Filipino y sobre las costumbres y prácticas supersticiosas de los infieles que existen aun por reducir en las principales montañas de las islas.* Tipografía del Colegio de Santo Tomás, Manila, 1883. 23 p. Br973.82 B228.

271. Baradère, H., ed. *Antiquités mexicaines; relation des trois expéditions du capitaine Dupaix, ordonnées en 1805, 1806, et 1807, pour la recherche des antiquités du pays, notamment celles de Mitla et de Palenque.* Bureau des Antiquités Mexicaines, Imprimerie de J. Didot l'aîné, Paris, 1834. 2 v. Br913.72 D927. Spanish text of the "Relation" of Dupaix with the French translation by Farcy in parallel columns.

272. Baraga, Frederic. *A Dictionary of the Otchipwe Language, Explained in English.* Printed for J. A. Hemann, Cincinnati, 1853. 662 p. Br497.11 CB232. Dictionary in Chippewa. "Frederic Baraga served as a missionary to Native Americans in Michigan and neighboring areas from 1831 until his death in 1868. In 1853 he was consecrated as bishop of Upper Michigan" (*Frank T. Siebert Library* 1999:1:309).

273. Baraga, Frederic. *A Dictionary of the Otchipwe Language, Explained in English; A New Edition by a Missionary of the Oblates.* Beauchemin and Valois, Montreal, 1878-1880. 2 v. Br497.11 CB232a.

274. Baraga, Frederic. *A Theoretical and Practical Grammar of the Otchipwe Language for the Use of Missionaries and Other Persons Living Among the Indians, by R. R. Bishop Baraga. 2 ed., By a Missionary of the Oblates.* Beauchemin and Valois, Montreal, 1878. 422 p. Br497.11 OB23.3. "This monumental work is one of the most significant nineteenth-century publications concerning Native American philology. This basic text is still consulted" (*Frank T. Siebert Library* 1999:1:311).

275. Baraga, Frederic. *Katolik anamie-masinaigan wetchipwewissing, by Frederic*

Baraga. Benziger Brothers, New York, 1874. 322 p. Br497.11 OR66. Catechism in Chippewa.

276. Baraga, Frederic. *Katolik gagikwe-masinaigan.* J. A. Hemann o gi-masinakisan mandan masinaigan, Cincinnati, 1858. 224 p. Br497.11 OB23. New Testament selections in Ojibwa.

277. Baraga, Frederic. *Kitchi mekatewik wanai; ó masinaigan.* Catholic Telegraph Book and Job Company, 1853. 10 p. Br497.11 OB23.4.

278. Barbará, Federico. *Manual ó vocabulario de la lengua pampa y del estilo familiar para el uso de los jefes y oficiales del ejército, y de las familias á cuyo cargo están los indígenas.* C. Casavalle, Buenos Aires, 1879. 178 p. Br498.977 AuB 23. Dictionary of Puelche and Tzoneca languages.

279. Barber, Edwin A. Aboriginal funeral customs in the United States. *American Naturalist* 9:197-204, 1875. Br572C An8141 v.35.

280. Barber, Edwin A. Ancient art in northwestern Colorado. *Bulletin of the United States Geological and Geographical Survey* 2(1): 65-66, 1876. Br572C An8141 v.35.

281. Barber, Edwin A. Bead ornaments employed by the ancient tribes of Utah and Arizona. *Bulletin of the United States Geological and Geographical Survey* 2(1): 67-69, 1876. Br572C An8141 v.35.

282. Barber, Edwin A. Catlinite: its antiquity as a material for tobacco pipes. *American Naturalist* 17(7): 745-764, 1883. Br572C An8141 v.13.

283. Barber, Edwin A. Indian music. *American Naturalist* 17(3): 267-274, 1883. Br572C An8141 v.13; Br572C An8141 v.65.

284. Barber, Edwin A. Language and utensils of the modern Utes. *Bulletin of the United States Geological and Geographical Survey* 2(1): 71-76, 1876. Br572C An8141 v.35.

285. Barber, Edwin A. Mound pipes. *American Naturalist* 16:265-281, 1882. Br572C An8141 v.13; Br572C An8141 v.39; Br572C An8141 v.139.

286. Barber, Edwin A. Pueblo pottery. *American Naturalist* 15:453-462, 1881. Br572C An8141 v.59.

287. Barber, Edwin A. Stone implements and ornaments. *American Naturalist* 11:254-275, 1877. Br572C An8141 v.35.

288. Barber, Edwin A. Traces of solar worship in North America. *American Naturalist* 10:228-232, 1878. Br572C An8141 v.35.

289. Barberena, Santiago. *Quicheísmos, contribución al estudio del folklore americano, por el Dr. Santiago I. Barberena.* Tipografía La Luz, San Salvador, 1894. 323 p. Br498.21KiB232.

290. Barboza Rodrigues, João. *Idolo amazonico.* Brown and Evaristo, Rio de Janeiro, 1875. 17 p. Br572C An8141 v.20.

291. Bárcena, Alonso. *Arte de la lengua toba; con vocabularios facilitados por los Sres. Dr. A. J. Carranza, Pelleschi y otros editados y comentados con un discurso preliminar por S. A. Lafone Quevedo.* Talleres de publicaciones del Museo, La Plata, 1893. 234 p. Br498.97 TB 233.

292. Bárcena, Mariano de la. Notice of some human remains found near the city of Mexico. *American Naturalist* 19:739–774, 1885. Br572C An8141 v.13.

293. Barchewitz, Ernst C. Über russische Racentypen. *Verhandlungen der Berliner Gesellschaft für Anthropologie, Ethnologie und Urgeschichte*, pp. 14–17, 1872. Br572C An8141 v.162.

294. Barnum, F. *Life on the Alaska Mission, With an Account of the Foundation of the Mission and the Work Performed.* Woodstock College Press, 1893. 39 p. Br572C An8141 v.119.

295. Barnum, F. Praeces in lingua Innuit vel Eskimo-Alaska. 1896. 4 p. Br572C An8141 v.146.

296. Barnum, F. Promises of Our Lord to B. Margaret Mary [in the Inuit language]. 1896. 1 p. Br572C An8141 v.146.

297. Barratt, Joseph. *The Indian of New-England, and the North-Eastern Provinces; A Sketch of the Life of an Indian Hunter, Ancient Traditions Relating to the Etchemin tribe, Their Modes of Life, Fishing, Hunting, &c.; With Vocabularies in the Indian and English, Giving the Names of the Animals, Birds, and Fish; the Most Complete that has Been Given for New-England, in the Languages of the Etchemin and Micmacs.* Charles H. Pelton, Printer, Middletown, CT, 1851. 24 p. Br497.11 MlB27. Includes a sketch of the life of Nicola Tenesles, as well as a grammatical analysis and vocabulary of the Micmac and Passamaquoddy.

298. Barreda, Nicolás de la. Doctrina christiana en lengua chinanteca añadida la explicación de los principales mysterios de la fee; modo de baptizar en caso de necessidad, y de ayundar á bien morir, y methodo de administración de sacramentos, por el Br. D. Nicolás de la Barrerda, cura beneficiado, juez ecclesiástico del beneficio de S. Pedro de Yolos de el obsipado de Oaxaca; dedicalo al muy Ill.re y vene cabildo de la Santa Iglesia de la ciudad de Antequera. Por los Herederos de la Viuda de Francisco Rodríguez Lupercio, en la Frente de Palacio, en México, año de 1730. 119 p. Br498.14 CB273. "Manuscript copy of the first and only edition of Barreda's work, and of the only copy known of it, which was obtained in Mexico by Dr. Berendt, and sold by him to Mr. John Carter Brown of Providence" (Brinton 1900).

299. Barreiro, Miguel. *Porvenir de Yucatán y ligera ojeada sobre su situación actual.* Imprenta de R. Pedreza, Mérida, 1864. 76 p. Br972.6 B27.

300. Barrera, Marciano. *Apuntes sobre los rios de Usumacinta.* Pedreza, Mérida, 1865. 136 p. Br972.6 B273.

301. Barros Arana, Diego, and Rodolfo Lenz. *La lingüística americana; su historia y su estado actual.* Imprenta Cervantes, Santiago de Chile, 1893. 49 p. Br572C An8141 v.123.

302. Barros Arana, Diego. *Notas para una bibliografía de obras anonimas i seudónimas sobre la historia, la jeografía i la literatura de America.* Imprenta Nacional, Santiago de Chile, 1882. 171 p. Br970B B275.

303. Bartels, Johann H. Ruinen von Zimbabwe in Süd-Afrika. *Verhandlungen der Berliner Anthropologischen Gesellschaft für Anthropologie, Ethnologie und Urgeschichte*, pp. 737–744, 1889. Br572C An8141 v.4.

304. Bartlett, John R. *Personal Narrative of Explorations and Incidents in Texas, New*

Mexico, California, Sonora, and Chihuahua Connected with the United States and Mexican Boundary Commission, During the Years 1850, '51, '52, and '53. D. Appleton, New York, 1854. 2 v. Br917.2 B28. "Bartlett, in addition to being the author of the first scholarly description of the Southwest, was an explorer and surveyor of the Mexican boundary, artist for most of the lithographed plates in this narrative and compiler of the first John Carter Brown Library catalogue" (*Frank T. Siebert Library* 1999:234).

305. Barton, Benjamin S. Observations concerning some remains of antiquity. *Transactions of the American Philosophical Society* 23:181-215, 1899. Br572C An8141 v.97. Barton, a professor at the University of Pennsylvania, was the first American with scientific training to consider the question of the antiquity of man in the Americas. He contended that American indigenous populations are descended ultimately from Asia.

306. Barton, George A. The kinship of gods and men among the early Semites. *Journal of Biblical Literature*, pp. 168-182, n.d. Br572C An8141 v.146.

307. Bartram, William. *Travels Through North and South Carolina, Georgia, East and West Florida, the Cherokee Country, the Extensive Territories of the Muscogulges or Creek Confederacy, and the Country of the Choctaws, Containing an Account of the Soil and Natural Productions of Those Regions; Together With Observations on the Manners of the Indians.* J. Moore, W. Jones, R. McAllister, and J. Rice, Dublin, 1798. 520 p. Br917.5 B283. "Written by naturalist William Bartram, son of the noted botanist John Bartram, this book is a classic of the Southern frontier, detailing plant and animal life, as well as recording the various Native American cultures" (*Frank T. Siebert Library* 1999:2:47).

308. Basadre, M. *Riquezas peruanas.* Imprenta de La Tribuna, Lima, 1884. 224 p. Br572C An8141 v.72.

309. Basalenque, Diego. *Arte de la lengua tarasca, dispuesto con nuevo estilo y claridad; con licencia, en Mexico, por Francisco Calderon, año de 1714; reimpreso en 1886, bajo el cuidado y corrección del Dr. Antonio Peñafiel.* Oficina Tipografica de la Secretaría de Fomento, México, 1886. 86 p. Br498.27 TB 292.

310. Bastian, Adolf, R. Virchow, and A. Voss. *Die Sprache der Caraya (Goyaz).* Verlag von A. Asher, Berlin, 1894. 32 p. Br572C An8141 v.137.

311. Bastian, Adolf. *Allgemeine Grundzüge der Ethnologie.* Dietrich Reimer, Berlin, 1884. 144 p. Br572C An8141 v.117. Bastian (1826-1905) began his academic training in law at Heidelberg, followed by studies in medicine and natural science at Berlin, Jena, and Würzburg. After completing his professional medical training in Prague in 1850, he began a series of lengthy voyages to Peru, the West Indies, Mexico, China, the Malay archipelago, Australia, India, and Africa as a ship's doctor. He published a series of descriptive works that laid the foundations for many of Bastian's later theoretical ethnological proposals. Noting similarities among the many culturers he had observed, he proposed a "psychic unity of mankind." Bastian was also the founder of the Königliche Museum für Völkerkunde in Berlin, and together with Rudolf Virchow was co-founder of the Berliner Gesellschaft für Anthropologie, Ethnologie und Urgeschichte.

312. Bastian, Adolf. *Controversen in der Ethnologie.* Weidmann, Berlin, 1893–1894. 4 v. Br572 B296. Contents include: 1. "Die geographischen Provinzen in ihren culturgeschichtlichen Berührungspuncten" (1893); 2. "Sociale Unterlagen für rechtliche Institutionen" (1894); 3. "Über Fetische und Zugehöriges" (1894); 4. "Fragestellungen der Finalursachen" (1894).

313. Bastian, Adolf. *Der Buddhismus als religions-philosophisches System.* Weidmannsche Buchhandlung, Berlin, 1893. 63 p. Br572C An8141 v.121.

314. Bastian, Adolf. *Die Aufgaben der Ethnologie.* Albrecht, Batavia, 1898. 28 p. Br572 B298.

315. Bastian, Adolf. *Die Denkschöpfung umgebender Welt, aus kosmogonischen Vorstellungen in Cultur und Uncultur.* Ferdinand Dümmlers Verlagsbuchhandlung, Berlin, 1896. 211 p. Br572C An8141 v.146.

316. Bastian, Adolf. *Die Samoanische Schöpfungs-Sage und Anschliessendes aus der Südsee.* Verlag von Emil Felber, Berlin, 1894. 50 p. Br572C An8141 v.133.

317. Bastian, Adolf. *Die Seele indischer und hellenischer Philosophie in den Gespenstern moderner Geisterseherei.* Weidmann, Berlin, 1886. 223 p. Br290 B29.

318. Bastian, Adolf. *Die Verbleibs-Orte der abgeschiedenen Seele.* Weidmannsche Buchhandlung, Berlin, 1893. 116 p. Br572C An8141 v.121.

319. Bastian, Adolf. *Die Welt in ihren Spiegelungen unter dem Wandel des Völkergedankens.* E. S. Mittler, Berlin, 1887. 480 p. Br572 B297.

320. Bastian, Adolf. *Ethnische Elementargedanken in der Lehre vom Menschen; Abtheilung I.* Weidmannsche Buchhandlung, Berlin, 1895. 16 p. Br572C An8141 v.138.

321. Bastian, Adolf. *Ethnische Elementargedanken in der Lehre vom Menschen; Abtheilung II.* Weidmannsche Buchhandlung, Berlin, 1895. 45 p. Br572C An8141 v.138.

322. Bastian, Adolf. Graphische Darstellung des buddhistischen Weltsystems. *Verhandlungen der Berliner Anthropologischen Gesellschaft für Anthropologie, Ethnologie und Urgeschichte* 26:203–210, 1894. Br572C An8141 v.133.

323. Bastian, Adolf. *Inselgruppen in Oceanien. Reiseergebnisse und Studien.* Dümmlers Verlagsbuchhandlung, Berlin, 1883. 282 p. Br572.99 B295.

324. Bastian, Adolf. *Lose Blätter aus Indien, II.* Albrecht, Batavia, 1897. 211 p. Br572C An8141 v.146.

325. Bastian, Adolf. *Lose Blätter aus Indien.* Albrecht and Company, Batavia, 1897–1899. 7 v. Br398.2 B296.

326. Bastian, Adolf. *Randglossen zur musealen Ethnologie.* Betrachtungen über offene Fragen in der Ethnologie. Berlin, 1894. 19 p. Br572C An8141 v.133.

327. Bastian, Adolf. *Steinsculpturen aus Guatemala.* Weidmannsche Buchhandlung, Berlin, 1882. 30 p. Br572C An8141 v.90.

328. Bastian, Adolf. Über Methoden in der Ethnologie. *Petermann's Mitteilungen* 8, 1893. 13 p. Br572C An8141 v.133.

329. Bastian, Adolf. *Vorgeschichtliche Schöpfungslieder in ihren ethnischen Elementargedanken.* Verlag von Emil Felber, Berlin, 1893. 146 p. Br572C An8141 v.133.

330. Bastian, Adolf. *Zur Mythologie und Psychologie der Nigritier in Guinea mit Bezugnahme auf socialistische Elementargedanken.* Geographische Verlagshandlung Dietrich Reimer, Berlin, 1894. 162 p. Br572C An8141 v.133.

331. Bastian, Adolf. *Zur naturwissenschaftlichen Behandlungsweise der Psychologie durch und für die Völkerkunde, einige Abhandlungen.* Weidmann, Berlin, 1883. 230 p. Br572 B295.

332. Batres, Leopoldo. *IV Tlalpilli, ciclo ó periodo de 13 años.* Piedra del Agua, Mexico, 1888. 28 p. Br572C An8141 v.44.

333. Bauer, Georg. Der Forschnitt der Weltsprache-Idée. 1888. 23 p. Br572C An8141 v.21.

334. Bauer, Georg. *Spelin:A Universal Language.* Charles T. Strauss, New York, 1888. 28 p. Br572C An8141 v.21.

335. Bauer, Georg. Welsprache-Prokekte: prospekt des Spelin-Wöterbuches. Agram, Suppan, 1891. 23 p. Br572C An8141 v.21.

336. Baume, Robert. *Die Kieferfragmente von la Naulette und aus der Schipkahöhle.* Leipzig, 1883. 46 p. Br572C An8141 v.24.

337. Baumgartner, Antione J. *Étude critique sur l'état du texte du Livre des Proverbs; d'après les principales traductions anciennes.* W. Drugulin, Leipzig, 1890. 282 p. Br220.33 B32.

338. Baxter, Joseph. *Journal of Several Visits to the Indians on the Kennebec River; by the Rev. Joseph Baxter, of Medfield, Massachusetts, 1717; With Notes by the Rev. Elias Mason.* David Clapp and Son, Boston, 1867. 18 p. Br572C An8141 v.81. Includes a short vocabulary.

339. Baxter, Sylvester. The old New World; an account of the explorations of the Hemenway Southwestern Archaeological Expedition in 1887–88, under the direction of Frank Hamilton Cushing. *Boston Herald,* April 15, 1888. 40 p. Br572C An8141 v.59.

340. Baye, Joseph de, baron de. Allocution prononcée à la séance du 12 août. *Souvenir de Congrès International d'Anthropologie et d'Archaeologie Préhistoriques, 11 session, Moscou, 1892,* pp. 5–9. Librarie Nilsson, Paris, 1893. Br572C An8141 v.120.

341. Baye, Joseph de, baron de. Contribution à l'étude du gisement Paléolithique de San-Isidro. *Bulletins d'Anthropologie de Paris* 14(4), 1893. 8 p. Br572C An8141 v.127.

342. Baye, Joseph de, baron de. La sculpture en France à l'âge de la pierre. *Souvenir de Congrès International d'Anthropologie et d'Archaeologie Préhistoriques, 11 session, Moscou, 1892,* pp. 10–21. Librarie Nilsson, Paris, 1893. Br572C An8141 v.116; Br572C An8141 v.120.

343. Baye, Joseph de, baron de. Note sur des Bijoux barbares en forme de mouches. *Mémoires de la Société Nationale des Antiquaries de France* 54, 1895. 22 p. Br572C An8141 v.138.

344. Baye, Joseph de, baron de. Note sur le gisement Paléolithique de San-Isidro, près Madrid. *Bulletins d'Anthropologie de Paris* 14(4): 391–396, 1893. Br572C An8141 v.127.

345. Baye, Joseph de, baron de. Origine orientale de l'orfèvrerie cloisonnée et son introduction en occident par les Goths. *Souvenir de Congrès International d'Anthropologie et d'Archaeologie Préhistoriques, 11 session, Moscou, 1892,* pp. 22–45.

Librarie Nilsson, Paris, 1893. Br572C An8141 v.116; Br572C An8141 v.120.

346. Baye, Joseph de, baron de. Un rapport archéologique entre l'ancien et le nouveau continent. *Revue Matériaux pour l'Histoire Primitive de l'Homme* 3:477-481, 1886. Br572C An8141 v.45.

347. Beach, William W., ed. *The Indian Miscellany; Containing Papers on the History, Antiquities, Arts, Languages, Religions, Traditions, and Superstitions of the American Aborigines; With Descriptions of Their Domestic Life, Manners, Customs, Traits, Amusements, and Exploits; Travels and Adventures in the Indian Country; Incidents of Border Warfare; Missionary Relations, etc.* J. Munsell, Albany, NY, 1877. 490 p. Br970.1 B352.

348. Beauchamp, William M. Earthenware of the New York aborigines. *Bulletin of the New York State Museum* 5(22): 73-146, 1898. Br913.747 B388.

349. Beauchamp, William M. Notes on David Cusick's Sketches of Ancient History of the Six Nations. In *The Iroquois Trail, or Foot Prints of the Six Nations In Customs, Traditions, and History*, pp. 39-150. Beauchamp, Fayetteville, NY, 1892. Br970.3 IrC963.

350. Beaumont, Pablo de la Purísima Concepción. *Crónica de la provincia de los santos apostoles S. Pedro y S. Pablo de Michoacan de la regular observancia de N. P. S. Francisco.* I. Escalante, México, 1873-1874. 5 v. Br972 B38.6.

351. Beauvois, Eugène. L'élysée transatlantique et l'Éden occidental. *Revue de l'Histoire des Religions* 7-8:273-375, 1884. Br572C An8141 v.22.

352. Beauvois, Eugène. L'histoire de l'ancien Mexique. *Revue des Questions Historiques*, pp. 109-165, 1885. Br572C An8141 v.18.

353. Beauvois, Eugène. *La découverte du Nouveau Monde par les Irlandais*, 1875. 93 p. Br572C An8141 v.22.

354. Beauvois, Eugène. *La grand terre de l'ouest dans les documents celtiques du Moyen Âge.* Madrid, 1882. 32 p. Br572C An8141 v.22.

355. Beauvois, Eugène. *La Norambègue.* Brussels, 1880. 42 p. Br572C An8141 v.22.

356. Beauvois, Eugène. *La vendette dans la Nouveau Monde.* Louvain, 1882. 28 p. Br572C An8141 v.22.

357. Beauvois, Eugene. Les Chretiens d'Islande au temps de L'odinisme. *Muséon* 8(3): 346-354, 1889; 8(4): 430-443, 1889. Louvain. Br572C An8141 v.7.

358. Beauvois, Eugène. Les colonie européenes du Markland et de l'Escoeiland, 14 siecle. 1877. 60 p. Br572C An8141 v.22.

359. Beauvois, Eugène. Les derniers vestiges du Christianisme, du 10 au 14 siecle, dans le Markland et la Grande Irlande. *Annales de Philosophie Chrétienne*, 1887. 27 p. Br572C An8141 v.22.

360. Beauvois, Eugène. Les premiers Chrétiens des Îles nordatlantiques. *Muséon* 8(3): 315-330, 1889; 8(4): 408-433, 1889. Br572C An8141 v.7.

361. Beauvois, Eugène. Les Skrälings: ancêtres des Esquimaux. *Revue Orientale et Américaine*, 1879. 48 p. Br572C An8141 v.22.

362. Beauvois, Eugène. Les voyages transatlantiques des Zeno. *Muséon* 9(3): 352-371, 1890; 9(4): 459-474, 1890. Br572C An8141 v.7.

Francisco Belmar (from Frederick Starr, Recent Mexican Study of the Native Languages of Mexico. *Chicago: University of Chicago Press, 1900. p. 8).*

363. Beauvois, Eugène. Origines et fondation du plus ancien Évêché du Nouveau Monde; le diuocèse de Gardhs en Groenland. *Mémoires de la Société d'Historie, d'Archéologie et de Littèrature de l'Arrondissement du Beanue*, pp. 109-140, 986-1126, 1878. Br572C An8141 v.22.

364. Beebe, William S. Plates illustrative of American archaeology. 1894. Br913.8 B394. Contents include: 1. General views, Peru, Bolivia, South America; 2. Great Dial, Tia-huanacu, Bolivia, South America; Cosmic theory of primes; 3. Series exhibiting the influence of the Tia-huanacu dial in both the Americas.

365. Belcourt, George A. *Anamihe-masinahigan; Jesus ot ijittwawin gaye anamihe-nakamunan takobihikatewan; mih' ejittwawad Ketolik-anamihadjik.* Côté et Cie. inahiganikkewinini endad, Kebekon [Québec] Jotenang, 1859. 209 p. Br497.11 OB41. Translation of hymns into Ojibwa.

366. Belcourt, George A. *Principes de la langue des sauvages appelés Sauteux.* Imprimerie de Fréchette, Québec, 1839. 146 p. Br497.11 OB41.2.

367. Bell, Alexander M. *Speech Tones.* The Volta Bureau, Washington, DC, 1893. 18 p. Br572C An8141 v.130.

368. Bell, Alexander M. *World English: The Universal Language.* Hodges, New York, 1888. 29 p. Br572C An8141 v.21.

369. Bellamy, Blanche W. *Governor's Island.* G. P. Putnam's Sons, New York, 1897. Br974.71 B414. Extract from *Historic New York* 12:141-181, 1897.

370. Belmar, Francisco. *Cartilla del idioma zapoteco serrano.* Imprenta de L. San-German, Oaxaca, 1890. 30 p. Br498.34 ZB 414.

371. Belmar, Francisco. *Ligero estudio sobre la lengua mazateca.* Imprenta del Comercio, W. Güendulain, Oaxaca, 1892. 135 p. Br498.34 MaB 415.

372. Beltrán de Santa Rosa María, Pedro. *Arte del idioma maya reducido a sucintas reglas, y semilexicón yucateco, por el R.P. Fr. Pedro Beltrán de Santa Rosa María, ex-custodio, lector, que sue de filosofía y teológica, revisor del santo oficio, e hijo de éste santa recolección franciscana de Mérida; formoló y dictolo, siendo maestro de lengua maya en el convento capitular de N. S. P. S. Francisco de dicha ciudad, año de 1742; y lo dedica a la glorioso, indiana Santa Rosa María de Lima.* 2d ed. Imprenta de J. D. Espinosa, Mérida de Yucatán, 1859. 242 p. Br498.21 MB418; Br498.21 MB418a. Two copies with Beltrán's original corrections carefully noted with a pen on the margin; the other with elaborate manuscript index by Karl H. Berendt. Beltrán was a native of Yucatan and taught Yucatec in Merida during the middle of the 18th century. His grammar was published in 1746.

373. Beltrán de Santa Rosa María, Pedro. *Declaración de la doctrina cristiana en el idioma yucateco.* Imprenta por J. D. Espinosa e hijos, Mérida, 1866. 32 p. Br498.21 MB 418.2. Text for instructing the Yucatec Maya in their religious duties.

374. Beltrán de Santa Rosa María, Pedro. Novena de Christo crucificado con otras oraciones en lengua maya. n.d. 105 p. Br498.21 MB418.3. Manuscript; transcription of *Novena de Christo crucificado, sus siete caidas, explanación de la eucharista, loa y demás metros y naciones, compuestos en el idioma maya, por el P. Fr. Pedro Beltrán de Santa Rosa* (En la Imprenta de Francisco Xavier Sánchez, México, 1740. 27 leaves).

375. Bengough, S. E. *Key to the Art of Expression in Reading and Composition.* Simpkin, Marshall, and Company, London, n.d. 16 p. Br572C An8141 v.71.

376. Ber, M. Les populations préhistoriques d'Ancon. *Revue d'Anthropologie* 4:55-68, 1875. Br572C An8141 v.20.

377. Berendt, Karl H. *Analytical Alphabet for the Mexican and Central American Languages.* American Ethnological Society, New York, 1869. 16 p. Br498 B45; Br572C An8141 v.52; Br572C An8141 v.55; Br572C An8141 v.81.

378. Berendt, Karl H. Apuntes sobre la lengua chaneabal, con un vocabulario. Tuxtla Gutiérrez, 1870. 7, 25 leaves. Br498.21 ChB 457. Manuscript containing a vocabulary of 416 words written in Berendt's analytical alphabet with a preface on the literature and geographical distribution.

379. Berendt, Karl H. Apuntes sobre la lengua mije, por C. H. Berendt, M.D. 1870. 16 leaves. Br498.35 MB 457. Manuscript; a sketch of the literature of Mixe, its geographical distribution, and a comparison with Zoque and Zapotec.

380. Berendt, Karl H. Apuntes y estudios sobre la lengua chiapaneca. Tuxtla Gutiérrez, 1869, 1870. 88 leaves. Br498.12 CB457. Rough manuscript draft with notes on the history, grammar, relationship, calendar, etc., of the Chiapanec.

381. Berendt, Karl H. Apuntes y estudios sobre la lengua zoque. Tuxtla Gutiérrez, 1869, 1870. 63 leaves. Br498.35 ZB 457.2. Rough working manuscript draft.

382. Berendt, Karl H. *Cartilla en lengua maya para la enseñanza de los niños indígenas, por C. H. B.* Imprenta de J. D. Espinosa e Hijos, Mérida, 1871. 14 p. Br498.21 MB456; Br498.21 MB456a. A second edition of Ruz's *Cartilla* revised and edited by Berendt at the request of the publishers.

383. Berendt, Karl H. Catalogue of his linguistic collection, by D. G. Brinton, 1884. 79 leaves. Br497B B456. Manuscript.
384. Berendt, Karl H. Comparative vocabulary of Darien and Costa Rican languages. New York, 1873. 6 leaves. Br498.21. Manuscript comparing approximately 150 words in Cholo, Cueva, Cuna, Tule, Sabanero, Bayano, San Blas, Boruca, and Viceita langauges; includes a regional map by Berendt showing the distribution of linguistic groups.
385. Berendt, Karl H. Diccionario español-huasteco, formado de las listas en la Noticia y doctrina de Tapia Zenteno, de la nueva redacción que los dio Don Marcelo Alejandre, etc. 84 leaves. Br498.21 HB457. Rough manuscript draft with approximately 2,759 words, including correspondence and vocabulary by Marcelo Alejandre, who published a paper on the Huastec in the *Boletín de la Sociedad Mexicana de Geografía.*
386. Berendt, Karl H. Drei tage auf der insel Cuba. 1860. 69 leaves. Br917.291 B457. Manuscript.
387. Berendt, Karl H. Languages of Chiriqui and Darien. n.d. Br498C L266. Manuscript, containing copies and extracts of various documents by Berendt, as follows: 1. Edward P. Lull, "Vocabulary of the Indians of San Blas and of Caledonia Bay [Isthmus of Darien]; recorded by Edward P. Lull, Commander, U.S.N.," 1870-1871. 31 p. Arranged English and Cuna; probably taken from Lull's, Vocabulary of the language of the Indians of San Blas and Caledonia Bay, Isthmus of Darien (*Transactions of the American Philological Association* 1873:103-109, 1874); 2. Alexander Henderson, "Words from the language of the San Blas Indians, communicated by the Rev. Alexander Henderson, of Belize," 1871. Includes 22 words, arranged English, San Blas, and Tule; 3. William M. Gabb, "Vocabulary of the San Blas Indians," 1874. 21 p. Manuscript; contains 333 words probably taken from William M. Gabb, On the Indian tribes and languages of Costa Rica (*Proceedings of the American Philosophical Society* 14:483-602, 1876); 4. Pedro Estala, "Voces de la lengua de los indios cunacunas, extractados del Viagero universal" (19 words, arranged English to Cunacuna, taken from an edition of Pedro Estala, *El Viagero universal; o, noticia del mundo antiguo y nuevo.* Atlas Ethnographique du Globe, Paris, 1876); 5. Lucien de Puydt, "Vocabulary and phrases of the Cuna language." 25 p. (vocabulary arranged English, Spanish, and Tule; from de Puydt's, "Account of scientific explorations in the Isthmus of Darien in the years 1861 and 1865." *Journal of the Royal Geographical Society* 38:69-110, 1869); 6. Lionel Wafer, "Voces de la lengua de los indios del Isthmo de Darien." 5 p. (arranged Darien and English; taken from Wafer's *A New Voyage and Description of the Isthmus of America.* Printed for J. Knapton, London, 1699); 7. Berthold Seeman, "Vocabulario de las lenguas de los indios sabaneros, cholos y bayanos en el isthmo de Panamá." 11 p. (arranged Spanish, Sabanero, Cholo, Bayano, Darien, and Tule; from Seeman's, "The aborigines of the isthmus of Panamá." *Transactions of the American Ethnological Society* 3(1): 173-182, 1853); 8. Berthold Seeman, "Vocabulario de la lengua de los Bayanos," 1856; 9. Edward Cullen, "Vocabulary of the language of the Cholo or Choco Indians, of the Isthmus of Darien, collected by Dr. Edward Cullen." 6 p. (from Cullen's, "Vocabulary of the

language of the Yule (Tule?) Indians who inhabit the rivers and the coast of Darien, from the mouth of the Astrato to the coast of San Blas." *Journal of the Royal Geographical Society* 21:241-242, 1851); 10. Berthold Seeman, "Vocabulario de la lengua de los indios cholos," 1875; 11. Karl H. Berendt, "Chiriqui words from various sources." 3 leaves; 12. Karl H. Berendt, "Cuera ó coiba," etc., from various sources, n.d. 14 p.; 13. Edward Cullen, "Vocabulary of the language of the Tule Indians (Darien), by Dr. Edward Cullen," 1851-1853. 23 p. (arranged English to Tule; from Cullen's, "The Darien Indians." *Transactions of the Ethnological Society of London* 5:150-175, 1868); 14. J. F. Bransford, "Vocabulary of the Huatuso Indians," 1875 (original manuscript containing 42 words); 15. W. Bollaert, "Vocabulary of the Muysca, Mosca or Chibcha language, collected from various authors and alphabetically arranged by Karl H. Berendt." 17 p.

388. Berendt, Karl H. Languages of Honduras, Nicaragua, and Costa Rica. n.d. Br498C L268. Manuscript, containing copies and extracts of various documents by Berendt, as follows: 1. George Henderson, "Mosquito vocabulary from Captain George Henderson's *An Account of the British settlement of Honduras.*" 4 p. (Arranged English and Mosquito; transcript from Henderson's, *An Account of the British Settlement of Honduras; Being A View of Its Commercial and Agricultural Resources, Soil, Climate, Natural History, etc.; To Which are Added, Sketches of the Manners and Customs of the Mosquito Indians, Preceded by the Journal of a Voyage to the Mosquito Shore; Illustrated By a Map; Second Edition, Enlarged, by Capt. Henderson, 44th Regt.* Printed for R. Baldwin, Paternoster Row, London, 1811); 2. Thomas Young, *Mosquito Vocabulary from Thomas Young's Narrative of a Residence on the Mosquito Shore.* London, 1842. 15 p. Arranged English and Mosquito. Transcript from Thomas Young's, *Narrative of a Residence on the Mosquito Shore, During the Years 1839, 1840, and 1841; with an Account of Truxillo, and the Adjacent Islands of Bonacca and Roatan* (Smith, Elder and Co., London, 1842. 172 p.); includes "Song in Mosquitian or Sambo language, with translation" (pp. 77-78), and "Vocabulary, Mosquitian and English" (pp. 170-172); 3. A. M. Fellechner, Dr. Muller, and C. L. C. Hesse, "Vocabulario de la lengua de los Moskitos, sacado de la relación de los Sres. Fellechner, Müller, y Hesse." Berlin, 1845. 25 p. (arranged Spanish to Moskito; taken from A. M. Fellechner, Dr. Muller, and C. L. C. Hesse, *Bericht über die im höchsten Auftrage seiner Königlichen Hoheit des prinzen Carl von Prüssen und Sr. Durchlaucht des Herrn Fürsten v. Schoenburg-Waldenburg bewirkte untersuchungeiniger Theile des Mosquitolandes, erstattet von der dazu ernannten Commission.* Alexander Duncker, Königlichen Hofbuchhandler, Berlin, 1845); 4. Alexander I. Cotheal, "A grammatical sketch of the language spoken by the Indians of the Mosquito Shore, by Alexander I. Cotheal." *Transactions of the American Ethnological Society* 2: 235-264, 1848. Includes Grammar of the Mosquito Indians (pp. 237-256), Lord's Prayer and Introduction to the Ten Commandments, with interlinear translation (p. 257), and Vocabulary (pp. 257-264); 5. Haly. "Short vocabulary of the Twaka Indians, together with a few words of the San Blas Indians, both tribes of the Moskito Coast…communicated by

Alexander Harrison," 1871; 6. Juan Galindo, "Vocabulary of the Caribs in Central America, by Col. Galindo; from the *Journal of the Royal Geographical Society*," 1833. 4 p. Transcript, probably taken from: Notice of the Caribs in Central America; communicated by Colonel Juan Galindo, F. R. G. S., dated Government House, Trugillo, 1833 (*Journal of the Royal Geographical Society of London* 3:290-291, 1834. London; including Carib vocabulary of 28 words on page 291); 7. Alexander Henderson, "Caribe vocabulary, by Alexander Henderson," 1870. 1 leaf. Manuscript; 8. Amory Edwards, "Vocabulario de los indios xicaques, por Amory Edwards." 5 p. Probably transcribed from E. G. Squier's, Noticias de los Indios Xicaques (*Nouvelles Annales des Voyages* 4:133-136. Paris, 1858; including a vocabulary of the Xicaque on page 135); 9. Julius Fröbel, "Some words of the Woolwa Indians at the headwaters of Blewfields River, Nicaragua; collected by Julius Fröbel," 1851. 2 leaves. Manuscript; transcript by Berendt from E. G. Squier's *Nicaragua, Its People, Scenery, Monuments, and the Proposed Interoceanic Canal* (New York: Appleton, 1852. 2 v.); 10. Paul Lévy, "Vocabulario de la lengua ulba, de los indios uluas en Nicaragua, por D. Pablo Lévy, colectado en el año de 1870. Matlack's Falls," 1874. 9 p. "Manuscript. This is the vocabulary printed in Lévy's work on Nicaragua, with some additions and many corrections obtained from him by Dr. Berendt, who met him at Granada in 1874. The words are written in Berendt's analytical alphabet" (Brinton 1900); 11. Karl H. Berendt, "Chorotega o diria comparada con chapaneca." 5 p. Manuscript, with approximately 100 terms arranged in three columns, English, Diria, and Chiapanec; 12. Karl Scherzer, "Vocabulario de la lengua de los indios blancos, valientes y talamancos en la costa oriental de Costa Rica, por Dr. Karl Scherzer." 12 p. Extract taken from Scherzer's *Sprachen der Indianer Central-Amerikas; Wahrend seinen mehrjahrigen Reisen in den verschiedenen Staaten Mittle-Amerika's aufgezeichnet und zusmmengstellt von Dr. Karl Scherzer* (Kaiserliche Akademie der Wissenschaften, Sitzungsberichte, Philosophisch-Historischen Classe 15:28-37, 1855. Wien). Contents of the original include: Sprache der wilden Indianerstamme der Blancos, Valientes und Talamancos, entlang der Ostkuste zwischen dem Río Zent und Bocco del Toro im Staate Costa Rica, as well as word lists for Pipil (Isalco, El Salvador), Quiché (Ixtahuacan), Pokomchí (Palin), Cakchiquel (Santa María); 13. Karl Scherzer, "Vocabulario de la lengua de los indios viceitas o blancos en Costa Rica; colectada por Karl Scherzer," 1853. 12 p. "Manuscript copies with notes and corrections" (Brinton 1900); 14. Lebkowitz, "Vocabulario y noticias de las biceitas, indios de Costa Rica, antigua provincia de la Talamanca, tomado por Lebkowitz," 1867. 5 leaves. Manuscript, original; 15. Vocabulario de los indios de San José de Costa Rica, 1867. 2 p. "Manuscript, original; contains 128 words; it is a dialect or corruption of the Talamanca" (Brinton 1900); 16. Phillip Valentini, "Vocabulario de la lengua de los indios de Boruca (costa pacifica de Costa Rica), colectada por D. Felipe Valentini," 1862. 11 p. A vocabulary of 126 words, arranged Spanish to Boruca; 17. Phillip Valentini, "Vocabulario de la lengua de las viceitas, en Costa Rica, por Ph. Valentini, Costa de Limón," 1866. 39 leaves. Leaf 34 is titled "Vocabularios de lengua indígena de la parte sureña de la provincia de Costarica, colectadas por F.V."; 18. Lucas Alvarado, "Vocabulario de la lengua de los indios del pueblo de Caché [Costa Rica], colectada por Dr. Lucas Alvarado, Cartago," 1866. 8 p. "Manuscript, a dialect of the Talamanca, 72 words" (Brinton 1900); 19. Girolamo Benzoni, "Lengua de suere o huetares, Girolamo Benzoni; words from his *Historia del mondo nuovo* (1572), with notes." Transcript by Berendt taken from Girolamo Benzoni, *La Historia del Mondo Nuovo; la qual tratta delle isole, et mari nouvamente ritrovati et delle nuove citta da lui propio vedute, per acqua, et per terra in quattordeci anni* (G. M. Bonelli, Venice, 1572).

389. Berendt, Karl H. Lengua chorotega, o mangue y lengua maribia de Subtiaba, por C. H. B. Nicaragua, 1874. 20 leaves. Br498.12 DB458.2. Manuscript including rough notes of vocabularies and grammatical rules; includes Berendt's, "Zur ethnologie von Nicaragua" (*Correspondenz-Blatt der Deutschen Gesellschaft für Anthropologie, Ethnologie und Urgeschichte* 9:70–72, 1874. Braunschweig).

390. Berendt, Karl H. Lengua maya, dialecto del Petén, Sacluk, 1866–1867. 9 leaves. Br498.21 MIB453. Manuscript.

391. Berendt, Karl H. Lengua maya, miscelanea. 3 v. Br498.21 MB456.5 v.2–3. Manuscript, containing copies and extracts of various documents by Berendt, as follows: 1(1). Vocabulario español-maya, copiado de Waldeck; 1(2). Frases de conversación, maya y español; 1(3). Nombres de pueblos; 1(4). Borrador de un sermón; 1(5). Vocabulario del dialecto de Petén; 1(6). Palabras del idioma Punc tunc; 1(7). Numerales en maya, kachiquel, huasteca, mexicano y othomi; 1(8). Numerales en maya; 1(9). Las profecias de los mayas; 1(10). Doctrina cristiana en el dialecto de la montana de Holmul (Petén); 1(11). Vocablos de la lengua de Yucatán en Oviedo; 1(12). Forma de administrar, etc., en lengua maya; 1(13). Tabla de multiplicar; 1(14). Acto de contrición en maya; 1(15). Modo de administrar etc, en maya; 1(16). El mismo abreviado; 1(17). Proclama a los indios sublevados; 1(18). Alocución de indios a Maximilian. v. 2(1). Epocas de la historia antigua de Yucatán del Chilam Balam de Mani, con traducción y notas de Pío Pérez (f. 1); 2(2). Epocas de la historia antigua de Yucatán; tres versiones del Chilam Balam de Chumayel (f. 24); 2(3). Las profecias de los mayas del Chilam Balam de Chumayel (f. 37); 2(4). Título de las tierras del pueblo Chacxulubchen (hoy Chixulub), 1542, traducción verbal por D. Manuel Encarnación Avila, Mérida; copiado en Mérida, octobre de 1868 (f. 47); 2(5). Fragmentos sobre la cronología de los mayas de la colección de mss. en lengua maya hecha por Pío Pérez (f. 85); 2(6). Las profecias de los mayas; dos versiones distintas de la colección de Pío Pérez (f. 107); 2(7). Parte del Chilam Balam de Maní en la colección de Pío Pérez (f, 185); 2(8). Pronósticos de los ahaues del Chilam Balam de Oxkutzcab (f, 185); 2(9). Historia de la doncella Teodora del Chilam Balam de Maní (f. 225).v. 3(1). Predicciones de los meses y fragmento de un calendario antiguo copiado de un manuscrito antiguo al parecer del año 1701 por D. Juan Pío Pérez (f. 1); 3(2). Fragmento de la historia sagrada traducido en lengua maya y copiado por Pío Pérez de un a libro de Chilam Balam que fué hallado en el pueblo de Yxil (f. 23); 3(3). Las épocas de la Historia antiguo de Yucatán, texto del Codice Pérez conforma de con el del Codice de Tizimín (f. 33); 3(4). Los años de la era cristiana, etc., arreglados al compuesto de los mayas por D. Juan Pío

Pérez (f. 49); 3(5). Caución amorosa, recogida en Izamal, 1864, traducida al frances y antotada por M. Brasseur de Bourbourg (f. 133); 3(6). Invocation au soleil (f. 137)[copied from Brasseur de Bourbourg]; 3(7). Título de un solar y monte en Acanceh, 1767, traducción de D. Manuel Encarnación, Mérida, 1870 (f. 145); 3(8). Dos piezas de los papeles de la Hacienda Xtepén (f. 155); 3(9). Una orden de gobernador de Yucatán respece del despacho punctual de los correos; dirigida a los subdelegados de Sierra Baja (Tecoh), Sierra Alta (Ticul), [Beneficios Bajos] (Sotutá), Costa (Izamal), Valladolid, Tizimín, [Beneficios Altos] (Tihosuco), y Bacalar, 1803 (f. 161) [original in Yucatec by Crescencio Carrillo]; 3(10). Dos oraciones en lengua maya, copiados de una hoja suelta numerada 21, que es de algun libro manuscrito en ecuarto, la poder de D. Crescencio Carrillo, Mérida, enero de 1871 (f. 169); 3(11). Proposiciones de los indios sublevados para un armisticio y tratado de paz al cura de Chemax, Fray Antonio García, Cruzchen, enero 24 de 1850 (f. 175).

392. Berendt, Karl H. Lista alfabetica de los pueblos de Guatemala, 1868. Br498.21 B454. Manuscript.

393. Berendt, Karl H. Los escritos de Joaquin García Icazbalceta, 1870. 8 leaves. Br972 Ic13.yB.

394. Berendt, Karl H. *Los trabajos lingüísticos de Joaquin Pío Pérez.* Leon y White, México, 1871. 6 p. Br498.21 P 41.YB.

395. Berendt, Karl H. Mayikanisse artikel, n.d. Br917.2 B457. Extract from *Deutsch-Amerikanisches Conversations-Lexikon* (A. J. Schem, ed. New York: F. Gerhard, 1869-1874. 11 v.).

396. Berendt, Karl H. Mexico. In *L'Histoire de l'ancien Mexique*, pp. 261-288. Palme, Paris, 1885. Br572C An8141 v.18.

397. Berendt, Karl H. Miscellanea centro-americana. 1 v. Br498C B457.2. Collection of handwritten notes, maps, and line drawings on a variety of subjects pertaining to Central America; contents include: "Bibliography of Central America" (f. 1); "Description of the Vera Paz, by K. H. Berendt" (f. 3); "Ruinas de Tabasco y Centla" (f. 5) [including several line drawings of pottery and a map of the lower drainage of the Usumacinta River with locations of settlements, archaeological sites, and transportation routes]; "Xicalango" (f. 14); "Ruinas de Chiapas" (f. 15); Totziles (f. 16) [including pencil drawings of stela and zoomorphs from the archaeological site of Quiriguá]; "Antiguedades de Yucatán" (f. 17); "Antiguedades de Centro America" (f. 19); "Etnografia de Nicaragua" (f. 21); "Antiguedades de Nicaragua" (f. 22) [including several line drawings of shoe-shaped pottery vessels from the Sarg and Berendt collections] (f. 25); "Figura from Verapaz" (f. 27); "Colored pottery from Nicaragua" (f. 29); "Rock inscriptions from Nicaragua" (f. 33); "Noticias de Palenque" (f. 35); "Noticias del Palenque" (f. 35); "Representaciones escencicas" (f. 36) [with texts of bailes de los Kekchís de Cobán, including Caxlan Queh, Baile de Moros y Cristianos, Baile de Huaxteca, and Baile de Cortes]; Native words [in Cueva and Chorotega] from Oviedo (f. 37); and *Boletin de la Sociedad Economica* (f. 38) [with selections from the early 1870s pertaining to Lacandon ethnography, Pedro de Alvarado and the conquest of Guatemala, and the Popol Vuh].

398. Berendt, Karl H. Miscellanea histórica el lingüística. 1 v. Museum Library Br498
CB457.3 v.1. Collection of miscellaneous handwritten notes, including word lists
and vocabularies, on a variety of subjects; contents include: Yucatán: bibliography
(f. 5), maps (f. 17), conquest (f. 18), discovery (f. 19), early notices (f. 20), Francisco
de Montejo (f. 21), Juan Pinzon (f. 22), missions of the Franciscans (f. 24), Indian
wars (f. 26), geography (f. 37); Guatemala: bibliography (f. 45), chronology (f. 47); Yucatán: Providencia dictionary (f. 50), Brasseuriana (f. 62), notes on Orozco y Berra
(f. 63), notes on Pedro Sánchez de Aguilar (f. 64); Cortes expedition to Honduras (f.
66); Carib and Kerif (f. 68); Chichimecas, Tultecos, Olmecos y Xicalancos (f. 72);
Relación de Tecuanapan (f. 73); Tehuantepec tribes (f. 74); Chiriquis (f. 80); Tribes of
southeastern Mexico (f. 82), Zoques (f. 83), Totonacs (f. 84), Popolucas (f. 86),
Cakchiquels (f. 89), Kiches (f. 91); also includes a collection of a handbills pertaining to the Caste War of Yucatán titled Cronica de la Campana. Periodico para noti-
ciar los sucesos de las lineas de defensa y estado de la guerra (no. 1, September 2,
1866 through no, 18, October 1, 1866).

399. Berendt, Karl H. Miscellanea maya. 1 v. Br498 CB457.3 v. Collection of miscellaneous handwritten notes, Spanish, English, and German, on Maya linguistics and
ethnography; contents include: "Gramatica: Analytical alphabet" (f. 4), "Comparative
alphabet of Maya languages" (f. 5), "Alfabeto de los lenguas metropolitanas" (f. 14),
"Charakter der amerikanischen Sprachen" (f. 22), "Wortbildung in Maya" (f. 24),
"Maya moderna y dialectos" (f. 34), "Formación del plural" (f. 36), "Adjectivas" (f. 39),
"Pronombres possessivos" (f. 42), "Preposiciones, conjugaciones, y interrogativos"
(f. 45), "Verbos" (f. 47); "Vocabularios: Maya: Partes sexuales, Koerpertheile, Nombres
de parentesco, Plantas, maiz, medidas" (f. 54), "Bebida y comida, mammalia, Pajaros,
Beleuchtung, insectos, aves" (f. 55), "Conversaciones" (f. 57); "Vocabularios: Comparativos: Maya und Nahuatl" (f. 58), "Mexicano-Maya-Otomi" (f. 59), "Maya-Cakchiquel"
(f. 60), "Maya-Natchez" (f. 62), "Maya-Apalahchi" (f. 63), "Maya-Chontal-Kiche-
Cakchiquel-Tzutuhil-Huasteca-Mam-Pokomchí" (f. 64), "Gramática comparativa de
las lenguas de la familia maya" (f. 66); "Ethnologica: Caracter de los indios de Yucatán" (f. 76), "Costumbres de los maya; supersticiones" (f. 77), "Calendarios" (f. 79),
"Jeroglificos" (f. 86), "Antiquedades" (f. 89), and "Mapa etnologica [of the Isthmus of
Tehuantepec]" (f. 92).

400. Berendt, Karl H. Miscellaneous collection of articles and notes on the Maya Indians,
n.d. Br498.21 MB 456.4. Manuscript.

401. Berendt, Karl H. Miscellaneous collection of articles and notes on the Indians of
Central America. n.d. Br498C B457. Manuscript.

402. Berendt, Karl H. More notes in Central America. n.d. Br913.728 B456. Manuscript.

403. Berendt, Karl H. Nombres propios en lengua maya. 150 leaves Br498.21 MB 456.3.
Manuscript; includes Nombres mitologicos, históricos, de personas, oficios, de fiestas, del calendario, etc.; Lists alfabetica de apellidos de los indios de Yucatán; Nombres geograficos en lengua maya; Verzeichnise geographischen Namen in der Maya
Sprache von Yucatán; Lista de nombres geograficos en lengua maya; Das Wort Maya
als Name der Sprache, oder des Volkes oder des Landes; La palabra Yucatán.

404. Berendt, Karl H. Notas gramaticales sobre la lengua maya de Yucatán. Providence, R.I., 1864. 43 p. Br498.21 MB456a. Manuscript.

405. Berendt, Karl H. Palabras y modismos de la lengua castellana según se habla en Nicaragua, colectados y coordinados por C. Hermann Berendt, M.D, 1874. 203 leaves. Br467 B457. Manuscript; a treatment of provincialisms in Nicaraguan Spanish.

406. Berendt, Karl H. Remarks on the centres of ancient civilization in Central America, and their geographical distribution; address read before the American Geographical Society, July 10, 1876. *Bulletin of the American Geographical Society* 2:4-15, 1875-1876. Br572C An8141 v.35; Br572C An8141 v.58.

407. Berendt, Karl H. Vocablos de la lengua huave, colectados por el Abate Brasseur de Bourbourg, comparados con los equivalentes en las principales lenguas de la América del sur y en las lenguas vecinas de Oaxaca y Chiapas. 15 p. Br498.18 HB738. Manuscript, compiled by Karl H. Berendt, contains Huave words collected by Mr. E. A. Fuertes in 1870 for the Smithsonian Institution. Page 4 begins a comparative vocabulary, which is six columns (occupying opposite pages), one for Spanish, one for Huave from Charles Etienne Brasseur de Bourbourg, "Coup d'oeil sur la nation et la langue des Wabi population maritime de la cote de Tehuanatec" (Mexique) (*Revue Orientale et Americaine* 5:261-271, 1861, Paris), interlined with Huave words, written in red ink, from the manuscript of E. A. Fuertes ("Vocabularies of the Chimalapa or Zoque; Guichiovian or Mixe; Zapoteco; and Maya." Manuscript, Bureau of American Ethnology, Washington, DC); one for Quechua from Clements R. Markham (*Contributions Towards a Grammar and Dictionary of Quichua, The Language of the Yncas of Peru*. Truebner, London, 1864); one for Aymara from David Forbes ("On the Aymara Indians of Bolivia and Peru." *Journal of the Ethnological Society of London* 2(3): 193-305, 1870. London); one for Araucana from Alcide Dessalines d'Orbigny (*Voyage dans l'Amerique Meridionale (le Brasil, la Republique Orientale de l'Uruguay, la Republique Argentine, la Patagonie, la Republique du Chili, la Republique de Bolivia, la Republique du Perou), execute pendant les annees 1826, 1827, 1828, 1829, 1830, 1831, 1832 et 1833*. Chez Pitois-Levrault et Cie., Paris, 1835-1847. 9 v.), interlined with words from the same language from Thomas Falkner (*A Description of Patagonie and the Adjoining Parts of South America*. C. Pugh, London, 1774), the latter written in red; and one for Guaraní words, which is blank. These vocabularies occupy pp. 4-9. "Los mismos vocablos comparados con sus equivalentes beginning on page 12, six columns occupying the two facing pages. Huave and Spanish in one column, Zoque, Mixe, Zapotec, Chinantec, Chiapanec (pp. 12-15).

408. Berendt, Karl H. Vocabulario de la lengua de los huatusos con apuntes. San Carlos, 1874. Br498.21. Manuscript.

409. Berendt, Karl H. Vocabulario de la lengua pocomam compilado de Gage y Scherzer, por C. H. B., Nueva York, 1867. 14 p. Br498.21 PoB457. Manuscript, with extracts from Thomas Gage's, *The English-American, His Travels by Sea and Land; Or a New Sur-*

vey of the West Indies (London, 1648) and Karl Scherzer's, *Sprachen der Indianer Central-Amerikas; Sprache der Indianer von Palin (Poconchi)* (Wien, 1855).

410. Berendt, Karl H. Vocabulario de la lengua popoluca de Oluta, recogido por C. Hermann Berendt, Frontera en Tabasco. 1862. 7 p. Br498.35 PB457. Manuscript.

411. Berendt, Karl H. Vocabulario de la lengua zoque de Tapijulapa, San Juan Bautista. 1862. 13 p. Br498.35 ZB457. Manuscript, containing approximately 180 words obtained from a Zoque-speaker from Tapijulapa.

412. Berendt, Karl H. Vocabularios comparativos de lenguas de Costa Rica. n.d. 17 p. Br498.21. Manuscript. Comparison of words in Vicieta, Cache, Valientes, Talamanca, Guatuso, Guaymí, and Boruca.

413. Berendt, Karl H. Vocabularios de lenguas de Honduras y de la parte septentrional de Nicaragua, 1873–1874. 6 leaves. Br498 B45.2. Manuscript. Comparative list of some 300 glosses in Lenca, Jicaque, Chontal, Ulua, Moskito, and Garifuna.

414. Berendt, Karl H. Vorläusige Liste der Völker, Stamme, Sprachen und Dialecte von Mexico und Central America. n.d. 27 leaves. Br498 B45.3. Manuscript.

415. Bérillon, Edgar. *L'onychophagie; sa fréquence chez les dégénérés et son traitement psycho-thérapique.* Maloine, Libraire-Éditeur, Paris, 1894. 23 p. Br572C An8141 v.123.

416. Beristáin de Souza, José Mariano. *Biblioteca hispano americana setentrional.* 2d ed. Tipografía del Colegio Catolico, Amecameca, 1883–1897. 4 v. Br972 B45.6.

417. Berkhan, Oswald. Alte braunschweigische Schädel. *Beiträge zur Anthropologie Braunschweigs* 21:107–121, 1898. Br572C An8141 v.164.

418. Berliner Gesellschaft für Anthropologie, Ethnologie und Urgeschichte. *Verhandlungen,* 1895/98, 1899, 1900, 1901/1902. Br572.06 B45.

419. Bernard, Augustin. Mythologie du monde minéral. *Revue des Traditions Populaires* 4(11): 551–566, 1889. Br572C An8141 v.49.

420. Bernhard, Herzog zu Sachsen-Weimar-Eisenach. *Reise Sr. Hoheit des Herzogs Bernhard zu Sachsen-Weimar-Eisenach durch Nord-Amerika in den Jahren 1825 und 1826.* W. Hoffman, Weimar, 1828. 2 v. Br917 L96. Author records observations made during travels through the American South, including Virginia, the Carolinas, Georgia, New Orleans, and a later visit to St. Louis after ascending the Mississippi, where his southern travels ended in April 1826.

421. Berthold, A. A. Über einen Schädel aus den Gräbern der alten Paläste von Mitla, in Staate von Oajaca. *Der Akademie Übergeben* 19(11): 443–454, 1841. Br572C An8141 v.95.

422. Bertholon, Arnold A. Conférence sur l'origine des Berbères. *La Revue Tunisienne* 4(15): 465–487, 1897. Br572C An8141 v.147.

423. Bertholon, Arnold A. *Résume de l'Anthropologie de la Tunisie.* Berger-Levrault et Cie., Paris, 1896. 44 p. Br572C An8141 v.147.

424. Bertholon, Lucien Joseph. Exploration anthropologique de l'Ile de Gerba (Tunisie). *L'Anthropologie* 8(3): 318–326, 1897. Br572C An8141 v.164.

425. Bertholon, Lucien Joseph. *Exploration anthropologique de la Khoumirie.* Imprimerie A. Burdin et Cie., Angers, 1892. 85 p. Br572C An8141 v.147.

426. Bertholon, Lucien Joseph. Formes de la famille chez les premiers habitants de l'Afrique du Nord. *La Revue Tunisienne*, 1893. 34 p. Br572C An8141 v.147.

427. Bertholon, Lucien Joseph. La race de Néanderthal dans l'Afrique du nord. *La Revue Tunisienne*, 1895. 8 p. Br572C An8141 v.147.

428. Bertholon, Lucien Joseph. Le secret du Lotophage. *La Revue Tunisienne*, 1895. 22 p. Br572C An8141 v.147.

429. Berthoud, Edward L. A sketch of the Natchez Indians. 1886. 11 p. Br572C An8141 v.23.

430. Bertonio, Ludovico. *Vocabulario de la lengua aymara*. B. G. Teubner, Leipzig, 1879. 2 v. Br498.71 AB 464; Br498.71 AB 464.2.

431. Bessels, Emil. The northernmost inhabitants of the earth. *American Naturalist* 18(9): 861–882, 1884. Br572C An8141 v.13.

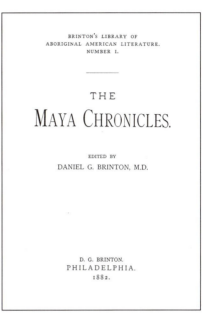

BRINTON'S LIBRARY OF ABORIGINAL AMERICAN LITERATURE. NUMBER I.

THE

MAYA CHRONICLES.

EDITED BY
DANIEL G. BRINTON, M.D.

D. G. BRINTON.
PHILADELPHIA.
1882.

Title page from Brinton's The Maya Chronicles *(1882).*

432. Biart, Lucien. *Les Aztèques; histoire, mœurs, coutumes*. A. Hennuyer, Paris, 1885. 304 p. Br970.3 AzB472.

433. *Bible Stories in the Mosquito Language, Old and New Testaments; biblia historia, testament almuk, raya sin; moskito bila*. J. F. Steinkopf, Stuttgart, 1863. 206 p. Br498.44 B 47.

434. Bibliografia indiana, 1847–1848. 130 leaves. Br970.1 B473. Manuscript, transcribed by Domingo del Monte; contents include: 1. Josef Rodrigues de Castro, "Manuscritos de la Real Biblioteca, Bibloteca Nacional, pertenecientes a la historia de Indios," 1788; 2. Antonio de Alcedo, "Memoria de don Antonio de Alcedo," 1812; 3. J. A. "Enriquez, memoria sobre manuscritos de Indias," 1779; 4. J. B. Muñoz, "Razon de los manuscritos que le guardaban en el archivo del ministerio universal de Indias," n.d.; 5. J. M. Navarro, "Indice de la colección de manuscritos pertenecientes á la historia de Indias que escriba... J. M. Muñoz," 1799.

435. *Bibliotheca Americana; Catalogue of a...Collection of Books and Pamphlets Relating to America*. Robert Clarke and Company, Cincinnati, 1886. 280, 51 p. Br970B C55a.

436. *Bibliotheca Americana; Catalogue of a...Collection of Books and Pamphlets Relating to America*; Supplement. Robert Clarke and Company, Cincinnati, 1887. 56 p. Br970B C55a Sup.

437. Biet, Antoine. Les Gabilis. *Revue Linguistique*, 1896. 106 p. Br572C An8141 v.147.

438. Biolley, Paul. *Costa Rica and Her Future, by Paul Biolley...Translated from the French by Cecil Charles, Study Accompanied by a Map...Drawn by F. Montesdeo- ca.* Judd and Detweiler, Printers, Washington, DC, 1889. 96 p. Br572C An8141 v.63. Br572C An8141 v.63.

439. Biondelli, Bernardino. *Evangeliarium Epistolarium et Lectionarium Aztecum sive Mexicanum ex antiquo codice Mexicano nuper reperto depromptum cum præfatione interpretatione adnotationibus glossario edidit Bernardinus Bion- delli.* Typis Jos. Bernardoni qm. Johannis, Mediolani, 1858. 574 p. Br498.22 AzB 473. Epistles and Gospels translated into Nahuatl.

440. Biondelli, Bernardino. *Glossarium azteco-latinum et latino-aztecum curâ et studio Bernardini Biondelli collectum ac digestum.* Valentiner et Mues, Medi- olani, 1869. 256 p. Br498.22 AzB 52. A reprint of the *Glossarium azteco-lat- inum in the Evangeliarium, Epistolarium et Lectionarium Aztecum sive Mexicanum ex antiquo codice mexicano nuper reperto depromptum cum præfatione interpretatione adnotationibus glossario edidit Bernardus Bion- delli*, Medioiani, 1858-1860, p. 427-553, with the addition of the *Glossarium latino-aztecum*, 1869.

441. Bissel, Johann. *Argonauticon America-norum, sive, historiae periculorum Petri de Victoria; ac sociorum eius, libri XV.* Straub for J. Wagner, Munich, 1647. 480 p. Br973.1 V835. The bibliographies falsely call this a translation of the pamphlet of Pedro Gobeo de Vitoria, Seville, 1610, via the German translation, Ingolstadt, 1622. Actually it is a novel of high literary accomplishment that uses Gobeo's simple, un- structured account merely as raw material.

442. Black, G. F. Notes on a silver-mounted charm-stone of rock-crystal from Inverleny. *Proceedings of the Society of Antiquaries of Scotland* 29:438-448, 1895. Br572C An8141 v.138.

443. Black, G. F. Notice of stone implements, etc., from Asia and Africa, in the National Collection. *Proceedings of the Society of Antiquaries of Scotland* 26:398-412, 1892. Br572C An8141 v.128.

444. Black, G. F. Notice of two sculptured stones at Kirk Andreas, Isle of Man. *Proceed- ings of the Society of Antiquaries of Scotland* 23:332-343, 1889. Br572C An8141 v.128.

445. Black, G. F. Report on the archaeological investigation of the Culbin Sands, Elgin- shire, obtained under the Victoria Jubilee Gift of His Excellency. *Proceedings of the Society of Antiquaries of Scotland* 25:485-511, 1891. Br572C An8141 v.128.

446. Black, G. F. Reports on local museums in Scotland. *Proceedings of the Society of An- tiquaries of Scotland* 22:331-422, 1888. Br572C An8141 v.128.

447. Black, G. F. Scottish charms and amulets. *Proceedings of the Society of Antiquaries of Scotland* 27:433-526, 1894. Br572C An8141 v.135.

448. Blackmar, Frank W. Indian education. *Annals of the American Academy of Politi- cal and Social Science* 2(6): 813-837, 1892. Br572C An8141 v.89.

449. Blake, John H. Notes on a collection from the ancient cemetery at the Bay of

Chacota, Peru. *Annual Reports of the Trustees of the Peabody Museum of American Archaeology and Ethnology* 2(2): 277-304, 1878. Br572C An8141 v.19; Br913.07 H265.

450. Blake, W.W. *Catalogue of the Collections, Historical and Archaeological, of the National Museum of Mexico.* Burlington: Hawkeye Job Print, 1864. 119 p. Br572C An8141 v.74.

451. Blanchard, Raphaël. *Traité zoologie médicale.* Paris, 1886. Br572C An8141 v.10.

452. Blasius, Wilhelm. Spuren paläolithischer Menschen in den Diluvial-Ablagerungen der Rübeländer Höhlen. *Beiträge zur Anthropologie Braunschweigs* 21:1-37, 1898. Br572C An8141 v.164.

453. Blatchford, Henry, and Sherman Hall. *Iu Otoshki-Kikindiuin au tebenimineng gaie bemajiineng Jesus Christ; ima Ojibue inuenining giizhitong; the New Testament of Our Lord and Saviour Jesus Christ; Translated into the Language of the Ojibwa Indians.* American Bible Society, New York, 1875. 717 p. Br497.11 OB47.

454. Bliss, John P. Vocablos de la lengua chontal de Oaxaca, recogidos en San Miguel Ecatepec, por John Porter Bliss, 1871; comparados con el chontal de otras partes. 3 p. Br498.21CoB614. Manuscript.

455. Blondell, Spire. *Recherches sur les bijoux des peuples primitifs.* Paris, 1876. 43 p. Br572C An8141 v.40.

456. Blumentritt, Ferdinand. *Alphabetisches verzeichnis der bei den philippinischen Eingebornen üblichen Eigennamen, welche auf Religion, Opfer und priesterliche Titel und Amtsverrichtungen sich Beziehen.* Germany?, 1894. 238 p. Br499.216B B 628.

457. Boardman, George D. *The Parliament of Religions; An Address Before the Philadelphia Conference of Baptist Ministers, October 23, 1893.* 2d ed. National Baptist Print, Philadelphia, 1893. 16 p. Br270 B63.

458. Boardman, Timothy. *Log-Book of Timothy Boardman; Kept on Board the Privateer Oliver Cromwell, During a Cruise from New London, Ct., to Charleston, S.C., and Return, in 1778; Also, a Biographical Sketch of the Author.* Joel Munsell's Sons, Albany, NY, 1885. 85 p. Br910.9 B63.

459. Boas, Franz. A year among the Eskimo. *Journal of the American Geographical Society* 19:383-402, 1887. Br572C An8141 v.23. Boas (1858-1942) was one of the most influential American anthropologists. He studied physics and geography at Heidelberg and Bonn before receiving his doctorate from Kiel. His interest in ethnography developed after observation of the Eskimos made during a scientific expedition to Baffin Island in 1883-1884. In 1886 he made the first of many trips to the North Pacific Coast to study the Kwakiutl and other tribes of British Columbia. In 1887 he became a permanent resident of the United States and in 1896 joined the faculty at Columbia University. He published widely on language, religion, and the material culture of North American Indians. During his tenure at Columbia, Boas created one of the foremost departments of anthropology in the United States, and trained or influenced many important ethnologists and linguists. Boas established the *International Journal of American Linguistics*, was one of

the founders of the American Anthropological Association, and president of the American Association for the Advancement of Science.

460. Boas, Franz. Anthropometrical observations on the Mission Indians of southern California. *Proceedings of the American Association for the Advancement of Science* 44:261-269, 1895. Br572C An8141 v.147.

461. Boas, Franz. Arctic exploration and its object. *Popular Science Monthly*:78-81, 1910. Br572C An8141 v.23.

462. Boas, Franz. Census and reservations of the Kwakiutl nation. *Bulletin of the American Geographical Society* 19(3): 225-232, 1887. Br572C An8141 v.23.

463. Boas, Franz. Chinook songs. *Journal of American Folk-Lore* 1:220-226, 1888. Br572C An8141 v.27.

464. Boas, Franz. *Chinook Texts.* Bulletin of the Bureau of Ethnology, 20. Smithsonian Institution, Washington, DC, 1894. 278 p. Br398.22 CB632.

465. Boas, Franz. Classification of the languages of the North Pacific Coast. *Memoirs of the International Congress of Americanists*, pp. 339-346. Schulte, Chicago, 1894. Br572C An8141 v.137.

466. Boas, Franz. Cranium from Progreso, Yucatan. *Proceedings of the American Antiquarian Society* 6(3): 350-357, 1890. Br572C An8141 v.12.

467. Boas, Franz. Der Eskimo-Dialekt des Cumberland-Sundes. *Mitteilungen der Anthropologischen Gesellschaft in Wien* 24:97-114, 1894. Br572C An8141 v.144.

468. Boas, Franz. Die Entwicklung der Geheimbünde der Kwakiutl-Indianer. In *Bastian Festschrift*, pp. 435-443. Verlag von Dietrich Reimer (Ernst Vohsen), Berlin, 1896. Br572C An8141 v.147.

469. Boas, Franz. Die Eskimos des Baffinlandes. *Verhandlungen des Fünften Deutschen Geographentages zu Hamburg* 1(1): 5-14, 1885. Br572C An8141 v.23.

470. Boas, Franz. Die religiösen Vorstellungen und einige Gebräuche der zentralen Eskimos. *Petermanns Mitteilungen* 10:302-316, 1887. Br572C An8141 v.96.

471. Boas, Franz. Die Tsimschian. *Zeitschrift für Ethnologie* 20:231-247, 1888. Br572C An8141 v.83.

472. Boas, Franz. Dissemination of tales among the natives of North America. *Journal of American Folk-Lore* 4:13-20, 1891. Br572C An8141 v.11.

473. Boas, Franz. Dr. William Townsend Porter's Untersuchungen über das Wachsthum der Kinder von St. Louis. *Correspondenz-Blatt der Deutschen Anthropologischen Gesellschaft* 6:42-46, 1895. Br572C An8141 v.144.

474. Boas, Franz. Eskimo tales and songs. *Journal of American Folk-Lore* 7:109-116, 1884. Br572C An8141 v.147.

475. Boas, Franz. Eskimo tales and songs. *Journal of American Folk-Lore* 10:45-50, 1887. Br572C An8141 v.137.

476. Boas, Franz. Gleanings from the Emmons Collection of ethnological specimens from Alaska. *Journal of American Folk-Lore* 1(3): 215-219, 1888. Br572C An8141 v.27.

477. Boas, Franz. Human faculty as determined by race. *Proceedings of the American Association for the Advancement of Science* 43, 1894. 29 p. Br572C An8141 v.137.

478. Boas, Franz. Introduction [to James Teit's Traditions of the Thompson River Indians

of British Columbia]. *Memoirs of the American Folk-Lore Society* 6, 1898, 18 p. Br398.22 NeB633.

479. Boas, Franz. Mythologie der Indianer von Washington und Oregon. *Globus* 63(10-12), n.d. 9 p. Br572C An8141 v.107.

480. Boas, Franz. Myths and legends of the Catlotq of Vancouver Island. *American Antiquarian* 20(4): 201-211, 1888. Br572C An8141 v.20; Br572C An8141 v.27.

481. Boas, Franz. Northern elements in the mythology of the Navajo. *American Anthropologist* 10:371-376, 1897. Br572C An8141 v.147.

482. Boas, Franz. Notes on Pacific Coast, 1891. *Verhandlungen der Berliner Anthropologischen Gesellschaft für Anthropologie, Ethnologie und Urgeschichte,* n.d. Br572C An8141 v.7. Br572C An8141 v.7.

483. Boas, Franz. Notes on the Chemakum language. *American Anthropologist* 5:37-444, 1892. Br572C An8141 v.48.

484. Boas, Franz. Notes on the Chinook language. *American Anthropologist* 6:55-63, 1893. Br572C An8141 v.115.

485. Boas, Franz. Notes on the Eskimo of Port Clarence, Alaska. *Journal of American Folk-Lore* 7(26): 205-208, 1894. Br572C An8141 v.137.

486. Boas, Franz. Notes on the Snanaimuq. *American Anthropologist* 2(4): 321-328, 1889. Br572C An8141 v.23.

487. Boas, Franz. On alternating sounds. *American Anthropologist* 2(1): 47-53, 1889. Br572C An8141 v.51.

488. Boas, Franz. Physical anthropology: the anthropology of the North American Indian. *Memoirs of the International Congress of Americanists,* pp. 37-49, n.d. Br572C An8141 v.137.

489. Boas, Franz. Physical characteristics of the Indians of the North Pacific Coast. *American Anthropologist* 4:25-32, 1891. Br572C An8141 v.10.

490. Boas, Franz. Reise im Baffinlande 1883 und 1884. *Verhandlungen der Gesellschaft für Erdkunde zu Berlin* 5-6, 1885. 10 p. Br572C An8141 v.23.

491. Boas, Franz. Sagen der Eskimos von Baffin-Land. *Verhandlungen der Berliner Anthropologischen Gesellschaft für Anthropologie, Ethnologie und Urgeschichte* 20:398-405, 1888. Br572C An8141 v.83.

492. Boas, Franz. Salishan texts. *Proceedings of the American Philosophical Society* 34:31-48, 1895. Br572C An8141 v.131.

493. Boas, Franz. Seventh Report on the North-Western tribes of Canada. n.d. Br572C An8141 v.10.

494. Boas, Franz. Songs of the Kwakiutl Indians. *Internationales Archiv für Ethnographie* 9:1-9, 1896. Br572C An8141 v.161.

495. Boas, Franz. Sprache der Bella-Coola-Indianer. *Verhandlungen der Berliner Anthropologischen Gesellschaft für Anthropologie, Ethnologie und Urgeschichte,* pp. 203-206, 1886. Br572C An8141 v.4.

496. Boas, Franz. The Central Eskimo. *Annual Report of the Bureau of Ethnology, Smithsonian Institution, for 1884-1885,* pp. 399-669, 1888. Br970.3 EB633.

497. Boas, Franz. The correlation of anatomical or physiological measurements. *Ameri-*

can Anthropologist 7:313–324, 1894. Br572C An8141 v.137.

498. Boas, Franz. The decorative art of the Indians of the North Pacific Coast. *Science* 4(82), 1896. 3 p. Br572C An8141 v.160.

499. Boas, Franz. The decorative art of the Indians of the North Pacific Coast. *Bulletin of the American Museum of Natural History* 9:123–176, 1897. Br572C An8141 v.147.

500. Boas, Franz. The doctrine of souls and of disease among the Chinook Indians. *Journal of American Folk-Lore* 6(20): 39–43, 1893. Br572C An8141 v.124.

501. Boas, Franz. The form of the head as influenced by growth. *Science* 4(80), 1896. 2 p. Br572C An8141 v.160.

502. Boas, Franz. The growth of Indian mythologies: a study based upon the growth of the mythologies of the North-Pacific Coast. *Journal of American Folk-Lore* 9(32): 1–11, 1896. Br572C An8141 v.147.

503. Boas, Franz. The half-blood Indian: an anthropometric study. *Popular Science Monthly*, October, 1894. 11 p. Br572C An8141 v.137.

504. Boas, Franz. The houses of the Kwakiutl Indians, British Columbia. *Proceedings of the United States National Museum, Smithsonian Institution* 12:197–213, 1888. Br572C An8141 v.23.

505. Boas, Franz. *The Indian Tribes of the Lower Fraser River*. Spottswoode and Company, London, 1894. 11 p. Br572C An8141 v.137.

506. Boas, Franz. The Indians of British Columbia. *Popular Science Monthly* 28(3): 229–243, 1899. Br572C An8141 v.23; Br572C An8141 v.147.

507. Boas, Franz. *The North-Western Tribes of Canada: Eleventh Report*. Spottiswoode and Company, London, 1896. 23 p. Br572C An8141 v.147.

508. Boas, Franz. Traditions of the Ts-ets'aut. *Journal of American Folk-Lore* 9:257–268, 1896. Br572C An8141 v.147.

509. Boas, Franz. *Tsimshian Texts*. Bulletin of the Bureau of Ethnology, 27. Smithsonian Institution, Washington, DC, 1902. 244 p. Br398.22 NB632.

510. Boas, Franz. Vocabularies of the Tlingit, Haida, and Tsimshian languages; read before the American Philosophical Society, October 2, 1891. *Proceedings of the American Philosophical Society* 29:173–208, 1891. Br572C An8141 v.48.

511. Boas, Franz. Vocabulary of the Kwakiutl language. *Proceedings of the American Philosophical Society* 30:34–82, 1892. Br572C An8141 v.115.

512. Boas, Franz. Zur Anthropologie der nordamerikanischen Indianer. *Verhandlungen der Berliner Anthropologischen Gesellschaft für Anthropologie, Ethnologie und Urgeschichte*, pp. 367–411, 1895. Br572C An8141 v.138.

513. Boban, Eugène. *Catalogue of the Extensive Archaeological Collection of Monsieur Eugène Boban, Comprising Antiquities of Mexico, Guatemala, Central and South America, Egypt, Greece, Rome and Gaul, Antique Gems, Cut and Polished Stones, Jade, Ivory, Jewelry Boxes, Curios, etc., Also Collections or Specimens Relating to Ethnography, Anthropology, Paleontology, Mineralogy, Geology, crystalography, etc., Pre-Historic Implements, Coins and Medals, etc., etc., etc.* George A. Leavitt and Company, New York, 1886–1887, 187 p. Br913.72B B633.

514. Bobán, Eugène. *Museo cientifico.* Tipografía de A. Vanegas, calle de la Encarnación, Mexico, 1885. Br572C An8141 v.71.

515. Boddam-Whetham, John W. *Across Central America.* Hurst and Blackett, London, 1877. 353 p. Br917.28 W576.

516. Boehmer, George H. Prehistoric naval architecture of the north of Europe. *Annual Report of the United States National Museum, Smithsonian Institution, for 1891,* pp. 527-647, 1893. Br572C An8141 v.120.

517. Boggiani, Guido. *Discusiones sobre filología etnográfica y geografía histórica.* Guido Boggiani, Asunción, 1899. 134 p. Br498.75 GB 63. An historical geography of Paraguay. Boggiani (1861-1901), trained in design and painting, spent six years in the interior of Paraguay and the Mato Grosso painting, collecting specimens, and gathering anthropological information on the Chamacoco people of the Paraguayan Gran Chaco and on the Caduveo of the Nabileque River of Brazil. He was killed in 1901 as he tried to penetrate the jungle of the Gran Chaco area to study the inhabitants of the Paraguay River. The rich ethnological collections gathered by Boggiani were acquired by the Museo Preistorico-Etnografico of Rome and by the Museum für Völkerlkunde of Berlin.

518. Boggiani, Guido. En favor de los indios. *Revista del Instituto Paraguayo* 2(11): 168-183, 1898. Br572C An8141 v.164.

519. Boggiani, Guido. Etnografia del alto Paraguay. *Boletin del Geografico Argentino* 18(10-12), 1898. 15 p. Br572C An8141 v.164.

520. Boggiani, Guido. *Guaicurú; sul nome posizione geografica e rapporti etnici e linguistici di alcune tribù.* Presso la Società Geografica Italiana, Roma, 1899. 55 p. Br498.97 B63.

521. Boggiani, Guido. *I caduvei.* Presso la Società Geografica Italiana, Roma, 1895. 59 p. Br572C An8141 v.144.

522. Boggiani, Guido. *I Ciamacoco; conferenza tenuta in Roma alla Società geografica italiana, il giorno 2 giugno, 1894.* Società Romana per l'Antropologia, Rome, 1894. 126 p. Br498.97 CB 63. Includes vocabulary of Chamacoco Indians on pp. 97-122.

523. Boggiani, Guido. *Nei dintorni di Corumbà (Brasile).* Presso la Società Geografica Italiana, Roma, 1897. 15 p. Br913.81 B633. Extract from *Bollettino della Società Geografica Italiana* (fascicles 10-11, 1897).

524. Boggiani, Guido. *Tatuaggio o pittura?* Stabilimiento Tipografico G. Civelli, Roma, 1895. 32 p. Br572C An8141 v.144.

525. Boggiani, Guido. *Viaggi d'un artista nell' America Meriodionale. I Caduvei (Mbayá o Guaycurú) con prefazio ed uno studio storico ed etnbografico dell dott. G.A. Colini, 112 figure intercalate nel testo ed una carta geografica; pubblicato col concorso della Società Geografica Italiana di Roma.* E. Loescher, Roma, 1895. 339 p. Br572.98 B63. Includes Vocabolario dell' idioma Caduevo (pp. 253-270); Notizie storiche ed etnografiche sopra i Guaycurú e gli Mbayá, studio del dott. G. A. Colini (pp. 285-335); Bibliografia sull'idioma Caduveo, Mbayá, Guaycurú, Eyiguayégi etc. (pp. 249-251). Ethnographic and linguistic notes on the Caduveo, Mbayá, and Guaycuru Indians.

526. Boggiani, Guido. Vocabulario dell'idioma Guana'. *Memorie della Classe di Scienze Morali, Storiche e Filologische* 3:57–80, 1895. Br572C An8141 v.144.

527. *Boletín de la Sociedad Geográfica de Lima: sumario.* Imprenta Liberal, Lima, 1893. 120 p. Br572C An8141 v.113.

528. Bollack, Léon. *Editions of the Blue Language; Bolak, International Practical Language.* P. Dupont, Paris, 1899. 8 p. Br409.9 L135. Includes The Blue language, by Raoul de LaGrasserie (pp. 3–7).

529. Bollack, Léon. *La langue Bleue-Bolak—langue internationale pratique.* Éditions de la Langue Bleue, Paris, 1899. 479 p. Br409.09 B63.

530. Bolles, T. Dix. Chinese relics in Alaska. *Proceedings of the United States National Museum, Smithsonian Institution* 15:221, 1899. Br572C An8141 v.82.

531. Bölsche, Wilhelm. *Das Liebesleben in der Natur.* Eugen Diederichs, Florenz, Leipzig, 1898–1900. 2 v. Br577 B633.

532. Bolton, H. Carrington. Abstracts of papers read before the New York Academy of Sciences, 1887–1888. *Transactions of the New York Academy of Sciences* 7, 1888. 15 p. Br572C An8141 v.29.

533. Bolton, H. Carrington. The language used in talking to domestic animals. *American Anthropologist* 10, 1897. 47 p. Br572C An8141 v.148.

534. Boltz, A. *Der Apollomythus, Die Engel und ihre Verehrer.* Verlag von L. Brill, Darmstadt, 1894. 58 p. Br572C An8141 v.132.

535. Boltz, A. *Hellas,* 1889. Br572C An8141 v.21.

536. Boltz, A. *Linguistiche Beitrage zur Frage nach der Urheimat der Arioeuropäer.* Verlag von L. Brill, Darmstadt, 1895. 32 p. Br572C An8141 v.138.

537. Boltz, A. *Vasantasena und die Hetären im indischen Drama: Das Vedavolk in seinen Gesamtverhältnissen.* Verlag von L. Brill, Darmstadt, 1894. 56 p. Br572C An8141 v.132.

538. Bompas, William C. *Epistles and Revelations, Translated into the Teni, or Slave Language.* British and Foreign Bible Society, London, 1891. 269 p. Br497.12 SIB 47.9. New Testament Epistles and Revelations translated into Ettchaottine.

539. Bompas, William C. *Hymns in the Tenni or Slavi Language of the Indians of Mackenzie River, in the North-West Territory of Canada.* Society for Promoting Christian Knowledge, London, 1890? 118 p. Br497.12 SIH 99. Hymnal translated into Ettchaottine language.

540. Bompas, William C. *Lessons and Prayers in the Tenni or Slave Language of the Indians of MacKenzie River in the North-West Territory of Canada.* Society for Promoting Christian Knowledge, London, 1890. 81 p. Br497.12 SIB 63.

541. Bompas, William C. *Lessons and Prayers in the Tenni or Slavi Language of the Indians of MacKenzie River, in the North-West Territory of Canada.* Society for Promoting Christian Knowledge, London, 1892. 126 p. Br497.12 SIB 63a.

542. Bompas, William C. *The Acts of the Apostles and the Epistles; Translated into the Tenni or Slave Language for Indians of Mackenzie River, North-West Canada by the Right Rev. the Bishop of Mackenzie River.* British and Foreign Bible Society, London, 1891. 374 p. Br497.12 SIB 47.9B.

543. Bompas, William C., and W. D. Reeve. *Gospel of St. John, Translated into the Slave Language...in the Syllabic Character, by W. C. Bompas and W. D. Reeve*. British and Foreign Bible Society, London, 1890. 67 p. Br497.12 SlB 47.4. New Testament Gospel of St. John translated into Ettchaottine.

544. Bompas, William C., and W. D. Reeve. *The Gospel of St. Luke Translated into the Slavé Language for Indians of North-West America; in the Syllabic Character*. Printed for the British and Foreign Bible Society, London, 1890. 92 p. Br497.12 SlB 47.3.

545. Bonaparte, Prince Roland Napoleon. La Lapone et la Corse. *Le Globe Journal Geographique* 4(8): 3-14, 1889. Br572C An8141 v.82.

546. Bonaparte, Prince Roland Napoleon. *La Nouvelle-Guinee*. Imprimé pour l'Autor, Paris, 1887. 14 p. Br572C An8141 v.3.

547. Bonaparte, Prince Roland Napoleon. *Le glacier de l'Aletsch et le Lac de Märjelen*. Imprimé pour l'Auteur, 1889. 27 p. Br572C An8141 v.3.

548. Bonaparte, Prince Roland Napoleon. *Le premier établissement des Néerlandais à Maurice*. Georges Chamerot, Paris, 1890. 60 p. Br572C An8141 v.3.

549. Bonaparte, Prince Roland Napoleon. *Les derniers voyages des Néerlandais à la Nouvelle-Guinée*. Imprimerie de E. Aubert, Versailles, 1884. 40 p. Br572C An8141 v.3.

550. Bonaparte, Prince Roland Napoleon. *Les premieres nouvelles concernant l'eruption du Krakatau en 1883*. Imprimerie Ch. Marechal et J. Montorier, Paris, 1884. 24 p. Br572C An8141 v.3.

551. Bonaparte, Prince Roland Napoleon. *Les premiers voyages des Néerlandais dans l'insulinde*. Imprimerie de E. Aubert, Versailles, 1884. 39 p. Br572C An8141 v.3.

552. Bonaparte, Prince Roland Napoleon. *Les récentes voyages des Néerlandais à la Nouvelle-Guinée*. Imprimé pour l'Auteur, Versailles, 1885. 16 p. Br572C An8141 v.3.

553. Bonaparte, Prince Roland Napoleon. Note on the Lapps of Finmark. *Journal of the Anthropological Institute of Great Britain and Ireland*, 1885. 12 p. Br572C An8141 v.3.

554. Bonnell, George W. *Topographical Description of Texas; To Which is Added an Account of the Indian Tribes*. Clark, Wing, and Brown, Austin, 1840. 150 p. Br917.64 B645.

555. Bordier, D. A. Laq milieu interieur et l'acclimatation. *Revue Menuselle de l'École d'Anthropologie de Paris*, pp. 129-142, 1891. Br572C An8141 v.8.

556. Borsari, Ferdinando. *Etruschi, Sardi e Siculi*. Marghieri, Napoli, 1891. 19 p. Br572C An8141 v.9.

557. Borsari, Ferdinando. *Geografia etnologica e storica della Tripolitania, Cirenaica e Fessan; con cenni sulla storia di queste regioni e sul silfio della Cirenaica*. Loescher, Torino, 1888. 278 p. Br572.9 B645.

558. Borsari, Ferdinando. *L'Atlantide saggio di geografia preistorica*, pp. 197-219. Stabilimento Tipografico dell'Iride, Napoli, 1889. Br572C An8141 v.7.

559. Borsari, Ferdinando. *La letteratura degl'i indigneni americani*. Luigi Pierro, Napoli, 1888. 76 p. Br572C An8141 v.60.

560. Borsari, Ferdinando. *Le zone colonizzabili dell' Etritrea e dell finitine regioni etiopiche*. Biblioteca Etopica, l. Ulrico Hoepli, Milano, 1890. 96 p. Br572C An8141 v.5.

Lorenzo Boturini Benaducci (from Justin Winsor, Aboriginal America. Cambridge, MA: Houghton, Mifflin, 1889. p. 160).

561. Borton, Frank. *A Few Valuable Books for Sale.* City of Mexico, 1892. 53 p. Br972B B648.

562. Borunda, Ignacio. *Clave general de jeroglíficos americanos de don Ignacio Borunda manuscrit inédit pub. le Duc de Loubat.* J. P. Scotti, Rome, 1898. 282 p. Br898.22 AzB648L.

563. Bossu, Jean B. *Nouveaux voyages dans l'Amerique septentrionale, contenant une collection de lettres ecrites sur les lieux, à son ami, M. Douin, chevalier, capitaine dans les troupes du roi, cide.* Chanuion, Amsterdam, 1777. 392 p. Br917.3 B655. "Captain Bossu's tour in Louisana from 1770 to 1771 is again related is epistolary form…His book provides additional information on the Arkansas and Louisana Indian tribes whom he befriended" (*Frank T. Siebert Library* 1999:2:110).

564. Boturini Benaducci, Lorenzo. *Idea de una nueva historia general de la America Septentrional; fundada sobre material copioso de figuras, symbolos, caractères, y geroglificos, cantares, y manuscritos de autores indios, ultimamente descubiertos.* En la Imprenta de Juan de Zuñiga, En Madrid, 1746. 40, 167, 96 p. Br980 B654.

565. Boturini Benaducci, Lorenzo. *Tezcoco en los últimos tiempos de sus antiguos reyes; ó sea Relación tomada de los manuscritos inéditos de Boturini.* Imprenta de M. Galvan Rivera, México, 1826. 276 p. Br972 B65.

566. Bouchard, A. America. *The Humming Bird*, pp. 105–120. n.d. Br572C An8141 v.153.

567. Boulet, Jean B. *Prayer Book and Catechism in the Snohomish Language.* Tulalip

Mission Press, Tulalip, W.T., 1879. 32 p. Br497.46 SnB664.

568. Bourgeois, L. Sur les silex considèrès comme portant les marques d'un travail humain découverte dans le terrain Miocène de Thenny, pp. 81–93. Bruxelles, 1873. Br572C An8141 v.58.

569. Bourke, John G. *Compilation of Notes and Memoranda Bearing Upon the Use of Human Ordure and Human Urine in Rites of a Religious or Semi-Religious Character Among Various Nations.* Washington, DC, 1888. 56 p. Br572C An8141 v.60. "Captain Bourke served with the Third United States Cavalry under [Brigadier General George] Crook in the Southwest for fourteen years" (*Frank T. Siebert Library* 1999:168).

570. Bourke, John G. Distillation by early American Indians. *American Anthropologist* 7:297–299, 1894. Br572C An8141 v.137.

571. Bourke, John G. Notes and news. *American Anthropologist* 8:192–196, 1895. Br572C An8141 v.138.

572. Bourke, John G. Notes upon the gentile organization of the Apaches of Arizona; delivered as a lecture before the Anthropological Society of Washington. *Journal of American Folk-Lore* 3(9): 111–126, 1890. Br572C An8141 v.20.

573. Bourke, John G. Popular medicine, customs, and superstitions of the Rio Grande. *Journal of American Folk-Lore* 7(25): 119–146, 1894. Br572C An8141 v.137.

574. Bourke, John G. *Scatalogic Rites of All Nations; A Dissertation Upon the Employment of Excrementitious Remedial Agents in Religion, Therapeutics, Divination, Witchcraft, Love-Philters, etc., In All Parts of the Globe.* W. H. Lowdermilk, Washington, DC, 1891. 496 p. Br394.4 B663.

575. Bourke, John G. The folk-foods of the Rio Grande Valley and of northern Mexico. *Journal of American Folk-Lore* 8:41–71, 1895. Br572C An8141 v.138.

576. Bourke, John G. The laws of Spain in their application to the American Indians. *American Anthropologist* 7:193–201, 1894. Br572C An8141 v.137.

577. Bourke, John G. *The Snake-Dance of the Moquis of Arizona; Being a Narrative of a Journey From Santa Fé, New Mexico, to the Villages of the Moqui Indians of Arizona, With a Description of the Manners and Customs of this Peculiar People, and Especially of the Revolting Religious Rite, the Snake-Dance; to Which is added a Brief Dissertation Upon Serpent-Worship in General, With an Account of the Tablet Dance of the Pueblo of Santo Domingo, New Mexico, etc.* C. Scribner's Sons, New York, 1884. 371 p. Br970.3 TB667.

578. Bourke, John G. *The Urine Dance of the Zuni Indians of New Mexico, From the Ethnological Notes Collected by Him Under the Direction of Lieutenant General P. H. Sheridan in 1861; Read before the American Association for the Advancement of Science.* Privately printed, 1885. 4 p. Br572C An8141 v.27.

579. Bourquin, Theodor. *Grammatik der Eskimo-Sprache wie sie im Bereich der Missions-Niederlassungen der Brüdergemeine an der Labradorküste gesprochen wird; Auf Grundlage der Kleinschmidtschen Grammatik der grönländischen Sprache, sowie älterer Labrador-Grammatiken zum Gebrauch der Labrador-Missionare.* Moravian Mission Agency, London, 1891. 415 p. Br497.25 LB66.

580. Bove, Giacomo. *Patagonia—Terra del Fucco, mari australi. Rapporto…al Comitato centrale por le esplorazioni antartiche. Parte I.*Tip. del R. Istituto de' Sordo-Muti, Genova, 1883. 150 p. Br918.2 B66.

581. Bowers, Stephen. Relics in a cave. *Pacific Science Monthly*:45-47, 1885. Br572C An8141 v.59.

582. Bowers, Stephen. Relics of the Santa Barbara Indians. *Kansas City Review* 7(12): 748-751, 1884. Br572C An8141 v.19.

583. Bowers, Stephen. *The Conchilla Valley and the Cahuilla Indians.* San Buena Ventura, CA, 1888. 7 p. Br572C An8141 v.23.

584. Boyd, Stephen G. *Indian Local Names With Their Interpretation.* York, PA, 1885. 70 p. Br497 B695.

585. Boyle, David. *Annual Archaeological Report, 1889.* Warwick Brothers and Rutter, Printers, Toronto, 1898. 118 p. Br572C An8141 v.15.

586. Boyle, David. *Annual Archaeological Report, 1896-1897.* Warwick Brothers and Rutter, Printers, Toronto, 1897. 116 p. Br572C An8141 v.148.

587. Boyle, David. *Annual Archaeological Report, 1897-1898.* Warwick Brothers and Rutter, Printers, Toronto, 1898. 87 p. Br572C An8141 v.148.

588. Boyle, David. *Annual Report of the Canadian Institute: Archaeological Report and Catalogue, 1888-1889.* Warwick Brothers and Rutter, Printers, Toronto, 1889. 118 p. Br572C An8141 v.28.

589. Boyle, David. Archaeological remains a factor in the study of history. *Transactions of the Canadian Institute* 1:67-71, 1889-1890. Br572C An8141 v.15.

590. Boyle, David. *Archaeological Report, 1894-1895: Appendix to the Report of the Minister of Education, Ontario.* Warwick Brothers and Rutter, Printers, Toronto, 1896. 79 p. Br572C An8141 v.138.

591. Boyle, David. *Catalogue of Specimens in the Ontario Archaeological Museum.* Warwick Brothers and Rutter, Printers, Toronto, 1897. 83 p. Br572C An8141 v.148.

592. Boyle, David. *Notes on Primitive Man in Ontario.* Warwick Brothers, and Rutter, Toronto, 1895. 98 p. Br572C An8141 v.134.

593. Brabrook, Edward W. *Address Delivered at the Anniversary Meeting of the Anthropological Institute of Great Britain and Ireland.* Harrison and Sons, London, 1896. 28 p. Br572C An8141 v.138.

594. Brabrook, Edward W. *Address Delivered at the Anniversary Meeting of the Anthropological Institute of Great Britain and Ireland, 1897.* Harrison and Sons, London, 1897. 16 p. Br572C An8141 v.148.

595. Brabrook, Edward W. *Address Delivered at the Anniversary Meeting of the Anthropological Institute of Great Britain and Ireland, January 25, 1898.* Harrison and Sons, London, 1898. 19 p. Br572C An8141 v.164.

596. Brabrook, Edward W. *Address to the Anthropological Section.* British Association for the Advancement of Science, Bristol, 1898. 12 p. Br572C An8141 v.164.

597. Brabrook, Edward W. Kent in relation to the ethnographic survey. *Archaeological Journal,* pp. 215-234, 1896. Br572C An8141 v.148.

598. Brabrook, Edward W. The literary treatment of history, 1893. 30 p. Br572C An8141 v.148.

599. Brackett, Albert G. The Sioux or Dakota Indians. *Annual Report of the United States National Museum, Smithsonian Institution, for 1876,* pp. 466–472, 1877. Br572C An8141 v.19.

600. Bradner, Nathaniel R. A history of a stone bearing Hebrew inscription, found in an American mound. 1873. 4 p. Br572C An8141 v.38.

601. Brandin, Abel-Victorin. L'Amèrique Espagnole en 1830. Paris, 1830. 48 p. Br572C An8141 v.40.

602. Branner, John C. Notes upon a native Brazilian language. *Proceedings of the American Association for the Advancement of Science* (August): 329–330, 1886. Br572C An8141 v.84.

603. Branner, John C. Rock inscriptions in Brazil. *American Naturalist* 18(12): 1187–1192, 1884. Br572C An8141 v.13.

604. Branner, John C. The Pororóca, or Bore of the Amazon. *Science,* 1884. 12 p. Br572C An8141 v.18.

605. Bransford, John F. *Archaeological Researches in Nicaragua.* Smithsonian Institution Contributions to Knowledge, 25, Washington, DC, 1881. 96 p. Br572C An8141 v.100.

606. Brasseur de Bourbourg, Charles E. *Bibliothèque mexico-guatémalienne; précédée d'un coup d'œil sur les études américaines dans leurs rapports avec les études classiques et suivie du tableau par ordre alphabétique des ouvrages de linguistique américaine contenus dans le même volume; rédigée et mise en ordre d'après les documents de la collection américaine.* Maisonneuve et Cie., Paris, 1871, 183 p. Br970B B73. An annotated catalog of the Brasseur de Bourbourg library. The collection was sold to Alphonse Pinart and eventually dispersed to Museum Library, University of Pennsylvania Museum; Bibliothèque Nationale, Paris; Newberry Library, Ayer Collection; Princeton University Library; and Bancroft Library, University of California at Berkeley. In 1855 Charles Etienne Brasseur de Bourbourg (1814-1874) was assigned as parish priest in Rabinal, a Quiché Maya town in the Guatemala highlands, where he began his studies of the Quiché language. He recorded the *Rabinal Achí,* a unique prehispanic drama, and later found copies of the *Popol Vuh,* possibly the greatest single work of native American literature, and the *Annals of the Cakchiquels (Memorial de Sololá).* In 1862 Brasseur discovered a manuscript copy of Bishop Diego de Landa's *Relación de las cosas de Yucatán.*

607. Brasseur de Bourbourg, Charles E. *Dictionnaire, grammaire et chrestomathie de la langue maya précédes d'une étude sur le systeme graphique des indigenes du Yucatán, (Mexique), par M. Brasseur de Bourbourg, ancien missionnaire.* Maisonneuve, Paris, 1872. 244, 464 p. Br498.21 MT742M.3.

608. Brasseur de Bourbourg, Charles E. *Gramatica de la lengua quichée; grammaire de la langue quichée, espagnole-française mise en parallèle avec ses deux dialectes, cakchiquel et tzutuhil, tirée des manuscrits des meilleurs auteurs*

guatémaliens; ouvrage accompagné de notes philologiques avec un vocabu-laire…et suivi d'un essai sur la poésie, la musique, la danse et l'art servant d'introduction au Rabinal-Achi, drame indigène avec sa musique originale, texte quiché et traduction français en regard. A. Bertrand, Paris, 1862. 2 v. Br498.21 KiB727. Contents include "Grammaire de la langue quichée suivie d'un vocabulaire," and "Rabinal-Achi ou Le drame-ballet du tun (quiché et français)." The Quiché grammar and vocabulary were taken from the Tesoro de las tres lenguas, quiché, cakchiquel y tzutuhil, of Father Francisco Ximénez. The indigenous dance drama of Rabinal Achí, according to the introduction written by Brasseur de Bourbourg, was collected by him from the natives of the parish of Rabinal. However, a note by Karl H. Berendt asserts that Brasseur found the manuscript of it complete in the hands of a haciendado on the road from Guatemala to Chiapas, and that the original still exists there.

609. Brasseur de Bourbourg, Charles E. *Histoire des nations civilisées du Mexique et de l'Amérique-Centrale, durant les siècles antérieurs à Christophe Colomb.* Bertrand, Paris, 1857–1859. 4 v. Br972 B72.5. A synthesis of the ancient history of Mexico and Guatemala based on manuscripts and copies in his own and other collections. Contents include: v. 1. "Les temps héroiques et l'histoire de l'empire des Toltèques"; v. 2. "L'histoire de l'Yucatán et du Guatémala; avec celle de l'Anahuac, durant le moyen âge aztèque, jusqu'à la fondation de la royauté à Mexico"; v. 3. "L'histoire des états du Michoacan et d'Oaxaca et de l'empire de l'Anahuac jusqu'à l'arrivée des Espagnols; Astronomie, religion sciences et arts des Aztèques, etc."; v. 4. "Conquète des états du Mexique et de Guatémala, etc."; "Établissement du gouvernement espagnol et de l'Église catholique; Ruine de l'idolatrie, déclin et abaissement de la race indigène."

610. Brasseur de Bourbourg, Charles E. Manuscrit cakchiquel, mémorial de Tecpan-Atitlan, Solola, histoire des deux familles royales du royaume des Cakchiquels d'Iximché ou Guatémala, rédigé en langue cakchiquèle…des rois Ahpozotziles, textes cakchiquel et essai de traduction française en regard faite à Rabinal par Brasseur de Bourbourg. 1856. 67 leaves. Br498.21 Car15a. Manuscript, transcribed by Brasseur de Bourbourg, containing selections from the larger original manuscript.

611. Brasseur de Bourbourg, Charles E. *Manuscrit troano; études sur le système graphique et la langue des Mayas.* Imprimerie Impériale, Paris, 1869–1870. 2 v. Br898.21 MT742M. Contents include: v.1. Rapport à son Excellence M. le ministre de l'instruction publique; Manuscrit troano, monographie et exposition du système graphiqu; Tableau des caractères phonétiques maya; v.2. Grammaire et chrestomathie; Vocabulaire général maya-français et espagnol; Langue des Mayas.

612. Brasseur de Bourbourg, Charles E. *Popol Vuh; le livre sacré et les mythes de l'antiquité américaine, avec les livres héroiques et historiques des quichés; ouvrage original des indigenes de Guatemala, texte quiché et traduction française en regard, accompagnée de notes philologiques et d'un commentaire sur la mythologie et les migrations des peuples anciens de l'Amérique, etc., compose sur des documents originaux et inedits, par l'Abbé Brasseur de Bourbourg, auteur.*

Charles Etienne Brasseur de Bourbourg (from Justin Winsor, Aboriginal America. *Cambridge, MA: Houghton, Mifflin, 1889. p. 170).*

Arthus Bertrand, Paris, 1861. 368 p. Br898.21 KP818a. Quiché text of the *Popol Vuh* with French translation.

613. Brasseur de Bourbourg, Charles E. *Recherches sur les ruines de Palenqué et sur les origines de la civilisation du Mexique, par M. l'abbé Brasseur de Bourbourg.* A. Bertrand, Paris, 1866. 83 p. Br913.72 B738a. Written to accompany the *Collection de vues, bas-reliefs, morceaux d'architecture [etc.] dessinés d'après nature et relevés par M. de Waldeck.*

614. Brasseur de Bourbourg, Charles E. *Vocabulaire général maya-français et espagnol.* Paris, 1870. Br498.21 MT742 M.3. This vocabulary forms the third part of Brasseur's *Études sur le systeme graphique et la langue des mayas.*

615. Brasseur de Bourbourg, Charles E. *Vocabulaire maya français d'apres divers auteurs anciens et modernes.* Paris, 1864. Br917.26 B23. Includes annotations by Karl H. Berendt.

616. Brasseur de Bourbourg, Charles E. *Voyage sur L'isthme de Tehuantepec dans l'état de Chiapas et la république de Guatémala, exécuté dans les années 1859 et 1860.* A. Bertrand, Paris, 1861. 209 p. Br917.27 B735.

617. Braunschweig, Johann D. von. *Über die Alt-Amerikanischen Denkmäler.* Reimer, Berlin, 1840. 188 p. Br572C An8141 v.70.

618. Brehm, Alfred E. Aus dem Leben des Chimpanse. *Verhandlungen der Berliner Anthropologischen Gesellschaft für Anthropologie, Ethnologie und Urgeschichte.* 1873. 6 p. Br572C An8141 v.162.

619. Breton, Raymond. *Dictionnaire caraibe-françois meslé de quantité de remarques historiques pour l'esclaircissement de la langue.* G. Bovqvet, Avxerre, 1892. 480, 70 p. Br498.78 B 758.

620. Breton, Raymond. *Grammaire caraibe...suivie du catécismé caraibe.* Bibliothèque Linguistique Américaine, 3. Maisonneuve, Paris, 1877. 73 p. Br497C Am3.

621. Breton, Raymond. Notice sur le dictionnaire caraïbe. *Actes de la Société Philologique* 12:30-38, 1883. Br572C An8141 v.84.

622. Brett, William H. *Legends and Myths of the Aboriginal Indians of British Guiana.* W.W. Gardner, London, 1880. 206 p. Br398.22 AaB758.

623. *Breve explicación en quichua, 1883; El via-crusis en quichua del S. Alfonso por un P. Redentorista.* Cordero, Cuenca, 1892. 32 p. Br498.7 KR 662.

624. Brewster, Edwin T. A measure of variability, and the relation of individual variations to specific differences. *Proceedings of the American Academy of Arts and Sciences* 32(15): 269-279, 1897. Br572C An8141 v.148.

625. Bridge, Cyprian A. G. Cruises in Melanesia, Micronesia, and western Polynesia, and visits to New Guinea and the Louisades. *Proceedings of the Royal Geographical Society,* pp. 545-567, 1886. Br572C An8141 v.44.

626. Bridges, Thomas. Notes on the structure of Yahgan. *Journal of the Anthropological Institute of Great Britain and Ireland* 23(1): 53-80, 1893. Br572C An8141 v.115. "The Rev. Thomas Bridges was easily the most important first-hand authority on the Yahgans' language and culture...Mr. Bridges first came into contact with the Yahgans in 1858 at the Keppel Island Mission in the Falkland [Malvina] Islands, whither he had come in 1856 as the adopted son of Rev. Mr. Despard. On the latter's departure for England in 1862, Mr. Bridges was left in charge of the mission Yahgans, of whose language he then began...a thorough study. After occasional visits to Fuegia from 1863 on, he took up permanent residence at Ushuaia in the heart of the Yahgan territory and at a time when the natives were comparatively untouched by the white man's culture. He remained continuously at Ushuaia from the time of his arrival there late in 1869 or early in 1870 until 1886, when he resigned from the South American Missionary Society and removed to Harberton (Downeast) about 30-35 miles east of Ushuaia on Beagle Channel. He lived here until his death in 1898" (Cooper 1917:74).

627. Brinton, Daniel G. A notice of some manuscripts in Central American languages. *American Journal of Science and Arts* 47:222-230, 1869. Br497C B775.2; Br572C An8141 v.50.

628. Brinton, Daniel G. *A Primer of Maya Hieroglyphics.* University of Pennsylvania, Series in Philology, Literature, and Archaeology 3(2). Philadelphia, 1894. 152 p. Br497 B775.2; Br498 B772.3.

629. Brinton, Daniel G. *A Record of Study in Aboriginal American Languages.* Printed for private distribution, Media, PA, 1898. 24 p. Br497 B77.3; Br497 B775.2. A bibliography of the author's own writings.

630. Brinton, Daniel G. A vocabulary of the Nanticoke dialect. *Proceedings of the American Philosophical Society* 32:325-333, 1893. Br572C An8141 v.127.

631. Brinton, Daniel G. *Aboriginal American Authors and Their Productions, Especially Those in the Native Languages; A Chapter in the History of Literature.* D. Brinton, Philadelphia, 1883. 63 p. Br897 B776.

632. Brinton, Daniel G. *Address Delivered on Columbus Day, October 21, 1892, at the*

Library and Museum Building of the University of Pennsylvania, Philadelphia. Philadelphia, 1892. 8 p. Br497 B775.2.

633. Brinton, Daniel G. Aims and traits of a world language; an address before the Nineteenth Century Club, New York. *Werner's Voice Magazine*, 1889. 23 p. Br497 B77.5; Br497 B775.2.

634. Brinton, Daniel G. Alphabets of the Berbers. *Proceedings of the Oriental Club of Philadelphia*, 1893. 11 p. Br913 B775.

635. Brinton, Daniel G. *American Hero-Myths. A Study in the Native Religions of the Western Continent.* H.C. Watts and Company, Philadelphia, 1882. 239 p. Br398.21B773.2.

636. Brinton, Daniel G. American languages and why we should study them. *Pennnsylvania Magazine of History and Biography* 9:15-35, 1885. Br497 B77.

637. Brinton, Daniel G. An inscribed table from Long Island. *The Archaeologist* 1(11): 201-203, 1893. Br913 B775.

638. Brinton, Daniel G. Analytical catalogue of works and scientific articles by Daniel G. Brinton, 1859-1892. 22 p. Br497 B77.5.

639. Brinton, Daniel G. *Ancient Nahuatl Poetry Containing the Nahuatl Text of XXVII Ancient Mexican Poems, With a Translation, Introduction, Notes, and Vocabulary.* Library of Aboriginal American Literature, 7. D. G. Brinton, Philadelphia, 1890. 177 p. Br897C B776. Includes a discussion of Nahuatl poetry; English translation of poems from the *Cantares de Nezahualcoyotl* and *Cantares mexicanos*, based on a copy by Brasseur de Bourbourg.

640. Brinton, Daniel G. Anthropology and ethnology. Iconographic Pub. Company, Philadelphia, 1886. 184 p. From the *Iconographic Encyclopaedia*, v. 1. Br571 B77.2.

641. Brinton, Daniel G. *Anthropology, As a Science and As a Branch of University Education.* Philadelphia, 1892. 15 p. Br913 B775.2 v.22.

642. Brinton, Daniel G. Articles and reviews published in *Science*, October 2, 1896-December 31, 1897. 62 p. Br572 B77.5. Collection of clippings arranged chronologically.

643. Brinton, Daniel G. Beginning of man and the age of the race, pp. 452-458. 1893. Br913 B775.

644. Brinton, Daniel G. Book reviews. n.d. Br497 B77; Br497 B775.

645. Brinton, Daniel G. Books of Chilam Balam, the prophetic and historic records of the Mayas of Yucatan. *Penn Monthly*, 1882. 19 p. Br497 B77.

646. Brinton, Daniel G. Books on American languages...duplicates from his library. 1891. 4 p. Br497 B77.5.

647. Brinton, Daniel G. Browning on unconventional relations, pp. 266-271. n.d. Br821 B82yBr.

648. Brinton, Daniel G. *Catalogue of the Berendt Linguistic Collection.* Department of Archaeology and Paleontology, University of Pennsylvania, Philadelphia, 1900. 32 p. Br497 B775.2.

649. Brinton, Daniel G. Characteristics of American languages. *American Antiquarian* 16, 1894. 8 p. Br497 B77.5.

650. Brinton, Daniel G. Collection of pamphlets. n.d. Br497 B77.

651. Brinton, Daniel G. Conception of love in some American languages. *Proceedings of the American Philosophical Society* 23:546-561, 1886. Br497 B77.

652. Brinton, Daniel G. Contributions to a grammar of the Muskokee language. *Proceedings of the American Philosophical Society* 11:301-309, 1870. Br497C B775.2; Br572C An8141 v.50.

653. Brinton, Daniel G. Critical remarks on the editions of Diego de Landa's writings. *Proceedings of the American Philosophical Society* 24:1-8, 1887. Br497 B77.

654. Brinton, Daniel G. Das Heidenthum in Christlichen Yucatan. *Globus* 59(7): 97-100, 1891. Br572C An8141 v.101.

655. Brinton, Daniel G. Dr. Allen's contributions to anthropology. *Proceedings of the Academy of Natural Sciences of Philadelphia*, pp. 522-529, 1897. Br497 B775.2.

656. Brinton, Daniel G. Epilogues of Browning; their artistic significance, pp. 57-64. n.d. Br821 B82yBr.

657. Brinton, Daniel G. *Essays of an Americanist: I. Ethnologic and Archaeologic; II. Mythology and Folk-Lore; III. Graphic Systems and Literature; IV. Linguistic.* Porter and Coates, Philadelphia, 1890. 489 p. Br497 B77.2; Br572C An8141 v.76.

658. Brinton, Daniel G. Ethnic affinities of the Quetares of Costa Rica. *Proceedings of the American Philosophical Society* 36:496-498, 1897. Br497 B77.5.

659. Brinton, Daniel G. Ethnologic affinities of the ancient Etruscans. *Proceedings of the American Philosophical Society* 27, 1889. 24 p. Br913 B775.

660. Brinton, Daniel G. Ethnologist's view of history. Address before the New Jersey Historical Society, 1896. 24 p. Br913 B775.

661. Brinton, Daniel G. Etrusco-Libyan elements in the song of the Arval brethern. *Proceedings of the American Philosophical Society* 31:317-324, 1893. Br497 B775.2.

662. Brinton, Daniel G. *Facettes of Love, From Browning; An Introductory Address at the Opening of the Browning Society of the New Century Club of Philadelphia, November 12, 1888.* Fell, Philadelphia, 1888. 35 p. Br821 B82yBr. Bound with: Daniel G. Brinton, Browning on unconventional relations, n.d.; Daniel G. Brinton, Epilogues of Browning, n.d.

663. Brinton, Daniel G. Folk-lore of the bones. *Journal of American Folk-Lore* 3(8): 17-22, 1890. Br497 B77.

664. Brinton, Daniel G. Folk-lore of Yucatan. *Folk-Lore Journal* 1(8): 244-256, 1883. Br497 B77.5; Br497 B775.2.

665. Brinton, Daniel G. Further notes on the Betoya dialects. *Proceedings of the American Philosophical Society* 30:271-278, 1892. Br497 B77.5.

666. Brinton, Daniel G. Further notes on the Fuegian languages, from unpublished sources. *Proceedings of the American Philosophical Society* 30:249-254, 1892. Br497 B77.5. "A notice of La Guilbaudiere's vocabulary of which 22 words are given…and a comparison of Yahgan words with Dr. [Polidoro A.] Seger's Ona vocabulary, which is given nearly in full…Dr. Brinton's conclusion is that the Onas are linguistically nearer to the Yahgans than to the Tehuelches is explained by the fact that Dr. Seger's list contains many errors and many Yahgan words"

(Cooper 1917:75).

667. Brinton, Daniel G. International Congress of Americanists. *American Anthropologist* 4, 1891. 5 p. Br913; Br497 B775.2.

668. Brinton, Daniel G. Language of Palaeolithic man. *Proceedings of the American Philosophical Society* 25, 1888. 16 p. Br913 B775; Br497 B775.2.

669. Brinton, Daniel G. Left-handedness in North American aboriginal art. *American Anthropologist* 9:175-181, 1896. Br913 B775; Br497 B775.2.

670. Brinton, Daniel G. *Library of Aboriginal American Literature*. D. G. Brinton, Philadelphia, 1882-1890. 8 v. Br897C B776.

671. Brinton, Daniel G. Lineal measures of the semi-civilized nations of Mexico and Central America. *Proceedings of the American Philosophical Society* 22:194-207, 1885. Br913 B775; Br497 B775.2.

672. Brinton, Daniel G. *Linguistic Cartography of the Chaco Region*. MacCalla, Philadelphia, 1898. 30 p. Br497 B775.2.

673. Brinton, Daniel G. *Maria Candelaria: An Historic Drama from American Aboriginal Life*. David McKay, Philadelphia, 1897. 98 p. Br812 B77M.

674. Brinton, Daniel G. Maria Candelaria: an historic drama from American aboriginal life. n.d. 122 leaves. Br812 B77Ma. Manuscript.

675. Brinton, Daniel G. Matagalpan linguistic stock of Central America. *Proceedings of the American Philosophical Society* 34:403-415, 1895. Br497 B77.5.

676. Brinton, Daniel G. Memoir of Karl Hermann Berendt. *Proceedings of the American Philosophical Society* 21:205-210, 1884. 8 p. Br913 B775.

677. Brinton, Daniel G. Memoir of S. S. Haldemann. *Proceedings of the American Philosophical Society* 18:279-285, 1881. Br497 B77.

678. Brinton, Daniel G. Miscellaneous collection of articles and notes on the Indians. n.d. Br497C B775. Manuscript.

679. Brinton, Daniel G. Miscellaneous pamphlets. n.d. Br913 B775.

680. Brinton, Daniel G. Missing authorities on Mayan antiquities. *American Anthropologist* 10:183-191, 1897. Br913 B775.

681. Brinton, Daniel G. Nagualism; a study in native American folk-lore and history. *Proceedings of the American Philosophical Society* 33, 1894. 65 p. Br289.1 B773.2.

682. Brinton, Daniel G. Names of the gods in the Kiche myths, Central America. *Proceedings of the American Philsophical Society* 19:613-647, 1881. Br497 B775.2.

683. Brinton, Daniel G. Natchez of Louisiana, an offshoot of the civilized nations of Central America. *Historical Magazine* 1:16-18, 1867. Br497C B775.2.

684. Brinton, Daniel G. Nation as an element in anthropology, presidential address before the International Congress of Americanists. *Memoirs of the International Congress of Americanists*, 1894. 16 p. Br913 B775.

685. Brinton, Daniel G. Nation as an element in anthropology. *Annual Report of the United States National Museum, Smithsonian Institution, for 1893*, pp. 589-600, 1894. Br497 B775.2.

686. Brinton, Daniel G. National legend of the Chahta-Muskokee tribes. *American Historical Magazine*, February, 1870. 13 p. Br497 B775.2.

687. Brinton, Daniel G. Native American stringed musical instruments. *American Antiquarian* 19:19–20, 1897. Br913 B775.

688. Brinton, Daniel G. *Native Calendar of Central America and Mexico: A Study in Linguistics and Symbolism.* MacCalla and Company, Philadelphia, 1893. 59 p. Br497 B775.2.

689. Brinton, Daniel G. Nomenclature and teaching of anthropology. *American Anthropologist* 5, 1892. 6 p. Br913 B775.

690. Brinton, Daniel G. Note on the classical murmex. *Bulletin of the Museum of Science and Art, University of Pennsylvania* 2(1), 1897. 2 p. Br913 B775; Br497 B775.2.

691. Brinton, Daniel G. Note on the Puquina language of Peru; read before the American Philosophical Society, November 21, 1890. *Proceedings of the American Philosophical Society* 28:242–248, 1890. Br497C B775.2; Br572C An8141 v.47.

692. Brinton, Daniel G. Notes on American ethnology. *American Antiquarian* 8, 1886. 3 p. Br497 B77; Br913 B775.

693. Brinton, Daniel G. Notes on the Codex Troano and Maya chronology. *American Naturalist* 15:719–724, 1881. Br497 B77; Br572C An8141 v.44.

694. Brinton, Daniel G. *Notes on the Floridian Peninsula, Its Literary History, Indian Tribes and Antiquities.* J. Sabin, Philadelphia, 1859. 202 p. Br975.9 B776.

695. Brinton, Daniel G. *Notes on the Floridian Peninsula, Its Literary History, Indian Tribes and Antiquities.* J. Sabin, Philadelphia, 1859. 202 p. Br975.9 B776a. Author's own copy interleaved with manuscript notes.

696. Brinton, Daniel G. Notes on the Mangue; an extinct dialect formerly spoken in Nicaragua. *Proceedings of the American Philosophical Society* 23, 1886. 22 p. Br497 B77.

697. Brinton, Daniel G. Notes. n.d. 3 p. Br924 B772.

698. Brinton, Daniel G. Obituary notice of Philip H. Law, Esq. *Proceedings of the American Philosophical Society* 25:225–231, 1888. Br913 B775; Br497 B775.2.

699. Brinton, Daniel G. Obituary notice of William Samuel Waithman Ruschenberger. *Proceedings of the American Philosophical Society* 34, 1895. 4 p. Br913 B775.

700. Brinton, Daniel G. Obituary of George de Benneville Keim. *Proceedings of the American Philosophical Society* 33:187–192, 1894. Br913 B775.

701. Brinton, Daniel G. Observations on the Chinantec language of Mexico and on the Mazatec language and its affinities. *Proceedings of the American Philosophical Society* 30:22–31, 1892. Br497C B775.2; Br498.6 B 77.

702. Brinton, Daniel G. On a petroglyph from the island of St. Vincent, West Indies. *Proceedings of the Academy of Natural Sciences of Philadelphia* 27:417–420, 1889. Br497 B77; Br572C An8141 v.11.

703. Brinton, Daniel G. On an ancient human footprint from Nicaragua. *Proceedings of the American Philosophical Society* 24:437–444, 1887. Br497 B77.

704. Brinton, Daniel G. On certain morphologic traits of American languages. *American Antiquarian* 16, 1894. 7 p. Br497 B77.5.

705. Brinton, Daniel G. On Etruscan and Libyan names; a comparative study. *Proceedings*

of the American Philosophical Society 28, 1890. 16 p. Br913 B775; Br497 B775.2.

706. Brinton, Daniel G. On polysynthesis and incorporation as characteristics of American languages. *Proceedings of the American Philosophical Society* 22:77-96, 1885. Br497 B77.

707. Brinton, Daniel G. On the Chane-abal, four language, tribe, and dialect of Chiapas. *American Anthropologist* 1:77-96, 1888. Br497 B77; Br572C An8141 v.51.

708. Brinton, Daniel G. On the cuspidiform petroglyphs, or so-called bird-track sculptures of Ohio. *Proceedings of the Academy of Sciences of Philadelphia*, pp. 275-277, 1884. Br497 B77.

709. Brinton, Daniel G. On the language of the Natchez. *Proceedings of the American Philosophical Society*, December, 1873. 17 p. Br497 B77.5; Br572C An8141 v.50.

710. Brinton, Daniel G. On the oldest stone implements in the eastern United States. *Journal of the Anthropological Institute of Great Britain and Ireland* 26(1): 59-64, 1896. Br497 B77.5.

711. Brinton, Daniel G. On the remains of the foreigners discovered in Egypt by Mr. Flinders-Petrie, 1895, now in the Museum of the University of Pennsylvania. *Proceedings of the American Philosophical Society* 35, 1896. 1 p. Br913 B775; Br497 B775.2.

712. Brinton, Daniel G. On the so-called Alagüilac language of Guatemala. *Proceedings of the American Philosophical Society* 24:366-377, 1887. Br497 B77.

713. Brinton, Daniel G. On the words Anahuac and Nahuatl. *American Antiquarian* 15:377-382, 1893. Br497 B77.5.

714. Brinton, Daniel G. On the Xinca Indians of Guatemala. *Proceedings of the American Philosophical Society* 21, 1884. 9 p. Br497 B77; Br572C An8141 v.52.

715. Brinton, Daniel G. On various supposed relations between the American and Asian races. *Memoirs of the International Congress of Anthropology*, pp. 145-151, 1894. Chicago. Br497 B77.5.

716. Brinton, Daniel G. Origin of sacred numbers. *American Anthropologist* 7(2): 168-173, 1894. Br913 B775.

717. Brinton, Daniel G. Origin of the sacred name Jahva. *Archiv für Religionswissenschaft* 2:225-236, 1899. Br492.133 B776.

718. Brinton, Daniel G. Pamphlets. n.d. Br497 B77.5.

719. Brinton, Daniel G. Pamphlets. n.d. Br497 B775.2.

720. Brinton, Daniel G. Pamphlets; Miscellaneous. n.d. Br497C B775.2.

721. Brinton, Daniel G. Philosophic grammar of American languages, as set forth by Wilhelm von Humboldt, with the translation of an unpublished memoir by him on the American verb. *Proceedings of the American Philosophical Society* 22:306-331, 1885. Br497 B77.5.

722. Brinton, Daniel G. Phonetic elements in the graphic system of the Mayas and Mexicans. *American Antiquarian* 8, 1886. 13 p. Br497 B77.

723. Brinton, Daniel G. Pillars of Ben. *Bulletin of the Museum of Science and Art, University of Pennsylvania* 1(1), 1897. 8 p. Br913 B775; Br497 B775.2.

724. Brinton, Daniel G. Popular superstitions of Europe, pp. 643-654. 1898. Br913 B775.

725. Brinton, Daniel G. Present status of American linguistics. *Memoirs of the International Congress of Anthropology*, pp. 335–338, 1894. Br497 B77.5.

726. Brinton, Daniel G. Primitive American poetry. *Poet-Lore*, pp. 329–331, 1892. Br497 B77.5.

727. Brinton, Daniel G. Protohistoric ethnography of western Asia. *Proceedings of the American Philosophical Society* 34, 1895. 32 p. Br913 B775; Br497 B775.2.

728. Brinton, Daniel G. *Races and Peoples; Lectures on the Science of Ethnography.* Hodges, New York, 1890. 313 p. Br572 B77.2.

729. Brinton, Daniel G. Recent European contributions to the study of American archaeology. *Proceedings of the Numismatic and Antiquarian Society of Philadelphia*, 1883. 3 p. Br497 B77.

730. Brinton, Daniel G. Relations of race and culture to degenerations of the reproductive organs and functions in women. *Medical News*, January, 1896. 6 p. Br913 B775.

731. Brinton, Daniel G. *Religions of Primitive Peoples.* G. P. Putnam, New York, 1897. 264 p. Br390 B776; Br390 B776.yA.

732. Brinton, Daniel G. Reminiscences of Pennsylvania folk-lore. *Journal of American Folk-Lore* 5(13): 177–185, 1892. Br497 B77.5.

733. Brinton, Daniel G. Report on the collections exhibited at the Columbian Historical Exposition. *Report of the Madrid Commission, 1892.* Government Printing Office, Washington, DC, 1895. 89 p. Br913 B775.

734. Brinton, Daniel G. Review of the data for the study of the prehistoric chronology of America; address by Daniel G. Brinton, M.D. *Proceedings of the American Association for the Advancement of Science* 36, 1887. 21 p. Br497 B77.

735. Brinton, Daniel G. *Rig Veda Americanus; Sacred Songs of the Ancient Mexicans, With a Gloss in Nahuatl, With Paraphrase, Notes, and Vocabulary.* Library of Aboriginal American Literature, 8. D. G. Brinton, Philadelphia, 1890. 95 p. Br897C B776. Publication of the twenty *Cantares a los Dioses* in Nahuatl and English translation based on the *Primeros memoriales* and *Codex Florentine* texts.

736. Brinton, Daniel G. So-called bow-puller identified as the Greek *uvpune. Bulletin of the Museum of Science and Art, University of Pennsylvania* 1(1), 1897. 6 p. Br913 B775; Br497 B775.2.

737. Brinton, Daniel G. Some words from the Andagueda dialect of the Chaco stock. *Proceedings of the American Philosophical Society* 34:401–402, 1895. Br497 B77.5; Br497 B775.2.

738. Brinton, Daniel G. Spelling reform, a dream and a folly. *Journal of Communication*, July, 1896. 3 p. Br422.34 B77; Br497 B77.5.

739. Brinton, Daniel G. Studies in South American native languages, from manuscripts and rare printed sources. *Proceedings of the American Philosophical Society* 30(137): 45–105, 1892. Br498.6 B 77.

740. Brinton, Daniel G. Study of the Nahuatl language. *American Antiquarian* 8, 1886. 7 p. Br497 B77.

741. Brinton, Daniel G. Ta ki, the svastika and the cross in America. *Proceedings of the*

Daniel G. Brinton (from Justin Winsor, Aboriginal America. *Cambridge, MA: Houghton, Mifflin, 1889. p. 165).*

American Philosophical Society 27, 1889. 13 p. Br497 B77.

742. Brinton, Daniel G. Taensa grammar and dictionary: a deception exposed. *American Antiquarian* 7:109-114, 1885. Br497 B77.

743. Brinton, Daniel G. *The Aims of Anthropology; Address Before the American Association for the Advancement of Science, at the Springfield Meeting, August 1895.* Aylward and Huntress, Salem, MA, 1895. 17 p. Br497 B775.2; Br572 B77.

744. Brinton, Daniel G. The American race. *Brighton Herald,* May 30, June 6, 1891. New York. 15 p. Br572C An8141 v.10.

745. Brinton, Daniel G. *The American Race; A Linguistic Classification and Ethnographic Description of the Native Tribes of North and South America.* N. D. C. Hodges, New York, 1891. 392 p. Br572.97 B77.

746. Brinton, Daniel G. The ancient phonetic alphabet of Yucatan. *American Historical Magazine,* 1870. 8 p. Br572C An8141 v.35.

747. Brinton, Daniel G. *The Annals of the Cakchiquels; The Original Text, With a Translation, Notes and Introduction.* Library of Aboriginal American Literature, 6. D. G. Brinton, Philadelphia, 1885. 234 p. Br498.21 Car15; Br897C B776.

748. Brinton, Daniel G. The Arawack language of Guiana in its linguistic and ethnological relations. *Transactions of the American Philosophical Society* 14(3): 427-444, 1871. Br498.77 ArB 775; Br572C An8141 v.93. Contains also Josef von Siemiradzki, Beiträge zur Ethnographie der südamerikanischen Indianer, n.d.

749. Brinton, Daniel G. The battle and ruins of Cintla. *American Antiquarian* 18, 1896. 10 p. Br913 B775.

750. Brinton, Daniel G. The chief god of the Algonkins, in his character as a cheat and liar. *American Antiquarian* 7(3): 137-139, 1885. Br497 B77.5.

751. Brinton, Daniel G. The cradle of the Semites; two papers read before the Philadelphia Oriental Club by Daniel G. Brinton; a reply by Morris Jastrow. Philadelphia, 1890. 26 p. Br492 B772.

752. Brinton, Daniel G. *The Güegüence; A Comedy Ballet in the Nahuatl-Spanish Dialect of Nicaragua.* Library of Aboriginal American Literature, 3. D. G. Brinton, Philadelphia, 1883. 94 p. Br897C B776. The text was obtained in Nicaragua by Karl H. Berendt.

753. Brinton, Daniel G. The International Congress of Americanists. *American Anthropologist* 4(1): 33-37, 1891. Br572C An8141 v.83.

754. Brinton, Daniel G. *The Lenâpé and Their Legends; With the Complete Text and Symbols of the Walam Olum, a New Translation, and an Inquiry Into Its Authenticity.* Library of Aboriginal American Literature, 5. D. G. Brinton, Philadelphia, 1885. 262 p. Br897C B776. The text of the Walam Olum (Red Score) is from a manuscript prepared by C. S. Rafinesque in 1833 from materials furnished by a Delaware Indian.

755. Brinton, Daniel G. The Library of Aboriginal American Literature [prospectus]. n.d. 8 p. Br497 B77.

756. Brinton, Daniel G. The Matagalpan linguistic stock of Central America. *Proceedings of the American Philosophical Society* 34:403-415, 1895. Br497 B775.2.

757. Brinton, Daniel G. *The Maya Chronicles.* Library of Aboriginal American Literature, 1. D. G. Brinton, Philadelphia, 1882. 279 p. Br897C B776. Includes selections from the books of Chilam Balam of Mani, Tizimin and Chumayel, respectively (pp. 79-185) including only the consecutive series of katuns that record ancient historical events in Yucatán. To these chronicles is added "The chronicle of Chac Xulub Chen [i.e. a history of the town of Chicxulub and of the conquest of the country] by N. Pech, 1562" (pp. 187-259). The Mayan text of each chronicle is followed by the editor's English translation and notes; in English and Mayan.

758. Brinton, Daniel G. *The Myths of the New World; A Treatise on the Symbolism and Mythology of the Red Race of America.* 3d ed. D. McKay, Philadelphia, 1896. 360 p. Br398.21 B773.

759. Brinton, Daniel G. *The Native Calendar of Central America and Mexico: A Study in Linguistics and Symbolism.* MacCalla and Company, Printers, Philadelphia, 1893. 59 p. "Read before the American Philosophical Society, Oct. 6, 1893." Br913.72 B776.

760. Brinton, Daniel G. The new poetic form as shown in Browning; read before the Browning Society of the New Century Club of Philadelphia, March 20, 1890. *Poet-Lore* 2:234-236, 1890. Br821 B82yBr2.

761. Brinton, Daniel G. The probable nationality of the Mound Builders. *American Antiquarian* 4(1): 9-18, 1881. Br572C An8141 v.59.

762. Brinton, Daniel G. *The Pursuit of Happiness; A Book of Studies and Strowings.* D.

McKay, Philadelphia, 1893. 292 p. Br143 B77.

763. Brinton, Daniel G. *The Religious Sentiment, Its Source and Aim; A Contribution to the Science and Philosophy of Religion*. Holt, New York, 1876. 284 p. Br201 B77.

764. Brinton, Daniel G. The Taensa grammar and dictionary, a deception exposed. *American Antiquarian* 7(2): 109-114, 1885. Br497 B77.5.

765. Brinton, Daniel G. The Taensa grammar and dictionary; a reply to M. Lucien Adam. *American Antiquarian* 7, 1885. 2 p. Br497 B77; Br572C An8141 v.47.

766. Brinton, Daniel G. Variations in the human skeleton and their causes. *American Anthropologist* 7:377-386, 1894. 10 p. Br913 B775.

767. Brinton, Daniel G. Vocabularies from the Mosquito Coast. *Proceedings of the American Philosophical Society* 29, 1891. 4 p. Br497 B77.5; Br572C An8141 v.47.

768. Brinton, Daniel G. Vocabulary of the Nanticoke dialect. *Proceedings of the American Philosophical Society* 31:325-333, 1893. Br497 B77.5.

769. Brinton, Daniel G. Vocabulary of the Noanama dialect of the Choco stock. *Proceedings of the American Philosophical Society* 35:202-204, 1896. Br497 B77.5.

770. Brinton, Daniel G. Were the Toltecs an historic nationality? *Proceedings of the American Philosophical Society* 24, 1887. 15 p. Br497 B77.

771. Brinton, Daniel G., and Albert S. Anthony. *A Lenapé-English Dictionary; From an Anonymous Manuscript in the Archives of the Moravian Church at Bethlehem, Pennsylvania; Edited With Additions, by Daniel G. Brinton...and Rev. Albert Seqaqkind Anthony*. Historical Society of Pennsylvania, Philadelphia, 1888. 236 p. Br497.11 DB77.

772. Brinton, Daniel G., and Morris Jastrow, *Cradle of the Semites; A Paper Read Before the Philadelphia Club*. Philadelphia, 1890. 26 p. Br497 B775.2.

773. Brinton, Daniel G., Henry Phillips, and J. Cheston Morris. The tribute roll of Montezuma. *Transactions of the American Philosophical Society* 17(2): 53-61, 1892. Br572C An8141 v.107.

774. Brinton, Daniel G., Henry Phillips, and Monroe B. Snyder. Report of the Committee appointed October 21, 1887, to examine into the scientific value of Volapük, presented to the American Philosophical Society, November, 1887. *Proceedings of the American Philosophical Society* 24, 1887. 12 p. Br497 B77.5; Br497 B775.2.

775. Brinton, Daniel G., Henry Phillips, and Monroe B. Snyder. Supplementary Report of the Committee appointed to consider an international language, read before the American Philosophical Society, December 7, 1888. Philadelphia, 1888. 8 p. Br497 B77.

776. Brintonia; three volumes of material relating to the Indians of America which form a part of the Daniel Garrison Brinton manuscript collection contained in the library of the University Museum, University of Pennsylvania. n.d. 3 v. Br497C B776. Manuscript; contents include: v.1. Bibliographical catalogue of American Indians and languages arranged alphabetically under name of tribe or language; v.2. Alphabetical list of authors which may have formed an author index to a portion of the collection of pamphlets which were later bound in more than one hundred volumes; v.3. Alphabetical list of subjects which may have formed a subject index to a portion of

the collection which were later bound in more than one hundred volumes.

777. Brisset, Jean-Pierre. *La science de dieu ou la création de l'homme*. Chamuel, Paris, 1900. 252 p. Br204.11 B778.

778. British and Foreign Aborigines Protection Society. *Report on the Indians of Upper Canada*. The British and Foreign Aborigines Protection Society, London, 1839. 52 p. Br572C An8141 v.34.

779. British Association for Advancement of Science. *Ethnographical Survey of the United Kingdom; Fourth Report of the Committee*, pp. 607–656, 1896. London. Br572.942 B77.

780. British Association for Advancement of Science. *Forms of Schedule, Prepared by a Committee of the British Association for the Advancement of Science Appointed to Organise an Ethnographical Survey of the United Kingdom*. London, 1893. 18 p. Br572.942 B77.2. Bound with: E. S. Hartland, Notes explanatory of the schedules, n.d.

781. British Association for the Advancement of Science. *Eighth Report on the North-Western tribes of Canada*. Spottswoode and Company, London, 1892. Br572C An8141 v.129.

782. British Association for the Advancement of Science. *Seventh Report on the North-Western tribes of Canada*. Spottswoode and Company, London, 1891. 43 p. Br572C An8141 v.10.

783. Broadhead, Garland C. Prehistoric evidences in Missouri. *Annual Report of the United States National Museum, Smithsonian Institution, for 1879–1880*, pp. 350–359, 1880. Br572C An8141 v.19.

784. Broca, Paul. *Instructions craniologiques et craniométriques de la Société d'Anthropologie de Paris*. G. Masson, Paris, 1875. 203 p. Br573.7 B782.

785. Broca, Paul. Populations préhistoriques d'Ancon. *Revue d'Anthropologie* 14(1): 55–69, 1875. Br572C An8141 v.20.

786. Broca, Paul. Sur l'origine et la répartition de la langue basque. *Revue d'Anthropologie* 14(1), 1875. 53 p. Br572C An8141 v.31.

787. Broca, Paul. Trepanning among the Incas. *Journal de la Société d'Anthropologique de Paris*, pp. 71–77, 1867. Br572C An8141 v.58.

788. Bromowicz, Franz. Vocabulario de la lengua pocomam de Jilotepec. 1878. 15 leaves. Br498.21. The rough notes of this journey, titled "Expedition nach Acasaguastlan und Jilotepec, Februar 8–23, 1878; Pocomam de Jilotepec," are contained in this manuscript; includes two vocabularies of approximately 200 words each.

789. Brooks, C. H., and A. Penny. *A Luku, a Ioane*. Society for Promoting Christian Knowledge, London, 1882. 153 p. Br497.54 B47.5. The Gospels of St. Luke and St. John translated into Timuquan.

790. Brooks, William K. On the Lucayan Indians. *Memoir of the National Academy of Sciences* 4:215–222, 1887. Br572C An8141 v.102.

791. Brown, Arthur E. The kindred of man. *Kansas City Review* 4(11): 628–636, 1883. Br572C An8141 v.13.

792. Brown, R. T. Ancient earthworks in Indiana. *Indianapolis Journal*, pp. 80–81, n.d. Br571.1 G89.5.

793. Brown, Robert. Euphratean stellar researches. *Proceedings of the Society of Biblical Archaeology*, pp. 16-36, 1895. Br572C An8141 v.138.

794. Brown, Robert. On the vegetable products used by the Northwest American Indians. *Pharmaceutical Journal and Transactions* 10(2): 89-94, 168-174, 1868. Br572C An8141 v.38.

795. Brown, Robert. *Semitic Influence in Hellenic Mythology, With Special Reference to the Recent Mythological Works of F. Max Müller and Andrew Lang.* Williams and Norgate, London, 1898. 228 p. Br282 B81.

796. Brown, W. W. Some indoor and outdoor games of the Wabanaki Indians. *Transactions of the Royal Society of Canada* 6(2): 41-46, 1888. Br572C An8141 v.96.

797. Browne, Mary E., ed. After the storm in St. Vincent. *Timenri; Being the Journal of the Royal Agricultural and Commercial Society* 5(2): 274-282, 1886. Br572C An8141 v.68.

798. Bruchmann, Kurt, Über mexikanische Poesie aus Anlass von Daniel G. Brinton *Ancient Nahuatl Poetry*, Philadelphia, 1887. *Prüssischen Jahrbüchern* 64(2): 196-211, n.d. Br572C An8141 v.48.

799. Brühl, Gustav. *Die Culturvölker alt-Amerika's.* Benziger Brothers, New York, Cincinnati, 1875-1887. 516 p. Br913.7 B83a.

800. Brühl, Gustav. On the pre-Columbian existence of syphilis in the western hemisphere. *Cincinnati Lancet Clinic*, May 29, 1880. 7 p. Br572C An8141 v.35.

801. Brühl, Gustav. Pre-Columbian syphilis in the western hemisphere. *Cincinnati Lancet Clinic*, March 8, 1890. 8 p. Br572C An8141 v.20.

802. Bruncken, Ernest. How Germans become Americans. *Proceedings of the State Historical Society of Wisconsin*, pp. 101-122, 1897. Br572C An8141 v.148.

803. Brunner, David B. *The Indians of Berks County, Pa.; Being A Summary of All the Tangible Records of the Aborigines of Berks County, and Containing Cuts and Descriptions of the Varieties of Relics Found Within the County; Written for the Society of Natural Sciences, Reading, Pa.* The Spirit of Berks Book and Job Printing Office, Reading, PA, 1881. 177 p. Br970.4 PB835.

804. Bruyas, Jacques. *Radices vberborum iroquaeorum.* Shea's Library of American Linguistics, 10. Cramoisy Press, New York, 1863. 123 p. Br497C Sh3; Br497C Sh3a.

805. Bryant, H. G. Abstract of a paper on the most northern Eskimos. *Sixth International Geographical Congress*, 1895. 3 p. Br572C An8141 v.138.

806. Brydges, J. *Aposl'ndfan u3tagu; The Acts of the Apostles, Translated into the Yahgan Language.* British and Foreign Bible Society, London, 1883. 118 p. Br498.9783 YB 47.6. New Testament Acts of the Apostles translated into Yahgan.

807. Brydges, J. *Gospl LYC ecamanaci, the Gospel of St. Luke, Translated into the Yahgan Language.* British and Foreign Bible Society, London, 1881. 120 p. Br498.9783 YB 47. New Testament Gospel of St. Luke translated into Yahgan.

808. Bucke, R. M. On sanity. *American Journal of Insanity* (July): 3-10, 1890. Br572C An8141 v.82.

809. Buckley, E. *Phallicism in Japan.* University of Chicago Press, Chicago, 1895. 34 p. Br572C An8141 v.138.

810. Buckner, Henry F., and Goliath Herrod. *A Grammar of the Masjwke, Or Creek Language To Which Are Prefixed Lessons in Spelling, Reading, and Defining.* The Domestic and Indian Mission Board of the Southern Baptist Convention, Marion, Alabama, 1860. 138 p. Br497.39 CrB85.

811. Büdinger, Max. *Acten zu Columbus; Geschichte von 1473 bis 1492.* Sitzungsberichte der Phil.–Hist. Classe der Kais. Akademie der Wissenschaften, 112(11). In Commission bei C. Gerold's Sohn, Wien, 1886. 53 p. Br572C An8141 v.40.

812. Buelna, Eustaquio. *La Atlántida y la última Tule.* Oficina Tipografica de la Secretaría de Fomento, México, 1895. 48 p. Br572C An8141 v.148.

813. Buelna, Eustaquio. *Luces del otomi ó, gramática del idioma que hablan los indios otomíes en la republica mexicana.* Imprenta del Gobierno Federal, Mexico, 1893. 303 p. Br498.23 OL 963.

814. Buelna, Eustaquio. *Peregrinación de los aztecas y nombres geográficos indígenas de Sinaloa.* Tipografía Literaria de Filomeno Mata, México, 1887. 140 p. Br572C An8141 v.61; Br572C An8141 v.119.

815. Bullock, William. *Voyage au Mexique, contenant des notions exactes et peu connues sur la situation physique, morale et politique de ce pays; accompagné d'un atlas de vingt planches par M. Beulloch…ouvrage traduit de l'anglais par M ***. Précédé d'une introd., et enrichi de pièces justificatives et de notes; par Sir John Bierley.* Lebigre Frères, Paris, 1831. 2 v. Br917.2 B463.

816. Bunyan, John. *The Pilgrim's Progress, by John Bunyan, In the Dakota Language; Translated by Stephen R. Riggs.* American Tract Society, New York, 1857. 264 p. Br497.5 DB88. Title in Dakota on verso of title page reads: Mahpiya ekta oicimani ya; John Bunyan oyaka, Dakota iapi en tamakoce okaga.

817. Burman, W. A. *Hanhanna qais Htayetu Cekiyapi; token ptecena eyapi kte cin, qa litany, qa nakun Dawid Tadowan kin etanhan, tonana Kahnigapi, qa Itancan Htayetu wotapi tawa kin, token wicaqupi kin, qa Omniciye kin en Hoksiyopa Baptisma wicaqupi kin, token eyapi kte hecetu.* Society for Promoting Christian Knowledge, London, 1889. 215 p. Br497.5 DB92. Printed for use at the Sioux mission, Manitoba, Canada, with the approval of the Lord Archbishop of Canterbury, and by direction of the Bishop of Rupert's Land. Church of England Book of Common Prayer translated into Dakota.

818. Burns, F. The Crump Burial Cave. *Annual Report of the United States National Museum, Smithsonian Institution, for 1892,* pp. 451-454, 1894. Br572C An8141 v.136.

819. Burton, Richard F. A day amongst the Fans. *Transactions of the Ethnological Society of London* 3:136-147, 1865. Br572C An8141 v.33. Sir Richard Burton (1821-1890) is today chiefly known for his attempt to discover the source of the Nile River yet in his day he helped found British anthropology.

820. Burton, Richard F. *The Jew, The Gypsy and El Islam.* Wilkins, Chicago, 1898. 351 p. Br270.4 B95.

821. Burton, Richard F. The primordial inhabitants of Minas Geraes, and the occupations of the present inhabitants. *Journal of the Anthropological Institute of Great*

Britain and Ireland 2(3): 407–423, 1873. Br572C An8141 v.33.

822. Busch, Friedrich. Über die Schädelbildung bei niederen Menschenrassen. *Verhandlungen der Deutschen Odontolog* 6(2), n.d. 79 p. Br572C An8141 v.138.

823. Busch, Friedrich. Über niedere Menschenrassen mit Vorführung einiger menschlicher Rassenschädel. *Verhandlungen der Deutschen Odontolog* 5(1–2), n.d. 69 p. Br572C An8141 v.138.

824. Busch, Friedrich. Über Verschmelzung und Verwachsung der Zähne des Michgenisses und des bleibenden Gebisses. *Verhandlungen der Deutschen Odontolog* 5(2), n.d. 58 p. Br572C An8141 v.138.

825. Buschan, Georg. Körpergewicht, Gewicht des ganzen Körpers und seiner Theile. *Real-Encyclopädie der Gesammten Heilkunde*, n.d. 34 p. Br572C An8141 v.148; Br573.6 B963.

826. Buschan, Georg. Körperlänge. In *Real-Encyclopädie der Gesammten Heilkunde*. Gistel, Wien, n.d. 25 p. Br572C An8141 v.148; Br573.6 B96.2.

827. Buschmann, Johann K. E. Der athapaskische Sprachstamm dargestellt von Hrn. Buschmann. *Abhandlungen der Königlichen Akademie der Wissenschaften zu Berlin* 1855:144–319, 1856. Br497.12 B96a. Buschmann (1805–1880) was educated at the Universities of Berlin and Göttingen and in 1832 was appointed librarian at the Royal Public Library in Berlin, a position he kept until his death. His outstanding contribution to anthropology was his comparative grammatical and lexical work on Northern and Mesoamerican Indian languages, which he attempted to classify genetically into large families. The "Athapascan" (Athabaskan) and the "Uto-Aztecan" families were defined by Buschmann prior to 1860.

828. Buschmann, Johann K. E. Die Sprachen Kizh und Netela von Neu-Californien dargestellt. *Abhandlungen der Königlichen Akademie der Wissenschaften zu Berlin*, pp. 501–531, 1855. Br572C An8141 v.92.

829. Buschmann, Johann K. E. *Die Spuren der aztekischen Sprache im nördlichen Mexico, und höheren amerikanischen Norden; zugleich eine Musterung der Völker und Sprachen des nördlichen Mexico's und der Westseite Nordamerika's von Guadalaxara an bis zum Eismeer.* Gedrukt in der Buchdrukerei der Königlichen Akademie der Wissenschaften, Berlin, 1859. 819 p. Br498.22 AzB 96.3.

830. Buschmann, Johann K. E. Die Völker und Sprachen Neu-Mexico's und der Westseite des britischen Nordamerika's. *Abhandlungen der Königlichen Akademie der Wissenschaften zu Berlin* 8:209–414, 1857. Br572C An8141 v.2.

831. Buschmann, Johann K. E. *Grammatik der sonorischen Sprachen; Vorzüglich der Tarahumara, Tepeguana, Cora und Cahita.* F. Dümmler's Verlags-Buchhandlung, 1864. Br498.22 B96.2. Extract from *Abhandlungen der Königlichen Akademie der Wissenschaften zu Berlin*, pp. 369–453, 1863.

832. Buschmann, Johann K. E. *Über die aztekischen Ortsnamen.* Gedrukt in der Druckerei der Königlichen Akademie der Wissenschaften zu Berlin, 1853. 206 p. Br498.22 AzB 96.

833. Byington, Cyrus. *Grammar of the Choctaw Language; Edited From the Original*

Manuscript by Daniel G. Brinton. McCalla and Stavely, Printers, Philadelphia, 1870. 56 p. Br497.39 ChB99.

834. Byington, Cyrus. Grammar of the Choctaw language; prepared by the Reverend Cyrus Byington, and edited by Dr. Brinton. *Proceedings of the American Philosophical Society* 1:317-367, 1871. Br572C An8141 v.50.

835. Byington, Cyrus. *The Books of Genesis, Exodus, Leviticus, Numbers, and Deuteronomy, Translated into the Choctaw Language; Chenesis, Eksotus, Lefitikus, Numbas, Micha Tutelonomi holisso aiena kut toshowut Chahta anumpa toba hoke.* American Bible Society, New York, 1867. 564 p. Br497.39 ChB46.2. Translation of selections from the Old Testament into Choctaw.

836. Caballero, Darío J. *Gramática del idioma mexicana segun el sistema de "Ollendorff".* Tipografía Literaría de F. Mata, México, 1880. 212 p. Br498.22 AzC 11.

837. Cadena de Vilhasanti, Pedro. *Beschreibung des portugiesischen Amerika vom Cudena [i.e. Cadena] ein spanisches Manuscript in der Wolfenbüttelschen Bibliothek; hrsg. vom Herrn Hofrath Lessing; mit Anmerkungen und Zusätzen begleitet von Christian Leiste.* Buchhandlung des Fürstl. Waysenhauses, Braunschweig, 1780. 160 p. Br498.6 C 892. Text on pp. 13-41, in Spanish and German, has title: Discripción de mil y treinta y ocho leguas de tierra del esto de Brasil, conquista del Marañon y Gran Pará...with dedication to Don Gaspar de Gusmann, dated "Madrid, 20 de septemb. 1634." The Wolfenbüttel manuscript includes an anonymous German translation, here attributed to Lessing, and corrected by Leiste. "Vorbericht des Herrn Hofrath Lessing": p. [3]-12. "Anmerkungen über vorstehenden spanischen Aufsatz des Cudena [sic]": p. 42-160.

838. Caland, W. *Die Altindischen Todten- und Bestattungsgebräuche mit benutzung Handschriftlicher Quellen.* Johannes Müller, Amsterdam, 1896. 190 p. Br572C An8141 v.160.

839. Calcaño, Julio. *Resumen de las actas de la Academia Venezolana.* Imprenta Nacional, Caracas, 1886. 86 p. Br572C An8141 v.51.

840. Calderon, Eustorgio. Ensayo lingüístico sobre el pupuluca y otra lengua india del sureste de Guatemala congénere del Pupuluca, precedido de un corto vocabulario de ambos idiomas. *Repertorio Salvadoreño* 5(1): 12-27, 119-153, 1891. Br572C An8141 v.48.

841. Calendario de los indios de Guatemala, 1685. Cakchiquel, copiado en la ciudad de Guatemala, marzo 1878. 27 p. Br498.21 KiC124. Manuscript. Added title page bears the notation "Copiado en la Ciudad de Guatemala. Marzo 1878." Karl H. Berendt's introduction indicates that the calendar was found in the "Chronica de la Santa Provincia del Santissimo Nombre de Jesús de Guatemala de la Orden de N. Serafico Padre San Francisco en el reino de la Nueva España." Portion of a manuscript from around 1685 containing the names of the days and months in the calendar of the Cakchiquel Indians. The first eight pages explain the history of the manuscript which was discovered in 1829 by Juan Gavarrete among the papers of the Franciscan convent in Guatemala City. They also include a description of the Cakchiquel year, arranged in eighteen months of twenty days each, with five extra days baldios

at the end of the year. Berendt makes various comparisons between the Mayan and Aztec calendars, and lists the names of the months in each calendar, as well as the names of the days and their meanings. Pages 9-27 contain the names and meaning of each month in the Cakchiquel calendar, and a list of the days with their corresponding dates in the Julian calendar.

842. Calendario de los indios de Guatemala, 1722. Kiche. 50 p. Br498.21 KiC124. Title page notation reads "Copiado en la ciudad de Guatemala, abril 1877." The introductory note by Karl H. Berendt contains a brief history of the original calendar, and an explanation of how the Quiché counted the days, weeks, and months of the year which for them began on February 21. There is a diagram of the Quiché calendar wheel, followed by a list of the days and months in Quiché and the Julian calendar equivalents in Spanish. Additional dates are given for the years 1723-1727.

843. Calleja, Felix M. Informé general, Colonia del Nuevo Santander y Nuevo Reino de Leon, 1795. 74 leaves. Br970.4 TC134. Manuscript; includes: 1. La descripzion ystorica, geografica, poblazion, bienes, industria, comercio, producto de meritas reales medios que para el fomento de arribas provincias pueden adaptarse tropas que tienen para su defensa y servicio de las veteranas; 2. Ystoria militar politica hasta el actual estado modo de tratar los yndios el en que hacen la guerra y el en que deve hacerseles, con reflexiones sobre estos puntos.

844. Calvert, Albert F. *The Aborigines of Western Australia*. Simpkin, Marshall, Hamilton, Kent and Company, Limited, London, 1894. 55 p. Br572.9 C13.

845. Camargo, Diego Muñoz. *Historia de Tlaxcala...por Diego Muñoz Camargo; publicada y anotada por Alfredo Chavero; se hace esta edición...para presentarla como un homenaje á Cristóbal Colón, en la exposición de Chicago. anotada por Alfredo Chavero*. Oficina Tipografica de la Secretaria de Fomento, 1892. 278 p. Br972.4 C14.

846. Campbell, John T. Traces of prehistoric man on the Wabash. *American Naturalist* 19:969-972, 1885. Br572C An8141 v.13.

847. Campbell, John. Asiatic tribes in North America. *Proceedings of the Canadian Institute* 3, 1881. 38 p. Br572C An8141 v.60.

848. Campbell, John. *Etruria Capta*. Copp, Clark, Toronto, 1886. 123 p. Br913.3791 C15.

849. Campbell, John. Hittites in America. *Canadian Naturalist* 9(6): 1-23, 1873. Br572C An8141 v.60.

850. Campbell, John. The affiliation of the Algonquin languages. *Proceedings of the Canadian Institute* 1:15-53, 1879. Br572C An8141 v.116.

851. Campbell, John. *Travels in South Africa Undertaken at the Request of the Missionary Society*. Printed for the author, London, 1815. 582 p. Br916.8 C15.

852. Canadian Institute. *Annual Archaeological Report of the Canadian Institute, Session 1891; Being An Appendix to the Report of the Minister of Education, Ontario*. Warwick and Sons, Toronto, 1892. 72 p. Br572C An8141 v.15.

853. Canadian Institute. *Annual Report of the Canadian Institute, Session 1886-1887; Being Part of Appendix to the Report of the Minister of Education, Ontario, 1887*. Warwick and Sons, Toronto, 1888. 58 p. Br572C An8141 v.15.

854. Canadian Institute. *Annual Report of the Canadian Institute, Session 1887-1888;*

Being Part of Appendix to the Report of the Minister of Education, Ontario, 1888. Warwick and Sons, Toronto, 1889. 118 p. Br572C An8141 v.15.

855. Canadian Institute. *Annual Report of the Canadian Institute, Session 1888-1889; Being Part of Appendix to the Report of the Minister of Education, Ontario, 1889.* Warwick and Sons, Toronto, 1890. 118 p. Br572C An8141 v.15.

856. Canadian Institute. *Fifth Annual Report of the Canadian Institute, Session 1892-1893; Being An Appendix to the Report of the Minister of Education.* Warwick and Sons, Toronto, 1893. 34 p. Br572C An8141 v.114.

857. Canadian Institute. *Fourth Annual report of the Canadian Institute, Session 1890-1891; Being An Appendix to the Report of the Minister of Education, Ontario.* Warwick and Sons, Toronto, 1891. 90 p. Br572C An8141 v.15.

858. Canadian Institute. General bibliography of original contributions to the publications of the Canadian Institute. *Transactions of the Canadian Institiute* 3:317-340, 1891-1892. Br572C An8141 v.114.

859. Canadian Institute. *Proceedings of the Canadian Institute*, v. 1, 1879. Toronto. Br980.3 GoC164.

860. Canadian Institute. *Proceedings of the Canadian Institute*, v. 7, 1888-1889, 1890. Toronto. Br572C An8141 v.67.

861. Canadian Institute. *Proceedings of the Canadian Institute*, v. 6, 1887. Toronto. Br572C An8141 v.65.

862. Canizzaro, F. A. *Genesi ed evoluzione del mito.* Tipi Extra Moenia, Messina, 1893. 44 p. Br572C An8141 v.129.

863. Cannizzaro, F. A. Daniel G. Brinton, *Nagualism: A Study in Native American Folklore and History* [review]. *Archivo per le Tradizioni Popolari* 15:447-449, 1896. Br572C An8141 v.164.

864. Cannizzaro, F. A. *Le Origini Religiose dell'India e Delta Grecia.* Tipografía dell'Unione Cooperativa Editrice, Roma, 1895. 27 p. Br572C An 8141 v.139.

865. Cannizzaro, F. A. *Scongiuri: raccolti nella provincia di Messina.* Archivo per le Tradizioni Popolari, 1896. 2 p. Br572C An8141 v.164.

866. Cano, Agustin. Informe dado al Rey, sobre la entrada que por la parte de la Verapaz se hizo al Petén el año 1695 y fragmento de una carta del mismo sobre el propio asunto. n.d. 19, 27 p. Br972.81 Sa53.

867. Cano, Agustin. Manche y Peten, 1696. 10, 47, 56 leaves. Br970.4 GC162. Manuscript.

868. *Canonicus Memorial Services of Sedication.* Rhode Island Historical Society, Province, 1883. 31 p. Br572C An8141 v.32.

869. Cantos en lengua mexicana, 17 cent. 18 leaves. Br498.22 AzC 168. Manuscript; transcribed by C. E. Brasseur de Bourbourg in Mexico City, February, 1865.

870. Capellini, Giovanni. *Relazione di un viaggio scientifico: nell'America settentrionale.* Tipi Gamberini e Parmegiani, Bologna, 1864. 44 p. Br572C An8141 v.7.

871. Cardim, Ferno. *Indios do Brazil.* Rio de Janeiro, 1881. 121 p. Br572C An8141 v.33.

872. Cardús, José. *Las misiones franciscanas entre los infieles de Bolivia; descripción del estado de ellas en 1883 y 1884, con una noticia sobre los caminos y tribus salvajes, una muestra de varias lenguas, curiosidades de historia natural, y un*

mapa para servir de ilustracion. Librería de la Inmaculada Concepción, Barcelona, 1886. 429 p. Br243.2 F84C.

873. Carnoy, Henry, and Stanislao Prato. *Le menuisier le tailleur et le sophta...notes comparatives.* Aux Bureau de La Tradition, Paris, 1891. 10 p. Br572C An8141 v.120.

874. Carnoy, Henry. *Le professeur Dr. Stanislas Prato...essai biographique et bibliographique.* Aux Bureau de La Tradition, Paris, 1889. 8 p. Br572C An8141 v.120.

875. Carochi, Horacio. *Arte de la lengva mexicana con la declaración de los adverbios della al Illustrisso. Y Reuerendisso.* Impresso con licencia por Iuan Ruyz, En Mexico, 1645. 132 leaves. Br498.22 AzC 223.2.

876. Carochi, Horacio. *Compendio del arte de la lengua mexicana del P. Horacio Carochi de la Compañia de Jesvs; dispuesto con brevedad, claridad, y propriedad, por el P. Ignacio de Paredes de la misma compañia...y dividido en tres partes, en la primera se trata de todo lo perteneciente à reglas del arte...en la segunda se enseña la formación de unos vocablos, de otros...en la tercera se ponen los adverbios más necessarios de la lengua.* En la Imprenta de la Bibliotheca Mexicana, México, 1759. 202 p. Br498.22 AzC 223.

877. Carpenter, Edward. *Civilisation, Its Cause and Cure and Other Essays.* Swan Sonnenschein and Company, Paternoster Square, London; S. Cowan and Company, General Printers, Perth, 1889. 156 p. Br301.1 C225a.

878. Carr, Lucien, and N. S. Shaler. On the prehistoric remains of Kentucky. *Memoirs of the Kentucky Geological Survey* 1(4): 3-31, 1876. Br572C An8141 v.97.

879. Carr, Lucien. Measurements of crania from California. *Annual Reports of the Trustees of the Peabody Museum of American Archaeology and Ethnology* 2(3): 497-505, 1880. Br913.07 H265.

880. Carr, Lucien. Notes on the crania of New England Indians. *Anniversary Memoirs of the Boston Society of Natural History*, 1880. 10 p. Br572C An8141 v.95.

881. Carr, Lucien. Observations on the crania from the stone graves in Tennessee. *Annual Reports of the Trustees of the Peabody Museum of American Archaeology and Ethnology* 2(2): 3612-384, 1878. Br913.07 H265.

882. Carr, Lucien. On the social and political position of woman among the Huron-Iroquois tribes. *Annual Reports of the Trustees of the Peabody Museum of American Archaeology and Ethnology* 3(3-4): 207-232, 1884. Br913.07 H265.

883. Carr, Lucien. Report on the exploration of a mound in Lee County, Virginia, conducted for the Peabody Museum. *Annual Reports of the Trustees of the Peabody Museum of American Archaeology and Ethnology* 2(1): 75-94, 1877. Br913.07 H265.

884. Carr, Lucien. The food of certain American Indians and their methods of preparing it. *Proceedings of the American Antiquarian Society* 10:155-190, 1895. Br572C An 8141 v.139.

885. Carr, Lucien. *The Mounds of the Mississippi Valley, Historically Considered.* Robert Clarke and Company, Cincinnati, 1883. 107 p. Br557 C23; Br572C An8141 v.97.

886. Carrera, Fernando de la. *Arte de la lengua yunga de los valles del obispado de Trujillo, con un confesonario* [sic] *y todas las oraciones cristianas y otras cosas, autor el beneficiado d. Fernando de la Carrera...dirijido al licenciado don Matías*

de Caravantes. Reimpreso en la Imprenta liberal, Lima, 1880. 130 p. Br498.73 MC233. "La obra ó 'El arte de la lengua yunga' se ha hecho tan rara que quizá no pasan de tres los ejemplares conocidos en las mejores bibliotecas de Europa y América; por esto...la reimprimimos en la 'Revista peruana y hemos hecho una edición especial de solo doscientos ejemplares."

887. Carriedo, Juan B. *Ensayo histórico-estadistico del Departamento de Oaxaca*. Imprenta del Estado, en la Escuela correccional de Artes y Oficios, Oaxaca, 1889. Br572C An8141 v.115.

888. Carriedo, Juan B. *Estudios históricos, y estadisticos del Estado Oaxaqueño*. Imprenta del autor, Oaxaca, 1847. 84 p. Br917.27 C233.

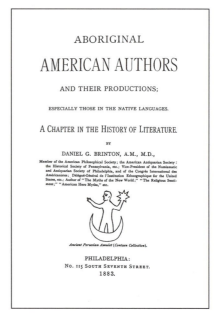

ABORIGINAL

AMERICAN AUTHORS

AND THEIR PRODUCTIONS;

ESPECIALLY THOSE IN THE NATIVE LANGUAGES.

A CHAPTER IN THE HISTORY OF LITERATURE.

BY

DANIEL G. BRINTON, A.M., M.D.,

Member of the American Philosophical Society; the American Antiquarian Society; the Historical Society of Pennsylvania, etc.; Vice-President of the Numismatic and Antiquarian Society of Philadelphia, and of the Congrès International des Américanistes; Délégué-Général de l'Institution Ethnographique for the United States, etc.; Author of "The Myths of the New World;" "The Religious Sentiment;" "American Hero Myths," etc.

Ancient Peruvian Amulet (Centum Collection).

PHILADELPHIA:
No. 115 South Seventh Street.
1883.

Title page from Brinton's Aboriginal American Authors *(1883).*

889. Carrillo y Ancona, Crescencio. *Carta sobre la historia primitiva de la fiebre amarilla*. Imprenta Mercantil de Ignacio L. Mena y Compañía, Mérida de Yucatán, 1892. 26 p. Br572C An8141 v.110. Crescencio Carrillo y Ancona (1837–1897) was appointed the thirty-sixth bishop of Yucatan in 1887. He founded an archaeological museum at Merida and also started several literary periodicals. He was a friend of Juan Pío Pérez and kept alive the Pérez tradition of Maya studies.

890. Carrillo y Ancona, Crescencio. *Compendio de la historia de Yucatan; precedido del de su geografía y dispuesto en forma de lecciones; para servir de texto á la enseñanza de ambos ramos en los establecimientos de instrucción primaria y secundaria por Don Crescencio Carrillo*. J. D. Espinosa é hijos, Mérida, 1871. 432 p. Br972.6 C233.

891. Carrillo y Ancona, Crescencio. *El obispado de Yucatán historia de su fundación y de sus obispos desde el siglo XVI hasta el XIX seguida de las constituciones sinodales de la diócesis y otros documentos relativos*. Imprenta y Lit. de Ricardo B. Caballero, Mérida de Yucatán, 1892–189. 2 v. Br972.6 C233.2.

892. Carrillo y Ancona, Crescencio. *Ensayo biografico del señor doctor D. José Canufo Vela*. Imprenta de Rafael Pedreza, Mérida, 1859. 24 p. Br572C An8141 v.119.

893. Carrillo y Ancona, Crescencio. *Estudio filologico sobre el nombre de America y el de Yucatan*. Imprenta Mercantil a cargo de José Gamboa Guzman, Mérida de Yucatan, 1890. 54 p. Br572C An8141 v.48.

894. Carrillo y Ancona, Crescencio. *Estudio histórico sobre la raza indígena de Yucatán.*Tipografía de J. M. Blanco,Veracruz, 1865. 26 p. Br572C An8141 v.64; Br980.3 MC233.

895. Carrillo y Ancona, Crescencio. *Historia antigua de Yucatán.* Imprenta de Espinosa y Compañía, Mérida, 1881. 671 p. Br972.6 C233.3.

896. Carrillo y Ancona, Crescencio. *Manual de historia y geografía de la peninsula de Yucatan.* Imprenta de J.D. Espinosa e hijos, Mérida de Yucatán, 1868. Br572C An8141 v.74.

897. Carrillo y Ancona, Crescencio. *Raza indígena de Yucatan.*Tipografía de J. M. Blanco,Veracruz, 1865. 26 p. Br572C An8141 v.128.

898. Carrillo y Ancona, Crescencio. *Undecima carta pastoral; el cuarto centenario del descubrimiento de la America*, pp. 299-314. Imprenta y litografía de R. Caballero, Mérida de Yucatán, 1892. Br572C An8141 v.110.

899. Carrington, Henry B.The Dacotah tribes: their beliefs, and our duty to them outlined. *Proceedings of the American Association for the Advancement of Science* 29:689-693, 1881. Br572C An8141 v.19.

900. *Carta enciclica su santidad Leon XIII Papa por la divina providencia a los patriarcos, primados, arzobispos, obispos, y demas ordinarios en paz y comunión con la Sede apostolica, acerca del rosario de la Virgen Maria*, pp. 315-329. Imprenta y litografia de R. Caballero, Mérida de Yucatán, 1892. Br572C An8141 v.110.

901. Cartailhac, Émile. *Les âges préhistoriques de l'Espagne et du Portugal.* C. Reinwald, Paris, 1886. 347 p. Br913.46 C24.

902. *Cartilla o silabario del uso de letras y raiz de palabras de que se compone el idioma mexicano, segun un manual de los llamados indigenas de Tlaxcala.* Imprenta de J. N. del Valle, Puebla, 1847. 80 p. Br498.22 TlSc 68.

903. Carvajal, Francisco L. Discurso para el descendimiento del Señor por D. Francisco Carvajal, presbitero; copiado del original, manuscrito en poder del parocco de Santiago en Mérida, Pbro. D. Nic Delgado, noviembre 1868, Dr. C.H. Berendt. 40 p. Br498.21 MC679. Manuscript; describes the crucifixion and suffering of Christ, and contains parenthetical instructions to the priest in Spanish for the reenactment in church of the descent of Christ from the cross; also included are a 3-page Maya-Spanish vocabulary list of some important words and phrases from the sermons, nine anonymous 18th-century sermons for the Sundays in Lent,Ash Wednesday, and Good Friday, as well as the "Sermón de Animas" and "Sermón de Difuntos," followed by a short vocabulary list.

904. Carvajal, Jacinto de. *Relación del descubrimiento del Rio Apure hasta su ingreso en el Orinoco.* Diputación provincial, Leon, 1892. 444 p. Br918.7 C24. "Apuntes biográficos": p. [399]-426. Title of codex: Jornadas nauticas, continuadas por el cappitan Miguel de Ochogauia, vezino y ecommendero de la muy celebrada çiudad de Barinas, governaçion de la muy noble çiudad de Mérida, en el descubrimiento que hiço de el çelebrado rio de Apúre, mediante las cappitulaçiones que hiço…el señor governador v cappitan general…Françisco Martinez de Espinossa, a cuyo nobillissimo sujéto se dedica…fray Jaçintho de Caruaja.

905. Casalis, Eugène. *Études sur la langue séchuana*. Imprimerie Royale, Paris, 1841. 103 p. Br496 C263. Sotho language.

906. Casas, Bartolomé de las. *Colección de las obras del venerable obispo de Chiapa...Enriquecida con 1. Dos obras ineditas de que no habia noticia exacta; 2. Traducción de otra que habia escrito en latin y no pudo imprimir en España sobre los derechos de las naciones para limitar el poder de los reyes, la cual obra impresa en Alemansia es ya mui rara; 3. Cuatro disertaciones sobre si el venerable Las Casas tuvo parte ó no en la introducción y el fomento del comercio de Negros en América; 4. Notas criticas y apéndices históricos del editor sobre las obras del venerable Las Casas; 5. Retrato del autor y su vida escritá por el editor*. En casa de Rosa, Paris, 1822. 2 v. Br972 L33.1. The two unedited works are: "Carta escrita al padre maestro fray Bartolomé Carranza de Miranda, residente en Inglaterra con el rey Felipe II, en el año 1555, sobre la perpetuación de las encomiendas de los Indios, que se intentó entonces," and "Respuesta de Don fray Bartolome de Las-Casas, a la consulta que se le hizo sobre los sucesos de la conquisto del Peru en 1564": v. II, cap. 7 and 8. The translation is "Sobre la potestad soberana de los reyes para enagenar vasallos, pueblos y jurisdicciones": v. II, cap. 6. The four dissertations are: "Memoria apologética del Señor Gregoire, antiguo obispo de Blois en que se procuró persuadir que el venerable Casas no tuvo parte en la introducción del comercio de Negros en América"; "Disertación del doctor Don Gregorio de Funes dean de Cordova de Tucuman en froma de carta escrita al Señor obispo Gregoire sobre el mismo asunto"; "Memoria del doctor Mier, natural, de Mégico, confirmando la apologia del obispo Casas, escrita por el reverendo obispo de Blois, monseñor Henrique Gregoire, en carta escrita à las Memorias de las señores Grégorire, Mier y Funes": v. II, cap. 8.

907. Casas, Bartolomé de las. *Historia de las Indias*. Paz, Mexico, 1777. 2 v. Br972 L33.

908. Castaing, A. *Ethnographie de la France, à l'usage des écoles*. Bibliothèque Ethnographique, 2. Maisonneuve et Ch. Leclerc, Paris, 1885. 116 p. Br572C R737.

909. Castellanzuelo, F. M. *Wörterbuch und gramatik der Inka-Group*. Caspboya, 1870. 75 p. Br498.7 IC 278. Manuscript.

910. Castillejo, Clemente. Frases en lengua zotzil, 1830; fragmento. 3 leaves. Br498.21 TC 278. "Manuscript, original. Stained and not vey legible. Bound with it is a "Proclamation" of the governor of Chiapas, addressed to the Indians, and printed in the Zotzil tongue. It is dated 1869, and has a Spanish translation" (Brinton 1900). The proclamation mentioned by Brinton is *Aguaiic iscotol lumalic te indioetic; oid los pueblos todos de indios sublevedos* (Tipografía del Porvenir, a Cargo de Manuel María Trujillo, San Cristóbal, 1869), a political broadside, arranged Spanish and Tzotzil in parallel columns, addressed to the rebellious Indians at Chamula and signed "San Cristobal, a veinte de octubre de 1869, Feliciano J. Lazos [..] Jovel San Cristobal, tom cocal octubre de 1869, Manuel L. Solórsano."

911. Castillo y Orosco, E. *Vocabulario paez-castellano...con adiciones, correcciones i un vocabulario castellano-paez*. Bibliothèque Linguistique Américaine, 2. Maisonneuve, Paris, 1877. Br497C Am3.

912. Castillo, Jerónimo del. *Diccionario histórico, biografico y monumental de Yucatán. Desde la conquista hasta el ultimo año de la dominación española en el pais, por D. Jerónimo Castillo.* Tomo I, A-E. Imprenta de Castillo y Compania, Mérida, 1866. 315 p. Br972.6 C277.

913. *Catalogo de aimara y quichua de las voces mas usuales en castellano.* 3d ed. Imprenta de El Progreso, La Paz, 1879. 22 p. Br498.71 AC 283.

914. *Catalogo de las voces usuales de aimará, con la correspondencia en castellano y quechua.* Garnier Hermano, Paris, 1894. 35 p. Br498.71 AC282.

915. *Catalogue of Books, Maps, Plates on America, And of a Remarkable Collection of Early Voyages, Offered For Sale by Frederik Muller, at Amsterdam, Literary Agent of the Smithsonian Institution at Washington; Including a Large Number of Books In All Languages With Bibliographical and Historical Notes.* Frederik Muller, Amsterdam, 1872. Br917B M91.

916. *Catalogue of Books, Pamphlets, Atlases, Maps, Plates, and Autobiographies Relating to North and South America, Including the Collection of Voyages by de Bry, Hulsius, Hartgers, Etc.* Frederick Muller, Amsterdam, 1877. 218 p. Br970.3 M913.

917. *Catalogue of Peruvian Antiquities.* The Messrs. Leavitt, Auctioneers, 1876. Br572C An8141 v.72.

918. *Catalogue of the Different Specimens of Cloth Collected in the Three Voyages of Captain Cook to the Southern Hemisphere, With a Particular Account of the Manner of the Manufacturing of the Same in the Various Islands of the South Seas; Partly Extracted From Mr. Anderson and Reinhold Forster's Observations, and the Verbal Account of Some of the Most Knowing of the Navigators, With Some Anecdotes That Happened to Them Among the Natives.* Shaw, London, 1788. 6 p. and 44 samples of cloth. Br572.993 C282.

919. *Catalogue of the S. D. Mitchell Archaeological Collection from Green Lake and Marquette Counties, Wisconsin.* Book and Job Printing, Ripon Commonwealth, 1888. Br572C An8141 v.71.

920. *Catechism of Christian Doctrine, Prepared and Enjoined by Order of the Third Plenary Council of Baltimore; Translated into Flat-head By a Father of the Society of Jesus.* Woodstock College, Granite, Maryland, 1891. 102 p. Br497.46 SC16. Catholic catechism translated into Kalispel.

921. *Catecismo de la doctrina christiana en idioma tacana, por un misionero del Colegio de Propaganda-Fide de La Paz de Ayacucho.* Vapor, Ayacucho, 1859. 41 p. Br498.94 TC 283.

922. *Catecismo pequeño en idioma español y tarasco, de todo lo que el cristiano debe saber y entender, creer y practicar para salvarse; traducción de S. O. R., Prseb.; catecismo zapichu catamba español ca tarasco himbó, yámendo ambeeri ynqui cristiano kuaninchca miteni ca curhánguni, hacáhcuni ca niátani euáhpequarentstani uécani; móngarhitqua S. O. B. Caszirequa.* Antigua Imprenta de Murguia, México, 1891. 32 p. Br498.27 TC284.

923. *Cathecismo romano.* F. De Rivera Calderon, Rome, 1723. 26, 248 p. Br498.22 AzR 66.2. Roman Catholic catechism translated into Nahuatl.

924. Catholic Church. Liturgy and ritual. Salishan. *Polyglott Manual*. Kamloops, B.C., 1896-1897. 1 v. Br497.46 SC284; Br497.46 SC284.1. Earlier editions published separately, translated by Bishop Durieu and transcribed in shorthand by Fr. Le Jeune; contents include: "Chinook manual, or prayers, hymns, and catechism in Chinook, with the approbation of Right Rev. P. Durieu" (pp. 43-100, 1896); "English manual, or prayers and catechism in English typography, with the approbation of Right Rev. P. Durieu" (1896. 19 p.); "Prayers and catechism in English" (pp. 21-40, 1896); "Lillooet manual, or prayers, hymns, and the catechism in the Lillooet or Stlatliemoch language, with the approbation of Right Rev. P. Durieu" (1897. 31 p.); "Thompson manual, or prayers, hymns and catechism in the Thompson or Ntla Kapmah language, with the approbation of Right Rev. P. Durieu" (1897. 3 p.); "Okanagan manual, or prayers and hymns and catechism in the Okanagan language, with the approbation of Right Rev. P. Durieu" (1897. 32 p.); "Sheshel manual, or prayers, hymns and catechism in the Sechel language" (pp. 57-109, 1896); "Shushwap manual, or prayers, hymns and catechism in Shushwap" (1896. 63 p.); "Slayamen manual, or prayers, hymns and catechism in the Slayamen language" (pp. 111-153, 1896); "Skwamish manual, or prayers, hymns and catechism in Skwamish" (1896. 56 p.); "Stalo manual, or prayers, hymns, and the catechism in the Stalo or Lower Frazer language; with the approbation of Rt. Rev. P. Durieu" (1897. 30 p.); "Latin manual, or hymns and chants in use by the Indians of British Columbia, with the approbation of Right Rev. Durieu" (pp. 103-183, 1896).

925. Catholic Church. Liturgy and ritual. Salishan. *Prayers in the Salishan Languages*. Kamloops, B.C., 1891-1896. Br497.46 SC284.2. Parts translated by Fr. Le Jeune or Bishop Durieu, and transcribed into shorthand by Fr. Le Jeune, editor and publisher of the *Kamloops Wawa*, who reproduced them by aid of the mimeograph; contents include: "First catechism in Thompson language" (1892. 32 p.); "Prayers in Thompson" (1891. 32 p.); "Prayers in Thompson or Ntlakapmah" (1892. 16 p.); "Stalo morning prayers" (1891. 16 p.); "Prayers in Shushwap: 1. Night prayers" (1892. 16 p.); "Skwamish morning prayers" (1891. 32 p.); "Sheshel manual, or prayers, hymns and catechism in the Sechel language" (pp. 57-109, 1896).

926. Catlin, George. *Catalogue: Descriptive and Instructive of Catlin's Indian Cartoons*. Baker and Goodwin, New York, 1871. 99 p. Br572C An8141 v.17. In 1830, after several years of painting portraits in Philadelphia and Albany, George Catlin (1796-1872) left for St. Louis, then the hub of the American fur trade, and for the next six years traveled the West, from the Plains to Lake Michigan and from North Dakota to the Gulf of Mexico. He hoped to visit "every nation of Indians on the continent of North America" and document Indian life and customs.

927. Catlin, George. *Letters and Notes on the Manners, Customs, and Condition of the North American Indians*. Chatto and Windus, London, 1866. 2 v. Br970.1 C284b. One of the most important works on American Indians published in the 19th century. Besides the descriptions of Catlin's travel's throughout the West, the book contains hundreds of line drawings of southern and western Indians, as well as two significant maps of Indian tribes.

928. Catlin, George. *The George Catlin Indian Gallery, in the United States National Museum (Smithsonian Institution);With Memoir and Statistics by Thomas Donaldson*. Government Printing Office,Washington, DC, 1887. 939 p., 150 leaves of plates. Br970.1 Sm68.

929. Cattell, J. McKeen, and Livingston Farrand. Physical and mental measurements of the students of Columbia University. *The Psychological Review* 3(6): 618-648, 1896. Br573.6 C291.

930. Cattell, J. McKeen. *Address of the President, Before the American Psychological Association: Physical and Mental Measurement of the Students of Columbia University*. Macmillan, New York, 1895. 15 p. Br572C An8141 v.149.

931. Cattell, J. McKeen. On reaction-times and the velocity of the nervous impulse. *Memoirs of the National Academy of Sciences* 7:393-415, 1895. Washington, DC. Br152.83 C2981a; Br572C An8141 v.161. Contains many references to America and manners and customs among the American Indians.

932. Cattell, J. McKeen. Psychology at the University of Pennsylvania. *American Journal of Psychology* 3(2): 281-283, 1890. Br572C An8141 v.88.

933. Caulin, Antonio. *Historia corográfica, natural y evangélica de la Nueva Andalucia, provincias de Cumaná, Nueva Barcelona, Guayana y vertientes del Río Orinoco*. Reimpresa por G. Corser, Caracas, 1841. 448, 12 p. Br980 C31.

934. Cavalcanti, Amaro. *The Brasilian Language and Its Agglutination*. Tipografia Nacional, Rio Janeiro, 1883. 179 p. Br498.75 C 316.

935. Celedon, R. *Gramatica, catecismo i vocabulario de la lengua goajire; con una introducción i un apéndice por Esquiel Uricoechea*. Bibliothèque Linguistique Américaine, 5. Maisonneuve, Paris, 1878. 179 p. Br497C Am3; Br498.77 C 33.

936. Celedón, Rafael. *Gramatica de la lengua köggaba, con vocabularios y catecismos*. Bibliothèque Linguistique Américaine, 10. Maisonneuve, Paris, 1886. 127 p. Br497C Am3; Br498.64 KC 33.

937. *Censo del Estado Libre y Soberano de Chiapas, 1862*. El Espiritu del Siglo, Imprenta del Gobierno, San Cristobal Las Casas, 1862. 10 p. Br572C An8141 v.106.

938. Cerna, D.The pilgrimage and civilization of the Toltecs. *Transactions of the Texas Academy of Science*, pp. 57-71, 1893. Br572C An8141 v.113.

939. Cervantes de Salazar, Francisco. *México en 1554; tres diálogos latinos que Francisco Cervántes Salazar escribió é imprimió en México en dicho año*. Andrade y Morales, México, 1875. 344 p. Br917.2 C337. Latin and Spanish text translated by Joaquin García Icazbalceta.

940. Ceuleneer, Adolphe de. L'Île de Crète. *Bulletin de la Société Royale de Géographie d'Anvers*, 1897. 39 p. Br572C An8141 v.149.

941. Ceuleneer, Adolphe de. *Type d'Indien du Nouveau Monde représenté sur un bronze antique du Louvre; nouvelle contribution à l'interpretation d'un fragment de Cornelius Nepos*. Mémoires Cauronné et Autres Mémoires par l'Académie Royale de Belgique, 1890. 34 p. Br572C An8141 v.10.

942. Chaix, Paul. *Étude sur l'ethnographie de l'Afrique*. Fick, Genéve, n.d. 89 p. Br572C An8141 v.26.

943. Chamberlain, Alexander F. A Mississagua legend of Na'nniboju. *Journal of American Folk-Lore* 5:291-292, 1892. Br572C An8141 v.124. Alexander Francis Chamberlain (1865-1914) received the first doctorate in anthropology in North America from Clark University in Worcester, Massachusetts, in 1892. He was renowned for his encyclopedic reading of ethnographic literature, and annually compiled bibliographies for *American Anthropologist, Current Anthropological Literature,* and the *Journal of American Folk-Lore,* which he edited. His most enduring contribution to anthropology was to develop the argument that race is distinct from culture, that cultures should be classified by the languages that people speak, not by the physical characteristics of their bodies.

944. Chamberlain, Alexander F. American Indian legends and beliefs about the squirrel and the chipmunk. *Journal of American Folk-Lore* 9(32): 48-50, 1896. Br572C An8141 v.149.

945. Chamberlain, Alexander F. American Indian names of white men and women. *Journal of American Folk-Lore* 12:24-31, 1899. Br929.4 C35.5.

946. Chamberlain, Alexander F. Beitrag zur pflanzenkunde der naturvölker America's. *Verhandlungen der Berliner Anthropologischen Gesellschaft für Anthropologie, Ethnologie und Urgeschichte* 19:551-556, 1895. Br572C An 8141 v.139.

947. Chamberlain, Alexander F. *Contributions Toward a Bibliography of the Archaeology of the Dominion of Canada and Newfoundland.* Canadian Institute Report, 1887-1889. 6 p. Br572C An8141 v.12.

948. Chamberlain, Alexander F. Einige Wurzeln aus der Sprache der Kitona'qa-Indianer von Britisch-Columbien. *Verhandlungen der Berliner Anthropologischen Gesellschaft für Anthropologie, Ethnologie und Urgeschichte,* pp. 419-425, 1893. Br572C An8141 v.123.

949. Chamberlain, Alexander F. In memoriam: Horatio Hale. *Journal of American Folk-Lore* 10(36): 60-66, 1897. Br572C An8141 v.149.

950. Chamberlain, Alexander F. New words in the Kootenay language. *American Anthropologist* 7(2): 186-192, 1894. Br572C An8141 v.136.

951. Chamberlain, Alexander F. Notes on the history, customs, and beliefs of the Mississagua Indians. *Journal of American Folk-Lore* 1(11): 150-160, 1888. Br572C An8141 v.11.

952. Chamberlain, Alexander F. *On the Chaneabal and Tzotzil languages.* Imrie and Graham, Toronto, 1888. 2 p. Br572C An8141 v.52.

953. Chamberlain, Alexander F. Record of American folk-lore. *Journal of American Folk-Lore* 10(37): 149-154, 1897. Br572C An8141 v.149.

954. Chamberlain, Alexander F. Record of American folklore. *Journal of American Folk-Lore* 10(36): 67-75, 1897. Br572C An8141 v.149.

955. Chamberlain, Alexander F. Record of American folklore. *Journal of American Folk-Lore* 15:317-322, 1902. Br572C An 8141 v.139.

956. Chamberlain, Alexander F. Sulle significazioni nella lingua degli indigeni americani. *Archivo per l'Antropologia e l'Etnologia* 23(3), 1893. 7 p. Br572C An8141 v.136.

957. Chamberlain, Alexander F. Tales of the Missassaguas. *Journal of American Folk-*

Lore 2:141–147, 1889; 3:149–154, 1890. Br572C An8141 v.11.

958. Chamberlain, Alexander F. The archaeology of Scugog Island. Read before the Canadian Institute, 1889. 3 p. Br572C An8141 v.59.

959. Chamberlain, Alexander F. The Aryan element in Indian dialects I. *Canadian Indian*, February, 1891. 8 p. Br572C An8141 v.48.

960. Chamberlain, Alexander F. *The Catawba Language*. Imrie and Graham, Toronto, 1888. Br572C An8141 v.52.

961. Chamberlain, Alexander F. *The Language of the Mississagua Indians of Skugog*. MacCalla and Company, Philadelphia, 1892. 84 p. Br572C An8141 v.84.

962. Chamberlain, Alexander F. The language of the Mississaguas of Scugog. *Proceedings of the Canadian Institute* 25:213–215, 1890. Br572C An8141 v.52; Br572C An8141 v.67.

963. Chamberlain, Alexander F. The maple amongst the Algonkian tribes. *American Anthropologist* 4(1): 39–43, 1891. Br572C An8141 v.11.

964. Chamberlain, Alexander F. The mythology and folk-lore of invention. *Journal of American Folk-Lore* 10(37): 89–100, 1897. Br572C An8141 v.149.

965. Chamberlain, Alexander F. The origin and development of grammatical gender. *Proceedings of the Canadian Institute* 25:216–217, 1890. Br572C An8141 v.52; Br572C An8141 v.67.

966. Chamberlain, Alexander F. The poetry of American aboriginal speech. *Journal of American Folk-Lore* 9(32): 43–47, 1896. Br572C An8141 v.149.

967. Chamberlain, Alexander F. The relationship of the American languages. *Proceedings of the Canadian Institute* 22:57–76, 1887. Br572C An8141 v.65.

968. Chamberlain, Alexander F. The Thunder-Bird amongst the Algonkins. *American Anthropologist* 3(1): 51–54, 1890. Br572C An8141 v.11.

969. Chamberlain, Alexander F. Words expressive of cries and noises in the Kootenay language. *American Anthropologist* 7:68–70, 1894. Br572C An8141 v.123.

970. Chamberlain, Isabel C. Contributions towards a bibliography of folk-lore relating to women. *Journal of American Folk-Lore* 12:32–37, 1899. Br396 C35.5.

971. Champlain, Samuel de. Champlain's expeditions to northern and western New York, 1609–1615, I, 1687. In *The Documentary History of the State of New York*, v. 3, pp. 1–24. Albany, NY, 1850. Br572C An8141 v.62.

972. Chantre, Ernest. *Anthropologie: conférence, leçon d'ouverture*. Faculté des Sciences de Lyon, 1881. 29 p. Br572C An8141 v.31.

973. Chantre, Ernest. *La Bijouterie Caucasienne de l'époque Scytho-Byzantine*. Imprimerie Alexandre Rey, Lyon, 1892. 40 p. Br572C An8141 v.109.

974. Chantre, Ernest. *Origine et ancienneté du premier age du fer au Caucase*. Imprimerie Alexandre Rey, Lyon, 1892. 24 p. Br572C An8141 v.109.

975. Chantre, Ernest. Projet de réforme dans la nomenclature des peuples de l'Asie, pp. 171–178. n.d. Br572C An8141 v.121.

976. Chapman, Henry C. The interpretation of certain verses of the first chapter of Genesis in the light of paleontology. *Proceedings of the Academy of Natural Sciences of Philadelphia* (February): 68–74, 1893. Br572C An8141 v.116.

977. Chapman, William. An ancient mine in Arkansas. Read before the Davenport Acad-

emy of Natural Sciences, pp. 29-32. 1886. Br572C An8141 v.12.

978. Chappell, Edward. *Narrative of a Voyage to Hudson's Bay in His Majesty's Ship Rosamond Containing Some Account of the North-Eastern Coast of America and of the Tribes Inhabiting That Remote Region.* Printed for J. Mawman…by R. Watts, London, 1817. 279 p. Br917.12 C368. Includes "A vocabulary of the language of the Cree or Knisteneaux Indians."

979. Charencey, Charles Félix Hyacinthe Gouhier, comte de. *Affinités de quelques légendes américaines avec celles de l'ancien monde.* Imprimerie de Mme. Vve. Bouchard Huzard, Paris, 1866. 16 p. Br572C An8141 v.78.

980. Charencey, Charles Félix Hyacinthe Gouhier, comte de. Cathecismo en lengua chuchona y castellana. 1888. 31 p. Br572C An8141 v.53.

981. Charencey, Charles Félix Hyacinthe Gouhier, comte de. *Chronologie des âges au soleils d'après la mythologie mexicaine.* Imprimerie de F. Le Blanc-Hardel, Caen, 1878. 31 p. Br572C An8141 v.31; Br572C An8141 v.79.

982. Charencey, Charles Félix Hyacinthe Gouhier, comte de. *Compte rendu du Congrès Scientifique International des Catholiques sur quelques étymologies de la langue Basque*, pp. 5-11. Alphonse Picard, Èditeur, Paris, 1891. Br572C An8141 v.87.

983. Charencey, Charles Félix Hyacinthe Gouhier, comte de. Confessionnaire en langue chanabal. Jacob, Orléans, n.d. 8 p. Br572C An8141 v.53.

984. Charencey, Charles Félix Hyacinthe Gouhier, comte de. *De la conjugaison dans les langues de la famille maya-quiché.* Typ. De Charles Peters, Louvain, 1885. 130 p. Br572C An8141 v.53.

985. Charencey, Charles Félix Hyacinthe Gouhier, comte de. *De quelques idées symboliques se rattachant au nom des douze fils de Jacob.* Maisonneuve et Cie., Paris, 1874. 104 p. Br572C An8141 v.78.

986. Charencey, Charles Félix Hyacinthe Gouhier, comte de. *Des affinités de la langue Basque avec divers idiomes des deux continents.* Secrétariat de l'Association Française pour l'Avancement des Sciences fusiónnée l'Association Scientifique de France, Paris, 1892. 17 p. Br572C An8141 v.127.

987. Charencey, Charles Félix Hyacinthe Gouhier, comte de. Des couleurs considérées comme symboles des points de l'horizon chez les peuples du Nouveau-Monde. *Actes de la Société Philologique* 6(3): 149-213, 1877. Br572C An8141 v.79.

988. Charencey, Charles Félix Hyacinthe Gouhier, comte de. *Des Nombrès symboliques chez les toltèques occidentaux.* Imprimerie Rousseau-Leroy, Amiens, 1893. 25 p. Br572C An8141 v.115.

989. Charencey, Charles Félix Hyacinthe Gouhier, comte de. *Des prefixes pejoratives en Basque.* Fribourg, Switzerland, 1898, 18 p. Br494.1 C375.

990. Charencey, Charles Félix Hyacinthe Gouhier, comte de. *Des signes de numération en maya.* E. Renaut-de Broise, Paris, 1881. 7 p. Br572C An8141 v.53.

991. Charencey, Charles Félix Hyacinthe Gouhier, comte de. Deux bluettes étymologiques. *Actes de la Société Philologique* 1(4): 62-71, 1872. Br572C An8141 v.78.

992. Charencey, Charles Félix Hyacinthe Gouhier, comte de. Deux poesies peruviennes, pp. 91-107. n.d. Br572C An8141 v.53.

993. Charencey, Charles Félix Hyacinthe Gouhier, comte de. Djemschid et Quetzalcoatl. *Revue des Traditions Populaires* 8(5), 1893. 7 p. Br572C An8141 v.123.

994. Charencey, Charles Félix Hyacinthe Gouhier, comte de. *Essai sur la symbolique dan l'Extreme-Orient*. Imprimerie de F. Le Blanc-Hardel, Caen, 1876. 26 p. Br572C An8141 v.79.

995. Charencey, Charles Félix Hyacinthe Gouhier, comte de. *Essai d'analyse grammaticale d'un texte en langue maya*. Imprimerie de F. Le Blanc-Hardel, Caen, 1873. 22 p. Br572C An8141 v.78; Br572C An8141 v.79.

996. Charencey, Charles Félix Hyacinthe Gouhier, comte de. *Essai d'analyse grammaticale d'un texte en langue maya*. Imprimerie Lepelletier, Havre, 1875. 9 p. Br498.21 MC37.3; Br572C An8141 v.50. "Une première fois déjà, nous avons donné dans les mémoires de l'Académie de Caen, un fragment de texte en langue Maya, avec expliction grammaticale" (p. 3).

997. Charencey, Charles Félix Hyacinthe Gouhier, comte de. Essai de déchiffrement d'un fragment d'inscription palenquéenne. *Actes de la Société Philologique* 1(3): 45–60, 1870. Br572C An8141 v.78.

998. Charencey, Charles Félix Hyacinthe Gouhier, comte de. Essai sur la symbolique des points de l'horizon dans l'extrême-orient. *Mémoires de l'Académie Nationale des Sciences, Arts et Belles-Lettres du Caen*, 1876. 26 p. Br572C An8141 v.50; Br572C An8141 v.79.

999. Charencey, Charles Félix Hyacinthe Gouhier, comte de. *Études de paléographie americaine: déchiffrement des écritures calculiformes, ou mayas; le bas-relief de la Croix de Palenque et le mss. Troano*. Archéologie Américaine de Broise, Alençon, 1879. 32 p. Br572C An8141 v.50; Br572C An8141 v.79.

1000. Charencey, Charles Félix Hyacinthe Gouhier, comte de. Études sur l'origine des Basques. *Revue de Linguistique et de Philologie Comparée*, n.d. 14 p. Br572C An8141 v.78.

1001. Charencey, Charles Félix Hyacinthe Gouhier, comte de. *Etymologies euskariennes*. Imprimerie de L. Marceau, Chalon-sur-Saone, n.d. 30 p. Br572C An8141 v.149.

1002. Charencey, Charles Félix Hyacinthe Gouhier, comte de. *Etymologies françaises*. Chartres, n.d. 9 p. Br572C An8141 v.53.

1003. Charencey, Charles Félix Hyacinthe Gouhier, comte de. Fragment de chrestomathie de la langue Algonquine. *Actes de la Société Philologique* 3(2): 39–50, 1873. Br572C An8141 v.78.

1004. Charencey, Charles Félix Hyacinthe Gouhier, comte de. *L'historien Sahagún et les migrations mexicaines*. A. Herepin, Alençon, 1898. 82 p. Br972 C373.

1005. Charencey, Charles Félix Hyacinthe Gouhier, comte de. L'office quotidien du culte brahmanique d'aprés Monier-Williams, n.d. Br572C An8141 v.53.

1006. Charencey, Charles Félix Hyacinthe Gouhier, comte de. *La langue Basque et les idiomes de l'Oural*. Imprimerie Georges Jacob, Orléans, n.d. 42 p. Br572C An8141 v.127.

1007. Charencey, Charles Félix Hyacinthe Gouhier, comte de. La Tula Votanide. *Bulletin de la Société de Linguistique* 25, n.d. 6 p. Br572C An8141 v.53.

1008. Charencey, Charles Félix Hyacinthe Gouhier, comte de. *Le fils de la Vierge.* Imprimerie Lepelletier, Havre, 1879. 28 p. Br572C An8141 v.79.

1009. Charencey, Charles Félix Hyacinthe Gouhier, comte de. *Le mythe d'Imos: traditions des peuples Mexicains.* Maisonneuve, Paris, 1873. 61 p. Br572C An8141 v.78.

1010. Charencey, Charles Félix Hyacinthe Gouhier, comte de. *Le mythe de Votan; étude sur les origines asiatiques de la civilisation américaine.* Imprimerie de E. de Broise, Alençon, 1871. 114 p. Br572C An8141 v.78.

1011. Charencey, Charles Félix Hyacinthe Gouhier, comte de. *Le pronom personnel dans les idiomes de la famille Tapachulane-Huastèque.* Imprimerie de F. Le Blanc-Hardel, Caen, 1868. 23 p. Br572C An8141 v.78.

1012. Charencey, Charles Félix Hyacinthe Gouhier, comte de. Les déformations craniennes et le Concile de Lima. *Revue des Religions,* pp. 17-57, 1894. Amiens. Br572C An8141 v.136.

1013. Charencey, Charles Félix Hyacinthe Gouhier, comte de. Les hommes-Chiens. *L'Athenée Oriental* 4, 1882. 28 p. Br572C An8141 v.53.

1014. Charencey, Charles Félix Hyacinthe Gouhier, comte de. Lettre a monsieur d'Abbadie sur l'origine asiatique des langues du nord de l'Afrique. *Actes de la Société Philologique* 1(2): 29-43, 1869. Br572C An8141 v.78.

1015. Charencey, Charles Félix Hyacinthe Gouhier, comte de. Lettres au Saint-Pere en lengue Kalispel, n.d. Br572C An8141 v.53.

1016. Charencey, Charles Félix Hyacinthe Gouhier, comte de. *Mélanges de philologie et de paléographie américaines.* E. Leroux, Paris, 1883 195 p. Br498 C37.

1017. Charencey, Charles Félix Hyacinthe Gouhier, comte de. *Melanges sur diférents idiomes de la Nouvelle Espagne.* Ernest Leroux, Paris, 1876. 31 p. Br572C An8141 v.18; Br572C An8141 v.53; Br572C An8141 v.79.

1018. Charencey, Charles Félix Hyacinthe Gouhier, comte de. *Notice sur quelques familles de langues du Mexique.* Imprimerie Lepelletier, Havre, 1870. 39 p. Br498.22 C37; Br572C An8141 v.78.

1019. Charencey, Charles Félix Hyacinthe Gouhier, comte de. *Phonétique souletine.* Imprimerie Georges Jacob, Orléans, 1891. 56 p. Br572C An8141 v.87.

1020. Charencey, Charles Félix Hyacinthe Gouhier, comte de. *Recherches sur les noms de nombres cardinaux, dans la famille Maya-Quiché.* Imprimerie Georges Jacob, Orleans, 1884. 15 p. Br498.21 KiC 373.

1021. Charencey, Charles Félix Hyacinthe Gouhier, comte de. *Recherches sur la familie des langues Américaines Pirinda-Othomi. Annales de Philosophie Chretienne,* 1867. 10 p. Br572C An8141 v.78.

1022. Charencey, Charles Félix Hyacinthe Gouhier, comte de. *Recherches sur le Codex Troano.* Ernest Leroux, Paris, 1876. 15 p. Br572C An8141 v.53; Br572C An8141 v.79; Br898.21 MT742.yC.

1023. Charencey, Charles Félix Hyacinthe Gouhier, comte de. *Recherches sur les dialectes tasmaniens.* De Broise, Alençon, 1880. 56 p. Br572C An8141 v.53.

1024. Charencey, Charles Félix Hyacinthe Gouhier, comte de. Recherches sur les lois phonétiques dans les idiomes de la familie mame-huastèque. *Revue de Linguis-*

tique 5:129-167, 1872. Br572C An8141 v.78.

1025. Charencey, Charles Félix Hyacinthe Gouhier, comte de. Recherches sur les noms d'animaux domestiques, de plantes cultivées et de metaux chez les Basques et les origines de la civilisation Européeme. *Actes de la Société Philologique* 1(1):3-28, 1869. Br572C An8141 v.78.

1026. Charencey, Charles Félix Hyacinthe Gouhier, comte de. Recherches sur les noms de nombres cardinaux dans la famille maya-quiche. *Revue Linguistique* 16:325-329, 1883. Br572C An8141 v.53.

1027. Charencey, Charles Félix Hyacinthe Gouhier, comte de. *Recherches sur les noms des points de l'espace.* Imprimerie de F. LeBlanc-Hardel, Caen, 1882. 86 p. Br572C An8141 v.53.

1028. Charencey, Charles Félix Hyacinthe Gouhier, comte de. *Sentences et réflexions.* Imprimerie G. Saint-Aubin et Thevenut, Paris, n.d. 28 p. Br572C An8141 v.127.

1029. Charencey, Charles Félix Hyacinthe Gouhier, comte de. *Sur la langue de Soconus-co.* Durand, Chartres, n.d. 7 p. Br572C An8141 v.53.

1030. Charencey, Charles Félix Hyacinthe Gouhier, comte de. *Symbolique romaine des couleurs affectées aux cochers du cirque.* Imprimerie de F. LeBlanc-Hardel, Caen, 1876. 35 p. Br572C An8141 v.79.

1031. Charencey, Charles Félix Hyacinthe Gouhier, comte de. *Textes en langue tarasque.* Orleans, 1886, 18 p. Br572C An8141 v.53.

1032. Charencey, Charles Félix Hyacinthe Gouhier, comte de. *Une legende cosmogo-nique.* Havre, 1884. 48 p. Br572C An8141 v.53.

1033. Charencey, Charles Félix Hyacinthe Gouhier, comte de. *Vocabulario tzotzil-es-panol, dialecto de los indios de la parte occidental del estado de Chiapas (Mex-ico).* G. Jacob, Orleans, 1890. 27 p. Br572C An8141 v.53.

1034. Charencey, Charles Félix Hyacinthe Gouhier, comte de. Xibalba, pp. 111-125, 1890. Br572C An8141 v.53.

1035. Charencey, Charles Félix Hyacinthe Gouhier, comte de. *Ymos-yima.* Imprimerie Lepelletier, Havre, 1876. 42 p. Br572C An8141 v.50; Br572C An8141 v.79.

1036. Charnay, Désiré. *Catalogue de la collection archéologique provenent des fouilles et explorations.* Paris, 1883. 14 p. Br572C An8141 v.44. Charnay (1828-1915) was educated at the Lycée Charlemagne in Paris and moved to the United States where, in 1850, he became a teacher in New Orleans. Charnay made several trips to Mexico between 1860 and 1882 during which he collected archaeological specimens and photographed ruins.

1037. Charnay, Désiré. *Cités et ruines américaines Mitla, Palenqué, Izamal, Chichén-Itzá, Uxmal.* Gide, Paris, 1863 543 p. Br913.7 V813. Includes "Antiquités améri-caines" by Eugène-Emmanuel Viollet-le-Duc" (pp. 1-104).

1038. Charnay, Désiré. La Ville Lorillard au pays des lacandons. *Revue d'Ethnographie* 2(6): 481-503, 1883. Br572C An8141 v.110.

1039. Charnay, Désiré. *Les anciennes villes du Nouveau Monde voyages d'explo-rations au Mexique et dan l'Amérique Centrale.* Hachette, Paris, 1900. 469 p. Br913.72 C385.

Désiré Charnay (from Justin Winsor,
Aboriginal America. *Cambridge, MA:*
Houghton, Mifflin, 1889. p. 187).

1040. Charnay, Désiré. *Viaje a Yucatan.* Mérida: Imprenta de la Revista de Mérida, 1888. 235 p. Br572C An8141 v.72.

1041. Chatelain, Héli. *Kimbundu grammar; grammatica elementar do Kimbundu ou lingua de Angola.* Typographie de C. Schuchardt, Genebra, 1888-1889. 172 p. Br496 C39.

1042. Chavero, Alfredo. *Calendario azteca; ensayo arqueológico.* 2d ed. Imprenta de Jens y Zapiain, México, 1876. 47 p. Br913.72 C395.2.

1043. *Cherokee Laws, Enacted by the General Council of Cherokees…Beginning in the Year 1808, and also the Laws Enacted by the Cherokees Known as the Old Settlers…Beginning in the Year 1824, Together With [the laws of] the United Cherokees, and Also the Constitution and Laws Here Enacted, Beginning With the Year 1839, and Continuing to 1849 [in Cherokee characters].* Tahlequah Cherokee Nation, Damaga, 1850. Br497.27 ChC 42.

1044. Chever, Edward E. The Indians of California. *American Naturalist* 5:129-148, 1871. Br572C An8141 v.38.

1045. Chilam Balam. Artículos y fragmentos de manuscritos antiguos en lengua maya, colectados por D. Juan Pío Pérez, 1868, y copiados en facsimile por C. Hermann Berendt, M.D., Mérida, 1870. 200 p., 1868. Br898.21 MC437. Manuscript.

1046. Chilam Balam. Artículos y fragmentos de manuscritos antiguos en lengua maya, colectados por D. Juan Pío Pérez, copiado en Mérida, 1870. 258 p. Br898.21 MC437.2. Manuscript in blank book, pp. 45-188, transcribed by Karl H. Berendt.

1047. Chilam Balam. Two books of Chilam Balam; manuscript copy of Chilam Balam of Chumayel and Chilam Balam of Tizimin, pp. 135-238, 141 leaves, n.d.

Br898.21 MC437.4. Manuscript.

1048. Chimalpopoca Galicia, Faustino. *Epítome ó modo fácil de aprender el idioma nahuatl ó lengua mexicana, por el Lic. Faustino Chimalpopoca.* Tipografía de la viuda de Murguía é hijos, Mexico, 1869. 124 p. Br498.22 AzC 44.

1049. Chimalpopoca Galicia, Faustino. Extracts from *Silabario del idioma mexicano*, of the edition of 1849, n.d. Br498.22 AzC 44.2. Manuscript.

1050. Chimalpopoca Galicia, Faustino. *Silabario de idioma mexicano, dispuesto par el Lic. Faustino Chimalpopoca[tl] Galicia.* Tipografía de M. Castro, Mexico, 1859. 32 p. Br498.22 AzC 44.2.

1051. Chimbaycela. *Cushiquilica*. Impreso por Andrés Cordero, Cuenca, 1884. Br572C An8141 v.115.

1052. Cholenec, Pierre. *Catherin Tekakouita; traduction iroquoise par J. Marcoux*. Tehoristorarakon J. Chapleau et fils, Tiohtiaki [Montréal, Québec], 1876. 52, 4 p. Br497.11 MnD93. Translation by père Flavien Durocher of a letter by père Pierre Cholenec, printed in the *Lettres édifiantes et curieuses* and prepared for printing by the abbé Jean André Cuoq. The text (p. 3-52) is entirely in the Montagnais language.

1053. Cholenec, Pierre. *Vie de Catherine teckak8[sic]ita; traduction iroquoise*. J. Chapleau, Tiohtiake [Montréal], 1876. 53 p. Br497.27 MC45. Text in Mohawk.

1054. Christison, David C. The gauchos of San Jorge, central Uruguay, pp. 34-52, 1881. Br572C An8141 v.33.

1055. Cieza de León, Pedro de. *Segunda parte de La crónica del Perú; que trata del señorío de los Incas yupanquis y de sus grandes hechos y gobernación.* Imprenta Manuel Gines Hernandez, Madrid, 1880. 279, 140 p. Br980.3 IC483. Ciudad Real, Antonio de. Diccionario de Motul; diccionaro de la lengua maya de Yucatán. Tomo I. Maya-Español, pp. viii, 1565. Tomo II. Español-Maya, pp. 508. Tomo III. Adiciones y correcturas. Unpaged; about 600 pp. Br498.21 MD543. Manuscript. The Motul dictionary is the most complete colonial period dictionary available for Yucatec Maya. While in México City in the 1850s, Brasseur de Bourbourg purchased a small quarto-sized dictionary, written in a very small and not very legible hand. He later sold this to John Carter Brown of Providence. In 1864 Berendt obtained permission to make a copy of it and in all his later studies of the language added to and emended the vocabulary, but using a different colored ink, so that the exact text of the original could be identified. The Yucatec-Spanish and Spanish-Yucatec dictionary was compiled during the late 16th and early 17th centuries. The Maya-Spanish dictionary (v. 3-6, 930 p.) has been identified as the Calepino compiled by Father Antonio de Ciudad Real between 1580 and 1617, in part while he resided at the Franciscan convent in Motul. His work includes 15,975 words from *aal* to *xuxek*, with words beginning with Parra letters following the B section. The Spanish-Maya vocabulary, bearing the caption title of Vocabulario en la lengua de maya (v. 1-2, 416 p.), was probably compiled somewhat later in the 17th century by an unidentified author. The approximately 11,180 entries list words and phrases in Spanish from *a* to *zorro*, followed by their equivalents in Maya.

1057. *Clara y sucinta exposición del pequeño catecismo impreso en el idioma mexi-*

cano siguiendo el orden mismo pregunytas y respuestas para la mejor instrucción de los feligreses indios, y de los que comienzan á aprender dicho idioma; por un sacerdote devoto de la madre santísima de la luz. Oficina del Oratorio de S. Felipe Néri, Puebla, 1819. 67 leaves. Br498.22 AzC 547.

1058. Clark, J. M. *The Functions of a Great University.* The Bryant Press, Toronto, 1895. 17 p. Br572C An8141 v.139.

1059. Clark, S. N. *Are the Indians Dying Out? Preliminary Observations Relating to Indian Civilization and Education.* Washington, DC, 1877. 42 p. Br572C An8141 v.32.

1060. Clark, William P. *The Indian Sign Language With Brief Explanatory Notes of the Gestures Taught Deaf-Mutes In Our Institutions For Their Instruction, And A Description of Some of the Peculiar Laws, Customs, Myths, Superstitions, Ways of Living, Code of Peace and War Signals of Our Aborigines.* L. R. Hamersly and Company, Philadelphia, 1885. 443 p. Br497.02 C54.

1061. Clarke, Hyde, and C. Staniland Wake. *Serpent and Siva Worship and Mythology, in Central America, Africa, and Asia, and the Origin of Serpent Worship; Two Treatises, by Hyde Clarke, M.A. I., and C. Staniland Wake, M.A. I.; edited by Alexander Wilder, M. D.* Trübner, London, 1876. 48 p. Br572C An8141 v.65.

1062. Clarke, Peter D. *Origin and Traditional History of the Wyandotts, and Sketches of Other Indian Tribes of North American; True Traditional Stories of Tecumseh and His League, in the Years 1811 and 1812.* Hunter, Rose, Toronto, 1870. 158 p. Br970.3 WC55.

1063. Clarke, Robert. *The Prehistoric Remains at Cincinnati, Ohio, and the "Cincinnati Tablet."* Cincinnati, 1876. 34 p. Br572C An8141 v.35.

1064. Clavigero, Francesco S. *Storica antica del Messico cavata da'migliori storici spagnuoli, e da'manoscritti, e dalle piture antiche degli Indiana.* Per Gregorio Biasini all'insegna di Pallade, Cesena, 1780. 4 v. Br972 C57.2. Clavigero (1731-1787), a Jesuit, was a native of Veracruz, Mexico, who spent thirty years of active research into the archaeology and antiquities of Mexico. His book is a mine of precious historical documents and contains lists of other manuscripts in the Mendoza, Vatican, and Boturini collections.

1065. Claypole, E. W. Human relics in the drift of Ohio. *American Geologist* 8:302-314, 1896. Br572C An8141 v.149.

1066. Claypole, E. W. Prof. G. F. Wright and his critics. *Popular Science Monthly,* 1893. 18 p. Br572C An8141 v.124.

1067. Clevenger, S. V. Disadvantages of the upright position. *American Naturalist* 18(1), 1884. 8 p. Br572C An8141 v.13.

1068. Clevenger, Shobal Vail. Origin and descent of the human brain. *American Naturalist* 15(7): 513-517, 1881. Br572C An8141 v.13.

1069. Closson, Carlos C. The hierarchy of European races. *American Journal of Sociology* 3(3): 314-327, 1897. Br572C An8141 v.149.

1070. Clozel, Marie François Joseph. Bibliographie des ouvrages relatifs à la Sénégambie et au Soudan occidental. *Revue de Géographie* 27-29, 1891. 60 p. Br572C An8141 v.7.

1071. Codex Becker no. 1. *Manuscrit mexicain; pub. par Henri de Saussure.* Imprimerie Aubert-Schuchardt, Genève, 1891. 8 p. and 18 facsimile plates. Br498.34 MS 88.

1072. Codex Boturini. *Reproduction of the Codex Boturini, by John Delafield.* Cincinnati, 1839. 1 folded leaf. Br898.22 AzB658D. Issued as supplement to *An Inquiry Into the Origin of the Antiquities of America,* by John Delafield (New York, 1839).

1073. Codex Cortesianus. *Codex Cortesianus; manuscrit hiératique des anciens Indiens de l'Amérique Centrale.* Maisonneuve et Cie., Paris, 1883. 50 p.; 42 plates in portfolio. Br898.21 MC817M. Edited by Léon Louis Lucien Prunol de Rosny; contains a list of Rosny's publications on American archaeology and the paleography of Yucatán.

1074. Codex Cortesianus. *Códice maya denominado cortesiano, que se conserva en el Museo Arqueológico Nacional (Madrid).* Madrid, 1892. 4 p. and scroll (col. facsim.) folded into 21 leaves, printed both sides. Br898.21 MC817M.2. Edited by Juan de Dios de la Rada and Jerónimo López Ayala y del Hierro.

1075. Codex Dresdensis Maya (R 310). *Die Mayahandschrift der Königlichen öffentlichen Bibliothèque zu Dresden, von prof. Dr. E. Förstemann...mit 74 tafeln in chrono-lichtdruck.* A. Naumann, Leipzig, 1880. 1 p., 18 facsimile plates. Br898.21 MD817. The facsimile is colored and mounted, forming 74 plates.

1076. Codex Fernández Leal. *Códice Fernández Leal; publicado por el Dr. Antonio Peñafiel.* Oficina Tipográfica de la Secretaria de Fomento, México, 1895. 8 p., 24 leaves of plates. Br898.34 ZC644. Facsimile of a Mexican picture-manuscript, recording the invasions of the Aztecs under Ahuitzolt; edited by Antonio Peñafiel.

1077. Codex Vaticanus Nr. 3738. *Il manoscritto messicano vaticano 3738, detto il Codice Rios.* Stabilimiento Danesi, Roma, 1900. 39 p., 96 facsimile plates. Br898.22 AzR475V. The Italian text, explanatory of the pictographs, is an amplified translation of the Spanish text of the Codex Telleriano-Remensis.

1078. Colburn, Richard T. Improvident civilization. *Proceedings of the American Association for the Advancement of Science* 46, 1897. 57 p. Br572C An8141 v.149.

1079. Colden, Cadwallader. *The History of the Five Indian Nations, Depending on the Province of New York in America.* William Bradford, New York, 1727. 119 p. Br970.3 IrC673b. Colden (1688-1776) came to Philadelphia from Scotland in 1710. His *The History of the Five Indian Nations* narrates the history of Indian affairs and the history of the Iroquois from the time of first contacts with Europeans through the Treaty of Ryswick in 1697.

1080. Colección de escritos menores en lengua kekchí de la Vera Paz, Cobán, 1875. 19 p. Br498.21 KC684. Manuscript; transcriptions of various document by Karl H. Berendt, including "Frases de conversación en lengua kekchí, copiado de un manuscrito en cuardo de año de 1819, propiedad de Francisco Poou, indio de Cobán, Cobán," 1875; "Sermón para el dia de San Juan en lengua kekchí, copiado de un manuscrito en cuarto del archivo de la parrochia de Cobán, transcrito por Juan de Morales, fiscal en San Juan Chamelco, 1741, por C. Hermann Berendt, M.D., Cobán," 1875; "Pláticas sobre los mandamientos de la ley de Dios en el idioma kekchí," n.d. 8 p.; "Sermon para el dia de San Juan en lengua kekchí. Cobán," n.d. 3 leaves.

1081. Colección de platicas doctrinales y sermones en lengua maya, 1868. 257 p. Br498.21 MC674. Manuscript, transcribed by Karl H. Berendt; contents include: Francisco E. Dominguez y Argaiz, "Platicas de los principales mysterios de Nuestra Santa Fee"; Francisco Carajal, "Discurso para el descendimiento del Señor"; "Sermones en lengua maya"; "Acuerdos del pecador repartidos en las dominicas de quaresma"; "Sermon de animas"; "Sermon de difuntos"; "Sermon para miercoles de ceniza"; "Modo de confesar en lengua maya."

1082. *Colección de poetas yucatecos y tabasqueños*. Merida, 1861. 252 p. Br572C An8141 v.63.

1083. Coleti, Giovanni D. *Dizionario storico-geografico dell'America meridionale*. Coleti, Venezia, 1771. Br980 C67.

1084. Colini, Giuseppe A. Osservazioni etnografiche sui givari. *Memorie della Classe di Scienze Morali, Storiche e Filologiche, Reale Accademia dei Lincei* 11:3-47, 1883. Roma. Br572C An8141 v.95.

1085. Colini, Giuseppe A. Scoperte paletnologiche nelle caverne dei Balzi Rossi. *Bullettino di Paletnologia Italiano* 19(7-12): 117-340, 1893. Br572C An8141 v.131.

1086. Colini, Giuseppe A., and R. Mengarelli. *La necropoli di villa Cavalletti nel comune di Grottaferrata*. Tipografía della R. Accademia dei Lincei, Roma, 1902. Br913.451 C68.

1087. *Collection of Ojibway hymns; Translated by Peter Jacobs, Jr. and Rev. Dr. O'Meara; With Additional Hymns by Peter Jones, Wm. Walker and John Jacobs; Re-Arranged, Revised and Published by John Jacobs*. 2d ed. J. Jacobs, Sarnia, Ontario, 1890. 324 p. Br497.11 OJ15.

1088. Collignon, René. Anthropologie de la France: Dorobgne, Charente, Corrèze, Creuse, Haute-Vienne. *Mémoires de la Société d'Anthropologie de Paris* 1(3): 3-79, 1894. Br572C An8141 v.132.

1089. Collignon, René. *Anthropologie du calvados et de la région environnante*. Typographie-Lithographie Ch. Valin, Caen, 1894. 29 p. Br572C An8141 v.143.

1090. Collignon, René. Considérations générales sur l'association respective des caractères anthropologiques. *L'Anthropologie* 3:43-54, 1892. Br572C An8141 v.122.

1091. Collignon, René. *Contribution al'étude anthropologique des populations françaises*. Secrétariat de l'Association Française pour l'Avancement des Sciences Fusiónnée l'Association Scientifique de France, Paris, 1892. Br572C An8141 v.127.

1092. Collignon, René. Cranes de la nécropole phénicienne de Mahédia (Tunisie). *L'Anthropologie* 3:163-173, 1892. Br572C An8141 v.122.

1093. Collignon, René. *L'anthropologie au conseil de revision: méthode a suivre*. A. Hennuyer, Paris, 1890. 63 p. Br572C An8141 v.8.

1094. Collignon, René. L'inscription de Temia découverte par le Capitaine Lefèvre; contribution à l'étude des Aïnos. *Revue d'Ethnographie*, pp. 449-454, 1888. Br572C An8141 v.164.

1095. Collignon, René. La Race Basque. *L'Anthropologie* 5:276-287, 1894. Br572C An 8141 v.139.

1096. Collignon, René. La race Lorraine; étudiée sur des ossements trouvés a Nancy. *Bul-*

letin de la Société des Sciences de Nancy, 1881. 20 p. Br572C An8141 v.164.

1097. Collignon, René. Les Basques. *Mémoires de la Société d'Anthropologie de Paris* 1(4), 1895. 129 p. Br572C An8141 v.149.

1098. Collignon, René. Les premiers habitants de l'Europe. *Les Sciences Biologiques,* pp. 296-320, n.d. Br572C An8141 v.102.

1099. Collignon, René. Observations ethnologiques, n.d. Br572C An8141 v.88.

1100. Collignon, René. Projet d'entente internationale pour arreter un programme commun de recherches anthropologiques a faire aux conseils de révision. *Mémoires de la Société Nationale des Sciences Naturelles et Mathématiques de Cherbourg,* 28, 1892. 11 p. Br572C An8141 v.88.

1101. Collin. *Instruments d' anthropologie.* Charriere, Paris, n.d. 8 p. Br572C An 8141 v.139.

1102. Collins, C. R. Report on the languages of the different tribes of Indians inhabiting the Territory of Utah, 1860. *Report of Explorations Across the Great Basin of the Territory of Utah,* pp. 465-474. United States War Department, Washington, DC, 1876. Br572C An8141 v.102.

1103. Collitz, Hermann. Über Ficks vergleichendes Wörterbuch der indogermanisch Sprachen. *American Journal of Philology,* pp. 293-309, 1891. Br572C An8141 v.46.

1104. Colomb, A. Vocabulaire Arorai, Iles Gilbert; précédés de notes grammaticales d'après un manuscrit du P. Latium Léveque, et le travail de Hale sur la langue Tarawa, par le P. A. C. *Actes de la Société Philologique* 15:123-228, 1887, 1887. Br499.24 G373C.

1105. Columbus, Christopher. *Voyages of Christopher Columbus.* United States Catholic Historical Society, New York, 1892. 290 p. Br572C An8141 v.118.

1106. Commuck, Thomas. *Indian Melodies, Harmonized by Thomas Hastings.* Lane, New York, 1845. 114 p. Br784.4 C73.

1107. *Compendio del confesonario en mexicano y castellano; para los que ignoren el primero puedan á lo menos en los cusos de necesidad administrar á los indígenas el sacramento de la Penitencia; por un sacerdote del Obispado de Puebla.* Imprenta antiqua en el portal de las Flores, México, 1840. 43 p. Br498.22 AzC 737.

1108. Conant, Alban Jasper. *Foot-Prints of Vanished Races in the Mississippi Valley; Being an Account of Some of the Monuments and Relics of Prehistoric Races Scattered Over Its Surface, With Suggestions as to their Origin and Uses.* C. R. Barns, St. Louis, 1879. 122 p. Br572 C74.

1109. Conant, Levi L. *The Number Concept; Its Origin and Development.* Macmillan, New York, London, 1896. 218 p. Br510.9 C74.

1110. Confesionario en castellano y pocomchí, Tactic, año de 1814. 2 leaves; 40 p. Br498.21 PC 763. Manuscript. Introduction signed by Karl H. Berendt; the full title given in the caption is "Dialogo entre confesor y penitente, o modo de confesar yndios en lengua poconchí, 1814." A note by Berendt states: "El original del presente confesionario es un manuscrito en 16mo. de 42 fajas utiles en el archivo parochial del pueblo de Tactic; y me lo presento para sacar copia para el cura de aquel pueblo, fray Silvestro Mijangos, dominico expulsado de Chiapas, Cobán, agosto de 1875."

1111. *Confesionario en lengua mixe; con una construcción de las oraciones de la Doctrina Christiana, y un Compendio de Voces Mixes, para enseñarse a pronunciar la dicha lengua; escrito todo por el P. Fr. Augustín de Quintana de la Orden de Predicadores, cura q. fué de la Doctrina de S. Juan Bautista de Xuquila. Dedicalo al Glorioso Apostol de la Europa, S. Vicente Ferrer.* Por la Viuda de Miguel de Ortega, Puebla, año de 1733. 148 p. Br498.35 MQ 45.

1112. *Congrès International des Sciences Ethnographiques.* Imprimerie Nationale, Paris, 1889. 60 p. Br572C An8141 v.98.

1113. Congrès Internationaux d'Anthropologie et d'Archéologique Préhistorique et de Zoologie. *Materiaux réunis par le comité d'organisation des congrès...a Moscou.* Moscou, 1893. Br572.06 C764.

1114. Congreso Científico Latino Americano, 1898. *Primera reunión celebrada en Buenos Aires del 10 al 20 de abril de 1898, por iniciativa de la Sociedad Científica Argentina; organización y resultados generales del Congreso.* Compañía Sud-Americana de Billetes de Banco, Buenos Aires, 1898. Br506 C76.

1115. Connelley, William E. *The Provisional Government of Nebraska Territory and the Journals of William Walker, Provisional Governor of Nebraska Territory; Edited by William E. Connelley.* Proceedings and collections of the Nebraska State Historical Society, 3. State Journal Company, Lincoln, Nebraska, 1899. 423 p. Br978.2 C767.

1116. Conover, George S. *Sayenqueraghta, King of the Senecas.* Waterloo, NY, 1885. 15 p. Br572C An8141 v.20; Br572C An8141 v.58.

1117. Conover, George S. *The Birthplace of Sa-go-ye-wat-ha, or the Indian Red Jacket, the Great Orator of the Senecas; With a Few Incidents of His Life.* Waterloo, NY, 1884. 22 p. Br572C An8141 v.32.

1118. Contreras y Muñoz, Rafael. *Estudio descriptivo de los monumentos árabes de Granada, Sevilla, y Córdoba; o, sea, la Alhambra, el Alcázar y la gran mezquita de occidente.* 3d ed. Estab. Tipografica de R. Fé, Madrid, 1885. 378 p. Br913.46 C764.

1119. Contreras, Rafael. Vocabulario de la lengua mam, por D. Rafael Contreras, cura de Chiantla, 1866; copiado del original en poder de D. Juan Gavarrette en Guatemala por Dr. C. H. Berendt, 1875. 7 p. Br498.21 MaC 768. Manuscript; transcript by Karl H. Berendt of a vocabulary in Mam of some eighty glosses.

1120. Contzen, L. *Der Titicaca und seine Erinnerungen. Jahresbericht über die Realschule I. Ordnung zu Köln für das Schuljahr Nr. 417.* Druck von J. P. Bachem, 1882. 40 p. Br572C An8141 v.109.

1121. Cooke, George H. Tte Pito te henua, known as Rapa Nui; commonly called Easter Island, south pacific Ocean, Latitude 27 10'S., longitude 109 26'W. *Annual Report of the United States National Museum, Smithsonian Institution, for 1897,* pp. 689-723, 1899. Br919.7 C78.

1122. Cope, Edward D. Applied metaphysics of sex. *American Naturalist* 19:820-823, 1885. Br173 C793. Edward Drinker Cope (1840-1897), a biologist and paleontologist, is best known for his research in vertebrate paleontology. In 1889 he became professor of geology and later zoology at the University of Pennsylvania. In 1896 he was elected president of the American Association for the Advancement of Science. Although a committed evolutionist, Cope rejected Darwin's idea that natural selection was the causal mechanism of evolution, and argued that modifications in individual embryological development caused important evolutionary changes. He did not explain the causes of embryological acceleration or retardation and maintained that God was ultimately responsible for the process and pattern of evolutionary change.

1123. Cope, Edward D. Catalogue and price-list of the papers of...Edward D. Cope; also price-list of plaster casts. Haverford, n.d. 31 p. Br590B C793.

1124. Cope, Edward D. Energy of life evolution. *Popular Science Monthly* 27(162): 789-800, 1885. Br573.2 C79.

1125. Cope, Edward D. Evolution of mind. *American Naturalist* 24:899-1016, 1890. Br575 C79.

1126. Cope, Edward D. Geneaology of man. *American Naturalist* 27:321-335, 1893. Br573 C79.

1127. Cope, Edward D. Inheritance in evolution. *American Naturalist* 23, 1889. 14 p. Br575.1 C79.

1128. Cope, Edward D. On lemurine reversion in human dentition. *American Naturalist* 20(11): 941-947, 1886. Br572C An8141 v.13.

1129. Cope, Edward D. On the material relations of sex in human society. *Monist*, pp. 38-47, 1890. Br173 C793.3.

1130. Cope, Edward D. On the remains of population observed on and near the Eocene plateau of northwestern New Mexico. *Proceedings of the American Philosophical Society* 14:475-482, 1875. Br572.9789 C79.4.

1131. Cope, Edward D. Origin of man and other vertebrates. *Popular Science Monthly*, pp. 605-614, 1885. Br572C An8141 v.58; Br573.2 C79.

1132. Cope, Edward D. Relation of the sexes to government. *Popular Science Monthly*, pp. 721-730, 1888. Br173 C793.2.

1133. Cope, Edward D. Sex as an intellect stimulant. *Applied Metaphysics of Sex*, pp. 491-492, 1885. Br173 C793.

1134. Cope, Edward D. The developmental significance of human physiognomy. Abstract of a lecture before the Franklin Institute of Philadelphia, June, 1883. Br572C An8141 v.31.

1135. Cope, Edward D. The evolutionary significance of human character. *American Naturalist* 17:907-919, 1883. Br572C An8141 v.13.

1136. Cope, Edward D. The Mesozoic and Cenozoic realms of the interior of North America. *American Naturalist* 21:445-462, 1887. Br572C An8141 v.149.

1137. Cope, Edward D. Topinard on genealogy of man. *American Naturalist* 22:660-663, 1888. Br572 T626yC.

1138. Copway, George. *The Traditional History and Characteristic Sketches of the Ojibway Nation.* C. Gilpin, London; A. and C. Black, Edinburgh, J.B. Gilpin, Dublin, 1850. 298, 24 p. Br970.3 OjKl23.

1139. Cora, Guido. *Il territorio contestato tra la Venezuela e la Guiana Inglese*. Cora, Torino, 1896. 7 p. Br987 C812.

1140. Cora, Guido. Le spedizioni di R. E. Peary nella Groenlandia Nord. *Cosmos di Guido Cora* 11(12): 360-368, 1892-1893. Br572C An8141 v.144.

1141. Corbusier, William H. The Apache-Yumas and Apache-Mojaves. *American Antiquarian* 8(5): 276-284, 1886. Br572C An8141 v.27.

1142. Cordier, Henri. État actuel de la question du Fou-Sang. *Journal de la Société des Americanistes de Paris* 1:33-41, 1895. Br572C An8141 v.144.

1143. Cordova, Juan de. *Arte del idioma zapoteco…reimpreso por acuerdo del C. General Mariano Jiminez, gobernador constitucional del Estado de Michoacan de Ocampo*. Imprenta del Gobierno, Morelia, 1886. 223 p. Br498.34 ZC 813.

1144. Coreal, Francisco. *Voyages de François Coreal aux Indes Occidentales, contenant ce qu'il y a vû de plus remarquable pendant son séjour depuis 1666. jusqu'en 1697. Traduite de l'Espagnol. Avec une rélation de la Guiane de Walter Raleigh, et le voyage de Narbrough à la mer du Sud par le détroit de Magellan, &c. Nouv. éd., rev., corr., et augm. d'une nouvelle découverte des Indes Meridionales et des Terres australes, enrichie de figures*. D. Horthemels, Paris, 1722. 2 v. Br918 C81.

1145. Cornalia, E. Illustrazione della mummia peruviana. *Revista Istituto Lombardo di Scienze e Lettere* 2:3-11, 1860. Br572C An8141 v.101.

1146. Corrado, Alejandro M. *Catecismo de la doctrina cristiana con varias oraciones y practicas devotas en lengua chiriguana, con su traducción literal al castellano*. Imprenta de Pedro España, Suere, Bolivia, 1871. 150 p. Br498.75 CiC 814.

1147. Corrado, Alejandro M. *El colegio franciscano de Tarija y sus misiones; noticias historicas recogidas por los misioneros del mismo colegio*. Colegio de S. Buenaventura, Quaracchi, 1884. 566 p. Br243.2 F84Co.

1148. Cortés, Hernán. *Carta q[ue] el muy ilustre senor don Hernando Cortes marques q[ue] luego fue d[e]l Valle, escriuio a la S.C.C.M. d[e]l emperador; dandole que[s]ta d[e] lo q[ue] [con]uenia p[ro]ueer e[n] aquellas p[ar]tes: [y] d[e] algunas cossas e[n] ellas acaescidas. Fecha e[n] la gra[n] cibdad d[e] Temistita[n] Mexico d[e] la Nueua Espana: a xv. dias del mes de otubre de M.d.xxiv. Anos*. Imprenta particular del editor [Ioaquin García Icazbalceta], En México, 1855. xiv leaves. Br972 C812.2.

1149. Cortés, Hernán. *Carta sexta de Hernando Cortés, escrita al emperador Carlos V*. Imprenta de S. W. Benedict, Nueva York, 1848. 138 p. Br972 C81.4.

1150. Cortés, Hernán. *Cartas y relaciones de Hernan Cortés al emperador Carlos V. colegidas é ilustradas por don Pascual de Gayangos*. A. Chaix, Paris, 1866. 575 p. Br972.02D C816.

1151. Cortés, Hernán. *Escritos sueltos de Hernan Cortés; colección formada para servir de complemento a las "Cartas de relacion" publicadas en el tomo I. de la Biblioteca*. I. Escalante, México, 1871. 401 p. Br972 C81.5.

1152. Cortés, Hernán. *Esta es vna carta que el muy ilustre senor don Hernando Cortes marques que luego fue d[e]l Ualle, escriuio a la S.C.C.M. d[e]l emperador; dandole que[s]ta d[e] lo q[ue] [con]uenia p[ro]ueer e[n] aquellas p[ar]tes: [y] de al-*

gunas cossas en ellas acaescidas. Fecha e[n] la gran cibdad de Temistitan Mexico d[e] la Nueva Espana: a xv. dias del mes d[e] otubre d[e] M.d.xxiv. anos. Agora nueuame[n]te imp[re]ssa por su original. En la imprenta particular de Joaquin García Icazbalceta, y a su costa, Mexico, 1865. xiv leaves. Br972 C812.2a.

1153. Coruja, Antônio A. P. *Collecção de vocabulos e frases usados na provincia de S. Pedro do Rio Grande do Sul no Brazil.* Trübner e Comp., Londres, 1856. 32 p. Br469.7 C818.

1154. Corzo, A. A. *Segunda reseña de sucesos ocurridos en Chiapas desde 1847 á 1867.* Neve, Ciudad de Mexico, 1868. 161 p. Br972 C815.

1155. Cotteau, Gustave H. *Le préhistorique en Europe: congrès, musées excursions.* J.-B. Baillière, Paris, 1889. 313 p. Br571 C82.

1156. Cotton States and International Exposition (Atlanta), 1895. Exhibition of the Smithsonian Institution. Washington, DC, 1895. Br606 At1895sm.

1157. Cotton, Josiah. *Vocabulary of the Massachusetts (or Natick) Indian Language.* Printed by E. W. Metcalf, Cambridge, 1829. 112 p. Br497.11 MaC82. "Edited from the 1708 manuscript by John Pickering. Joshiah Cotton was the son of John Cotton, who helped [John] Eliot translate the Bible" (*Siebert Library* 1999:1:324).

1158. Coudreau, Henri A. *Voyage à Itaboca et à l'Itacayuna, Ier juillet 1897-11 octobre 1897.* A. Lahure, Paris, 1898. 158 p. Br918.1 C83.4.

1159. Coudreau, Henri A. *Voyage au Tapajoz, 28 juillet 1895-7 janvier 1896…illustré de 37 vignettes et d'une carte.* A. Lahure, Paris, 1897. 213 p. Br918.1 C83.

1160. Coudreau, Henri A. *Voyage au Tocantins-Araguaya, 31 décembre 1896-23 mai 1897…illustré de 87 vignettes et d'une carte des rivières "Tocantins-Araguaya."* A. Lahure, Paris, 1897. 298 p. Br918.1 C83.3.

1161. Coudreau, Henri A. *Voyage au Xingú 30 mai 1896-26 octobre 1896…illustré de 68 vignettes et d'une carte.* A. Lahure, Paris, 1897. 230 p. Br918.1 C83.2.

1162. Coudreau, Henri. *Vocabulaires méthodiques des langues Ouayana, Aparaï, Oyampi, Emérillon…précédés d'une introduction par Lucien Adam.* Bibliothèque Linguistique Américaine, 15. Maisonneuve, Paris, 1892. Br497C Am3.

1163. *civilisatrices. Cour de Tezcuco.* Lith. Desportes à l'Institut Royal des Sourds Muets, Paris, 1886. Br898.22 AzQ45. Includes map measuring 49 x 86 cm.

1164. Court, J. *Catalogue de la précieuse bibliothèque de feu m. le docteur J. Court, comprenant une collection unique de voyageurs et d'historiens relatifs à l'Amerique.* Charles Leclerc, Paris, 1884. 2 v. in 1. Br970B C83.

1165. Courtonne, E. Dictionnaire monosyllabique. *Bulletin de la Société Niçoisé des Sciences Naturalles, Historiques et Geographiques,* 1884. Br572C An8141 v.21.

1166. Courtonne, E. *Langue internationale Neo-Latine.* Librarie Europeene de Baudry, Paris, 1881. 43 p. Br572C An8141 v.21.

1167. Courtonne, E. Spécimen des dictionnaires international français et français international, n.d. Br572C An8141 v.21.

1168. Courtonne, E. Traductions diverses en prose et en vers. *Bulletin de la Société Niçoisé des Sciences Naturalles, Historiques et Geographiques,* pp. 1-24, 33-80, n.d. Br572C An8141 v.21.

1169. Couto de Magalhães, José V. *O selvagem. I. Curso da lingua geral segundo Ollendorf, comprehendendo o texto original de lendas tupìs. II. Origens, costumes, região selvagem, methodo a empregar para amansalos por intermedio das colonias militares e do interprete militar.* Livrària Popular, Rio de Janeíro, 1876. 281, 194 p. Br498.75 GC 83.

1170. Coville, Frederick V. *Directions for Collecting Specimens and Information Illustrating the Aboriginal Uses of Plants.* Government Printing Office, Washington, D.C, 1895. 8 p. Br572C An 8141 v.139.

1171. Coville, Frederick V. Notes on the plants used by the Klamath Indians of Oregon. *Contributions from the United States National Herbarium* 5(2): 87-108, 1897. Br572C An8141 v.149.

1172. Cox, C. F. *Faith-Healing in the Sixteenth and Seventeenth Centuries.* De Vine Press, New York, 1891. 21 p. Br572C An8141 v.82.

1173. Cox, George W. *An Introduction to the Science of Comparative Mythology and Folklore.* C. K. Paul and Company, London, 1881. 380 p. Br398 C83.

1174. Coy, José Domingo. Frases de conversación en lengua quecchi; apuntadas por Domingo Coy, indio de Cobán, 1868. 7 p. Br498.21 KC838. Manuscript, copied in Cobán. Phrases, arranged double column in Spanish and Kekchí (pp. 3-7); bound with "Via sacra en lengua cacchí, 1875." 30 p.

1175. Coy, José Domingo. Ortografia en lengua ccechi, traducida por José Domingo Coy, en la ciudad de Cobán, año de 1870. 16 p. Br498.21 KC838.2a. An original manuscript in Kekchí; pages 12-16 are in double columns.

1176. Coy, José Domingo. Ortografia en lengua kekchi, traducida por José Domingo Coy, indio de Cobán, en la ciudad de Cobán, año de 1870; copiado de su original en Cobán, abril de 1875, por Dr. C. H. Berendt. 33 p. Br498.21 KC838.2. Manuscript; bound with "Via sacra en lengua kekchí, 1861"; transcription by José Domingo Coy.

1177. Coyne, J. H. *The Country of the Neutrals from Champlain to Talbot.* Times Print, St. Thomas, 1895. 44 p. Br572C An 8141 v.139.

1178. Cramer, Narine-Prediger. Über die Reise der kaiserlichen Corvette *Hertha,* insbesondere nach Korea. *Verhandlungen der Berliner Gesellschaft für Anthropologie, Ethnologie und Urgeschichte,* pp. 1-9, 1873. Br572C An8141 v.162.

1179. Crane, Agnes. The American race. *Brighton Herald,* May 30, June 6, 1891. 15 p. Br572C An8141 v.10.

1180. Cresson, Hilbourne T. Aztec music. *Proceedings of the Academy of Natural Sciences in Philadelphia,* pp. 86-94, 1883. Br572C An8141 v.65.

1181. Cresson, Hilbourne T. Construction of ancient Mexican terra-cotta pitch-pipes and flageolets. *American Naturalist* 18:498-510, 1884. Br572C An8141 v.13.

1182. Cresson, Hilbourne T. Fallen forest layer underlying aqueous deposits in Delaware. *Bulletin of the Geological Society of America* 2:640-642, n.d. Br572C An8141 v.119.

1183. Cresson, Hilbourne T. *Report Upon Pile-Structures in Naaman's Creek, Near Claymont, Delaware.* Salem Press Publishing and Printing, Salem, MA, 1892. 22 p. Br572C An8141 v.110.

1184. Crevaux, J. N., P. A. Sagot, and L. Adam. *Grammaires et vocabulaires roucouyenne, arrouague, piapoco et d'autres langues de la région des Guyanes.* Bibliothèque Linguistique Américaine, 8. Maisonneuve, Paris, 1882. Br497C Am3.

1185. Crookes, William. Address by the President. *Proceedings of the Society for Pyschical Research* 12:337-355, 1897. Br572C An8141 v.149.

1186. *Crozet's Voyage to Tasmania, New Zealand, the Ladrone Islands, and the Philippines in the Years 1771-1772; Translated by H. Ling Roth; With a Preface and a Brief Reference to the Literature of New Zealand, by James R. Boosé.* Truslove and Shirley, London, 1891. 148 p. Br919 C888.

1187. Cruikshank, E. Early traders and trade-routes in Ontario and the West, 1760-1783. *Transactions of the Canadian Institute* 3:253-274, 1891-1892. Br572C An8141 v.114.

1188. Cuervo Márquez, Carlos. *Prehistoria y viajes: Tierradentro, Los Paeces, San Agustín, El Llano, etc.* Tipografía La Luz, Bogotá, 1893. 248 p. Br913.7 M346.

1189. Cuesta, Felipe Arroyo de la. *A Vocabulary or Phrase Book of the Mutsun Language of Alta California.* Shea's Library of American Linguistics, 8. Cramoisy Press, New York, 1862. 96 p. Br497C Sh3; Br497C Sh3a.

1190. Cuesta, Felipe Arroyo de la. *Extracto de la gramatica mutsum, ó de la lengua de los naturales de la mision de San Juan Bautista, compuesta por el Rev. Padre Felipe Arroyo de la Cuesta.* Shea's Library of American Linguistics, 4. Cramoisy Press, New York, 1861. 48 p. Br497C Sh3; Br497C Sh3a.

1191. Cueva, R. P. de la. *Principes et dictionnaire de la langue yuracare ou yurujure, composés par le R. P. de la Cueva et publiées copnformément au manuscrit de A. d'Orbigny por Lucien Adam.* Bibliothèque Linguistique Américaine, 16. J. Maisonneuve, Paris, 1893. 122 p. Br497C Am3; Br498.92 YC 896.

1192. Culin, Stewart. American Indian games: Presidential address, American Folk-Lore Society, Baltimore, Maryland, December, 1897. 14 p. Br572C An8141 v.164. Stewart Culin (1858-1929) had no formal education in anthropology but had a significant impact on the discipline through his work with the University of Pennsylvania Museum and the Brooklyn Museum. He was a founding member of the American Anthropological Association and the American Folklore Society. His main research interests were in games and museum work.

1193. Culin, Stewart. American medals, paper money, and books concerning the currency of American money. In *Archaeological Objects Exhibited by the Department of Archaeology and Palaeontology, University of Pennsylvania, Philadelphia*, pp. 194-207. Government Printing Office, Washington, DC, 1895. Br572C An8141 v.139.

1194. Culin, Stewart. Archaeological objects exhibited by the Department of Archaeology and Palaeontology, University of Pennsylvania, Philadelphia. In *Report of the Madrid Commission, 1892*, pp. 194-211. Government Printing Office, Washington, DC, 1895. Br572C An 8141 v.139.

1195. Culin, Stewart. *China in America: A Study in the Social Life of the Chinese in the Eastern Cities of the United States.* Philadelphia, 1887. 16 p. Br572C An8141 v.82.

1196. Culin, Stewart. Chinese drug stores in America. *Journal of Pharmacology*, December, 1887. 6 p. Br572C An8141 v.82.

1197. Culin, Stewart. Chinese games with dice and dominoes. *Annual Report of the United States National Museum, Smithsonian Institution, for 1893,* pp. 489-537, 1895. Br572C An 8141 v.139.

1198. Culin, Stewart. *Hawaiian Games.* G. P. Putnam's Sons, New York, 1899. Br394.3 C895. Extract from *American Anthropologist* 1:201-247, 1899.

1199. Culin, Stewart. Mancala, the national game of Africa. *Annual Report of the United States National Museum, Smithsonian Institution, for 1894,* pp. 595-607, 1896. Br572C An8141 v.149.

1200. Culin, Stewart. The gambling games of the Chinese in America; fán t'an, the game of repeatedly spreading out; pák kòp piú, or the game of the white pigeon ticket. *University of Pennsylvania Series in Philology, Literature, and Archaeology* 1(4): 1-17, 1891. Philadelphia. Br572C An8141 v.82.

1201. Culin, Stewart. The museums of archaeology of the University of Pennsylvania, 1893. 7 p. Br572C An8141 v.136.

1202. Culin, Stewart. *The Religious Ceremonies of the Chinese in the Eastern Cities of the United States.* Franklin Printing House, Philadelphia, 1887. 23 p. Br286.1 C895.

1203. Cunow, Heinrich. *Die Soziale Verfassung des Inkareichs.* Verlag von J. H. W. Dietz, Stuttgart, 1896. 118 p. Br572C An8141 v.149.

1204. Cuoq, Jean A. *Aiamie tipadjiimosin masinagan ka ojitogobanen kaiat ka niinasisi mekatesikonaiesgobanen kanaetaqeng, saksi enasindibanen.* Mekatesikonaiesikamikong kanactageng, Moniang [Montreal], 1859. 339 p. Br497.11 NiB 45. Christian doctrine translated into Nipissing language. "Father Cuoq published his first philological study under the initials of the names given him by the Indians among whom he worked for twenty years at the Lake of Two Mountains Mission in Canada" (*Siebert Library* 1999:1:77).

1205. Cuoq, Jean A. *Jugement erroné de M. Ernest Renan sur les langues sauvages, par l'auteur des Études Philologiques.* Dawson Brothers, Montreal, 1870. 113 p. Br572C An8141 v.50.

1206. Cuoq, Jean A. *Kaiatonsera ionteweienstakwa kaiatonserase; nouveau syllabaire Iroquois.* Tehoristorarakon John Lovell, Tiohtiake [i.e. Montreal], 1873. 69 p. Br497.27 MC92. Prayer book and devotionary in the Mohawk language.

1207. Cuoq, Jean A. *Lexique de la langue algonquine.* J. Chapleau, Montréal, 1886. 446 p. Br497.11 A1 C92.

1208. Cuoq, Jean A. *Lexique de la langue iroquoise; avec notes et appendices.* J. Chapleau et Fils, Montréal, 1882. 215 p. Br497.27 MC92.2.

1209. Cuoq, Jean A. *Quels étaient les sauvages que rencontra Jacq. Cartier sur les rives du Saint-Laurent.* Imprimerie Beau, Versailles, France, 1869. 7 p. Br970.1 C925.

1210. Cuoq, Juan A. *Études philologiques sur quelques langues sauvages de l'Amerique, par N.O., ancien missionaire.* Dawson Brothers, Montreal, 1866. 160 p. Br497.11 Al C92.2.

1211. Curtis, Mattoon M. An outline of philosophy in America. *Western Reserve Univer-*

sity Bulletin, March, 1896. 16 p. Br572C An8141 v.144.

1212. Curtis, William E. *Christopher Columbus; His Portraits and His Monuments: A Descriptive Catalogue, Part II.* W. H. Lowdermilk Company, Chicago, 1893. 72 p. Br572C An8141 v.118.

1213. Curtis, William E. Recent disclosures concerning pre-Columbian voyages to America in the archives of the Vatican. *National Geographic Magazine* 5:197-234, 1893. Br572C An8141 v.123.

1214. Curtis, William E. *Relics of Columbus: An Illustrated Description of the Historical Collection in the Monastery of La Rabida.* W. H. Lowdermilk Company, Chicago, 1893. 224 p. Br572C An8141 v.118.

1215. Cushing, Frank H. *Katalog einer Sammlung von Idolen, Fetischen und priesterlichen Ausrüstungsgegenständen der Zuñi oder Ashiwi-Indianer von Neu-Mexiko (U.S. Am.); Altindianische Ansiedelungen in Guatemala und Chiapas, von Carl Sapper; Alterthümer aus Guatemala, von Ed. Seler.* Geographische Verlagshandlung D. Reimer, Berlin, 1895. 53 p. Br970.3 ZC954.2. A member of the first Bureau of American Ethnology expedition to the American Southwest in 1879, Cushing (1857-1900) is credited with the first scientific study of the ethnology and archaeology of the region. The first anthropologist to study a culture as participant observer, he remained at Zuni Pueblo from 1879 to 1884. In addition to his ethnographic work among the Zuni, Cushing is known for his pioneering the experimental reproduction of indigenous material culture.

1216. Cushing, Frank H. Manual concepts: a study of the influence of the hand-usage on culture-growth. *American Anthropologist* 5(4): 289-317, 1892. Br572C An8141 v.124.

1217. Cushing, Frank H. Outlines of Zuni creation myths. *Annual Report of the Bureau of Ethnology, Smithsonian Institution, for 1893-1894,* pp. 321-447, 1896. Br970.6 C95.6.

1218. Cushing, Frank H. Primitive copper working: an experimental study. *American Anthropologist* 7:93-117, 1894. Br572C An8141 v.123.

1219. Cushing, Frank H. *Primitive Handicraft and Arts of America: Syllabus of a Course of Five Lectures.* Drexel Institute of Art, Science, and Industry, Philadelphia, n.d. 13 p. Br572C An8141 v.136.

1220. Cushing, Frank H. The Pepper-Hearst Expedition: a preliminary report on the exploration of ancient key-dweller remains on the Gulf Coast of Florida. *Proceedings of the American Philosophical Society* 35(153), 1897. 120 p. Br572C An8141 v.149.

1221. Cushing, Frank H. Zuni fetishes. *Annual Report of the Bureau of Ethnology, Smithsonian Institution, for 1880-1881,* pp. 3-45, 1883. Br970.6 C95.

1222. Cusick, David. *Sketches of Ancient History of the Six Nations.* Beauchamp, Fayetteville, NY, 1894. 54 p. Br970.3 IrC963.

1223. D'Eichthal, Gustave. Étude sur les origines Bouddhiques de la civilisation Américaine. *Revue Archéologique*, 1865. 85 p. Br572C An8141 v.26.

1224. Dahlberg, Robert N., and Charles L. Dahlberg. Composition of ancient pottery found near the mouth of Chequest Creek at Pittsburgh. *Annual Report of the Smithsonian Institution, for 1879*, pp. 349-350, 1880. Br572C An8141 v.19.

1225. Dall, William H. Notes on the paleontological publications of Professor William Wagner. *Transactions of the Wagner Free Institute of Science* 5:7-11, 1898. Br572C An8141 v.160. Through exploration sponsored by the Western Union Telegraph, the United States Coast and Geodetic Survey, the United States Geological Survey, the Smithsonian Institution, and E. H. Harriman, Dall (1845-1927) traveled repeatedly to Alaska between 1865 and 1899 and became one of the leading scientists concerned with Alaska. He assembled a large collection of Eskimo and Athabaskan artifacts, recorded some linguistic data, and carried out archaeological investigations on the Aleutians.

1226. Dall, William H. On some peculiarities of the Eskimo dialect. *Proceedings of the American Association for the Advancement of Science* 19:332-349, 1871. Br572C An8141 v.52.

1227. Dall, William H. *On the Remains of Later Pre-Historic Man Obtained From Caves in the Catherina Archipelago, Alaska Territory, and Especially From the Caves of the Aleutian Islands.* Smithsonian Institution Contributions to Knowledge, 22. Washington, DC, 1878. 35 p. Br572C An8141 v.100.

1228. Dall, William H. On the so-called Chukchi and Namollo people of eastern Siberia. *American Naturalist* 14:857-868, 1881. Br572C An8141 v.13.

1229. Dall, William H. Pearls and pearl fisheries. *American Naturalist* 17:579-586, 1883. Br572C An8141 v.13.

1230. Dall, William H. Social life among our aborigines. *American Naturalist* 12(1): 1-10, 1878. Br572C An8141 v.27.

1231. Dall, William H. The native tribes of Alaska; an address before the section of anthropology of the American Association for the Advancement of Science. *Proceedings of the American Association for the Advancement of Science* 34, 1885. 19 p. Br572C An8141 v.23.

1232. Dall, William H. *Tribes of the Extreme Northwest.* Smithsonian Institution, Contributions to American Ethnology, 1(1). Government Printing Office, Washington, DC, 1877. 156 p. Br557.3 Un319. Includes "On the distribution and nomenclature of the native tribes of Alaska and the adjacent territory, with a map. On succession in the shell-heaps of the Aleutian Islands. On the origin of the Innuit." Appendices include J. Furnhelm, "Notes on the natives of Alaska"; William H. Dall, "Terms of relationship used by the Innuit"; and George Gibbs and William H. Dall, "Comparative vocabularies."

1233. Danforth, E. *The Indians of New York.* Oneida Historical Society, Oneida, NY, 1894. 52 p. Br572C An8141 v.134.

1234. Danielli, I. *Crani ed ossa lunghe di Abitanti dell'Isola d'Engano.* Tipografia di Salvatore Landi, Firenze, 1894. 37 p. Br572C An8141 v.135.

1235. Daniels, Arthur H. *The New Life: A Study of Regeneration.* F. S. Blanchard, Worcester, 1893. 48 p. Br572C An8141 v.120.

1236. Danielsson, Olaf A. Epigraphica. *Uppsala Universitets Årsskrift*, 1890. 65 p. Br572C An8141 v.56.

1237. Danielsson, Olaf A. Zur Argivischen Bronzeinschrift der Sammlung Tyskiewicz. *Erani* 1, 1896. 10 p. Br572C An8141 v.139.

1238. Darapsky, L. Estudios lingüísticos americanos. *Boletin del Instituto Geografico Argentino* 10(9): 276-289, 1889. Br572C An8141 v.49.

1239. Darapsky, L. *La lengua araucana.* Imprenta Cervantes, Santiago de Chile, 1888. 35 p. Br572C An8141 v.49.

1240. Darwin, Charles. *The Descent of Man, and Selection in Relation to Sex.* 2d ed. John Murray, London, 1883. 693 p. Br575.5 D25b.

1241. Davidson, Thomas. *Giordano Bruno and The Relation of His Philosophy to Free Thought; A Lecture Delivered Before the New York Liberal Club, Oct. 30, 1885.* Index Association, Boston, 1886. 45 p. Br119 B83yB.

1242. Davis, Solomon. *Prayer Book, in the Language of the Six Nations of Indians; Containing the Morning and Evening Catechism, Some of the Collects, and the Prayers and Thanksgivings Upon Several Occasions, in the Book of Common Prayer of the Protestant Episcopal Church; Together With Forms of Family and Private Devotion; Compiled From Various Translations, and Prepared for Publication by Request of the Domestic Committee of the Board of Missions of the Protestant Episcopal Church in the United States of America; by the Rev. Solomon Davis, Missionary to the Oneidas, at Duck-Creek, Territory of Wisconsin.* Swords, Stanford and Company D. Fanshaw, Printer, New York, 1837. 168 p. Br497.27 OP94.

1243. Dawkins, William B. Early man in America. *Kansas City Review of Science* 7(6): 344-351, 1883. Br572C An8141 v.20.

1244. Dawkins, William B. The tools of the pyramid builders. *Kansas City Review of Science* 7(6): 336-344, 1883. Br572C An8141 v.20.

1245. Dawson, George M. Geological notes on some of the coasts and islands of Bering Sea and vicinity. *Bulletin of the Geological Society of America* 5:117-146, 1894. Br572C An8141 v.123.

1246. Dawson, George M. Note on the occurrence of jade in British Columbia and its employment by the natives; with quotations and extracts from a paper by Prof. A. B. Meyer, on nephrite and analogous minerals. *Canadian Record of Science* 2(6), 1887. 15 p. Br572C An8141 v.59.

1247. Dawson, George M. Notes and observations on the Kwakiool people of Vancouver Island. *Transactions of the Royal Society of Canada* 5(2): 1-36, 1887. Br572C An8141 v.92.

1248. Dawson, George M. Notes on the Indian tribes of the Yukon District and adjacent northern portion of British Columbia. *Annual Report of the Geological Survey of Canada,* 1887. 23 p. Br572C An8141 v.32.

1249. Dawson, George M. Notes on the Shuswap people of British Columbia. *Transactions of the Royal Society of Canada,* pp. 3-44, 1891. Br572C An8141 v.105.

1250. Dawson, George M. On the glaciation of the northern part of the cordillera, with an attempt to correlate the events of the glacial period in the cordillera and Great Plains. *The American Geologist,* September, pp. 153-162, 1890. Br572C An8141 v.7.

1251. Dawson, George M. On the later physiographical geology of the Rocky Mountain region in Canada, with special reference to changes in elevation and the history of the glacial period. *Transactions of the Royal Society of Canada* 8(4): 3-74, 1890. Br557.1 D327.

1252. Dawson, George M. Some observations tending to show the occurrence of secular climatic changes in British Columbia. *Transactions of the Royal Society of Canada* 4:159-166, 1896. Br572C An8141 v.150.

1253. Dawson, George M. The physical geography and geology of Canada. *The Handbook of Canada*. Rowsell and Hutchinson, Toronto 1897. 48 p. Br572C An8141 v.150.

1254. Dawson, George M. The progress and trend of scientific investigation in Canada; being the presidential address delivered at the annual meeting of the Royal Society of Canada, May 22, 1894. *Transactions of the Royal Society of Canada*, 1894. 17 p. Br572C An8141 v.144.

1255. Dawson, J. William. Address. *Report of the British Association for the Advancement of Science*, 1886. 34 p. Br572C An8141 v.41. John W. Dwason was a geologist and principal of McGill College and University, who attempted to link artifacts excavated in western Montreal with the Iroquois village of Hochelaga. His work is considered to have been the beginning of Canadian archaeology.

1256. Dawson, J. William. *Fossil Men and Their Modern Representatives; An Attempt to Illustrate the Characters and Condition of Prehistoric Men in Europe, by Those of the American Races*. Hodder and Stoughton, London, 1880. 348 p. Br571 D32.

1257. DeBeaujeu, M. *Le héroes de la Monongahela*. Desauliniers et Cie., Montreal, 1892. 26 p. Br572C An8141 v.128.

1258. DeCosta, Benjamin F. The Pre-Columbian voyages of the Welsh to America; Myryrian Archaeology. *Winsor Collection* 1(3), 1891. 12 p. Br572C An8141 v.10.

1259. DeForest, John W. *History of the Indians of Connecticut From the Earliest Known Period to 1850*. William James Hamersley, Hartford, 1852. 509 p. Br970.4 CD362. Consideration of Mohegan and Pequot Indians.

1260. DeGregorio, Giacomo. *Glottologia*. Hoepli, Milan, 1896. 318 p. Br409.02 G863.

1261. DeGregorio, Giacomo. *Letterature neo-latine, per la storia comparata delle letterature neo-latine, considerazioni introduttive ed accenni; su qualche tema speciale*. Clausen, Palermo, 1893. 65 p. Br879.01 G865.

1262. DeGregorio, Giacomo. *Studi glottologici italiani*. Loescher, Torino, 1899. Br451G865.

1263. DeGregorio, Giacomo. *Ultima parola sulla varia origine del Sanfratellano, Nicosiana e Piazzese*. Paris, 1899. 23 p. Br457.5 G863.

1264. Dellenbaugh, F. S. Death-masks in ancient American pottery. *American Anthropologist* 10:48-53, 1897. Br572C An8141 v.150.

1265. Dellenbaugh, F. S. The true route of Coronado's march. *Bulletin of the American Geographical Society* 29:399-431, 1897. Br572C An8141 v.150.

1266. Demoor, Jean, Jean Massart, and Emile Vandervelde. *L'évolution régressive en biologie et en sociologie*. F. Alcan, Paris, 1897. 324 p. Br575 D394.

1267. Dencke, Christian. *Nek nechenenawachgissitschik bambilak naga geschiechauch-*

John W. Dawson (from Justin Winsor, Aboriginal America. *Cambridge, MA: Houghton, Mifflin, 1889. p. 380).*

sitpanna Johannessa elekhangup; gischitak elleniechsink untschi C. F. Dencke. Printed for the American Bible Society, New York, 1818. 21, 21 p. Br497.11 DB47.4. Epistles of St. John translated into Delaware.

1268. Deniker, Joseph, and R. Boulart. *Sur divers points de anatomie de l'Orang-Outan.* Gauthier-Villars et Fils, Imprimeurs, Paris, 1894. 4 p. Br572C An8141 v.145.

1269. Deniker, Joseph. Les Ghiliaks d'après les derniers renseignements. *Revue d'Ethnographie* 2(4): 289-310, 1883. Br572C An8141 v.31.

1270. Deniker, Joseph. Les indigènes de Lifou (Iles Loyauté). *Bulletins de la Société d'Anthropologie de Paris,* pp. 791-804, 1893. Br572C An8141 v.131.

1271. Denis, Ferdinand. *Arte plumaria: les plumes.* Paris, 1875. 76 p. Br572C An8141 v.40.

1272. Denis, Ferdinand. *Une fête brésilienne célébrée à Rouen en 1550; suivie d'un fragment du XVIe siècle roulant sur la théogonie des anciens peuples du Brésil, et des poésies en langue tupique de Christovam Valente; par Ferdinand Denis.* J. Techener, Paris, 1850. 104 p. Br980.4 BD413.

1273. Denton, D. *Brief Description of New York, Formerly Called New Netherlands With the Places Thereunto Adjoining; Likewise a Brief Relation of the Customs of the Indians There By Daniel Denton; A New Edition with an Introduction and Notes by Gabriel Furman.* Gowans, New York, 1845. 214 p. Br974.7 D434.

1274. Derby, Orville A. The artificial mounds of the Island of Marajó, Brazil. *American Naturalist* 13(4): 224-229, 1879. Br572C An8141 v.19.

1275. Desjardins, Ernest E. A. *Rapport sur les deux ouvrages de bibliographie américaine de M. Henri Harrisse; par M. Ernest Desjardins, lu à la séance de la commission centrale, le 18 janvier 1867; Extrait du Bulletin de la Société de Géographie.* Imprimerie de E. Martinet, Paris, 1867. 20 p. Br572C An8141 v.40; Br985 D463.

1276. Desor, Edouard. *L'homme pliocène de la Californie.* Nice, 1849. 16 p. Br572C An8141 v.41.

1277. Devéria, M. G., and Willy Bang. Notes d'epigraphie Mongole-Chinoise. *Journal Asiatique,* 1896. 87 p. Br572C An8141 v.146.

1278. Dewitz, Hermann. Über altpreussische Begräbnisstätten an der Samländischen Küste und in Masuren. *Verhandlungen der Berliner Gesellschaft für Anthropologie, Ethnologie und Urgeschichte,* pp. 3–9, 1872. Br572C An8141 v.162.

1279. Di Priuli, Constantino. *Copia di una lettera venuta d'India, indrizzata al magnifico M. Constantino Di Priuli, nella quale si leggono cose maravigliose e varie di quelli paesi, scritta nel 1557, ricevuta nel 1539.* Danese-Buri-Giovanelli, Venezia, 1824. 40 p. Br572C An8141 v.69.

1280. Dias, Antônio Gonçalves. *Diccionario da lingua tupy: chamada lingua geral dos indigenas do Brazil.* Bibliotheca linguistica, 1. F. A. Brockhaus, Lipsia, 1858. 191 p. Br498.75 G 583.

1281. Díaz del Castillo, Bernal. *Histoire véridique de la conquête de la Nouvelle-Espagne; écrite par le capitaine Bernal Diaz del Castillo l'un de ses conquistadores; traduction par D. Jourdanet. 2. éd. cor., précédée d'une étude sur les sacrifices humains et l'anthropophagie chez les Aztèques.* Masson, Paris, 1877. 952 p. Br972D D542.FJ.

1282. Diaz del Castillo, Bernal. *Historia verdadera de la conquista de la Nueva España.* Imprenta de L. Escalante, México, 1870. 3 v. Br972 D542a.

1283. Díaz del Castillo, Bernal. *Historia verdadera de la conquista de la Nueua España; escrita por el capitan Bernal Diaz del Castillo, vno de sus conquistadores; sacada a luz, por el P. M. Fr. Alonso Remon, predicador y coronista general del Orden de N. S. de la Merced, redención de cautiuos.* En la emprenta del reyno, Madrid, 1632. 256 leaves. Br972 B542.

1284. Diaz del Castillo, Bernal. *The Memoirs of the Conquistador Bernal Diaz del Castillo, Written by Himself, Containing a True and Full Account of the Discovery and Conquest of Mexico and New Spain.* J. Hatchard and Son, London, 1844. 2 v. Br972 D542b.

1285. Diccionario de San Francisco. tomo I: Diccionario maya-español del convento de San Francisco en Mérida. 364 p.; tomo II: Diccionario español-maya del convento de San Francisco en Mérida. 386 p. Br498.21 MD542. "According to the most skillful Maya scholars, this dictionary was composed in the seventeenth century, and is older than that of Ticul. When, in 1820, the Franciscan convent of Mérida was closed, the original manuscript was presented to a citizen of Mérida, and passed through various hands until it reached those of Don Juan Pío Pérez. He made a faithful copy of it, from which the present one was taken in 1870 by Dr. Berendt. The original could nowhere be found at that date, nor is there any intimation who the author was, nor the exact date of his labors" (Brinton 1900).

1286. Diccionario de Ticul; diccionario español-maya. 268 p.; Diccionario maya-español. 241 p. Bound in one volume. Br498.21 Md544. "In 1836 the cura of Ticul, don Estanislas Carrillo, found among the baptismal archives of his parish a manuscript of

154 leaves with the title "Vocabulario de la lengua maya que comienza en romance, compuesto de varios autores de esta lengua." It bore as the date of completion January 26, 1690. He presented it to his friend, Don Juan Pío Pérez, the distinguished Yucatecan linguist. The latter copied it, after which the original, not being cared for, was lost. In 1847 he made another copy, and either gave away or otherwise disposed of that of 1836. From that of 1847, the present one was made by Dr. Berendt in Mérida in 1870, with the utmost care" (Brinton 1900).

1287. Diccionario pocomchi-castellano y castellano-pocomchi de S. Cristobal Cahcoh; fragmentos en todo 145 fojas utiles, San Cristobal Cahcoh, 16 cent. 151 leaves. Br498.21 PD568. An original manuscript written at the end of the 16th century by a Dominican, and obtained by Karl H. Berendt from the cura of San Cristobal Cahcoh in 1875; photostatic copy of a manuscript with the same title in Tulane University attributed to Dionisio de Zuniga.

1288. Dictionaire française walla walla klikatak, n.d. Br497.48 WD567.

1289. *Die Zeugung in Sitte, Brauch und Glauben der Südslaven.* Kruptadia, recueil de documents pour servir à l'étude des traditions populaires, v. 6, pp. 193-384. H. Welter, Paris, 1899. 3 v. Br392.6 Z28.

1290. Dieseldorff, Erwin P. Alte Bemalte Thongefässe von Guatemala. *Verhandlungen der Berliner Anthropologischen Gesellschaft für Anthropologie, Ethnologie und Urgeschichte* 25:547-550, 1893. Br572C An8141 v.137.

1291. Dieseldorff, Erwin P. Ausgrabungen in Coban. *Verhandlungen der Berliner Anthropologischen Gesellschaft für Anthropologie, Ethnologie und Urgeschichte* 25:374-382, 1893. Br572C An8141 v.137.

1292. Dieseldorff, Erwin P. Das Gefäss von Chamá. *Verhandlungen der Berliner Anthropologischen Gesellschaft für Anthropologie, Ethnologie und Urgeschichte* 21:770-776, 1895. Br572C An8141 v.150.

1293. Dieseldorff, Erwin P. Ein Bemaltes Thongefäss mit figülichen Darstellungen aus einem Grabe von Chamá. *Verhandlungen der Berliner Anthropologischen Gesellschaft für Anthropologie, Ethnologie und Urgeschichte* 26:372-378, 1894. Br572C An8141 v.137.

1294. Dieseldorff, Erwin P. Ein Thongefäss mit Darstellung einer vampyrköpfigen Gottheit. *Verhandlungen der Berliner Anthropologischen Gesellschaft für Anthropologie, Ethnologie und Urgeschichte* 26:575-576, 1894. Br572C An 8141 v.139.

1295. Dieseldorff, Erwin P. Reliefbild aus Chipolém. *Verhandlungen der Berliner Anthropologischen Gesellschaft für Anthropologie, Ethnologie und Urgeschichte* 21:777-783, 1895. Br572C An8141 v.150.

1296. Dieseldorff, Erwin P. Wer waren die Tolteken?, 1896. 4 p. Br572C An8141 v.150.

1297. Dietrich, Adolf. Les parlers créoles des Mascareignes. *Romania* 20:216-276, 1891. Br572C An8141 v.46.

1298. *Directory of the Scientific Societies of Washington.* Gibson Brothers, Printers, Washington, DC, 1897. Br572C An8141 v.136.

1299. Distel, Theodor. *Aus Wilhelm von Humboldt's lekten Lebensjahren.* Leipzig, 1883. 44 p. Br572C An8141 v.54.

1300. *Dix ans sur la cote du Pacifique par un missionaire canadien.* Quebec, 1873. 100 p. Br572C An8141 v.71.

1301. Dobritzhofer, Martin. *An Account of the Abipones; An Equestrian People of Paraguay.* Murray, London, 1822. 3 v. Br980.3 AD652. Martin Dobrizhofer was born in 1717, entered the Jesuit order in 1736, and began extensive missionary activities in eastern South America in 1749.

1302. Doctrina christiana en lengua ccacchi; trasladada por mano y pluma de José Secundino Paccay en 15 de septiembre del año de 1861, y copiado por C. Hermann Berendt, abril de 1875. 114 p. Br498.21 KD654. Manuscript; transcription by Karl H. Berendt of an early Kekchí *doctrina*.

1303. Doctrina christiana en lengua chapaneca; fragmento de un manuscrito anónimo, copiado en facsimile por C. Hermann Berendt, M.D. Tuxtla Gutiérrez, 1869. 67 p. Br498.12 CD653. Manuscript; in the introduction by Berendt, "El original de este manuscrito es un cuaderno en cuarto, papel, y letra del siglo XVII o XVIII; escritura muy clara y regular. Le fáltan la portada y las primeras veinte páginas, que parece han contenido la parte principal de la doctrina cristiana la qual concluye en la pagina 36. Siguen despues 14 fojas más en la lengua, faltando uno el principio de este parte, que contiene oraciones en versos acrósticos y anagramas y concluye con una alocución o sermón. El resto es en castellano; dos fojas con una disertación sobre el lugar del paraiso, que pone el cerro Gólgota, tres fojas tablas de los evangelios y epistolas y en 136 paginas de nueva numeración los evangelios de todos los Domingos. Las epístolas se encuentran en ocho fojas sin numeración, en parte destruidos y seguidas por una fojas blanca que en el reverso del pedazo que se conservo muestra un pedazo de una rubrica y algunas palabras, que parece una advertencia ritual. Solo las 44 páginas en lengua chapaneca van copiados aquí. Este manuscrito es propriedad de D. Angel Carnas en la ciudad de Chiapa, en cuya familia lo han conservado desde muchos años y me lo consiguió para estudiar y copiaro mi amigo D. Francisco Amado Calebró de esta ciudad.

1304. Doctrina christiana en lengua zoque, año de 1736. 51, 7 leaves. Br498.35 ZD653. Manuscript; fragments of a doctrina written early in the last century, and presented to Karl H. Berendt by Don José María Sánchez, cura of Ocosocantla.

1305. Doctrina christiana en pocomchí, año de 1810. 2 preliminary leaves and 39 p. Br498.21 PD 653. Manuscript; introduction signed by Karl H. Berendt, states: "La presente doctrina se ha copiada de un cuaderno en [octavo] con 22 fajas útiles. Lleva la inscripción 'para el uso de Basilio Co, año de 1810.' El cura del pueblo de Tactic me lo consiguó prestado de un indio en el barrio de San Jacinto en el mismo pueblo. Va copioso aqui con la ortografia de su original, Cobán, agosto de 1875."

1306. Doctrina christiana y confesionario en lengua kekchi y castellano, con un pequeo vocabulario del archivo de la parroquia de Cobán, copiado por C. Hermann Berendt, M. D., Cobán, febrero de 1875. 51 p. Br498.21 KD653. Manuscript.

1307. Doctrina y confesionario en lengua ixil; precedidos de un corto modo para aprenderla, y ritual de matrimonio, por el cura párroco de Nebah, 1824. 28 leaves. Br498.321 ID653. Manuscript; a handbook containing an Ixil grammar and vocabulary; a bilingual transcription of the marriage service in Spanish and Ixil; and various prayers and responses, compiled in 1824 by the parish priest of the village of Nébaj in the province of Quiché, Guatemala. The Ixil grammar is followed by a short Spanish-Ixil vocabulary containing some basic terms relating to parts of the body and family relationships; temporal expressions; and pronouns and conjunctions. The text of the marriage service is given in Spanish and Ixil, arranged in parallel columns on each page. The section entitled "Doctrina en lengua Yxil" contains Ixil versions of the Lord's Prayer, the Apostles' Creed, the Ave María and Salve Regina, the commandments, the sacraments of the church, and articles of faith. A general confession in Spanish and Ixil appears in double columns on each page. Also included in the notebook are the parish accounts of contributions received by the priest from the villages of Nébaj, Cotzal, and Chajul for the celebration of monthly masses and church feasts of Epiphany, St. Sebastián, St. Vincent, and St. Anthony. He also records the quantities of chickens, corn, chiles, frijoles and other food he has received in payment of his salary.

1308. Documentos historicas, n.d. Br972 D653. Manuscript; contents include: 1. Francisco de Montejo, Carta al emperador, 1545; 2. Francisco de Montejo, Carta al emperador, 1547; 3. Francisco de Montejo, Carta al emperador, 1547; 4. Estevan Inigues de Castañeda, Carta al emperador, 1547; 5. Juan de Puerta, Carta al Consejo de Indias, 1547; 6. Lorenzo de Bienvenida, carta, 1548; 7. Cerrato, Carta al emperador, 1548; 8. Pedrarias Davila, Relación dirigida al Rey, 1529; 9. Juan Estrada de Salvago, Descripción de las provincias de Costa Rica, Guatemala, Honduras, Nicaragua, 1572; 10. Juan Vasquez de Coronado, Relación mui circunstanciada, 1562.

1309. Documentos politicos de Yucatán, 1837-1876. 2 v. Br917.27 D663.2. Manuscript; contents include: volume 1; 1. Yucatán, Junta: Trabajo hechos por la comisión sobre la división provincial de este departamento que previene la constitución, 1837; 2. Yucatán, Congreso; Proyecto que comprende la división del territorio del estado de Yucatán, presentado al augusto congreso, 21 setiembre de 1840, 1840; 3. Justo Sierra, Oración circa y popular pronunciada el 16 de setiembre de 1841, aniversario del glorioso Grito de Dolores, 1841; 4. Yucatán, Gobernador: Representación dirige al congreso constituyente de republica mejicana en cumplimiento del acuerdo de la legislatura del estado de 2 junio de 1842, 1842; 5. Yucatán, Gobernador: Discurso por Miguel Barbachano, 1849-1853;6. Mexico, Dirección General de Estadistico: Memoria sobre el estado de la agricultura e industria de la republica, 1844, 1845; 7. Estevan de Antuño, Documentos para la historia de la industria moderna de Mejico, 1845; 8. Yucatán, Secretaria General: Piezas justificativas de la conducta politica de Yucatán al observar la del gobierno de Mejico respecto de los convenios de 14 diciembre de 1843, 1843; 9. S. L. de Llergo, Manifiesto respecto a la época en que ha ejercido el mando principal de las armas, 1850; 10. Yucatán, Gobernador: Discurso por Miguel Barbachano, 1849-1853; 11. Yucatán, Gobernador: Discurso por Miguel Barbachano, 1849-1853; 12. Yucatán, Gobernador: Discurso por Miguel Barbachano, 1849-1853; 13. Francisco Martínez de Arredondo, Memoria con que dió cuenta a las honorables camaras del estado de Yucatán el secretario del despacho el 10 de enero de 1883, en cumplimiento del articulo 160 del reglamento interior de H. congreso de 28 setiembre de 1852, 1853; 14. Yucatán, Gobernador: Discurso pronunciado por Santiago Mendez, 1857; 15. Mexico: Reglamento para la organización de la Guardia Nacional expedido en 11 setiembre de 1846, y mandado observar por decreto de 14 de enero de 1856; 16. Mexico: Reglamentos Santiago Mendez, 1856; 17. Mexico, Secretaria de Fomento: Documentos e Informés relativos a la proyectada población del Progreso, 1856; 18. Juan Suarez y Navarro, Refutación de las exposiciones hechas...pretendiendo la nulidad de las elecciónes de diputados al congreso de la union verificadas el 20 de enero ultimo, 1861; 19. Yucatán, Ministerio de Fomento: Balanza mercantil del puerto de Sisal en el primer semestre de 1861 en esta capital, 1861. Volume 2, 1. Yucatán: Constitución política del estado de Yucatán sancionada en 21 abril de 1862; 2. Yucatán, Gobernador: Reglamento del hospital de San Juan de Dios en Mérida de Yucatán, 1862; 3. Yucatán, Congreso: ley constitucional para el gobierno interior de los pueblos de Yucatán, 1862; 4. Mexico, Junta Superior: El supremo poder ejecutivo provisional de la nación a los habitantes de ella, saber: Que la junta superior de gobierno hecho la siguiente elección, n.d.; 5. Campeche y la intervención, n.d.; 6. M. von Hippel, Nachrichten für Auswanderer über die Colonisation von Yucatán, n.d.; 7. A SS. MM. II por su viaje a Yucatán, n.d.; 8. Viva la emperador, n.d.; 9. Exposición dirigida a S. M. el emperador Maximiliano por los habitantes de la villa de Sisal y otros pueblos de Yucatán sobre la cuestion del ferrocarril que debe unir a Mérida con el litoral, 1866; 10. Mexico, Secretaria de Fomento: Documentos e informes relativos a la proyectada población del Progreso publicados en 1866, segunda edición por J. M. Castro, 1869; 11. Rafael de Portas, Sisal y el Progreso, defensa de los intereses generales de Yucatán, n.d.; 12. Yucatán, Vice-Gobernador: Expediente de la visita oficial del estado hecha por el C. Lic. Manuel Cirerol, vice-gobernador constitucional del mismo, en cumplimiento del articulo 56 de la constitución política de Yuctan, n.d.; 13. J. M. Castro, El triunfo de la verdad en favor de la Progreso, 1870; 14. Yucatán: Documentos justificativos de esta publicación, 1870; 15. J. M. Castro, Documentos relativos a la cuestion de translación de la aduana de Sisal al Progreso, 1870; 16. Pedro Lavalle, Revista de la exposición de los productos de las artes y de la industria de Yucatán, 1871; 17. Yucatán: Instrucción publica: Consejo de presidente del H.: Memoria de las escuelas especiales del estado verificada el 30 de julio de 1876; 18. Yucatán: Instituto Literario del Estado: Informé del ciudadno director, 1876; 19. Yucatán, Conservatorio: Composiciones...el 16 de setiembre de 1876, aniversario III de su instalación, 1876; 20. R. G. Canton, Proyecto sobre la formación de una sociedad y banco agricola y varias indicaciones relativos al henequen, 1876; 21. Yucatán, Conservatorio: Informé leido por el C. director general...en la junta general celebrada el domingo de 23 de julio de 1876.

1310. Documentos politicos de Yucatán, 1845-1868. Br917.26 D663. Manuscript. Contents include: 1. Yucatán, Secretaria general: Memoria leida ante la Excma. Asemblea del departamento de Yucatán, 1845-1846; 2. Yucatán, Gobernador: Documentos relativos a los creditos de Yucatán, 1868; 3. Yucatán: Censo del estado de Yucatán por A. G. Rejon, 1845, 1862; 4. Apolinar García y García, Historia de la guerra de castas de Yucatán, 1865; 5. Crescencio Carrillo y Ancona, Observación critico-historica ó defensa del clero yucateco, 1866; 6. La cola del mus v.1(1–4), 1866.

1311. Documents in Spanish and early tongues of Florida. Br970.4 FD653. Manuscript. Contents include: 1. Diego de Quiroga y Lossada, Carta; 2. Marcelo de San Joseph, Carta; 3. Matheo Chuba, Car lus adulu pin holahta pula qui achit; 4. Matheo Chuba, Carta…Carlos segunda Nro. Casique principal y Nro. Mayor Rey; translated from the Apalachian language by Marcelo de San Joseph; 5. Francisco de Roxas, Carta; 6. Francisco de San Matheo, Carta e reihe ca anaconica; 7. Francisco de San Matheo, Carta al Rey Nro. Señor; translated from the Timuquamam language by Francisco de Rojas.

1312. *Documents Relating to the Colonial, Revolutionary, and Post-Revolutionary History of the State of New Jersey.* New Jersey Historical Society, Newark, 1880. v. 1–7, 19. Br974.9 N463.2.

1313. Dolby-Tyler, C. H., and Enrico H. Giglioli. Di alcuni strumenti litici tuttora in uso presso certe tribú del Río Napo, pp. 283–294, n.d. Br572C An8141 v.152.

1314. Domenech, Emmanuel. *Manuscrit pictographique américain, précédé d'une notice sur l'idéographie des Peaux-Rouges.* Gide, Paris, 1860. 119 p. Br497.01 D71. Reproduction of a manuscript (no. 8022) preserved in the Bibliothèque de l'Arsenal at Paris and designated by the title "Livre des sauvages".

1315. Domínguez y Argaiz, Francisco Eugenio. *Pláticas de los principales mysterios de nuestra ste. Fe, con una breve exortación al fin, del modo con que deben exitarse al dolor de las culpas; hechas en el ydioma yucateco, por orden del Illmo. Y Rmo. Sr. Dr. Y Mtro. D. F. Ignacio de Padilla, del sagrado orden de San Augustín, digníssimo arzobispo obispo de estas provincias de Yucatán, de el consejo de Su Majestad, por el Doctor D. Francisco Eugenio Dominguez y Argaiz, cura propio de la parrochial del Santo Nombre de Jesús, intramuros de la ciudad, y examinador synodal del obispado de Yucatán; quien las dedica al dicho Illmo. y Rmo. Señor; contiene seis pláticas; la 1. La explicación de N. Santa Fee; la 2. El mysterio de la SS. Trinidad; la 3. El de la encarnación del verbo divino; la 4. El de la eucharistía; la 5. La explicación del fin último para que fué criado el hombre; que es solo dios; la 6. La explicación del modo con que deben excitarse al dolor de las culpas.* En la Imprenta del Real y Mas Antiguo Colegio de S. Yldefonso, México, año de 1758. 24 p. Br498.21 MD713. Translated "por orden del illmo. D.F. Ignacio de Padilla…arzobispo obispo de estas provincias de Yucatán." Karl H. Berendt copied only the first two of the six sermons in Maya of Dominguez y Argaiz's "Pláticas de los principales misterios de nuestra Santa Fee" of 1757. The first explains basic ideas of the Catholic faith, while the second focuses on the mysteries of the Trinity. He also copied the preliminary materials from the edition of the sermons published in Mexico in 1758 by the Colegio de San Ildefonso, including the author's letter to Bishop Ignacio Padilla; his note to the readers; requests for permission to publish the sermons; and approval from ecclesiastical officials.

1316. Dominguez, Francisco. *Catecismo de la doctrina cristiana puesto en el idioma totonaco de la cierra baja de Naolingo, distinto del de la cierra alta de Papantla, por el Lic. D. Francisco Dominguez, cura interino de Xalpan.* En la imprenta del Hospital de San Pedro, Puebla, 1837. 28 p. Br498.29 ToD 713.

1317. Donaldson, Thomas C. *Eastern Band of Cherokees of North Carolina.* United States Census Printing Office, Washington, DC, 1892. 24 p. Br970.3 ChD713; Br572C An8141 v.102; Br572C An8141 v.108.

1318. Donaldson, Thomas C. *Moqui Pueblo Indians of Arizona and Pueblo Indians of New Mexico.* United States Census Printing Office, Washington, DC, 1893. 136 p. Br970.3 TD713; Br572C An8141 v.108.

1319. Donaldson, Thomas C. *North American Indians in the United States, Alaska Excepted.* Government Printing Office, Washington, DC, 1893. 46 p. Br970.5 D714.

1320. Donaldson, Thomas C. *The Six Nations of New York; Cayugas, Mohawks (Saint Regis), Oneidas, Onondagas, Senecas, Tuscarora.* United States Census Printing Office, Washington, DC, 1892. 89 p. Br970.3 IrD713; Br572C An8141 v.102; Br572C An8141 v.108.

1321. Donath, Julius. *Die Anfänge des menschlichen Geistes.* Verlag von Ferdinand Enke, Stuttgart, 1898. 47 p. Br572C An8141 v.164.

1322. Dondé Ibarra, Joaquin. *Lecciones de botanica, arregladas segun los principios admitidos por Guibourt, Richard, Duchartre, De Candolle y otros.* Imprenta de J. F. Molina, Mérida de Yucatán, 1876. 259 p. Br580 D712.

1323. Dónde Ibarra, Joaquín. Noticias de varias plantas y sus virtudes, 1868. 29 p. Br498.21 MN848. A note on page 2, signed by Karl H. Berendt and dated September, 1868, states that he copied the manuscript from an original ca. 1850 document owned by Pedro de Regil y Paon of Mérida, nephew of Juan Pío Pérez The author describes 140 plants and herbs native to the Yucatán, including a brief mention of their uses as medical remedies. There is also an index listing all the plants mentioned in the notebook.

1324. Dorsey, George A. A bibliography of the anthropology of Peru. *Anthropological Series, Field Columbian Museum* 2(2): 51-206, 1898. Br572C An8141 v.166. In 1894 George Dorsey (1868-1931) received the first doctorate awarded in anthropology in the United States. He was selected to do fieldwork in South America and to make anthropological investigations and collections for the 1893 World's Columbian Exposition. His work took him to Peru, Ecuador, Chile and Bolivia during 1891-1892 and in 1893 was appointed Superintendent of Archaeology at the Exposition's Department of Anthropology. He was Instructor of Anthropology at Harvard during 1895-1896 and in 1896 became Assistant Curator in charge of physical anthropology at the Field Columbian Museum in Chicago. In 1898 he was made Curator, a position he held until 1915. He amassed a large anthropological collection and published widely on the Plains Indians.

1325. Dorsey, George A. A ceremony of the Quichuas of Peru. *Journal of American Folk-Lore* 7:307-309, 1894. Br572C An8141 v.134.

1326. Dorsey, George A. A copper mask from Chimbote, Peru. *American Anthropologist*

10:413-414, 1887. Br572C An8141 v.150.

1327. Dorsey, George A. A cruise among the Haida and Tlingit villages about Dixon's Entrance. *Appleton's Popular Science Monthly*, June, 1898. 15 p. Br572C An8141 v.166.

1328. Dorsey, George A. A Maori skull with double left parietal bone. *Chicago Medical Recorder* 12, 1897. 4 p. Br572C An8141 v.150.

1329. Dorsey, George A. A Peruvian cranium with suppressed upper lateral incisors. *Dental Cosmos*, March, 1897. 3 p. Br572C An8141 v.150.

1330. Dorsey, George A. Crania from the necropolis of Ancon, Peru. *Proceedings of the American Association for the Advancement of Science* 63, 1894. 12 p. Br572C An8141 v.134.

1331. Dorsey, George A. History of the study of anthropology at Harvard University. *Denison Quarterly* 4(2): 77-97, 1896. Br572C An8141 v.150.

1332. Dorsey, George A. Notes on the numerical variations of the teeth in fifteen Peruvian skulls. *Dental Cosmos*, 1897. 3 p. Br572C An8141 v.150.

1333. Dorsey, George A. Numerical variations in the molar teeth of fifteen New Guinea crania. *Dental Review* 11, 1897. 7 p. Br572C An8141 v.150.

1334. Dorsey, George A. Observations on a collection of Papuan crania. *Anthropological Series, Field Columbian Museum* 2(1): 7-39, 1897. Br572C An8141 v.150.

1335. Dorsey, George A. The character and antiquity of Peruvian civilization. *Denison Quarterly* 3(1), 1895. 10 p. Br572C An8141 v.134; Br572C An 8141 v.139.

1336. Dorsey, George A. The geography of the Tsimshian Indians. *American Antiquarian* 19, 1897. 7 p. Br572C An8141 v.150.

1337. Dorsey, George A. The long bones of Kwakiutl and Salish Indians. *American Anthropologist* 10:174-182, 1887. Br572C An8141 v.150.

1338. Dorsey, George A. The lumbar curve in some American races. *Bulletin of the Essex Institute* 27:53-73, 1895. Br572C An8141 v.150.

1339. Dorsey, George A. The photograph and skeleton of a native Australian. *Bulletin of the Essex Institute* 28:57-69, 1896. Br572C An8141 v.166.

1340. Dorsey, George A. Wormian bones in artificially deformed Kwakiutl crania. *American Anthropologist* 10:169-182, 1897. Br572C An8141 v.150.

1341. Dorsey, James O. An account of the war customs of the Osages. *American Naturalist* 18(2): 115-133, 1884. Br572C An8141 v.13; Br572C An8141 v.32.   An Episcopal minister, James Dorsey (1848-1895), was primarily an ethnological and linguistic fieldworker. He began research on the Siouan-speaking tribes of the northern Plains as a missionary to the Ponca (1871-1873). Dorsey later joined John Wesley Powell's Geological and Geographical Survey of the Rocky Mountain Regions as an ethnologist and continued at the Bureau of American Ethnology until his death. Most of his work concentrated on the Omaha, Kansa, Osage, Quapaw, Iowa, Oto, Winnebago, and Dakota, although he also worked on Athabaskan and Caddoan languages.

1342. Dorsey, James O. Books on myths and mythology. *American Anthropologist* 9:40-41, 173-174, 1887. Br572C An8141 v.51.

1343. Dorsey, James O. Dhegiha language and myths. *American Antiquarian* 8:285, 286, 366–368, 1886. Br572C An8141 v.51.

1344. Dorsey, James O. Indians of Siletz Reservation, Oregon. *American Anthropologist* 2(1): 55–62, 1889. Br572C An8141 v.27.

1345. Dorsey, James O. Migrations of Siouan tribes. *American Naturalist* 20:211–222, 1886. Br572C An8141 v.13; Br572C An8141 v.23.

1346. Dorsey, James O. Mourning and war customs of the Kansas. *American Naturalist* 19(7): 670–680, 1885. Br572C An8141 v.13; Br572C An8141 v.23.

1347. Dorsey, James O. *Omaha and Ponka Letters.* Government Printing Office, Washington, DC, 1891. 127 p. Br398.22 OmD737; Br572C An8141 v.48. Omaha, Ponca, and Dhegiha language.

1348. Dorsey, James O. Omaha clothing and personal ornaments. *American Anthropologist* 3(1): 71–77, 1890. Br572C An8141 v.23.

1349. Dorsey, James O. Omaha sociology. *Annual Report of the Bureau of Ethnology, Smithsonian Institution, for 1881-1882*, pp. 205–370, 1885. Br970.3 OmD738.

1350. Dorsey, James O. On the comparative phonology of four Siouan languages. *Annual Report of the United States National Museum, Smithsonian Institution, for 1883*, pp. 919–929, 1885. Br572C An8141 v.51.

1351. Dorsey, James O. Osage traditions. *Annual Report of the Bureau of Ethnology, Smithsonian Institution, for 1884-1885*, pp. 373–397, 1888. Br970.3 OD738.

1352. Dorsey, James O. Siouan onomatopes. *American Anthropologist* 5(1): 1–8, 1892. Br572C An8141 v.84.

1353. Dorsey, James O. Teton folk-lore. *American Anthropologist* 2(2): 144–158, 1889. Br572C An8141 v.51.

1354. Dorsey, James O. The Biloxi Indians of Louisiana. *Proceedings of the American Association for the Advancement of Science* 62:3–23, 1893. Br572C An8141 v.115.

1355. Dorsey, James O. *The Cegiha Language.* Smithsonian Institution, Contributions to American Ethnology, 6. Government Printing Office, Washington, DC, 1890. 794 p. Br557.3 Un319.

1356. Dorsey, James O. The places of gentes in Siouan camping circles. *American Anthropologist* 2(4): 375–379, 1889. Br572C An8141 v.51.

1357. Dorsey, James O. The social organization of the Siouan tribes. *Journal of American Folk-Lore* 4(14): 257–266, 331–342, 1891. Br572C An8141 v.110.

1358. Douay, L. *Études étymologiques sur l'antiquité Américaine.* J. Maisonneuve, Paris, 1891. 158 p. 159 p. Br572C An8141 v.47; Br572C An8141 v.115.

1359. Doughty, F.W. *Evidences of Man in the Drift.* New York, 1892, 18 p. Br572C An8141 v.82; Br572C An8141 v.109.

1360. Douglas, James. The consolidation of the Iroquois Confederacy; or, what happened on the St. Lawrence between the times of Cartier and Champlain. *Bulletin of the American Geographical Society* 29(1): 41–54, 1897. Br572C An8141 v.155.

1361. Douglass, Andrew E. A find of ceremonial weapons in a Florida mound. *Proceedings of the American Association for the Advancement of Science* 31:584–592, 1882. Br572C An8141 v.59.

1362. Douglass, Andrew E. A table of the geographical distribution of American Indian relics in a collection exhibited in the American Museum of Natural History, New York, with explanatory text. *Bulletin of the American Museum of Natural History* 8:199-220, 1896. Br572C An8141 v.150.

1363. Douglass, Andrew E. Some characteristics of the Indian earth and shell mounds of the Atlantic coast of Florida. *American Antiquarian*, pp. 76-82, 141-148, 1885. Br572C An8141 v.39.

1364. Drake, Samuel G. *The Aboriginal Races of North America; Comprising Biographical Sketches of Eminent Individuals, and an Historical Account of the Different Tribes, From the First Discovery of the Continent to the Present Period; With a Dissertation on Their Origin, Antiquities, Manners and Customs, Illustrative Narratives and Anecdotes, and a Copious Analytical Index.* 15th ed. Hurst and Company, New York, 1880. 787 p. Br970.2 D78.2. Drake (1798-1875) briefly served as a school teacher before a career as the proprietor of a rare book shop in Boston. He developed an interest in the American Indians, particularly those in New England, and became one of the foremost Indian historians of his day.

1365. Dubois, Eugène. *Pithecanthropus erectus. Eine menschenaehnliche Übergangsform aus Java.* Landesdruckerei, Batavia, 1894. 39 p. Br573.2 D85. Dubois (1858-1940) earned world-wide fame through his discovery of *Pithecanthropus erectus* (*Homo erectus*). Supported by the Dutch colonial government, Dubois searched for fossil remains between 1888-1895 in Sumatra and Java in the Netherlands East Indies. The famous remains of *Pithecantropus* and other vertebrate fossils were discovered near the village of Trinil, Java, during 1891-1893. Dubois' pioneering efforts influenced the rising science of paleoanthropology.

1366. Dubois, Eugène. Über die Abhängigkeit des Hirngewichtes von der Körpergrösse bei den Säugethieren. *Archiv für Anthropologie* 25(1-2), 1897. 28 p. Br572C An8141 v.150.

1367. Duckworth, Wynfrid L. H. An account of skulls from Madagascar in the Anatomical Museum of Cambridge University. *Journal of the Anthropological Institute of Great Britain and Ireland* 2(3): 285-293, 1897. Br572C An8141 v.150.

1368. Duckworth, Wynfrid L. H. Foetus of *Gorilla savagei. Journal of Anatomy and Physiology* 33:82-90, 1892. Br599.8 D85.

1369. Duckworth, Wynfrid L. H. Note on an anthropoid ape. *Proceedings of the Zoological Society of London*, pp. 989-994, 1898. Br599.8 D851.

1370. Duckworth, Wynfrid L. H. Notes on the anthropological collection in the Museum of Human Anatomy, Cambridge University, 1899. n.p. Br572 C14.

1371. Duges, Alfred, and José Ramirez. *Informé que rinde á la Secretaria de Fomento...sobre algunas excursiones á las montañas de Ajusco y serranía de la Cruces.* Secretaria de Fomento, México, 1895. 64 p. Br508.72 D873.

1372. Dumble, W. J. Notes on the geology of the valley of the middle Rio Grande. *Bulletin of the Geological Society of America* 3, 1891. 1 p. Br572C An8141 v.125.

1373. Dumont, Arsene. Essai sur la natalité au Massachusetts. *Journal de la Société de Statistique de Paris*, 1898. 40 p. Br572C An8141 v.150.

1374. Dumoutier, Gustave. *Les stations de l'homme préhistorique sur les plateaux du Grand-Morin*. Paris, 1882. 98 p. Br572C An8141 v.24.

1375. Dunbar, John B. *The Pawnee Indians; A Sketch*. New York, 1883? 90 p. Br970.3 PD914. Sketches reprinted from the *Magazine of American History*, April, November, 1880; November, 1882.

1376. Dunn, Henry. *Guatemala, or, the United Provinces of Central America, in 1827-8, Being Sketches and Memorandums Made During a Twelve Months' Residence in that Republic*. G. and C. Carvill, New York, 1828. 318 p. Br917.28 D923.

1377. Dunning, E. O. Account of antiquities in Tennessee. *Annual Report of the United States National Museum, Smithsonian Institution, for 1870*, pp. 376-380, 1872. Br572C An8141 v.19.

1378. Düntzer, H. Die Ara Ubiorum und das Legionslager beim Oppidum Ubiorum. In *Festschrift zum Fünfzigjährigen Jubiläum des Vereins von Alterthumsfreunden im Rheinlande*, pp. 35-61. Gedruckt auf Kosten des Vereins, Bonn, 1891. Br572C An8141 v.98.

1379. Duponceau, Peter S. *Mémoire sur la systeme grammatical des langues de quelques nations indiennes de l'Amerique du Nord; ouvrage qui, à la séance publique annuelle de l'Institut Royal de France le 2 mai 1835, a remporté le prix fondé par M. le comte de Volney*. À la Librairie de A. Pihan de la Forest, Paris, 1838. 464 p. Br497 D926. "One of the first attempts subsequent to that of Mr. Gallatin to systematize the aboriginal languages, and determine the laws of their construction" (Field 1873:111). Duponceau (1760-1844) emigrated to America from France in 1777 and soon developed an interest in American Indian languages. He was honored for this essay on the grammatical typology of American Indian languages, based on Algonquian.

1380. Dupont, E. *D'Omalius d'Halloy, 1783-1875*. Polleunis et Ceuterick, Bruxelles, 1897. 95 p. Br572C An8141 v.150; Br925.7 H155D.

1381. Dupont, P. *Notes et observations sur la côte orientale d'Amérique*. Boehm et Files, Imprimeurs de l'Académie, Montpellier, 1868. 84 p. Br572C An8141 v.98.

1382. Durán, Diego. *Historia de las Indias de Nueva-España y islas de Tierra Firme, por el padre Fray Diego Durán*. Imprenta de J. M. Andrade y F. Escalante, México, 1867-1880. 2 v. and 1 atlas of facsims. Br972 D93. "Apéndice. Explicación del códice geroglífico de M. Aubin, por Alfredo Chavero" (172 p. at end of v. II). The Atlas contains the reproductions of the colored designs in the 3 parts of the manuscript, and facsimile of the "Códice geroglifico de M. Aubin" (known as the "Codex Ixtlilxochitl," now in the Bibliothèque Nationale in Paris, Mss. Mex. 65-71).

1383. Durocher, Flavien. *Aiamie kushkushkutu mishinaigan*. Nte etat W. Neilson, Ka iakonigants, nte opishtikoiats [Quebec], 1847. 67 p. Br497.11 MnD 93.2.

1384. Durocher, Flavien. *Aiamieu kushkushkutu mishinaigan*. Nte etat A. Cote, Ka iakonigants nte opistikoiats [Québec], 1856. 104 p. Br497.11 MnD 93.2a. Translated into the Montagnais language by Flavien Durocher, with sub-titles in Latin.

1385. Dwight, T. Methods of estimating the height from parts of the skeleton. *Medical Record*, 1894. 16 p. Br572C An8141 v.135.

1386. Dwight, T. *The Shattuck Lecture: The Range and Significance of Variation in the Human Skeleton.* David Clapp and Son, Boston, 1894. 29 p. Br572C An8141 v.135.

1387. Dyneley, John. Notes on the language of the eastern Algonkin tribes. *American Journal of Philology* 9(3), 1888. 7 p. Br572C An8141 v.157.

1388. Eakins, T. The differential action of certain muscles passing more than one joint. *Proceedings of the Academy of Natural Sciences of Philadelphia*, 1894. 9 p. Br572C An8141 v.131.

1389. Eames, Wilberforce. *Bibliographic Notes on Eliot's Indian Bible, And On His Other Translations and Works in the Indian Language of Massachusetts; Extract From A Bibliography of the Algonquian Languages, by J. C. Pilling.* United States Government Printing Office, Washington, DC, 1890. 58 p. Br497.11 MaEl 4VP.

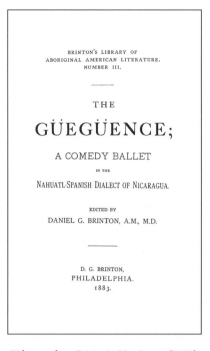

Title page from Brinton's Güegüence (1883).

1390. Eastman, Mary H. *Dahcotah; Or, Life and Legends of the Sioux Around Fort Snelling.* J. Wiley, New York, 1849. 268 p. Br970.3 DEa7. "Mrs. Eastman's…narratives of Indian life and legend were largely based on her first-hand contact with the Mdwekanton people of the Dakotas during the period that her husband was the commander of Fort Snelling, between the Minnesota and Mississippi Territory" (*Siebert Library* 1999:2:232).

1391. Echeverria y Reyes, Aníbal. *La lengua araucana; notas bibliográficas.* Imprenta Cervantes, Santiago de Chile, 1889. 32 p. Br498.977 AEc 43. Mapuche language.

1392. Eckarti, Anselmi. *Specimen linguae brasilicae vulgaris; editionem separatam alias immutatam, curavit Julius Platzmann.* In Aedibus B. G. Teubneri, Lipsiae, 1890. 19 p. Br572C An8141 v.84.

1393. Ecker, Alexander. Zur Kenntniss des Körperbaues früherer Einwohner der Halbinsel Florida. *Archiv für Anthropologie* 10:101–114, 1878. Braunschweig. Br572C An8141 v.96.

1394. Eder, Francisco Javier. *Descripción de la provincia de los mojos en el reino del Perú; sacada de los escritos póstumos del P. Francisco Javier Eder; arreglada e ilustrada con notas por el abate y consejero real, Mako; traducida del latin por Fray Nicolás Armentia.* Imprenta de El Siglo Industrial, La

Paz, 1888. 178 p. Br918.5 Ed2. Translation of Descriptio provinciae Moxitarum in regno peruano.

1395. *Edición bi-lingual guaraní y español; el sermón de Jesu-Cristo en la montaña; ó sean los capitulos v, vi, vii del santo evangelio...según San mateo, el texto español...revisada, traducido a la lengua guaraní por un paraguayo.* Sociedad Biblica é Estrangera, London, n.d. 31 p. Br498.75 GB 47. New Testament Gospel of St. Matthew translated into Guaraní.

1396. Edwards, Jonathan. *Memoir of J. Brainerd, Missionary to the Indians.* Baynes, Edinburgh, 1826. 426 p. Br922 B73.

1397. Eells, Myron. The Twana Indians of the Skokomish Reservation in Washington Territory, by Rev. M. Eells, missionary among these Indians. *Bulletin of the United States Geological and Geographical Survey of the Department of the Interior* 3(1): 57-114, 1877. Br572C An8141 v.32. Eells (1843-1907) was a Congregational missionary on the Skokomish Reservation in western Washington. He was a prolific writer on the ethnology and history of the Pacific Northwest Indian missions.

1398. Egede, Hans P. *Pok, kalelek avalangnek, nunalikame nunakatiminut okalugtuartok.* Bertelson, n.p., 1857, 18 p. Br497.25 GEg22. Hans Egede (1686-1758) initiated the Danish-Norwegian colonization of Greenland. As a Lutheran minister in northern Norway he became interested in the fate of the Christian Norse population in Greenland. He settled in West Greenland with his family in 1721, and conducted missionary work there until 1736.

1399. Ehrenreich, Paul M. A. *Anthropologische Studien über die Urbewohner Brasiliens vornehmlich der Staaten Matto Grosso, Goyaz und Amazonas (Purus-gebeit); nach eigenen Aufnahmen und Beobachtungen in den Jahren 1887 bis 1889.* F. Vieweg und Sohn, Braunschweig, 1897. 165 p. Br572.981 Eh83.

1400. Ehrenreich, Paul M.A. Beiträge zur Völkerkunde Brasiliens. *Veröffentlichungen aus dem Königlichen Museum für Völkerkunde* 2(1-2): 4-80, 1891. Br572C An8141 v.91; Br572C An8141 v.105.

1401. Ehrenreich, Paul M.A. Die Einteilung und Verbreitung der Völkerstämme Brasiliens nach dem gegenwärtigeen Stande unser Kenntnisse. *Petermanns Mitteilungen* 4(5): 1-19, 1891. Br572C An8141 v.91.

1402. Ehrenreich, Paul M.A. *Die Sprache der Akuä. Zeitschrift für Ethnologie,* 1895. 88 p. Br572C An 8141 v.139.

1403. Ehrenreich, Paul M.A. Die Sprache der Caraya (Goyaz). *Zeitschrift für Ethnologie,* pp. 33-57, 1894. Br572C An 8141 v.137.

1404. Ehrenreich, Paul M.A. Ein Beitrag zur Characteristik der botokudischen Sprache. *Bastian-Festschrift,* pp. 605-630. Verlag von Dietrich Reimer (Ernst Vohsen), Berlin, 1896. Br572C An8141 v.150.

1405. Ehrenreich, Paul M.A. Geographie Central-Brasiliens. *Zeitschrift der Gesellschaften für Erdkunde zu Berlin,* pp. 167-191, n.d. Br572C An8141 v.7.

1406. Ehrenreich, Paul M.A. Materialen zur Sprachenkunde Brasiliens: 6. Vokabulare von Purus-Stämmen. *Zeitschrift für Ethnologie* 26:89-101, 1894. Br572C An8141 v.137; Br572C An8141 v.150.

1407. Eichhorn, A. *Naual; oder die Hohe Wissenschaft (scientia mirabilis) der architectonischen und künstlerischen Composition bei den Maya-Völkern deren Descendenten und Schülern.* Buchhandlung für Architectur und Kunstgewerbe, Berlin, 1896. 128 p. Br572C An8141 v.161.

1408. Eisen, Gustavus A. On some ancient sculptures from the Pacific slope of Guatemala. *Memoirs of the California Academy of Sciences* 2(2): 9–20, 1888. Br572C An8141 v.90.

1409. Eliot, John. *The Indian Primer, or, the Way of Training Up of Our Indian Youth in the Good Knowledge of God, by John Eliot, To Which is Prefixed the Indian Covenenting Confession, Reprinted From the Originals in the Library of the University of Edinburgh.* Andrew Elliot, Edinburgh, 1880. 124 p. Br497.11 MaEl4. John Eliot (1604–1690), commonly referred to as the Apostle to the Indians, maintained a career as missionary to the Indians of Massachusetts. He translated the Old and New Testaments into Massachusett and had them published in one volume in 1663, the first complete Bible printed anywhere in the New World. He also translated a primer, a grammar, a logic manual, and some sermons as further aids in converting the Indians.

1410. Eliot, John. *The Logick Primer; Some Logical Notions to Initiate the Indians in the Knowledge of the Rule of Reason and to Know How to Make Use Thereof; Especially for the Instruction of Such As Are Teachers Among Them.* Printed by M. J., Cambridge, MA, 1672. 75 p. Br497.11 MaEl 4.2. Text in the Massachusett language with interlinear English translation. "The use of this iron key is to open the rich treasury of the Holy Scripture."

1411. *Eliza Marpicokawin, raratonwan oyate en wapiye sa; qa Sara Warpanica qon, he nakun ikcewicaxta oyate wan etanhan.* Published for the American Tract Society by Crocker and Brewster, Boston, 1842. 12 p. Br497.5 DSQ14. Tract in Santee.

1412. Elliott, Aaron M. Contributions to a history of the French language of Canada, 1800. 16 p. Br572C An8141 v.55.

1413. Elliott, Aaron M. The Nahuatl-Spanish dialect of Nicaragua. *American Journal of Philology* 5(1), n.d. 15 p. Br572C An8141 v.52.

1414. Elliott, Aaron M. University work in the Romance languages; an address delivered on the 15th anniversary of the Johns Hopkins University, February 22, 1891. Baltimore, 1891. 16 p. Br572C An8141 v.46.

1415. Ellis, A. C., and G. S. Hall. A study of dolls. *Pedagogical Seminary* 4(2): 129–175, 1896. Br572C An8141 v.150.

1416. Ellis, Alexander J. On the conditions of a universal language. *Transactions of the Philological Society,* pp. 59–98, 1888. Br572C An8141 v.21.

1417. Ellis, Havelock. *Man and Woman; A Study of Human Secondary Sexual Characters.* 4th ed. Scott, London, 1904. 488 p. Br173 El54a.

1418. Ellis. Nez Perce laws, n.d. 8 p. Br497.48 CEl57.

1419. Ely, William D. *A Keyhole for Roger Williams Key, Or, A Study of Suggested Misprints, in its Sixteenth Chapter, "Of the Earth and the Fruits Thereof, etc."* Rhode Island Historical Society, Providence, 1892. 41 p. Br572C An8141 v.123.

1420. Emerson, E. R. The Book of the Dead and rain ceremonials. *American Anthropologist* 7:233-259, 1894. Br572C An8141 v.136.

1421. Emory, William H. *Notes of a Military Reconnaissance From Fort Leavenworth, in Missouri, to San Diego, in California, Including Parts of the Arkansas, Del Norte, and Gila Rivers.* Wendell and Van Benthuysem, Washington, DC, 1848. 614 p. Br917.8 Em61; Br917.8 Em61a. Includes Report of Lt. J. W. Abert of his examination of New Mexico in the years 1846-1847 (pp. 417-548); Report of Lt. Col. P. St. George Cooke of his march from Santa Fe, New Mexico, to San Diego, Upper California (pp. 549-562); Journal of Capt. A. R. Johnston (pp. 565-614).

1422. Emory, William H. *Report on the United States and Mexican Boundary Survey, Made Under the Direction of the Secretary of the Interior, by William H. Emory, Major First Cavalry, and United States Commissioner.* A. O. P. Nicholson, Washington, DC, 1857-1859. 2 v. Br917.8 Em61.2a.

1423. Enault, Louis. *L'Amérique Centrale et Méridionale.* Dessins de MM. Jules Noel, Lebreton et Gustave Janet. F. de P. Mellado et Cie., Paris, 1867. 444 p. Br918 En16.

1424. Endlich, Frederic M. Barbados. *American Naturalist* 16:210-222, 1882. Br572C An8141 v.13.

1425. Endlich, Frederic M. Demerara. *American Naturalist* 15(12): 937-946, 1881. Br572C An8141 v.13.

1426. *Ensaios de sciencia por diversos amadores.* Rio de Janiero. v. 1 (1876)-v. 3 (1880). Br913.8 En76.

1427. Erdmann, Freidrich. *Eskimoisches Wörterbuch; gesammelt von den Missionaren in Labrador; revidirt und herausgegeben von Friedrich Erdmann.* E. M. Monse, Budissin, Germany, 1864. 360 p. Br497.25 LEr 24. Text in Inuit and German in double columns.

1428. Erlingsson, Thorstein, and Ernest D. Grand. *Ruins of the Saga Time; Being an Account of Travels and Explorations in Iceland in the Summer of 1895.* D. Nutt, London, 1899. 112 p. Br913.491 Er5.

1429. Erman, Georg A. Über Beschaffenheit und Alter einiger asiatischen Industrien. *Verhandlungen der Berliner Gesellschaft für Anthropologie, Ethnologie und Urgeschichte*, pp. 3-6, 1872. Br572C An8141 v.162.

1430. Ernst, Adolf. Bilder und Schalensteine von Venezuela. *Verhandlungen der Berliner Gesellschaft für Anthropologie, Ethnologie und Urgeschichte,* pp. 371-373, 1886. Br572C An8141 v.4.

1431. Ernst, Adolf. Drei Nephrit-Beile aus Venezuela. *Verhandlungen der Berliner Gesellschaft für Anthropologie, Ethnologie und Urgeschichte*, pp. 36-38, 1895. Br572C An 8141 v.139.

1432. Ernst, Adolf. Etymologisches von Venezuela's Nord-Küste. *Verhandlungen der Berliner Gesellschaft für Anthropologie, Ethnologie und Urgeschichte*, pp. 32-26, 1895. Br572C An 8141 v.139.

1433. Ernst, Adolf. Motilonen-Schädel aus Venezuelas. *Verhandlungen der Berliner Anthropologischen Gesellschaft für Anthropologie, Ethnologie und Urgeschichte*, pp. 296-301, 1887. Br572C An8141 v.110.

1434. Ernst, Adolf. Notes on some stone-yokes from Mexico. *Internationales Archiv für Ethnographie* 5:71-76, 1892. Br572C An8141 v.105.

1435. Ernst, Adolf. On the etymology of the word tobacco. *American Anthropologist* 2(2): 133-141, 1889. Br572C An8141 v.51.

1436. Ernst, Adolf. Petroglyphen aus Venezuela. *Verhandlungen der Berliner Gesellschaft für Anthropologie, Ethnologie und Urgeschichte*, pp. 651-655, 1889. Br572C An8141 v.4.

1437. Ernst, Adolf. Proben venezuelanischer Volksdichtung. *Verhandlungen der Berliner Gesellschaft für Anthropologie, Ethnologie und Urgeschichte*, pp. 525-534, 1889. Br572C An8141 v.4.

1438. Ernst, Adolf. Tio Tigre und Tio Canejo. *Verhandlungen der Berliner Anthropologischen Gesellschaft für Anthropologie, Ethnologie und Urgeschichte* 30:274-278, 1888. Br572C An8141 v.83.

1439. Ernst, Adolf. Über die Reste der Ureinwohner in den Gebirgen von Mérida. *Zeitschrift für Ethnologie* 17:190-197, 1885. Br572C An8141 v.4.

1440. Ernst, Adolf. Über einige weniger bekannte Sprachen aus der Gegend des Meta und oberen Orinoco. *Zeitschrift für Ethnologie* 23:1-13, 1891. 13 p. Br572C An 8141 v.47.

1441. Ernst, Adolf. Upper Orinoco vocabularies. *American Anthropologist* 3(4): 393-401, 1895. Br572C An 8141 v.139.

1442. *Erstes Lesebuch in der Mosquito Sprache*. Monse, Budissin, 1899. 16 p. Br498.44 Er 8.

1443. Escard, F. *Prince Roland Bonaparte en Laponie*. Imprimé pour l'Autor, Paris, 1886. 60 p. Br572C An8141 v.3.

1444. Esperanto. *Langue internationale*. Varsovie, 1887. 48 p. Br572C An8141 v.21.

1445. Espinosa, José D. *Apuntaciones para la estadistica de la provincia de Yucatán*. Espinosa e Hijos, Mérida, 1871. 55 p. Br572C An8141 v.18.

1446. Ethnographic Survey of Great Britain, Report 27, n.d, 18 p. Br572C An8141 v.150.

1447. *Ethnographische Sammlung. Berlin-Königliche Museen-Museums für Völkerkunde-Ethnologische Abtheilung*, 1872. Br572C An8141 v.17.

1448. *Ethnologisches Notizblatt, Königlichen Museums für Völkerkunde in Berlin*. Heft 1. Druck und Verlag von A. Haack, Berlin, 1894. 68 p. Br572C An8141 v.133.

1449. *Ethnologisches Notizblatt, Königlichen Museums für Völkerkunde in Berlin*. Heft 2. Druck und Verlag von A. Haack, Berlin, 1895. 159 p. Br572C An8141 v.150.

1450. *Ethnologisches Notizblatt, Königlichen Museums für Völkerkunde in Berlin*. Heft 3. Druck und Verlag von A. Haack, Berlin, 1896. 135 p. Br572C An8141 v.150.

1451. Ettrenreich, P. Beiträge zur Völkerkunde Brasiliens. *Veröffentlichungen aus dem Königlichen Museum für Völkerkunde* 2(1-2): 3-80, 1891. Br572C An8141 v.105.

1452. Ettwein, John. Ein delawarisches Wörterbuch, n.d. 84 leaves. Br497.11 Det78. Manuscript, copied from an original manuscript in the archives of the Moravian Church, Bethlehem, PA.

1453. Étude sur les Kalmoucks. *Revue d'Anthropologie*, pp. 505-510, n.d. Br572C An8141 v.40.

1454. Evans, John. *The Ancient Bronze Implements, Weapons, and Ornaments of Great Britain and Ireland.* D. Appleton, New York, 1881. 509 p. Br571.3 Ev14a.

1455. Evers, Edward. The ancient pottery of southeastern Missouri. In *Contributions to the Archaeology of Missouri, by the Archaeological Section of the St. Louis Academy of Science*, pp. 21-30. George A. Bates, Naturalist's Bureau, Salem, 1880. Br572C An8141 v.90.

1456. Exposición Centro-Americana de Guatemala, 1897. *Sección de Costa Rica. Documentos relativos a la participación de Costa Rica en dicho certasmen.* Tipografía Nacional, San José de Costa Rica, 1896. n.p. Br606 G93.

1457. *Exposición del Gobierno del Estado de Chiapas contra la desmembración de una oarte considerable de su territorio interntada por el Exmo. Sr. Gobernador de Tabasco.* Imprenta del Gobierno de Chiapas, dirigida por Manuel Maria Trujillo, 1856. 17 p. Br572C An8141 v.69.

1458. Exposición Histórico-Americana (1892 Madrid). Sección de México. *Catálogo de la sección de México.* Est. Tipografica "Sucesores de Rivadeneyra", Madrid, 1892. 432 p. Br606 M892m.

1459. Extracts from various works on the Indians. n.d. 12 leaves. Br970.1 Ex88. Manuscript.

1460. Fabié, Antonio M. *Estudio filológico.* Madrid, 1885. 143 p. Br572C An8141 v.55.

1461. Fabricus, Otho. *Testamentitokamit mosesism aglegej siurdleet; kaladlin okauzeennut nuktersimarsut narkiutingoaenniglo sukkuiarsimarsut pellesiunermit ottomit Fabriusimit, attuaegek saukudlugit innungnut koisimarsunnut.* Illiarsuin igloaenne nakkittarsimarsut, Kiöbenhavnime, 1822. 202 p. Br497.25 GB46.1. Book of Genesis translated into Greenland Eskimo by a Danish missionary.

1462. Fages, Eduardo. *Noticias estadisticas sobre el Departamento de Tuspan*, 1856. 126 p. Br572C An8141 v.18.

1463. Faidherbe, Louis L. C. *Instructions sur l'anthropologie de l'Algérie: considérations générales.* A. Hennuyer, Paris, 1874. 60 p. Br572C An8141 v.9.

1464. Faidherbe, Louis L. C. Sur l'ethnographie du Nord de l'Afrique et sur les tombeaux megalithiques de cette contrée. *Bulletin de la Société Algerienne de Climatologique* 1:4-18, 1869. Br572C An8141 v.58.

1465. Famous Toltec smiling heads in the Petich's Old Mexican Collection. Commercial prospectus, 1898. 4 p. Br572C An8141 v.99.

1466. Fancourt, Charles Saint John. *The History of Yucatán; From its Discovery to the Close of the Seventeenth Century; By Charles St. John Fancourt, Recently H.M. Superintendent of the British Settlements in the Bay of Honduras.* J. Murray, London, 1854. 340 p., 32 p. Br972.6 F212. "This volume is devoted almost entirely to the aboriginal history of the peninsula of Yucatan, the wars, treaties, and association of the Spaniards, and the missions established by them. The author's long residence in the country should, however, have afforded him more material for a general view of the peculiarities, language, and condition of its aboriginal inhabitants" (Field 1873:126).

1467. Faraud, Henri. *Dix-huit ans chez les sauvages; voyages et missions de Mgr. Hen-*

ry Faraud, *évêque d'Anemour, vicaire apostolique de Mackensie, dans l'extrême nord de l'Amerique Britannique; d'après les documents de Mgr. L'évêque d'Anemour par Fernand-Michel.* R. Ruffet et Cie., Paris, 1866. 465 p. Br970.1 F222. "Faraud was at the Red River Settlement in 1844, located at the junction of the Red and Assiniboine Rivers in Manitoba. He was one of three bishops to administer to the territories that stretched from Hudson's Bay to the Rocky Mountains. His account details his travels among the Indians at Ile-à-la Crosse, Lake Athabaska, Fort Resolution, Great Slave Lake, the Peace River country. It documents a peace conference with the Sioux, Faraud's frustrations in converting the 'Sauteaux' (a branch of Ojibwa), and contains a brief analysis of the Cree and Montagais languages" (Siebert Library *1999:1:*39).

1468. Farmacopea mexicana: tabla alfabética de los medicamentos simples mas usuales, 1846. 60 p. Br572C An8141 v.128.

1469. Fay, E. W. Agglutination and adaptation. *American Journal of Philology* 15(60): 409–442; 16(61): 1–27, 1895. Br572C An 8141 v.139.

1470. Feaux, Maurice. *La vallée de l'Isle dans les environs de Périgueux aux temps préhistoriques.* Perigueux, 1880. 10 p. Br572C An8141 v.24.

1471. Febrés, Andrés. *Arte de la lengua general del reyno de Chile, con un dialogo chileno-hispano muy curioso; a que se añade la Doctrina christiana, esto es, rezo, catecismo, coplas, confesionario, y plàticas; lo mas en lengua chilena y castellana; por fin un Vocabulario hispano-chileno, y un Calepino chileño-hispano mas copioso.* En la calle de la Encarnaçion, Lima, 1765. 682 p. Br498.977 AF 31. Contents include: 1. "Arte de la lengua general de Chile. Dialogo entre dos caciques. Exemplo de un Coyaghtun. Breve diccionario de algunas palabras mas usuales"; 2. "Doctrina christiana en Chilli Dugu"; 3. "Vocabulario hispano-chileno"; 4. "Calepino chileno-hispano."

1472. Febrés, Andrés. *Diccionario araucano-español; ó sea, Calepino chileno-hispano.* Impreso por J.A. Alsina, Buenos Aires, 1882. 282, 104 p. Br498.977 AF31.2. Reprint of the fourth part (p. 415–682) of the author's *Arte de la lengua general del reyno de Chile* (Lima, 1765). "Apéndice sobre las lenguas quichua, aimará y pampa y fragmento de un Vocabulario de los idiomas alikhulip y tekinica, y algunas palabras pertenecientes á los Patagones Tehueiches y á los Chonos."

1473. Feer, L. *Le Tibet; le pays, le peuple, la religion.* Bibliothèque Ethnographique, 7. Maisonneuve et Ch. Leclerc, Paris, 1886. 107 p. Br572C R737.

1474. Fellechner, A., Dr. Müller, and C. L. C. Hesse. *Bericht über die im böchsten Auftrage Seiner Königlichen Hoheit des Prinzen Carl von Preufsen und Sr. Durchlaucht des Herrn Fürsten v. Schoenburg-Waldenburg bewirkte Untersuchung einiger Theile des Mosquitolandes, erstattet von der dazu ernannten Commission.* Verlag von Alexander Duncker, Berlin, 1845. 274 p. Br572C An8141 v.25.

1475. Fenollosa, Ernest F. *Review of the Chapter on Painting in Gonsel's L'Art Japonais.* James R. Osgood and Company, Boston, 1885. 54 p. Br572C An8141 v.151.

1476. Feria, Pedro de. Doctrina xpiana en lengua çapoteca, compuesta por el muy R.P. Fray Pedro d'Feria, 1567. 24 p. Br498.34 ZF384. Manuscript; transcript by Karl H.

Berendt of *Doctrina christiana en lengua castellana y çapoteca; compuesta por el Rev. Padre Fray Pedro de Feria, provincial de la Orden de Sancto Domingo, en la provincia de Sanctiago de la Nueva Hispana* (En Casa de Pedro Ocharte, México, 1567. 116 p.) in the John Carter Brown Library.

1477. Fernández de Oviedo y Valdés, Gonzalo. *Historia general y natural de las Indias, islas y tierre-firme del mar océano, por el capitan Gonzalo Fernández de Oviedo y Valdés...publicala la Real Academia de la Historia, cotejada con el códice original, enriquecida con las enmiendas y adiciones del autor, é ilustrada con la vida y el juicio de las obras del mismo por d. José Amador de los Ríos...primera [-tercera] parte.* Imprenta de la Real Academia de la Historia, Madrid, 1851-1855. 4 v. Br972.9 Ov42. The first complete publication of this famous 16th century chronicle. It is an important source for the history of early exploration and conquest of the Spaniards in the period to ca. 1530. Oviedo's account of events differs considerably from that of Las Casas; the two found themselves on opposite sides in many matters, including the debate concerning the nature and rights of the Indians.

1478. Fernández Ferraz, Juan. *Informe eleva á la Secretaria de Instrucción Pública [del Congreso pedagógico hispano portugués americano, 1893].* Tipografia Nacional, San José de Costa Rica, 1893. 122 p. Br370.6 C76.

1479. Fernández Ferraz, Juan. *Nahuatlismos de Costa Rica; ensayo lexicográfico acerca de las voces mejicanas que se hallan en el habla corriente de los Costarricenses.* Tipografía Nacional, San José de Costa Rica, 1892. 148 p. Br498.22 F41.

1480. Fernández Nodal, José. *Elementos de gramática quichua; o, idioma de los Yncas, por José Fernaández Nodal.* Fernández Nodal, Cuzco, 1872. 441 p. Br498.7 IN 672.

1481. Fernández y González, Francisco. *Los lenguas hablados por los indígenas del norte y centro de América.* Establecimiento Tipográfico Sucesores de Rivadeneyra, Madrid, 1893. 120 p. Br572C An8141 v.113.

1482. Fernández, Juan P. *Relazione istorica della nuova christianità degl'Indiani detti Cichiti; scritta in spagnuolo dal P. Gio. Patrizio Fernández, e tradotta in Italiano da Gio. Battista Memmi.* Per Antonio de'Rossi, Roma, 1729. 233 p. Br980.3 GF392.

1483. Fernández, Leon. *Colección de documentos para la historia de Costa Rica.* Imprenta Nacional, San José de Costa Rica, 1881-1883. 3 v. Br972.86 F39.2.

1484. Fernández, León. *Lenguas indigenas de Centro America en el siglo XVIII. según copia del Archivo de Indias.* Tipografía Nacional, San José de Costa Rica, 1892. 110 p. Br498 F395. List of 440 Spanish words provided with their equivalents in 21 dialects of Central America in compliance with a request of Catherine II of Russia.

1485. Ferraz de Macedo, Francisco. *Ethnogenie bresilienne; essay critique sur les ages prehistoriques du Bresil et l'autochthonie polygeniste.* Imprimerie Nationale, Lisbonne, 1887. 130 p. Br572C An8141 v.1.

1486. Ferraz, Juan F. *Informe relativo al año de 1897 á 1898 presentado al señor Secretario de Fomento.* Tipografia Nacional, San José, 1898. 16 p. Br572C An8141 v.166.

1487. Ferree, Barr. Comparative architecture. *Journal of the American Institute of Architects*, 1892. 15 p. Br572C An8141 v.116.

1488. Ferree, Barr. Institute organization: the plan and scope of the Brooklyn Institute and its application to other cities. New York, 1898. 20 p. Br572C An8141 v.151.

1489. Ferree, Barr. Primitive architecture: 1. Sociological influences. *American Naturalist* 23:25-32, 1889. Br572C An8141 v.28.

1490. Ferree, Barr. Primitive architecture: 2. Climatic influences. *American Naturalist* 24:147-158, 1890. Br572C An8141 v.28.

1491. Ferree, Barr. The element of terror in primitive art. *American Antiquarian* 11(6): 331-346, 1889. Br572C An8141 v.28.

1492. Feuling, J. B. On the place of the Indian languages on the study of ethnology. *Wisconsin Academy of Sciences, Arts, and Letters* 1:178-181, 1872. Br572C An8141 v.84.

1493. Fewkes, Jesse W. A Central American ceremony which suggests the Snake Dance of the Tusayan villagers. *American Anthropologist* 6(3): 285-306, 1893. Br572C An8141 v.124; Br572C An8141 v.125. Jesse Walter Fewkes (1850-1930), a marine biologist and anthropologist, was appointed ethnologist with the Smithsonian Institution Bureau of American Ethnology in 1895. In search of the origin of the Hopi clans, he excavated near Awatobi and Sikyatki, and later extended his research into southwestern Colorado. Following the establishment of American influence in the Caribbean after the Spanish-American War, Fewkes conducted archaeological investigations in Puerto Rico, Cuba, the Isle of Pines, the Cayman Islands, the west coast of Florida, and the Gulf Coast of Mexico. Fewkes served as president of the American Anthropological Association in 1911-1912, and in 1911 and 1915 he was vice president for the anthropology section of the American Association for the Advancement of Science. In 1914 he became a member of the National Academy of Science. Fewkes was one of the chief 19th-century students of Hopi culture who furthered the protection of antiquities and successfully argued that stabilization should follow the disturbance of archaeological sites.

1494. Fewkes, Jesse W. A Comparison of Sia and Tusayan snake ceremonials. *American Anthropologist* 8:118-141, 1895. Br572C An 8141 v.139.

1495. Fewkes, Jesse W. A contribution to ethnobotany. *American Anthropologist* 9(1): 14-21, 1896. Br572C An 8141 v.139.

1496. Fewkes, Jesse W. A few Tusayan pictographs. *American Anthropologist* 5(1): 9-26, 1892. Br572C An8141 v.12.

1497. Fewkes, Jesse W. *A Journal of American Ethnology and Archæology.* Houghton, Mifflin and Company, Boston, New York, 1891-1908. 3 v. Br572.97 F43. Contents include: 1. Jesse W. Fewkes, "A few summer ceremonials at Zuñi pueblo"; B. I. Gilman, "Zuñi melodies"; Jesse W. Fewkes, "Reconnaissance of ruins in or near the Zuni reservation"; 2. Jesse W. Fewkes, "A few summer ceremonials at the Tusayan pueblos"; J. G. Owens, "Natal ceremonies of the Hopi Indians"; Jesse W. Fewkes, "A report on the present condition of a ruin in Arizona called Casa Grande"; 3. Adolf

F. Bandelier, "An outline of the documentary history of the Zuñi tribe"; H. F. C. ten Kate, "Somatological observations on Indians of the Southwest."

1498. Fewkes, Jesse W. A study of certain figures in a Maya codex. *American Anthropologist* 7(3): 260–274, 1894. Br572C An8141 v.134.

1499. Fewkes, Jesse W. A study of summer ceremonials at Zuni and Moqui Pueblos; Hemenway Southwestern Archaeological Expedition. *Bulletin of the Essex Institute* 22(7–9): 89–113. Br572C An8141 v.11.

1500. Fewkes, Jesse W. A-wá-to-bi: an archaeological verification of a Tusayan legend. *American Anthropologist* 6:363–375, 1893. Br572C An8141 v.114; Br572C An8141 v.125.

1501. Fewkes, Jesse W. Contribution to Passamaquoddy folk-lore. *Journal of American Folk-Lore*. October-December, 1890. 24 p. Br572C An8141 v.48.

1502. Fewkes, Jesse W. Dolls of the Tusayan Indians. *Internationales Archiv für Ethnographie* 7:45–74, 1894. Leiden. Br970.3 TF436.

1503. Fewkes, Jesse W. Morphology of Tusayan altars. *American Anthropologist* 10:129–145, 1897. Br572C An8141 v.151; Br970.3 TF436.2.

1504. Fewkes, Jesse W. On certain personages who appear in a Tusayan ceremony. *American Anthropologist* 2(1): 32–52, 1894. Br572C An8141 v.125.

1505. Fewkes, Jesse W. On zemes from Santo Domingo. *American Anthropologist* 4(2): 167–175, 1891. Br572C An8141 v.11.

1506. Fewkes, Jesse W. Pacific Coast shells from prehistoric Tusayan pueblos. *American Anthropologist* 9:359–367, 1896. Br572C An8141 v.151.

1507. Fewkes, Jesse W. Prehistoric culture of Tusayan. *American Anthropologist* 9:151–173, 1896. Br917.2 F43.6.

1508. Fewkes, Jesse W. Preliminary account of an expedition to the cliff villages of the Red Rock Country, and the Tusayan ruins of Sikyatki and Awatobi, Arizona, in 1895. *Annual Report of the United States National Museum, Smithsonian Institution for 1895,* pp. 557–588, 1896. Br572C An8141 v.151.

1509. Fewkes, Jesse W. Preliminary account of an expedition to the pueblo ruins near Winslow, Arizona. *Annual Report of the United States National Museum, Smithsonian Institution, for 1896,* pp. 517–539, 1898. Br913.791 F43.7.

1510. Fewkes, Jesse W. Preliminary account of archæological field work in Arizona in 1897. *Annual Report of the United States National Museum, Smithsonian Institution, for 1897,* pp. 601–623, 1898. Br913.791 F43.6.

1511. Fewkes, Jesse W. The ceremonial circuit among the village Indians of northeastern Arizona. *Journal of American Folk-Lore* 5(16): 33–42, 1892. Br572C An8141 v.110.

1512. Fewkes, Jesse W. The feather symbol in ancient Hopi designs. *American Anthropologist* 11, 1898. 14 p. Br572C An8141 v.151.

1513. Fewkes, Jesse W. The God 'D' in the Codex Cortesianus. *American Anthropologist* 8:205–222, 1895. Br572C An 8141 v.139.

1514. Fewkes, Jesse W. The kinship of the Tusayan Indains. *American Anthropologist* 7(4): 394–417, 1894. Br572C An8141 v.134.

1515. Fewkes, Jesse W. The Miconinovi flute altars. *Journal of American Folk-Lore* 9(35):

241-255, 1896. Br572C An8141 v.151.

1516. Fewkes, Jesse W. The Oraibi flute altar. *Journal of American Folk-Lore* 8(31): 265-282, 1895. Br572C An 8141 v.139.

1517. Fewkes, Jesse W. The prehistoric culture of Tusayan. *American Anthropologist* 9:151-173, 1896. Br572C An8141 v.151.

1518. Fewkes, Jesse W. The sacrificial element in Hopi worship. *Journal of American Folk-Lore* 10(38): 187-201, 1897. Br572C An8141 v.151.

1519. Fewkes, Jesse W. The Tusayan new fire ceremony. *Proceedings of the Boston Society of Natural History* 26:422-458, 1895. Br572C An8141 v.134.

1520. Fewkes, Jesse W. The Tusayan ritual: a study of the influence of environment on aboriginal cults. *Annual Report of the United States National Museum, Smithsonian Institution, for 1895*, pp. 683-700, 1896. Br572C An8141 v.151.

1521. Fewkes, Jesse W. The Walpi flute observance: a study of primitive dramatization. *Journal of American Folk-Lore* 7(26): 265-288, 1894. Br572C An8141 v.134.

1522. Fewkes, Jesse W. The winter solice ceremony at Walpi. *American Anthropologist* 11, 1898. 38 p. Br572C An8141 v.166.

1523. Fewkes, Jesse W. The winter solstice altars at Hano pueblo. *American Anthropologist* 1:251-276, 1899. Br913.791 F43.

1524. Fewkes, Jesse W. Tusayan katcinas. *Annual Report of the Bureau of Ethnology, Smithsonian Institution, for 1894-1895*, pp. 245-313, 1897. Br970.3 TF436.3.

1525. Fewkes, Jesse W. Tusayan snake ceremonies. *Annual Report of the Bureau of Ethnology, Smithsonian Institution, for 1894-1895*, pp. 269-326, 1897. Br970.6 F436.2.

1526. Fewkes, Jesse W. Tusayan totemic signatures. *American Anthropologist* 10(1): 1-11, 1897. Br572C An8141 v.151.

1527. Fewkes, Jesse W., and A. M. Stephen. The Na-ac-nai-ya: a Tusayan initiation ceremony. *Journal of American Folk-Lore* 5:189-221, 1892. Br572C An8141 v.124.

1528. Fewkes, Jesse W., and A. M. Stephen. The Pá-lü-lü-kon-ti: a Tusayan ceremony. *Journal of American Folk-Lore* 6:269-282, 1893. Br572C An8141 v.125.

1529. Fewkes, Jesse W., and J. G. Owens. The La-la-kon-ta: a Tusayan dance. *American Anthropologist* 5:105-129, 1892. Br572C An8141 v.110.

1530. Field Columbian Museum. Annual report of the Director to the Board of Trustees for the year 1896-1897. *Report Series, Field Columbian Museum* 1(3): 170-256, 1897. Br572C An8141 v.151.

1531. Field, Thomas W. *An Essay Toward an Indian Bibliography; Being a Catalogue of Books, Relating to the History, Antiquities, Languages, Customs, Religion, Wars, Literature, and Origin of the American Indians, in the Library of Thomas W. Field; With Bibliographical and Historical Notes, and Synopses of the Contents of Some of the Works Least Known.* Scribner, Armstrong, and Company, New York, 1873. 430 p. Br970.aB F456.

1532. Finsch, Otto. *Reise in der Südsee und dem Malayischen Archipel in den Jahren 1879-1882.* Verlag von A. Asher, Berlin, 1884. 78 p. Br572C An8141 v.4.

1533. Fischer, Heinrich. Bericht über eine Anzahl Steinsculpturen aus Costa Rica. *Ab-*

handlungen der Naturhist. Vereins zu Bremen 7:153-175, 1881. Br572C An8141 v.44.

1534. Fischer, Heinrich. Die Nephritefrage. *Verhandlungen der Berliner Gesellschaft für Anthropologie, Ethnologie und Urgeschichte*, pp. 9-11, 1875. Br572C An8141 v.162.

1535. Fischer, Heinrich. *Nephrit und Jadeit nach ihren mineralogischen Eigenschaften sowie nach ihrer urgeschichtlichen und ethnographischen Bedeutung. Einführung der Mineralogie in das Studium der Archaeologie. 2. durch Zusätze und ein alphabetisches Sachregister vermehrte Ausgabe.* E. Schweizerbart'sche Verlagshandlung (E. Koch), Stuttgart, 1880. 411 p. Br913 F523.

1536. Fisk, James L. *Expedition of Captain Fisk to the Rocky Mountains; letter from the Secretary of War [Edwin M. Stanton], in Answer to a Resolution of the House of February 26, Transmitting Report of Captain Fisk of His Late Expedition to the Rocky Mountains and Idaho.* Washington, DC, 1864. 38 p. Br328.7326.2 Sd.

1537. *Flateyjarbók; the "Flatey book", written between 1380 and 1400 for John Hakonsson.* Royal Danish General Staff, Topographical Department, Copenhagen, 1893. 27 p. Br973.1 F618.2.

1538. Fleming, John. *A Short Sermon, Also Hymns, in the Muskokee or Creek Language.* Crocker and Brewster, Boston, 1835. 35 p. 240. Br497.39 CrF62.

1539. Fletcher, Alice C. Notes on certain beliefs concerning will power among the Siouan tribes. *Proceedings of the American Academy for the Advancement of Science*, 1896. 4 p. Br572C An8141 v.151. Alice Fletcher (1838-1923) was a member of the first generation of professional anthropologists in the United States. A pioneering fieldworker, she is known for her studies of Indian music and Plains Indians religious ceremonialism. Fletcher also worked actively to reform United States Indian policy. In 1890 Fletcher was awarded a lifetime Mary C. Thaw Fellowship at the Peabody Museum of Amerrican Archaeology and Ethnology at Harvard University, thus becoming the first women to have a paid professional position at Harvard.

1540. Fletcher, Alice C. The Elk Mystery or festival; Ogallala Sioux. *Annual Reports of the Trustees of the Peabody Museum of American Archaeology and Ethnology* 3(3-4): 276-288, 1884. Br913.07 H265.

1541. Fletcher, Alice C. The emblematic use of the tree in the Dakotan group. *Proceedings of the American Academy for the Advancement of Science* 45:3-21, 1896. Br572C An8141 v.151.

1542. Fletcher, Alice C. *The Import of the Totem: A Study From the Omaha Tribe.* Salem Press, Salem, MA, 1897. 12 p. Br572C An8141 v.151.

1543. Fletcher, Alice C. The phonetic alphabet of the Winnebago Indians. *Proceedings of the American Association for the Advancement of Science* 5(38): 354-357, 1890. Br572C An8141 v.51.

1544. Fletcher, Alice C. The religious ceremony of the Four Winds or quarters, as observed by the Santee Sioux. *Annual Reports of the Trustees of the Peabody Museum of American Archaeology and Ethnology* 3(3-4): 289-307, 1884. Br913.07 H265.

1545. Fletcher, Alice C. The significance of the scalp-lock: a study of Omaha ritual. *Journal of the Anthropological Institute* 27:436–450, 1898. Br572C An8141 v.166.

1546. Fletcher, Alice C. The Sun Dance of the Ogalalla Sioux. *Proceedings of the American Association for the Advancement of Science* 31:580–584, 1882. Br572C An8141 v.32.

1547. Fletcher, Alice C. The Wawan, or Pipe Dance of the Omahas. *Annual Reports of the Trustees of the Peabody Museum of American Archaeology and Ethnology* 3(3–4): 308–333, 1884. Br913.07 H265.

1548. Fletcher, Alice C. The White Buffalo Festival of the Uncpapas. *Annual Reports of the Trustees of the Peabody Museum of American Archaeology and Ethnology* 3(3–4): 260–275, 1884. Br913.07 H265.

1549. Fletcher, E. T. On language as evincing special modes of thought. *Transactions of the Literary and Historical Society of Quebec* 4:51–69, 1861. Br572C An8141 v.55.

1550. Fletcher, Richard. *Breve devocionario para todos los dias de la semana; payalchioob utial tulacal le u kiniloob ti le semana.* W. M. Watt, Londres, 1865, 18 leaves. Br498.21 MF638. "These works…printed without name of author by W. M. Watts, Crown Court, Temple Bar, London, were written by the Rev. Richard Fletcher, Methodist missionary at Corozal, in the English section of Yucatán" (Brinton 1900).

1551. Fletcher, Richard. *Catecismo de los metodistas. no. 1. Para los niños de tierna edad. Catecismo ti le metodistaoob. no. 2. Utial mehen palaloob.* London: W. W. Watts, 1865, 18 p. Br498.21 MF638.2. Spanish and Yucatec Maya on opposite pages.

1552. Fletcher, Richard. *Leti u ebanhelio Hezu Crizto hebix Mateo.* British and Foreign Bible Society, London, 1900. 104 p. Br498.21 MB473. The Gospel of St. Matthew translated into Yucatec Maya.

1553. Fletcher, Robert. *On Prehistoric Trephining and Cranial Amulets.* Smithsonian Institution, Contributions to American Ethnology, 5(2). Government Printing Office, Washington, DC, 1882. 32 p. Br557.3 Un319.

1554. Fletcher, Robert. Paul Broca and the French School of Anthropology; read before the United States National Museum, Washington, DC, April 15, 1882. Br572C An8141 v.26.

1555. Fleury, Claude. *Catecismo histórico ó Compendio de la istoria sagrada, y de la doctrina cristiana; con preguntas y respuestas, y lecciones seguidas…y traducidas del castellano al idioma yucateco, con un breve exorto para el entrego del santo cristo á los enformos por…Joaquin Ruz…para instrucción de los naturales.* En la oficina á cargo de D. Canton, Mérida de Yucatán, 1822, 186 p. Br498.21 MF 639.

1556. Fleury, Claude. *Catecismo histórico que contiene en resumen la historia santa y la doctrina cristiana con las pruebas de la religión con laminas.* Rosa, n.p., 1867. 211 p. Br262.8 F633.

1557. Fligier, Cornelius. *Zur Prähistorischen Ethnologie Italiens.* Alfred Holder, Wien, 1877. 55 p. Br572C An8141 v.56.

1558. Flinders Petrie, W. M. *Catalogue of a Collection of Egyptian Antiquities Discov-*

ered in 1895, Between Ballas and Nagada, Exhibited at University College, Gower Street, London, July 1 to July 27 J. H. Deakin, London, n.d. 19 p. Br572C An8141 v.143.

1559. Flinders Petrie, W. M. Catalogue of antiquities from Thebes; exhibited at University College, Gower Street, London, July 6th to August 1st, 1896. 15 p. Br572C An8141 v.99.

1560. Flores, Ildefonso José. *Arte de la lengua metropolitana del reyno cakchiquel, o guatemalico, con un parallelo de las lenguas metropolitanas de los reynos kiche, cakchiquel, y zutuhil, que hoy integran el reyno de Guatemala; compuesto por el P. F. Ildefonso Ioseph Flores.* Con licencia de los Sup. por S. de Arebal, En Guatemala [Antigua], 1753. 388 p. Br498.21 CF667.

1561. Flower, William H. *Anthropometric Laboratory.* Spottiswoode, London, 1893. 9 p. Br572C An8141 v.123.

1562. Foledo, Roderico. *Geografía de Centro-América; adoptada por el supremo gobierno como testo de enseñanza en la república.* Guatemala, 1874. 271 p. Br917.28 F694.

1563. Foley, Antoine E. Des trois grandes races humanines. Conference faite au profit des Écoles Laïques de Vincennes. Paris, 1880. 61 p. Br572C An8141 v.26.

1564. Folklore Society. *Fifteenth Annual Report of the Council,* 1893. 7 p. Br572C An8141 v.129.

1565. Forbes, David. On the Aymara Indians of Bolivia and Peru. *Journal of the Ethnological Society of London* 2(3): 193–206, 1870. Br572C An8141 v.67.

1566. Force, Manning F. Some early notices of the Indians of Ohio; read before Historical and Philosophical Society of Ohio. Cincinnati, 1879. 40 p. Br572C An8141 v.32.

1567. Force, Manning F. Some observations on the letters of Amerigo Vespucci. International Congress of Americanists. Brussels, 1879. Cincinnati, 1885. 24 p. Br572C An8141 v.40.

1568. Force, Manning F. To what race did the Mound Builders belong? *Proceedings of the International Congress of Americanists,* pp. 41–75, 1877. Br572C An8141 v.32.

1569. Förstemann, Ernst W. Aus dem Inschriftentempel von Palenque. *Globus* 75(5): 77–80, 1899. Br497.21 F68. Ernst Wilhelm Förstemann (1822-1906) was head librarian of the Königliche Öffentliche Bibliothek in Dresden from 1865 to 1887. In addition to his official duties as librarian, Förstemann produced numerous works on the decipherment of Maya hieroglyphic writing, working first with the Codex Dresden and later the Codex Madrid and Codex Paris, and inscriptions on stone. He succeeded in deciphering the Maya celendrical system, identifying the hieroglyphs for the months, the numbers zero and twenty, and the 260-day cycle. Förstemann recognized that the Maya calendar was founded on a vigesimal system.

1570. Förstemann, Ernst W. Das Gefäss von Chamá. *Verhandlungen der Berliner Anthropologischen Gesellschaft für Anthropologie, Ethnologie und Urgeschichte* 15:573–576, 1894. Br572C An 8141 v.139.

1571. Förstemann, Ernst W. Das mittelamerikanische Tonalamatl. *Globus* 67(18), 1895. 3 p. Br572C An8141 v.144.

1572. Förstemann, Ernst W. Der Maya-Apparat in Dresden. *Centralblatt für bibliiothekswesen* 2:181–192, 1885. Br572C An8141 v.39.

1573. Förstemann, Ernst W. Die Kreuz-Inschrift von Palenque. *Globus* 72(3), 1897. 5 p. Br572C An8141 v.160.

1574. Förstemann, Ernst W. Die Mayahieroglyphen. *Globus* 71(5), 1897. 4 p. Br572C An8141 v.160.

1575. Förstemann, Ernst W. *Die Tagegötter der Mayas*. F. Vieweg und Sohn, Braunschweig, 1898. Br913.726 F68. 4 p. Extract from *Globus*. Bd. 73, Nr. 9, 4 p, 1898.

1576. Förstemann, Ernst W. *Erlauterungen zur Mayahandschrift der Königlichen Offentlichen Bibliothek zu Dresden*. Warnatz und Lehmann, Dresden, 1886. 80 p. Br572C An8141 v.1.

1577. Förstemann, Ernst W. Neue Mayaforschungen. *Globus* 70(3), 1896. 3 p. Br572C An8141 v.160.

1578. Förstemann, Ernst W. *Schildkröte und Schnecke in der Mayaliteratur: III. Zur Entzifferung der Mayahandschriften*. Druck von Heinrich, Dresden, 1892. 8 p. Br572C An8141 v.110.

1579. Förstemann, Ernst W. Zeitperioden der Mayas. *Globus* 63(2): 29–32, 1893. Br572C An8141 v.107.

1580. Förstemann, Ernst W. *Zur Entzifferung der Mayahandschriften*. Druck von C. Heinrich, Dresden, 1895. 19 p. Br572C An 8141 v.47; Br572C An 8141 v.139.

1581. Förstemann, Ernst W. *Zur Entzifferung der Mayahandschriften: VII. Die Reihe Dresd. 51 bis 58*. C. Heinrich, Dresden, 1898. 12 p. Br572C An8141 v.166.

1582. Förstemann, Ernst W. *Zur Entzifferung der Mayahandschriften; Notizblatt 24 der Dresdener Mayahandschrift*. Druck von C. Heinrich, Dresden, 1894. 17 p. Br572C An8141 v.136.

1583. Förstemann, Ernst W. *Zur Entzifferung der Mayanhandschriften; VI. Dresd. 31a bis 32a*. Druck von C. Heinrich, Dresden, 1897. Br572C An8141 v.151; Br572C An8141 v.166.

1584. Förstemann, Ernst W. Zur Maya-Chronologie. *Zeitschrift für Ethnologie* 23:141–155, 1891. Br572C An8141 v.12.

1585. Fort y Roldán, Nicolás. *Cuba indígena*. Imprenta de R. Moreno y R. Rojas, Madrid, 1881. 200 p. Br917.291 F778.

1586. Fortnightly Club for the Study of Anthropology. *Program*. Yonkers, NY, 1898. 98 p. Br572.06 Y84.

1587. *Forty-Six Select Scripture Narratives From the Old Testament; Embellished with Engravings, for the Use of Indian Youth; Newinachke & guttasch pipinasiki gisehekhasiki elekpanni wendenasiki untschi Mechoweki Nachgundowoagani bambil*. Daniel Fanshaw, New York, 1838. 304 p. Br497.11 DL96. Delaware language reader.

1588. Foster, George E. *Se-quo-yah, The American Cadmus and Modern Moses; A Complete Biography of the Greatest of Redmen, Around Whose Wonderful*

Life Has Been Woven the Manners, Customs and Beliefs of the Early Chero-kees, Together With a Recital of Their Wrongs and Wonderful Progress Toward Civilization. Office of the Indian Rights Association, Philadelphia, 1885. 244 p. Br970.2 F81.

1589. Foster, John W. *Prehistoric Races of the United States of America.* 2d ed. S. C. Griggs, Chicago, 1873. 415 p. Br573 F81a.

1590. Fouillée, Alfred. *Psychologie du peuple français.* 2d ed. F. Alcan, Paris, 1898. 391 p. Br160 F825.

1591. *Four Chapters of Lucas; the Joaquin Ruz, John Kingdon Translation, Corrected by...Alexander Henderson.* Baptist Bible Translation Society, London, 1870. 14 p. Br498.21 MB473. New Testament Gospel of St. Luke partially translated into Yucatec Maya.

1592. Fowke, Gerard. Aboriginal remains of the piedmont and valley region of Virginia. *American Anthropologist* 6:415–422, 1893. Br572C An8141 v.123.

1593. Fowke, Gerard. *Archeological Investigations in James and Potomac Valleys.* Government Printing Office, Washington, DC, 1894. 80 p. Br572C An 8141 v.139.

1594. Fowke, Gerard. Notes on Ohio archaeology, 1894. 85 p. Br572C An8141 v.136.

1595. Fowke, Gerard. Pre-glacial and recent drainage channels in Ross County, Ohio. *Bulletin of the Scientific Laboratories of Denison University* 9:15–24, n.d. Br913.771 F822.

1596. Fraipont, Julien Jean Joseph. *Le tibia dans la race de Neanderthal.* G. Masson, Paris, 1888. 16 p. Br572C An8141 v.8.

1597. Fraipont, Julien Jean Joseph. *Les Néolithiques de la Meuse.* Imprimerie Hayez, Bruxelles, 1900. Br571.2 F847. Extract from *Bulletin de la Société d'anthropologie de Bruxelles,* 1898. t. 16.

1598. França, Ernesto Ferreira. *Chrestomathia da lingua brazilica.* Bibliotheca Linguistica, 2. F. A. Brockhaus, Leipzig, 1859. 230 p. Br498.75 GF 41.

1599. Franck, Adolphe. Réflexiones sur le Bouddhisme. *Annales de l'Alliance Scientifique,* pp. 57–60, 1891. Br572C An8141 v.9.

1600. Franco, Blas José. *Noticias de los indios del Departamento de Veragua, y vocabularios de las lenguas guaymi, norteño, sabanero y dorasque.* Colección de lingüística y etnografía americanas, 4. Imprenta de A.L. Bancroft y Ca., San Francisco, 1882. 73 p. Br498.13 GP65. Transcribed by A. L. Pinart from the original manuscript by Blas José Franco.

1601. Frantzius, Alexander von. Der geographish-kartographische Standpunkt von Costa-Rica. *Petermann's Geographischen Mitteilungen* 15:81–84, 1869. 11 p. Br572C An8141 v.69.

1602. Frantzius, Alexander von. Die Säugethiere costaricas; ein Beitrag zur Kenntniss der geographischen Verbreitung der Säugethiere Amerikas. *Archiv für Naturgeschichte* 35(1): 247–325, 1869. Br572C An8141 v.69.

1603. Frantzius, Alexander von. Die warmen mineralquellen in Costarica, pp. 496–510, 1862. Br572C An8141 v.69.

1604. Frantzius, Alexander von. Über die whare Lage der in Costarica vergeblich gesuchten reichen Goldminen von Tisingal und Estrella. *Zeitschrift der Gesellschaft für Erdkunde* 4:1–30, 1869. Br572C An8141 v.69.

1605. Frantzius, Alexander von. Vergiftete Wunden bei Thieren und Menschen durch den Biss der in Costarica vorkommenden Minirspinne (Mgale). *Virchow's Archiv für Pathologische Anatomie und Physiologie und für klinische Medicin* 47, n.d. 8 p. Br572C An8141 v.69.

1606. Fregni, A. Giuseppe. *Delle piu celebre iscrizioni etrusche ed umbre.* Tipo-Litografia Angelo Namias E.C., Modena, 1897. Br572C An8141 v.151.

1607. Frémont, John C. *Report of the Exploring Expedition to the Rocky Mountains in the Year 1842 and to Oregon and North California in the Years 1843-44.* Gales and Seaton, Washington, DC, 1845. 693 p. Br917.8 F89. Contents include: A report on an exploration of the country lying between the Missouri River and the Rocky Mountains, on the line of the Kansas and Great Platte rivers; John Torrey, Catalogue of plants collected by Lieutenant Frémont, in his expedition to the Rocky Mountains; A report of the exploring expedition to Oregon and north California, in the years 1843-'44 (with appendices); Astronomical observations made during the expedition to the Rocky Mountains in the year 1842; Meteorological observations.

1608. Friedreich, J. B. Schädels von Chiriqui (Panama). *Berliner Gesellschaft für Anthropologie, Ethnologie und Urgeschichte* 12:1–8, 1871. Br572C An8141 v.165.

1609. Fritz, Johann F. *Orientalisch- und occidentalischer Sprachmeister, welcher nicht allein hundert Alphabete nebst ihrer Aussprache, so bey denen meisten europaisch-asiatisch-africanisch- und americanischen völckern und nationen gebräuchlich sind, auch einigen Tabulis polyglottis verschiedener Sprachen und Zahlen vor Augen leget, sondern auch das Gebet des Herrn, in 200 Sprachen und Mund-arten mit dererselben Characteren mittheilet...aus glaubwürdigen auctoribus zusammengetragen.* C. F. Gessner, Leipzig, 1748. 219, 128 p. Br409.8 F918.

1610. Fry, Carlos. *La gran región de los bosques, o, ríos peruanos navegables, Urubamba, Ucayali, Amazonas, Pachitea y Palcazu; diario de viajes y exploraciones.* Imprenta de B. Gil, Lima, 1889. 2 v. Br918.5 F946.

1611. Fuensanta del Valle, A., J. S. Rayon, and Francisco de Zabalburn, eds. *Colección de documentos inéditos para la historia de España.* Ginesta, Madrid, 1892. Br946 C67. v. 104 only.

1612. Fuentes y Guzmán, Francisco Antonio de. *Historia de Guatemala, ó, recordación florida.* L. Navarro, Madrid, 1882–1883. 2 v. Br972.81 F95.

1613. Fuertes, E.A. Algunos vocablos de al lengua huave, colectados en el pueblo de San Dionisio de la Mar, Oaxaca, 1870. 2 leaves. Br498.18 HF953. Manuscript.

1614. Fuertes, E.A. Vocabularies of the Zapoteco from Suchitán, Zoque from Chimalapa, and Mixe from Guichicore, 1871. 53 p. Br498.34 ZF 953. Extracted by Karl H. Berendt from J. C. Spear, "Report on the geology, mineraology, natural history, inhabitants, and agriculture of the isthmus of Tehuantepec," (In R. W. Shufeldt, *Reports of Explorations and Surveys, Isthmus of Tehuantepec*, pp. 99-139. Washington, DC, 1872; the section Languages of the aboriginal tribes, p. 128, contains vocabularies of the Zapoteco (Tehuantepec), Loque (Zoque)(San Miguel and Chimalapa). Fuertes accompanied this expedition as civil engineer and he probably had much to do with the collection of the vocabularies.

1615. Fulton, Alexander R. *The Red Men of Iowa; Being a History of the Various Aboriginal Tribes Whose Homes Were in Iowa; Sketches of Chiefs, Traditions, Indian Hostilities, Incidents and Reminiscences; With a General Account of the Indians and Indian Wars of the Northwest; and Also an Appendix Relating to the Pontiac War.* Mills and Company, Des Moines, 1882. 559 p. Br970.4 IoF954.

1616. Furtwängler, A. Die Bronzeeimer von Mehrum. In *Festschrift zum Fünfzigjährigen Jubiläum des Vereins von Alterthumsfreunden im Rheinlande,* pp. 23-34. Gedruckt auf Kosten des Vereins, Bonn, 1891. Br572C An8141 v.98.

1617. Gabb, William M. On the Indian tribes and languages of Costa Rica. *Proceedings of the American Philosophical Society* 14:483-602, 1875. Br572C An8141 v.50.

1618. Gabb, William M. *On the Indian Tribes and Languages of Costa Rica.* Philadelphia, 1875. 120 p. Br498 G11.4. Manuscript; arranged English to San Blas; taken from "On the Indian tribes and languages of Costa Rica" (*Proceedings of the American Philosophical Society* 14:483-602, 1875).

1619. Gabelentz, Georg von der Handbuch zur aufnahme fremder Sprachen. *Im Auftrage der Kolonial-Abtheilung des Auswärtigen amts.* E.S. Mittler und Sohn, Berlin, 1892. 272 p. Br402 G11. "Wörterbuch" (p. 21-272) consists of lists of German words, arranged with blank space after each.

1620. Gabelentz, Georg von der. Baskisch und Berberisch. *Sitzungsberichte der Königlich Prüssuschen Akademie der Wissenschaften zu Berlin* 31:593-613, 1893. Br572C An8141 v.113.

1621. Gabelentz, Hans G. C. von der. *Grammatik der Dakota-Sprache.* F. A. Brockhaus, Leipzig, 1852. 64 p. Br572C An8141 v.51; Br572C An8141 v.81.

1622. Gabelentz, Hans G. C. von der. *Grammatik der Dayak-Sprache.* F. A. Brockhaus, Leipzig, 1852. 48 p. Br572C An8141 v.87.

1623. Gabelentz, Hans G. C. von der. *Grammatik der Kiriri-Sprache.* F. A. Brockhaus, Leipzig, 1852. 62 p. Br572C An8141 v.51; Br572C An8141 v.81.

1624. Gaffarel, P. Jean de Lévy. *La langue tupí.* Maisonneuve et Cie., Libraires-Éditeurs, Paris, 1877. 29 p. Br572C An8141 v.60.

1625. Gage, Thomas. *A New Survey of the West-Indies Being a Journal of Three Thousand and Three Hundred Miles Within the Main Land of America; The Fourth Edition Enlarg'd by the Author, With an Accurate Map.* Printed by M. Clark, for J. Nicolson...and T. Newborough, London, 1699. 475 p. Br917.29 G123. The book created a sensation when it was first published in 1648. In it Gage describes Mexico and the wealth of South America, commenting upon the ease with which it could be conquered. Gage originally belonged to the Dominican order and served as a missionary in Mexico. He later joined the Church of England and was appointed chaplain to the forces which captured Jamaica, where he died in 1656.

1626. Gagern, Carlos de. Charakteristik der Indianischen Bevölkerung Mexikos. *Mit-*

teilungen der Geographisches Gesellschaft Nr. 2, 1873. 29 p. Br572C An8141 v.58; Br572C An8141 v.165.

1627. Gala, Leandro R. de la. *U tz'ibhuun hach noh tzic benil Ahaucaan.* José D. Espinosa, Ho U Calhuun, 1870. 8 p. Br498.21 MG132. A pastoral letter by Leandro R. de la Gala which was put into Maya by the prysbyter, D. José Pilar Vales; full title: "U tz'ibhuun hach noh tzicbenil ahaucaan ahmiatz Leandro R. de la Gala, ti u hach yamailoob mohenoob yanoob tu nachilcahtaliloob nohol y chikin ti le luumcabil Yucatán laa. Ho [Mérida]: U tzcalhuun José D. Espinosa, tu hunpic cabak catac oxhal lahunpiz u habiloob, 1870, cristo ahlohil." Translation: Letter of the illustrious Sr. Bishop Dr. D. Leandro R. de la Gala to his well-beloved sons, who live apart or segregated in the cantons of the south and east of this territory of Yucatán. Mérida: In the printing house of José D. Espinosa, in the year of Christ the Redeemer, 1870.

1628. Gallatin, Albert. Hale's Indians of North-West America, and vocabularies of North America; with an introduction. *Transactions of the American Ethnological Society* 2:1–130, 1848. Br497 H13. Albert Gallatin (1761–1849) had a lengthy government career that included positions as state legislator, Congressman, Secretary of the Treasury, and diplomat in Russia, France, and England. When he retired from public service he concentrated on the study of American Indian languages. His *A Table of Indian Languages in the United States*, published in 1826, provided the first tribal language map and was the first attempt to designate language groups using the comparative method. In 1843 Gallatin was a force in the founding of the American Ethnological Society and served as its first president.

1629. Galles, René. Monuments en Basse-Bretagne et Algerie. *Bulletin de la Société Algerienne de Climatologique* 1:31–57, 1869. Br572C An8141 v.58.

1630. Galton, Francis. *Hereditary Genius; An Inquiry Into Its Laws and Consequences.* Macmillan, London, 1892. 379 p. Br172 G13a.

1631. Gámez, José D. *Historia de Nicaragua; desde los tiempos prehistóricos hasta 1860; en sus relaciones con España, México y Centro-America.* Tipografía de "El Pais," Managua, 1889. 855 p. Br972.85 G14.

1632. Ganong, William F. A monograph of the place-nomenclature of the province of New Brunswick. *Transactions of the Royal Society of Canada* 2:175–289, 1896. Br572C An8141 v.152.

1633. Gaono, Juan. *Colloquios de la paz y tranquilidad christiana, en lengua mexicana.* En casa de Pedro Ocharte, México, 1582. 121 p. Br498.22 AzG 155.

1634. García de Palacio, Diego. *Carta dirijida al rey de España.* C. B. Norton, London, 1860. 129 p. Br913.7281 G163. From a manuscript copy made by the historian Muñoz, and preserved in the Royal Academy of History at Madrid; Spanish and English on opposite pages.

1635. García de Palacio, Diego. *San Salvador und Honduras im Jahre 1576; Amtlicher bericht des licenciaten Dr. Diego García de Palacio an den König von Spanien über die centralamerikanischen provinzen San Salvador und Honduras im Jahre 1576; Aus dem spanischen übersetzt und mit erklärewnden anmerkun-*

Joaquín García Icazbalceta (from Justin Winsor, Aboriginal America. Cambridge, MA: Houghton, Mifflin, 1889. p. 163).

gen und einer Karte versehen von Dr.A. von Frantzius. Dietrich Reimer, Berlin; B.Westermann, New York; Nicholas Truebner, London, 1873. 70 p. Br572C An8141 v.61.This is a description of the ancient provinces of Guazacapan, Cuzcatlan, and Chiquimula, in the audiencia of Guatemala.

1636. García Icazbalceta, Joaquín. *Apuntes para un catálogo de escritores en lenguas indígenas de América*. En la imprenta particular del autor, México, 1866. 157 p. Br498B Ic18.

1637. García Icazbalceta, Joaquín. *Colección de documentos para la historia de México*. J. M. Andrade, México, 1858-1866. 2 v. Br972 G164.2.

1638. García Icazbalceta, Joaquín. *De la destrucción de antigüedades mexicanas*. Diaz, Mexico, 1881. 72 p. Br572C An8141 v.44.

1639. García Icazbalceta, Joaquín. *Nueva colección de documentos para la historia de México*. Andrade y Morales, sucesores, México, 1886. v. 1. Br972 G164.

1640. García Peláez, Francisco de Paula. *Memorias para la historia del antiguo reyno de Guatemala, redactadas por...Francisco de Paula García Pelaez*. Establecimiento tip. de L. Luna, Guatemala, 1851-1852. 3 v. Br972.81 P36a.

1641. García Peláez, Francisco de Paula. *Sermón del glorioso apóstol Santiago el Mayor, predicado el día 25 de julio de 1858*. Imprenta de la Paz, en el Palacio del Gobierno, Guatemala, 1858. 15 p. Br257.3 P364.

1642. García, Bartholomé. *Manual para administrar los santos sacramentos de penitencia, eucharistia, extramaunción, y matrimonio; dar gracias despues de comulgar, y ayudar a bien morir a los indios de las naciones; pajalates, orejones, pacaos, pacóas, tilijayas, alasapas, pausanes, y otras muchas diferentes, que se hallan en las misiones del Rio de San Antonio, y Rio Grande, pertenecientes à el Colegio de la Santissima Cruz de la ciudad de Queretaro, como son; los pacuâches, mescâles, pampôpas, tâcames, chayopînes, venados, pamâques, y toda la juventud de pihuiques, borrados, sanipaos, y manos de perro.* Imprenta de los Herederos de Doña Maria de Rivera, México, 1760. 512 p. Br262.3 G16.

1643. García, Gregorio. *Origen de los indios de el Nuevo Mundo e indias occidentales.* 2d ed. Madrid, 1729. 416 p. Br970.1 G16.

1644. García, Manuel. *El toro de Sinkeuel; leyenda hípica, político-tauromaquica.* Imprenta a Cargo de Isac Manuel Avila, Mérida, 1856. 32 p. Br498.21 MG 163. "A political squib, said in a note of Dr. Berendt's to be wriiten by Manuel García and directed against General Ampudia. It is interesting in this connection for the many Maya words used by the writer, and as indicating the general familiarity with that tongue which he takes for granted among his readers" (Brinton 1900).

1645. Garcilaso de la Vega, El Inca. *La Florida del Inca. Historia del adelantado, Hernando de Soto, governador, y capitan general del reino de la Florida.* En la Oficina Real...Nicholas Rodriguez Franco, Madrid, 1723. 2 v. Br973.1 G163. "Garcilaso de la Vega was the son of the Spanish conquistador Sebastián Garcilaso de la Vega, and of princess Isabel Chimpu Ocllo, granddaughter of the last Inca emporer...His *Florida* is an account of Hernando de Soto's 1539-1542 expedition from Florida throughout the entire southeastern United States as far as Texas and Oklahoma. It is based on the old-age reminiscences of several survivors, one an anonymous *hidalgo*, and the two others common soldiers" (*Siebert Library* 1999:2:11).

1646. Gariel, M. L'électricité dans ses rapports avec l'hygiène. *Revue Scientifique* 23:705-716, 1885. Br572C An8141 v.95.

1647. Garrioch, Alfred C. *Manual of Devotion in the Beaver Indian Language.* Society for Promoting Christian Knowledge, London, 1886. 87 p. Br497.12 SlG 19.

1648. Garrioch, Alfred C. *The Gospel According to St. Mark, Translated by the Rev. Alfred C. Garrioch...Into the Langauge of the Beaver Indians of the Diocese of Athabasca.* Society for Promoting Christian Knowledge, London, 1886. 47 p. Br497.12 SlB47.2G. Translation of the Gospel of St. Mark into Tsattine.

1649. Garrioch, Alfred C. *The Gospel According to St. Mark, Translated Into the Beaver Indian Language, by the Rev. Alfred C. Garrioch.* Society for Promoting Christian Knowledge, London, 1886. 79 p. Br497.12 SlB47.2Ga. Translation of the Gospel of St. Mark into Tsattine.

1650. Gates, William E. *Maya and Tzental Calendars, Comprising the Complete Series of Days, With Their Positions in the Month, for Each of the Fifty-Two Years of the Cycle, According to Each System.* Cleveland, 1900. 114 p. Br913.726 G22.

1651. Gatschet, Albert S. Adjectives of color in Indian languages. *American Naturalist* 13:475-485, 1879. Br572C An8141 v.52. Gatschet (1832-1907) was educated in his native Switzerland and after coming to the United States in 1869, he worked on the American Indian vocabularies collected by Oscar Loew, of the United States Geological Survey West of the 100th Meridian (Wheeler Survey). John Wesley Powell later hired him as an ethnologist with the United States Geographical and Geological Survey of the Rocky Mountain Regions. He joined the staff of the Bureau of American Ethnology when it was founded in 1879, and continued there until he retired in 1905. During his career he fieldwork among the Klamath, Biloxi, Tunica, Natchez, Tonkawa, Chitimacha, and the Atakapa in the United States, and the Comecrudo and other small groups in northern Mexico.

1652. Gatschet, Albert S. Analytical report upon Indian dialects spoken in Southern California, Nevada, and on the Lower Colorado River, etc., based upon vocabularies collected by the expeditions for Geographical Surveys West of 100th Meridian. *Annual Report of the Chief of Engineers for 1876, Appendix JJ.* p. 550-563. Washington, DC. Br572C An8141 v.52.

1653. Gatschet, Albert S. Classification into seven linguistic stocks of western Indian dialects contained in forty vocabularies. In *Reports Upon Archaeological and Ethnological Collections From the Vicinity of Santa Barbara,* F.W. Putnam, ed., pp. 403-485. Washington, DC, 1879. Br572C An8141 v.92.

1654. Gatschet, Albert S. Ein Sturmrennen am Horizonte; Zwei Indianer-Mythen aus Isleta, Neu-Mexiko, übertragen von A. S. Gatschet, n.d. 5 p. Br572C An8141 v.110.

1655. Gatschet, Albert S. Ethnographic notes. *American Antiquarian* 5(1), 1883. 2 p. Br572C An8141 v.48.

1656. Gatschet, Albert S. Indian languages of the Pacific states and territories and of the pueblos of New Mexico. *Magazine of American History* 8:254-263, 1882. Br572C An8141 v.49.

1657. Gatschet, Albert S. Indian notes. *American Antiquarian* 1:267-269, 1878; 2:76-79, 171-174, 236-238, 318-319, 1879; 3:66, 249-252, 337-338, 1880; 4:73-77, 235-281, 337-340, 1882; 5:85-88, 191-193, 283-286, 354-356, 1883; 6:63, 1884. Br572C An8141 v.52.

1658. Gatschet, Albert S. Linguistic notes. *American Antiquarian* 5(1), 1883. 4 p. Br572C An8141 v.48.

1659. Gatschet, Albert S. *Migration Legend of the Creek Indians; With a Linguistic, Historic, and Ethnographic Introduction.* Library of Aboriginal American Literature, 4. D. G. Brinton, Philadelphia, 1884-1888. 2 v. Br897C B776.

1660. Gatschet, Albert S. *Promenade onomatologique sur les bords du lac Léman.* J. Allemann, Berne, 1867. 38 p. Br409.04 G22.

1661. Gatschet, Albert S. Recent literature: *The Annals of the Cakchiquels. American Naturalist* 20:414-425, 1886. Br572C An8141 v.13.

1662. Gatschet, Albert S. Specimen of the Chúmeto language I. *American Antiquarian* 5(1): 71-73, 1883. Br572C An8141 v.48.

1663. Gatschet, Albert S. Specimen of the Chúmeto language II. *American Antiquarian* 5(2): 173-180, 1883. 3 p. Br572C An8141 v.48.

1664. Gatschet, Albert S. *Tchikilli's Kasihta Legend in the Creek and Hitchiti Languages With a Critical Commentary and Full Glossaries to Both Texts.* R. P. Studley, St. Louis, 1888. 207 p. Br897.39 CrT213.

1665. Gatschet, Albert S. The Aruba language and the Papiamento jargon. *Proceedings of the American Philosophical Society* 21:229-305, 1884. Br572C An8141 v.52.

1666. Gatschet, Albert S. The Karankawa Indians, the coast people of Texas: notes by

Charles A. Hammond and Alice W. Oliver, and a vocabulary contained from Alice W. Oliver. *Archaeological and Ethnological Papers of the Peabody Museum of American Archaeology and Ethnology, Harvard University* 1(2): 69-167, 1891. Br572C An8141 v.110.

1667. Gatschet, Albert S. *The Klamath Indians of Southwestern Oregon*. Smithsonian Institution, Contributions to American Ethnology, 2(1). Government Printing Office, Washington, DC, 1890. 711 p. Br557.3 Un319.Vol. 2(2) includes "Dictionary: Klamath-English; English-Klamath."

1668. Gatschet, Albert S. The numeral adjective in the Klamath language of southern Oregon. *American Antiquarian* 2(3): 210-217, 1879-1880. Br572C An8141 v.52.

1669. Gatschet, Albert S. The Shetimasha Indians of St. Mary's Parish, southern Louisiana. *Transactions of the Anthropological Society of Washington* 2:148-158, 1883. Br572C An8141 v.52.

1670. Gatschet, Albert S. The test of linguistic affinity. *American Antiquarian* 2(2): 163-165, 1879. Br572C An8141 v.52.

1671. Gatschet, Albert S. *The Timucua Language*. Philadelphia, 1880. Br497.54 G22. Extract from *Proceedings of the American Philosophical Society* 17:90-504, and 18:465-502; excepting the first article, which is reprinted with new paging from 16:625-642.

1672. Gatschet, Albert S. Volk und Sprache der Timucua. *Zeitschrift für Ethnologie* 13:189-200, 1881. Br572C An8141 v.4.

1673. Gatschet, Albert S. *Zwölf Sprachen aus dem südwesten Nordamerikas (Pueblos- und Apache-mundarten; Tonto, Tonkawa, Digger, Utah.) Wortverzeichnisse herausgegeben, erläutert und mit einer Einleitung über Bau, Begriffsbildung und locale Gruppirung der amerikanischen Sprachen*. H. Böhlau, Weimar, 1876. 150 p. Br497 G224.3. Includes "Felsinschrift südöstlich von Tsitsúmovi, Arizona" (p. 149) and "Felsinschrift an der Mesa pintada" (p. 150). "Literatur": p. 5-6.

1674. Gaudry, Albert. *Matériaux pour l'histoire des temps quaternaires*. Librairie F. Savy, Paris, 1876-1892. 130 p. Br566 G23. Contents include: 1. "Preliminaires; Fossiles quaternaires de la Mayenne, par A. Gaudry," 1876; 2. "De l'existence des saïgas en France à l'époque quaternaire, par A. Gaudry," 1880; 3. "L'elasmotherium, par A. Gaudry et M. Boule," 1888; and 4. "Les oubliettes des Gargas, par A. Gaudry et M. Boule," 1892.

1675. Gavarrete, Francisco. *Catecismo de geografía de Guatemala; para el uso de las escuelas de primeras letras de la República*. Imprenta de la Paz, Guatemala, 1860. 100 p. Br917.281 G24.2.

1676. Gavarrete, Francisco. *Geografía de la República de Guatemala*. 3d ed. Emilio Goubaud, Guatemala, 1874. 128 p. Br917.281 G24a.

1677. Gavarrete, Francisco. *Geografía de la República de Guatemala; 2 ed. corregida y aumentada con muchos datos y especialmente con un bosquejo histórico desde los tiempos mas remotos hasta nuestros dias. Para el uso de los colegios y escuelas*. Imprenta de La Paz, Guatemala, 1868, 110 p. Br917.281 G24.

1678. Gay, José A. *Historia de Oaxaca*. Imprenta del Comercio de Dublan, México, 1881. 2 v. Br972 G25.

1679. Geneva Oriental Congress. *Asiatic Quarterly Review*, 1894. 16 p. Br572C An8141 v.132.

1680. Génin, Auguste. *Collection Boturini-Aubin-Goupil de manuscrits figuratifs mexicains*. Ernest Leroux, Paris, 1892. 8 p. Br572C An8141 v.152.

1681. Genin, Auguste. *Poemes azteques, par Auguste Genin, 1884-1889; lettre-preface de Clovis Hugues*. Fischbacher, Paris, 1890. 255 p. Br848 G282P.

1682. Geographical Club of Philadelphia. *Bulletin*, 1893-1896. 2 v. Br910.6 P53.

1683. Geographical Club of Philadelphia. *Charter, by-laws, List of members*, 1894-95, 1898. 3 v. Br910.6 P53.

1684. Gerland, Georg K. C. Amerikanische Journale: Die Eskimo. *Bericht über die Ethnographische Forschung*, pp. 217-265, 285-306, 1894-1895. Br572C An8141 v.152.

1685. Gerland, Georg K. C. *Anthropologische Beiträge, 1*. Lippert (M. Niemeyer), Halle, 1875. 424 p. Br572 G31.

1686. Gerland, Georg K. C. *Atlas der Völkerkunde; 15 kolorierte Karten in Kupferstich mit 49 Darstellungen*. J. Perthes, Gotha, 1892. 15 p. 15 double maps. Br572 G31.2.

1687. Gerland, Georg K. C. Bericht über die ethnologische Forschung, 1896-1897. *Geographisches Jahresberichte* 32:184-219, 1884. Br572B G313.

1688. Gerland, Georg K. C. Bericht über die ethnologische Forschung. *Geographisches Jahrbuch* 10:249-322, 408-476, 1888. Br572C An8141 v.31.

1689. Gheyn, Joseph van den. *Essais de mythologie et de philologie comparée*. Société Belge de Librairie; V. Palmé, Paris, 1885. 431 p. Br270 G34.

1690. Gibbs, George. *A Dictionary of the Chinook Jargon, or Trade Language of Oregon*. Shea's Library of American Linguistics, 12. Cramoisy Press, New York, 1863. 43 p. Br497C Sh3; Br497C Sh3a; Br497.19 CG353. Rejecting a career as librarian of the New York Historical Society, Gibbs (1815-1873) explored the Pacific slope from 1849 to 1860. Travels through northern California, Oregon, and Washington provided the opportunity for linguistic and ethnographic studies and his annually shipped artifacts to the Smithsonian Institution. In the 1860s he settled in Washington, DC, and published linguistic studies on Yakima, Chinook, Chinook Jargon, Clallam, Lummi, and Nisqually. He also studied Northwest Coast mythology and was a founder of the Anthropological Institute of New York and the American Philological Society.

1691. Gibbs, George. *Alphabetical Vocabulary of the Chinook Language*. Shea's Library of American Linguistics, 11. Cramoisy Press, New York, 1863. 23 p. Br497C Sh3; Br497C Sh3a.

1692. Gibbs, George. *Alphabetical Vocabulary of the Clallam and Lummi*. Shea's Library of American Linguistics, 13. Cramoisy Press, New York, 1863. 40 p. Br497C Sh3; Br497C Sh3a. "Both vocabularies were collected by Mr. Gibbs during a residence of a few months at Port Townshend and its adjacent territory" (Field 1873:147).

1693. Gibbs, George. *Instructions for Research Relative to the Ethnology and Philology of America*. Smithsonian Institution, Miscellaneous Contributions, 160. Washington, DC, 1863. 51 p. Br572C An8141 v.58; Br572C An8141 v.70.

1694. Gibbs, George. *Tribes of Western Washington and Northwestern Oregon, With a Map*, pp. 157-361. Smithsonian Institution, Contributions to American Ethnology, 1(2). Government Printing Office, Washington, DC, 1877. 361 p. Br557.3 Un319.

1695. Gibson, George. Report of a finding of pottery on Fox River, near Green Bay, Wisconsin. *Proceedings of Central Ohio Scientific Association* 1(1): 62-65, 1878. Br572C An8141 v.59.

1696. Giddings, Franklin H. *Outline of Lectures on Sociology*. William J. Dornan, Philadelphia, 1891, 18 p. Br572C An8141 v.88.

1697. Giddings, Franklin H. Sociology as a university study. *Political Science Quarterly* 6(4): 635-655, 1891. Br572C An8141 v.88.

1698. Giddings, Franklin H. The theory of sociology. *Annals of the American Academy of Political and Social Science,* 1894. 80 p. Br572C An8141 v.131.

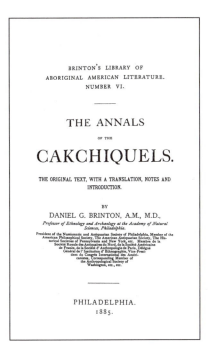

Title page from Brinton's The Annals of the Cakchiquels *(1885).*

1699. Gigault de la Bedelliere, Emile. *Les Llanos de Venezuela*, n.d. 362 p. Br918.7 G363. Br919 C888.

1700. Giglioli, Enrico H. Album von Celébes-Typen, 1890. 2 p. Br572C An8141 v.9. In 1865 Enrico Hillyer Giglioli (1845-1909) served as an assistant on the first voyage around the world sponsored by the Italian government. He spent three years on the ship *Magenta* visiting Brazil, Uruguay, Malaysia, Indochina, Japan, China, and Patagonia. In 1869 he began teaching at the University of Florence and was instrumental in founding the Società di Antropologia. In subsequent years Giglioli published on material culture, especially stone tools. He also studied the Negrito, a group of Negroid peoples of small stature found in Oceania and southeastern Asia, contributed to racial classification and the field of museum studies.

1701. Giglioli, Enrico H. Alcune notizie intorno agli ariani primitivi detti Siah Posh. *Archivo per l'Antropologia e la Etnologia* 19, 1889. 7 p. Br572C An8141 v.9.

1702. Giglioli, Enrico H. Alcuni cenni ai Dajak. *Archivo per l'Antropologia e la Etnologia* 13, 1883. 7 p. Br572C An8141 v.9.

1703. Giglioli, Enrico H. Alla Nuova Guinea. *Archivo per l'Antropologia e la Etnologia* 19, 1889. 20 p. Br572C An8141 v.9.

1704. Giglioli, Enrico H. Di alcune maschere fatte colla porzione anteriore di cranii umani...Nuova Bretagna. *Archivo per l'Antropologia e la Etnologia* 17, 1887. 12 p. Br572C An8141 v.9.

1705. Giglioli, Enrico H. Due singolarissime e rare trombe da guerra guernite di ossa umane dell'Africa e dell'America meridionale, n.d. 8 p. Br572C An8141 v.152.

1706. Giglioli, Enrico H. I cacciatori di teste alla Nuova Guinea, pp. 311-318, n.d. Br572C An8141 v.152.

1707. Giglioli, Enrico H. L'età della pietra nella Nuova Caledonia. *Archivo per l'Antropologia e la Etnologia* 26(3), 1896. 12 p. Br572C An8141 v.152.

1708. Giglioli, Enrico H. La moneta nella Melanesia. *Archivo per l'Antropologia e la Etnologia*, 17, 1887. 6 p. Br572C An8141 v.9.

1709. Giglioli, Enrico H. La trebbiatrice guernita di pietre in uso presso alcune tribù Berbere nella Tunisia, 1893. 4 p. Br572C An8141 v.152.

1710. Giglioli, Enrico H. Le mazze con testa sferoidale di Pietra della nuova gli ultimi giorni dell' eta della Pietra (Melanesia), n.d. 28 p. Br572C An8141 v.152.

1711. Giglioli, Enrico H. Maschere della Nuova Guinea e dell-Archipelago Bismarck. *Archivo per l'Antropologia e la Etnologia*, 20, 1890. 4 p. Br572C An8141 v.9.

1712. Giglioli, Enrico H. Note etnologische dalle Isole Marchesi. *Archivo per l'Antropologia e la Etnologia*, 18, 1888. 5 p. Br572C An8141 v.9.

1713. Giglioli, Enrico H. Note intorno ad alcuni oggetti interessanti. *Archivo per l'Antropologia e la Etnologia*, 17, 1887. 7 p. Br572C An8141 v.9.

1714. Giglioli, Enrico H. Note su du pipe singolari dell'America boreale. *Archivo per l'Antropologia e la Etnologia* 17:426-430, 1887. 6 p. Firenze. Br572C An8141 v.9.

1715. Giglioli, Enrico H. Notes on a remarkable and very beautiful ceremonial stone adze from Kapsu, New Ireland. *Internationales Archiv für Ethnographie* 3:181-186, 1890. Br572C An8141 v.91.

1716. Giglioli, Enrico H. Notes on a singular mask from Boissy Island, northeastern New Guinea; and queries on the lizard in the folk-lore of Australasia. *Internationales Archiv für Ethnographie* 1:184-187, 1888. Br572C An8141 v.91.

1717. Giglioli, Enrico H. Notizie ethnografiche dalle isole Nicobar. *Archivo per l'Antropologia e la Etnologia*, 17, 1887. 5 p. Br572C An8141 v.9.

1718. Giglioli, Enrico H. Notizie intorno ai Djelma o Baduvi ed ai Tenger montanari non-Islamiti. *Archivo per l'Antropologia e la Etnologia*, v. 8, 1878. 7 p. Br572C An8141 v.9.

1719. Giglioli, Enrico H. Notizie sugli indigeni delle isole Nicobar. *Archivo per l'Antropologia e la Etnologia*, v. 15, 1885. 4 p. Br572C An8141 v.9.

1720. Giglioli, Enrico H. Nuove notizie sui popoli Negroidi dell'Asia. *Archivo per l'Antropologia e la Etnologia*, v. 9, 1879. 8 p. Br572C An8141 v.9.

1721. Giglioli, Enrico H. On a remarkable stone axe and stone chisel in actual use amongst the Chamacocos of southeast Bolivia. *Internationales Archiv für Ethnographie* 2:272-277, 1889. Br572C An8141 v.91.

1722. Giglioli, Enrico H. On a singular obsidian scraper used at present by some of the Galla tribes in southern Shoa. *Internationales Archiv für Ethnographie* 2:212-214, 1889. Br572C An8141 v.91.

1723. Giglioli, Enrico H. On two ancient Peruvian masks made with the facial portion of human skulls. *Internationales Archiv für Ethnographie* 4:83-86, 1891. Br572C An8141 v.91.

1724. Giglioli, Enrico H. Ossa umane portate come ricordi o per ornamento y usate come utensili od armi. *Archivo per l'Antropologia e la Etnologia*, v, 18, 1888. 8 p. Br572C An8141 v.9.

1725. Giglioli, Enrico H. Ragazzi allevati e conviventi con lupi nell-Hindustan. *Archivo per l'Antropologia e la Etnologia*, v. 12, 1882. 8 p. Br572C An8141 v.9.

1726. Giglioli, Enrico H. Studi etnologici in Siberia. *Archivo per l'Antropologia e la Etnologia* 15(1), 1885. 14 p. Br572C An8141 v.9.

1727. Giglioli, Enrico H. Ulteriori notizie intorno agli Akka dell-Africa centrale. *Archivo per l'Antropologia e la Etnologia*, v, 18, 1888. 3 p. Br572C An8141 v.9.

1728. Giglioli, Enrico H. Ulteriori notizie: intorno ai Negriti. *Archivo per l'Antropologia e la Etnologia*, v. 10, 1880. 8 p. Br572C An8141 v.9.

1729. Giglioli, Enrico H., and A. Zannetti. *Istruzioni per fare le osservazioni antropologische ed etnologiche*. Roma, 1880. 45 p. Br572C An8141 v.9.

1730. Giglioli, Enrico H., and Francesco Sacramucci. Notizie sui Danakil e piu specialmente su quelli di Assab. *Archivo per l'Antropologia e la Etnologia*, v. 14, 1884. 30 p. Br572C An8141 v.9.

1731. Gilbert, G. K. Niagara Falls and their history. *National Geographic Magazine* 1(7): 203-236, 1895. Br572C An8141 v.144.

1732. Gilbert, Grove K. *The History of the Niagara River*. Sixth Annual Report of the Commissioners of the State Reservation at Niagara, Albany, NY, 1889. p.60-84. Br572C An8141 v.41.

1733. Gilberti, Maturino. *Arte de la lengua tarasca ó de Michoacán*. N. León, ed. Tipográfia de la oficina impresora del Timbre, México, 1898. 344 p. Br498.27 TG 37.

1734. Gillan, M. M. North and South America for 1,000 years, n.d. 44 p. Br970 G413.

1735. Gillman, Henry. Certain characteristics pertaining to ancient man in Michigan. *Annual Report of the United States National Museum, Smithsonian Institution, for 1875*, pp. 234-245, 1876. Br572C An8141 v.20.

1736. Gillman, Henry. The mound builders and platycnemism in Michigan. *Annual Report of the United States National Museum, Smithsonian Institution, for 1873*, pp. 364-390, 1874. Br572C An8141 v.20.

1737. Gilman, Benjamin I. Chinese musical system. *Philosophical Review* 1(1): 54-178, 1892. Br572C An8141 v.82.

1738. Gilman, Daniel C. *The Sheffield Scientific School of Yale University: A Semi-Centennial Historical Discourse*. Sheffield Scientific School, New Haven, 1897. 39 p. Br572C An8141 v.152.

1739. Gilmour, Richard. History of the New Testament, translated into Chinook by Paul Durieu, 1894. 20 p. Br497.19 CG425.

1740. Gilmour, Richard. History of the Old Testament, translated into Chinook by Paul Durieu. n.d. 24 p. Br497.19 CG425.

1741. Giorda, Joseph. *A Dictionary of the Kalispel or Flat-Head Indian Language*. St. Ignatius Print, St. Ignatius, Montana, 1877-1879. 2 v. Br497.46 KG43. Based on the manuscript dictionary of Rev. Gregory Mengarini, comprises Kalispel to English and English to Kalispel dictionaries, and was printed by Indian boys at the Saint Ignatius Mission School at Flathead Agency on the Jocko Resdervation in Montana.

1742. Giral del Pino, Hipólito San Joseph. *A Dictionary, Spanish and English, and English and Spanish; Containing the Signification of Words, With Their Different Uses; the Terms of Arts, Sciences, and Trades; the Constructions, Forms of Speech, Idioms Used in Both Languages, and Several Thousand Words More Than Any Other Dictionary; With Their Proper, Figurative, Burlesque, and Cant Significations, &c.; Also the Spanish Words Accented and Spelled According to the Modern Observations of the Royal Spanish Academy of Madrid.* Printed for A. Millar, J. Nourse, and P. Vaillant, in the Strand, London, 1763 2 v. Br463.1 D37.

1743. Girard de Rialle, Julien. *La mythologie comparée.* C. Reinwald, Paris, 1878. 363 p. Br270.1 R35.

1744. Giraud, Léopold. L'homme fossile, 1860. 30 p. Br572C An8141 v.24.

1745. Gomme, Laurence. On the method of determining the value of folklore as ethnological data. *Report of the Ethnographical Survey of the United Kingdom*, pp. 626-656. Spottiswoode, London, 1896. Br572C An8141 v.150.

1746. González Holguín, Diego. *Gramática y arte neuva de la lengua general de todo el Peru llamada lengua qquichua o lengua del inca.* Nueva ed. rev. y corr. Pagano, Genova, 1842. 320 p. Br498.7 KG 585.2.

1747. González Holguín, Diego. *Vocabvlario dela lengva general de todo el Perv llamada lengua quichua, o del Inca; corregido y renovado conforme ala propriedad cortesana del Cuzco; diuidido en dos libros, que son dos vocabularios enteros en que salen a luz de nueuo las cosas q[ue] faltauan al vocabulario; y la suma de las cosas que se aumentan se vea enla hoja siguiente.* Por Francisco del Canto, Impresso enla Ciudad de los Reyes, 1608. 375, 332 p. Br498.7 KG 585.

1748. González Suarez, Federico. *Estudio histórico sobre los Cañaris, antiguos habitantes de la provincia del Azuay en la República del Ecuador.* Quito, 1878. 54 p. Br572C An8141 v.95.

1749. González, Darío. *Lecciones de geografía.* San Salvador, 1877. 243 p. Br917.28 G583.

1750. Good, John B. *The Office for Public Baptism and the Order of Confirmation, With Select Hymns and Prayers, Translated Into the Neklakapamuk or Thompson Tongue for the Use of the Indians of the St. Paul's Mission, Lytton, British Columbia.* Printed by the St. Paul's Mission Press (S.P.C.K.), Victoria, B.C., 1879. 32 p. Br497.46 NC433.

1751. Goode, George B. *An Account of the Smithsonian Institution; Its Origin, History, Objects, and Achievements.* City for Washington for Distribution at the Atlanta Exposition, Washington, DC, 1895. n.p. Br61 Sm5.22.

1752. Goode, George B. Report upon the condition and progress of the United States National Museum (during the year ending June 30, 1888). *Annual Report of the United States National Museum, Smithsonian Institution, for 1888*, pp. 3-84, 1890. Br572C An8141 v.17.

1753. Goode, George B. The museums of the future. *Annual Report of the United States*

National Museum, Smithsonian Institution, for 1889, pp. 427–445, 1891. Br572C An8141 v.17.

1754. Gordon, George B. *Caverns of Copán, Honduras; Report on Explorations by the Museum, 1896–1897.* Memoirs of the Peabody Museum of American Archaeology and Ethnology, Harvard University, 1(5), 1898. 12 p. Br913.7283 G653.2. George Byron Gordon (1870–1927) was born in New Perth, Prince Edward Island, Canada. His archaeological career began in 1892 when he was appointed surveyor for the Peabody Museum's second expedition to the Maya site of Copán, Honduras. He returned to Copán as the director of the Peabody Museum's Fourth Copán Expedition. In 1903 he became assistant curator of the Free Museum of Science and Art (University of Pennsylvania Museum) and the following year was made curator of anthropology and lecturer in anthropology. In 1907 he was promoted to assistant professor of anthropology, a position he held until 1915. As one of the first doctorates in anthropology in the United States, Gordon (Harvard, 1903) was instrumental in the professionalization of anthropology. In 1910 Gordon was appointed director of the University of Pennsylvania Museum and, under his guidance, the Museum became known as one of the world's foremost scientific institutions.

1755. Gordon, George B. *Prehistoric Ruins of Copán, Honduras: A Preliminary Report of the Explorations by the Museum, 1891–1895.* Memoirs of the Peabody Museum of American Archaeology and Ethnology, Harvard University, 1(1), 1896. Cambridge, MA. Br572C An8141 v.161.

1756. Gordon, George B. *Researches in the Uloa Valley, Honduras.* Memoirs of the Peabody Museum of American Archaeology and Ethnology, Harvard University, 1(4), 1898. 44 p. Br913.7283 G653.

1757. *Gospel Jon ecamanaci; The Gospel of S. John, Translated into the Yahgan Language.* The British and Foreign Bible Society, London, 1886. 94 p. Br498.9783 YB 47.4.

1758. *Gospel of St. Matthew Translated into the Slave Language for the Indians of North-West America, in the Syllabic Character.* Printed for the British and Foreign Bible Society, London, 1886. 86 p. Br497.12 SlB 47.1.

1759. *Gospels According to St. Matthew, St. Mark, St. Luke, and St. John, Translated into the Language of the Esquimaux Indians, On the Coast of Labrador; By the Missionaries of the Unitas Fratrum; or, United Brethren, Residing at Nain, Okkak, and Hopedale.* Printed for the use of the mission, by the British and Foreign Bible Society. Printed by W. M'Dowall, London, 1813. 416 p. Br497.25 LB 47.5. Translation of the Gospels into Innuit.

1760. Gosse, Louis A. Instructions ethnologiques pour le Mexique, pp. 211–236, 1862. Br572C An8141 v.10.

1761. Gosse, Louis A. Sur les anciennes races du Pérou. *Bulletin de la Société d'Anthropologie de Paris* 1:549–557, 1860. Br572C An8141 v.10.

1762. Gosse, Louis A. Sur les races qui composaient l'ancienne population du Pérou. *Memoirs de la Société d'Anthropologie de Paris* 1:149–176, 1863. Br572C An8141 v.10.

1763. Goupil, E. Eugène. *Documents pour servir à l'histoire du Mexique; catalogue raisonné de la collection de m. E.-Eugène Goupil (ancienne collection J.-M.-A. Aubin); manuscrits figuratifs, et autres sur papier indigène d'agave mexicana et sur papier européen antérieures et portérieures à la conquête du Mexique (XVIe siècle)... avec une introduction de m. E.-Eugène Guopil et une lettre-préface de m. Auguste Génin.* Jean Maisonneuve, Paris, 1891. 2 v. and atlas of 80 plates. Br972D B63.4.

1764. Gourgues, Dominique de. La reprinse de la Florida, par le cappitaine Gourgue, 1875. Br917.57 G744. Extract from *Historical collections of Louisiana and Florida*, Benjamin F. French, ed., 2d ser., pp. 265–289. New York, 1875.

1765. Grabowsky, F. Die Lübbensteine bei Helmstedt. *Beiträge zur Anthropologie Braunschweigs* 21:39–58, 1898. Br572C An8141 v.164.

1766. Graffarel, Paul. Les Irlandais en Amérique. *Revue de Géographie*, 1890. 35 p. Br572C An8141 v.7.

1767. *Gramática de la lengua zapoteca.* Oficina Tipografica de la Secretaría de Fomento, México, 1887. 148 p. Br498.34 ZG 765.

1768. *Gramatica frases, oraciones, cathezismos, confessonario y vocabulario de la lengua chibcha*, pp. 231–295. Quijano, Bogotá, 1620. Br498.64 MG 763.

1769. Gramatzky, Dr. Bulletin critique. *T'oung Pao; archives pour servir à l'etude de l'histoire des langues, de la géographie et de l'ethnographie de Asie Orientale.* n.d. 20 p. Br572C An 8141 v.139.

1770. *Grammar of the Cakchiquel Language of Guatemala; Translated From a Manuscript in the Library of the American Philosophical Society, With an Introduction and Additions by Daniel G. Brinton.* McCalla and Stavely, Philadelphia, 1884. 72 p. Br498.21 Car 78 EB. This translation originally appeared in the *Proceedings of the American Philsosophical Society*, no. 115.

1771. Granados y Gálvez, José Joaquín. *Tardes americanas; gobierno gentil y catolico; breve y particular noticia de toda la historia indiana; sucesos, casos notables, y cosas ignoradas, desde la entrada de la gran nación tulteca á esta tierra de Anahuac, hasta los presentes tiempos.* En la nueva imprenta matritense de D. F. de Zúñiga y Ontiveros, México, 1778. 540 p. Br970.4 MG766. Written in form of a dialogue between an Indian and a Spaniard.

1772. Granger, Frank S. *The Worship of the Romans Viewed in Relation to the Roman Temperament.* Methuen and Company, London, 1895. 313 p. Br282 G76.

1773. Granger, Henry G., and Edward B. Treville Quibdo. Mining districts of Colombia. *Transactions of the American Institute of Mining Engineers*, 1898. 51 p. Br572C An8141 v.166.

1774. Gratacap, Louis P. Opinions upon clay stones and concretions. *American Naturalist* 18:882–892, 1884. Br572C An8141 v.13.

1775. Gratiolet, Louis P. Description d'un crane de mexicain Totonaque des environs d'Orizaba. *Memoirs de la Société d'Anthropologie de Paris* 1:391–398, 1860–1863. Br572C An8141 v.12.

1776. Gratiolet, Louis P. Sur un crane de Totonaque, pp. 561–565, 1860. Br572C An8141 v.12.

1777. Gravier, Gabriel. Étude sur le sauvage du Brésil. *Bulletin de la Société Normande de Géographie*, 1880, 1881. 63 p. Br572C An8141 v.37.

1778. Gregor, Walter. Preliminary report on folklore in Galloway, Scotland. *Report of the Ethnographical Survey of the United Kingdom*, pp. 612–626. Spottiswoode, London, 1896. Br572C An8141 v.150.

1779. Griffis, William E. *The Influence of the Netherlands in the Making of the English Commonwealth and the American Republic*. De Wolfe, Fiske, Boston, 1891. 40 p. Br572C An8141 v.7.

1780. Grimes, J. S. *Mental Anthropology*. R. R. Donnelley and Sons, The Lakeside Press, Chicago, 1887. 16 p. Br572C An8141 v.129.

1781. Grosse, E. *Die Anfänge der Kunst*. Akademische Verlagsbuchhandlung von J. L. B. Mohr, Freiburg I. B. und Leipzig, 1894. 301 p. Br572C An8141 v.133.

1782. Grosse, Ernst. Über den ethnologischen Unterricht, n.d. 10 p. Br572C An8141 v.152.

1783. Grossi, Vicenzo. Antropofagia e sacrifizi umani nell America precolombina. *Proceedings of the International Congress of Americanists* (7 session, Berlin, 1888), 1888. Br572C An8141 v.11.

1784. Grossi, Vicenzo. Corso libero con effeti legali di etnologia americana. Genova, 1889. 3 p. Br572C An8141 v.122.

1785. Grossi, Vicenzo. Diritto e morale nel Messico antico. *Proceedings of the International Congress of Americanists* (7 session, Berlin, 1888), 1888. 349 p. Br572C An8141 v.11.

1786. Grossi, Vicenzo. Elenco delle pubblicazioni scientifico-letterarie. Genova, 1891. 3 p. Br572C An8141 v.122.

1787. Grossi, Vicenzo. *Folk-lore brasiliano*. Tipografía di Angelo Ciminago, Genova, 1891. 22 p. Br572C An8141 v.122.

1788. Grossi, Vicenzo. *Folk-lore peruviano*. Filotechnico, fasc I–III, 1888. 22 p. Br572C An8141 v.37.

1789. Grossi, Vicenzo. Fra gli eschimesi delle Isole Aleutine. *Ateneo Ligure*, fasc. I–III. Genova, 1890. 23 p. Br572C An8141 v.11.

1790. Grossi, Vicenzo. *Geografia commerciale dell'America del Sud. Italo-Americana esposizione comerciale*. Stabilimento Artisti Tipografi, Genova, 1890. 63 p. Br572C An8141 v.7.

1791. Grossi, Vicenzo. *Geografia medica del Brasile*. Tipografia di Angelo Ciminago, Genova, 1890. 44 p. Br572C An8141 v.7.

1792. Grossi, Vicenzo. *L'idrografia dello stato brasiliano di S. Paolo e l'esplorazione dei fiumi Itapetininga e Paranapanema*. Tipografía G. Derossi, Torino, 1892. 15 p. Br572C An8141 v.122.

1793. Grossi, Vicenzo. La cremazione fra i moderni non-Europei. *Rivista di Filosofia Scientifica*, serie 2, v. 7, 1888. 43 p. Br572C An8141 v.11; Br572C An8141 v.29.

1794. Grossi, Vicenzo. *La cremazione nell'antichità storica e preistorica*. Tipografia Insubria, Milano, 1893. 27 p. Br572C An8141 v.122.

1795. Grossi, Vicenzo. *La questione dei cosidetti precursori di Colombo in America; conferenza tenuta alla sede Società Geografica di Rio de Janeiro la sera delli 19 settembre 1891*. Tipografía G. Derossi, Torino, 1892. 19 p. Br572C An8141 v.122.

1796. Grossi, Vicenzo. *La relazione e la carta dei viaggi dei fratelli Zeno nel nord*. Tipografía G. Derossi, Torino, 1887. 23 p. Br572C An8141 v.122.

1797. Grossi, Vicenzo. *Le leggende delle piramidi*. Tipografía di Angelo Ciminago, Genova, 1890. 38 p. Br572C An8141 v.122.

1798. Grossi, Vicenzo. *Le mummie nell'antico e nel Nuovo Mondo*. Torino, 1888. Br572C An8141 v.11.

1799. Grossi, Vicenzo. Lingue, letteratura e tradizione popolari degli indigeni d'America. *Ateneo Ligure*, fasc. I–III, 1890. 59 p. Br572C An8141 v.11.

1800. Grossi, Vicenzo. *Relazione sommaria del VI Congresso Internazionale degli Americanisti*. Presso la Societa Geografica Italiana, Roma, 1886. Br572C An8141 v.83.

1801. Grossi, Vicenzo. *Teocalli e piramidi*. Torino, 1888. 17 p. Br572C An8141 v.11.

1802. Grossi, Vicenzo. *Una questione du geografia antropologica (l'origine degli americani)*. Tipografía G. Derossi, Torino, 1891. 16 p. Br572C An8141 v.122.

1803. Grossman, F. E. The Pima Indians of Arizona. *Annual Report of the United States National Museum, Smithsonian Institution, for 1871*, pp. 407-419. Br572C An8141 v.19.

1804. Grote, August R. On the peopling of America. *Bulletin of the Buffalo Society of Natural Sciences*, 1877. 6 p. Br572C An8141 v.58.

1805. Grote, Augustus R. Stone Age of North America. *Popular Science Monthly*, pp. 78-79, n.d. Br571.1 G89.5.

1806. Guede, Henry. Aide-mémoire d'antropologie et d'ethnographie. J.B. Baillière et fils, Paris, 1898. 282 p. Br572 G933.

1807. Guerra, José María. *Pastoral del illustrisimo señor obispo D. José María Guerra, dirigida a los indígenas de esta diócesis; traducida en lengua maya por J. C. Vela*. Impreso por Antonio Petra Mérida de Yucatán, 1848. 8 p. Br498.21 MG93. A pastoral letter to the rebel Maya, in Spanish and Yucatec, by Bishop José María Guerra, and translated into Yucatec by José Canuto Vela.

1808. Guest, W. E. Ancient Indian remains near Prescott, C.U. *Annual Report of the United States National Museum, Smithsonian Institution, for 1857*, pp. 271-276, 1857. Br572C An8141 v.19.

1809. Gumilla, Joseph. *El Orinoco, ilustrado y defendido, historia natural, civil, y geographica de este gran rio y de sus caudalosas vertientes; govierno, usos y costumbres de los Indios sus habitadores*. Fernandez, Madrid, 1745. 412 p. Br918.7 G955. "Gumilla was born in 1690 and appointed Superior of the Missions of Orinoco, and more than once traveled along the shores of almost the entire course of this great river. As late as 1745 he returned from Spain to America, but the period and place of his death is unknown" (Field 1873:151).

1810. Gummere, Francis B. *On the Symbolic Use of the Colors Black and White in German Tradition*. Haverford College Studies, 1, n.d. 52 p. Br572C An8141 v.29.

1811. Gunckel, Lewis W. Analysis of the deities of Mayan inscriptions. *American Anthropologist* 10:397-412, 1897. Br572C An8141 v.152.

1812. Gunckel, Lewis W. The direction in which Maya inscriptions should be read. *American Anthropologist* 10:146-162, 1897. Br572C An8141 v.152.

1813. Gunckell, Lewis W. The study of American hieroglyphs. *American Antiquarian* 19, 1897. 16 p. Br572C An8141 v.152.

1814. Gurdon, Eveline C. *Suffolk*. Publications of the Folk-Lore Society 37(2). D. Nutt, London, 1893. 202 p. Br398.3 G963.

1815. Guss, Abraham L. Early Indian history on the Susquehanna. *Historical Register* 1(3-4), 1883. 32 p. Br572C An8141 v.27.

1816. Guss, Abraham L. Early view of the Pennsylvania interior: the Juniata and the Tuscarora Indians; explorations of the Indian traders. In *History of Juniata and Other Counties in Pennsylvania*, pp. 25-80, 1883. Br572C An8141 v.96.

1817. Guyot, Arnold H. *Maka-oyakapi, Elementary Geography in the Dakota Language, Translated by S. R. Riggs and A. S. Riggs*. Scribner, New York, 1876. 83 p. Br497.5 DSG99.

1818. Guyot, Arnold H. *Makoce wowapi wakan kin en cajeyatapi kin, Geography of the Bible Lands*. Scribner, New York, 1876. 4 p. Br497.5 DSG99.

1819. Guzmán, Pantaleón de. Libro yntitulado Compendio de nombres en lengua cakchiquel y significados de verbos por ymperativo y aculativos reciprocos en doce tratados por el Pe. Predicador. F. Pantaleón de Guzmán; cura doctrinero por el real patronato de esta doctrina y curato de Santa María de Jesús Paché; en veinte dias del mes de octubre, de mil setecientos y quatro años. 323 p. Br498.21 CG999. Manuscript, transcribed by Karl H. Berendt. Comprises a vocabulary list, dated October 20, 1704, of terms in Cakchiquel with their Spanish equivalents, compiled by Father Pantaleon de Guzmán of Santa María de Jesús in Sacatepequez, Guatemala. The list is arranged in twelve sections, with each section containing nouns relating to a particular topic, such as the botany, zoology, or customs of the Cakchiquel Indians. Topics include types of trees, edible and medicinal herbs, precious stones, flints, metals, planets, animals, snakes, fish, birds, illnesses, parts of the body, and common proverbs. There are also sections containing imperative and reflexive verb forms, family relationships, prayers and devotions, creeds, catechisms, religious songs, and riddles. The manuscript concludes with a list of addenda and a table of contents.

1820. Guzmán, Pantaleón de. Traslado este vocabulario el sobredicho Pe. el año de 1620 años en la provincia de los Tzeldales en el pueblo de Taquinvitz, n.d. 221 leaves. Br498.21 TzG 999. Manuscript.

1821. Habel, M.A. *Voyage dans la partie tropicale des deux Amériques*. Gauthier-Villars, Imprimeur-Librarie des comptes rendus de l'Académie des Sciences, 1869. 4 p. Br572C An8141 v.93.

1822. Habel, S. *The Sculptures of Santa Lucia Cosumalwhuapa* [sic] *in Guatemala; With an Account of Travels in Central America and on the Western Coast of South America*. Smithsonian Institution, Contributions to Knowledge, 269. Washington, DC, 1878. 90 p. Br572C An8141 v.93.

1823. Habenicht, Hermann. Einige Gedanken über die hauptsächlichsten recenten Veränderungen der Erdoberfläche, 1882. 31 p. Br572C An8141 v.26.

1824. Haberlandt, Michael. *Völkerkunde*. G. J. Göschen, Leipzig, 1898. 200 p. Br572 H112.

1825. Haddon, Alfred C. *Evolution in Art; as Illustrated by the Life-Histories of Designs*. The Walter Scott Press, Newcastle-on-Tyne, 1895. 364 p. Br701 H115. A. C. Haddon (1855-1940) is generally regarded as the father of anthropology at Cambridge University. Initially interested in marine biology, Haddon gradually involved himself in anthropology. During 1888-1889 he visited the Torres Straits between New Guinea and Australia. His second trip to the Torres Straits in 1898-1899 was the first multidisciplinary expedition of its kind and was a milestone in the history of anthropology. At Cambridge Haddon was a major force in the development of an anthropological curriculum and was an important figure in the Museum of Archaeology and Ethnology. His chief scholarly interests were in physical anthropology and the decorative arts.

1826. Haddon, Alfred C. *The Study of Man*. G. P. Putnam's Sons; Bliss, Sands, and Company, New York, London, 1898. 410 p. Br572 H115.

1827. Haddon, Alfred C. Woodcarving in the Trobriands. *Illustrated Archaeologist*, pp. 107-112, 1893. Br572C An8141 v.113.

1828. Haebler, K. Die Maya-Litteratur und der Maya-Apparat zu Dresden. *Centrallblatt für Bibliothekswesen* 12(12): 537-576, 1895. Br572C An8141 v.140.

1829. Haefkens, J. *Centraal Amerika uit een geschiedkundig, aardrijkskundig en statistiek oogpunt beschouwd*. Bij Blussé en Van Braam, Te Dordrecht, 1832. 488 p. Br972.8 H13.

1830. Haeser, Heinrich. Lehrbuch der Geschichte der Medicin und der Volkskrankheiten. Mauke, Jena, 1845. 922 p. Br619.9 H115.2.

1831. Hahn, E. *Demeter und Baubo versuch einer Theorie der Entstehung unseres Uckerbaus*. Druck von Max Schmidt, Lübeck, 1896. 77 p. Br572C An8141 v.153.

1832. Hahn, J. G. von. *Mythologische Parallelen*. F. Mauke, Jena, 1859. 191 p. Br270 H123. Analysis of parallels in Norse and Greek mythology.

1833. Halbert, Henry S. Courtship and marriage among the Choctaws of Mississippi. *American Naturalist* 16:222-224, 1882. Br572C An8141 v.13.

1834. Halcombe, J. J. *Stranger Than Fiction*. S. P. C. K., London, 1882. 275 p. Br970.1 H127.

1835. Haldeman, Samuel S. On a polychrome bead from Florida. *Annual Report of the United States National Museum, Smithsonian Institution, for 1877*, pp. 302-305, 1878. Br572C An8141 v.39.

1836. Haldeman, Samuel S. On the contents of a rock retreat in south-eastern Pennsylvania. *Transactions of the American Philosophical Society* 15(4b): 351-368, 1878. Br572C An8141 v.97.

1837. Hale, Edwin M. Anhalonium, mescal buttons. *Hahnemannian Monthly*, 1896. 8 p. Br615.781 H13.

1838. Hale, Edwin M. *Ilex cassine: The Aboriginal North American Tea; Its History, Distribution, and Use Among the Native North American Indians*. United States Department of Agriculture, Division of Botany, Bulletin 14, 1891. Washington, DC. 22 p. Br572C An8141 v.11.

1839. Hale, Horatio E. An Iroquois condoling council: A study of aboriginal American society and government. *Transactions of the Royal Society of Canada* 1(2): 45-65,

1895. Br572C An8141 v.140. After graduation from Harvard in 1837, Hale (1817-1896) was appointed philologist of the United States South Seas Exploring Expedition. During this voyage (1838-1842) he collected vocabularies and sketched grammars of various Oceanic dialects. He confirmed the affinity of Malayan and Polynesian languages and advanced a theory based on phonetic shifts to establish the eastward migration of Polynesian peoples. After a career as a lawyer and administrator, Hale concentrated on the Iroquoian linguistics. He demonstrated that Tutelo was a Siouan language and discovered Mohawk and Onondaga versions of the ritual texts of the Iroquois ceremony for mourning and installing League chiefs (*The Iroquois Book of Rites*).

1840. Hale, Horatio E. Fourth report of the Committee on the northwestern tribes of the Dominion of Canada, 1885. 23 p. Br572C An8141 v.57.

1841. Hale, Horatio E. Indian migrations, as evidenced by language. *American Antiquarian* 5:18-28, 108-124, 1883. Br572C An8141 v.55; Br572C An8141 v.57.

1842. Hale, Horatio E. Language as a test of mental capacity; being an attempt to demonstrate the true basis of anthropology. *Transactions of the Royal Society of Canada* 9(2): 77-11, 1891. Br572C An8141 v.107.

1843. Hale, Horatio E. On some doubtful or intermediate articulations: an experiment in phonetics. *Journal of the Anthropological Institute* 14(3): 233-243, 1885. Br572C An8141 v.57.

1844. Hale, Horatio E. Race and language. *Popular Science Monthly*, January, pp. 340-351, 1888. Br572C An8141 v.57.

1845. Hale, Horatio E. *Remarks on North American Ethnology, Introductory to the Report on the Indians of British Columbia.* British Association for the Advancement of Science, Committee…on the…Northwestern Tribes of the Dominion of Canada, Report 5. London, 1889. 5 p. Br572C An8141 v.57.

1846. Hale, Horatio E. *Report on the Blackfoot Tribes.* British Association for the Advancement of Science, 1885. 12 p. Br572C An8141 v.57.

1847. Hale, Horatio E. The Aryans in science and history. *Popular Science Monthly* 34(5): 672-686, 1889. Br572C An8141 v.57.

1848. Hale, Horatio E. *The Development of Language.* Copp, Clark Company, Toronto, 1888. 45 p. Br572C An8141 v.57; Br572C An8141 v.84.

1849. Hale, Horatio E. *The Iroquois Book of Rites.* Library of Aboriginal American Literature, 2. D. G. Brinton, Philadelphia, 1883. 222 p. Br897C B776. Contents include: Mohawk text with English translation of the ancient rites of the condoling council (pp. 116-139), and Onondaga text with English translation of the Book of the Younger Nations (pp. 140-145).

1850. Hale, Horatio E. The Iroquois sacrifice of the white dog. *American Antiquarian* 7:7-14, 1885. Br572C An8141 v.57.

1851. Hale, Horatio E. The origin of languages and the antiquity of speaking man; an address before the American Association for the Advancement of Science, at Buffalo, August 1886. *Proceedings of the American Association for the Advancement of Science* 35, 1886. 47 p. Br572C An8141 v.57.

1852. Hale, Horatio E. The Tutelo tribe and language. *Proceedings of the American Philosophical Society* 21:1–47, 1883. Br572C An8141 v.57.

1853. Hale, Horatio E. *United States Exploring Expedition; During Two Years 1838, 1839, 1840, 1841, 1842; Under the Command of Charles Wilkes, United States Navy; v. II: Ethnography and Philology, by Horatio Hale, Philologist of the Expedition.* C. Sherman, Philadelphia, 1846. 666 p. Br572 H13. Charles Wilkes, a standard bearer of Manifest Destiny, was appointed to command the United States Exploring Expedition in 1838. The Expedition surveyed and charted islands and harbors around the world as well as 800 miles of coastal and inland waterways of Oregon Territory. The Wilkes Expedition helped to establish the United States Navy as a presence in the Pacific and in the world.

1854. Hale, Horatio. The origin of primitive money. *Popular Science Monthly*, January, pp. 296–307, 1886. Br572C An8141 v.57.

1855. Halfmoon, Charles. *A Collection of Muncey and English Hymns, for the Use of the Native Indians.* Missionary Society of the Wesleyan Methodist Church in Canada, Toronto, 1842. 206 p. Br497.11 MuH 13.

1856. Haliburton, Robert G. *How A Race of Pygmies Was Found in North Africa and Spain With Comments of Professors Virchow, Sayce and Starr; and Papers on Other Subjects.* Arbuthnot, Toronto, 1897. 147 p. Br573.8 H13.

1857. Haliburton, Robert G. *The Dwarfs of Mount Altas; With Notes as to Dwarfs and Dwarf Worship.* Alexander and Shepheard, London, 1891. 41 p. Br572C An8141 v.135.

1858. Haliburton, Robert G. *The Holy Land of Punt and Racial Dwarfs in the Atlas and the Pyrennes, Etc.* Alexander and Shepheard, London, 1893. 17 p. Br572C An8141 v.135.

1859. Hall, Alfred J. A grammar of the Kwagiutl language. *Transactions of the Royal Society of Canada* 6(2): 59–105, 1888. Br572C An8141 v.92.

1860. Hall, Alfred J. *A Kwagutl Version of the Book of Common Prayer.* Society for Promoting Christian Knowledge, London, 1891. 62 p. Br497.59 KwC47. Church of England Book of Common Prayer translated into Kwakiutl.

1861. Hall, C. W., and F. W. Sardeson. Paleozoic formations of southeastern Minnesota. *Bulletin of the Geological Society of America* 3, 1891. Br572C An8141 v.125.

1862. Hall, J. Yucatan. *American Monthly*, pp. 107–125, 1864. Br572C An8141 v.165.

1863. Halloy, Jean Baptiste, d'Omalius d'. *Manuel pratique d'ethnographie, ou description des races humaines, les différents peuples, leurs caracteres naturels, leurs caracteres sociaux, divisions et subdivisions des différentes races humaines.* 5th ed. Lacroix, Paris, 1864. 127 p. Br572 H154; Br572 H154a.

1864. Hamilton, James C. The Great Center; an astronomical study. *Transactions of the Canadian Institute* 3:189–194, 1891–1892. Br572C An8141 v.114.

1865. Hamilton, James C. The Panis: an historical outline of Canadian Indian slavery in the 18th century. *Proceedings of the Canadian Institute* 1(1): 19–27, 1897. Br572C An8141 v.153.

1866. Hammond, William A. The disease of the Scythians. American Neurological Association, June 23, 1882. 17 p. Br572C An8141 v.40.

1867. Hamy, Ernest T. An interpretation of one of the Copán monuments (Honduras). *Journal of the Anthropological Institute* 16(3): 242-247, 1887. Br572C An8141 v.44. Trained as a physician, in 1868 Hamy (1842-1908) became Paul Broca's assistant at the École des Hautes Études and began teaching a course on comparative anatomy at the Sorbonne. His publication of *Crania Ethnica* in 1873 constituted the apex in the development of craniometry. Hamy later worked at the Muséum d'Histoire Naturelle and Palais du Trocadero in Paris. In 1882 he founded the *Revue d'Ethnographie*.

1868. Hamy, Ernest T. *Anthropologie du Mexique; recherches zoologiques pour servir à l'histoire de la faune de l'Amérique Centrale et du Mexique*. Imprimerie Nationale, Paris, 1884. 40 p. Br572C An8141 v.104.

1869. Hamy, Ernest T. Commentaire sur un bas-relief Aztéque de la Collection Uhde. *Revue d'Ethnographie* 2(4), 1883. 14 p. Br572C An8141 v.40.

1870. Hamy, Ernest T. Contribution à l'anthropologie du Nayarit. *Bulletin du Muséum d'Histoire Naturelle* 6:190-192, 1897. Br572C An8141 v.153.

1871. Hamy, Ernest T. Étude sur les collections américaines réunies a Gênes. *Journal de la Société des Américanistes de Paris* 1, 1896. Br913.7 H188.2.

1872. Hamy, Ernest T. *Étude sur les collections américaines; réunies a gènes à l'occasion du IVe Centenaire de la Découverte de l'Amérique*. Société des Americainistes, Paris, 1895. 31 p. Br572C An8141 v.144.

1873. Hamy, Ernest T. *Étude sur les peintures ethniques d'un Tombeau Thébain de la XVIII dynastie*. Ernest Leroux, Paris, 1885. Br572C An8141 v.82.

1874. Hamy, Ernest T. Francisque et André d'Albaigne, cosmographes lucquois au service de la France. *Bulletin de Géographie Historique et Descriptive*, 1894. 34 p. Br572C An8141 v.140.

1875. Hamy, Ernest T. L'age de la pierre dans l'arrondissement de Bien-Hoa. *Bulletin du Muséum d'Histoire Naturelle* 2:48-52, 1897. Br572C An8141 v.153.

1876. Hamy, Ernest T. L'Age de pierre au Gabon. *Bulletin du Muséum d'Histoire Naturelle* 5:154-156, 1897. Br572C An8141 v.153.

1877. Hamy, Ernest T. *L'Oeuvre ethnographique de Nicolas-Martin Petit*. Librarie de l'Académie de Medecine, Paris, 1891. 24 p. Br572C An8141 v.83.

1878. Hamy, Ernest T. La Collection Piñedo, n.d. 1 p. Br572C An8141 v.44.

1879. Hamy, Ernest T. La croix de Téotihuacan. *Revue d'Ethnographie* 5, 1882. 23 p. Br572C An8141 v.40.

1880. Hamy, Ernest T. Le fleuriste Pierre Morin Le Jeune, dit troisième. *Bulletin du Muséum d'Histoire Naturelle* 6:186-190, 1897. Br572C An8141 v.153.

1881. Hamy, Ernest T. *Le pays des Troglodytes*. Typographie de Firman-Didot et Cie., Paris, 1891. 17 p. Br572C An8141 v.103.

1882. Hamy, Ernest T. Le petit vase a figurine humaine de Santiago Tlaltelolco. *Journal de la Société des Américanistes de Paris*, 1903. 5 p. Br913.7 H188.2.

1883. Hamy, Ernest T. *Les origines du Musée d'Ethnographie histoire et documents*.

E. Leroux, Paris, 1890. 321 p. Br572 H187.

1884. Hamy, Ernest T. Les premiers habitants du Mexique. *Revue d'Anthropologie*, pp. 56–65, 1878. Br572C An8141 v.110.

1885. Hamy, Ernest T. Les races humaines de Madagascar. *Revue Scientifique*, 1895. 26 p. Br572C An8141 v.140.

1886. Hamy, Ernest T. Les races Malaïques et Américaines. *L'Anthropologie* 7(2): 129–146, 1896, 18 p. Br572C An8141 v.153.

1887. Hamy, Ernest T. *Les races nègres, leçon d'ouverture du cours d'anthropologie du museum.* Imprimerie de A. Burdin, Angers, 1897. 15 p. Br572C An8141 v.153.

1888. Hamy, Ernest T. Note sur d'anciennes peintures sur peaux des Indiens Illinois. *Journal de la Société des Américanistes de Paris*, 1899. Br913.7 H188.2.

1889. Hamy, Ernest T. Note sur la mappemonde de Diego Ribero. *Bulletin de Géographie Historique et Descriptive* 1, 1887. 10 p. Br572C An8141 v.24.

1890. Hamy, Ernest T. Note sur un masque en pierre des Indiens de la Riviére Nass, Colombie Britannique. *Journal de la Société des Américanistes de Paris*, pp. 167–170, 1897. Br572C An8141 v.160.

1891. Hamy, Ernest T. Note sur un wampum représentant les quatre-nations des Hurons. *Journal de la Société des Américanistes de Paris,* pp. 163–166, 1897. Br572C An8141 v.160.

1892. Hamy, Ernest T. Note sur une inscription chronographique de la période aztéque; appartenant au Musée du Trocadero par le Dr. E.T. Hamy, conservateur du Musée. *Revue d'Ethnographie* 2:191–202, 1883. Br572C An8141 v.40.

1893. Hamy, Ernest T. Notes sur les collections ethnographiques du Joseph Muneraty. *Journal de la Société des Américanistes de Paris*, 1898. 14 p. Br913.7 H188.2.

1894. Hamy, Ernest T. Notice sur une mappemonde portugaise anonyme de 1502. *Bulletin de Géographie Historique et Descriptive* 4, 1887. 16 p. Br572C An8141 v.24.

1895. Hamy, Ernest T. Pamphlets, 1896–1903. Br913.7 H188.2.

1896. Hamy, Ernest T. Quelques notes: La mort et la succession de Guy de la Brosse. *Bulletin du Muséum d'Histoire Naturelle* 5:152–154, 1897. Br572C An8141 v.153.

1897. Hamy, Ernest T. *Quelques observations sur l'Anthropologie des Comalis.* Typographie A. Hennuyer, Paris, 1883. 12 p. Br572C An8141 v.82.

1898. Hamy, Ernest T. Six anciens portraits d'Incas du Pérou. *Comptes Rendus de l'Académie des Inscriptions et Belles-Lettres,* 1897. 8 p. Br572C An8141 v.153.

1899. Hamy, Ernest T. *Sur lâge des anthropolithes de la Guadeloupe.* Gauthier-Villars, Imprimeur libraire des comptes rendus des Séances de l'Académie des Sciences, n.d. 3 p. Br572C An8141 v.97.

1900. Hamy, Ernest T., Abel Hovelacque, and Elie Vinson. Questionnaire de sociologie et d'ethnographie. *Bulletin de la Société d'Anthropologie de Lyon*, 1883. 24 p. Br572C An8141 v.26.

1901. Hannezo, M. Note sur des ssépultures phéniciennes; découvertes près de Mahédia (Tunisie). *L'Anthropologie* 3:161–162, 1892. Br572C An8141 v.122.

1902. Hänselmann, Ludwig. Die eingemauerten mittelalterischen Thongeschirre Braunschweigs. *Beiträge zur Anthropologie Braunschweigs* 21:91–105, 1898. Br572C An8141 v.164.

1903. Hansen, Soren. *Lagoa Santa Racen*. Bianco Lunos Kgl. Hof-Bogtrykkeri, Kjoben-havn, 1887. 37 p. Br572C An8141 v.96.

1904. Hardy, Michel. Explication de l'apparence de taille de certains silex tertiaires, 1881. 8 p. Br572C An8141 v.24.

1905. Harris, George H. *Aboriginal Occupation of the Lower Genesee Country*. D. Mason and Company, Rochester, NY, 1884. 96 p. Br572C An8141 v.1.

1906. Harrison, Charles. Haida grammar. *Transactions of the Royal Society of Canada* 1:123–266, 1895. Br497.51 HH24; Br572C An8141 v.153.

1907. Harrison, Charles. *Saint Matthew gie giatlan las; The Gospel According to St. Matthew Translated into the Haida by Charles Harrison*. British and Foreign Bible Society, London, 1891. 143 p. Br497.51 HB47.1.

1908. Harrison, J. Park. On the relative length of the first three toes of the human foot. *Journal of the Anthropological Institute of Great Britain and Ireland* 13(3): 258–269, 1884. Br572C An8141 v.67.

1909. Harrison, William H. *A Discourse on the Aborigines of the Valley of the Ohio in Which the Opinions of the Conquest of That Valley by the Iroquois, or Six Nations, in the Seventeenth Century, Supported by Cadwallader Colden, Governor Pownal, Dr. Franklin, the Hon. De Witt Clinton and Judge Haywood, Are Examined and Contested; To Which Are Prefixed Some Remarks on the Study of History*. Printed at the Cincinnati Express, Cincinnati, 1838. 51 p. Br913 H24.5. Harrison (1773–1841) served as a military officer in the Northwest Indian Wars (1791–1794), as Indiana territorial governor (1800–1813), and as Indian treaty negotiator (1814–1815)

1910. Harrisse, Henry. *A Brief Disquisition Concerning the Early History of Printing in America*. Privately Printed at the Bradstreet Press, New York, 1866, 18 p. Br655.173 H245. Extract from the *Bibliotheca Americana vetustissima*, pp. 365–377.

1911. Harrisse, Henry. *Bibliotheca Americana Vetustissima; A Description of Works Relating to America Published Between the Years 1492 and 1551*. G. Philes, New York, 1866. 519 p. Br970B H245.

1912. Harrisse, Henry. New York book stalls, 1864. 29 p. Br90 H245. Bound with: Books grand and peculiar; and Columbus in a nutshell.

1913. Harrisse, Henry. *Notes pour servir à l'histoire, à la bibliographie et à la cartographie de la Nouvelle-France et des pays adjacents 1545-1700*. Tross, Paris, 1872. 367 p. Br971B H245.

1914. Harrisse, Henry. When did John Cabot discover North America. *Forum*, pp. 463–476, 1897. Br973.1 H247.

1915. Harshberger, John W. A botanical excursion to Mexico, 1896. *American Journal of Pharmacy* 68(11), 1896. 5 p. Br572C An8141 v.153.

1916. Harshberger, John W. Maize: a botanical and economic study. *Contributions from the Botanical Laboratory of the University of Pennsylvania* 1(2): 75–202, 1893. Br572C An8141 v.113.

1917. Harshberger, John W. The purposes of ethno-botany. *Botanical Gazette* 21:146-154, 1896. Br572C An8141 v.140.

1918. Hart, Charles H. Memoir of Lewis H. Morgan of Rochester, New York. *Proceedings of the Numismatic and Antiquarian Society of Philadelphia for 1882*, pp. 3-12, 1883. Br572C An8141 v.58.

1919. Hartland, E. Sidney. Ethnographical survey of the United Kingdom. *Transactions of the Bristol and Gloucestershire Archaeological Society*, n.d. 11 p. Br572C An8141 v.153.

1920. Hartland, E. Sidney. On an inscribed leaden tablet found at Dymock, in Gloucestershire. *Reliquary and Illustrated Archaeologist*, 1897. 11 p. Br572C An8141 v.153.

1921. Hartland, Edwin S. *The Science of Fairy Tales; An Inquiry Into Fairy Mythology*. Scribner and Welford, New York, 1891. 372 p. Br398.4 H263.

1922. Hartmann, Robert. Anthropoiden Mafuca des Dresdener zoologischen Gartens. *Verhandlungen der Berliner Gesellschaft für Anthropologie, Ethnologie und Urgeschichte*, pp. 20-26, 1875. Br572C An8141 v.162.

1923. Hartt, Charles F. Brazilian rock inscriptions. *American Naturalist* 5(3): 139-147, 1871. Br572C An8141 v.37.

1924. Hartt, Charles F. Descripção dos objectos de pedra de origem indigena conservados no Museu nacional. *Archivos do Museu Nacional do Rio de Janeiro* 1:45-75, 1876. Br572C An8141 v.90.

1925. Hartt, Charles F. Notes on the Lingoa Geral or modern Tupí of the Amazonas. *Transactions of the American Philological Association*, 1872. 20 p. Br572C An8141 v.52; Br572C An8141 v.81.

1926. Hartt, Charles F. O mytho do Curupira. *Aurora Brasiliera; journal dos estudantes brasileiros na Universidade de Cornelli* 1-2:1-12, 1873. Br572C An8141 v.60.

1927. Haumonté, J. D., J. Parisot, and L. Adam, *Grammaire et vocabulaire de la langue taensa*. Bibliothèque Linguistique Américaine, 9. Maisonneuve, Paris, 1882. 111 p. Br497C Am3.

1928. Haupt, Paul. Report of the International Congress of Orientalists. *Annual Report of the United States National Museum, Smithsonian Institution, for 1890*, pp. 85-92, 1891. Br572C An8141 v.86.

1929. Haupt, Paul. Wo lag das Paradies? *Sonder-Abdruck aus Über Land und Meer, Deutsche Illustrirte Zeitung* 15, 1894-1895. 8 p. Stuttgart. Br572C An8141 v.144.

1930. Hauser, O. *Das Amphitheater Vindonissa*. Zürich: E. Hull, 1898. 15 p. Br572C An8141 v.153.

1931. Hauser, Otto. Die neuesten Ausgrabungen in Baden. *Anzeiger für Schweizerische Altertumskunde*, 1896. 4 p. Br571.3 H295.

1932. Hauthal, Rodolfo, Santiago Roth, and Robert Lehmann-Nitsche. *El Mamífero misterioso de la Patagonia Grypotherium domestixum*. Publicaciones del Museo, La Plata, 1899. 65 p. Br913.82 H297. Contents include: 1. R. Hauthal, "Reseña de los hallazgos en las cavernas de Ultima Esperanza, Patagonia austral"; 2. S. Roth, "Descripción de los restos encontrados en la caverna de Ultima Esperanza"; 3. R. Lehmann-Nitsche, "Coexistencia del hombre con un gran desdentado y un

Samuel F. Haven (from Justin Winsor, Aboriginal America. *Cambridge, MA: Houghton, Mifflin, 1889. p. 374).*

equino en las cavernas patagónicas"; 4. Christfried Jacob, "Exámen microscópico de la pieza cutánea del mamifero misterioso de la patagonia, Grypotherium domesticum."

1933. Havard, V. The mezquit. *American Naturalist* 18:451-459, 1884. Br572C An8141 v.13.

1934. Haven, Samuel F. *Archaeology of the United States; or, Sketches, Historical and Bibliographical, of the Progress of Information and Opinion Respecting Vestiges of Antiquity in the United States.* Smithsonian Institution Contributions to Knowledge, 8. Washington, DC, 1856. 168 p. Br572C An8141 v.100. Samuel Foster Haven (1806-1881), librarian at the American Antiquarian Society in Worcester, Massachusetts, is best known for his *Archaeology of the United States*, a collection of historical and bibliographical essays.

1935. Havestadt, Bernhard. *Chilidúgu, sive Tractatus linguae chilensis, Editionem novam immutatam curavit dr. Julius Platzmann.* In aedibus B. G. Teubneri, Lipsiae, 1883. 2 v. Br498.977 AH 294. Reprint of the original edition (1777); Araucanian language.

1936. Hawkins, Benjamin. *A Sketch of the Creek Country in the Years 1798 and 1799, by Col. Benjamin Hawkins, United States Agent for Indian Affairs; With An Introduction and Historic Sketch of the Creek Confederacy, by W. B. Hodgson, of Savannah, Georgia.* Bartlett and Welford, New York, 1848. 88 p. Br572C An8141 v.35. "The author of this treatise weas for more than thirty years employed by the government of the United States in its intercourse with the Indians. He was styled by the Creeks, Choctaws, Chickasaws, and Cherokees, the Beloved Man of the Four Nations…This treatise is filled with sketches of all these partriculars as existing in the Creek nation" (Field 1873:162).

1937. Hayden, Ferdinand V. A sketch of the Mandan Indians, with some observations illustrating the grammatical structure of their language. *American Journal of Science and Arts* 34(100): 57–66, 1862. Br572C An8141 v.81.

1938. Hayden, Ferdinand V. Brief notes on the Pawnee, Winnebago, and Omaha languages. *Proceedings of the American Philosophical Society* 10:389–424, 1869. Br572C An8141 v.81.

1939. Hayden, Ferdinand V. Contributions to the Ethnography and Philology of the Indian Tribes of the Missouri Valley. *Transactions of the American Philosophical Society* 12: 233–461. Br497 H328; Br572C An8141 v.93.

1940. Hayes, C.W. An expedition through the Yukon District. *National Geographic Magazine* 4:117–162, 1892. Br572C An8141 v.83.

1941. Haynes, Henry W. Agricultural implements of the New England Indians. *Proceedings of the Boston Society of Natural History* 22:436–443, 1883. Br572C An8141 v.39.

1942. Haynes, Henry W. Discovery of Palaeolithic flint implements in Upper Egypt. *Memoirs of the American Academy of Arts and Sciences* 10:357–361, 1881. Br572C An8141 v.90; Br572C An8141 v.161.

1943. Haynes, Henry W. Notes upon the ancient soap-stone quarries worked for the manufacture of cooking utensils. *Proceedings of the American Antiquarian Society* 2(3): 364–365, 1883. Br572C An8141 v.39.

1944. Haynes, Henry W. Some indications of an early race of men in New England. *Proceedings of the Boston Society of Natural History* 21:382–390, 1882. Br572C An8141 v.41.

1945. Haynes, Henry W. Some new evidences of cannibalism among the Indians of New England. *Proceedings of the Boston Society of Natural History* 22:60–63, 1882. Br572C An8141 v.39.

1946. Haynes, Henry W. The bow and arrow unknown to Palaeolithic man. *Proceedings of the Boston Society of Natural History* 23, 1886. 6 p. Br572C An8141 v.41.

1947. Haynes, Henry W. The prehistoric archaeology of North America. In *Narrative and Critical History of America*, J. Winsor, ed., v. 1, pp. 329–368. Boston, 1889. Br572C An8141 v.1.

1948. Hazard, Willis H. A Syriac charm. *Journal of the American Oriental Society* 15:284–296, 1893. Br572C An8141 v.116.

1949. Hazeu, G.A.J. *Bijdrage tot de kennis van het Javaansche tooneel*. E. J. Brill, Leiden, 1897. 203 p. Br572C An8141 v.153.

1950. Heath, Edwin R. Dialects of Bolivian Indians; a philological contribution from material gathered during three years' residence in the Department of Beni, Bolivia. *Kansas City Review of Science and Industry* 6(12): 679–687, 1883. Br572C An 8141 v.47.

1951. Heaviside, John T. C. *American Antiquities; Or, The New World the Old, and the Old World the New*. Trübner, London, 1868. 43 p. Br572C An8141 v.38.

1952. Heckewelder, John G. E. *Comparative Vocabulary of Algonquin Dialects, from Heckewelder's Manuscripts in the Collections of the American Philosophical Society, Philadelphia*. J. Wilson and Son, University Press, Cambridge, MA, 1887. 7 p. Br497.11 H35; Br572C An8141 v.96. Heckewelder, professionally trained as a cooper, worked as Rev. Zeisberger's assistant at the Moravian Mission on the Muskingum in Ohio, 1771-1786.

1953. Heckewelder, John G. E. *History, Manners, and Customs of the Indian Nations Who Once Inhabited Pennsylvania and the Neighboring States*. New and revised ed. The Historical Society of Pennsylvania, Philadelphia, 1876. 465 p. Br970.4 PH353a.

1954. Heger, F. Aderlassgeräthe bei Indianern und Papuas. *Mitteilungen der Anthropologischen Gesellschaft in Wein* 23, 1893. 4 p. Br572C An8141 v.144.

1955. Heger, F. Altmexikanische Reliquien aus dem Schlosse Ambras in Tirol. *Annalen des K. K. Naturhistorischen Hofmuseums* 7(4): 379-400, 1892. Br572C An8141 v.109.

1956. Heierli, Jakob. *Nachträge zur archäologische Karte des Kantons Zürich*. Zürich, 1897. 4 p. Br572C An8141 v.143.

1957. Heierli, Jakob. *Die archäologischen Funde des Kantons Schaffhausen in ihrer Beziehung zur Urgeschichte der Schweiz*. Druck von H. R. Saverländer, Aarau, 1896. 31 p. Br572C An8141 v.153.

1958. Heierli, Jakob. Die Näfelser Letzi, n.d. 15 p. Br572C An8141 v.153.

1959. Heierli, Jakob. Die neuesten Ausgrabungen in Baden. *Anzeiger für Schweizerische Alterthumskunde* 2, 1895. 7 p. Br572C An8141 v.140.

1960. Heierli, Jakob. Die Verbreitung der Pfahlbauten ausserhalb Europa's. *Antiqua*, pp. 5-12, 1890-1891. Br572C An8141 v.12.

1961. Heierli, Jakob. Ein Blick in die Urgeschichte der Schweiz. Schweiz. *Pädagog Zeitschrift* 2:96-105, 1892. Br572C An8141 v.82.

1962. Heierli, Jakob. Ein bronzezeitlicher Grabfund. *Anzeiger für Schweizerische Altertumskunde*, 1896. 2 p. Br571.3 H367.

1963. Heierli, Jakob. *Erklärungen und Register zur Archäologischen Karte des Kantons Zürich*. Druck von A. Coradi-Stahl, Zürich, n.d. 47 p. Br572C An8141 v.143.

1964. Heierli, Jakob. Pfahlbauern. *Mitteilungen der Antiquarischen Gesellschaft* 22(2): 33-98, 1888. Br572C An8141 v.101.

1965. Heierli, Jakob. *Urgeschichte der Schweiz*. Buchdruckerei W. Hepting, Andelfikgen, 1901. 453 p. Br572C An8141 v.127.

1966. Hein, Alois R. *Die Bildenden Künste bei den Dayaks auf Borneo*. Alfred Hölder, Wien, 1890. Br572C An8141 v.107.

1967. Hein, Alois R. *Meander, Kreuze, Hakenkreuze...in Amerika*. Wien, 1891. 48 p. Br572C An8141 v.11.

1968. Hein, Wilhelm. Die Todtenbretter im Böhmerwalde. *Mitteilungen der Anthropologische Gesellschaft in Wien* 21:85-100, 1891. Br572C An8141 v.91.

1969. Hein, Wilhelm. Die Verwendung der Menschengestalt in Flechtwerken. *Mitteilungen der Anthropologische Gesellschaft in Wien* 21:45-56, 1891. Br572C An8141 v.101.

1970. Hein, Wilhelm. Ornamentale Parallelen. *Mitteilungen der Anthropologische Gesellschaft in Wien* 20:50-58, 1890. Br572C An8141 v.97.

1971. Hellmann, Gustav. Der achte internationale Amerikanisten-Kongress in Paris. *Verhandlungen der Deutsche Gesellschaft für Erdkunde*, 1890. Br572C An8141 v.83.

1972. Hellmann, Gustav. *Meteorologische Volksbücher*. Verlag von Hermann Paetel, Berlin, 1891. 53 p. Br572C An8141 v.5.

1973. Hellwald, Friedrich von. Der Tanz im Lichte der Völkerkunde. *Globus* 59(7): 100-102, 1891. Br572C An8141 v.101.

1974. Hellwald, Friedrich von. *Die amerikanische Völkerwanderung*. Wien: Druck und Verlag von Adolf Holzhausen, 1866. 54 p. Br572C An8141 v.72.

1975. Hellwald, Friedrich von. *Die Erde und ihre Völker ein geographisches Hausbuch Dritte, gänzlich umgearb*. W. Spemann, Berlin, 1884. 914 p. Br572 H367.

1976. Helmolt, Hans F. *Der Begriff Weltgeschichte*. Bibliographisches Institut, Leipzig, 1899. 20 p. Br572 H36. Contents include: J. Kohler, "Grundbegriffe einer Entwicklungsgeschichte der Menschheit"; 2. Friedrich Ratzel, "Die Menschheit als Lebenserscheinung der Erde"; 3. Johannes Ranke, "Die vorgeschichte der Menschheit"; 4. Konrad Häbler, "Amerika."

1977. Helps, Arthur. *The Spanish Conquest in America; And Its Relation to the History of Slavery and to the Government of Colonie*. Harper and Brothers, New York, 1856-1868. 4 v. Br973.1 H367. "The whole of this noble work is devoted to a history of the relations of the Indians of America to its Spanish invaders, and the effect of their occupation and conquest upon the population, religion, and manners of the aborigines" (Field 1873:166).

1978. Hempstead, G. S. B. *Antiquities of Portsmouth and Vicinity; With Some Speculations Upon the Origin and Destiny of the Mound Builders*. Portsmouth, 1875. 19 p. Br572C An8141 v.39.

1979. Henderson, Alexander, and Richard Fletcher. *Leti u ebanhelio Hezo Crizto hebix Huan*. Printed for the British and Foreign Bible Society by J. C. Clay...at the University Press, London, 1869. 83 p. Br498.21 MB4. Alexander Henderson, a Baptist missionary who came to Belize in 1834, prepared several religious tracts in Yucatec Maya and Moskito languages.

1980. Henderson, Alexander. *A Grammar of the Moskito Language, by Alexander Henderson*. Belize, Honduras. Printed by John Gray, New York, 1846. 47 p. Br498.44 H 383.

1981. Henderson, Alexander. *Araidatiu-iumurau segung Madeju*. Printed by Thomas Constable, Edinburgh, 1847. 88 p. Br498.11 CB47.1. Gospel of St. Matthew translated into Carib.

1982. Henderson, Alexander. Dictionary of the Karif language as spoken in the Bay of Honduras, by Alexander Henderson. Belize, 1872; newly arranged by Dr. C. H. Berendt. New York, December 1873. 232 p. Br498.11 MH383. Manuscript; transcript by Karl H. Berendt; includes a number of autograph letters from Henderson.

1983. Henderson, Alexander. Grammar of the Karif language as spoken in the Bay of Honduras. Belize, 1872. 110 p. Br498.11 MH383.2. Manuscript; transcript of an original apparently in the library of the Bureau of American Ethnology.

1984. Henderson, Alexander. *The Maia Primer, by Alexander Henderson, Belize, Honduras, etc.* Printed by J. Showell, Birmingham, England, 1852. 12 p. Br498.21 MH38.

1985. Henry, Victor. *Dom Parisot ne produira pas le manuscrit Taensa.* Paris, 1885. 13 p. Br572C An8141 v.47.

1986. Henry, Victor. Esquisse d'une grammaire de la langue innok. *Revue de Linguistique*, 1878. 38 p. Br572C An8141 v.52.

1987. Hensel, Reinhold. Die Coroados der brasilianischen provinz Rio Grande do Sul, 1867. 12 p. Br572C An8141 v.33; Br572.981 H394.

1988. Hensel, Reinhold. Die Schädel der Corosados, pp. 195-204, 1867. Br572.981 H394.

1989. Henshaw, Henry W. *Perforated Stones from California.* Bureau of Ethnology, Smithsonian Institution, Bulletin 2. Washington, DC, 1887. 34 p. Br572C An8141 v.14; Br572C An8141 v.140.

1990. Henshaw, Henry W. Who are the American Indians? *American Anthropologist* 2(3): 193-214, 1889. Br572C An8141 v.27.

1991. Hermes, F. Über natur der amerikanischen Indianersprachen. *Herrig's Archiv für das Studium der Neuern Sprachen* 29:231-254, 1861. Br497 H425.

1992. Hernández, Eusebio, and Alphonse L. Pinart. *Pequeño vocabulario de la lengua lenca (dialecto de Guajiquiro).* Petite Bibliothèque Américaine, 8. E. Leroux, Paris, 1897. 25 p. Br498.19 LGH43.

1993. Hernández, Francisco. *Cuatro libros de la naturaleza y virtudes de las plantas y animales, de la Nueva España; extracto de las obras del Dr. Francisco Hernández; anotados, traducidos y publicados en México el ano de 1615, por Fr. Francisco Ximenez; ahora por primera vez reimpreso mediante la protección del C. Lic. Agustin Canseco... bajo la dirección del Dr. Nicolás León.* J. R. Bravo, Morelia, 1888. 300 p. Br615.32 H425. A translation of the author's *Rerum medicarum Novae Hispaniae thesaurus; seu, Plantarum, animallum, mineralium mexicanorum historia* (México, 1615).

1994. Hernández, Francisco. *Francisci Hernandi, medici atque historici Philippi II Hisp. et Indiar. Regis, et totius novi orbis archiatri, opera, cum edita, tum inedita, ad autographi fidem et integritatem expressa, impensa et jussu region.* Ex Typographia Ibarrae Heredum, Matriti, 1790. 3 v. Br581.972 H43.

1995. Herranz y Quiros, Diego N. *Compendio mayor de gramatica castellana para uso de los niños que concurren a las escuelas dispuesto en dialogo para la mejor instrucción de la juventud.* Viana, Madrid, 1856. 110 p. Br468 H43.

1996. Herrera y Tordesillas, Antonio de. *Historia general de los hechos de los castellanos en las Islas i Tierra Firme del Mar Oceano.* Franco, Madrid, 1726-1730. 8 v. Br973.1 H434b. This primary account of the early Spanish conquest of the New World was originally published in Madrid in 1601-1615. Herrera was the official historian to Felipe II, and was able to examine many documents which were later destroyed, making his work a primary document in its own right. It is one of the most basic of New World histories.

1997. Herrera, José de. *Via sacra del divino arnante corazon de Jesús, dispuesta por las cruces del Calvario...traducida al idioma yucateco por Joaquín Ruz*. Novelo, Mérida, 1849. 34 p. Br498.21 MH 435.

1998. Herrero, Andres. *Doctrina y oraciones cristianas en lengua Mosetena; y traducidas en español palabra por palabra para la mejor inteligencia de los demas misioneros que de nuevo vayan a catequizar en aquella nacion*. En la Imprenta de Propaganda, Roma, 1834 20 p. Br498.93 H 437.

1999. Herzog, Wilhelm. Über die Wandtschaftsbeziehungen der costaricensischen Indianer-Sprachen mit denen von Central und Süd-Amerika. *Kleiner Mitteilungen*, pp. 623-627, n.d. Br572C An8141 v.92.

2000. Hesselmeyer, Ellis. Die Pelasger und Etruskerfrage. *Neues Korrespondenzblatt* 9:373-388, 1895. Br572C An8141 v.153.

2001. Hesselmeyer, Ellis. *Die Pelasgerfrage und ihre Lösbarkeit*. Verlag von Franz Fues, Tübingen, 1890. 162 p. Br572C An8141 v.5.

2002. Hesselmeyer, Ellis. *Die Ursprünge der Stadt Pergamos in Kleinasien*. Verlag und Druck von Franz Fues, Tübingen, 1885. 46 p. Br572C An8141 v.5.

2003. Hesselmeyer, Ellis. Zu Herodot; Birket-el-Kerun und Möris. *Neues Korrespondenzblatt* 6:217-232, 1896. Br572C An8141 v.153.

2004. Heuzey, Leon. *Le tresor de Cuenca*. Imprimerie de J. Claye, Paris, 1870. 16 p. Br572C An8141 v.1.

2005. Hewitt, J. N. B. Polysynthesis in the languages of the American Indians. *American Anthropologist* 6:381-407, 1893. Br572C An8141 v.125.

2006. Hilder, Frank F. *Notes on the Archaeology of Missouri; A Paper Read Before the Missouri Historical Society*. Missouri Historical Society, Publication 6. Missouri Historical Society, St. Louis, 1881. 17 p. Br572C An8141 v.19.

2007. Hill, Alfred J. Captain Glazier's claim to the discovery of the source of the Mississippi River. *Magazine of Western History*, March, 1887. 8 p. Br572C An8141 v.7.

2008. Hill, H. A., W. Hess, and J. A. Wilkes. *Ne Tsinihhoweyea-nenda-onh orighwa do geaty, roghyadon royadado geaghty, Saint Luke; The Gospel According to Saint Luke*. Printed for the American Bible Society, New York, 1827. 157, 157 p. Br497.27 MB 47.3. Translation of the Gospel of St. Luke into Mohawk; English King James version.

2009. Hill, Richard, and George Thornton. *Notes on the Aborigines of New South Wales; by the Hon. richard Hill, M.L.C., and the Hon. George Thornton, M.L.C. With Personal Reminiscences of the Tribes Formerly Living in the Neighbourhood of Sydney and the Surrounding Districts*. Charles Potter, Government Printer, Phillip-Street, Sydney, 1892. 8 p. Br572C An8141 v.121.

2010. Hillman, Frederic G, 1897. A contribution to Australasian and Polynesian archaeology. *Natural Science Journal* 1(2): 38-39, 1897. Br572C An8141 v.153.

2011. Hills, R. E. A pilgrimage to Teotihuacan. *American Naturalist* 16(12): 933-937, 1882. Br572C An8141 v.13.

2012. Hill-Tout, Charles. Oceanic origin of the Kwakiutl-Nootka and Salish stocks of British Columbia, and fundamental unity of same, with additional notes on the Déné. *Transactions of the Royal Society of Canada* 4(2): 187-231, 1898. Br497.46 ST64.

2013. Hilprecht, H.V. Die Votiv-Inschrift eines nicht erkannten Kassitenkönigs. *Zeitschrift für Assyriologie* 7:305-318, 1892. Br572C An8141 v.116.

2014. Hilprecht, H.V. Zur Lapislazuli-Frage in Babylonischen. *Zeitschrift für Assyriologie*, pp. 185-193, n.d. Br572C An8141 v.116.

2015. Hind, Henry Y. *Explorations in the Interior of the Labrador Peninsula, the Country of the Montagnais and Nasquapee Indians.* Longman, Green, Longman, Roberts and Green, London, 1863. 2 v. Br917.19 H58. In 1861, the Canadian government appointed Hind, a geologist and professor of chemistry, to conduct a survey of the Labrador Peninsula, including the Montagnais route from the Bay of Seven Islands on the north shore of the Gulf of St. Lawrence, overland by the Moisie River, to the Hamilton River. Hind provides a history of the various religious missions in the region, and evokes a sympathetic account of the dwindling Indian population, made sparse or forced to migrate northwards, because of the fur trade's enroachment on their hunting grounds.

2016. Hindley, John I. Indian Legends: Nanahush (The Ojiboeway Savior) and Moosh-Kuh-Ung (The Flood), 1885. 22 p. Br572C An8141 v.11.

2017. Hinman, Samuel D. *Ikee wocekiye wowapi; qa isantanka makoce; kin en token wohduze, qa okodakiciye wakan en tonakiya woecon kin, hena de he wowapi kin.* Pioneer Printing Company, St. Paul, 1865. 321 p. Br497.5 DSH59. Episcopal Church Book of Common Prayer translated into Santee. Hinman was a missionary to the Dakota at the Lower Sioux Agency, Minnesota. He helped defend Fort Ridgely during the Sioux Uprising of 1862 and then accompanied the captive Sioux to Crow Creek, Dakota Territory, where he remained as their missionary until 1865, when he was stationed with the Santee Sioux near Niobrara, Nebraska. Hinman was Santee interpreter at the Treaty of Fort Rice in 1868 and was United States commissioner to purchase the Black Hills from the Indians in 1874.

2018. *Histoire de l'empire mexicain, representée par figures; Relation du Mexique, ou de la Nouvelle Espagne, par Thomas Gage.* Cramoisy, Paris, 1696. 58, 40 p. Br898.22 AzH628. Extract from M. Thevenot, *Relations de divers voyages*, pt. 4.

2019. *Histoire des Aztecs.* Morris, Paris, 1855. 24 p. Br970.3 AzH625.

2020. *Histoire du royaume d'Acolhuacan ou de Tezcuco, n.d. Bibliothèque nationale (France). Mss. (Mex. 373). Mappe Tlotzin. Histoire du royaume d'Acolhuacan ou de Tezcuco (peinture non chronologique) Établissements ou cavernes chichimèques. Vie sauvage et arrivée des Chichimèques. Dynastie Tezcucane. Villes des lagunes.* Lith. de J. Desportes à l'Inst[itut] Roy[al] des S[ourds] M[uets], Paris, 1886. fold plate. 49 x 139 cm. fold. to 49 x 35 cm. Br898.22 NH628. Published in the *Anales of the Museo Nacional de México* [ser. 1], v.3.

2021. Historia de los mexicanos por sus pinturas; notes upon the Codex Ramirez, with a translation of the same, by Henry Phillips, Jr. *Proceedings of the American Philosophical Society* 21:616-651, 1884. Br898.22 AzH625. Translation of a Spanish anonymous history of the Aztecs, apparently based upon a series of hieroglyphic paintings, now lost. The original was first published with title as above, by García Icazbalceta in the *Anales del Museo Nacional de México* (1882), and later in the

Nueva colección de documentos para la historia de México (1891), together with various pieces selected from a codex in his possession entitled by one of its former owners "Libro de oro y tesoro indico." The *Historia*, the first piece in the codex, is a copy of the original work that was accompanied by paintings and presumably composed upon the order of Bishop Sebastian Ramírez de Fuenleal who took it with him to Madrid.

2022. *Historia del descubrimiento de las regiones austriales hecho por el general Pedro Fernández de Quirós publicada por Don Justo Zaragoza.* Imprenta de M. G. Hernandez, Madrid, 1876–1882. 2 v. Br918 F392. Attributed by Justo Zaragoza to Luis de Belmonte y Bermúdez; This collection includes Gallego's Relation of Mendaña's first voyage, 1567–68; Relation of Mendaña's and Pedro Fernandes de Quiros' voyage to Santa Cruz in 1595; and Quiros' voyage to the Tierra Austral del Espirito Santo [New Hebrides], including the discovery of La Sagittaria [Tahiti], in 1606.

2023. Hitchcock, Romyn. Ancient burial mounds of Japan. *Annual Report of the United States National Museum, Smithsonian Institution, for 1891,* pp. 511–523, 1893. Br572C An8141 v.120.

2024. Hitchcock, Romyn. Shinto, or the mythology of the Japanese. *Annual Report of the United States National Museum, Smithsonian Institution, for 1891,* pp. 489–509, 1893. Br572C An8141 v.120; Br572C An8141 v.130.

2025. Hitchcock, Romyn. Some ancient relics in Japan. *Annual Report of the United States National Museum, Smithsonian Institution, for 1891,* pp. 525–526, 1893. Br572C An8141 v.120.

2026. Hitchcock, Romyn. The Ainos of Yezo, Japan. *Annual Report of the United States National Museum, Smithsonian Institution, for 1890,* pp. 429–502, 1892. Br572C An8141 v.86.

2027. Hitchcock, Romyn. The ancient pit-dwellers of Yezo, Japan. *Annual Report of the United States National Museum, Smithsonian Institution, for 1890,* pp. 417–427, 1892. Br572C An8141 v.86.

2028. Ho, Silverio. *Pequeño catecismo, traducido en lengua k'ak'chi, dialecto de Cobán.* Petite Bibliothèque Américaine, 7. Paris, 1897. 28 p. Br498.21 KH793.

2029. Hochstetter, Ferdinand von. *Mexikanische Reliquien aus der Zeit Montezuma's in der K. K. Ambraser Sammlung.* In Commission bei Carl Gerold's Sohn, Wien, 1884. 24 p. Br572C An8141 v.90.

2030. Hodge, Frederick W. Bandelier's researches in Peru and Bolivia. *American Anthropologist* 10:303–311, 1897. Br572C An8141 v.153. Frederick Webb Hodge (1864–1956) was a prolific scholar and a major influence on the development of anthropology in the United States. Hodge was employed variously by the United States Geological Survey, Bureau of American Ethnology, Hemenway Southwestern Archaeological Expedition, Museum of the American Indian/Heye Foundation, and the Southwest Museum. Hodge's anthropological and historical fieldwork on the American Southwest took place at intervals between 1886 and 1947. His major contributions to anthropology were as an organizer and editor. He helped found the American Anthropological Association and served as editor of *The Masterkey* and *American Anthropologist*.

2031. Hodge, Frederick W. *List of Publications of the Bureau of Ethnology...With Index to Authors and Subjects.* United States Government Printing Office, Washington, DC, 1894. Br572C An8141 v.131; Br572C An8141 v.140.

2032. Hodge, Frederick W. *List of Publications of the Bureau of Ethnology...With an Index to Authors and Titles.* Bulletin of the Bureau of Ethnology, Smithsonian Institution, 24. Washington, DC, 1897. 25 p. Br572B Sm65b.

2033. Hodge, Frederick W. Prehistoric irrigation in Arizona. *American Anthropologist* 6:323-330, 1893. Br572C An8141 v.124.

2034. Hodge, Frederick W. Pueblo Indian clans. *American Anthropologist* 9:345-352, 1896. Br572C An8141 v.153.

2035. Hodge, Frederick W. Pueblo snake ceremonials. *American Anthropologist* 9:133-136, 1896. Br572C An8141 v.140.

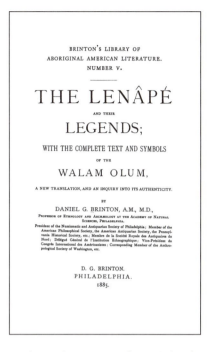

BRINTON'S LIBRARY OF
ABORIGINAL AMERICAN LITERATURE.
NUMBER V.

THE LENÂPÉ

AND THEIR

LEGENDS;

WITH THE COMPLETE TEXT AND SYMBOLS

OF THE

WALAM OLUM,

A NEW TRANSLATION, AND AN INQUIRY INTO ITS AUTHENTICITY.

BY

DANIEL G. BRINTON, A.M., M.D.,

Professor of Ethnology and Archæology at the Academy of Natural Sciences, Philadelphia.

President of the Numismatic and Antiquarian Society of Philadelphia ; Member of the American Philosophical Society, the American Antiquarian Society, the Pennsylvania Historical Society, etc.; Membre de la Société Royale des Antiquaires du Nord ; Délégué Général de l'Institution Ethnographique ; Vice-Président du Congrès International des Américanistes ; Corresponding Member of the Anthropological Society of Washington, etc.

D. G. BRINTON.
PHILADELPHIA.
1885.

Title page from Brinton's The Lenâpé and Their Legends *(1885).*

2036. Hodge, Frederick W. The early Navajo and Apache. *American Anthropologist* 8:223-240, 1895. Br572C An8141 v.140.

2037. Hodge, Frederick W. The Enchanted Mesa. *National Geographical Magazine* 8:273-284, 1897. Br572C An8141 v.153.

2038. Hodge, Frederick W. The first discovered city of Cibola. *American Anthropologist* 8(2): 142-152, 1895. Br572C An8141 v.136.

2039. Hodge, Frederick W. The verification of a tradition. *American Anthropologist* 10:299-302, 1897. Br572C An8141 v.153.

2040. Hodgson, William B. The Creek Confederacy. *Collections of the Georgia Historical Society* 3(1): 13-18, 1848. Br572C An8141 v.35.

2041. Hoernes, Moritz. *Die Urgeschichte des Menschen nach dem heutigen Stande der Wissenschaft.* A. Hartleben, Wien, 1892. 672 p. Br572 H673.

2042. Hoernes, Moritz. *Urgeschichte der bildenden Kunst in Europa von den Anfängen bis um 500 vor Chr.* A. Holzhausen, Wien, 1898. 709 p. Br913.4 H67.

2043. Hoffman, Walter J. Antiquities of New Mexico and Arizona. *Proceedings of the Davenport Academy of Natural Sciences* 3:108-127, 1881. Br572C An8141 v.20.

2044. Hoffman, Walter J. Bird names of the Selish, Pah-Uta, and Shoshoni Indians. *The Auk* 2(1), 1885. 10 p. Br572C An8141 v.52.

2045. Hoffman, Walter J. Comparison of Eskimo pictographs with those of other American aborigines. *Transactions of the Anthropological Society of Washington* 2:128–146, 1883. Br572C An8141 v.59.

2046. Hoffman, Walter J. Folk-lore of the Pennsylvania Germans. *Journal of American Folk-Lore* 2(4): 23–35, 125–136, 1889. Br572C An8141 v.29.

2047. Hoffman, Walter J. Folk-medicine of the Pennsylvania Germans. *Proceedings of the American Philosophical Society* 27:329–352, 1889. Br572C An8141 v.29.

2048. Hoffman, Walter J. Hugo Reid's account of the Indians of Los Angeles County, California. *Bulletin of the Essex Institute* 17(1), 1885. 33 p. Br572C An8141 v.27.

2049. Hoffman, Walter J. Miscellaneous ethnographic observations on Indians inhabiting Nevada, California, and Arizona. *Annual Report of the United States Geological and Geographical Survey of the Territories for the Year 1876*, pp. 461–478, Washington, DC, 1878. Br572C An8141 v.35.

2050. Hoffman, Walter J. Notes on Ojibwa folk-lore. *American Anthropologist* 2(3): 215–223, 1889. Br572C An8141 v.27.

2051. Hoffman, Walter J. Remarks on aboriginal art in California and Queen Charlotte's Island. *Proceedings of the Davenport Academy of Natural Sciences* 4:105–122, 1884. Br572C An8141 v.39; Br572C An8141 v.58; Br572C An8141 v.117.

2052. Hoffman, Walter J. Remarks on Ojibwa ball play. *American Anthropologist* 3(2): 133–135, 1890. Br572C An8141 v.23.

2053. Hoffman, Walter J. Report on the Chaco cranium. *Annual Report of the United States Geological and Geographical Survey of the Territories for the Year 1876*, pp. 453–461. Washington, DC, 1878. Br572C An8141 v.35.

2054. Hoffman, Walter J. The Carson footprints. *Transactions of the Anthropological Society of Washington* 2:34–38, 1883. Br572C An8141 v.20.

2055. Hoffman, Walter J. Vocabulary of the Selish [sic] language. *Proceedings of the American Philosophical Society* 23(123): 261–380, 1886. Br572C An8141 v.84.

2056. Holbrook, W. C. Prehistoric altars of Whitesides County, Illinois. *Proceedings of the American Association for the Advancement of Science* 29:722–724, 1894. Br572C An8141 v.19.

2057. Holden, Luther, and James Shuter. *Human Osteology, Comprising a Description of the Bones with Delineations of the Attachments of the Muscles, the General and Microscopic Structure of Bone and Its Development*. 6th ed. Presley Blakiston, Philadelphia, 1882 309 p. Br591.49 H713.

2058. Holder, C. F. The ancient islanders of California. *Appleton's Popular Science Monthly* 48(5): 658–662, 1896. Br572C An8141 v.141.

2059. Holm, Gustaf F. Bidrag til kjendskabet om Eskimoernes Herkomst. *Geografisk Tidskrift* 1–2:1–13, 1891. Br572C An8141 v.101.

2060. Holm, Gustaf F. *Ethnologisk skizze af angmagsalikerne*. Bianco Lunos Kgl. Hof-Bogtrykkeri, Kobenhavn, 1887. 164 p. Br572.998 H73.

2061. Holm, Gustaf F. Resumé des communications sur le Grønland, pp. 364–400, n.d. Br572C An8141 v.10.

2062. Holm, Gustaf F. *Sagn og fortællinger fra Angmagsalik; samlede af G. Holm; be-*

maerkninger til Sagnsamlingen af H. Rink. Blanco Lunos Kgl., Hofbogtrykkeri, Kjobenhavn, 1887. 124 p. Br572C An8141 v.11.

2063. Holmberg, Heinrich J. *Ethnographische Skizzen: über die Völker des russischen Amerika.* Gedruckt bei H. C. Friis, Helsingfors, 1855-1862. 142 p., 67 p. Br572C An8141 v.95.

2064. Holmes, Nathaniel. Geological and geographical distribution of the human race. *Transactions of the Academy of Sciences of St. Louis* 4(1), 1879. St. Louis. 42 p. Br572C An8141 v.117.

2065. Holmes, William H. *An Ancient Quarry in Indian Territory.* Bureau of American Ethnology, Bulletin 21. Government Printing Office, Washington, DC, 1894. 19p. Br572C An8141 v.131. Holmes (1846-1933) made significant contributions to the archaeological study of North American Indians and played a major role in the world of Washington anthropology in the last decades of the 19th and the first decades of the 20th century. His first professional position was as an artist for the Smithsonian Institution and for Hayden's Geological and Geographical Survey of the Territories. He later worked for the United States Geological Survey and the United States National Museum. In 1903 he was appointed John Wesley Powell's successor at the Bureau of American Ethnology. Holmes was a major force behind the censure in 1919 of Franz Boas by the American Anthropological Association. This action was primarily the result of Boas' pacifism during World War I.

2066. Holmes, William H. Ancient pottery of the Mississippi Valley: a study of the collection of the Davenport Academy of Sciences. *Proceedings of the Davenport Academy of Natural Sciences* 4:123-196, 1884. Br572C An8141 v.117.

2067. Holmes, William H. *Archeological Studies Among the Ancient Cities of Mexico.* Field Columbian Museum, Chicago, 1895-1897. 2 v. Br913.726 H733. Contents include, 1. Monuments of Yucatán; 2. Monuments of Chiapas, Oaxaca and the valley of México.

2068. Holmes, William H. Are there traces of man in the Trenton Gravels? *Journal of Geology* 1(1): 15-37, 1893. Br572C An8141 v.124.

2069. Holmes, William H. Art in shell of the ancient Americans. *Annual Report of the Bureau of Ethnology, Smithsonian Institution, for 1880-1881*, pp. 179-365, 1883. Br913.7 H733.

2070. Holmes, William H. Caribbean influence on the prehistoric ceramic art of the southern states. *American Anthropologist* 7:71-79, 1894. Br572C An8141 v.123.

2071. Holmes, William H. Examples of iconoclasm by the conquerors of Mexico. *American Naturalist* 19:1032-1037, 1885. Br572C An8141 v.13.

2072. Holmes, William H. Prehistoric textile art of eastern United States. *Annual Report of the Bureau of Ethnology, Smithsonian Institution, for 1896*, pp. 3-46, 1896. Br571.54 H733.

2073. Holmes, William H. Preservation and decorative features of Papuan crania. *Anthropological Series, Field Columbian Museum* 2(1): 41-48, 1897. Br572C An8141 v.150.

2074. Holmes, William H. Stone implements of the Potomac-Chesapeake tidewater province. *Annual Report of the Bureau of Ethnology, Smithsonian Institution, for 1894-1895*, pp. 3-152, 1897. Washington, DC. Br571.15 H733.

2075. Holmes, William H. *Textile Fabrics of Ancient Peru*. Bureau of Ethnology, Smithsonian Institution, Bulletin 7. Washington, DC, 1889. 17 p. Br572C An8141 v.14; Br572C An8141 v.20.

2076. Holmes, William H. *The Use of Gold and Other Metals Among the Ancient Inhabitants of Chiriqui, Isthmus of Darien*. Bureau of Ethnology, Smithsonian Institution, Bulletin 3. Washington, DC, 1887. 27 p. Br572C An8141 v.14.

2077. Holmes, William H. The World's Fair Congress of Anthropology. *American Anthropologist* 6:423-434, 1893. Br572C An8141 v.124.

2078. Holmes, William H. Traces of glacial man in Ohio. *Journal of Geology* 1(2): 147-163, 1893. Br572C An8141 v.124.

2079. Holmes, William H. Vestiges of early man in Minnesota. *American Geologist* 11(4): 219-240, 1893. Br572C An8141 v.124.

2080. *Hommages a M. le Prof. Guido Cora pour son XXVe Anniversaire Géographique; première liste.* Imprimerie Vincent Bona, Turin, n.d. Br572C An8141 v.144.

2081. Hommel, Fritz. *Hethiter und Skythen und das erste Auftreten der Iranier in der Geschichte.* Verlag der Königl. Böhmischen Gesellschaft der Wissenschaften, Prag, 1898. 28 p. Br572C An8141 v.166.

2082. Honegger, Johann J. *Allgemeine Kulturgeschichte.* J. J. Weber, Leipzig, 1882-1886. 2 v. Br572 H755.

2083. *Hoosier Mineralogist and Archaeologist* 1(5-8, 10-12), 1885-1886. Br572C An8141 v.71.

2084. Hopkins, E. Washburn. Ancient and modern Hindu gilds. *Yale Review*, pp. 24-42, 1898. Br572C An8141 v.166.

2085. Hopkins, E. Washburn. Ancient and modern Hindu gilds: II. fines, revenues, and expenditures. *Yale Review*, pp. 197-212, 1898. Br572C An8141 v.166.

2086. Hopkins, E. Washburn. *The Religions of India.* Handbooks on the History of religions, 1. Ginn, Boston, 1895. 612 p. Br281 H77.

2087. Horden, John, and John Sanders. *The Book of Common Prayer and Administration of the Sacraments, and Other Rites and Ceremonies of the Church According to the Use of the Church of England; Translated into the Language of the Ojibbeway Indians in the Diocese of Moosonee, by the Right Rev. the Bishop of Moosonee and the Rev. J. Sanders, of Matawakumma.* Society for Promoting Christian Knowledge, London, 1880. 152 p. Br497.11 CC475.2; Br497.11 OC47. Church of England Book of Common Prayer translated into Ojibwa.

2088. Horden, John, and John Sanders. *The Moosonee Hymnal, Translated into the Ojibbeway Language, by the Right Rev. the Bishop of Moosonee and the Rev. John Sanders.* Society for Promoting Christian Knowledge, London, 1879. 112 p. Br497.11 CH7831. Text in syllabic characters.

2089. Horden, John. *A Collection of Psalms and Hymns in the Language of the Cree Indians of North-West America.* Society for Promoting Christian Knowledge, London, 1890. 76 p. Br497.11 CrH78.2.

2090. Horden, John. *Bible and Gospel History in Saulteux.* W. M. Watts, London, 1860. 72 p. Br497.11 OH77. Text in Ojibwa.

2091. Horden, John. *Bible and Gospel History in the Moose Dialect.* W. M. Watts, London, 1860. 83 p. Br497.11 CrH78.3.

2092. Horden, John. *Book of Common Prayer and Administration of the Sacraments and Other Rites and Ceremonies of the Church; According to the Use of the Church of England; Together With the Psalter or Psalms of David; Translated into the Language of the Cree Indians.* Society for Promoting Christian Knowledge, London, 1890. 152 p. Br497.11 CrC47.2. Church of England Book of Common Prayer translated into Cree.

2093. Horden, John. *Grammar of the Cree Language, As Spoken by the Cree Indians of North America.* Society for Promoting Christian Knowledge, London, 1875. 238 p. Br497.11 CrH78. "First edition, by the first bishop of Moosonee, diocese of Rupert's Land. Hordon, an English ironworker, received his calling to Canada in 1851, and was given two weeks to find a wife and board ship" (Siebert Library 1999:1:66).

2094. Horden, John. *Proper Lessons From the Old Testament for the Sundays and Other Holy Days Throughout the Year, in the Cree Language, by the Right Rev. J. Horden.* Printed for the Society for Promoting Christian Knowledge, London, 1878. 317 p. Br497.11 CrB46.9.

2095. Horden, John. *St. Matthew's Gospel, Translated Into the Language of the Ojibbeway* [sic] *Indians in the Diocese of Moosonee.* Society for Promoting Christian Knowledge, London, 1880. 140 p. Br497.11 CrB47. Gospel of St. Matthew translated into Cree.

2096. Horden, John. *The Book of Common Prayer and Administration of the Sacraments, and Other Rites and Ceremonies of the Church, According to the Use of the Church of England; Translated into the Language of the Ojibbeway Indians in the Diocese of Moosonee.* Society for Promoting Christian Knowledge, London, 1880. 152 p. Br497.11 OC47. Church of England Book of Common Prayer translated into Chippewa.

2097. Horden, John. *The New Testament in Moose Cree.* British and Foreign Bible Society, London, 1876. 424 p. Br497.11 CrB47.

2098. Horsford, Cornelia. *An Inscribed Stone.* John Wilson, and Son, Cambridge, MA, 1895. 22 p. Br572C An8141 v.145.

2099. Horsford, Cornelia. Dwellings of the saga-time in Iceland, Greenland, and Vineland. *National Geographic Magazine* 9(3): 73-84, 1898. Br572C An8141 v.153.

2100. Horsford, Eben N. *John Cabot's Landfall in 1497, and the Site of Norumbega; A Letter to Chief-Justice Daly, President of the American Geographical Society.* J. Wilson, Cambridge, MA, 1886. 42 p. Br973.1 H786.1.

2101. Horsford, Eben N. *The Defences of Norumbega and a Review of the Reconnaissances of Col. T. W. Higginson, Professor Henry W. Haynes, Dr. Justin Winsor, Dr. Francis Parkman, and Rev. Dr. Edmund F. Slafter; A Letter to Judge Daly...by Eben Norton Horsford.* Houghton, Mifflin and Company, Boston, New York, 1891. 84 p. Br974.44 H78.7.

2102. Horsford, Eben N. *The Discovery of the Ancient City of Norumbega; A Communication to the President and Council of the American Geographical Society at Their Special Session in Watertown, November 21, 1889*. Privately printed, Cambridge, 1889. 63 p. Br973.1 H786.

2103. Horsford, Eben N. *The Indian Names of Boston, and Their Meaning*. John Wilson and Son, Cambridge, 1886. 26 p. Br497.11 H781; Br572C An8141 v.104.

2104. Horsford, Eben N. *Watertown, The Site of the Ancient City of Norumbega; Remarks by Eben Norton Horsford at the Second Anniversary of the Watertown Historical Society, November 18, 1890*. Watertown, MA, 1890. 12 p. Br974.44 H78.6.

2105. Houdas, O. V. *Ethnographie de l'Algérie*. Bibliothèque Ethnographique, 5. Maisonneuve et Ch. Leclerc, Paris, 1886. 124 p. Br572C R737.

2106. Hough, Walter. An Eskimo strike-a-light from Cape Bathurst, British America. *Proceedings of the United States National Museum, Smithsonian Institution* 11:181-184, 1889. Br572C An8141 v.19.

2107. Hough, Walter. Environmental interrelations in Arizona. *American Anthropologist* 11:133-155, 1898. Br572C An8141 v.166.

2108. Hough, Walter. Music of the Hopi flute ceremony. *American Anthropologist* 10:162-163, 1897. Br572C An8141 v.153.

2109. Hough, Walter. The Columbian Historical Exposition in Madrid. *American Anthropologist* 6:217-277, 1893. Br572C An8141 v.124.

2110. Hough, Walter. The Hopi in relation to their plant environment. *American Anthropologist* 10:33-44, 1897. Br572C An8141 v.153.

2111. Hough, Walter. The lamp of the Eskimo. *Annual Report of the United States National Museum, Smithsonian Institution, for 1896*, pp. 1025-1057, 1898. Br970.3 EH814.

2112. Hough, Walter. The methods of fire-making. *Annual Report of the United States National Museum, Smithsonian Institution, for 1890*, pp. 395-409, 1892. Br572C An8141 v.86.

2113. Hough, Walter. The origin and range of the Eskimo lamp. *American Anthropologist* 11:116-122, 1898. Br572C An8141 v.166.

2114. Hovelacque, Abel, and G. Hervé. *Précis d'anthropologie*. Bibliothèque Anthropologique, 4. Vigot Frères, Paris, 1887. 651 pp. Br572 H82.

2115. Hovelacque, Abel, and G. Herve. Recherches ethnologiques sur le Morvan. *Mémoires de la Société d'Anthropologie de Paris* 5(2): 3-256, 1894. Br572C An8141 v.132.

2116. Hovelacque, Abel. L'évolution du language. *Revue Scientifique* 23:716-736, 1885. Br572C An8141 v.95.

2117. Hovelacque, Abel. *La linguistique*. 3. éd. C. Reinwald, Paris, 1881. 435 p. Br409 H82.

2118. Hovelacque, Abel. Limite du Catalan et du Languedocien. *Revue Mensuelle de l'Ecole d'Anthropologie de Paris*, pp. 143-145, 1891. Br572C An8141 v.8.

2119. Hovelacque, Abel. *Notre ancêtre; recherches d'anatomie et d'ethnologie sur le precurseur de l'homme*. Paris, 1877. 43 p. Br572C An8141 v.31.

2120. Hovey, Horace C. On the alabaster quarries, flint mines, and other antiquities of Wyandot Cave. *Proceedings of the American Association for the Advancement of Science* 29:725-731, 1880. Br572C An8141 v.19.

2121. Howitt, A. W. Remarks on the class systems collected by Mr. Palmer. *Journal of the Anthropological Institute of Great Britain and Ireland* 13(3): 335-346, 1884. Br572C An8141 v.67.

2122. Howse, Joseph. *A Grammar of the Cree Language; With Which is Combined an Analysis of the Chippeway Dialect.* Rivington, London, 1865. 324 p. Br497.11 CrH 84a. "One of the most comprehensive of Cree grammars by a fur trader who had spent twenty years among the Cree in Prince Rupert's Land" (*Frank T. Siebert Library* 1999:1:84).

2123. Hoy, Philo R. Dr. Koch's Missourium. *American Naturalist* 5:147-158, 1871. Br572C An8141 v.39.

2124. Hoyos Sáinz, Luis, and Telesforo de Aranzadi. *Un avance a la antropologia de España.* Establecimiento tipografico de Fortanet, Madrid, 1892. 71 p. Br572C An8141 v.121. Hoyos Sáinz (1868-1951) was a Spanish physical anthropologist, ethnologist, folklorist, and archaeologist. His early work was dedicated almost exclusively to craniology although his largest body written work espoused the fundamental idea that it was necessary to develop an anthropological knowledge of the different racial and cultural groups that inhabited the Iberian peninsula.

2125. Hrdlicka, Aleš. *Anthropological Investigations on One Thousand White and Colored Children of Both Sexes, the Inmates of the New York Juvenile Asylum, With Additional Notes on One Hundred Colored Children of the New York Colored Orphan Asylum.* New York, 1898. 86 p. Br573.6 H8. Hrdlicka (1869-1943) was Curator of the Anthropological Division of the Smithsonian Institution, where he assembled the most complete collection of human skeletal materials of all races. He advocated the theory of the Asiatic origins of American Indians, and between 1926 and 1938 undertook ten expeditions to Alaska, Kodiak Island, and the Aleutian Islands. Hrdlicka founded the *American Journal of Physical Anthropology* as well as the American Association of Physical Anthropologists. Hrdlicka's interests spread over the entire range of physical anthropology, the primary focus of his scientific work was the origin and antiquity of the aboriginal population of the Americas.

2126. Hrdlicka, Aleš. Study of the normal tibia. *American Anthropologist* 11:307-312, 1898. Br611.71 H855.

2127. Hubbard, Gardiner G. Discoverers of America: annual address by the President. *National Geographic Magazine* 5:1-20, 1893. Br572C An8141 v.122.

2128. Hubbard, Gardiner G. South America; annual address by the President. *National Geographic Magazine* 3:1-30, 1891. Br572C An8141 v.83.

2129. Humboldt, Friedrich Heinrich Alexandre, Freiherr von. *Kleinere Schriften, Erster band. Geognostische und physikalische Erinnerungen; mit einem Atlas.* J. G. Cotta'scher Verlag, Stuttgart, Tübingen, 1853. 474 p. Br551.04 H88.2. Baron Alexandre von Humboldt (1769-1859) was a naturalist, geographer, and explorer. Between 1799 and 1804 Humboldt undertook geographical and botanical studies in the

Caribbean, and North, Middle, and South America. He also studied indigenous populations and antiquities from these regions and published his findings. His collection of artifacts and pictorial manuscripts from Mexico, together with his publications, laid the foundation of anthropological research in Berlin.

2130. Humboldt, Karl Wilhelm von. *Briefe von Wilhelm von Humboldt an eine Freundin.* F. A. Brockhau, Leipzig, 1860. 531 p. Br925.7 H88H. Letters to Charlotte Diede, most of them written from 1822 to 1835, edited by her, and published after her death by Frau von Lützow (Therese con Bacheracht) under the title *Briefe an eine Freundin* (Leipzig, 1847).

2131. Humboldt, Karl Wilhelm von. *Die sprachphilosophischen Werke Wilhelm's von Humboldt; Hrsg. und erklärt von Dr. H. Steinthal.* Ferd. Dümmlers Verlagsbuchhandlung, Berlin, 1883. 699 p. Br409 St48. Karl Wilhelm von Humboldt (1767-1835) was a statesman, political philosopher, educational reformer, anthropologist, and linguist. He made a political career in the Prussian government, serving as envoy to Rome, Vienna, and London. He reformed Prussia's educational system and founded the University of Berlin. Among Humboldt's varied interests were comparative anthropology, and the study of American Indian languages. Humboldt extended his studies to ancient Egyptian, Sanskrit, Chinese, Japanese, Southeast Asian, and Pacific languages.

2132. Humboldt, Karl Wilhelm von. On the verb in American languages, translated by Daniel G. Brinton. *Proceedings of the American Philosophical Society* 22:332-354, 1885. Br497 B77.5.

2133. Humboldt, Karl Wilhelm von. Über das Verbum in den Americanischen Sprachen, n.d. 57 p. Br572C An8141 v.106. Manuscript, copied from the original in the Royal Library at Berlin, March 1884, for Daniel G. Brinton.

2134. Humboldt, Karl Wilhelm von. *Vues des cordillères, et monumens des peuples indigènes de l'Amérique.* N. Maze, Paris, 1824. 2 v. Br913.7 H88. Abridged from the folio edition (*Atlas pittoresque*) which was issued to accompany pt. 1 of the *Voyage de Humboldt et Bonpland* (Paris, 1814-1834).

2135. Humboldt, Karl Wilhelm von. *Wilhelm von Humboldt's Gesammelte Werke.* G. Reimer, Berlin, 1841-1852. 3 v. Br409.7 H88.1.

2136. Hunt, Jerome. *Katholik wocekiye wowapi.* Brown, Sioux Falls, 1890. 125 p. Br497.5 DH91. Prayers, instructions and hymns in the Sioux Indian language.

2137. Hunter, A. F. National characteristics and migrations of the Hurons as indicated by their remains in North Simcoe. *Transactions of the Canadian Institute* 3:225-228, 1891-1892. Br572C An8141 v.114.

2138. Hunter, James, and J. Sanders. *St. Matthew's Gospel; Translated into the Language of the Ojibbeway Indians in the Diocese of Moosonee, by the Right Rev. the Bishop of Moosonee and the Rev. J. Sanders, of Matawakumma.* Society for Promoting Christian Knowledge, London, 1880. 140 p. Br497.11 OB47.1. New Testament Gospel of St. Matthew translated into Ojibwa. Hunter and his wife were "a missionary couple who worked among the Indians near the Grand Rapids on Red River and Fort Simpson on the Mackenzie River" (*Frank T. Siebert Library* 1999:1:67).

2139. Hunter, James. *A Lecture on the Grammatical Construction of the Cree Language; Delivered by the Ven. Archdeacon Hunter...Also Paradigms of the Cree Verb With Its Various Conjugations.* Printed for the Society for Promoting Christian Knowledge, London, 1875. 267 p. Br497.11 CrH91.

2140. Hunter, James. *Ayumehawe mussin'ahikun, mena ka isse makinanew'ukee kunache k'eche iss'etwawina, mena ate'et kotuka iss'etwawina ayumehawin'ik, ka isse aputch'etanew'ukee akayasewe ayumehawin'ik; ussitche David oo Nikumoona...a isse mussin'ah'uk naheyowe isse keeswawin'ik, akayasewe mussin'ahikun'ik oche, the Ven. Archdeacon Hunter.* Printed for the Society for Promoting Christian Knowledge, London, 1877. 739 p. Br497.11 CrC47.3. Church of England Book of Common Prayer traslated into Cree.

2141. Hunter, James. *Nikumoowe mussinàhikun; The Book of Psalms, Translated Into the Language of the Cree Indians.* British and Foreign Bible Society, London, 1876. 271 p. Br497.11 CrB46.3. Old Testament Psalms translated into Cree.

2142. Hunter, James. *Oo meyo achimoowin St. John; The Gospel According to St. John; Translated Into the Language of the Cree Indians, of the Diocese of Rupert's Land, North-west America, by the Venerable James Hunter.* Printed for the British and Foreign Bible Society, London, 1876. 126 p. Br497.11 CrB47.4. New Testament Gospel of St. John translated into Cree; includes "Nistum oo mamowe mussinahumakawin John, the First Epistle General of John" (pp. 111–126).

2143. Hunter, James. *Oo meyo achimoowin St. Mark; The Gospel According to St. Mark; Translated Into the Language of the Cree Indians, of the diocese of Rupert's Land, North-West America, by the Venerable James Hunter.* British and Foreign Bible Society, London, 1876. 89 p. Br497.11 CrB47.2. New Testament Gospel of St. Mark translated into Cree.

2144. Hunter, James. *Oo meyo achimoowin St. Matthew; The Gospel According to St. Matthew; Translated Into the Language of the Cree Indians, of the Diocese of Rupert's Land, North-West America, by the Venerable James Hunter.* The British and Foreign Bible Society, London, 1877. 136 p. Br497.11 CrB47.1. New Testament Gospel of St. Matthew translated into Cree.

2145. Hunter, James. *Oo tapwatumoowin mena oo tipetotumoowin ootayumehaw; The Faith and Duty of a Christian; Translated Into the Language of the Cree Indians, of the Diocese of Rupert's Land, North-West America.* Society for Promoting Christian Knowledge, London, 1855. 54 p. Br497.11 CrH91.2.

2146. Hunter, James. *The Book of Common Prayer, and Administration of the Sacraments and Other Rites and Ceremonies of the Church According to the Use of the United Church of England and Ireland, Translated Into the Language of the Cree Indians of the Diocese of Rupert's Land, Northwest America.* Printed for the Society for Promoting Christian Knowledge, London, 1884. 190 p. Br497.11 CrC47. Church of England Book of Common Prayer translated into Cree.

2147. Hunter, Jean R. *Kukwachetoowe mussinahikun; A Catechism for the Cree Indians of Rupert's Land (North-West America), by Mrs. Hunter.* Society for Promoting Christian Knowledge, London, 1874. 8 p. Br497.11 CrH915.2.

2148. Hunter, Jean R. *Kunache nikumoowina, a ke mussinahuk naheyowe keeswawinik, Mrs. Hunter*, pp. 741–828. Gilbert and Rivington, London, 1877. Br497.11 CrH915. Collection of 100 hymns in Cree, with English captions; appended to and paged continuously with some copies of James Hunter, *Ayumehawe mussinahikun* (1877).

2149. Hurlbut, George C. Krakatau. *Bulletin of the American Geographical Society* 19 (3): 233–253, 1887. Br572C An8141 v.23.

2150. Hyades, Paul D. Observations anthropologiques et ethnographiques à la Baie Orange, Terre de Feu, 24 avril 1883. pp. 564–576, n.d. Br572C An8141 v.44.

2151. Hyades, Paul D., and J. Deniker. *Anthropologie, ethnographie*. Gauthier-Villars, Paris, 1891. 422 p. Br508.3 F84. Comprises v. 7 of *Mission scientifique du Cap Horn, 1882-1883*, 1891.

2152. Iles, George. *The Appraisal of Literature*. International Library Conference, London, 1897. 16 p. Br572C An8141 v.166.

2153. Iles, George. The appraisal of literature: address to the American Library Association, 1896. 7 p. Br572C An8141 v.153.

2154. Iles, George. Why human progress is by leaps. British Association for the Advancement of Science, Toronto, 1897. 7 p. Br572C An8141 v.166.

2155. Iles, George. Why progress is by leaps. *Appleton's Popular Science Monthly*, 1896. 15 p. Br572C An8141 v.153.

2156. Iles, George. Why progress is by leaps. *Appleton's Popular Science Monthly*, 1896. 62 p. Br572C An8141 v.166.

2157. Im Thurn, Everard F. *Among the Indians of Guiana; Being Sketches Chiefly Anthropologic From the Interior of British Guiana, by Everard F. Im Thurn*. K. Paul, Trench and Company, London, 1883. 445 p. Br980.3 GubIm88. Everard F. Im Thurn's (1852-1932) account of the forest and remote interior savanna country of British Guiana (Guyana) is a classic of anthropology. Based on almost five years there presented the first satisfactory account of the botany and zoology of the region, and the first observations of the culture of the Indians there.

2158. Im Thurn, Everard F. Notes on the plants observed during the Roraima Expedition of 1884. *Timenri; Being the Journal of the Royal Agricultural and Commercial Society* 5(2): 145–223, 1886. Br572C An8141 v.68.

2159. Im Thurn, Everard F. On some stone implements from British Guiana. *Journal of the Anthropological Institute of Great Britain and Ireland* 11:444–452, 1882. 9 p. Br572C An8141 v.68.

2160. Im Thurn, Everard F. On the animism of the Indians of British Guiana. *Journal of the Anthropological Institute of Great Britain and Ireland* 11:360–382, 1882. Br572C An8141 v.68.

2161. Im Thurn, Everard F. On the races of the West Indies. *Journal of the Anthropological Institute of Great Britain and Ireland* 16:190–196, 1886. Br572C An8141 v.19.

2162. Im Thurn, Everard F. Primitive games. *Timenri; Being the Journal of the Royal Agricultural and Commercial Society*, pp. 270–307, 1890. Georgetown. Br572C An8141 v.68.

2163. Im Thurn, Everard F. *West Indian Stone Implements*. Argosy Office, Demerara, 1883; extract from: *Timenri; Being the Journal of the Royal Agricultural and Commercial Society* 2(2): 1–63, 1882. Br572C An8141 v.68.

2164. Indian Rights Association. *Fifteenth Annual Report of the Executive Committee of the Indian Rights Association*. Office of the Indian Rights Association, Philadelphia, 1898. 68 p. Br572C An8141 v.153.

2165. Indiana. Department of Geology and Natural History. *Annual Report*, 12, 1883. Indianapolis. Br557.72 In25.2.

2166. *Indicazione degli Oggetti piu importanti*...1882. 87 p. Br572C An8141 v.17.

2167. *Informé que acerca del Congreso Pedagógico Hispano Portugués Americano eleva á la Secretaría de instrucción pública*. Tipografía Nacional, San José de Costa Rica, 1893. 122 p. Br370.6 C76.

2168. Ingersoll, Ernest. Wampum and its history. *American Naturalist* 17:467–480, 1883. Br572C An8141 v.13.

2169. Innokentt, Metropolitan of Moscow. *Opyt grammatiki aleutsko-li'evskago iazyka*, 1846. 120 p. Br497.25 AlIn67. Includes Aleutian-Russian and Russian-Aleutian vocabularies.

2170. Inscripciones, medallas, edificios, templos, y antigüedades y monumentos del Peru, n.d. 107 p. Br572C An8141 v.106. Manuscript, copy of an original in the British Museum Library.

2171. Instituto Medico Nacional (Mexico). *Datos para la materia medica mexicana*. México, 1894–1898. 5 v. Br615.1 M578.

2172. International Catalogue of Scientific Literature. *Rapport de la Commission Locale Néerlandaise*. 2 session. 1898. 31 p. Br500B In83.2.

2173. International Congress of Americanists (1 session, Nancy, 1875). *Invitation*, 1875. 6 p. Br572C An8141 v.35.

2174. International Congress of Americanists (3 session, Brussels, 1879). *Compte-rendu de l'Assemblée Générale du Comité Central d'Organisation de la 3e Session du Congrès International des Américanistes*. Typographie Ve. Ch. Vanderauwera, Bruxelles, 1879. Br572C An8141 v.111.

2175. International Congress of Americanists (5 session, Copanhagen, 1883). *Notice sur les musées ethnographiques et archéologiques de Copenhagen*, 1883. 15 p. Br572.06 In8.5.2.

2176. International Congress of Americanists (5 session, Copenhagen, 1883). *Procès-verbal*. Copenhagen, 1883. 38 p. Br572.06 In8.5.3.

2177. International Congress of Americanists (9 Session, Huelva, 1892). *Reunion del año de 1892 en el Convento de Santa Maria de la Raboda*. Tipografía de Manuel Gines Hernandez, Madrid, 1891. Br572C An8141 v.83.

2178. International Congress of Americanists (11 session, Mexico, 1897). *Reunion en México del 15 al 20 de octubre de 1895; programa*. Oficina Tipografica de la Secretaría de Fomento, México, 1895. 35 p. Br572C An8141 v.142.

2179. International Congress of Anthropology and Prehistoric Archaeology (7 session, Stockholm, 1874). *Compte rendu*. Norstedt, Stockholm, 1876. 2 v. Br572.06 In83.7.

2180. International Congress of Anthropology and Prehistoric Archaeology (11 session, Moscow, 1892). *Compte rendu*. Imprimerie de l'Université Impériale, 1892-1893. 2 v. Br572.06 In83.11.

2181. International Congress of Orientalists (12 session, Rome, 1899). *Bulletin*, 2. Br490.6 In8.102.

2182. *Itse Kanohedv Datlohisdv Ugvwiyuhi Igatseli Tsisa Galonedv utseliga; Digalvquodi Goweli Diniyelihisdisgi Unadatlegv Watsiniyi tsunileyvtanvhi. Nuyagi Digaleyvtanvhi.* American Bible Society, New York, 1860. 408 p. Br497.27 ChB 47. New Testament translated into Cherokee.

2183. Ives, J. C. *Report Upon the Colorado River of the West, Explored in 1857 and 1858 by Lieutenant Joseph C. Ives... Under the Direction of the Office of Explorations and Surveys*. Government Printing Office, Washington, DC, 1861. Br917.8 Iv37.

2184. Jack, E. The Abenakis of Saint John River. *Transactions of the Canadian Institute* 3:195-205, 1891-92. Br572C An8141 v.114.

2185. Jackson, Sheldon. *Introduction of Reindeer Into Alaska; Preliminary Report of the General Agent of Education for Alaska to the Commissioner of Education, 1890.* Washington, DC, 1891. 15 p. Br572C An8141 v.10. Jackson (1834-1909), a Presbyterian clergyman, served as an educator and missionary in Alaska and, with representatives of other denominations, worked out a division of mission fields in the territory. In the 1880s he established a mission school and anthropological museum in Sitka.

2186. Jackson, Sheldon. The native tribes of Alaska. In *Christian Educators in Council: Sixty Addresses*, J. C. Hartzell, ed., pp. 118-127. Phillipp and Hunt, New York, 1883. Br572C An8141 v.32.

2187. Jacquet, Eugéne V. *Considerations sur les alphabets des Philippines*. Imprimerie Royale, 1831. 30 p. Br499.216 PJ 168.

2188. Janssen, Karl E. *Elementarbog i eskimoernes sprog til brug for Europaeerne ved colonierne I Grønland.* Louis Kleins Bogtrykkeri, Kjøbenhavn, 1862. 92 p. Br497.25 GJ26.

2189. Jastrow, Joseph. *Address Before the Section of Anthropology, American Association for the Advancement of Science*. Salem Press, Salem, MA, 1891. 23 p. Br572C An8141 v.8.

2190. Jastrow, Morris. A new fragment of the Babylonian Etana legend. *Beiträge zur Semitsche Sprachwissenschaft* 3:363-383, n.d. Br572C An8141 v.140. After graduation from the University of Pennsylvania in 1881, Jastrow (1861-1921) began rabbinical studies at the Jewish Theological Seminary in Breslau, and later studied Oriental languages at Breslau, Leipzig, Strasbourg, and Paris. He received his doctorate from Leipzig in 1884. In 1891 he was appointed professor of Semitics. As University Librarian (1898-1919) Jastrow supported the growth of many new academic subjects. He established at the University of Pennsylvania a major American center for Oriental studies, and for the academic study of religion and the ancient Near East.

2191. Jastrow, Morris. A Phoenician seal. *Hebraica* 7:258-267, 1891. Br572C An8141 v.5.

2192. Jastrow, Morris. Marduktabikzirim or Marduksapikzirim? pp. 214-219, n.d. Br572C An8141 v.116.

2193. Jastrow, Morris. On ikonomatic writing in Assyria. *Proceedings of the American Oriental Society* 13:18-22, 1887. Br572C An8141 v.12.

2194. Jastrow, Morris. On the founding of the city of Carthage (review). *Proceedings of the American Oriental Society,* n.d. 28 p. Br572C An8141 v.5.

2195. Jastrow, Morris. Recent movements in the historical study of religions in America. *Biblical World,* pp. 24-32, n.d. Br572C An8141 v.124.

2196. Jastrow, Morris. The letters of Abdiheba. *Hebraica,* pp. 24-46, n.d. Br572C An8141 v.116.

2197. Jastrow, Morris. The Men of Judah in the El-Amarna tablets. *Journal of Biblical Literature,* pp. 61-72, n.d. Br572C An8141 v.116.

2198. Jastrow, Morris. The origin of the form "yud-hey" of the divine name. *Zeitschrift für die Alttestamentliche Wissenschaft* 16, 1896. 16 p. Br572C An8141 v.140.

2199. Jastrow, Morris. The two copies of Rammannirari's inscription. *Zeitschrift für Assyriologie und Verwandte Gebiete* 10:35-48, 1895. Br572C An8141 v.131.

2200. Jensen, Peter. The solution of the Hittite question. *The Sunday School Times,* 1893. 16 p. Br572C An8141 v.122.

2201. Jewitt, John R. *Narrative of Adventures and Sufferings of John R. Jewett, Only Survivor of the Crew of the Ship Boston During a Captivity of Nearly Three Years Among the Savages of Nootka Sound; With an Account of the Manners, Mode of Living, and Religious Opinions of the Natives.* New York, 1824. 166 p. Br970.3 ToJ553.

2202. Jiménez de la Espada, Marcos, ed. *Tres relaciones de antigüedades peruanas.* Imprenta de M. Tello, Madrid, 1879. 328 p. Br913.85 Sp16. Includes: "Carta al excmo. Sr. D. F. de B. Queipo de Llano, conde de Toreno"; "Relación del orígen, descendencia, política y gobierno de los Incas, por el licenciado Fernando de Santillan"; "Relación de las costumbres antiguas de los naturales del Pirú"; and "Relación de antigüedades deste reyno del Pirú por don Joan de Santacruz Pachacuti Yamqui."

2203. Johnson, Elias. *Legends, Traditions and Laws, of the Iroquois, or Six Nations, and History of the Tuscarora Indians, by Elias Johnson, A Native Tuscarora Chief.* Union Printing and Publishing Company, Lockport, NY, 1881. 234 p. Br398.22 IJ635.

2204. Jomard, Edmé F. Seconde note sur une pierre gravée. *L'Académie des Inscriptions et Belles-Lettres,* 1845. 30 p. Br572C An8141 v.24.

2205. Jones, Charles C. Aboriginal structures in Georgia. *Annual Report of the United States National Museum, Smithsonian Institution, for 1877,* pp. 278-289, 1878. Br572C An8141 v.58.

2206. Jones, Charles C. Ancient tumuli in Georgia. *Proceedings of the American Antiquarian Society,* 1869. 29 p. Br572C An8141 v.38.

2207. Jones, Charles C. *Antiquities of the Southern Indians, Particularly of the Georgia Tribes.* D. Appleton, New York, 1873. 532 p. Br970.6 J72.

2208. Jones, Charles C. Canoe in Savannah River swamp. *Journal of the Anthropological Institute of New York* 1:67–70, 1871–1872. Br572C An8141 v.58.

2209. Jones, Charles C. *Hernando De Soto; The Adventures Encountered and the Route Pursued by the Adelantado During His March Through Georgia*. Savannah, 1880. 42 p. Br572C An8141 v.35.

2210. Jones, Charles C. *Historical Sketch of Tomo-chi-chi, Mico of the Yamacraws*. J. Munsell, Albany, NY, 1868. 133 p. Br970.2 T595.yJ.

2211. Jones, Charles C. *Indian Remains in Southern Georgia: Address Delivered Before the Georgia Historical Society*. Steam Press of John M. Cooper, Savannah, 1859. 25 p. Br572C An8141 v.70.

2212. Jones, Charles C. *Monumental Remains of Georgia*. John M. Cooper and Company, Savannah, 1861. 119 p. Br572C An8141 v.38; Br572C An8141 v.70.

2213. Jones, Joseph. *Explorations of the Aboriginal Remains of Tennessee*. Smithsonian Institution, Contributions to Knowledge, 22(1). Washington, DC, 1876. 171 p. Br913.768 J713. While practicing medicine in Tennessee between 1866 and 1868, Jones (1833-1896) conducted archaeological investigations of local earthworks, and conducted paleopathological examinations of early skeletal populations.

2214. Jones, Joseph. The aboriginal Mound Builders of Tennessee. *American Naturalist* 3:57–73, 1869. Br572C An8141 v.38.

2215. Jones, Peter, James Evans, and George Henry. *A Collection of Ojibway and English Hymns, for the Use of the Native Indians; Translated by the Late Rev. Peter James, Wesleyan Indian Missionary; to Which are Added a Few Hymns Translated by the Rev. James Evans and George Henry*. Printed for the Wesleyan Missionary Society, Toronto, 1869. 236 p. Br497.11 OJ71.

2216. Jones, Peter. *History of the Ojebway Indians; With Especial Reference to the Conversion to Christianity, by Rev. Peter Jones (Kahkewaquonaby), Indian Missionary; With a Brief Memoir of the Writer; and Introductory Notice by the Rev. G. Osborn, D. D., Secretary of the Weslayan Methodist Missionary Society*. A. W. Ben-

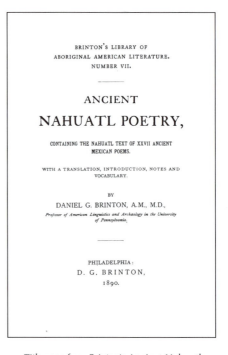

BRINTON'S LIBRARY OF
ABORIGINAL AMERICAN LITERATURE.
NUMBER VII.

ANCIENT

NAHUATL POETRY,

CONTAINING THE NAHUATL TEXT OF XXVII ANCIENT
MEXICAN POEMS.

WITH A TRANSLATION, INTRODUCTION, NOTES AND
VOCABULARY.

BY

DANIEL G. BRINTON, A.M., M.D.,
*Professor of American Linguistics and Archæology in the University
of Pennsylvania.*

PHILADELPHIA:
D. G. BRINTON,
1890.

Title page from Brinton's Ancient Nahuatl Poetry *(1890).*

nett, London, 1861. 278 p. Br970.3 OjJ72. Peter Jones was both a ruling chief of the Chippewa and a minister in the Wesleyan Methodist Church from 1833 until his death in 1856.

2217. Jordan, Francis. The remains of an aboriginal encampment at Rehoboth, Delaware; a paper read before the Numismatic and Antiquarian Society of Philadelphia, February 5, 1880. 7 p. Philadelphia, 1880. Br572C An8141 v.19.

2218. *Journal of the Anthropological Institute of Great Britain and Ireland* 23(2-3), 1894. Br572C An8141 v.130.

2219. *Journal of the Anthropological Institute of New York* 1(1), 1871-1872. 100 p. Br572.06 An88; Br572C An8141 v.35; Br572C An8141 v.37.

2220. *Journal of the Cincinnati Society of Natural History* 9(4): 226-244, 1887. Br572C An8141 v.19.

2221. Juarros, Domingo. *Compendio de la historia de la ciudad de Guatemala; escrito por Domingo Juarros.* Imprenta de Luna, Guatemala, 1857. 2 v. Br972.81 J877. Contents include: 1. "Descripción geográfica del reyno de Guatemala; geografía eclesiástica"; 2. "Cronicón de la ciudad de Guatemala"; 3. I"ndice cronológico de los varones ilustres, que ha tenido esta ciudad"; 4. "Parte 1a, en que se discurre sobre algunos puntos de la historia de este reyno en general; De la historia de las provincias, que se hallan situadas en la parte austral del reyno de Guatemala"; 5. "De las provincias situadas ácia la mar del Norte"; 6. "De las provincias…situadas en el medio."

2222. Kain, John H. An account of several ancient mounds and of two caves in east Tennessee. *American Journal of Science* 1:428-430, 1819. Br572C An8141 v.19.

2223. Kalendario conservado hasta el dia por los sacerdotes del sol en Yxtlavacam e pueblo descendiente de la nación kiche, descubierto por el presbitero Vicente Hernandez Spina, Santa Catarina Yxtlavacam (Ixtlahuacan), agosto 12 de 1854. 13 leaves. Br913.7281 K127.

2224. Kalvun, S. J. Araukanische Märchen und Erzählungen; gesammelt und übersetz von Rudolf Lenz, 1896. Br498.977 L545.

2225. *Kamloops Wawa; A Newspaper in Shorthand.* v. 4(7), 1895. Kamloops, British Columbia. Br572C An8141 v.149. Monthly periodical in Chinook edited by Fr. John M. Le Jeune.

2226. *Kamloops Wawa; A Newspaper in Shorthand.* v. 7(2), 1898; v. 10(3), 1901. Kamloops, British Columbia. Br497.19 K124. Monthly periodical in Chinook edited by Fr. John M. Le Jeune.

2227. Kanda, T. *Notes on Ancient Stone Implements, etc., of Japan.* Kokubunsha, Tokio, 1884. 8 p. Br572C An8141 v.103.

2228. Kane, Paul. *Les Indiens de la baie d'Hudson, promenades d'un artiste parmi les Indiens de l'Amerique du Nord.* Amyot, Paris, 1861. 273 p. Br970.1 K122.FD.

2229. Kane, Paul. *Wanderings of an Artist Among the Indians of North America from Canada to Vancouver's Island and Oregon, Through the Hudson's Bay Company's Territory and Back Again.* Longman, London, 1859. 455 p. Br970.1 K133. "The author, after four years study of art in Europe, returned to Canada filled with the determination to fulfill an early formed design of executing a series of drawings, of scenes in Indian life. To accomplish this, he traversed almost alone, the territories of the Red River Settlement, the valley of the Saskatchewan, across the Rocky Mountains, down the Columbia River, the shores of Puget Sound, and Vancouver's Island. The book is a transcript of his daily journal" (Field 1873:199).

2230. Kastner, Adolphe. *Analyse des traditions religieuses des peuples indigènes de l'Amérique, par Adolphe Kastner.* C. J. Fonteyn, Louvain, 1845. 120 p. Br398.21 K157.

2231. *Katalog der Ethnographischen Sammlung in Museum des Missionshauses zu Basel.* Basel, 1883. 65 p. Br572C An8141 v.71.

2232. Kawczynski, Maximilien. *Essai comparatif sur l'origine el l'histoire des rythmes.* Bouillon, Paris, 1889. 220 p. Br416 K174.

2233. Kay, Charles de. On a bronze Buddha in the United States National Museum. *Annual Report of the United States National Museum, Smithsonian Institution, for 1889,* pp. 427–445, 1891. Br572C An8141 v.17.

2234. Keane, Augustus H. *Ethnology.* University Press, Cambridge, 1896. 442 p. Br572 K196.

2235. Keary, Charles F. *Outlines of Primitive Belief Among the Indo-European Races.* C. Scribner's Sons, New York, 1882. 534 p. Br280 K21.

2236. Kellor, F.A. Sex in crime. *International Journal of Ethics* 9(1): 74–85, 1899. Br572C An8141 v.166.

2237. Kelton, Dwight H. *Indian Names of Places Near the Great Lakes.* Detroit Free Press, Detroit, 1888. 55 p. Br497.11K27.

2238. Kengla, Louis A. *Contributions to the Archaeology of the District of Columbia; An Essay to Accompany a Collection of Aboriginal Relics Presented for the Toner Medal, 1882.* Washington, DC, 1883. 42 p. Br572C An8141 v.59.

2239. Kennedy, James. *Essays Ethnological and Linguistic, By the Late James Kennedy, Esq., Formerly Her Brittanic Majesty's Judge at the Havana; Edited by C. M. Kennedy, B.A.* Williams and Norgate, London, 1861. 230 p. Br572 K38. Includes Carib words showing African affinities (pp. 120–121).

2240. Keys, D. R. et al. General bibliography of original contributions to the publications of the Canadian Institute. *Transactions of the Canadian Institute* 3:317–340, 1891–1892. Br572C An8141 v.114.

2241. Keyser, C. S. *Minden Armais; The Man of the New Race.* Press of American Printing House, Philadelphia, 1892. 125 p. Br572C An8141 v.89.

2242. *Ki-Eyboróri-gun poh eygamánin serra main. Totsarorona "Bible" yawon káreta Moses neméynogahpu, itéyzek "Genesis".* Society for Promoting Christian Knowledge, London, 1856, 189 p. Br498.78 AcB 45.9. First part of Genesis and the Gospel of St. Matthew, with supplementary extracts from the other Gospels, translated into Acawoio.

2243. Kingdon, John. *Leti u cilich evangelio jesu cristo hebix San Lucas.* W. M. Watts, Crown Court, Temple Bar, London, 1865. 90 p. Br498.21 MB47.2. Translation of the Gospel of St. Luke into Yucatec. Kingdon, a Baptist missionary, arrived in Belize in

1845 and founded several missions and translated the Yucatec Maya grammar of Joaquin Ruz (Tozzer 1921:145-146).

2244. Kirkby, William W. *A Manual of Prayer and Praise for the Cree Indians of North-West America*. Society for Promoting Christian Knowledge, London, 1879. 127 p. Br497.11 CrK63.

2245. Kirkby, William W. *Hymns and Prayers for the Private Devotions of the Slave Indians of McKenzie's River.* Rennie, Shea and Lindsay, New York, 1862. 16 p. Br497.12 SlK 63.

2246. Kirkby, William W. *Hymns, Prayers and Instruction in the Chipewyan Language.* Society for Promoting Christian Knowledge, London, 1881. 91 p. Br497.11 OK63.

2247. Kirkby, William W. *Manual of Devotion and Instruction, in the Chipewyan Language, for the Indians of Churchill.* Church Missionary House, London, 1872. 113 p. Br497.11 OK63.2.

2248. Kirkby, William W. *Portions of the Book of Common Prayer, Hymns, etc., in the Chipewyan Language; by Archdeacon Kirkby; Printed at the Request of the Bishop of Rupert's Land.* Society for Promoting Christian Knowledge, London, 1879. 195 p. Br497.12 CK633a.

2249. Kirkby, William W. *The New Testament, Translated into the Chipewayan Language by the Ven. Archdeacon Kirby.* Printed for the British and Foreign Bible Society, London, 1881. 396 p. Br497.12 CB473. New Testament translated into Chippewa.

2250. Kirkby, William W., and William C. Bompas. *Manual of Devotion in the Beaver Indian Dialect.* Society for Promoting Christian Knowledge, London, 1880. 48 p. Br497.12 SlK 63.2. Hymns, prayers, catechisms and lessons of the Church of England in the Tsattine language. Text in syllabic characters.

2251. Kirkby, William W., and William C. Bompas. *Portions of the Book of Common Prayer, Hymns, etc., in the Chipewyan Language; by Archdeacon Kirkby; Adapted for the Use of the Slavi Indians by the Right Rev. W. C. Bompas.* Society for Promoting Christian Knowledge, London, 1879. 175 p. Br497.12 CK633.

2252. Klein, J. *Drei römische Bleitafelchen. In Festschrift zum Fünfzigjährigen Jubiläum des Vereins von Alterthumsfreunden im Rheinlande*, pp. 129-146. Gedruckt auf Kosten des Vereins, Bonn, 1891. Br572C An8141 v.98.

2253. Kleinschmidt, G. Zwei Lemnische Inschriften. *Zeitschrift des Insterburger Alterhumsvereins* 3, 1893. 19 p. Br572C An8141 v.116.

2254. Kleinschmidt, Samuel. *Grammatik der grönlandischen Sprache mit theilweisen Einschluss des Labradordialects von Samuel Kleinschmidt*. Druch und Verlag von G. Reimer, Berlin, 1851, 182 p. Br497.25 GK675.

2255. Kloos, J. H. Die braunschweigischen Jadeitbeile. *Beiträge zur Anthropologie Braunschweigs* 21:59-68, 1898. Br572C An8141 v.164.

2256. Knipe, C. *Some Account of the Tahkaht Language, as Spoken by Several Tribes of the Western Coast of Vancouver Island.* Hatchard and Company, London, 1868. 80 p. Br497.59 TK74. Includes a Tahkaht grammar (pp. 9-31), and Tahkaht-English and English-Tahkaht dictionaries (pp. 31-80).

2257. Knortz, Karl. *Aus der Mappe eines Deutsch-Amerikaners; Frommes und Gottloses.* C. Schneider Verlag, Bamberg, 1893. 124 p. Br917.3 K754.

2258. Knortz, Karl. *Die Kolonie der Rappisten in Pennsylvanien.* Verlag von Ernst Wiest, Leipzig, 1892. 31 p. Br572C An8141 v.89.

2259. Knortz, Karl. *Folklore, von Karl Knortz, mit dem Unhange: Amerikanische Kinderreime.* Verlag der Druckerei Glöss, 1896. 85 p. Br572C An8141 v.140.

2260. Knortz, Karl. *Mythologie und Civilization der Nordamerikanischen Indianer.* Leipzig, 1882. 76 p. Br572C An8141 v.65.

2261. Kohl, Johann G. *Kitchi-gami; Wanderings Round Lake Superior.* Chapman and Hall, London, 1860. 428 p. Br970.3 OjK824. "An exhaustive and valuable treatise on Native American life, considered to be one of the best books on the Lake Superior country" (*Frank T. Siebert Library* 1999:1:285).

2262. Kohl, Johann G. *Reisen im Nordwesten der Vereinigten Staaten.* D. Appleton and Company, New York, 1857. 534 p. Br917.3 K823.

2263. Kollmann, Julius. Die Formen des Ober- und Unterkiefers bei den Europäern. *Schweizerischen Vierteljahrsschrift für Zahnheilkunde* 2(2), 1892. 32 p. Br572C An8141 v.121.

2264. Kollmann, Julius. Die Menschenrassen Europas und die Frage nach der Kerkunst der Arier. *Correspondenz-Blatt der Deutschen Anthropologischen Gesellschaft* 10:102-106, 1892. Br572C An8141 v.107.

2265. Kollmann, Julius. Flöten und Pfeifen aus Alt-Mexico. In *Bastian Festschrift.* Verlag von Dietrich Reimer (Ernst Vohsen), Berlin, 1896. 18 p. Br572C An8141 v.166.

2266. Kollmann, Julius. Pygmäen in Europa. *Verhandlungen der Anatomischen Gesellschaft* 13-16:206-216, 1894. Br572C An8141 v.136.

2267. Kollmann, Julius. Schädel aus alten Gräben bei Genf. *Verhandlungen der Naturforschenden Gesellschaft in Basel* 8(1): 204-241, 1886. Br572C An8141 v.88.

2268. Kollmann, M. S. Les races humaines de l'Europe et la question Arienne. *Berichten des Moskauer Congresses für Anthropologie und Urgeschichte,* pp. 249-262, n.d. Br572C An8141 v.132.

2269. Kongeligt Nordiske Oldskrift Selskab (Copenhagen). *Mémoires,* 1866-1893, 1895-1898. Br913.489 C793.

2270. Kongeligt Nordiske Oldskrift Selskab (Copenhagen). *Nordiske fortidsminder; antiquités scandinaves, résumés en français,* 1890. Br571.3 C793.

2271. Köppen, W. *Die Schreibung geographischer Namen.* Gustav W. Seitz, Hamburg, 1893. 39 p. Br572C An8141 v.122.

2272. Korajar, Vilim. *Die Pfahlbauern: Silhouetten aus slavonischen Ursitzen.* C. Daberkow's Verlag, Wien, 1882. 84 p. Br572C An8141 v.166.

2273. Krall, Jakob. *Die etruskischen Mumienbinden des Agramer National-Museums; beschrieben und hrsg. von prof. J. Krall; mit 10 Lichtdrucktafeln und 1 Abbildung im Texte.* Wien, F. Tempsky, Wien, 1892. 70 p. Br913.3791 K85.

2274. Krall, Jakob. *Die Etruskischen Mumienbinden.* Akademie der Wissenschaften, Wien, 1892. 11 p. Br572C An8141 v.82.

2275. Krause, Aurel. *Die Tlinkit-Indianer; Ergebnisse einer Reise nach der Nord-West-*

küste von Amerika und der Beringstrasse, ausgeführt im Auftrage der Bremer Geographischen Gesellschaft in der Jahren 1880-1881 durch die Doctoren Arthur und Aurel Krause; geschildert von dr. Aurel Krause. H. Costenoble, Jena, 1885. 420 p. Br970.3 KoK868.

2276. Krause, Ernst H. L. Ein archäologischer Beitrag zur nordeutschen Flora. *Botanisches Centralblatt* 65(6-7), 1896. 2 p. Br572C An8141 v.140.

2277. Krauss, Friedrich S. Abderiten von heute. *Am Ur- Quell: Monatschrift für Völkskunde* 7:117-119, 1891. Br572C An8141 v.5.

2278. Krauss, Friedrich S. Bojagic Alile's Glück und Grab; Zwei Moslimische Guslarenlieder, von Dr. Friedrich S. Krauss, in Wien. *Internationales Archiv für Ethnographie* 9:6-45, 1896. Br572C An8141 v.144.

2279. Krauss, Friedrich S. Der Tod in Sitte, Brauch und Glauben der Südslaven. *Zeitschrift des Vereins für Völkskunde* 2:177-189, 1892. Br572C An8141 v.82.

2280. Krauss, Friedrich S. Die Kosmogonie der Cherokee. *Am Ur-Quell Monatsschrift für Völkskunde*, pp. 86-100, 1891. Br572C An8141 v.110.

2281. Krusenstern, Adam J. von. *Wörter-Sammlungen aus den Sprachen einiger Völker des Östlichen Asiens und der Nordwest-Küste von Amerika; Bekannt gemacht von A. L. v. Krusenstern, Capitain der Russisch Kaiserlichen Marine.* Gedrukt in der Druckerey der Admiralität, St. Petersburg, 1813. 69 p. Br572C An8141 v.2.

2282. Kuhlenbeck, L. *Der Occultismus der nördamerikanischen Indianer.* Verlag von Wilhelm Friedrich, Leipzig, n.d. 60 p. Br572C An8141 v.153.

2283. Kunz, George F. Gold and silver ornaments from mounds of Florida. *American Antiquarian* 9(4): 219-227, 1887. Br572C An8141 v.59.

2284. *L'Homme: Journal Illustré des Sciences Anthropologiques.* no. 12, 1884. Paris. Br572C An8141 v.31; no, 18, 1886. Br572C An8141 v.24.

2285. La Borde, Sieur de. *History of the Origin, Customs, Religion, Wars, and Travels of the Caribs, Savages of the Antilles in America.* J. Thomson, Demerara, 1886. Br572C An8141 v.68. Extract from *Timenri; being the journal of the Royal Agricultural and Commercial Society* 5(2): 224-273, 1886. Abridged version of *Voyage qui content un relation exacte de l'origine moeurs, coutomes, réligiuon, guerres et voyages des Caraibes, sauvages des isles Antilles de l'Amerique, faite para le Sieur de la Borde, employé à la conversion des Caraibes* (Voyage ou Nouvelle Decouverte. L. Hennipin, ed., pp. 517-604. Amsterdam, 1704).

2286. La Grasserie, Raoul de, and N. Leon. *Langue tarasque.* Bibliothèque Linguistique Américaine, 19. Maisonneuve, Paris, 1896. 293 p. Br497C Am3.

2287. La Grasserie, Raoul G. de. *Catégorie des cas.* Jean Maisonneuve, Paris, 1890. 351 p. Br572C An8141 v.6.

2288. La Grasserie, Raoul G. de. *Cinq langues de la Colombie britannique.* Bibliothèque Linguistique Américaine, 24. Maisonneuve, Paris, 1902. Br497C Am3.

2289. La Grasserie, Raoul G. de. *De l'infixation.* Imprimerie P. Pigelet, Orléans, n.d. 27 p. Br572C An8141 v.135.

2290. La Grasserie, Raoul G. de. *De l'origine et de l'évolution premiére des racines des langues.* J. Maisonneuve, Paris, 1895. 174 p. Br572C An8141 v.152.

2291. La Grasserie, Raoul G. de. De la categorie des cas. In *Études de grammaire comparée*. Maisonneuve et Ch. Leclerc, Paris, 1890. 344 p. Br572C An8141 v.6.

2292. La Grasserie, Raoul G. de. *De la catégorie des modes*. Imprimerie J.B. Istas, Louvain, 1891. 111 p. Br572C An8141 v.6.

2293. La Grasserie, Raoul G. de. De la categorie des modes. In *Études de grammaire comparée*. Maisonneuve et Ch. Leclerc, Paris, 1891. 111 p. Br572C An8141 v.6.

2294. La Grasserie, Raoul G. de. De la categorie du nombre. In *Études de grammaire comparée*. Maisonneuve et Ch. Leclerc, Paris, 1887. 112 p. Br572C An8141 v.6.

2295. La Grasserie, Raoul G. de. De la classification de langues. pp. 296-338, 374-387, n.d. Br572C An8141 v.6.

2296. La Grasserie, Raoul G. de. *De la familie linguistique Pano*. Maisonneuve, Paris, 1888. 12 p. Br572C An8141 v.51.

2297. La Grasserie, Raoul G. de. De la véritable nature du pronom. *Études de Grammaire Comparée*, 1888. 50 p. Br572C An8141 v.87.

2298. La Grasserie, Raoul G. de. *Des recherches récentes de la linguistique relatives aux langues de l'Extreme Orient*. Imprimerie Nationale, Paris, 1891. 31 p. Br572C An8141 v.6.

2299. La Grasserie, Raoul G. de. Du syncrétisme pronominal. *La Revue de Linguistique*, pp. 3-72, 1895. Br572C An 8141 v.139.

2300. La Grasserie, Raoul G. de. *Esquisse d'une grammaire du Timucua langue de la Floride*. Jacob, Orleans, n.d. 44 p. Br572C An8141 v.52.

2301. La Grasserie, Raoul G. de. *Essai d'une grammaire et d'un vocabulaire de la langue Baniva*. Ernest Leroux, Paris, 1892. Br572C An8141 v.115.

2302. La Grasserie, Raoul G. de. *Études de grammaire comparée de la catégorie du temps*. Maisonneuve et Ch. Leclerc, Paris, 1888. 195 p. Br572C An8141 v.66.

2303. La Grasserie, Raoul G. de. *Études de grammaire comparée de la conjugaison objective*. Maisonneuve et Ch. Leclerc, Paris, 1888. 39 p. Br572C An8141 v.66.

2304. La Grasserie, Raoul G. de. *Ètudes de grammaire comparée de la possibilité et des conditions d'une langue internationale*. J. Maisonneuve, Libraire-Èditeur, 1892. 56 p. Br572C An8141 v.87.

2305. La Grasserie, Raoul G. de. *Études de grammaire comparée des divisions de la linguistique*. Maisonneuve et Ch. Leclerc, Paris, 1888. 164 p. Br572C An8141 v.66.

2306. La Grasserie, Raoul G. de. *Études de grammaire comparée du verbe: être: considéé comme instrument d'abstraction et de ses diverses fonctions*. Maisonneuve et Ch. Leclerc, Paris, 1887. 128 p. Br572C An8141 v.66.

2307. La Grasserie, Raoul G. de. Études de grammaire comparée: de l'inclusif et de l'exclusif. *Muséon*, 1893. 15 p. Louvain. Br572C An8141 v.132.

2308. La Grasserie, Raoul G. de. *Grammaire comparée de la psychologie du langue*. Maisonneuve et Ch. Leclerc, Paris, 1889. 108 p. Br572C An8141 v.87.

2309. La Grasserie, Raoul G. de. *Grammaire comparée de la véritable nature du pronom*. Imprimerie Lefever frères et soeur, Louvain, 1888. 50 p. Br572C An8141 v.87.

2310. La Grasserie, Raoul G. de. *Langue auca, ou langue indigène du Chili*. Bibliothèque Linguistique Américaine, 21. Maisonneuve, Paris, 1898. Br497C Am3.

2311. La Grasserie, Raoul G. de. *Langue puquina: textes puquina contenus dans le Rituale seu manuale peruanum de Gerónimo de Oré, publié à Naples en 1607; d'ápres un exemplaire trouvé à la Bibliotèque Nationale de Paris; avec texte espagnole en regard. traduction analytique interlinéaire, vocabulaire et essai de grammaire.* K. F. Köhler, Leipzig, 1894. 67. p. Br498.72 L 134.

2312. La Grasserie, Raoul G. de. *Langue zoque et langue mixe.* Bibliothèque Linguistique Américaine, 22. Maisonneuve, Paris, 1898. 168 p. Br497C Am3.

2313. La Grasserie, Raoul G. de. Langues de l'extreme orient. In *Études de grammaire comparée,* pp. 5-31. Maisonneuve et Ch. Leclerc, Paris, 1891. Br572C An8141 v.6.

2314. La Grasserie, Raoul G. de. Voca*bulaire timucua.* Georges Jacob, Orleans, n.d. 16 p. Br572C An8141 v.52.

2315. La Rochefoucauld, François A., duc de. *Palenqué et la civilisation maya, avec des croquis et indications à la plume par l'auteur.* E. Leroux, Paris, 1888. 192 p. Br498.21 ML324.

2316. Labarthe, Jean F. C. de. Documents inédits sur l'empire des Incas. Maisonneuve, Paris, 1861. 23 p. Br572C An8141 v.37.

2317. Laborde, D. Les fonctions intellectuelles et instinctives. *Revue Mensuelle de l'Ecole d'Anthropologie de Paris,* pp. 33-45, 1891. Br572C An8141 v.8.

2318. Lacombe, Albert. *Dictionnaire de la langue des Cris, par Alb. Lacombe.* C.O. Beauchemin et Valois, Montreal, 1874. 709 p. Br498.11 CrL11. Beauchemin, Montreal, 1874. 190 p. Lacombe (1827-1916) was an Oblate priest in the Canadian West who published a Cree grammar and dictionary as well as other volumes in Cree and Blackfoot. Between 1861 and 1895 he founded missions for Cree and Métis Indians.

2319. Lacombe, Albert. *Livre de prières, etc.,…en Sauteux.* Beauchemin, Montreal, 1880. 382 p, 1881 Br497.11 OR66.2.

2320. Lacombe, E. La fortaleza de Huichay y el arte de la fortificatión en el tiempo de los Incas. *Boletin de la Sociedad Geográfica de Lima* 2(4-6): 144-147, 1892. Br572C An8141 v.109.

2321. Lafitau, Joseph F. *Moeurs des sauvages ameriquains, comparées aux moeurs des premiers temps; par le P. Lafitau, de la Compagnie de Jesus.* Chez Saugrain l'aîné, Quay des Augustins, prés la ruë pavée, à la Fleur de Lys. Charles-Estienne Hochereau, Imprimerie à Rouen, et se vend A Paris, à l'entrée du Quay des Augustins, au Phénix, Rouen. 1724. 4 v. Br970.1 L132a. Lafitau (1681-1746), a French Jesuit, was assigned to Sault-Saint-Louis (Caughnawaga) and remained nearly six years. He studied the Iroquoian language and made studies of the customs of the Iroquois.

2322. Lafone y Quevedo, Samuel A. Colectores de vocabularios indígenas. *Revista del Museo de La Plata* 3, 1892. 16 p. Br572C An8141 v.109.

2323. Lafone y Quevedo, Samuel A. El culto de Tonapa. *Revista del Museo de La Plata* 3, 1892. 59 p. Br572C An8141 v.109.

2324. Lafone y Quevedo, Samuel A. El pueblo de Batungasta. *Anales del Museo de La Plata* 2:5-11, 1892. Br572C An8141 v.104.

2325. Lafone y Quevedo, Samuel A. El verbo; estudio filológico-gramático. *Revista del Museo de La Plata* 3, 1892. 55 p. Br572C An8141 v.109.

2326. Lafone y Quevedo, Samuel A. Huacas de Chañar-Yaco: catálogo descriptivo é ilustrado. *Revista del Museo de La Plata* 3, 1892. 31 p. Br572C An8141 v.109.

2327. Lafone y Quevedo, Samuel A. *Idioma abipón; ensayo fundado sobre el de Abiponibus de Dobrizhoffer y los manuscritos del J. Brignier; con introducción, mapa, notas y apéndices.* Coni, Buenos Aires, 1896. 371 p. Br498.97 AQ38.

2328. Lafone y Quevedo, Samuel A. *Idioma mbaya; llamado guacururú según Hervas gilü y castelnau, con introducción, notas y mapa.* Imprenta de P. E. Coni é Hijos, Buenos Aires, 1896. 62 p. Br498.97 MbQ 38.2.

2329. Lafone y Quevedo, Samuel A. Las huacas de Chanar-Yaco. *La Nacion*, pp. 353–360, 1891. Br572C An8141 v.119.

2330. Lafone y Quevedo, Samuel A. *Las migraciones de los indios en la America meridional.* Pirciao, 1895. Br980.4 SQ38.

2331. Lafone y Quevedo, Samuel A. *Lenguas argentinas; idioma abipón; ensayo fundado sobre el "De Abiponibus" de Dobrizhoffer y los manuscritos del padre J. Brigniel, S. J. con introducción, mapas, notas y apéndices.* Imprenta de P. E. Coni, Buenos Aires, 1896. 371 p. Br498.97M Q 38. Contents include: Alonso Barcena, "Arte y vocabulario de la lengua toba; con un lexicon toba-catellano y otras piezas por Samuel A. Lafone y Quevedo"; Samuel A. Lafone y Quevedo, "La lengua vilela ó chulupí; estudio de fiología chaca-argentina fundado sobre los trabajos de Hervas adelung y Pelleschi," 1895; Samuel A. Lafone y Quevedo, "Observaciones sobre el vocabulario del Giovanni Pelleschi"; Giovanni Pelleschi, "Vocabulario chulupí ó vilela"; Samuel A. Lafone y Quevedo, "Apendice vocabularios de los indios chunupus chaco austral"; Samuel A. Lafone y Quevedo, "Tesoro de Catamarqueñismos, nombres de lugar y apellidos indios con etimologias y eslabones aislados de la lengua cacama"; Joaquín Remedi, "Los indios matacos y su lengua, con vocabularios ordenados [mataco-castellano] por Samuel A. Lafone y Quevedo," 1896; A. D. d'Orbigny, "Dialecto vejoz, vocabulario y apuntes, con introducción, notas…por Samuel A. Lafone y Quevedo," 1896; Samuel A. Lafone y Quevedo, "Idioma mbaya según Hervas Gilu y castelnau," 1896; Inocencio Massei, "Dialecto nocten; pater noster y apuntes, con introducción y notas por Samuel A. Lafone y Quevedo," 1896; Samuel A. Lafone y Quevedo, "Los indios chanases y su lengua con apuntes sobre los Guerandíes, Yarós, Boanes, Güenoas ó Minuanes y un mapa etnico," 1897; Samuel A. Lafone y Quevedo, "Idioma abipón, ensayo fundado sobre el De Abiponibus de Dobrifhoffen y los manuscritos del…J. Brigniel, con introducción, mapa, notas y apéndices," 1896; Guido Boggiani, "Importante correspondencia apuntes sueltos de la lengua de los indios caduveos del Chaco paraguayo," 1897.

2332. Lafone y Quevedo, Samuel A. *Los lules; estudio filológico y calepino lule-castellano; seguido del catecismo; vade mecum para el arte y vocabulario del…Antonio Machoni.* Imprenta y Encuadernación Roma, Buenos Aires, 1894. 145 p. Br498.971 LQ 38.

2333. Lafone y Quevedo, Samuel A. *Mocoví ms. del P. Francisco Tavolini (Biblioteca del Gen-*

eral Mitre) y otros documentos. Biblioteca Lingüística del Museo de La Plata. Sección del Chaco, Talleres de Publicaciones del Museo, La Plata, 1893. 573 p. Br498.97 MbQ 38. Includes S. Lafone y Quevedo, "Introducción al arte Mocoví del Padre Tavolini, estudio de gramática comparada; Fr. Francisco Tavolini, Reglas para aprender á hablar la lengua moscovítica"; S.A. Lafone y Quevedo, "Notas ó sea principios de gramática Mocoví segun ellos se desprenden de los trabajos de Tavolini, Dobrizhoffer, Barcena y otros"; S.A. Lafone y Quevedo, "Vocabulario mocoví-español fundado en los del P. Tavolini."

2334. Lafone y Quevedo, Samuel A. *Tesoro de catamarqueñismos nombres de lugares y apellidos indios con etimologías y eslabones aislados de la lengua cacana.* Imprenta de Pablo e Coni e Hijos, Buenos Aires, 1898 377 p. Br498.975 CQ 38.

2335. Lafone y Quevedo, Samuel A. Vocabulario toba-castellano-ingles; fundado en el vocabulario y arte del...A. Bárcena, con equivalencias del indio sopez en 1888. In *Arte de la languae toba*, Alonso Bárcena, ed., pp. 157–234. Talleres de Publicaciones del Museo,.La Plata, 1893. Br498.97 TQ 38.

2336. Lagunas, Juan Baptista de. *Arte y diccionario tarascos por el P. Fr. Juan Bautista de Lagunas, impresos en México el año 1574; los reimprimé por vez primera el Doctor Nicolás León.* Imprenta y lit. en la Escuela de Artes, Morelia, 1890. 168 p. Br498.27 L133.

2337. Lahitte, Charles de. *La teo-cosmogonía, base de la filosofía positiva explicada racionalmente según el Guaraní.* Establecimiento Tipográfico Cangallo, Buenos Aires, 1899. 66 p. Br498.75 GL 133.

2338. Lahontan, Louis Armand, baron de. Woordenboek van de taal der wilden. Extract from his *Reizen...in het noordelyk Amerika*, v.2, pp. 524–552, 1739. Br497.11 Al L134. Lahontan, a French soldier serving in Canada, fought the Iroquois, commanded a frontier fort in present-day Michigan, and claimed to have ascended the Mississippi, though a stretch of the imagination, it was probably the Minnesota River" (Siebert Library 1999:2:104).

2339. Lallemant, German A. Sobre la cordillera de Mendoza. *Boletín del Instituto Geográfico Argentino* 10:351–380, 1889. Br572C An8141 v.38.

2340. Lambert, T. H. *America: A Name of Native Origin.* C. T. Dillingham, New York, 1893. 27 p. Br572C An8141 v.153.

2341. Lanciani, Rodolfo A. *Forma urbis Romae.* Apud Ulricum Hoepli, Mediolani, 1893–1901. 8 v. Br913.371 R55L.1.

2342. Landa, Diego de. *Relation des choses de Yucatán de Diego de Landa; texte espagnol et traduction française en regard comprenant les signes du calendrier et de l'alphabet hieroglyphique de la langue maya accompagne de documents divers historiques et chronologiques, avec une grammaire et un vocabulaire abreges français-maya; precedes d'un essai sur les sources de l'histoire primitive du Mexique, et de l'Amerique Centrale etc., apres les monuments egyptiens et de l'histoire primitive de l'Egypt d'apres les monuments américains, par l'Abbe Brasseur de Bourbourg, ancien administrateur ecclesiastique des indiens de Rabinal (Guatemala), membre de la Commission Scientifique du Mexique, etc.* Arthus Bertrand, Paris, 1864. 516 p. Br917.26 L23. Includes "Esquisse d'une grammaire de la langue maya d'apres celles de Beltrán et de Cruz" (pp. 459–479) and "Vocabulaire maya-français d'apres divers auteurs anciens et modernes" (pp. 480–512). Bishop Diego de Landa, the second bishop of Yucatan, was a central figure in Mayan history.

2343. Lang, Andrew. *Custom and Myth*. Harper, New York, 1885. 312 p. Br398 L25. Andrew Lang (1844-1912) was a Scottish folklorist, ethnologist and poet who demonstrated that similar myths are found in cultures separated by space and language. He argued further that myths reflect how people think and are, in some sense, a form of history.

2344. Lang, John D., and Samuel Taylor. *Report of A Visit to Some of the Tribes of Indians Located West of the Mississippi River.* M. Day, New York, 1843. 34 p. Br572C An8141 v.32.

2345. Lange, G. Las ruinas de la fortaleza del Pucara. *Anales del Museo de La Plata* 3:3-12, 1892. Br572C An8141 v.104.

2346. Lange, G. Las ruinas del pueblo de Watungasta. *Anales del Museo de La Plata* 2:3-4, 1892. Br572C An8141 v.104.

2347. Lanman, Charles R. The beginnings of Hindu pantheism; read before American Philological Association, 22 annual meeting, July 8, 1890. 24 p. Br572C An8141 v.9.

2348. Lanning, C. M. *A Grammar and Vocabulary of the Blackfoot Language, Being a Concise and Comprehensive Grammar for the Use of the Learner, to Which is Added an Exhaustive Vocabulary, Containing Upwards of Five Thousand Words, Phrases, and Sentences, Compiled by C. M. Lanning From Original Translations by Joseph Kipp and W.S. Gladston, Jr.* Lanning, Fort Benton, Montana Territory, 1882. 143 p. Br497.11 SiL 28. "Lanning, a Montana Territory merchant, wrote this Blackfoot grammar; 'It is for those who wish to be able to exchange ideas with those people of the prairie, that this little volume has been published' " (*Frank T. Siebert Library* 1999:2:324).

2349. Lanzi, Luiz. *El devoto instruido en el santo sacrificio de la misa; traducción libre al idióma Yucateco, con unos afectos por el P. Fr. Joaquín Ruz, con las licencias necessarias.* José Antonio Pino, Mérida de Yucatán, 1835, 18 p. Br498.21 ML 299.

2350. Lapham, Increase A. *The Antiquities of Wisconsin, As Surveyed and Described by I. A. Lapham.* Smithsonian Institution, Contributions to Knowledge, v. 7. Washington, DC, 1855. 95 p. Br913.775 L314.

2351. Lapham, Increase A., Levi Blossom and George G. Dousman. A paper on the number, locality, and times of removal of the Indians of Wisconsin, 1870. 27 p. Br572C An8141 v.32.

2352. Lapouge, Georges Vacher, comte de. L'anthropologie et la science politique. *Revue d'Anthropologie*, 1887. 22 p. Br572C An8141 v.31.

2353. Latham, Robert G. *Opuscula Essays, Chiefly Philological and Ethnographical.* Williams and Norgate, London; R. Hartmann, Leipzig, 1860. 418 p. Br409.7 L34. Essays on North and Central American languages.

2354. Laudonnière, René Goulaine de. *L'histoire notable de la Floride; situèe es Indes Occidentales; contenant les trois voyages faits en icelle par certains capitaines et pilotes françois, descrits par le capitaine Laudonnière, qui y a commandé l'e-*

Increase A. Lapham (from Justin Winsor, Aboriginal America. Cambridge, MA: Houghton, Mifflin, 1889. p. 400).

space d'un an trois moys; à laquelle a esté adjousté un quatriesme voyage fait par le capitaine Gourgues. Mise en lumière par M. Basanier. P. Jannet, Paris, 1853. 228 p. Br917.59 L36.

2355. Laverlochère, Jean N., and André M. Garin, trans. *Catechisme, recueil de prières et de cantiques à l'usage des sauvages d'Albany, (Baie-d'Hudson).* L. Perrault, Montreal, 1854. 94 p. Br497.11 CrL38. Text in the Cree language, syllabic characters.

2356. Lawrence, Robert M. *The Magic of the Horse-Shoe; With Other Folk-Lore Notes.* Gay and Bird, London, 1898. 344 p. Br398 L43.

2357. Laws, Edward. Report of the Ethnographic Survey of Pembrokeshire. *Report of the Ethnographical Survey of the United Kingdom,* pp. 610-612, 1896. Br572C An8141 v.150.

2358. Lawson, Andrew C. Ancient rock inscriptions of the Lake of the Woods. *American Naturalist* 19(7): 654-657, 1885. Br572C An8141 v.13.

2359. LeBeau, Claude. *Avantures du Sr. C. Le Beau, avocat en parlement, ou voyage curieux et nouveau, parmi les sauvages de l'Amérique septentrionale; dans le quel on trouvera une description du Canada, avec une relation très particulière des anciennes coutumes, moeurs et façons de vivre des barbares qui l'habitent et de la manière dont ils se comportent aujourd'hui.* Chez Hermann Uytwerf, Amsterdam, 1738. 2 v. Br970.1 L49. "The writer had some acquaintance certainly with the peculiar habits of American savages, but whether the result of personal experience or derived from others, and where the boundary line is to be drawn between the incidents of intercourse with them, and the offspring of his imagination, we are left without any guide to determine" (Field 1873:229–230).

2360. LeBon, Gustave. *Lois psychologiques de l'évolution des peuples.* 2d ed. F. Alcan, Paris, 1895, 186 p. Br140 L49.

2361. *Lecciones espirituales para las tandas de ejercicios de S. Ignacio, dadas a los In-*

dios en el idioma mexicano, compuestas por un sacerdote del obispado de la Puebla de los Angeles. Imprenta Antigua, Puebla, 1841. 213 p. Br498.22 AzP 11.

2362. Leclerc, Charles. *Arte de la lengua de los indios Antis o Campas...con un vocabulario metodico i una introducción comparative por Lucien Adam.* Bibliothèque Linguistique Américaine, 13. Maisonneuve, Paris, 1890. Br497C Am3.

2363. Leclerc, Charles. *Bibliotheca americana; catalogue raisonné d'une très-précieuse collection de livres anciens et modernes sur l'Amerique et les Philippines, classés par ordre alphabétique de noms d'auteurs; rédigé par Ch. Leclerc.* Maisonneuve et Cie., Paris, 1867. 424 p. Br970B L493.

2364. LeConte, John L. On the distinctive characteristics of the Indians of California. pp. 378-382, 1852. Br572C An8141 v.19.

2365. Lefèvre, André. *Du cri à la parok.* Ancienne Librarie Germerr-Bailliere, Paris, 1891. 19 p. Br572C An8141 v.8.

2366. Legoff, Laurent. *Cours d'instructions en langue montagnaise par le Rev. pere Legoff.* Imprimerie J. Fournier, Montreal, 1889. 444 p. Br497.12 MnL52.

2367. Legoff, Laurent. *Katolik deneya 'tiye dittlisse; livre de prieres en langue montagnaise par le Rev. pere Legoff.* C.O. Beauchemin et Fils, Montreal, 1890. 404 p. Br497.12 MnR66.

2368. Legoff, Laurent. *Livre des prières en langue montagnaise...par le Rév. père Legoff.* C.O. Beauchemin et Fils, Montreal, 1890. 440 p. Br497.12 MnR66.2.

2369. Lehmann-Nitsche, Robert. Antropología y craneología: conferencia dada en la sección antropológica del primer Congreso Científico Latino-Americano, Buenos Aires, 10-20 de abril de 1898. *Revista del Museo de La Plata* 9:3-20, 1898. Br572C An8141 v.99. Lehmann-Nitsche (1872-1938) studied anthropology and medicine at Freiburg im Breisgau, Berlin, and Munich. In 1898 he was awarded the Goddard Prize by the French Anthropological Society for his dissertation on long bones found in Bavarian line graves. He published extensively on the folklore, ethnography, archaeology, and linguistics of the original inhabitants of Argentina. In 1897 he was appointed director of the anthropology department at the museum in Buenos Aires, and in 1906 he received the first professional chair in physical anthropology established in South America at La Plata University.

2370. Lehmann-Nitsche, Robert. *Beiträge zur prähistorischen Chirurgie nach Funden aus Deutscher Vorzeit.* Buchdruck. von Fessel und Mengen, Buenos Aires, 1898. 28 p. B5617.09 L52.

2371. Lehmann-Nitsche, Robert. *Lepra precolombiana; ensayo critico.* Talleres de Publicaciones del Museo, La Plata, 1898. 34 p. Br572.97 L524a.

2372. Lehmann-Nitsche, Robert. *Quelques observations nouvelles sur les Indiens Guayaquis du Paraguay.* Publicaciones del Museo de La Plata, La Plata, 1899. 12 p. Br980.3 GuL524.

2373. Lehmann-Nitsche, Robert. *Trois crânes, un trépané, un lésionné, un perforé, conservés au Musée de La Plata et au Musée National de Buenos Aires.* Talleres de Publicaciones del Museo, La Plata, 1899. 42 p. Br572.97 L524a; Br573.7 L527.

2374. Leidy, Joseph. Notice of some fossil human bones. *Transactions of the Wagner*

Free Institute of Science 2:9–12, 1889. Br572C An8141 v.98.

2375. Leidy, Joseph. Remarks on the nature of organic species. *Transactions of the Wagner Free Institute of Science* 2:51–53, 1889. Br572C An8141 v.98.

2376. Leitner, Gottlieb W. A secret religion in the Hindukush (the Pamir region) and in Lebanon. *Asiatic Quarterly Review,* April, 1893. 14 p. Br572C An8141 v.116.

2377. Leitner, Gottlieb W. An appeal of Orientalists in favour of the maintenance of the original principles of the 1889 International Congress of Orientalists…followed by a declaration signed by 161 Orientalists, n.d. 8 p. Br572C An8141 v.29.

2378. Leitner, Gottlieb W. *Anthropological Observations on…Dards and Kafirs Being Appendix V, A Supplement to the Second Edition of the Hunza and Nagyr Handbook.* Oriental Nobility Institute, Woking, England, 1893. 8 leaves. Br572C An8141 v.117.

2379. Leitner, Gottlieb W. *Muhammadanism.* Oriental Nobility Institute, Woking, England, 1889. 36 p. Br572C An8141 v.29.

2380. Leitner, Gottlieb W. *On the Sciences of Language and of Ethnography with General Reference to the Language and Customs of the People of Hunza.* Harvard Publishing Union, London, 1890. 16 p. Br572C An8141 v.29.

2381. Leitner, Gottlieb W. The Kelám-I-Pir and esoteric Muhammadism. *Asiatic Quarterly Review,* pp. 159–167, n.d. Br572C An8141 v.116.

2382. Leland, Charles G. *Song of the Bees.* Campbello, New Brunswick, 1883. 2 p. Br497.11 AL53.

2383. Leland, Charles G. *The Algonquin Legends of New England; Or, Myths and Folklore of the Micmac, Passamaquoddy, and Penobscot Tribes.* Houghton, Mifflin and Company, Boston, 1884. 379 p. Br398.22 AeL534.

2384. Leland, Charles G. The mythology, legends, and folk-lore of the Algonkins. *Transactions of the Royal Society of Literature* 24(1), 1887. 24 p. Br572C An8141 v.110.

2385. LeMoine, James M. *The Scot in New France; An Ethnological Study; Inaugural Address, Lecture Season, 1880–81; Read Before the Literary and Historical Society of Quebec, 29th November, 1880.* Dawson Brothers, Montreal, 1881. 83 p. Br971 L54.

2386. Lengua maya de Yucatán. n.d. 53 p. Br498.21 ML 545. Manuscript; transcribed by Karl H. Berendt; followed by manuscript notes.

2387. Lentzner, Karl A. *Bemerkungen über die spanische Sprache in Guatemala.* Ehrhardt Karras' Verlag, Halle-Leipzig, 1892. Br572C An8141 v.84.

2388. Lentzner, Karl A. *Colonial English: A Glossary of Australian, Anglo-Indian, Pidgin English, West Indian, and South African Words.* Kegan Paul, Trench, Trübner, London, 1891. 237 p. Br572C An8141 v.117.

2389. Lentzner, Karl A. *Das Kreuz bei den Angelsachen.* O. R. Reisland, Leipzig, 1890. 28 p. Br572C An8141 v.85.

2390. Lentzner, Karl A. *Der Berlinische Dialekt; Untersucht und nach aufzeichnungen Richtiger Berliner herausgegeben.* Williams and Norgate, London, 1893. 15 p. Br572C An8141 v.116.

2391. Lentzner, Karl A. *Edward Thring, The Classics.* Max Niemeyer, Halle, 1890. 32 p. Br572C An8141 v.85.

2392. Lentzner, Karl A. *Ophelia und Porzia.* O. R. Reisland, Leipsig, 1890. Br572C An8141 v.85.

2393. Lentzner, Karl A. Robert Browning's Sonettdichtung. *Zeitschrift Anglia*, pp. 500-517, 1889. Br572C An8141 v.85.

2394. Lentzner, Karl A. *Tesoro de voces y provincialismos hispano-americanos, pub. por Carlos Lentzner; tomo I, pte. 1. La región del Rio de la Plata.* E. Karras, Halle a. S., Leipzig, 1892. 63 p. Br467.1 L544.

2395. Lentzner, Karl A. *Three Essays.* Max Niemeyer, Halle, 1890. Br572C An8141 v.85.

2396. Lentzner, Karl A. *Über das Sonett und seine Gestaltung in der englischen Dichtung bis Milton.* Max Niemeyer, Halle, 1886. 81 p. Br572C An8141 v.85.

2397. Lentzner, Karl A. *Über einige von Shakepeare's Frauen-Charakteren.* E. C. Brunn's Buchdruckerei, Münster, 1885. 29 p. Br572C An8141 v.85.

2398. Lentzner, Karl A. *Zur Shakespeare-Bacon Theorie.* Max Niemeyer, Halle, 1890. 48 p. Br572C An8141 v.85.

2399. Lenz, Rudolf. *Critica de la langue auca del...R. G. de la Grasserie.* Cervantes, Santiago de Chile, 1898. 21 p. Br498.977 AuG 766yL.

2400. Lenz, Rudolf. *De la literatura araucana; discurso leido en la sesión pública de la Facultad de Filosofía I Humanidades de la Universidad de Chile el 1 de octubre de 1897.* C. F. López S., Chillán, 1897. 44 p. Br498.977 L545.

2402. Lenz, Rudolf. Der Ausbruch des Vulcans Calbuco; nach der Beschreibung eines Indianers von Orinoco. *Verhandlungen des Deutschen Wissenschaftlichen Vereins zu Santiago* 3:133-139, 1895. Br498.977 L545.

2402. Lenz, Rudolf. Dialogos en dialecto noluche; segun dictado del indio Juan Calvun de Cholchol, Araucania central. *Anales de la Universidad de Chile* 97:448-485, 1895-1897. Br498.977 ML 542.

2403. Lenz, Rudolf. *Estudios araucanos materiales para el estudio de la lengua, la literatura i las costumbres de los indios mapuche o araucanos; diálogos en cuatro dialectos, cuentos populares, narraciones históricas i descriptivas, i cantos de los indios de Chile en lengua mapuche.* Imprenta Cervantes, Santiago de Chile, 1895-1897. 485 p. Br498.977 L545. German version, by Lenz, of the tales contributed by Calvun appeared first in *Verhandlungen des Deutschen Wissenschaftlichen Vereins zu Santiago de Chile*, Bd. 3, pp. 169-238, under the title Araukanische märchen und erzählungen mitgeteilt von Segundo Jara (Kalvun) Araucanian Indians; contents include: 1. "Introducción a los estudios araucanos," 1896; 2. "Viaje al pais de los Manzaneros," 1895; 3. "Diálogos araucanos en dialecto hulliche," n.d.; 4. "Diálogos araucanos en dialecto picunche," 1895; 5. "Diálogos en dialecto pehuenche chileno," 1896; 6-9. "Cuentos araucanos referidos por el indio Calvun," 1896-1897; 10. "Cantos araucanos en moluche i pehuenche chileno," 1897; 11. "Trozos descriptivos documentos para el estudio del folk-lore araucano en dialecto pehuenche chileno," 1897.

2404. Lenz, Rudolf. *Kritik der Langue auca des Herrn Dr. jur. Raoul de la Grasserie; eine Warnung für Amerikanisten, von Rudolf Lenz.* Imprenta del Universo de Gmo. Helfmann, Valparaiso, 1898. 53 p. Br498.977 AuG 766yLa.

2405. León Pinelo, Antonio de. El prospero o Lacandon, 1639. 22 leaves. Br572C An8141 v.106. Manuscript, transcribed by Karl H. Berendt.

2406. León y Gama, Antonio de. *Descripción histórica y cronológica de las dos piedras que con ocasión del nuevo empedrado que se está formando en la plaza principal de México, se hallaron en ella el año de 1790; explícase el sistema de los calendarios de los Indios, el método que tenian de dividir el tiempo, y la corrección que hacian de él para igualar el año civil, de que usaban, con el año solar trópico. Noticia muy necesaria para la perfecta inteligencia de la segunda piedra: á que se añaden otras curiosas é instructivas sobre la mitología de los Mexicanos, sobre su astronomía, y sobre los ritos y ceremonias que acostumbraban en tiempo de su gentilidad.* 2d ed. Imprenta del Ciudadano A. Valdés, México, 1832. 114, 148 p. Br913.72 L55.

2407. León y Gama, Antonio de. *Saggio dell'astronomia, cronologia e mitologia degli antichi Messicani.* Presso il Salomoni, Roma, 1792, 184 p. Br913.72 L55.2. Translation by Pietro Giuseppe Marquez of *Descripción histórica y cronológica de las dos piedras.*

2408. León, Martín de. *Camino del cielo en lengva mexicana, con todos los requisitos necessarios para conseguir este fin, co[n] todo lo que vn Xp[r]iano deue creer, saber, y obrar, desde el punto que tiene vso de razon, hasta que muere; co[m]puesto por el P. F. Martin de Leo[n].* En la Emprenta de Diego López Daualos, en México, an[n]o de 1611. 160 leaves. Br498.22 AzL 555.

2409. León, Nicolás. *Anomalies et mutilations ethniques du systeme dentaire ches les Tarasques pre-colombiens.* Imprimerie et Litographie de l'Ecole des Arts et Metiers, Morelia, México, 1890. 9 p. Br572C An8141 v.101.

2410. León, Nicolás. *Apuntes para la historia de la medicina en Michoacan.* Imprenta del Gobierno en la Escuela de Artes, Morelia, 1886 47 p. Br610.9 L554.

2411. León, Nicolás. *Biblioteca botánico-mexicana; catalogo bibliográfico, biográfico y critico de autores y escritos referentes a vegetales de México y sus aplicaciones, desde la conquista hasta el presente; suplemento a la materia médica mexicana publicada por el Instituto Médico Nacional.* Oficina Tipografica de la Secretaría de Fomento, México, 1895. 372 p. Br581.972B L552.

2412. León, Nicolás. *Diccionario popular y manual historia antigua de México* [prospectus]. W. J. Agüeros, Santo Domingo, 1896. 8 p. Br913.72 L553.

2413. León, Nicolas. La catedral de Patzcuaro. *Memorias de la Sociedad Cientifica Alzate de Mexico* 11:75-79, 1897. Br572C An8141 v.166.

2414. León, Nicolás. *La moneda del General Insurgente Don José Maria Morelos; ensayo numismático.* Tipografía del Gobierno de Morelos, Cuernavaca, 1897. 40 p. Br572C An8141 v.154.

2415. León, Nicolás. *Noticia descripción de un codice del Ilmo. D. Fr. Bartolomé de Las Casas.* Morelia, 1886. 10 p. Br572C An8141 v.71.

2416. León, Nicolás. *Piedad heroica de D. Fernando Cortes, marques del Valle.* 2d ed. Talleres de la Librería Religiosa, Mexoco, 1898. Br572C An8141 v.154.

2417. León, Nicolás. *Silabario del idioma tarasco o de Michoacán.* Imprenta de Don José Rosario Bravo, Morelia, 1886. 15 p. Br498.27 TL 555.

Nicolás León (from Frederick Starr, Recent Mexican Study of the Native Languages of Mexico. *Chicago: University of Chicago Press, 1900. p. 5).*

2418. León, Nicolás. *Tres obras de Sigüenza y Góngora.* Imprenta del Gobierno, en la Escuela de Artes, Morelia, 1886. 10 p. Br572C An8141 v.71.

2419. León, Nicolás. *Un impreso mexicano del siglo XVI.* Imprenta de J. R. Bravo, Morelia, 1887. 2 p. Br572C An8141 v.71.

2420. León, Nicolás. Un nuevo documento geroglífico maya. *Memorias de la Sociedad Cientifica Alzate de Mexico* 10(21): 355-358, 1896. Br572C An8141 v.154.

2421. León, Nicolás. Una respuesta y una pregunta al Sr. Profesor D. Alonso L. Herrera, 1895. 3 p. Br572C An8141 v.140.

2422. LePlongeon, Alice D. *Here and There in Yucatán Miscellanies.* J. W. Bouton, New York, 1886. 146 p. Br917.26 L554.

2423. LePlongeon, Augustus. *Sacred Mysteries Among the Mayas and the Quiches, 11,500 Years Ago; Their Relation to the Sacred Mysteries of Egypt, Greece, Chaldea and India; Free Masonry in Times Anterior to the Temple of Solomon.* R. Macoy, New York, 1886. 163 p. Br289.4 L554. Augustus LePlongeon (1825-1908) is remembered for his theorizing on how the ancient Maya were linked to the people of the lost city of Atlantis. He also argued fore the existence of Masonic orders among the ancient Maya, and that Maya mariners had traveled the world establishing civilizations in India, Egypt, and Burma. However, he did provide his predecessors with many excellent photographs of the Maya site Chichén Itzá in northern Yucatan.

2424. LePlongeon, Augustus. *Vestiges of the Mayas or, Facts Tending to Prove That Communications and Intimate Relations Must Have Existed, In Very Remote Times, Between the Inhabitants of Mayab and Those of Asia and Africa.* J. Polhemus, Printer, New York, 1881. 86 p. Br970.3 MaL554.

2425. Lepsius, R. *Über die Tyrrhenischen Pelasger in Etrurien und über die Verbreitung des Italischen Münzsystems von Etrurien aus.* Georg Wigand, Leipzig, 1842. 80p. Br572C An8141 v.82.

2426. Lery, Jean de. *Histoire d'un voyage faict en la terre du Bresil, autrement dite Amerique; contenant la navigation et choses remarquables, veues sur mer par auteur; le comportement de Vullegagnon en ce pays la; les moeurs et façons de viure estranges des sauvages bresiliens; avec un collogue de leur langage; ensamble la description de plusieurs animaux, arbres, herbes.* 3d ed. Chuppin, n.p., 1585. 427 p. Br918.1 L566. "The author sailed for Brazil in 1563 and after a residence of nearly eighteen years returned to France, and from his journals and writings composed this book. It has a high value as a historical work being the results of a long experience among the savages of South America" (Field 1873:235).

2427. *Leti u cilich ebanhelio hezu-clizto hebix Zan Lucas.* Baptist Bible Translation Society, London, 1870. 14 p. Br498.21 MB472. Contains chapters 5, 11, 15, and 23 of the Gospel of Luke in the Maya language, taken almost bodily from the 1865 edition, the principal changes being in dropping the accents, changing the reverse c to s, and the initial y to i. A note by Berendt states "Printed from a corrected text of the Reverend [Joaquín] Ruz's translation, corrected by the Rev. Alexander Henderson, Baptist Translation Society, London, 1878."

2428. *Leti u ebanheles Hezu Crizto helix Marcoz.* British and Foreign Bible Society, London, 1900. 67 p. Br497.21 MB473. New Testament Gospel of St. Mark translated into Yucatec.

2429. Letourneau, Charles J. M. *L'évolution de l'éducation dans les diverses races humaines.* Bibliothèque Anthropologique, 19. Vigot Frères, Paris, 1898. 617 p. Br370.9 L563.

2430. Letourneau, Charles J. M. *L'évolution de l'esclavage dans les diverses races humaines.* Bibliothèque Anthropologique, 17. Vigot Frères, Paris, 1897. 538 p. Br326.9 L56.

2431. Letourneau, Charles J. M. *L'évolution du commerce dans les diverses races humaines.* Bibliothèque Anthropologique, 18. Vigo Frères, Paris, 1897. 581 p. Br380 L56.

2432. *Lettres édifiantes et curieuses; écrites des missions étrangères, par quelque missionnaires de la Compagnie de Jésus.* LeClerc, Paris, 1738. v. 23 only. Br241.2 L566a.

2433. Leupp, Francis E. *Notes of a Summer Tour Among the Indians of the Southwest.* Office of the Indian Rights Association, Philadelphia, 1897. 26 p. Br572C An8141 v.154.

2434. Levanto, Leonardo. Cathecismo de la doctrina christiana, en lengua zaapoteca; dispuesto por el M. R. P. Mró. Fr. Leonardo Levanto…impreso con las licencias necesarias en la Puebla por la viuda de Miguel de Ortega; y por su original en la oficina Palafoxiana de dicha ciudad, ao de 1776. 82 p. Br498.34 ZL573a. Manuscript; copy by Karl H. Berendt with the addition of other material, also in Zapotec, including: L. Levanto, "Cathecismo de la doctrina christiana," n.d.; L. Levanto, "Expolicación de la doctrina christiana," n.d.; Jacinto Vilches, "Mysterios del santisimo rosario," n.d.

2435. Levanto, Leonardo. *Cathecismo de la doctrina christiana, en lengua zaapoteca; dispuesto por el M. R. P. Mró. Fr. Leonardo levanto, provincial que fue dos veces de la provincia de S. Hypolito Martyr de Oaxaca, y una de la de S. Miguel, y Santos Angeles de la Puebla, prior tres veces del Convento grande, y otras tres del convento de recolección de N. P. Sto. Domingo Soriano, comisario del Smo. Rosario, asistenmte real, examinador synodal del obispado de Oaxaca, consultor del santo oficio, y su corrector de libros, etc.* Impreso con las licencias necesarias en la Puebla por la viuda de Miguel de Ortega; y por su original en la oficina Palafoxiana de dicha ciudad, ano de 1776. 32 p. Br498.34 ZL573.

2436. Levanto, Leonardo. Cathecismo de la doctrina christiana, en lengua zapoteca; dispuesto por el M. R. P. Fr. Leonardo Levanto, provincial que fué dos veces de la provincia de S. Hypolito Martír de Oaxaca, etc. 82 p. Br498.34 ZL578. Transcription by Karl H. Berendt of *Cathecismo de la doctrina christiana, en lengua zaapoteca; dispuesto por el M. R. P. Mró. Fr. Leonardo levanto, provincial que fue dos veces de la provincia de S. Hypolito Martyr de Oaxaca, y una de la de S. Miguel, y Santos Angeles de la Puebla, prior tres veces del Convento grande, y otras tres del convento de recolección de N. P. Sto. Domingo Soriano, comisario del Smo. Rosario, asistenmte real, examinador synodal del obispado de Oaxaca, consultor del santo oficio, y su corrector de libros, etc.* (Por la Viuda de Miguel de Ortega, Puebla, 1776); arranged Zapotec and Spanish in double columns.

2437. Lévy, Paul. *Notas geográficas y económicas sobre la república de Nicaragua y una exposición completa de la cuestion del canal interoceánico y de la de inmigración, con una lista bibliográfica, las mas completa hasta el dia, de todos los libros y mapas relativos á la América central y general y á Nicarrgua [sic] en particular.* E. Denné Schmitz, Paris, 1873. 627 p. Br972.85 L57.

2438. Lévy, Paul. Vocabulario de la lengua ulba, de los indios uluas en Nicaragua, por D. Pablo Lévy, colectado en el año de 1870. Matlack's Falls, 1874. 9 p. Br498.3 UL578. Manuscript; trancription, with corrections and additions by Karl H. Berendt.

2439. Lewis, Benjamin F. The Madog tradition. *Utica Morning Herald*, April 11, 1894. 7 p. Br572C An8141 v.140.

2440. Lewis, Henry C. The geology of Philadelphia. *Journal of the Franklin Institute*, 1883. 21 p. Br572C An8141 v.58.

2441. Lewis, Theodore H. A new departure in effigy mounds. *Science* 13(318): 187, 1889. Br572C An8141 v.36.

2442. Lewis, Theodore H. Ancient fire-places on the Ohio. *American Antiquarian* 8(3): 167-168, 1886. Br572C An8141 v.36.

2443. Lewis, Theodore H. Ancient rock inscriptions in eastern Dakota. *American Naturalist* 20(5): 423-425, 1886. Br572C An8141 v.13; Br572C An8141 v.20; Br572C An8141 v.36.

2444. Lewis, Theodore H. Boulder outline figures in the Dakotas, surveyed in the summer of 1890. *American Anthropologist* 4(1): 19-24, 1891. Br572C An8141 v.36.

2445. Lewis, Theodore H. Cave drawings. *Appleton's Annual Cyclopedia*, 1889. 10 p. Br572C An8141 v.36.

2446. Lewis, Theodore H. Copper mines worked by the Mound Builders. *American Antiquarian* 11(5): 293–296, 1889. Br572C An8141 v.36.

2447. Lewis, Theodore H. Cup-stones near Old Fort Ransom, North Dakota. *American Naturalist* 25, 1891. 7 p. Br572C An8141 v.36.

2448. Lewis, Theodore H. *Description of Some Copper Relics of the Collection of T. H. Lewis in the Macalester Museum of History and Archaeology.* Macalester College Contributions, 6. St. Paul, Minnesota, 1890. Br572C An8141 v.36.

2449. Lewis, Theodore H. Effigy mounds in Iowa. *Science*, 146, 1885. 3 p. Br572C An8141 v.20; Br572C An8141 v.36.

2450. Lewis, Theodore H. Effigy mounds in northern Illinois. *Science*, September 7, 1888. 3 p. Br572C An8141 v.36.

2451. Lewis, Theodore H. Effigy-mound in the valley of the Big Sioux River, Iowa. *Science* 15(278): 275, 1890. Br572C An8141 v.36.

2452. Lewis, Theodore H. *History of the Northwestern Archaeological Survey.* Pioneer Press, St. Paul, MN, 1898. 16 p. Br572C An8141 v.166.

2453. Lewis, Theodore H. Incised boulders in the Upper Minnesota Valley. *American Naturalist* 21(7): 639–642, 1887. Br572C An8141 v.19; Br572C An8141 v.36.

2454. Lewis, Theodore H. Minor antiquarian articles. *St. Paul Pioneer Press, At Home,* and *American Antiquarian,* 1880–1884. 7 p. Br572C An8141 v.36.

2455. Lewis, Theodore H. Mounds of the Mississippi basin. *Magazine of American History,* 1882. 6 p. Br572C An8141 v.36.

2456. Lewis, Theodore H. Mounds on the Red River of the North. *American Antiquarian* 8(6): 369–371, 1886. Br572C An8141 v.36.

2457. Lewis, Theodore H. Notice of some recently discovered effigy mounds. *Science* 106, 1885. 3 p. Br572C An8141 v.36; Br572C An8141 v.39.

2458. Lewis, Theodore H. Old French post at Trempeleau, Wisconsin. *Magazine of American History,* 1889. 5 p. Br572C An8141 v.36.

2459. Lewis, Theodore H. Quartz-workers of Little Falls. *American Antiquarian* 9(2): 105–107, 1887. Br572C An8141 v.36.

2460. Lewis, Theodore H. Sculptured rock at Trempeleau, Wisconsin. *American Naturalist* 23(273): 782–784, 1889. Br572C An8141 v.36.

2461. Lewis, Theodore H. Snake and snake-like mounds in Minnesota. *Science* 10(220): 393, 1887. Br572C An8141 v.19; Br572C An8141 v.36.

2462. Lewis, Theodore H. Stone monuments in northwestern Iowa and southwestern Minnesota. *American Anthropologist* 3(1): 43–46, 1890. Br572C An8141 v.36.

2463. Lewis, Theodore H. Stone monuments in southern Dakota. *American Anthropologist* 2(2): 159–164, 1889. Br572C An8141 v.36.

2464. Lewis, Theodore H. The "Old Fort" earthworks of Greenup County, Kentucky. *American Journal of Archaeology* 3(3–4): 375–382, 1887. Br572C An8141 v.36.

2465. Lewis, Theodore H. The effigy mounds of Buffalo Lake, Marquette County, central Wisconsin. *American Antiquarian* 13(2): 115–117, 1891. Br572C An8141 v.36.

2466. Lewis, Theodore H. The monumental Tortoise Mounds of De-coo-tah. *American Journal of Archaeology,* January, 1886. 5 p. Br572C An8141 v.20; Br572C An8141 v.36.

2467. Lewis, Theodore H. The silver find in Kentucky. *American Naturalist* 9(4): 234-236, 1887. Br572C An8141 v.36.

2468. Libro de cuentas de la Cofradía del Rosario en el pueblo de Suchiapa desde 1796 hasta 1821, en lengua chapaneca. 1796 hasta 1821. 243 p. Br498.12 CL614. Added note on page 2 "Este libro contiene muchos apuntes en lengua chapaneca relativos a las contribuciones de los cofrades y a los gastos de la Cofradía. Nota de Dr. Berendt." An account book in Spanish and Chiapanec for the Cofradía de Nuestra Señora del Rosario in Suchiapa, México, containing a record of contributions and expenses of the society for the years 1796-1821. A financial accounting is given for each year, including the balance on hand; a list of the names of members of the society and the amount contributed by each; and an itemization of expenditures by the society for alms, special masses, candles, and Christmas gifts (*aguinaldos*).

2469. Libro de estado del convento de Nuestra Señora de Belem, n.d. 36 leaves. Br243 B413. Manuscript.

2470. Libro en pocomchí y kekchí. 194 leaves. Br498.21 PV427. Manuscript, original, from the parochial archives of Cobán in Vera Paz. The volume contains a large assortment of *sermons, confesionarios, doctrinas, frases, catecismos*, and other religious and grammatical matter in and on the two dialects. Most of the leaves are in good condition and quite legible. They date from various periods in the 18th century. Among the articles are the original Doctrina and various sermons of Fr. Hippolito de Aguilera; and "Arte de lengua cakchi."

2471. Lidzbarski, Mark. Einige Bemerkungen zu Stumme's Tunisischen Märchen. pp. 666-668, n.d. Br572C An8141 v.142.

2472. Lincke, Arthur A. *Bericht über die Fortschrifte der Assyriologie in den Jahren 1886-1893*. Druck von Bär und Hermann, Leipzig, 1894. 124 p. Br572C An8141 v.140.

2473. Lincke, Arthur A. *Die neuesten Rübezahlforschungen*. Verlag von V. Zahn und Jänsch, Dresden, 1896. Br572C An8141 v.154.

2474. Lincke, Arthur A. Kambyses in der Sage, Litteratur und Junst des Mittelalters. *Ägyptica* 1:41-61, 1897. Br572C An8141 v.154.

2475. Lincke, Arthur A. *Über den gegenwärtigen Stand der Völkskunde im Allgemeinen und der Sachsen's im Besonderen*. Druck von Bär und Hermann, Leipzig, 1897. Br572C An8141 v.154.

2476. Liorel, Jules. *Kabylie du Jurjura*. E. Leroux, Paris, 1892. 544 p. Br496 L66.

2477. List of publications of the Bureau of Ethnology, Smithsonian Institution. *Annual Report of the Bureau of Ethnology, Smithsonian Institution*, pp. 101-129, n.d. Br572B Sm65b.

2478. Litanies at baptism; in the language of the Lenape Indians, 1899. 18 p. Br497.11 DL71. Text in a Delaware dialect with captions and commentary in English or German; found in an old Moravian church in Moraviantown, Kent County, Ontario.

2479. Literatura yucateca, n.d. Br868.1C L71. Contents include: 1. El le-deum laudamus glosado en veinte y nueve sonetos que dan a luz, varios aficionados, por una señora americana, 1832; 2. J. A. Diego Cisneros, El mulato, drama en tres actos, en verso,

1846; 3. Cipriano Arias, Una noche de 1843, ó, el honor yucateco; ensayo dramatico en un acto escrito en variedad de metros, 1846; 4. Baranda, Alegre viaje de cuatro amigos las ruinas de Uxmal, en 18 de mayo de 1852; refexiones sobre los arquitectos de los antiguos edificios de Yucatan y de sus ultimos moradores, 1852; 5. M.Y. Escoffié de Aubry, Seilam, hija de Jepthe, juez de Israel, en tres cantos, 1854; 6. Ley que establece el Instituto Campechano y su reglamento, 1859; 7. Asociación catolica formada para subvenir a los gastos del culto divino en la santa iglesia catedral de Mérida, y curato del sagrario de la misma con su auxiliar S. Sebastian, 1861; 8. Corona funebre a la memoria del...Justo Sierra, 1861; 8. El album yucateco, periodico literario, n.d.; 9. Eligio Ancona, Modo de atrapar a un novio, comedia en dos actos, 1862; Fabian Carrillo, Discurso pronunciado en el palacio del ayuntamiento de Mérida el 16 de setiembre de 1864; aniversario de la independencia de Mejico, 1864; 10. Crescencio Carrillo y Ancona, Oración funebre del...J. M. Guerra, obispo de Yucatan, 1864; 11. Leandro Rodríguez de la Gala, Carta pastoral, 1864; 12. J. M. García Montero, Juicia critico de la revista escrita, bajo el seudonimo de Antruejo, 1864; 13. Justo Sierra, Ensayo biografico, n.d.; Registro catolico, publicación extraordinaria del Colegio Católico de Mérida de Yucatan; con motivo de la solemnidad del 8 de diciembre de 1869, 1869; 14. J. Estrada y Zenca, Yucatan; romance histórico y geografico, 1870; Programa de los examenes de estatuto del Colegio catolico de instrucción primaria y secundaria de San Ildefonso, 1872; Composiciones leidas en el Conservatorio Yucateca en 16 de setiembre de 1876; aniversario III de su instalación, 1876.

2480. Livermore, Abiel A. *The War with México Reviewed*. W. Crosby and H.P. Nichols, Boston, 1850. 298 p. Br972 L75.2.

2481. *Livre des morts des anciens Égyptiens*. Bibliothèque orientale elzévirienne, 33. Ernest Leroux, Paris, 1882 661 p. Br893 B648.FP.

2482. Lizana, Bernardo de. *Historia de Yucatán; devocionario de Ntra. Sra. de Izamal y conquista espiritual, por el P. Fr. Bernardo de Lizana...impresa en 1633 y ahora nuevamente por el Museo Nacional de México*. Imprenta del Museo Nacional, México, 1893. 12, 127 p. Br972.6 L76.

2483. Llisa, Pedro de. *Pequeño catecismo cristiano; dios onamaque carta chenicua; traducido en la lengua cuna o de los indios del Darien...y revisto por...A. L. Pinart y...Diego Carranza*. Panama, 1884. 17 p. Br572C An8141 v.106. Facsimile of a Pinart manuscript.

2484. Löffelholz, Karl, freiherr von. *Die Zoreisch indianer der Trinidad-Bai*, 1893. Br970.3 L82.4.

2485. Loga del Niño Dios; presentación escenica de los mangues en Namotivá. Santa Catarina, 1874. 10 p. Br498.12 ML823. Manuscript; this loga or play of the Baby God is written in Spanish with some Mangue words; transcribed by Karl H. Berendt.

2486. Logan, W. S. *The Siege of Cuautla: the Bunker Hill of Mexico*. The Knickerbocker Press, New York, 1893. 27 p. Br572C An8141 v.128.

2487. Long, John. *Voyages and Travels of an Indian Interpreter and Trader, Describing the Manners and Customs of the North American Indians; With an Account of the Posts Situated on the River Saint Laurence, Lake Ontario, &c.; To Which Is Added a Vocabulary of the Chippeway Language...A List of Words in the Iroquois, Mohegan, Shawanee, and Esquimeaux Tongues, and a Table, Showing the Analogy Between the Algonkin and Chippeway Languages.* Printed for the author, and sold by Robson, London, 1791. 295 p. Br970.1 L85. "The author engaged in the service of the Hudson's Bay Company in 1768 and journeyed as a fur trader among the Indians of Canada for nineteen years. His knowledge of the character, customs, and domestic life of the Indians was therefore the most thorough and intimate" (Field 1873:245).

2488. Longpérier, Henri A. de. *Notice des monuments*, 1850. 130p. Br572C An8141 v.28.

2489. López de Cogolludo, Diego. *Historia de Yucatán.* 3d ed. Imprenta de M. Aldana Rivas, Mérida, 1867–1868. 2 v. Br972.6 C65.4.

2490. López de Gómara, Francisco. *Historia de las conquistas de Hernando Cortés.* Imprenta de la Testamentaría de Ontiveros, México, 1826. v. 1 only. Br972.02 L88.

2491. López Yepes, Joaquín. *Catecismo y declaración de la doctrina cristiana en lengua otomí, con un vocabulario del mismo idioma.* Impreso en la Oficina de A. Valdés, Megico, 1826 254 p. Br498.23 OL 88.

2492. López, Carlos A. *Navegación de los rios afluentes del Plata.* El Orden, Buenos Aires, 1857. 48 p. Br572C An8141 v.7.

2493. López, M. S. Miti e leggende degli indigeni americani. *Revista Natura ed Arte* 4:3-12, 1894. Br572C An8141 v.113.

2494. Löschcke, G. Kopf der Athena Parthenos des Pheidas. In *Festschrift zum Fünfzigjährigen Jubiläum des Vereins von Alterthumsfreunden im Rheinlande,* pp. 1-22. Gedruckt auf Kosten des Vereins, Bonn, 1891. Br572C An8141 v.98.

2495. Loskiel, George H. *Geschichte der Mission der evangelischen Brüder unter den Indianern in Nordamerika.* Zu finden in den Brüdergemeinen; In Commission bey Paul Gotthelf Kummer, Leipzig, 1789. 783 p. Br970.6 L893. "This is the 'official history of the missionary work of the United Brethren among the North American Indains in Georgia, Pennsylvania, New York, and the Middle West, 1735-1787, based on the journals and letters of the missionaries, particularly those of David Zeisberger and Gottlieb Spangeberg'...It presents the most accurate account of the Iroquois, Delawares, Shawnees, etc., including a narrative of the travels of the missionaries and of the massacre of the peaceful Indians of Gnadenhütten and Salem" (*Frank T. Siebert Library* 1999:1:224).

2496. Lott, Julius. *Eine Compromiss-Sprache.* Lentze, Leipzig, 1889. 30 p. Br572C An8141 v.21.

2497. Lott, Julius. *Grammatik der Weltsprache (Mondolingue).* Druck von Frankenstein und Wagner, Leipzig, n.d. 35 p. Br572C An8141 v.87.

2498. Lott, Julius. Suplent folie and mie internazional lingue, 1891. 16 p. Br572C An8141 v.21.

2499. Lott, Julius. *Über Volapuk.* Wien, 1888. Br572C An8141 v.21.

2500. Lott, Julius. *Un lingua internazional; grammatika et vokabular pro angleses, germanes, romanes et pro kultivates de tut mond.* Frankenstein et Wagner, Leipzig, 1890. 46 p. Br572C An8141 v.73.

2501. Loughridge, Robert M. *Cesus klist em opunubu-heru maro coyvte, Gospel According to St. Matthew; Translated from the Original Greek into the Muskokee Language.* American Bible Society, New York, 1867. 92 p. Br497.39 CrB47.1. New Testament Gospel of St. Matthew translated into Creek; also includes W. S. Robertson, "Coku enhutecesky mekusapulke utekat cane ohtotute" [New Testament Gospel of St. John translated into Creek].

2502. Loughridge, Robert M. *Nakcokv esyvhiketv Muskokee hymns.* 5th ed. Presbyterian Board of Publication and Sabbath-School Work, Philadelphia, 1868. 221 p. Br497.39 CrL92. Includes "Temperance pledge" in English and Creek (p. 93) and "Temperance songs" in Creek (p. 206–212).

2503. Loughridge, Robert M., and David Winslett. *Nakcokv setempohetv; Introduction to the Shorter Catechism; Translated into the Creek Language, by Rev. R. M. Loughbridge, A. M., and David Winslett.* 2d ed. Presbyterian Board of Publication, Philadelphia, 1858. 34 p. Br497.39 CrP92.

2504. Lovisato, Domenico. Appunti etnografici con accenni geologici sulla terra del fuoco. *Cosmos di Guido Cora* 8(4–5), 1884. 34 p. Br572C An8141 v.1.

2505. Lovisato, Domenico. Di alcune armi e utensili dei Fueghini, e degli antichi Patagoni. *Memorie della Classe di scienze morali, storiche e filologiche* 11:3–11, 1883. Br572C An8141 v.96. "A valuable detailed description of the material culture of the Yahgans and…the Alacaluf and Onas" (Cooper 1917:107).

2506. Lubbock, John. *The Pleasures of Life.* J. Fitzgerald, New York, 1888. 45 p. Br572C An8141 v.120.

John Lubbock (from Justin Winsor, Aboriginal America. Cambridge, MA: Houghton, Mifflin, 1889. p. 379).

2507. Luckenbach,Abraham. Acts of the Apostles, translated into Delaware. New Fairfield, 1843. 83 leaves. Br497.11 DB47. Manuscript. New Testament Acts of the Apostles translated into Delaware. "Abraham Luckenbach (1777-1854) was a Moravian missionary among the Delaware at the village of Woapikamikunk in present-day Madison County, Indiana, on the upper section of the west fork of the White River. The missionary station operated there from 1801 to 1806" (*Frank T. Siebert Library* 1999:2:336).

2508. Lucy-Fossarieu, Pierre H. R. de. Ethnographie de l'Amérique antarctique: Patagons, Araucaniens, Fuégiens. *Mémoires de la Société d'Ethnographie* 4:103-179, 1884. Br572C An8141 v.103. "An extensive monograph, the Fuegian section...of which is based on a comprehensive study of the then extant written sources and on personal observation of the group of eleven Alacaluf in the Jardin d'Acclimatation at Paris" (Cooper 1917:108).

2509. Lucy-Fossarieu, Pierre H. R. de. *Les langues indiennes de la Californie; étude de philologie ethnographique.* Imprimerie Nationale, Paris, 1881. 55 p. Br572C An8141 v.49; Br572C An8141 v.55.

2510. Ludecus, Eduard. *Reise durch die mexikanischen Provinzen Tumalipas*[sic], *Cohahuila und Texas im jahre 1834 in Briefen an seine Freunde.* J. F. Hartknoch, Leipzig, 1837. 356 p. Br917.64 L96.

2511. Ludewig, Hermann E., and William W. Turner. *The Literature of American Aboriginal Languages, by Hermann E. Ludewig; With Additions and Corrections by Professor Wm. W. Turner; Edited by Nicholas Trübner.* Trübner, London, 1858. 258 p. Br497B L963. Ludewig, trained in the legal profession, came to the United States in 1844, and was considered one of the earliest professional bibliographers. His *Literature of the American Aboriginal Languages* was published after his death in 1858.

2512. Lumholtz, Carl S. Explorations in the Sierra Madre. *Scribner's Magazine* 10(5): 531-548, 1891. Br572C An8141 v.12.

2513. Lumholtz, Carl S. The Huichol Indians of Mexico. *Bulletin of the American Museum of Natural History* 10(1): 1-14, 1898. Br572C An8141 v.154.

2514. Lumholtz, Carl S., and Ale? Hrdlicka. Marked human bones from a prehistoric Tarasco Indian burial place in the State of Michoacan, Mexico. *Bulletin of the American Museum of Natural History* 10:61-79, 1898. Br572C An8141 v.166.

2515. Lumholtz, Carl S., and Ale? Hrdlicka. Trephining in Mexico. *American Anthropologist* 10:389-396, 1897. Br572C An8141 v.154.

2516. Luschan, Felix von. Abbildungen eines Knaben aus Deutsch-Neu-Guinea. *Verhandlungen der Berliner Anthropologischen Gesellschaft für Anthropologie, Ethnologie und Urgeschichte,* pp. 273-275, 1893. Br572C An8141 v.123. Luschan (1854-1924) was a radical social Darwinist who is best known for his activities as curator and later director of the Berlin Museum für Völkerkunde. His research conducted while professor of anthropology at the University of Berlin foreshadowed the disciplines of anthropobiology and human genetics.

2517. Luschan, Felix von. Ausgrabungen von Sendschiri. *Verhandlungen der Berliner*

Anthropologischen Gesellschaft für Anthropologie, Ethnologie und Urgeschichte, pp. 488-495, 1894. Br572C An8141 v.140.

2518. Luschan, Felix von. Beitrag zur Kenntnis der Tättowirung in Samoa. *Zeitschrift für Ethnologie* 31:551-561, 1899. Br572C An8141 v.154.

2519. Luschan, Felix von. Beiträge zur Ethnographie von Neu-Guinea. *Bibliothek der Länderkunde* 5-6:440-524, 1899. Br572.96 L977.

2520. Luschan, Felix von. *Beiträge zur Völkerunde der Deutschen Schutzgebiete.* D. Reimer (E.Vohsen), Berlin, 1897. 87 p. Br572 L975.

2521. Luschan, Felix von. Bogenspannen. *Verhandlungen der Berliner Anthropologischen Gesellschaft für Anthropologie, Ethnologie und Urgeschichte* 18:670-678, 1891. Br572C An8141 v.83.

2522. Luschan, Felix von. Das Hakenkreuz in Africa. *Verhandlungen der Berliner Anthropologischen Gesellschaft für Anthropologie, Ethnologie und Urgeschichte* 25:137-141, 1896. Br572C An8141 v.154.

2523. Luschan, Felix von. Das Wurfholz in Neu Holland und in Neu-Holland, und in Oceanien. In *Bastian-Festschrift,* pp. 131-155, 1896. Br572C An8141 v.154.

2524. Luschan, Felix von. Defecte des Os tympanicum an künstlich deformirten Schädeln von Peruanern. *Verhandlungen der Berliner Anthropologischen Gesellschaft für Anthropologie, Ethnologie und Urgeschichte* 25:69-73, 1896. Br572C An8141 v.154.

2525. Luschan, Felix von. *Die Altertümer von Benin.* Vereinigung wissenschaftlicher Verleger, Berlin, Leipzig, 1919. 522 p. and two portfolios of 129 plates. Br913.665 L978.

2526. Luschan, Felix von. Die Tachtadschy und andere Überreste der alten Bevölkerung. *Archiv für Anthropologie* 19(1-2), 1890. Br572C An8141 v.103.

2527. Luschan, Felix von. Drei trepanirte Schädel von Tenerife. *Verhandlungen der Berliner Anthropologischen Gesellschaft für Anthropologie, Ethnologie und Urgeschichte* 25:63-69, 1896. Br572C An8141 v.154.

2528. Luschan, Felix von. Einen Zusammengesetzten Bogen aus der Zeit Rhamses II. *Verhandlungen der Berliner Anthropologischen Gesellschaft für Anthropologie, Ethnologie und Urgeschichte,* pp. 266-271, 1893. Br572C An8141 v.123.

2529. Luschan, Felix von. Instruktion für ethnographische Beobachtungen und sammlungen in Deutsch-Ostafrika. *Mitteilungen aus den Deutschen Schutzgebieten* 19(2), 1896. 29 p. Br572C An8141 v.154.

2530. Luschan, Felix von. Sechs Mandragora-Wurzeln. *Verhandlungen der Berliner Anthropologischen Gesellschaft für Anthropologie, Ethnologie und Urgeschichte* 17:726-746, 1891. Br572C An8141 v.83.

2531. Luschan, Felix von. Trinkschalen aus menschlichen Schäden in Ober-Guinea. *Verhandlungen der Berliner Anthropologischen Gesellschaft für Anthropologie, Ethnologie und Urgeschichte,* pp. 271-273, 1893. Br572C An8141 v.123.

2532. Luschan, Felix von. Über den antiken Bogen. pp, 189-197, 1894. Br572 L976.

2533. Luschan, Felix von. Zur Ethnographie der Matty-Insel. *Internationales Archiv für Ethnographie* 8:41-56, 1895. Br572.95 L97.5.

2534. Luther, Martin. *Lutheri Catechismus, öfwersatt på American-Virginiske Språket.*

Ttryckt vthi thet af Kongl. Maytt. privileg. Burchardi Tryckeri, af J. J. Genath, Stockholm, 1696, 160 p. Br497.11. Catechism in Delaware and Swedish.

2535. Lyman, Benjamin S. Metallurgical and other features of Japanese swords. *Journal of the Franklin Institute,* 1895. 14 p. Br572C An8141 v.140.

2536. Lyman, Benjamin S. The character of the Japanese. *Journal of Speculative Philosophy,* 1885. 40 p. Br572C An8141 v.58.

2537. MacDonald, Arthur. *Abnormal Man, Being Essays on Education and Crime and Related Subjects, With Digests of Literature and a Bibliography.* Government Printing Office, Washington, DC, 1893. 495 p. Br339.1 M146.1.

2538. MacDonald, Arthur. *Criminology.* Funk and Wagnalls, New York, 1893. 416 p. Br175.5 M14.

2539. MacDonald, Arthur. Growth of Children in Germany. *Pediatrics* 7(12), 1899. 4 p. Br573.6 M146.

2540. Macedo, Joaquim Manuel de. *Geographische beschreibung Brasiliens.* Druck von F. A. Brockhaus, Leipzig, 1873. 535 leaves. Br918.1 M15.

2541. Macedo, José M. Catalogue des antiquities peruviennes, 1881.13 p. Br572C An8141 v.20.

2542. MacFarlane, A. On exact analysis as the basis of language. *Transactions of the Texas Academy of Science,* pp. 5–10, 1892. Br572C An8141 v.89.

2543. Machoni de Cerdeña, Antonio. *Arte y vocabulario de la lengua lule y tonocoté; compuestos con facultad de sus superiores.* P. E. Coni, Buenos Aires, 1877. 361 p. Br498.971 LM 185. Originally published in 1732 at Madrid.

2544. Mackay, John A. *Family Prayers for the Use of the Cree Indians; Compiled and Translated into the Syllabic Character of the Cree Language.* Printed for the Society for Promoting Christian Knowledge, London, 1881. 32 p. Br497.11 CrM19.2.

2545. Mackay, John A. *Psalms and Hymns in the Language of the Cree Indians of North-West America.* Printed for the Society for Promoting Christian Knowledge, London, 1877. 108 p. Br497.11 CrM 19.

2546. Mackay, John A. *Psalms and Hymns in the Language of the Cree Indians of the Diocese of Saskatchewan, North-West America.* Printed for the Society for Promoting Christian Knowledge, London, 1891. 111 p. Br497.11 CrM19a.

2547. Mackenzie, Alexander. Descriptive notes on certain implements, weapons, etc., from Graham Island, Queen Charlotte Island, B. C. *Transactions of the Royal Society of Canada* 2:45–59, 1891. Br572C An8141 v.107.

2548. Mackenzie, Alexander. *Voyages from Montreal, on the River St. Lawrence, Through the Continent of North America, to the Frozen and Pacific Oceans, in the Years 1789 and 1793 With a Preliminary Account of the Rise, Progress, and Present State of the Fur Trade of that Country.* T. Cadell, Jun. and W. Davies, London, 1801. 412 p. Br917 M192a. Compiled by William Combe from Mackenzie's notes; includes Examples of the Knisteneaux and Algonquin tongues (pp. 108–116) and Example of the Chepewyan tongue (pp. 129–132). "The classic account of the first crossing of the continent north of Mexico by a European. Mackenzie's dual expeditions were intended to expand the field of trade for the

North West Company, of which he was a member. His travel narrative is renowed for the accuracy of his investigation and observation. Brief vocabularies of the Cree, Algonquin, and Chipewyan, all of whom Mackenzie traded with, are included" (*Frank T. Siebert Library* 1900:2:179).

2549. MacLean, John P. A study of American archaeology: the literature on the subject. *Universalist Quarterly* 37-38, 1880-1881. 23 p. Boston. Br572C An8141 v.59.

2550. MacLean, John P. *Jewish Nature Worship; The Worship of the Reciprocal Principles of Nature Among the Ancient Hebrews*. R. Clarke and Company, Cincinnati, 1882. 22 p. Br274 M22.

2551. MacLean, John P. The Great Serpent Mound. *American Antiquarian* 7(1): 44-47, 1885. Br572C An8141 v.39.

2552. MacLean, John P. *The Mound Builders; Being an Account of a Remarkable People That Once Inhabited the Valleys of the Ohio and Mississippi, Together With an Investigation into the Archaeology of Butler County, Ohio*. R. Clarke and Company, Cincinnati, 1879. 233 p. Br571.91 M22.

2553. Macritchie, David. Notes on a Finnish boat preserved in Edinburgh. *Proceedings of the Society of Antiquaries of Scotland* 24:353-369, 1890. Br572C An8141 v.128.

2554. Macritchie, David. The historical aspect of folk-lore. *Transactions of the International Folk-Lore Congress*, pp. 103-112, 1891. Br572C An8141 v.116.

2555. Macritchie, David. *The Underground Life*. T. and A. Constable, Edinburgh University Press, Edinburgh, 1892. 47 p. Br572C An8141 v.128.

2556. Magio, A. *Arte de la lengua de los indios baures de la provincia de los Moxos, conforme al manuscrito original...por Lucien Adam y Charles Leclerc*. Bibliothèque Linguistique Américaine, 7. Maisonneuve, Paris, 1880. Br497C Am3.

2557. Maillard, Antoine S. *Grammaire de la langue mikmaque, par M. l'abbe Maillard, redigée et mise en ordre par Joseph M. Bellenger*. Shea's Library of American Linguistics, 9. Cramoisy Press, New York, 1864. 101 p. Br497C Sh3; Br497C Sh3a.

2558. Makuen, G. Hudson. Interesting case of rapid speech development...in an adult following operation for the tongue-tied, 1895. 3 p. Br613.91 M283.

2559. Maler, Teobert. Yukatekische Forschungen. *Globus* 68(16): 247-259, 1895. Br572C An8141 v.161. Maler (1842-1917) accompanied Archduke Maximilian (later Emperor Maximilian of Mexico) in 1864 as a cadet and served in the Imperial Mexican Army. Maler traveled throughout southern Mexico and in 1874 began photographing city scenes, buildings, and indigenous people. In 1875 he directed archaeological excavations in Tehuantepec and later explored some 100 Maya ruins in Chiapas, Yucatan, and the Petén region of northern Guatemala. At times he worked on behalf of the Peabody Museum of American Archaeology and Ethnology at Harvard University.

2560. Maler, Teobert. Yukatekische Forschungen. *Globus* 68(18): 277-292, 1895. Br572C An8141 v.161.

2561. Mallat de Bassilan, Marcel Jacques Saint-Ange. *L'Amérique inconnue d'aprés le journal de voyage de J. de Brettes; chargé d'un mission scientifique...Mallat de Bassilan; dessins de M. Gaston Bonfils d'aprés les documents de l'explorateur.*

Firmin-Didot et Cie., Paris, 1892. 280 p. Br918 M294. Narrative of the exploration of the Gran Chaco.

2562. Mallery, Garrick. A calendar of the Dakota nation. *Bulletin of the United States Geological and Geographical Survey of the Territories* 3(1): 3-25, 1877. Br572C An8141 v.50.

2563. Mallery, Garrick. Greeting by gesture. *Popular Science Monthly,* February-March, pp. 477-490, 1891. Br572C An8141 v.9.

2564. Mallery, Garrick. *Introduction to the Study of Sign Language Among the North American Indians as Illustrating the Gesture Speech of Mankind.* Bureau of Ethnology, Smithsonian Institution, 1880. 72 p. Br572C An8141 v.93; Br572C An8141 v.96.

2565. Mallery, Garrick. Israelite and Indian: a parallel in planes of culture; address before the American Association for the Advancement of Science, delivered at the Toronto meeting, August 1889. *Proceedings of the American Association for the Advancement of Science,* 1899. 47 p. Br572C An8141 v.23.

2566. Mallery, Garrick. Pictographs of the North American Indians; a preliminary paper. *Annual Report of the Bureau of Ethnology, Smithsonian Institution, for 1882-1883,* pp. 3-256, 1886. Br497.01 M29. Includes: James G. Swan, Tattoo marks of the Haida Indians of Queen Charlotte Islands, B.C., and the Prince of Wales Archipelago, Alaska (pp. 66-73).

2567. Mallery, Garrick. Some common errors respecting the North American Indians. *Bulletin of the Philosophical Society of Washington* 2:175-180, 1877. Br572C An8141 v.27.

2568. Mallery, Garrick. The former and present number of our Indians. *Proceedings of the American Association for the Advancement of Science* 26:340-366, 1877. Br572C An8141 v.23.

2569. Mallery, Garrick. The gesture speech of man; address before the American Association for the Advancement of Science at Cincinnati, Ohio, August 1881. *Proceedings of the American Association for the Advancement of Science* 30, 1882. 21 p. Br572C An8141 v.51.

2570. Maminai della Rovere, Lodovico V. *Arte de grammatica da lingua brazilica da nação kiriri.* 2d ed. Brown, Rio de Janiero, 1877. 101 p. Br498.79 M 315.

2571. Manouvrier, L. Classification naturelle des sciences; position et programme de l'anthropologie. *Association Française pour l'Avancement des Sciences,* 1889. 21 p. Br572C An8141 v.140.

2572. Mansilla, Lucio V. *Una escursion a los indios ranqueles, por Lucio V. Mansilla...Buenos Aires, 1870.* Imprenta, litografía y fundición de tipos, Buenos Aires, 1870. 2 v. in 1. Br980.3 RM315. Letters concerning the Ranqueles Indians published in the *Tribuna* of Buenos Aires in 1870.

2573. Mantia, P. *L'eridita e l'origine delle specie.* Libreria Carlo Clausen, Palermo, 1894. 43 p. Br572C An8141 v.135.

2574. *Manualito para administrar el viatico y extremaunción en idioma mexicano; con las licencias necesarias.* En la Oficina de D. Alexandro Valdés, México, 1817. 9 p. Br498.22 AzR 66.

2575. *Manuscrit dit mexicain no 2 de la Bibliothèque Impériale; photographie sans reduction.* Imprimerie Bonaventure et Ducessois, Paris, 1864. Portfolio with 23 mounted photographs. Br898.21 MP214. Photographic prints of originals in the 1864 Paris edition of the Maya Codex Peresianus.

2576. *Manuscrito mexicano.* J. M. Melgar y Serrano, Veracruz, 1875. 29 plates Br898.22. AzM578M. From the Boban Collection.

2577. *Mapa de la isla de Cuba.* J. S. Smith, Philadelphia, n.d. Br912.729 Sm5.

2578. *Mappe de Tepechpan; histoire synchronique et seigneuriale de Tepechpan et de México.* Lith. de J. Desportes, Paris, 1855. 1 map. Br498.22 AzM 327a.

2579. *Mappe dit de Tepechpan; histoire synchronique et seigneuriale de Tepechpan et de México,* n.d. 12 maps. Br498.22 AzM 327. After a document in the Aubin Collection.

2580. Marbán, Pedro. *Arte de la lengva moxa, con su vocabulario, y cathecismo; compuesto por el M. R. P. Pedro Marban de la Compañia de Jesvs, superior, que fue, de las missiones de infieles, que tiene la Compañia de esta provincia de el Perù en las dilatadas regiones de los indios moxos, y chiquitos; dirigido al Excmo. Sr. D. Melchor Portocarrero Lasso, de la Vega, conde de la Monclova, comendador de la Zarza, del orde de Alcantara, del consejo de guerra, y Junta de guerra de Indias, virrey, governador, y capitan general, que fue del reyno de la Nueva España, y actual, q es de estos reynos, y provincias del Peru. Con licencia de los svperiores.* En la Imprenta Real de Joseph de Contreras, Lima, 1702. 664, 142, 202 p. Br498.77 MM 327. Bound with *Cathecismo menor en lengua española y moxa,* n.d. 203 p.

2581. Marcano, Gaspar. *Ethnographie précolombienne du Venezuela région des raudals de l'orénoque.* A. Hennuyer, Paris, 1890 123 p. Br572.987 M33.

2582. Marcel, Gabriel. Les Fuégiens au XIIe siécle. *Revue de Géographie* 14:104-111, 1891. Br572C An8141 v.7.

2583. Marcoux, J. *Lettres de Feu M. Jos. Marcoux, missionnaire du Sault, aux chefs Iroquois du Lac des Deux Montagnes.* Tehoristorakon John Lovell, Tiohtiake, 1869. Br572C An8141 v.74.

2584. Marcoy, Paul. *Voyage à travers l'Amérique du Sud; de l'Océan Pacifique à l'Océan Atlantique, par Paul Marcoy; illustré de 626 vues, types et payages par E. Riou et accompagné de 20 cartes gravées sur les dessins de l'auteur.* L. Hachette et Cie., Paris, 1869. 2 v. Br918 M33. Originally published serially in *Le tour du monde,* v. 6-16, 1862-1867. Contents include: 1. Islay; Arequipa; Lampa; Acopia; Cuzco; Écharati; Chulituqui; Tunkini; Sarayacu; 2. Tierra-Blanca; Nauta; Tabatinga; Santa Maria de Belem do Para.

2585. Marcy, Randolph B., and George B. McClellan. *Exploration of the Red River of Louisiana, in the Year 1852.* Government Printing Office, Washington, DC, 1854. 286 p. Br508.763 M33. Includes: Vocabularies of words in the languages of the Comanches and Wichitas, by Capt. R. B. Marcy; with remarks on the preceding vocabularies by Prof. W. Turner (pp. 273-276). "Captain Marcy's report affords the reader some authentic information regarding the peculiar customs of the Indians of the southern Plains. Their mode of warfare, their invariable violation of the chastity of female prisoners, and the construction of their dwellings and villages, are more particularly described in Chapters VIII and X. The appendix contains a comparative vocabulary of the Comanches and Wichitas, of five pages; and one of the plates is a view of a Wichita village" (Field 1873:260).

2586. Marde, Charles C. Some Mexican versions of the Brer Rabbit stories. *Modern Language Notes* 11(1): 22–23 1896. Br572C An8141 v.144.

2587. Marden, Charles C. *The Phonology of the Spanish Dialect of Mexico City; Dissertation Presented to the Board of University Studies of the Johns Hopkins University for the Degree of Doctor of Philosophy*. Modern Language Association of America, Baltimore, 1896. 66 p. Br572C An8141 v.140.

2588. Margry, Pierre. *Mémoires et documents*. Maisonneuve, Paris, 1882. 10 p. Br572C An8141 v.20. A valuable compilation of journals, correspondence, and reports by French explorers, missionaries, traders, and government officials from the St. Lawrence to the Rocky Mountains.

2589. Marina, Giuseppe. Das Italienische Anthropologische Institut zu Livorno. *Zeitschrift für Ethnologie* 1:55–58, 1898. Br572C An8141 v.99.

2590. Marina, Giuseppe. *Richerche antropologiche ed etnografiche sui Ragazzi*. Fratelli Bocca Editori, Torino, 1896. 86 p. Br572C An8141 v.99.

2591. Marina, Giuseppe. *Studi antropologici sugli adulti (Italiani e Stranieri)*. Fratelli Bocca Editori, Torino, 1897. 38 p. Br572C An8141 v.99.

2592. Marina, Giuseppe. *Sulle curvature della colonna vertebrale; contributo di studi de anatomia normale e patologica*. Tipografia di Raffaello Giusti, Livorno, 1897. 35 p. Br616.73 M33.

2593. Markham, Clements R. *Contributions Towards a Grammar and Dictionary of Quichua, the Language of the Yncas of Peru*. Trübner and Company, London, 1864. 223 p. Br498.7 M 34. "Pages 1 to 61, are occupied with a grammar, and pages 63 to 195, with a dictionary of Quichua, Spanish, and English, while the remainder of the book is devoted to a dictionary of Quichua and English alone. The learned author was secretary to the French Royal Society of Geography, and composed his work during a long residence in Peru" (Field 1873:261).

2594. Markham, Clements R. Note on the ancient Ynca drama: a reply to a criticism of *Ollantay* by Bartolomé Mitré, n.d. 26 p. Br572C An8141 v.60.

2595. Markham, Clements R. *Ollanta, An Ancient Ynca Drama; Translated From the Original Quichua*. Trübner and Company, London, 1871. 128 p. Br898.7 IO.EM. Translation in parallel columns. "This remnant of the literature of the Incas, was preserved until about 1770, by the *quipus*, or knotted calendar; when Dr. Valdoz, who had often witnessed the representation of the drama by Indian actors, before the ill-fated Inca, Tupac Amaru, reducing it to writing. From this copy, written by the *cura* in pure Quichua, Mr. Markham has translated this English version. Its great antiquity is authenticated, not so much by the existence of several copies in MS as by the conformity of the widespread traditions, and the entire absence of every Spanish word. There is not the slightest trace of ideas, derived from, civilization or Christianity. It has received the sanction of such scholars as Drs. Riviero, Tschudi, and Barranca, who were convinced that it was composed long before the conquest of Peru by Pizarro" (Field 1873:261).

2596. Marquez, Pedro. *Due antichi monumenti di architettura messicana, illustrati da d. Pietro Marquez*. Presso il Salomoni, Roma, 1804. 47 p. Br572C An8141 v.64.

2597. Marsh, Othniel C. Description of an ancient sepulchral mound near Newark, Ohio. *American Journal of Science and Arts*, v. 42, 1866. 11 p. Br572C An8141 v.19; Br572C An8141 v.38. The most enduring legacy of Othniel Charles Marsh (1831-1899) is the collections he acquired for the United States Geological Survey during his ten years as the government's first vertebrate paleontologist.

2598. Marsh, Othniel C. On the Pithecanthropus erectus, Dubois, from Java. *American Journal of Science* 69:144-147, 1895. Br572C An8141 v.132.

2599. Marshall, William E. *Travels Amongst the Todas, Or the Study of a Primitive Tribe in South India, Their History, Character, Customs, Religion, Infanticide, Polyandry, Language; With Outlines of the Tuda Grammar*. Longmans, Green, London, 1873. 271 p. Br915.4 M35. Includes "A brief outline of the grammar of the Tuda language by the Rev. G. U. Pope…from a collection of Tuda words and sentences presented by the Rev. Friedrich Metz" (pp. 239-269).

2600. Martin, C. *Die Krankheiten im Südliche Chile*. Berlin, 1885. 85 p. Br572C An8141 v.18.

Clements R. Markham (from Justin Winsor, Aboriginal America. Cambridge, MA: Houghton, Mifflin, 1889. p. 272).

2601. Martin, Ernst. *Les déformations craniennes en Chine*, pp. 504-506. Mémoires Originaux 2. 1893. Br572C An8141 v.110.

2602. Martin, Felix, ed. *Mission du Canada; relations in édites de la Nouvelle-France (1672-1679); pour faire suite aux anciennes relations (1615-1672)*. Voyages et Travaux des Missionaires de la Compagnie de Jésus, 3-4. C. Douniol, Paris, 1861. 2 v. Br970.6 J498.

2603. Martin, Rudolf. Altpatagonische Schädel. *Vierteljahrsschrift der Naturforschenden Gesellschaft* 41(11): 496-537, 1896. Br572C An8141 v.154.

2604. Martin, Rudolf. Aus der englischen and amerikanischen Literatur. *Archiv für Anthropologie* 22:141-153, 1893. Br572C An8141 v.145.

2605. Martin, Rudolf. Ein Beitrag zur Osteologie Alakaluf. *Vierteljahrsschrift der Naturforschenden Gesellschaft* 3(4): 1-12, 1892. Br572C An8141 v.129. "Description and measurements of the complete skeletons of two Alacaluf men and three Alacaluf women, four of whom died at Zurich" (Cooper 1917:110).

2606. Martin, Rudolf. Kritische Bedenken gegen den *Pithecanthropus erectus* Dubois. *Globus* 67(14), 1895. 5 p. Br572C An8141 v.144.

2607. Martin, Rudolf. Über die Weddas der Gebrüder Sarasin. *Archiv für Anthropologie* 22:316-351, 1893. Br572C An8141 v.145.

2608. Martin, Rudolf. *Weitere Bemerkungen zur Pithecanthropus-Frage*. Zürich, 1896, 18 p. Br572C An8141 v.140.

2609. Martin, Rudolf. Ziele und Methoden einer Rassenkunde der Schweiz. *Schweizerischen Archiv für Völkskunde* 1(1), 1896. 15 p. Br572C An8141 v.154.

2610. Martin, Rudolf. Zur Frage von der Vertretung der Anthropologie an unsern Universitäten. *Globus* 66(19), 1894. 2 p. Br572C An8141 v.160.

2611. Martin, Rudolf. Zur physischen Anthropologie der Feuerländer. *Archiv für Anthropologie* 22(3): 155-218, 1893. Br572C An8141 v.107. "A very important monograph coordinating all the then extant sources on Yahgan and Alacalufan anatomy. Of these 21 skeletons and 58 skulls included, the great majority were Yahgan, the rest Alacalufan. Dr. Martin's conclusion was that the Alacaluf differ from the Yahgans by a slighter tallerr stature and by a slightly greater tendency to dolichocephalism" (Cooper 1917:111).

2612. Martínez de Lejarza, Juan J. *Análisis estadístico de la provincia de Michuacan, en 1822*. Imprenta Nacional del Supremo Gobierno de los Estados-Unidos, México, 1824. 281 p. Br917.23 M36.

2613. Martínez Gracida, Manuel. *Catálogo etimológico de los nombres de los pueblos, haciendas y ranchos del estado de Oaxaca, formado por el C. Manuel Martinez Gracida*. Imprenta del estado en el ex-obispado, dirigida por I. Candiani, Oaxaca, 1883. 142 p. Br572C An8141 v.64.

2614. Martínez Gracida, Manuel. *El rey cosijoeza y su familia; reseña histórico y legendaria de los últimos soberanos de Zachila*. Oficina Tipografica de la Secretará de Fomento, México, 1888, 182 p. Br572C An8141 v.16.

2615. Martínez López, José. Vocablos conversaciones en lengua maya, 1866. n.p. Br498.21 ML 883. Manuscript.

2616. Martínez,Alonso. Manual breve y compendioso para enpezar a aprender lengua zapoteca y administrar en casa de necessidad; lo escribio Fr. Alonso Martínez de la Orden de Santo Domingo y lo sujeta a la Santa Madre Yglesia católica romana y a su corrección y censura, año de 1633; copiado en Verapaz, 1871, año de 1633. 74 leaves. Br498.34 ZM 363. Spanish and Zapotec, with some selections in Latin. Introduction by Karl H. Berendt describes the original as: "El original de este confesionario y arte se halla en un manuscrito en curato menor de 83 fojas sin numeración, letra y papel del siglo XVI; no tiene portada y le faltan las últimas hojas. Contiene entre materias religiosas, noticias sobre historia natural, poesias, etc., en castellano y latín el confesionario en fojas 13-29 y el arte en fojas 36-48. Es propriedad de J.e M.e Melgar en Vera Cruz quien lo compró en una libreria antiquaria de la ciudad de México. Va copiado linea por linea y páginas por páginas, lo zapoteco en letra redonda y lo Castellano en cursiva ordinaria; Vera Cruz, enero 22 de 1871; Dr. C. H. Berendt."

2617. Martius, Karl F. P. von. *Beiträge zur Ethnographie und Sprachenkunde Amerika's zumal Brasiliens.* F. Fleischer, Leipzig, 1867. 2 v. Br498 M365. Contents include: 1. "Zur Ethnographie"; 2. "Zur Sprachenkunde"; "Wörtersammlung brasilianischer Sprachen."

2618. Martius, Karl F. P. von. *Von dem Rechtszustande unter den Ureinwohren Brasiliens: Eine Abhandelung.* Friedrich Fleischer, Munich, 1832. 85, 20 p. Br572C An8141 v.2.

2619. Maryland Historical Society. *Fund Publications,* 1874. v. 7. Br975.2C M366. Contents include: Andrew White, "Realtio itineris in Maryland...narrative of a voyage to Maryland"; Cecil C. Baltimore, "Declaratio colonial domini baronis de Baltimore"; E. A. Dalrymple, ed. "Excerpta ex diversis litteris missionariarum ab anno 1635 ad annum 1638."

2620. Mason, Otis T. Aboriginal American zoötechny. *American Anthropologist* 1(1): 45-81, 1899. Br799 M38. In 1884 Mason (1838-1908) was appointed curator in ethnology in the United States National Museum. He was acting head curator of anthropology in 1902-1903, and head curator in 1904-1908. He spent much of his career classifying and describing material culture. He was a proponent of evolutionary ideas of culture history but was among the first to advance the culture area concept.

2621. Mason, Otis T. Basketwork of the North American aborigines. *Annual Report of the United States National Museum, Smithsonian Institution, 1884,* pt. 2, pp. 291-309, 1884. Br572C An8141 v.10.

2622. Mason, Otis T. Geographical distribution of the musical bow. *American Anthropologist* 10:377-380, 1897. Br572C An8141 v.155.

2623. Mason, Otis T. Influence of environment upon human industries of arts. *Annual Report of the United States National Museum, Smithsonian Institution, for 1895,* pp. 639-665, 1896. Br572C An8141 v.155.

2624. Mason, Otis T. Introduction of the Iron Age in America. *American Anthropologist* 9:191-215, 1896. Br572C An8141 v.155.

2625. Mason, Otis T. Migration and the food quest: a study in the peopling of America. *American Anthropologist* 6:275-292, 1894. Br572C An8141 v.137.

2626. Mason, Otis T. Migration and the food-quest: a study in the peopling of America. *Feestbundel van Taal-, Letter-, Geschied- en Aardrijkskundige Bijfragen ter Gelegenheid van zijn Tachtigsten Geboortedag aan Dr. P. J. Veth*, pp. 253-256, 1894. Leiden. Br572C An8141 v.144.

2627. Mason, Otis T. North American bows, arrows, and quivers. *Annual Report of the United States National Museum, Smithsonian Institution, for 1893*, pp. 631-679, 1894. Br572C An8141 v.137.

2628. Mason, Otis T. Overlaying with copper by the American aborigines. *Proceedings of the United States National Museum, Smithsonian Museum* 17(1015): 475-477, 1894. Br572C An8141 v.137.

2629. Mason, Otis T. Primitive travel and transportation. *Annual Report of the United States National Museum, Smithsonian Institution, for 1894*, pp. 239-593, 1896. Br656 M38.

2630. Mason, Otis T. Similarities in culture. *American Anthropologist* 8(2): 101-117, 1895. Br572C An8141 v.137.

2631. Mason, Otis T. Technogeography or the relation of the earth to the industries of mankind. *American Anthropologist* 6(2): 137-161, 1894. Br572C An8141 v.137.

2632. Mason, Otis T. The archaeology of the Potomac tidewater region. *Proceedings of the United States National Museum, Smithsonian Institution* 12:367-376, 1889. Br572C An8141 v.41.

2633. Mason, Otis T. The birth of invention. *Annual Report of the United States National Museum, Smithsonian Institution, for 1892*, pp. 603-611, 1893. Br572C An8141 v.137.

2634. Mason, Otis T. The Guesende Collection of antiquities in Pointe-a-Pitre, Guadaloupe, West Indies. *Annual Report of the United States National Museum, Smithsonian Institution, for 1899*, pp. 729-837, 1899. Br572C An8141 v.30.

2635. Mason, Otis T. The Latimer Collection of antiquities from Porto Rico in the National Museum at Washington, DC. *Annual Report of the United States National Museum, Smithsonian Institution, for 1876*, pp. 371-393, 1877. Br572C An8141 v.30.

2636. Mason, Otis T. The man's knife among the North American Indians; a study in the collections of the United States National Museum. *Annual Report of the United States National Museum, Smithsonian Institution, for 1897*, pp. 725-745, 1899. Br970.6 M38.2.

2637. Mason, Otis T. The progress of anthropology in 1892. *Annual Report of the United States National Museum, Smithsonian Institution, for 1892*, pp. 465-512, 1893. Br572C An8141 v.137.

2638. Mason, Otis T. The Ray Collection from Tupa Reservation. *Annual Report of the United States National Museum, Smithsonian Institution, for 1886*, pp. 205-239, 1886. Br572C An8141 v.30.

2639. Mason, Otis T. The scope and value of anthropological studies. *Proceedings of the American Association for the Advancement of Science*, pp. 367-383,

1884. Salem, MA. Br572C An8141 v.30.

2640. Mason, Otis T. The ulu, or woman's knife, of the Eskimo. *Annual Report of the United States National Museum, Smithsonian Institution, for 1890*, pp. 411-416, 1892. Br572C An8141 v.86.

2641. Mason, Otis T. Throwing-sticks from Mexico and California. *Proceedings of the United States National Museum, Smithsonian Institution* 16(932): 219-221, 1894. Br572C An8141 v.124.

2642. Mason, Otis T. Throwing-sticks in the National Museum. *Annual Report of the United States National Museum, Smithsonian Institution, for 1884*, pt. 2, pp. 279-289, 1885. Br572C An8141 v.10.

2643. Mason, Otis T. *Tribe, Stock, Reservation, and Agency of Indians in the United States*. Smithsonian Institution, Washington, DC, 1892. 8 p. Br572C An8141 v.101; Br572C An8141 v.104.

2644. Mason, William. *Kanachi kichi masinaikan, kayasi testement, mina oski testement, ketipeyichikeminow mina kipimachiyiweminow Chisas Knist; emiskochitasinahat neiyawenik issi; William Mason, ayamiewikimaw*. Printed for the British and Foreign Bible Society, London, 1861. 855 p. Br497.11 CrB45. Old and New Testament translated into Cree. "Printed entirely in the Cree syllabary, except for the English imprints on the title pages and on the final leaf. The bible was translated by William Mason, a missionary in Prince Ruprert's Land, with the assidstance of his wife (who was the daughter of the governor of Red River), an Indian pastor, and several native speakers" (Siebert Library 1999:1:65).

2645. Mason, William. *Oski testement, ketipeyichikeminow mina kipimachiyiweminow Chisas Knist; emiskochitasinahat neiyawenik issi; William Mason, ayamiewikimaw*. Printed for the British and Foreign Bible Society, London, 1862. 292 p. Br497.11 CrB45. New Testament translated into Cree.

2646. Mason, William. *The Book of Common Prayer, and Administration of the Sacraments, and Other Rites and Ceremonies of the Church, According to the Use of the United Church of England and Ireland; Translated into the Language of the Cree Indians of the Diocese of Rupert's Land, North-West America*. Society for Promoting Christian Knowledge, London, 1881. 190 p. Br497.11 CrC47.

2647. Masse, R. P. *L'oraison dominicale et autres prières traduites en langage des Montagnards de Canada; extraites des Voyages au Canada du Sieur de Champlain*. H. Herluison, Orléans, 1865. 12 p. Br572C An8141 v.60.

2648. Mateos, Juan A. *Composición leida*. Imprenta a Cargo de L. Ancona, Merida, 1866. 10 p. Br572C An8141 v.69.

2649. Mathevet, Jean C. *Aiamie-tipadjimowin masinaigan ka ojitogobanen kaiat nainawisi mekatewikonaiewigobanen. L'histoire sainte en algonquin par un ancien missionnaire*. 2d ed. J. M. Valois, Montreal, 1890. 334 p. Br497.11 A1 B473.

2650. Mathevet, Jean C. Cantique en langue Algonquine. *Actes de la Sociètè Philologique* 1(4) 1872. 3 p. Br572C An8141 v.78.

2651. Mathevet, Jean C. *Ka titc Jezos tebeniminang ondaje aking...vie de Notre-Seigneur Jésus-Christ; deuxième édition, revue...A. Cuoq*. 2d ed. J. M. Valois, Montreal, 1892. 384 p. Br497.11 NiM 42. The life of Christ in Algonquin-Nipissing.

2652. Mathieu, L. Catalogue des instruments anthropologiques, 1873. 30 p. Br572C An8141 v.31.

2653. *Matiu*, n.d. 136 p. Br498.78 BB 47.1. New Testament Gospel of St. Matthew translated into Bakairi.

2654. Matthews, Washington, Jacob L. Wortman, and John S. Billings. The human bones of the Hemenway Collection in the United States Army Medical Museum at Washington. *Memoirs of the National Academy of Sciences* 6:139-286, 1893. Br573.7 M433.

2655. Matthews, Washington. *Ethnography and Philology of the Hidatsa Indians*. United States Geological and Geographical Survey of the Territories, Miscellaneous Publication, 7. Washington, DC, 1877. 239 p. Br497.5 HM43. Includes Hidatsa grammar (pp. 87-121), Hidatsa-English dictionary (pp. 123-212), and English-Hidatsa vocabulary (pp. 213-239).

2656. Matthews, Washington. *Grammar and Dictionary of the Language of the Hidatsa (Minnetarees, Grosventres of the Missouri), With an Introductory Sketch of the Tribe.* Shea's Library of American Linguistics, ser. 2, v. 1-2. Cramoisy Press, New York, 1873-1874. 2 v. Br497C Sh3.

2657. Matthews, Washington. Mythic dry-paintings of the Navajos. *American Naturalist* 19:931-939, 1885. Br572C An8141 v.13.

2658. Matthews, Washington. Navajo gambling songs. *American Anthropologist* 2(1): 1-20, 1889. 19 p. Br572C An8141 v.27.

2659. Matthews, Washington. Navajo names for plants. *American Naturalist* 20(1): 841-850, 1886. Br572C An8141 v.13.

2660. Matthews, Washington. Navajo silversmiths. *Annual Report of the Bureau of Ethnology, Smithsonian Institution, for 1880/1881,* pp. 167-178, 1883. Br970.6 M43.2.

2661. Matthews, Washington. Some deities and demons of the Navajos. *American Naturalist* 20:841-850, 1886. Br572C An8141 v.13.

2662. Matthews, Washington. The Catlin Collection of Indian paintings. *Annual Report of the United States National Museum, Smithsonian Institution, for 1890,* pp. 593-610, 1892. Br572C An8141 v.86.

2663. Matthews, Washington. The gentile system of the Navajo Indians; delivered as a lecture before the Anthropological Society, Washington, 1890. *Journal of American Folk-Lore* 3(9): 89-110, 1890. Br572C An8141 v.20.

2664. Matthews, Washington. The Inca bone and kindred formations among the ancient Arizonians. *American Anthropologist* 2(4): 337-345, 1889. Br572C An8141 v.27.

2665. Matthews, Washington. The prayer of a Navaho shaman. *American Anthropologist* 1(2): 5-26, 1888. Br572C An8141 v.60.

2666. Matthews, Washington. The suppressed part of the mountain chant. *Annual Report of the Bureau of Ethnology, Smithsonian Institution, for 1892,* pp. 2-4, 1888. Br572C An8141 v.110.

2667. Matthews, Washington. Two Mandan chiefs. *American Anthropologist* 10(5): 269-272, 1888, Br572C An8141 v.27.

2668. Maudslay, Alfred P. A Maya calendar inscription, interpreted by Goodman's Tables. *Proceedings of the Royal Society* 62:67–80, 1897. Br572C An8141 v.155. Maudslay (1850-1931) was educated at Cambridge University and spent five years in the colonial service in Trinidad, Samoa, Tonga, and Fiji. In Fiji he collected ethnographic material which, with other collections, became the core of the University Museum of Archaeology and Ethnology at Cambridge. In 1880 he traveled to Guatemala and visited Maya ruins at Copán, Quirigua, and Tikal. In subsequent expeditions he recorded sculpture and mapped at Yaxchilán, Palenque, and Chichén Itzá. Pieces of sculpture brought back by Maudslay from Copán and Yaxchilán were exhibited at the British Museum. Maudslay's *Archaeology* (1889-1902) in *Biologia Centrali-Americana* remains an essential reference work.

2669. Maudslay, Alfred P. *Archæology*. R. H. Porter and Dulau and Company, London, 1889-1902. 5 v. Br913.72 M443. At head of title: *Biologia Centrali-Americana; or, Contributions to the Knowledge of the Fauna and Flora of Mexico and Central America*, edited by F. Ducane Godman and Osbert Salvin.

2670. Maudslay, Alfred P. Exploration of the ruins and site of Copán, Central America. *Proceedings of the Royal Geographical Society* 8:568, 595, 1886. Br572C An8141 v.44.

2671. Maudslay, Alfred P. Explorations in Guatemala. *Proceedings of the Royal Geographical Society*, pp. 185-204, 1882. Br572C An8141 v.44.

2672. Maurault, Joseph Pierre A. *Histoire des Abenakis, depuis 1605 jusqu'à nos jours; par l'abbé J.A. Maurault*. Imprimé à l'atelier typographique de la "Gazette de Sorel," Sorel, Quebec, 1866. 631 p. Br970.3 AbM447.

2673. Maury, L.-F.-Alfred. *La magie el l'astrologie dans l'antiquité et au moyen âge, ou étude sur les superstitions païennes qui se sont perpétuées jusqu'à nos jours*. Didier, Paris, 1860 450 p. Br291 M446.

2674. Maya-English dictionary. n.d. 200 p. Br498.21 MM317. Manuscript; possible working dictionary by Daniel G. Brinton or by some member of the Collins family.

2675. Mayer, Brantz. *Observations on Mexican History and Archaeology, with Special Notice of Zapotec Remains, as Delineated in Mr. J. G. Sawkin's Drawings of Mitla, etc.* Smithsonian Institution Contributions to Knowledge, 9, 1856. 33 p. Washington, DC. Br572C An8141 v.100.

2676. Mayer, Brantz. *Tah-gah-jute; or, Logan and Cresap, An Historical Essay*. J. Munsell, Albany, NY, 1867. 204 p. Br975.2 M454a.

2677. Mays, Thomas J. An experimental inquiry into the chest movements of the Indian female; read before the College of Physicians, Philadelphia, April 6, 1887. *Therapeutic Gazette*, 1887. 11 p. Br572C An8141 v.27.

2678. Mays, Thomas J. Does pulmonary consumption tend to exterminate the American Indian? *New York Medical Journal*, 1887. 8 p. Br572C An8141 v.27.

2679. Mazuchelli, Samuel C. *Ocangra aramee Wawakakara, or Winnebago Prayer Book, by Samuel Mazzuchelli*. George L. Whitney, Printer, Waiastanoeca [Detroit], 1833. 23 p. Br497.5 Woc12. A Catholic prayer book and catechism in Winnebago. "Mazzuchelli, a member of a prominent Milanese family, served as a Roman Catholic missionary to Iowa and Wisconsin, and is considered to be one of the greatest western missionaries" (Siebert Library 1999:2:128).

2680. McAdams, William. Ancient mounds of Illinois. *Proceedings of the American Association for the Advancement of Science* 29:710–718, 1880. Br572C An8141 v.19.

2681. McCoy, Isaac. *History of Baptist Indian Mission; Embracing Remarks on the Former and Present Condition of the Aboriginal Tribes, Their Settlement Within the Indian Territory, and Their Future Prospects.* William M. Morrison, Washington, DC; H. and S. Raynor, New York, 1840. 611 p. Br970.6 M13. "A missionary to the Indians in the Arkansas Territory and present-day Kanasa, McCoy was motivated by the desire 'to meliorate and substantially improve the condition of the aborigines of our country" (Siebert Library 1999:2:196).

2682. McCoy, Isaac. The annual register of Indian affairs, no. 1, 1835. 50 p. Br572C An8141 v.34.

2683. McDonald, Robert. *Chilig Takidh tshah zit; Hymns in Takudh Language; Composed and Translated by the Ven. Archdeacon McDonald, D.D.* Society for Promoting Christian Knowledge, London, 1890. 89 p. Br497.12 TuM 14.2.

2684. McDonald, Robert. *Ettunetle tutthug enjit gichinchik ako sakrament rsikotitinyoo ako chizi thlelchil nutinde ako kindi kwunttlutritili Ingland thlelchil tungittiyin kwikit; takudh tsha zit thleteteitazya ven archdeacon McDonald D.D. kirke.* Society for Promoting Christian Knowledge, London, 1885. 221 p. Br497.12 TuC47. Church of England Book of Common Prayer translated into Tukkuthkutchin.

2685. McDonald, Robert. *Fourth and Fifth Books of Moses, Called Numbers and Deuteronomy, Moses vit ettunetle ttyig ako ttankthut nikendo…Translated into Tukudh.* British and Foreign Bible Society, London, 1891. 191 p. Br497.25 GB46.9. Old Testament Books of Numbers and Deuteronomy translated into Tukudh.

2686. McDonald, Robert. *Hymns and Canticles in the Tukudh or Soucheux Dialect.* Society for Promoting Christian Knowledge, London, 1885. 74 p. Br497.12 TuM14. Hymns translated into Tukkuthkutchin.

2687. McDonald, Robert. *Mosis vit ettunettle ttyig Genesis, Exodus, Levitikus…Archdeacon McDonald, D.D., kirkhe thleteteitzaya.* Printed for the British and Foreign Bible Society, London, 1890. 282 p. Br497.12 TuB46. Translation of the Old Testament Pentateuch into Tukkuthkutchin.

2688. McDonald, Robert. *Selection from the Book of Common Prayer, According to the Use of the United Church of England and Ireland; Translated into Tukudh.* Society for Promoting Christian Knowledge, London, 1873. 123 p. Br497.12 TuM 14.3. Translation of selections of the Book of Common Prayer into Tukkuthkutchin.

2689. McDonald, Robert. *Syllabarium for the Tukudh Language.* Society for Promoting Christian Knowledge, London, n.d. 1 p. Br497.12 TuM 14.4; Br497.12 TuM 14.4a.

2690. McDonald, Robert. *The Books of the Twelve Minor Prophets; O musinaiiguniwan igiw mitaswi ashi nizh anwajigewininwug noondash opitendagozijig; Translated into Otchipwe by the Rev. Robert McDonald.* Printed at the University Press for the British and Foreign Bible Society, London, 1874. 171 p. Br497.11

CB474.Translation of the minor prophets of the Old Testament into Chippewa.

2691. McDonald, Robert. *The New Testament of Our Lord and Saviour Jesus Christ; Translated into Takudh by Ven. Archdeacon McDonald, D. D.* Printed for the British and Foreign Bible Society, London, 1886. 576 p. Br497.12 TuB47.

2692. McDougall, Alan. The Beothick Indians. *Transactions of the Canadian Institute* 2(1): 98-102, 1891. Br572C An8141 v.10.

2693. McGee, Anita N. An experiment in human stirpiculture. *American Anthropologist* 4(4): 319-325, 1891. Br572C An8141 v.8.

2694. McGee, William J. A fossil earthquake. *Bulletin of the Geological Society of America* 4:411-414, 1892. Br572C An8141 v.125. McGee (1853-1912) was a prolific scholar who is best remembered for his organizational and leadership abilities. He was influential in the Anthropological Society of Washington and was one of the founders of the American Anthropological Association. In 1902 he became the Association's first president. He was also vice-president of the Archaeological Institute of America, a founder of the Geological Society of America, and vice-president of the National Geographic Society.

2695. McGee, William J. A Muskwaki bowl. *American Anthropologist* 11(1): 88-91, 1898. Br970.6 M17.2.

2696. McGee, William J. An account of the progress in geology for the years 1887, 1888. *Annual Report of the United States National Museum, Smithsonian Institution, for 1888*, pp. 217-260, 1890. Br572C An8141 v.125.

2697. McGee, William J. An obsidian implement from Pleistocene deposits in Nevada. *American Anthropologist* 2(4): 301-312, 1889. Br572C An8141 v.41.

2698. McGee, William J. Annotations and remarks on C. C. Baldwin, *Man and the Glacial Period. American Anthropologist* 6, 1893. 22 p. Br572C An8141 v.124.

2699. McGee, William J. Anthropology of the Madison meeting. *American Anthropologist* 6:435-448, 1893. Br572C An8141 v.125.

2700. McGee, William J. Areal work of the United States Geological Survey. *Transactions of the American Institute of Mining Engineers*, 1892. 10 p. Br572C An8141 v.125.

2701. McGee, William J. Bureau of Ethnology. In *The Smithsonian Institution, 1846-1896; The History of Its First Half-Century*, pp. 367-396. Washington, DC, 1897. Br61 M17.

2702. McGee, William J. Classification of geographic forms by Genesis. *National Geographic Magazine* 11(1): 27-36, 1888. Br572C An8141 v.125.

2703. McGee, William J. Comparative chronology. *American Anthropologist* 5(4): 327-344, 1892. Br572C An8141 v.125.

2704. McGee, William J. Encroachments of the sea. *The Forum*, pp. 437-449, 1890. Br572C An8141 v.125.

2705. McGee, William J. Man and the glacial period. *American Anthropologist* 6(1): 85-98, 1893. Br572C An8141 v.125.

2706. McGee, William J. Neocene and Pleistocene continent movements. *Proceedings of the American Association for the Advancement of Science* 60:253, 1891. Br572C An8141 v.125.

2707. McGee, William J. On the meridional deflection of ice-streams. *American Journal of Science* 29:386-392, 1885. Br572C An8141 v.125.

2708. McGee, William J. Ovibos cavifrons from the loess of Iowa. *American Journal of Science* 34:217-220, 1887. Br572C An8141 v.125.

2709. McGee, William J. Palaeolithic man in America: his antiquity and environment. *Popular Science Monthly*, November, pp. 20-36, 1888. Br572C An8141 v.41; Br572C An8141 v.125.

2710. McGee, William J. Piratical acculturation. *American Anthropologist* 11:243-249, 1898. Br970.6 M17.

2711. McGee, William J. Reports to the delegates to the Congrès Géologique International. *American Anthropologist* 5(1): 45-51, 1892. Br572C An8141 v.125.

2712. McGee, William J. Some principles of evidence relating to the antiquity of man. *Proceedings of the American Association for the Advancement of Science* 38, 1889. Br572C An8141 v.125.

2713. McGee, William J. The drainage system and the distribution of the loess of eastern Iowa. *The Messenger Book and Job Print*, Fort Dodge, 1884. 14 p. Br572C An8141 v.125.

2714. McGee, William J. The evolution of serials published by scientific societies. *Bulletin of the Philosophical Society of Washington* 11:221-246, 1890. Br572C An8141 v.125.

2715. McGee, William J. The field of geology and its promise for the future. *Bulletin of the Minnesota Academy of Natural Sciences* 3(2): 191-206, 1888. Br572C An8141 v.125.

2716. McGee, William J. The flood plains of rivers. *The Forum*, pp. 221-234, 1891. Br572C An8141 v.125.

2717. McGee, William J. The geologic antecendents of man in the Potomac Valley. *American Anthropologist* 2(3): 227-234, 1889. Br572C An8141 v.41; Br572C An8141 v.125.

2718. McGee, William J. The Gulf of Mexico as a measure of isostasy. *American Journal of Science* 64:177-192, 1892. Br572C An8141 v.125.

2719. McGee, William J. The relations of geology and agriculture. *Transactions of the Iowa State Horticultural Society* 16:227-240, 1884. Br572C An8141 v.125.

2720. McGee, William J. The remains of don Francisco Pizarro. *American Anthropologist* 7, 1894. 25 p. Br572C An8141 v.125.

2721. McGee, William J. The science of humanity; an address...before the section anthropology, American Association for the Advancement of Science. *Proceedings of the American Association for the Advancement of Science* 46, 1897. 34 p. Br572 M175.

2722. McGee, William J. The Siouan Indians, a preliminary sketch. *Annual Report of the Bureau of Ethnology, Smithsonian Institution, for 1894-1895*, pp. 153-204, 1897. Br970.3 SiM183.

2723. McGee, William J. The southern extension of the Appomattox formation. *American Journal of Science* 60:15-41, 1890. Br572C An8141 v.125.

2724. McGee, William J. The southern old fields (abstract). *Proceedings of the American*

Association for the Advancement of Science v. 60, 1891. 1 p. Br572C An8141 v.125.

2725. McGuffey, William H. *Laguna Indian Translation of McGufeyf's* [sic] *New First Eclectic Reader. Laguna, New Mexico, 1882. 162 p.* Br497.3 LM17. English and Laguna dialect of Keres on facing pages.

2726. McGuffey, William H. *McGuffey's New First Eclectic Reader for Young Learners.* Van Antwerp, Bragg and Company, Cincinnati, New York, 1885. 84 leaves. Br497.3 LM17a.

2727. McGuire, Joseph D. A study of the primitive methods of drilling. *Annual Report of the United States National Museum, Smithsonian Institution, for 1894,* pp. 623-756, 1896. Br571.25 M175; Br572C An8141 v.154.

2728. McGuire, Joseph D. Aboriginal quarries-soapstone bowls and the tools used in their manufacture. *American Naturalist* 17(6): 587-595, 1883. Br572C An8141 v.13; Br572C An8141 v.59.

2729. McGuire, Joseph D. Classification and development of primitive implements. *American Anthropologist* 9:227-236, 1896. Br572C An8141 v.154.

2730. McGuire, Joseph D. Materials, apparatus, and processes of the aboriginal lapidary. *American Anthropologist* 5:165-176, 1892. Br572C An8141 v.110.

2731. McGuire, Joseph D. On the evolution of the art of working in stone. *American Anthropologist* 6:307-319, 1893. Br572C An8141 v.124.

2732. McGuire, Joseph D. The development of sculpture: a preliminary paper. *American Anthropologist* 7:358-366, 1894. 9 p. Br572C An8141 v.134.

2733. McGuire, Joseph D. The stone hammer and its various uses. *American Anthropologist* 4(4): 301-312, 1891. Br572C An8141 v.12.

2734. McKenney, Thomas L. Cherokee alphabet. Report of Thomas L. McKenney, Superintendent of Indian Affairs in the War Department, September 1825. Br572C An8141 v.52. McKenney (1785-1859) was for many years Superintendent of Indian Affairs and met with representatives of numerous American Indian tribes and nations.

2735. McLaury, W. M. Hallucinations and delusions. *The Alienist and Neurologist,* 1894. 26 p. Br572C An8141 v.131.

2736. McLean, John P. A study of American archaeology. *Universalist Quarterly* 37-38, 1880-1881. Boston. Br572C An8141 v.58.

2737. McLennan, John F. *Studies in Ancient History. The Second Series, Comprising an Inquiry into the Origin of Exogamy.* Macmillan, London, New York, 1896. 605 p. Br392.5 M225. John Ferguson McLennan (1827-1881) was a lawyer and ethnologist whose work on social evolution, kinship, and the origin of religion contributed to the development of social anthropology.

2738. McPherson, G. *La cueva de la mujer, descripción de una caverna conteniendo restos prehistóricos, descubierta en las inmediaciones de Alhama de Granada.* Velasco, Cadiz, 1871. 7 p. Br913.46 M24.

2739. Meacham, Alfred B. *Wi-ne-ma (The Woman-Chief) and Her People, by Hon. A. B. Meacham.* American Publishing Company, Hartford, 1876. 168 p. Br970.2 M46. Study of Modoc chieftainess Winema (1842-1932).

2740. Medina, José Toribio. *Los aboríjenes de Chile.* Imprenta Gutenberg, Santiago, 1882. 427 p. Br913.83 M46. "This classic, though treating chiefly Araucanian anthropology, sums up or quotes literally almost all the Chonoan material contained in the earlier sources" (Cooper 1917:111).

2741. Meigs, James A. *Catalogue of Human Crania, in the Collection of the Academy of Natural Sciences of Philadelphia; Based upon the Third Edition of Dr. Morton's "Catalogue of Skulls", by J. Aitken Meigs*. J. B. Lippincott, Philadelphia, 1857. 112 p. Br573.7 P53.

2742. Meitzen, Friedrich E. A. Über Bildung von Dörfern und deren nationale Bedeutung. *Verhandlungen der Berliner Gesellschaft für Anthropologie, Ethnologie und Urgeschichte*, pp. 4–16, 1872. Br572C An8141 v.162.

2743. Meitzen, Friedrich E. A. Über die schlesische Preseka und andere Grenzverhaue des Mittelalters. *Verhandlungen der Berliner Gesellschaft für Anthropologie, Ethnologie und Urgeschichte*, pp. 12–19, 1873. Br572C An8141 v.162.

2744. Melgar, J. M. Antiguedades mexicanas, 1870. 4 p. Br572C An8141 v.165.

2745. Melgar, J. M. *Examen comparativo entre los signos simbolicos de las teogonias y cosmogonias antiguas y los que existen en los manuscritos mexicanos publicados por Kingsborough y los bajos relieves de una pared de Chichen-Itza*. R. Laine y Ca., Veracruz, 1872. 26 p. Br572C An8141 v.165.

2746. Membreño, Alberto. *Hondureñismos; vocabulario de los provincialismos de Honduras; 2 ed. corregida y aumentada y con un apéndice que contiene vocabularios de los idiomas indígenas de Honduras*. Tipografía Nacional, Tegucigalpa, 1897. 269 p. Br467.1 M51. Appendix includes vocabularies of Moreno, Zambo, Sumo, Paya, Jicaque, Lenca and Chorti.

2747. *Memoirs of an Eventful Expedition in Central America, Resulting in the Discovery of the Idolatrous City of Iximaya, Described by John L. Stephens and Other Travelers*. New York, 1850. 35 p. Br572C An8141 v.34.

2748. *Memorial de Sololá. Annals of the Cakchiquels; The Original Text, With a Translation, Notes and Introduction* [by Daniel G. Brinton]. Philadelphia, 1885. 234 p. Br498.21 Car 15.

2749. Memorial de Solola. Manuscrito cakchiquel o sea memorial de Tecpan-Atitlan (Solola). Historia del antiguo reino del Cakchiquel, dicho de Guatemala; escrito en lengua Cakchiquel por don Francisco Ernantez Arana Xahila Xahila y continuado por don Francisco Diaz Gebuta Queh. Atitlan, 1650? 96 p. Br498.21 Car 15. Manuscript.

2750. Memorial de Solola. Memorial de Tecpan-Atitlan…completé par F. D. G. Queh et traducit de la langue cakchiquèle en français par Brasseur de Bourbourg, 1855, Mérida, 1870. 165 p. Br498.21 Car 15.2. Manuscript transcribed by Karl H. Berendt from Brasseur's copy.

2751. *Memorias de la Sociedad Económica*. num. 2, 1861. Br572C An8141 v.69.

2752. Menaul, John, ed. Laguna hymns, n.d. Br572C An8141 v.155.

2753. Menaul, John. *Child's Catechism in English and Laguna; Translated and Printed at the Laguna Mission School*. Valencia Company, Laguna, NM, 1880. 69 p. Br497.3 LM52.

2754. Mendieta, Gerónimo de. *Historia eclesiástica indiana, obra escrita á fines del siglo XVI*. México, 1870. 790 p. Br972 M52.4.

2755. Mendoza, J. El pueblo de Cacaopera. *La Universidad* 10:436-448, 1895. San Salvador. Br572C An8141 v.142.

2756. Mengarini, Gregory. *Grammatica linguae selocae; auctore P. Gregorio Mengarini*. Shea's Library of American Linguistics, 2. Cramoisy Press, New York, 1861. 122 p. Br497C Sh3; Br497C Sh3a.

2757. Mengarini, Gregory. Indians of Oregon, etc. *Journal of the Anthropological Institute of New York* 1:81-88, 1871-1872. Br572C An8141 v.19.

2758. Mercer, Henry C. A new investigation of man's antiquity at Trenton. *Science* 6(149):675-682, 1897. Br572C An8141 v.155. Until the late 1890s Henry Chapman Mercer (1856-1930), a gentleman farmer focused his interest on the material culture of the New World and the existence of original man in the Delaware valley of eastern Pennsylvania. Between 1891 and 1897 he was on the curatorial staff of the University of Pennsylvania Museum's newly formed Department of Archaeology and Paleontology, and explored sites in the Delaware valley looking for evidence of early man. He later excavated archaeological sites in Maine, Indiana, Ohio, Virginia, and Tennessee. In 1895 he led the Corwith Expedition to the Yucatan peninsula of southern Mexico, publishing his findings in 1896. He established the Moravian Pottery and Tile Works in Doylestown, and developed a handwork system of manufacturing relief-decorated tiles. Mercer played an important role in the revitalization of the decorative ceramic tile as an element of architecture, was a major promoter of the Arts and Crafts Movement's handicraft ideology, wrote seminal books on the material culture of colonial America that remains standard references in the field.

2759. Mercer, Henry C. A preliminary account of the re-exploration in 1894 and 1895 of the Bone Hole, now known as Irwin's Cave, at Port Kennedy, Montgomery County, Pennsylvania. *Proceedings of the Academy of Natural Sciences of Philadelphia*, pp. 443-446, 1895. Br572C An8141 v.140.

2760. Mercer, Henry C. Cave exploration in the eastern United States. *The Archaeologist* 2, 1894. 2 p. Br572C An8141 v.144.

2761. Mercer, Henry C. Cave exploration in the eastern United States: preliminary report, 1896. 3 p. Br572C An8141 v.160.

2762. Mercer, Henry C. Cave hunting in Yucatan. *Technology Quarterly* 10(4): 353-371, 1897. Br572C An8141 v.155.

2763. Mercer, Henry C. Chipped stone implements in the Columbian Historical Exposition at Madrid. *Report of the Madrid Commission, 1892*, pp. 367-397. United States Government Printing Office, Washington, DC, 1895. Br572C An8141 v.140.

2764. Mercer, Henry C. Exploration by the University of Pennsylvania in West Florida. *American Naturalist* 30:691-693, 1896. Br572C An8141 v.155.

2765. Mercer, Henry C. Fashion's holocaust. *City and State*, pp. 3-12. 1897. Br572C An8141 v.155.

2766. Mercer, Henry C. Indian jasper mines in the Lehigh Hills. *American Anthropologist* 7(1): 80-91, 1894. Br572C An8141 v.127.

2767. Mercer, Henry C. Jasper and stalagmite quarried by Indians in the Wyandotte

Cave. *Proceedings of the American Philosophical Society* 34:396-400, 1895. Br572C An8141 v.140.

2768. Mercer, Henry C. *Light and Fire Making; With Forty-Five Illustrations Explaining the Rubbing of Fire From Wood, the Striking of Flint and Steel, and Some of the Lamps, Candles, Torches, and Lanterns of the American Pioneer.* Contributions to American History, Bucks County Historical Society, 4, Doylestown, PA, 1898. 29 p. Br572C An8141 v.99.

2769. Mercer, Henry C. Notes taken at random; read before the Bucks County Historical Society, at the annual meeting at Newton, July 21, 1898, 1896. Br572C An8141 v.155.

2770. Mercer, Henry C. Notes taken in December, 1892, and March, 1893, at the Quaternary gravel pits of Abbeville, St. Acheul and Chelles. *The Archaeologist* 1(7): 121-127, 1893. Br572C An8141 v.127.

2771. Mercer, Henry C. Observations on the scapulae of Northwest Coast Indians. *American Naturalist* 31:736-745, 1897. Br572C An8141 v.155.

2772. Mercer, Henry C. Pebbles chipped by modern Indians as an aid to the study of the Trenton gravel implements. *Proceedings of the American Association for the Advancement of Science* 41:287-289, 1892. Br572C An8141 v.119.

2773. Mercer, Henry C. Prehistoric jasper mines in the Lehigh Hills. *Popular Science Monthly*, pp. 662-672, 1893. Br572C An8141 v.119.

2774. Mercer, Henry C. Professor W. Boyd Dawkins on Paleolithic man in Europe. *American Naturalist* 28:448-451, 1894. Br572C An8141 v.136.

2775. Mercer, Henry C. Re-exploration of Hartman's Cave, near Stroudsburg, Pennsylvania, in 1893. *Proceedings of the Academy of Natural Sciences of Philadelphia*, pp. 96-104, 1894. Br572C An8141 v.136.

2776. Mercer, Henry C. Relative efficiency of animals as machines. *American Naturalist* 30:784-795, 1896. Br572C An8141 v.155.

2777. Mercer, Henry C. *Researches Upon the Antiquity of Man in the Delaware Valley and the Eastern United States, by Henry C. Mercer.* Publications of the University of Pennsylvania. Series in Philology, Literature and Archaeology, 6. Ginn and Company, Boston; M. Niemeyer, Halle a S., 1897. 178 p. Br572 M535. Contents include: H. C. Mercer, "The antiquity of man in the Delaware Valley"; H. C. Mercer, "Exploration of an Indian ossuary on the Choptank River, Dorchester County, Maryland"; E. D. Cope, "Physical characters of the skeletons found in the Indian ossuary on the Choptank estuary, Maryland"; R. H. Harte, "Traces of disease in the human remains found in Indian ossuary on the Choptank estuary, Maryland"; H. C. Mercer, "An exploration of aboriginal shell heaps revealing traces of cannibalism on York River, Maine"; H. C. Mercer, "The discovery of aboriginal remains at a rockshelter in the Delaware Valley known as the Indian House"; and H. C. Mercer, "An exploration of Durham Cave in 1893."

2778. Mercer, Henry C. The bone cave at Port Kennedy, Pennsylvania, and its partial excavation in 1894, 1895 and 1896. *Journal of the Academy of Natural Sciences of Philadelphia* 11(2): 270-285, 1899. Br560.974 M536.

2779. Mercer, Henry C. The decorated stove plates of Durham. *Contributions to Ameri-*

can History, Bucks County Historical Society, 3, 1897. 4 p. Br572C An8141 v.99.

2780. Mercer, Henry C. *The Decorated Stove Plates of the Pennsylvania Germans.* McGinty's Job Press, Doylestown, PA, 1899. 26 p. Br973.03 M537.

2781. Mercer, Henry C. The finding of the remains of the fossil sloth at Big Bone Cave, Tennessee, in 1896. *Proceedings of the American Philosophical Society* 36(154): 5-39, 1897. Br572C An8141 v.155.

2782. Mercer, Henry C. *The Hill-Caves of Yucatán; A Search for Evidence of Man's Antiquity in the Caverns of Central America; Being an Account of the Corwith Expedition of the Department of Archaeology and Palaeontology of the University of Pennsylvania.* J. B. Lippincott, Philadelphia, 1896 183 p. Br913.726 M53.1.

2783. Mercer, Henry C. The kabal, or potter's wheel of Yucatan. *Bulletin of the Free Museum of Science and Art, University of Pennsylvania* 1(2): 63-70, 1897. Br572C An8141 v.155.

2784. Mercer, Henry C. *The Lenape Stone; or the Indian and the Mammoth.* Putnam, New York, 1885. 95 p. Br970.3 DeM537.

2785. Mercer, Henry C. The Red Man's Bucks County; a paper by Henry C. Mercer, read before the Bucks County Historical Society, at Wolf Rocks, Buckingham, July 16, 1895. Bucks County Historical Society, 1895. 3 p. Br572C An8141 v.140.

2786. Mercer, Henry C. The survival of the mediaeval art of illuminative writing among Pennsylvania Germans. *Proceedings of the American Philosophical Society* 36(156): 423-432, 1897. Br572C An8141 v.155.

2787. Mercer, Henry C. *Tools of the Nation Maker.* Office of the Bucks County Intelligence, Doylestown, PA, 1897. 87 p. Br572C An8141 v.155.

2788. Mercer, Henry C. Trenton and Somme gravel specimens compared with ancient quarry refuse in America and Europe. *American Naturalist* 27:962-978, 1893. Br572C An8141 v.113.

2789. Mérida, Libreria Meridiana. *Catalogo de los libros, que se hallan de centa en la Libreria Meridiana de Canton*, n.d. Br972.6 M543. Bound with: *Arancel para el cobro de arbitrios en las mercados publicos de esta ciudad.* Guzmán, Mérida, 1856. 13 p.; and *Reglamento de policia de la ciudad de Mérida, capital de Yucatán.* Espinosa, Mérida, 1858. 15 p.

2790. Merrill, Moses. *Wdtwhtl wdwdklha tva eva wdhonetl; Marin Awdofka; Otoe Hymn Book.* J. Meeker, Printer, Shawannoe Mission, 1834. 12 p, 1834 Br497.5. OtM55.

2791. Merrit, J. K. Report on the huacals, or ancient graveyards of Chiriqui. American Ethnological Society, 1860. 14 p. Br572C An8141 v.165.

2792. Method of writing, practised by ther Seneka Indians of New York. *Medical and Philosophical News*, pp. 83-86, 1808. Br572C An8141 v.60.

2793. Mexico. Dirección General de Estadistica. *Anuario estadistico de la república mexicana, 1895-1898.* México, 1896-1899. v. 3-6. Br317.2 M576.2.

2794. Mexico. Dirección General de Estadistica. *Boletin demografico de la republica mexicana*, 1896, 1898. México, 1897, 1898. v. 1, v. 3. Br317.2 M576.3.

2795. Mexico. Dirección General de Estadistica. *Estadistica general de la república mexicana.* México, 1884-1896. v. 5. Br317.2 M577.

2796. Meye, Heinrich, and Julius Schmidt. *Die Steinbildwerke von Copán und Quiriguá*. A. Asher, Berlin, 1883. 16 p. Br913.728 Sch54.

2797. Meyer, Adolf B. von. *Die Nephritfrage kein ethnologisches Problem: Vortrag*. Berlin, 1883. 24 p. Br572C An8141 v.24.

2798. Meyer, Adolf B. von. Notizen über das Feilen der Zähne bei den Völken des ostindischen archipels. *Mitteilungen der Anthropologische Gesellschaft in Wien* 7:214-216, 1878. Br572C An8141 v.82.

2799. Meyer, Adolf B. von. *The Distribution of the Negritos in the Philippine Islands and Elsewhere*. Stengel and Co., Dresden, 1899. 92 p. Br572.9914 M577. A revised translation of two chapters from a larger work on the Negritos in v. 9 of the Publications of the Royal Ethnographical Museum of Dresden.

Essays of an Americanist.

I. ETHNOLOGIC AND ARCHÆOLOGIC.
II. MYTHOLOGY AND FOLK LORE.
III. GRAPHIC SYSTEMS AND LITERATURE.
IV. LINGUISTIC.

BY

DANIEL G. BRINTON, A. M., M. D.,

PROFESSOR OF AMERICAN ARCHÆOLOGY AND LINGUISTICS IN THE UNIVERSITY OF PENNSYL-
VANIA, PRESIDENT OF THE NUMISMATIC AND ANTIQUARIAN SOCIETY OF PHILADEL-
PHIA, PRESIDENT OF THE AMERICAN FOLK-LORE SOCIETY, MEMBER OF THE
AMERICAN ANTIQUARIAN SOCIETY, THE AMERICAN PHILOSOPHICAL
SOCIETY, THE SOCIÉTÉ ROYALE DES ANTIQUAIRES DU NORD,
THE SOCIÉTÉ AMÉRICAINE DE FRANCE, THE BER-
LINER ANTHROPOLOGISCHE GESELLSCHAFT,
THE REAL ACADEMIA DE HIS-
TORIA, MADRID, ETC., ETC.

PHILADELPHIA:
PORTER & COATES.
1890.

Title page from Brinton's Essays of an Americanist *(1890).*

2800. Meyer, Adolf B. von. Über den Ursprung von Rechts und Links. *Verhandlungen der Berliner Gesellschaft für Anthropologie, Ethnologie und Urgeschichte*, pp. 2-13, 1873. Br572C An8141 v.162.

2801. Meyer, Hermann A. H. Bows and arrows in central Brazil. *Annual Report of the United States National Museum, Smithsonian Institution, for 1896*, pp. 549-590, 1898. Br913.81 M313. Translated from the original German *Bogen und Pfeil in central-Brasilien* (Druck vom Bibliographischen Institut, Leipzig, 1896).

2802. Michael, Helen C. de S. A. A chemical study of *Yucca augustifolia*. *Transactions of the American Philosophical Society* 16(3): 254-284, 1888. Br584.32 M583.

2803. Michel, Henri. *Les projectiles rotatoires chez les peuples primitifs*. Association Française pour l'Avancement des Sciences, Paris, 1894. 10 p. Br572C An8141 v.99.

2804. Michel, Henri. Note sur les propulseurs à crochet. *Association Française pour l'Avancement des Sciences, Congrès de Saint-Etienne*, 1897. 4 p. Br572C An8141 v.99.

2805. Michel, Henri. Présentation de deux cranes de l'epoque incasique. *Association Française pour l'Avancement des Sciences, Congrès de Besançon*, 1893. 6 p. Br572C An8141 v.99.

2806. Michelena y Rojas, Francisco. *Exploración oficial por la primera vez desde el norte de la America del Sur siempre por rios, entrando por las bocas del Orinóco, de los valles de este mismo y del Meta, Casiquiare, Rio-Negro ó Guaynia y Amazónas, hasta Nauta en el alto Marañon ó Amazónas, arriba de las bocas del Ucayali bajada del Amazonas hasta el Atlántico...viaje a Rio de Janeiro desde Belen en el Gran Pará, por el Atlántico, tocando en las capitales de las principales provincias del imperio en los años, de 1855 hasta 1859.* A. Lacroix, Erboeckhoven y C., Bruselas, 1867. 684 p. Br918 M585.

2807. Middendorf, Ernst W. *Die einheimischen Sprachen Perus.* Brockhaus, Leipzig, 1890-1892. 6 v. Br498.6 M58. Contents include: v. 1. Das Runa Simi oder die Keshua-Sprache, wie sie gegenwärtig in der Provinz von Cusco gesprochen wird; v. 2. Wörterbuch des Runa Simi oder der Keshua-Sprache; v. 3. Ollanta, ein Drama der Keshuasprache; v. 4. Dramatische und lyrische Dichtungen der Keshua-Sprache; v. 5. Die Aimará-Sprache; v. 6. Das Muchik oder die Chimu-Sprache.

2808. Milfort, General. *Mémoire au coup-d'oeil rapide sur mes différens voyages et mon séjour dans la nation Crëck; par la gal. Milfort, Tastanégy ou grand chef de guerre de la nation Crëck, et général de brigade au service de la République française.* De l'Imprimerie de Giguet et Michaud, an XI, Paris, 1802. 331 p. Br970.3 CrM593. "The narrative of this extraordinary man's career among the Creek Indians, has so much of the romantic in the design of the author, that the reader is at first predisposed to think lightly of its veracity. There are, however, corroborative circumstances which confirm his statements, and induce us to give a fair degree of credence to his narrative. At the time of his arrival among the Creeks, a half breed names McGillivray had obtained so great an influence over them by his talent for organization, that he had actually acquired the rank of head chief. Milfort was received by McGillivray with great cordiality, married his Indian sister, and in a short time was made the commander of the warriors of the nation. He led them against both the Spaniards and the Americans, and by his aid the Indians defeated the forces of each in several skirmishes. Milfort remained with the Creeks until the breaking out of the Revolution in his own country. His memoir affords us some general information of the tribes he visited, but not of such value as we might have anticipated from his opportunities" (Field 1873:275).

2809. Mill, Hugh R. The geographical work of the future. *Scottish Geographical Magazine* 11:49-56, 1895. Br572C An8141 v.99.

2810. Mill, Hugh R. The principles of geography. *Scottish Geographical Magazine* 8:1-7, 1892. Br572C An8141 v.99.

2811. Miller, Merton L. *A Preliminary Study of the Pueblo of Taos, New Mexico.* University of Chicago Press, Chicago, 1897. 48 p. Br572C An8141 v.155.

2812. Miller, W. J. *King Philip and the Wampanoags of Rhode Island; With Some Account of a Rock Picture on the Shore of Mount Hope Bay in Bristol.* 2d ed. Sidney S. Rider, Providence, 1885. 148 p. Br572C An8141 v.112.

2813. Mindeleff, Cosmos. Aboriginal remains in Verde Valley, Arizona. *Annual Report of the Bureau of Ethnology, Smithsonian Institution for 1893-1894,* pp. 179-261, 1896. Br913.791 M66.

2814. Mindeleff, Cosmos. The influence of geographic environment. *Bulletin of the American Geographical Society* 29(1), 1897. 12 p. Br572C An8141 v.155.

2815. *Ethnology, Smithsonian Institution for 1893-1894,* pp. 317-349, 1896. Br913.791 M66.1.

2816. Ministerio de Fomento (Mexico). *Departamento de Censo General de la Republica Mexicana,* v. 1-26, 1897-1899. Br317.2 M577.4.

2817. Ministerio de Fomento (Spain). *Relaciones geográficos de Indias: Peru.* Tipografía de M. G. Hernández, Madrid, 1881-1897. v. 1. Br985D Sp12.

2818. Misterios del Smo. Rosario en lengua cakchi del archivo parroquial en Cobán. 17 p. Br498.21 KM698. Manuscript.

2819. Mitre, Bartolomé. *Las ruinas de Tiahuanaco; arqueologia americana.* Buenos Aires, 1879. 67 p. Br572C An8141 v.37.

2820. Mitre, Bartolomé. *Lenguas americanas; el mije y el zoque.* Imprenta de La Nación, Buenos Aires, 1895. 39 p. Br498.35 MM 694.

2821. Mitre, Bartolomé. *Lenguas americanas; estudio bibliográfico-lingüístico de las obras del P. Luis de Valdivia sobre el araucano y el allentíak, con un vocabulario razonado del allentíak.* Talleres de publicaciones del Museo, La Plata, 1894. 153 p. Br498.977 GV23yM.

2822. Mitre, Bartolomé. Los bibliofagos; estracto de una bibliografía americana. *Nueva Revista de Buenos Aires,* 1881. 22 p. Br572C An8141 v.37.

2823. Mitre, Bartolomé. Ollantay: estudio sobre el drama quechua. *Nueva Revista de Buenos Aires,* 1881. 44 p. Br572C An8141 v.37.

2824. Modern Language Association of America. *Programme of the Thirteenth Annual Meeting Held at Yale University, December 26-28, 1895,* 1895. Br420.6 M726.

2825. Modern Language Association of America. Report of the Committee of the Twelve. pp. 1391-1433. Government Printing Office, Washington, DC, 1899. Br420.6 M721. A chapter from a report of the United States Commissioner of Education.

2826. Modo de administrar los sacramentos en castellano y tzendal, 1707. Tuxtla Gutiérrez, 1870. 44 p. Br498.21 TzM 725. Transcript by Karl H. Berendt of a manuscript on the administration of the sacraments in Tzeltal and Spanish originally in the possession of José Hilario Aguilar, the cura of Chiapas.

2827. Modo de confesar en lengua maya, año de 1803, obsequio de Dn. Florentino Gimeno Echeverría en Campeche, septiembre de 1870. 38 leaves. Br498.21 MM725. "Manuscript, original; written in a clear, small hand, Spanish in one column, Maya in the other. The name of the author is carefully blotted on the first page and is illegible. The questions and answers extend over a wide variety of topics, and form a valuable means of studying the language. The manuscript was [probably written by a Franciscan at the convent in Tixcacalcupul and] obtained in Campeche by Dr. Berendt" (Brinton 1900).

2828. Molee, Elias. *Nu English Herald* v. 1, no. 1, 1891. Br409.09 N88; Br572C An8141 v.21.

2829. Molee, Elias. *Plea for an American Language, or Germanic-English.* J. Anderson, Chicago, 1888. 303 p. Br409.09 M733.3.

2830. Molina Solís, Juan Francisco. *Historia del descubrimiento y conquista de Yucatán, con una reseña de la historia antigua de esta peninsula; por Juan Francisco Molina Solis.* Imprenta R. Caballero, Mérida de Yucatán, 1896. 911 p. Br972.6 So44.

2831. Molina, Alonso de. Aqui comienca un vocabulario en la lengua castellana y mexicana, 1871. Br498.22 AzM 73 1555 facsim. Transcript of *Aqui comiença un vocabulario en la lengua castellana y mexicana, compuesta por el...padre fray Alonso de Molina* (A. de Spinosa, México, 1571).

2832. Molina, Alonso de. *Arte de la lengua mexicana y castellana.* Escalante, México, 1886. 222 p. Br498.22 AzM 73.3.

2833. Molina, Alonso de. *Vocabulario de la lengua mexicana, compuesto por el P. Fr. Alonso de Molina; publicado de nuevo por Julio Platzmann.* B. G. Teubner, Leipzig, 1880. Br498.22 AzM 73.2a.

2834. Molina, Alonso de. *Vocabvlario en lengva castellana y mexicana; compuesto por el muy Reuerendo Padre Fray Alonso de Molina de la Orden del Bienuenturado Nuestro Padre Sant Francisco; dirigido al Mvy Excelente Señor Don Martin Enriquez, Visorrey desta Nueua España.* En Casa de Antonia de Spinosa en México, 1571. 121, 162 leaves. Br498.22 AzM 73.2.

2835. Molina, Luis. El cultivo del añil en la India Oriental; traducción del inglés. In *Instrucción para el cultivbo del añil en la república,* by José Avila and Jorge Ponce, pp. 27–34. Imprenta de la Paz, Guatemala, 1869. Br572C An8141 v.69.

2836. Molinero, Caralampio. *Cartas de D. Caralampio Molinero del Cerro a Doña Bibiana Cerezo, su mujer, vecinos de las Batuecas mas remotas é ignoradas, sobre la felicidad y ventura de vivir en la corte; recopiladas por El Cronista; edición de la "Biblioteca Universal" de M. Villanueva.* M. Villanueva, México, 1868. 403 p. Br917.2 M733.

2837. Monardes, Nicolás. *Primera y segunda y tercera partes de la historia medicinal de las cosas que se traen de nuestras Indias Occidentales que sirven en medicina; tratado de la piedra Bezaar, y dela yerva Escuerçonera; dialogo de las grandezas del hierro, y de sus virtudes medicinales; tratado de la nieve, y del bever frio.* F. Diaz, Sevilla, 1580. 162 leaves. Br615 M742.

2838. Montelius, Oscar. Sur les souvenirs de l'Age de la Pierre des lapons en Suede, n.d. 16 p. Br572C An8141 v.82.

2839. Montero Barrantes, Francisco. *Elementos de historia de Costa Rica, por Francisco Montero Barrantes.* Tipografía Nacional, San José de Costa Rica, 1892. 349 p. Br972.86 B27.

2840. Montgomery, George W. *Narrative of a Journey to Guatemala, in Central America, in 1838.* Wiley and Putnam, New York, 1839. 195 p. Br917.281 M76.

2841. Moody, Dwight L. *Meyoo-achimoowin mena numoweya pa-petoosayimowuk.* Methodist Mission Room, Toronto, 1885? 20 p. Br497.11 CrM77. Two of Moody's sermons translated into the Cree language.

2842. Moody, J. D. The Rockford tablet, n.d. 5 p. Br572C An8141 v.35.

2843. Mooney, James. Cherokee and Iroquois parallels. *Journal of American Folk-Lore* 3, 1890. 1 p. Br572C An8141 v.110. Mooney (1861-1921), an ethnologist at the Bureau of American Ethnology, was an outstanding authority on American Indians. Although his research emphasized Cherokee and Kiowa ethnography, he also investigated and collected among the Arapaho, Cheyenne, Apache, Dakota, Plains Apache, Wichita, Comanche, Hopi, Paiute, Shoshoni, Caddo, and other groups in northern Mexico and the American Southeast.

2844. Mooney, James. Cherokee theory and practice of medicine. *Journal of American Folk-Lore* 3:44-50, 1890. Br572C An8141 v.23.

2845. Mooney, James. Die Kosmogonie der Cherokee. *Der Urquell* 2:85-87, 1891. Br572C An8141 v.110.

2846. Mooney, James. Improved Cherokee alphabets. *American Anthropologist* 5(1): 63-65, 1892. Br572C An8141 v.110.

2847. Mooney, James. Myths and folk-lore of Ireland, by Jeremiah Cutin [Book notice]. *American Anthropologist* 3:191-194, 1890. Br572C An8141 v.29.

2848. Mooney, James. Notes on the Cosumnes tribes of California. *American Anthropologist* 3:259-262, 1890. Br572C An8141 v.110.

2849. Mooney, James. The Cherokee ball play. *American Anthropologist* 3(2): 105-132, 1890. Br572C An8141 v.23.

2850. Mooney, James. The sacred formulas of the Cherokees. *Seventh Annual Report of the Bureau of Ethnology, Smithsonian Institution*, pp. 307-397, 1891. Br572C An8141 v.105.

2851. Mooney, James. *The Siouan Tribes of the East*. Bureau of American Ethnology, Bulletin 22. United States Government Printing Office, Washington, DC, 1894. 101 p. Br572C An8141 v.140.

2852. Moorehead, Warren K. *Fort Ancient, The Great Prehistoric Earthwork of Warren County, Ohio; Comp. From a Careful Survey, With an Account of Its Mounds and Graves, a Topographical Map, Thirty-Five Full-Page Phototypes, and Surveying Notes in Full*. Miss Millard, Teddington, Middlesex, 1890. 129 p. Br572C An8141 v.12; Br913.771 M784.2.

2853. Moorehead, Warren K. *Handybook for Collectors; Illustrations, Descriptions, and Prices of Rare Indian and Mound Builder Relics*. A. H. Pugh Printing, Cincinnati, n.d. 24 p. Br572C An8141 v.71.

2854. Moorehead, Warren K. *Primitive Man in Ohio*. Putnam Knickerbocker Press, New York, 1892. 246 p. Br913.771 M784.

2855. Moorehead, Warren K. Report of field work carried on in the Muskinggum, Scioto, and Ohio valleys during the season of 1896. *Ohio State Archaeological and Historical Society, Annual Publications* 5:165-274, 1897. Br572C An8141 v.156.

2856. Morán, Francisco. Arte en lengua choltí; con fragmentos de doctrina christiana y confesionario en la misma lengua; copia de 1685. 80 p. Br498.21ClM 797.2. A work on the Choltí dialect of Maya by Francisco Morán. It is a small quarto of 92 leaves. Marginal note on page 1 indicates that manuscript was presented to the

American Philosophical Society on Sept. 16, 1836 by Maríano Gálvez, governor of Guatemala. The first three pages contain a narrative in Spanish, difficult to decipher, by Thomas Murillo, a layman, touching the missions in 1689-1692. Then comes one leaf not numbered, with notes on the verso in Choltí, nearly illegible. On the recto of the fourth leaf is "Arte en lengua choltí que quiere decir lengua de milperos" (32 p.). In a clear hand, ornamented with scroll work and pen sketches of birds and grotesque animals). On page 35 is "Libro de lengua choltí que quiere decir lengua de milperos" (24 p.). At the end is the colophon: "Fin del arte q.e trae no. M. R.do P.e Frai Fran.co Morán en un libro de quartilla grande alto, que enquaderno u recogio de nuestro religiosos i barias cosas (añadio), el R.do P.e Frai Alonso de Triana; requiescant in pace todos. Amen, Jesus, María, Joséph." This is a duplicate of the preceeding arte, differing from it in several particulars, being more full and accurate. Both seem to be copies of the original Morán, not the one of the other. After the libro follow eight leaves of questions and answers at the confessional, etc., in Choltí. On page 77 begins "Confessionario en lengua choltí, escrito en el pueblo de San Lucas Salac de el Chol, año de 1685." Three leaves ending with a catchword, indicating that it is but a fragment. The remaining leaves are occupied by a vocabulary, Spanish and Choltí, chiefly on the rectos only. At the commencement is the following marginal note: "Todo el vocabulario grande de No. M.R. P.e Fr. Fran.co Morán esta tradusido en este libro, por el Abesedario, i algunos bocablos más." The colophon reads "En este pueblo de lacandones llamado de Nta. Señora de los Dolores en 24 de junio dia de S.n Juan de 1695 años."

2857. Morán, Francisco. Vocabulario en lengua choltí, extractado del Vocabulario que compuso el R.P. Fray Francisco Morán, Dominicano. 12 leaves. Br498.21ClM 797. Vocabulary based on entry above with the addition of Chorti words collected by John L. Stephens in Zacapa, Guatemala.

2858. Morelet, Arthur. *Voyage dans l'Amérique Centrale, l'île de Cuba et le Yucatán, par Arthur Morelet.* Gide et J. Baudry, Paris, 1857. 2 v. Br917.2 M812.

2859. Moreno, Francisco J.P. El origen del hombre sud-americano. *Anales de la Sociedad Científica Argentina*, pp. 182-223, 1882. Br572C An8141 v.28.

2860. Moreno, Francisco J.P. Esploración arqueologica de la provincia de Catamarca. *Revista del Museo de La Plata* 1, 1890-1891. 36 p. Br572C An8141 v.98.

2861. Moreno, Francisco J. P. Projet d'une exposition rétrospective argentine à l'occasion du quatriènne centenaire de la découverte de l'Amérique. *Revista del Museo de La Plata*, pp. 1-7, 1890. Br572C An8141 v.98.

2862. Moreno, Francisco J.P. Rapide coup d'oeil sa fondation et son développement. *Revista del Museo de La Plata,* 1890. 31 p. Br572C An8141 v.98.

2863. Moreno, Francisco J.P. *Viaje á la Patagonia austral, emprendido bajo los auspicios del gobierno nacional, 1876-1877, por Francisco P. Moreno.* Imprenta de La Nación, Buenos Aires, 1879. 460 p. Br918.21 M812.

2864. Moreno, Francisco P. Le Musée de la Plata. *Revista del Museo de la Plata* 1, 1890. 31 p. Br572C An8141 v.98.

2865. Morgan, J. de. *Les premiers ages des métaux dans l'Arménie, Russe; Mission Sci-*

entifique au Caucase, études archéologiques et historiques. Ernest Leroux, Paris, 1889. 209 p. Br572C An8141 v.103.

2866. Morgan, Lewis H. *Ancient Society, or, Researches in the Lines of Human Progress from Savagery Through Barbarism to Civilization.* H. Holt, New York, 1878. 560 p. Br301.2 M82a. Lewis Henry Morgan (1818–1881), trained as a lawyer, collected and studied Iroquois material culture in response to an appeal from the Regents of the University of the State of New York for artifacts to form a state collection. Between 1859 and 1862 Morgan made four trips to the West, going to Kansas and Nebraska Territories, up the Missouri River to the Rockies, and to Lake Winnipeg in Canada. During these trips he collected information on indigenous classifications of kin for some 200 genealogical positions among 80 nations. Morgan's fieldwork in the West and among the Iroquois led to a series of important publications on social structure and religion. *Ancient Society* is Morgan's grand synthesis, tracing "the lines of human progress from savagery through barbarism to civilization." He deploys the stages-of-development idea to the problems first posed for him by Iroquois matrilineal clans, classificatory kinship, and communal living.

2867. Morgan, Lewis H. *Houses and House-Life of the American Aborigines.* Smithsonian Institution, Contributions to American Ethnology, 4. Government Printing Office, Washington, DC, 1881. 281 p. Br557.3 Un319.

2868. Morgan, Lewis H. *Laws of Consanguinity and Descent of the Iroquois, by Lewis H. Morgan, Corresponding Member of the New York Historical Society, of the American Ethnological Society, etc.* Steam Press of A. Strong, Rochester, NY, 1859. 12 p. Br572C An8141 v.32.

2869. Morgan, Lewis H. *League of the Ho-dé-no-sau-nee, or Iroquois.* Sage and Brother, Rochester, 1851. 477 p. Br970.3 IrM66. Morgan's *League of the…Iroquois* remains the best overall ethnography of the Iroquois.

2870. Morgan, Lewis H. On the ruins of a stone pueblo on the Animas River in New Mexico, with a ground plan. *Annual Reports of the Trustees of the Peabody Museum of American Archaeology and Ethnology* 2(3): 536–556, 1880. Br913.07 H265.

2871. Morgan, Lewis H. *Systems of Consanguinity and Affinity of the Human Family.* Smithsonian Institution, Contributions to Knowledge, 17. Washington, DC, 1871. 590 p. Br572 M82. In his *Systems of Consanguinity* Morgan argues that the "classificatory" kinship system in the Americas and Asia may be interpreted as an evolutionary stage leading to the "descriptive" kinship system of Europe and the Near East through a series of different forms of marriage from primitive promiscuity to monogamy.

2872. Morgan, Lewis H. The stone and bone implements of the Arickarees. *Annual Report of the Regents of the University of the State of New York, on the Condition of the State Cabinet of Natural History, for 1867,* pp. 25–46. Albany, NY, 1871. Br572C An8141 v.32.

2873. Morhardt, J. L., and F. Erdmann. *Testamentetokak, Hiobib aglangit, Salomoblo imgerusersoanga tikkilugit.* G. Winerib nênerlauktangit, Stolpen, Germany, 1871. 274 p. Br497.25 LB46.9. Translation of Psalms and Proverbs, Job, Ecclesiastes, and the Song of Solomon, and from Job to the Song of Songs, into Inuktitut.

2874. Morice, Adrien G. *Carrier Reading-Book, by Rev. A. G. Morice.* 2d ed. Stuart's Lake Mission, British Columbia 1894. 192 p. Br497.12 DM82.2. Revised and enlarged edition of the author's Carrier primer; title also in the Déné syllabic characters. Morice (1859-1938) joined the Oblates of Mary Immaculate in 1877 and then spent nearly 30 years in British Columbia and Manitoba working with the Indians. He made basic contributions to the study of Athapaskan languages.

2875. Morice, Adrien G. Carrier sociology and mythology. *Transactions of the Royal Society of Canada* 2:109-126, 1892. Br572C An8141 v.105.

2876. Morice, Adrien G. Déné roots. *Transactions of the Canadian Institute* 3:145-164, 1891-1892. Br572C An8141 v.115.

2877. Morice, Adrien G. *Le petit catéchisme à l'usage des sauvages porteurs; texte et traduction avec notes suivi des prières du matin et du soir par le R. P. Morice.* Mission du Lac Stuart, 1891. 144 p. Br497.12 DM82. Text in French and Carrier; includes "Cantiques" (pp. 96-143).

2878. Morice, Adrien G. *Lœkateshisyaz keikœz; Jezi kli hwœztli et hwotsœn.* Stuart's Lake, British Columbia, 1890. 300 p. Br497.12 DM82.1. Translation of title: The-little-catechism drawn-on (written); Jesus Christ was-born then since with it 1890-times it- annually-revolved Stuart's Lake there Father Morice made it.

2879. Morice, Adrien G. *New Improved and Easy Alphabet or Syllabary Suggested to the Cherokee Nation By a Friend and Earnest Sympathiser.* Stuart's Lake Mission, British Columbia, 1890. 1 leaf. Br497.27 ChM 822.

2880. Morice, Adrien G. *Pe toestloes oetsôtoeléh.* Stuart's Lake Mission, Stuart Lake, British Columbia, 1890. 32 p. Br497.12 DM 82.4. Primer containing spelling and elementary reading with text in Déné syllabic characters.

2881. Morice, Adrien G. The Dené languages, considered in themselves and incidentally in their relations to non-American idioms. *Transactions of the Canadian Institute* 1:170-212, 1889-1890. Br572C An8141 v.48.

2882. Morice, Adrien G. *The New Methodical, Easy and Complete, Déné Syllabary.* Stuart's Lake Mission, Stuart Lake, British Columbia, 1890. 3 p. Br497.12 DM82.3.

2883. Morillot, L. Mythologie et légendes des Esquimaux du Groenland. *Actes de la Société Philologique* 4:215-288, 1875. Br572C An8141 v.52.

2884. *Morning and Evening Prayers, the Administration of the Sacraments, and Other Rites and Ceremonies of the Church; According to the Use of the United Church of England and Ireland.* Printed for the Society for Promoting Christian Knowledge, London, 1847. 157, 34 p. Br497.11 MuC47. Church of England Book of Common Prayer translated into Munsee; text of prayer book in English and Munsee on opposite pages; hymnal (Minseeweh nuhkoomwawaukunol) on 34 p. at end in Munsee only.

2885. Morris, Charles. The making of man. *American Naturalist* 20(6): 493-502, 1886. Br572C An8141 v.13.

2886. Morris, J. Cheston. Relation of the pentagonal dodecahedron found near Marietta, Ohio, to shamanism. *Proceedings of the American Philosophical Society* 36, 1897. 15 p. Br572C An8141 v.156.

2887. Morse, Edward S. A curious Aino toy. *Bulletin of the Essex Institute* 25:1-7, 1893. Br572C An8141 v.121. Edward Sylvester Morse (1838–1925), a biologist and expert on Japanese culture, served as an assistant to zoologist Louis Agassiz in the Museum of Comparative Anatomy at Harvard University. In 1863–1864 he joined the Essex Institute in Salem, Massachusetts, and was professor of zoology and comparative anatomy at Bowdin College from 1871 to 1874. Between 1880 and 1916 Morse was director of the Peabody Museum in Salem. Between 1877 and 1880, Morse served as professor of zoology at Imperial University in Tokyo. During this time he developed an interest in the ethnography ands material culture of Japan.

2888. Morse, Edward S. *Address Delivered at the New York Meeting, August, 1887.* Salem Press, Salem, MA, 1887. 43 p. Br506 M837.

2889. Morse, Edward S. Ancient and modern methods of arrow release. *Bulletin of the Essex Institute* 17, 1885. 53 p. Br572C An8141 v.31.

2890. Morse, Edward S. Korean interviews. *Appleton's Popular Science Monthly*, 1897. 16 p. Br572C An8141 v.156.

2891. Morse, Edward S. Latrines of the East. *American Architect*, March, 1893. 18 p. Br572C An8141 v.123; Br572C An8141 v.129.

2892. Morse, Edward S. Man in the tertiaries. *American Naturalist* 18:1001-1012, 1884. Br572C An8141 v.13.

2893. Morse, Edward S. *Natural Selection and Crime*. D. Appleton and Company, New York, 1892. 14 p. Br572C An8141 v.88.

2894. Morse, Edward S. On the older forms of terra-cotta roofing tiles. *Bulletin of the Essex Institute* 24:1-72, 1892. Br572C An8141 v.83.

2895. Morse, Edward S. *On the So-Called Bow-Pullers of Antiquity*. Salem, MA, 1894. Br572C An8141 v.156; Br913.369 M813. Extract from *Essex Institute Bulletin* 26:141-155, 1894.

2896. Morse, Edward S. Shell mounds of Omori. *Memoirs of the College of Science, Imperial University of Japan* 1(1), 1879. 36 p. Br571.93 M837.

2897. Morse, Edward S. Some recent publications on Japanese archaeology. *American Naturalist* 14:656-662, 1880. Br572C An8141 v.131.

2898. Morse, Edward S. The Omori shell middens. *Nature*, April, pp. 657-662, 1890. Br572C An8141 v.131.

2899. Morse, Edward S. *Was Middle America Peopled from Asia?* Appleton and Company, New York, 1898. 16 p. Br572.9728 M837. Reprinted from *Appleton's Popular Science Monthly*, November, 1898.

2900. Morse, Jedidiah. *A Report to the Secretary of War of the United States on Indian Affairs; Comprising a Narrative of a Tour Performed in the Summer of 1820, Under a Commission From the President of the United States, for the Purpose of Ascertaining, for the Use of the Government, the Actual State of the Indian Tribes in Our Country; Illustrated by a Map of the United States; Ornamented by a Correct Portrait of a Pawnee Indian, by the Rev. Jedidiah Morse, Late Minister of the First Congregational Church in Charlestown, Near Boston, Now resident in New Haven.* S. Converse, New Haven, 1822. 400 p. Br970.5 M83. "Thomas

Field considered Morse's report to Secretary of War John C. Calhoun 'certainly the most complete and exhaustive report of the condition, numbers, names, territory, and general affairs of the Indians, ever made'...Morse's relatively brief report is followed by a massive appendix of original documentation, all of which supports the idea of a forced removal of all Indians to lands west of the Mississippi" (*Frank T. Siebert Library* 1999:2:195).

2901. Morselli, Enrico. Osservazioni, critiche sulla parte antropologico-preistorica. pp. 123-140, 1896. Br572C An8141 v.156.

2902. Mortillet, Adrien de. Evolution quaternaire de la pierre. *Revue Mensuelle de l'École d'Anthropologie de Paris* 7(1): 18-26, 1897. Br572C An8141 v.99.

2903. Mortillet, Adrien de. Figures gravées et sculptées sur des monuments mégalithiques des environs de Paris. *Bulletins d'Anthropologie de Paris* 4: 657-668, 1893. Br572C An8141 v.127.

2904. Mortillet, Adrien de. Les monuments mégalithiques christianisés. *Revue Mensuelle de l'Ecole d'Anthropologie de Paris* 7(11): 321-338, 1897. Br572C An8141 v.156.

2905. Mortillet, Adrien de. Les petits silex tailles a contours geometriques trouves en Europe, Asie et Afrique. *Revue Mensuelle de l'École d'Anthropologie de Paris* 6(11): 377-405, 1896. Br572C An8141 v.99.

2906. Mortillet, Gabriel de. Anthropologie de la Haute-Savoie. *Bulletin de la Société d'Anthropologie*, 1892. 11 p. Br572C An8141 v.121. Gabriel de Mortillet (1821-1898) studied geology and engineering in his native France until 1848 when he fled to Switzerland and Italy. In the late 1850s, together with Eduoard Desor, Mortillet began excavating a Neolithic settlement at Lake Varese, Italy. In 1864 he returned to Paris and began work at the Museum of National Antiquities. In 1876 he became a professor of prehistoric anthropology at the School of Anthropology in Paris. Mortillet is best known for developing a chronological classification system of the prehistoric cultural development of humankind. This model served as the basis for the concept of linear evolution.

2907. Mortillet, Gabriel de. Chronique préhistorique. *Revue Mensuelle de l'École d'Anthropologie de Paris*, pp. 20-27, 46-64, 146-160, 1891. Br572C An8141 v.8.

2908. Mortillet, Gabriel de. *Formation de la nation française; textes, linguistique, palethnologie, anthropologie.* Bibliothèque scientifique internationale, 86. F. Alcan, Paris, 1897. 336 p. Br572.944 M841.

2909. Mortillet, Gabriel de. Formation des variétés albinisme et gauchissement. *Bulletin de la Société d'Anthropologie*, 1890. Br572C An8141 v.8.

2910. Mortillet, Gabriel de. *Le préhistorique; antiquité de l'homme.* 2d ed. C. Reinwald, Paris, 1885. 658 p. Br571 M84.

2911. Mortillet, Gabriel de. Les sepultures de Solutré Reponse à l'abbe Ducrost. *Bulletin de la Société d'Anthropologie de Lyon* 7, 1888. Br572C An8141 v.26.

2912. Mortillet, Gabriel de. *Musée préhistorique.* C. Reinwald, Paris, 1881. 407 p. Br571 M84.1.

2913. Mortillet, Gabriel de. Nouveau caveau funéraire dolménique de Crécy (Seine-et-Marne). *L'Homme* 3(23): 705-712, 1886. Br572C An8141 v.156.

2914. Mortillet, Gabriel de. *Réforme de la Chronologie*. Saint-Germain-en-Laye, 1893. 3 p. Br572C An8141 v.127.

2915. Mortillet, Gabriel de. Station paléolithique sous marine du Havre (Seine-Inférieure). *Bulletins de la Société d'Anthropologie de Paris*, pp. 369–380, 1894. Br572C An8141 v.131.

2916. Morvillo, Anthony. *A Numipu, or, Nez-Perce Grammar*. Indian Boys' Press, Desmet, ID, 1891. 255 p. Br497.48 CM84.

2917. Moschen, L. Crani moderni di Bologna. *Atti della Societa Romana di Antropologia*, 1899. 23 p. Br573.7 M85.

2918. Moschen, L. Il metodo naturale in craniologia. *Monitore Zoologico Italiano* 6(5), 1895. 26 p. Br572C An8141 v.140.

2919. Moschen, L. Note di craniologia trentina. *Atti della Società Romana di Antropologia* 5(1), 1898. 15 p. Br572C An8141 v.156.

2920. Moschen, L. Quattro decadi di crani moderni della Sicilia e il metodo naturales nella determinazione della varieta del cranio umano. *Atti della Società Veneto-Trentina di Scienze Naturali* 1(2): 3–53, 1893. Br572C An8141 v.127.

2921. Moschen, L. *Una centuria di crani umbri moderni*, pp. 5–35. Tipografia dell'Umone Cooperativa Editrice, Roma, 1896. Br572C An8141 v.156.

2922. Moscow Imperatorsky Universitet. *Imperatorskoje obscestvo ljubiteley jestestroznaniya antropologyi i etnografyi*. Comite d'organisation des Congres Internationaux d'Archeologie Préhistorique et d'Anthropologie et de Zoologie. Moscow, 1892. n.p. Br572.06 M841.

2923. Moser, Hans J. *Geschichte der Weltsprache*. Heuser, Berlin, 1888. 70 p. Br572C An8141 v.21.

2924. Moser, Hans J. *Zur Universal-Sprache*. Heuser, Berlin, 1887. 32 p. Br572C An8141 v.21.

2925. Moses, Thomas F. Antiquities of Mad River Valley, Ohio. *Proceedings of Central Ohio Scientific Association of Urbana* 1(1): 23–46, 1878. Br572C An8141 v.39; Br572C An8141 v.59.

2926. Moses, Thomas F. Shell heaps on the coast of Maine. *Proceedings of the Central Ohio Scientific Association of Urbana* 1(1): 70–76, 1878. Br572C An8141 v.59.

2927. Mott, F. T. The hairless condition of the human skin; read before Section D of the Leicest Literary and Philosophical Society, July 21, 1886, n.d. 3 p. Br572C An8141 v.121.

2928. Moure, Amadée. *Les Indiens de la province de Mato-Grosso (Brésil); observations, par Amédée Moure*. A. Bertrand, Paris, 1862. 56 p. Br980.4 M866; Br572C An8141 v.33.

2929. Moussy, Martin de. De l'industrie indienne dans le Bassin de La Plata. *Annuaire du Comité d'Archéologie Américaine*, 1866. 38 p. Br572C An8141 v.33.

2930. Moxó, Benito María de. *Cartas mejicanas*. 2d ed. Tipografía de L. Pellas, Genova, 1839. 415 p. Br913.72 M87.

2931. Mühlenpfordt, Eduard. *Versuch einer getreuen Schilderung der Republik Mejico, besonders in Beziehung auf Geographie, Ethnographie und Statistik*. C. F. Kius,

Hannover, 1844. 2 v. Br917.2 M884. Contents include: Bd. 1. "Überblick über das Land im Allgemeinen"; Bd. 2. "Beschreibung der einzelnen Landestheile."

2932. Müller, Friedrich M. *Allgemeine Ethnographie*. A. Hölder, Wien, 1873. 550p. Br572 M88a.

2933. Müller, Friedrich M. *Bemerkungen über das Verbum der koloschischen Sprache, von Friedrich Müller.* In commission bei C. Gerold's Sohn, Wien, 1884. 12 p. Br497.33 SM88; Br572C An8141 v.51. Analysis of the verb in the Tlingit language.

2934. Müller, Friedrich M. *Der grammatische Bau der Algonkin-Sprachen: Ein Beitrag zur amerikanischen Linguistik.* Aus der K. K. Hof- und Staatsdruckerei in Commission bei Karl Gerold's Sohn, Wien, 1867. 23 p. Br572C An8141 v.51.

2935. Müller, Friedrich M. Der Ursprung der indischen Schrift. *Kaiserlichen Akademie der Wissenschaften in Wien* 212-221, 1897. Br572C An8141 v.156.

2936. Müller, Friedrich M. *Die Äquatoriale Sprachfamilie in Central-Afrika.* Sitzungsberichte der Kais. Akademie der Wissenschaften in Wien, Philosophisch-Historische Classe, 119. F. Tempsky, Wien, 1889. Br572C An8141 v.46.

2937. Müller, Friedrich M. *Grundriss der Sprachwissenschaft.* A. Hölder, Wien, 1876-1888. 4 v. Br409.4 M88. Issued in ten parts, each part with general and special title page; includes linguistic material on Aleut, Algonkin, Arawak, Athapaskan, Bribri, Cherokee, Choctaw, Dakota, Innuit (Eskimo), Iroquois, Kalingo, Karina, Matlatzinga, Maya, Mixtec, Moskito, Mutsun, Nahuatl, Sonora, Otomi, Salish, Sahaptin, Tarascan, Tlingit, Totonac, and Zapotec.

2938. Müller, Friedrich M. *Lectures on the Science of Religion with a Paper on Buddhist Nihilism; and a Translation of the Dhammapada or "Path of Virtue."* Charles Scribner, New York, 1872. 300 p. Br201 M88.

2939. Müller, Friedrich M. *Nachträge zur Abhandlung: Die Äquaroriale Sprachfamilie in Central-Afrika. Sitzungsberichte der Kais.* Akademie der Wissenschaften in Wien, Philosophisch-Historische Classe, 127(10), 1892. 6 p. Br572C An8141 v.132.

2940. Müller, Friedrich M. *Three Lectures on the Science of Language and Its Place in Education.* 2d ed. Longmans, Green, and Company, London, New York, 1889. 73 p. Br409.9 M88.

2941. Müller, Friedrich M. *Über den Ursprung der gruzinischen Schrift.* Sitzungsberichte Band 137, 1897. 12 p. Br572C An8141 v.156.

2942. Muller, Hendrick C. *Beiträge zur Lehre der Wortsusammensetzung im Griechischen.* A. W. Sijthoff, Leiden, 1896. 57 p. Br572C An8141 v.156.

2943. Muller, Hendrick C. Lijst der voornaamste Geschriften, n.d. 7 p. Br572C An8141 v.99.

2944. Müller, J. G. *Geschichte der amerikanischen Urreligionen.* Schweighauser, Basel, 1855. 706 p. Br289 M88.

2945. Müller, Karl O. *Die Etrusker.* A. Heitz, Stuttgart, 1877. 2 v. Br913.3791 M88a.

2946. Müller, Sophus. Colliers de la fin de l'Age de Bronze et du premier Age de Fer. pp. 32-34, n.d. Br572C An8141 v.91.

2947. Müller, Sophus. Nogle halsringe fra slutningen af bronzalderen og fra aeldste jernalder. pp. 19-31, n.d. Br572C An8141 v.91.

2948. Müller, Wilhelm Max. A contribution to the Exodus geography. *Proceedings of the Society of Biblical Archaeology*, 1888. 11 p. Br572C An8141 v.116.

2949. Müller, Wilhelm Max. *Asien und Europa nach altägyptischen Denkmälern mit einem Vorwort von Georg Ebers.* W. Engelmann, Leipzig, 1893. 403 p. Br913.01 M88.

2950. Müller, Wilhelm Max. Das Ideogramm. *Zeitschrift für Ägyptische Sprache und Alterthumskunde* 3(4): 1-3, 1886. Br572C An8141 v.107.

2951. Müller, Wilhelm Max. Deux petits textes provenant de Thèbes. pp. 171-172, n.d. Br572C An8141 v.107.

2952. Müller, Wilhelm Max. Ein Hieroglyphenzeichen. *Travaux relatifs à la Philologie et à l'Archéologie Egyptiennes et Assyriennes* v. 14, n.d. 3 p. Br572C An8141 v.107.

RACES AND PEOPLES:

LECTURES

ON THE

SCIENCE OF ETHNOGRAPHY.

BY

DANIEL G. BRINTON, A.M., M.D.,

PROFESSOR OF ETHNOLOGY AT THE ACADEMY OF NATURAL SCIENCES, PHIL-
ADELPHIA, AND OF AMERICAN ARCHÆOLOGY AND LINGUISTICS IN THE
UNIVERSITY OF PENNSYLVANIA; PRESIDENT OF THE AMERICAN
FOLK-LORE SOCIETY AND OF THE NUMISMATIC AND ANTI-
QUARIAN SOCIETY OF PHILADELPHIA; MEMBER OF THE AN-
THROPOLOGICAL SOCIETIES OF BERLIN AND VIENNA AND
OF THE ETHNOGRAPHICAL SOCIETIES OF PARIS AND
FLORENCE, OF THE ROYAL SOCIETY OF ANTIQUAR-
IES, COPENHAGEN, THE ROYAL ACADEMY OF
HISTORY OF MADRID, THE AMERICAN
PHILOSOPHICAL SOCIETY, THE
AMERICAN ANTIQUARIAN
SOCIETY, ETC., ETC.

NEW YORK:
N. D. C. HODGES, PUBLISHER,
47 LAFAYETTE PLACE,
1890.

Title page from Brinton's Races and Peoples *(1890).*

2953. Müller, Wilhelm Max. Eine Hieroglyphe. *Travaux relatifs à la Philologie et à l'Archéologie Egyptiennes et Assyriennes* v. 15, n.d. 4 p. Br572C An8141 v.107.

2954. Müller, Wilhelm Max. Einige Griechsch-Demotische Lehnwörter. pp. 172-178, 1886. Br572C An8141 v.107.

2955. Müller, Wilhelm Max. Erklärung des grossen Dekrets des Königs. *Zeitschrift für Ägyptische Sprache und Alterthumskunde* 2(3), 1888. 25 p. Br572C An8141 v.107.

2956. Müller, Wilhelm Max. Geographische Einzelheiten. pp. 273-278, 1897. Br572C An8141 v.156.

2957. Müller, Wilhelm Max. Studien zur ägyptischen Formenlehre. *Zeitschrift für Ägyptische Sprache* 29, n.d. 17 p. Br572C An8141 v.107.

2958. Müller, Wilhelm Max. The sign papyrus of Tanis. *Proceedings of the Society of Biblical Archaeology*, 1891. 2 p. Br572C An8141 v.116.

2959. Müller, Wilhelm Max. Über einige hieroglyphenzeichen. pp. 157-176, 1888. Br572C An8141 v.107.

2960. Müller, Wilhelm Max. Zur Etymologie des koptischen αγω:ογξ. *Zeitschrift für Ägyptische Sprache und Alterthumskunde* 2(3): 1-2, 1888. Br572C An8141 v.107.

2961. Muñoz, Manuel A., and W. J. McGee. Primitive trephining in Peru. *Annual Report of the Bureau of Ethnology, Smithsonian Institution, for 1894-1895*, pp. 3-72, 1897. Br913.85 M9231.

2962. Munro, Robert. A sketch of lake-dwelling research. *Proceedings of the Royal Soci-*

ety of Edinburgh 20:385–411, 1894–1895. Br572C An8141 v.140.

2963. Munro, Robert. Some further notes on otter and beaver traps. *Journal of the Proceedings of the Royal Society of Antiquaries of Scotland* 8(3): 245–249, 1898. Br571.51 M92.4.

2964. Muratori, Lodovico A. *Il Cristianesimo felice nelle missioni de' padri della Compagnia di Jesunel paraguai*. Pasquali, Venezia, 1743. 196 p. Br918.9 M933.

2965. Murdoch, John. A few legendary fragments from the Point Barrow Eskimos. *American Naturalist* 20:593–599, 1886. Br572C An8141 v.13; Br572C An8141 v.23.

2966. Murdoch, John. A study of the Eskimo bows in the United States National Museum. *Annual Report of the United States National Museum, Smithsonian Institution, for 1884*, pp. 307–316, 1895. Br572C An8141 v.10.

2967. Murdoch, John. Dr. Rink's Eskimo tribes. *American Anthropologist* 1(2): 125–133, 1888. Br572C An8141 v.10.

2968. Murdoch, John. Notes on counting and measuring among the Eskimo of Point Barrow. *American Anthropologist* 3(1): 37–43, 1890. Br572C An8141 v.10.

2969. Murdoch, John. On the Siberian origin of some customs of the Western Eskimos. *American Anthropologist* 1(4): 325–336, 1888. Br572C An8141 v.27.

2970. Murdoch, John. The history of the throwing stick which drifted from Alaska to Greenland. *American Anthropologist* 3:230–233, 1890. Br572C An8141 v.10.

2971. Murphy, Henry C. *Catalogue of the Magnificent Library…Consisting Almost Wholly of Americana or Books Relating to America*. George A. Leavitt and Company, New York, 1884. 434p. Br970B M95.

2972. Murphy, Henry C. *The Voyage of Verrazzano; A Chapter in the Early History of Maritime Discovery in America*. New York, 1875. 198 p. Br917 M95.

2973. Murr, Christoph G. von. *Reisen einiger Missionarien der Gesellschaft Jesu in Amerika; Aus ihren eigenen Aufsätzen hrsg. von Christoph Gottlieb von Murr. Johann Eberhard Zeh*, Nürnberg, 1785. 614 p. Br918 M962. Contents include: F. X. Viegl, "Gründliche Nachrichten über die Verfassung der Landschaft von Maynas, in Süd-Amerika, bis zum Jahre 1768"; F. X. Viegl, "Nachricht von den Sprachen der Völker am Orinokoflusse; aus dem Saggio di storia americana…des Herrn abbate F.S. Gilii"; "Des Herrn P. Anselm Eckart…zusätze zu Pedro Cudena's Beschreibung der länder von Brasilien, und zu Herrn rectors C. Leiste Anmerkungen im sechsten Lessingischen Beytrage zur geschichte und litteratur."

2974. Museum des Missionshauses zu Basel. *Katalog der Ethnographischen Sammlung im Museum des Missionshauses zu Basel*. Verlag der Missionsbuchhandlung, Basel, 1883. 68 p. Br572C An8141 v.71.

2975. Museum of American Archaeology. *Annual Report of the Curator of the Museum of American Archaeology, v. 1, no. 1*. University Press, Philadelphia, 1890. 54 p. Br572C An8141 v.17.

2976. Musters, George C. *Unter den Patagoniern; Wanderungen auf unbetretenem Boden von der Magalhäesstrasse bis zum Rio Negro; von George Chaworth Musters; aus dem Englischen von J. E. A. Martin*. 2. Aufl., Wohlfeile Volksausg. Bibliothek geographischer Reisen und Entdeckungen älterer und neuerer Zeit, Bd. 11.

H. Costenoble, Jena, 1877. 341 p. Br918.21 M978. Translation of *At Home with the Patagonian*; includes "Kurzes Verzeichnis von Wörtern aus der Tsoneca-Sprache, wie die nördlichen Tehuelchen sie sprechen" (pp. 338-341).

2977. Myer, I. Anniversaries: the proper time for the celebration of and especially of Washington's Birthday. *The American Historical Register*, February, 1895. 12 p. Br572C An8141 v.136.

2978. Myer, I. Qabbalah: quotations from the Zohar and other writings, treating of the Qabbalistic or divine philosophy. *Oriental Quarterly Review*, 1893. 7 p. Br572C An8141 v.130.

2979. *Na lei kokoeliulivuti; Prayers in the Florida Language*. Society for Promoting Christian Knowledge, London, 1882. 141 p. Br497.54 N11. Church of England prayer book and devotionary translated into Timucua.

2980. Nadaillac, Jean François Albert du Pouget, marquis de. Anthropologie del'Amerique du Nord; les nations indiennes. *Revue d'Anthropologie*, pp. 685-702, 1885. Br572C An8141 v.45.

2981. Nadaillac, Jean François Albert du Pouget, marquis de. Colonies françaises et colonies anglaises. *Correspondant*, 1897. 32 p. Br572C An8141 v.156.

2982. Nadaillac, Jean François Albert du Pouget, marquis de. De l'affaiblidssement progressif de la Natalité en France, ses causes et ses conséquences. *Bulletin de la Sociéte Archéologique, Scientifique et Littérature du Vendomois*, 1885. 30 p. Br572C An8141 v.45.

2983. Nadaillac, Jean François Albert du Pouget, marquis de. De la période glaciaire de l'existence de l'homme durant cette période en Amérique. *Revue Matériaux pour l'Histoire Primitive de l'Homme*3(1), 1884. 16 p. Br572C An8141 v.45.

2984. Nadaillac, Jean François Albert du Pouget, marquis de. Découvertes dans la grotte de Spy, province de Namur. *Revue Matériaux pour l'Histoire Primitive de l'Homme* 3:491-494, 1886. Br572C An8141 v.45.

2985. Nadaillac, Jean François Albert du Pouget, marquis de. Discours prononcé à l'Assemblée Générale de la Société de l'Histoire de France. *Bulletin de la Société de l'Histoire de France*, 1896. 15 p. Br572C An8141 v.156.

2986. Nadaillac, Jean François Albert du Pouget, marquis de. Empreintes de pieds humains découvertes dans une carrière auprès de Carson (Nevada). *Revue Matériaux pour l'Histoire Primitive de l'Homme* 18, 1882. 11 p. Br572C An8141 v.45.

2987. Nadaillac, Jean François Albert du Pouget, marquis de. Étude sur l'anthropologie. *Bulletins de la Sociéte d'Anthropologie,* 1888. 19 p. Br572C An8141 v.45.

2988. Nadaillac, Jean François Albert du Pouget, marquis de. Expéditions polaires. *Correspondant*, 1896. 46 p. Br572C An8141 v.156.

2989. Nadaillac, Jean François Albert du Pouget, marquis de. *Foi et science*. Soye et Fils, Paris, 1895. 39 p. Br572C An8141 v.141.

2990. Nadaillac, Jean François Albert du Pouget, marquis de. Grotte de la Biche aux Roches, Province de Namur (Belgique). *Revue d'Anthropologie*, pp. 744-747, n.d. Br572C An8141 v.45.

2991. Nadaillac, Jean François Albert du Pouget, marquis de. *Intelligence et instinct*. De

Soye et Fils, Imprimeurs, Paris, 1892. 75 p. Br572C An8141 v.88.

2992. Nadaillac, Jean François Albert du Pouget, marquis de. L'Art préhistorique en Amérique. *La Revue des Deux Mondes*, November, 1883. 30 p. Br572C An8141 v.45.

2993. Nadaillac, Jean François Albert du Pouget, marquis de. L'Atlantide et les oscillations de l'écorce terrestre. *Correspondant*, 1882. 24 p. Br572C An8141 v.45.

2994. Nadaillac, Jean François Albert du Pouget, marquis de. L'époque glaciaire. *Revue des Questions Scientifiques*, 1886. 40 p. Br572C An8141 v.45.

2995. Nadaillac, Jean François Albert du Pouget, marquis de. *L'évolution du mariage*. De Soye et Fils, Paris, 1893. 58 p. Br572C An8141 v.121.

2996. Nadaillac, Jean François Albert du Pouget, marquis de. L'évolution et le dogme. *Revue des Questions Scientifiques*, 1896, 18 p. Br572C An8141 v.156.

2997. Nadaillac, Jean François Albert du Pouget, marquis de. L'Homme tertiaire. *Annales de la Sociéte Scientifique de Bruxelles,* 1884. 14 p. Br572C An8141 v.45.

2998. Nadaillac, Jean François Albert du Pouget, marquis de. *La Chine du XXe siècle*. De Soye et Fils, Paris, 1899. 46 p. Br915.1 N12.

2999. Nadaillac, Jean François Albert du Pouget, marquis de. La fin de l'humanité. *Correspondant*, 1897. 41 p. Br572C An8141 v.156.

3000. Nadaillac, Jean François Albert du Pouget, marquis de. La grotte de Montgaudier (Charente). *Comptes Rendus de l'Académie des Inscriptions et Belles-Lettres*, 1887. 8 p. Br572C An8141 v.45.

3001. Nadaillac, Jean François Albert du Pouget, marquis de. La Guadeloupe préhistorique. *Revue Matériaux pour l'Histoire Primitive de l'Homme* 3:1-15, 1886. Br572C An8141 v.45.

3002. Nadaillac, Jean François Albert du Pouget, marquis de. La peche préhistorique en Europe et dans l'Amérique du Nord. *Revue Matériaux pour l'Histoire Primitive de l'Homme* 4:93-110, 1887. Br572C An8141 v.45.

3003. Nadaillac, Jean François Albert du Pouget, marquis de. La poterie chez les anciens habitantes de l'Amérique. *Revue d'Anthropologie* 2(4): 639-680, n.d. Br572C An8141 v.45.

3004. Nadaillac, Jean François Albert du Pouget, marquis de. La poterie de la vallée du Mississippi. *Revue Matériaux pour l'Histoire Primitive de l'Homme* 4:373-383, 1887. Br572C An8141 v.45.

3005. Nadaillac, Jean François Albert du Pouget, marquis de. La station préhistorique de Lengyel (Hongrie). *Bulletins de la Sociéte d'Anthropologie*, 1890. 11 p. Br572C An8141 v.45; Br572C An8141 v.88.

3006. Nadaillac, Jean François Albert du Pouget, marquis de. *L'Amérique préhistorique*. G. Masson, Imprimeurs, Paris, 1883. 588 p. Br571 N12.2.

3007. Nadaillac, Jean François Albert du Pouget, marquis de. Le Moshonaland. *Correspondant*, 1894. 42 p. Br572C An8141 v.131.

3008. Nadaillac, Jean François Albert du Pouget, marquis de. *Le péril national*. De Soye et Fils, Imprimeurs, Paris, 1890. 46 p. Br572C An8141 v.88.

3009. Nadaillac, Jean François Albert du Pouget, marquis de. Le Préhistorique américain. *Revue des Questions Scientifiques*, October, 1893. 27 p. Br572C An8141 v.123.

3010. Nadaillac, Jean François Albert du Pouget, marquis de. Le royaume de Bénin; massacre d'une Mission Anglaise. *Correspondant*, 1898. 32 p. Br572C An8141 v.156.

3011. Nadaillac, Jean François Albert du Pouget, marquis de. *Les agglomérations urbaines*. De Soye et Fils, Imprimeurs, Paris, 1898. 32 p. Br572C An8141 v.99.

3012. Nadaillac, Jean François Albert du Pouget, marquis de. Les anciennes populations de la Colombie. *Revue Matériaux pour l'Histoire Primitive de l'Homme* 2:49-61, 1885. Br572C An8141 v.45.

3013. Nadaillac, Jean François Albert du Pouget, marquis de. Les archives de Dropmore. *Correspondant*, 1896. 48 p. Br572C An8141 v.156.

3014. Nadaillac, Jean François Albert du Pouget, marquis de. Les barrows dans les Iles Britanniques. *Revue d'Anthropologie*, pp. 300-314, 1885. Br572C An8141 v.45.

3015. Nadaillac, Jean François Albert du Pouget, marquis de. Les dates préhistoriques. *Correspondant*, 1893. 41 p. Br572C An8141 v.127.

3016. Nadaillac, Jean François Albert du Pouget, marquis de. Les découvertes récentes en Amérique. *Revue Matériaux pour l'Histoire Primitive de l'Homme* 1:433-447, 1884. Br572C An8141 v.45.

3017. Nadaillac, Jean François Albert du Pouget, marquis de. *Les Mound-Builders: une monographie*. Imprimerie Polleunis et Ceuterick, Louvain, 1895. 93 p. Br572C An8141 v.141.

3018. Nadaillac, Jean François Albert du Pouget, marquis de. Les pétroglyphes. *Revue des Sciences et de Leurs Applications aux Arts et à l'Industrie,* 18 année, no. 888, 1890. 16 p. Br572C An8141 v.98.

3019. Nadaillac, Jean François Albert du Pouget, marquis de. Les pierres a cupules. *Revue d'Anthropologie* 1:93-110, 1886. Br572C An8141 v.45.

3020. Nadaillac, Jean François Albert du Pouget, marquis de. Les pipes et le tabac. *Revue Matériaux pour l'Histoire Primitive de l'Homme* 2:497-517, 1885. Br572C An8141 v.45.

3021. Nadaillac, Jean François Albert du Pouget, marquis de. *Les plus anciens vestiges de l'homme en Amérique*. Imprimerie Polleunis et Ceuterick, Bruxelles, 1891. 23 p. Br572C An8141 v.88.

3022. Nadaillac, Jean François Albert du Pouget, marquis de. Les populations lacustres de l'Europe. *Revue des Questions Scientifiques*, 1894. 44 p. Br572C An8141 v.131.

3023. Nadaillac, Jean François Albert du Pouget, marquis de. Les premières populations de l'Europe. *Correspondant*, 1889. 71 p. Br572C An8141 v.45.

3024. Nadaillac, Jean François Albert du Pouget, marquis de. *Les progrès de l'anthropologie*. De Soye et Fils, Imprimeurs, Paris, 1891. 39 p. Br572C An8141 v.88.

3025. Nadaillac, Jean François Albert du Pouget, marquis de. *L'Homme et le Singe*. Polleunis et Ceuterick, Louvain, 1898. 88 p. Br575 N12.

3026. Nadaillac, Jean François Albert du Pouget, marquis de. *Ménélik II négûs négûsti roi des rois de l'Éthiopie*. De Soye et Fils, Imprimeurs, Paris, 1898. 39 p. Br913.397 N12.

3027. Nadaillac, Jean François Albert du Pouget, marquis de. *Moeurs et monuments des peuples préhistoriques; par le marquis de Nadaillac...avec 113 figures dans le texte.* G. Masson, Paris, 1888. 312 p. Br571 N121.

3028. Nadaillac, Jean François Albert du Pouget, marquis de. Nouvelles découvertes préhistoriques aux États-Unis. *Bulletins de la Sociéte d'Anthropologie*, 1883. 12 p. Br572C An8141 v.45.

3029. Nadaillac, Jean François Albert du Pouget, marquis de. Resume des premiers temps de l'homme sur la terre. *Annales de la Sociéte Scientifique de Bruxelles*, 1884. 3 p. Br572C An8141 v.45.

3030. Nadaillac, Jean François Albert du Pouget, marquis de. Revue critique [of Boyd Dawkins]. *Revue d'Anthropologie* 2(7): 311-331, n.d. Br572C An8141 v.40.

3031. Nadaillac, Jean François Albert du Pouget, marquis de. *Un Diplomate Aaglais au début du siecle.* Soye et Fils, Paris, 1895. 51 p. Br572C An8141 v.141.

3032. Nadaillac, Jean François Albert du Pouget, marquis de. Unité de l'espèce humaine. *Revue des Questions Scientifiques*, 1897. 38 p. Br572C An8141 v.156.

3033. Nahuatl de San Augustín Acasaguastlán, 16 leaves. Br498.22N N145. Manuscript; contains four leaves of a legal document in Nahuatl, dated 1636, from the archives of the parish of San Cristóbal Acasaguastlán, presented to Karl H. Berendt by the cura, and a vocabulary at San Augustín Acasaguastlán by M. Franz Bromowicz in 1878.

3034. Nájera, Manuel de San Juan Crisóstomo. *Disertación sobre la lengua othomi; leida en latín en la Sociedad Filosófica Americana de Filadelfia y publicada en su orden en el tomo 5o. de la nueva serie de sus actas.* En la Imprenta del Aguila, México, 1845. 145 p. Br498.23 ON 23.

3035. Nájera, Manuel de San Juan Crisóstomo. *Gramática del tarasco; compuesta por el M. R. P. prior del Cármen Fr. Manuel de S. Juan Crisóstomo Nájera; copiada del autógrafo por Agustín F. Villa.* Imprenta de O. Ortiz, Morelia, 1870. 45 p. Br498.27 N14.

3036. Native American dogs. *Kansas City Review*, pp. 239-243, n.d. Br572C An8141 v.20.

3037. Naue, Julius. Armi italiane della collezione Nave in Monaco. *Bulletino di Paletnologia Italiano* 22(4-6): 94-104, 1896. Br572C An8141 v.156.

3038. Naue, Julius. *Die bronzezeit in Oberbayern; Ergebnisse der Ausgrabungen und Untersuchungen von Hügelgrägern der Bronzezeit zwischen Ammer- und Staffelsee und in der Nähe des Starnbergersees.* Piloty und Löhle, München, 1894. 292 p. Br571.3 N22.

3039. Naue, Julius. L'époque de Hallstatt en Bavière, particuliérement dans la Haute-Baviere et le Haut-Palatinat. *Revue Archéologique*, 1895. 39 p. Br572C An8141 v.141.

3040. Naue, Julius. Nouvelles trouvailles préhistorqiues de la Haute-Bavière. *L'Anthropologie* 8:641-666, 1897. Br572C An8141 v.99.

3041. Navarro, José M. *Memoria de San Miguel Milpas Duenas, formada por su cura encargado presbítero José María Navarro.* Imprenta de Luna, Guatemala, 1874. 134 p. Br917.281 N22.

3042. Navarro, José M. *Memoria del estado actual de la parroquia de Aurora, Guatemala de Concepción de Villa Nueva.* Aurora, Guatemala, 1868. 245 p. Br917.281 N22.2.

3043. Naxera, E. De lingua othomitorum dissertatio. *Transactions of the American Philosophical Society* 5(3): 249–296, 1835. Br572C An8141 v.93.

3044. Neill, Edward D. Memoir of the Sioux; a manuscript in the French archives, now first printed with introduction and notes. *Macalester College Contributions* 10:224–240, 1890. St. Paul, MN. Br572C An8141 v.10.

3045. Nelson, Edward T. Unsymmetric lance-points. *American Naturalist* 14, 1880. 1 p. Br572C An8141 v.19.

3046. Nelson, William. *The Indians of New Jersey; Their Origin and Development; Manners and Customs; Language, Religion and Government; With Notices of Some Indian Place Names.* The Press Printing and Publishing Company, Paterson, NJ, 1894. 168 p. Br970.4 NN335.

3047. Neumann, Carl F. *Mexico in fünften Jahrhundert inseren Zeitrechnung nach chinesischen Quellen.* Munchen, 1845. 30 p. Br572C An8141 v.44.

3048. Neumann, R. *Nordafrika (mit Ausschluss des Milgebietes) nach Herodot.* Verlag von Gustav Uhl, Leipzig, 1892. 165 p. Br572C An8141 v.126.

3049. Neve y Molina, Luis de. *Grammatica della lingua otomi; esposta in italiano; secondo la traccia del licenziato Luis de Neve y Molina col vocabulario spagnuolo-otomi spiegato in italiano.* Tipografia di Propaganda Fide, Roma, 1841. 82 p. Br498.23 OP 583.

3050. Neve y Molina, Luis de. *Reglas de ortografia, diccionario y arte del idioma othomi; breve instrucción para los principiantes.* Imprenta de Bibliotheca Mexicana, México, 1767. 254 p. Br498.23 ON 413.

3051. *New Testament of Our Lord and Saviour Jesus Christ; Translated into the Choctaw Language; Pin chitokaka pi okchalinchi Chisvs Klaist in testament himona, chahta anumpa atoshowa hoke.* 2d ed. American Bible Society, New York, 1854. 818 p. Br497.39 ChB47.

3052. Newbold, Michael E. *Catalogue of His Celebrated Indian Collection.* New Jersey, 1888. 48 p. Br572C An8141 v.59.

3053. Newcomb, Cyrus F. *The Book of Algoonah; Being a Concise Account of the History of the Early People of the Continent of America, Known as Mound Builders.* Little and Becker, St. Louis, 1884. 353 p. Br571.9 N43.

3054. Newcomb, Simon, and W. J. McGee. The elements which make up the most useful citizen of the United States. *American Anthropologist* 7:345–351, 1894. Br572C An8141 v.141.

3055. Newman, F.W. *First Steps in Etruscan.* Kegan Paul, Trench, Trübner, and Co., Limited, London, 1892. 32 p. Br572C An8141 v.116.

3056. Nicaise, Auguste. Sur un buste antique en marbre trouvé au chatelet, Haute-Marne. *Gazette Archéologique*, 1886. 6 p. Br732 N51.

3057. *Nican ycuiliuhtic ayninxi tlapoval catca mexica ça nauhtetl yniuhquitova ceacatl quitlamia xiij acatl ce tecpatl quitlami a xiij tecpatl ce acatl iqui tlamia xiij calli ce tpocchtli quitlamia xiij tochtlictuh yni quac otlami to nauhte ixtin in mamolpia in toxiuh ypan yn ome acatl xi vitl ompavalxiuhtica onimatpia ypan onxivitl, velcen veueti litztli quimomicuitlo nican mexi-*

co a xxvij dias del mes de setiembre de 1576 as. Litho. J. Desportes, Paris. 79 leaves. Br898.22 AzN51. Photographic reproduction of an original pictorial chronicle in the British Museum (Add. MS 31219) and accompanying text in Nahuatl, compiled between 1576 and 1596 by one Indian scribe, with subsequent additions made between 1597 and 1607 by various other scribes, documenting the early history of the Aztecs, their migration from Aztlan, Mexica dynastic history, conquest by the Spaniards, and colonial events to the early 17th century. The codex also includes descriptions of the pre- and post-Conquest rulers of Tenochtitlán, their dates in office, and names of Spanish viceroys.

3058. Nican ycuiliuhtic ayninxi tlapoval catca mexica ça nauhtetl; Historia del imperio azteco, continudad hasta el año de 1607, documento pictográfico con texto en lengua nahuatl, 1873. 19 p. Br898.22 AzN51.2. Manuscript transcribed by Karl H. Berendt, New York, 1873.

3059. Niceforo, Alfredo. *Le varietà umane pigmee e microcefaliche della Sardegna*. Tipografía dell'Unione Cooperativa Edirice, Roma, 1896. 24 p. Br572C An8141 v.99.

3060. Nicolar, Joseph. *The Life and Traditions of the Red Man*. C. H. Glass, Bangor, ME, 1893. 147 p. Br398.21 N544. Abnaki Indians.

3061. Nicoli, J. P. *Yaquis y mayos; estudio histórico*. Imprenta de Francisco Diaz de León, México, 1885. 102 p. Br572C An8141 v.110.

3062. Nicollet, Joseph N. *Report Intended to Illustrate a Map of the Hydrographical Basin of the Upper Mississippi River, Made by J. N. Nicollet, While in the Employ Under the Bureau of the Corps of Topographical Engineers, February 16, 1841*. Blair and Rives, Washington, DC, 1843. 170 p. Br328.73 26.2SD.

3063. Nicolucci, Giustiniano. *Antropologia dell'Etruria; memoria di Giustiniano Nicolucci*. Stamperia del Fibreno, Napoli, 1869. 60 p. Br572.9 N543.

3064. Niederle, Lubor. Les derniers résultats de l'archéologie préhistorique en Bohême et ses rapports avec l'Europe orientale. pp. 75–86, n.d. Br572C An8141 v.99.

3065. Niederle, Lubor. *Über den Ursprung der Slaven*. Vieweg, Braunschweig, 1897. 2 p. Br572.491 N55.

3066. Niederle, Lubor. *Zur Frage über den Ursprung der Slaven*. Wiesner, Prag, 1899. 15 p. Br572.491 N55.2.

3067. Nield, William, comp. *Bibliotheca Americana; Catalogue of Books Relating to America, Canada, the West Indies, and Containing Early Voyages and Travels, Old Maps, Rare Tracts, Printed in America*. Nield, Bristol, 1885. 28 p. Br970B N55.

3068. Nieremberg, Juan E. *Historia natvrae, maxime peregrinae, libris XVI distincta Accedunt de miris & miraculosis naturis in Europa libri duo; item de iisdem in Terra Hebraeis promissa libe vnus*. Ex officina Plantiniana Bathasaris Moreti, Antverpiae, 1635. 502 p. Br508.3 N55.

3069. Nijhoff, M. Catalogue of books relating to America. *Americana* 207, 1888. 32 p. Br572C An8141 v.60.

3070. Niven, William. Omitlán, a prehistoric city in Mexico, 1897. 6 p. Br572C An8141 v.157.

3071. Noack, Ferdinand. Über eine alte Ansiedelung am Mühlenbach unterhalb Cöslin und einige andere Alterthumsfunde aus der Nachbarschaft. *Verhandlungen der Berliner Gesellschaft für Anthropologie, Ethnologie und Urgeschichte*, pp. 4-10, 1872. Br572C An8141 v.162.

3072. Nodal, J. F. *Los vínculos de Ollanta Y Cusi-Kcuylor: drama en Quichua*. En el depósito del Autor, Ayacucho, 1870?. 70 p. Br572C An8141 v.115.

3073. Noguera, Victor J. Vocabulario de la lengua popoluca ó chontal de Matagalpa [Nicaragua], por D. Víctor Noguera, cura de Matagalpa, 1855; copiado en Masaya, marzo de 1874. 6 leaves. Br498.35 PN 685. Vocabulary, arranged in double column, Spanish and Popoluca, pp. 1-6; on page 6 are a few phrases followed by the note, "El Padre Noguera, hizo en 1855 una colección de frases en popoluca, de 3 o 4 fojas en folio la cual en el transcurso del tiempo se perdió. La presente habia conservado en la memoria. B[erendt]."

3074. Noguera, Víctor J. Vocabulario y apuntes del idioma llamado parrastah, un dialecto de la lengua ulba, por don Víctor Jesús Noguera, presbitero. Santo Tomás Loviguisca, 1874. 15 p. Br498.35 P N685. Original manuscript prepared at the request of Karl H. Berendt.

3075. Noire, L. *On the Origin of Language and the Logos Theory*. Open Court Publishing Company, Chicago, 1895. 57 p. Br572C An8141 v.135.

3076. Nolan, Edward J. A biographical notice of W. S. W. Ruschenberger, M. D. *Proceedings of the Academy of Natural Sciences of Philadelphia,* pp. 452-462, 1895. Br572C An8141 v.141.

3077. Nolan, Edward J. Proceedings of a meeting held in commemoration of Harrison Allen, M. D., and George Henry Horn, M.D. *Proceedings of the Academy of Natural Sciences of Philadelphia*, December, pp. 505-535, 1897. Br572C An8141 v.146.

3078. Nolasco de los Reyes, Pedro. El ejercicio del santo via crucis puesto en lengua maya y copiado de un antiguo manuscrito. Mérida, 1869. 31 p. Br498.21 Mej 36. Probably a transcript copy of Pedro Nolaco de los Reyes, *El ejercicio del santo viacrucis puesto en lengua maya y copiado de un antiguo manuscrito; lo da a la prensa con superior permiso el Dr. D. J. Vicente Solís Rosales, quien desea se propage esta devoción entre los fieles, principalmente de la clase indígena; va corregida por el R.P. Fr. M. Antonio Peralta* (Mérida: Imprenta de J.D. Espinosa e Hijos, 1869. 32 p). From a note it appears that the manuscript was completed by Damian Chim, a Yucatec Maya. By another title which appears after the frontispiece it seems that the author of this work was Sr. D. Pedro Nolasco de los Reyes, "A devoción del Dr. D. Pedro Nolasco de los Reyes, cura interino de la parroquia de Santiago. Hele en 30 de enero de 1826 años."

3079. Nordenskiöld, Adolf E., baron. *Trois cartes précolombiennes représentant une partie de l'Amérique*. Typographie de l'Imprimerie Centrale, Stockholm, 1883. Br572C An8141 v.89.

3080. Nordenskiöld, Gustaf. *Cliff-Dwellers of the Mesa Verde, Southwestern Col-*

orado; Their Pottery and Implements. Norstedt, Stockholm, 1893. 189 p. Br571.84 N75.5.

3081. Nordiska Museet (Stockholm). *Guide to the Collections of the Northern Museum in Stockholm, Published by Artur I. Hazelius; Translated by Isabel C. Derby.* P. A. Norstedt, Stockholm, 1889. 52 p. Br572.07 St63.2 ED.

3082. Nordiska Museet (Stockholm). *Nordiska Museets Framjande,* 1881, 1883, 1885, 1886, 1889. Br572.07 St63.

3083. Nordiska Museet (Stockholm). *Stimmen aus der Fremde als Beilage, Führer durch die Sammlungen des Museums.* P. A. Norstedt, Stockholm, 1888. 122 p. Br913.06 St6. Contents include: Ferdinand Krauss, Österich, 1887; Johanne Mestorf, Deutschland, 1874; Felix Liebrecht and Reinhold Mejborg, Belgien und Dänemark, 1887; W. Q. von Ufford, Holland, 1876; Jachris Topelius, Finnland, 1885.

3084. Norman, Benjamin M. *Rambles by Land and Water; or, Notes of Travel in Cuba and Mexico, Including a Canoe Voyage Up the River Panuco, and Researches Along the Ruins of Tamaulipa.* Paine and Burgess, New York; B. M. Norman, New Orleans, 1845. 216 p. Br917.291 N78.

3085. Norman, Benjamin M. *Rambles in Yucatán, or, Notes of Travel Through the Peninsua, Including a Visit to the Remarkable Ruins of Chi-Chen, Kabak, Zayi, and Uxmal.* J. and H.G. Langley, New York; Thomas, Cowperthwait and Company, Philadelphia, 1843. 304 p. Br917.26 N78.

3086. Notice sur plusieurs langues Indiennes de la Nouvelle-Grenade, aujourd'hui États-Unis de la Colombie, Amérique du Sud, Paris, 1899. 8 p. Br572C An8141 v.50.

Adolf E. Nordenskjöld (from Justin Winsor, Aboriginal America. Cambridge, MA: Houghton, Mifflin, 1889. p. 113).

3087. Nuix, Juan. *Reflexîones imparciales sobre la humanidad de los Españoles en las Indias, contra los pretendidos filósofos y políticos. Para ilustrar las historias de MM. Raynal y Robertson. Escritas en italiano por el abate Don Juan Nuix, y traducidas con algunas notas por D. Pedro Varela y Ulloa*. J. Ibarra, Madrid, 1782. 315 p. Br972 N91.5.

3088. Numismatic and Antiquarian Society of Philadelphia. *Report of the Proceedings of the Numismatic and Antiquarian Society of Philadelphia, 1887-1889*. 86 p. Br572C An8141 v.12.

3089. Núñez Cabeza de Vaca, Alvar. The narrative of Alvar Nuñez Cabeça de Vaca; translated by Buckingham Smith. Washington, DC, 1851. 138 p. Br973.1 N923.ES. Translation of the first part *La relación y comentariõs*, (Valladolid, 1555).

3090. Nuttall, Zelia. A note on ancient Mexican folk-lore. *Journal of American Folk-Lore* 8(29): 117-129, 1895. Br572C An8141 v.157. Zelia Nuttall (1857-1933) was the first woman scholar to study Mesoamerica and published commentaries on prehispanic manuscripts, correctly identified a large piece of featherwork in the Vienna Museum as a headdress, possibly Motecuhzoma's, and offered hypotheses of Mesoamerican calendrical systems. She was instrumental in setting up the International School of American Archaeology and Ethnology in Mexico City.

3091. Nuttall, Zelia. Ancient Mexican Feather Work at the Columbian Historical Exposition at Madrid. *Report of the Madrid Commission, 1892*, pp. 329-337. Government Printing Office, Washington, DC, 1895. Br572C An8141 v.141.

3092. Nuttall, Zelia. Ancient Mexican superstitions. *Journal of American Folk-Lore* 10(39): 265-281, 1897. Br572C An8141 v.99.

3093. Nuttall, Zelia. Coyote versus long-tailed bear. *Internationales Archiv für Ethnographie* 6:95-97, 1893. Br572C An8141 v.109.

3094. Nuttall, Zelia. *Note on the Ancient Mexican Calendar System*. Printed by Bruno Schulze, Dresden, 1894. 36 p. B4913.72 N962.2; Br572C An8141 v.136.

3095. Nuttall, Zelia. On ancient Mexican shields: an essay. *Internationales Archiv für Ethnographie* 5:34-53, 1892. Br572C An8141 v.105.

3096. Nuttall, Zelia. Preliminary note of an analysis of the Mexican codices and graven inscriptions. *Proceedings of the American Association for the Advancement of Science* 35:325-326, 1886. Br572C An8141 v.28.

3097. Nuttall, Zelia. Standard or head-dress? An historical essay on a relic of ancient Mexico. *Archaeological and Ethnological Papers of the Peabody Museum of American Archaeology and Ethnology, Harvard University* 1(1): 1-52, 1888. Br572C An8141 v.28.

3098. Nuttall, Zelia. *The Atlatl or Spear-Thrower of the Ancient Mexicans*. Archaeological and Ethnological Papers of the Peabody Museum of American Archaeology and Ethnology, Harvard University 1(3): 173-197, 1891. Br572C An8141 v.110.

3099. Nuttall, Zelia. The terracotta heads of Teotihuacan. *American Journal of Archaeology* 2(2): 157-178, 1886. Br572C An8141 v.28.

3100. *Offices for the Solemnization of Matrimony, the Visitation of the Sick, and the*

Burial of the Dead. St. Paul's Mission Press, Victoria, B.C., 1880. 15 p. Br497.46S C47. Church of England Book of Common Prayer translated into Ntlakyapamuk.

3101. Ohio. Centennial, Board of Managers. Final Report. Columbus, OH, 1877. 167 p. Br606 Ph1876yO.

3102. Oliveira Cezar, Filiberto. *La vida en los vosques sud-americanos; viaje al oriente de Bolivia*. Jacobo Peuser, Buenos Aires, 1891. 164 p. Br572C An8141 v.149.

3103. Ollanta; ein altperuanisches Drama aus der Kechuasprache; Übersetzt und Commentirt von J. J. von Tschudi. *Denkschriften der Philosophisch-Historische Klasse, Kaiserlichen Akademie der Wissenschaften, Wien* 24:167–384, 1876. Br898.7 IO.GT. Quechua and German arranged in parallel columns.

3104. *Ollantai; drame en vers quechuas du temps des Incas*. Bibliothèque Linguistique Américaine, 4. Maisonneuve, Paris, 1878. 265 p. Br497C Am3.

3105. Olmos, Andrés de. *Arte para aprender la lengua mexicana; compuesto por fr. Andres del Olmos; publicado por Mr. Rémi Siméon. Imprenta nacional, Paris. MDCCCLXXV; reimpreso en México, 1885. Imprenta de Ignacio Escalante, México*, 1885. 125 p. Br498.22 AzOl 5.

3106. Olmos, Andrés de. *Grammaire de la langue nahuatl ou mexicaine; composée en 1547 par le franciscain André de Olmos; et publieé avec notes, éclaircissements, etc. par Rémi Siméon*. Imprimerie Nationale, Paris, 1875. 273 p. Br498.22 AzOl 5.2.

3107. Omalius d'Halloy, Jean Julien, baron d'. Observations sur la distribution ancienne des peuples de la race blanche. *Académie Royale de Bruxelles* 15(5), 1848. 16 p. Br572C An8141 v.31.

3108. Onasakenral, Joseph. *The Holy Gospels; Translated from the Authorized English Version into the Iroquois Indian Dialect, Under the Supervision of the Montreal Auxiliary to the British and foreign Bible Society; Neh nase tsi shok8atak8en ne sonk8aianer Iesos-Keristos. Tsiniiot tsi teho8ennatenion oni tsi roiahton ne Sose Onasakenrat*. Printed by J. Lovell, for the British and Foreign Bible Society, Montreal, 1880. 324 p. Br497.27 MB47.5. Translation of the Gospels into Iroquois.

3109. Onnis, E. Ardu. *Contributo all'antropologia della Sardegna*. Tipographia dell'Unione Cooperativa Editivce, Roma, 1896. Br572C An8141 v.99.

3110. Onnis, E. Ardu. La Sardegna preistorica; note di paletnologia. *Atti del Società Romana di Antropologia* 5(3), 1898. 82 p. Rome. Br913.379 On52.

3111. Oraciones en lengua quiché de Rabinal, con unos fragmentos en lengua cuchechi (Cagchi), n.d. 7 leaves. Br498.21 Kor13. Manuscript.

3112. *Oraciones y meditaciones, según S. Alfonso; traducido al Inca por los PP. Redentoristas*. Cordero, Cuenca, 1884. 57 p. Br498.7 KR 662.

3113. Orbigny, Alcide Dessalines d'. *Fragment d'un voyage au centre de l'Amérique Méridionale; contenant des considérations sur la navigation de l'Amazone et de la Plata, et sur les anciennes missions des provinces de Chiquitos et de Moxos (Bolivia)*. P. Bertrand, Paris, 1845. 584 p. Br918 Or13.

3114. Orbigny, Alcide Dessalines d'. *Lenguas argentinas grupo mataco-mataguayo del*

Chaco; dialecto vejoz vocabulario y apuntes. Imprenta Roma de Juan Carbone, Buenos Aires, 1896. 55 p. Br498.97 AQ 38.

3115. Orbigny, Alcide Dessalines d'. *L'homme américain (de l'Amérique Méridionale), considéré sous les rapports physiologiques et moraux.* Chez Pitois-Levrault et Cie., Pari; Chez F. G. Levrault, Strasbourg, 1839. 2 v. Br572.98 Or12.

3116. Orcutt, Samuel. *The Indians of the Housatonic and Naugatuck Valley.* Press of the Case, Lockwood and Brainard Company, Hartford, CT, 1882. 220 p. Br970.4 COr13.

3117. Organization and historical sketch of the Women's Anthropological Society of America, 1889. 22 p. Br572C An8141 v.29.

3118. Oriental Club of Philadelphia. *Oriental Studies; A Selection of the Papers Read Before the Oriental Club of Philadelphia, 1888-1894.* Ginn and Company, Boston, 1894. 278 p. Br490.6 P533. Contents include: Morton W. Easton, "The physical geography of India"; Marcus Jastrow, "An interpretation of Psalms LXXI-II and XC"; Stewart Culin, "Literature of Chinese laborers"; Daniel G. Brinton, "The alphabets of the Berbers"; W. Max Müller, "Who were the ancient Ethiopians?"; George A. Barton, "Native Israelitish deities"; Morris Jastrow, "A legal document of Babylonia"; H. V. Hilprecht, "A numerical fragment from Nippur"; Edward W. Hopkins, "The holy numbers of the Rig-Veda"; Benjamin Smith Lyman, "The change from surd to sonant in Japanese compounds"; H. Collitz, "The Aryan name of the tongue"; Sara Yorke Stevenson, "The feather and the wing in early mythology"; and Paul Haupt, "The book of Ecclesiastes."

3119. *Original Mitteilungen aus der Ethnologischen Abtheilung.* Verlag von W. Spemann, Berlin, 1885. 234 p. Br572C An8141 v.1.

3120. Orozco y Berra, Manuel. *Geografía de las lenguas y carta etnográfica de México; precedidas de un ensayo de clasificación de las mismas lenguas y de apuntes para las inmigraciones de las tribus.* Imprenta de J. M. Andrade y F. Escalante, México, 1864. 392 p. Br498 Or62.

3121. Orozco y Berra, Manuel. *Historia antigua y de la conquista de México.* Tipografía de G. A. Esteva, México, 1880. 4 vols; atlas. Br972 Or64.

3122. Ortega, Joseph de. *Vocabulario de las lenguas castellana y cora, reimpreso...conforme al ejemplar que existe en la biblioteca publica de Guadalajara y cuya carátula se reproduce textualmente.* Segaspi, Tepic, 1888. 90 p. Br498.22 CoOr 88.

3123. *Os indios bravos.* Lima, 1867. 124 p. Br572C An8141 v.33.

3124. Osborn, Henry F. Memorial tribute to Prof. Thomas H. Huxley. *Transactions of the New York Academy of Sciences* 15:40-50, 1895. Br119 H983.yO. Henry Fairfield Osborn (1857-1935), paleontologist and science administrator accepted a joint appointment at Columbia University and the American Museum of Natural History in 1891. In 1908 Osborn became museum president and promoted expeditions and exhibits on a grand scale. His interest in paleoanthropology led to the exploration of Cro-Magnon and Neanderthal sites in Europe and the development of a large Hall of the Age of Man. He actively supported Roy Chapman Andrews's explorations in Mongolia, and he sent other expeditions to the Congo, Micronesia, and the Northwest Territories of

Canada. Discoveries from these expeditions were displayed in large dioramas, habitat groups, and exhibit halls throughout the museum. Osborn made the American Museum of Natural History the largest and most famous science museum in the United States.

3125. Osborn, Henry F. The Cartwright lectures, 1892: Present problems in evolution and heredity; I. The contemporary evolution of man; II. Difficulties in the heredity theory; III. Heredity and the germ cells. *The Medical Record*, 1892. 71 p. Br572C An8141 v.88; Br572C An8141 v.121.

3126. Osborn, Henry F. The history and homologies of the human molar cusps. *Anatomischer Anzeiger* 7(23-24): 740-747, 1892. Jena. Br572C An8141 v.121.

3127. Osborn, Henry F. The history of the cusps of the human molar teeth. *International Dental Journal*, July, 1895. 26 p. Br572C An8141 v.157.

3128. Osborn, Henry F. The Huerfano Lake Basin, southern Colorado, and its Wind River and Bridger fauna. *Bulletin of the American Museum of Natural History* 9:247-258, 1897. Br572C An8141 v.157.

3129. Osborn, Henry F. The rise of the Mammalia in North America. *Studies from the Biological Laboratories of Columbia College, Zoology* 1(2): 61-103, 1893. Br572C An8141 v.123.

3130. Osorio, Lope de. Auto de la real visita en el pueblo de Chiapa de la Real Corona, a favor de los indios de dicha comunidad, fecho en Guathemala, a 24 de junio de 1665. 54 leaves. Br970.4 Cos55. Manuscript.

3131. Osten-Sacken, T. Chronique des congrès. *Société Impériale des Amis des Sciences Naturelles, d'Anthropologie et d'Ethnographie de l'Université de Moscou* 6:1-4, 1892. Br572C An8141 v.102.

3132. Osterwald, Jean F. *Ettunetle choh kwunduk nyukwun treltsei Rev. M. Osterwald...Ven archdeacon McDonald*. Society for Promoting Christian Knowledge, London, 1885. 23 p. Br497.12 TuOs76.

3133. Otis, Fessenden. The new gold discoveries on the Isthmus of Panama. *Harper's Weekly*, August, 1859. 5 p. Br572C An8141 v.77.

3134. *Our Forest Children*. Shingwauk Home, Owen Sound, Ontario, 1887-1890. 4 v. Br371.95 Ou73. no. 6. Published in the interest of Indian education and civilization; Museum Library has v.1 (1-7, 10) and v. 2(1-6)

3135. Outes, Félix F. *Etnografía argentina, segunda contribucíon al estudio de los Indios Querandíes*. Buenos Aires, 1898 15 p. Br498.977 Qou 8.

3136. Outes, Félix F. Los Querandíes. *Breve contribución al estudio de la etnografía argentina*. Imprenta de M. Biedma, Buenos Aires, 1897. 202 p. Br498.977 Qou 8.2.

3137. Oviedo y Banos, José de. *Historia de la conquista y población de la provincia de Venezuela, escrita por D. José de Oviedo y Banos; ilustrada con notas y documentos por el capitán de navio Cesareo Fernández Duro*. L. Navarro, Madrid, 1885. 2 v. Br987 Ov44a.

3138. Owen, Edward T. The meaning and function of thought-connectives. *Transactions of the Wisconsin Academy of Sciences, Arts, and Letters* 12(1): 1-48, 1898. Br572C An8141 v.99.

3139. Oxenden, Ashton. *Zzebkko enjit gichinchik nekwazzi ttrin ihtblog kenjit ako gichinchik ttrin kittekookwichiltsej kenjit kah.* Society for Promoting Christian Knowledge, London, 1885. 50 p. Br497.12 TuOs76.

3140. Packard, Alpheus S. Ascent from the volcano of Popocatepetl. *American Naturalist* 20:109-123, 1886. Br572C An8141 v.157.

3141. Packard, Alpheus S. Memoir of Jeffries Wyman, 1814-1874. *Memoirs of the National Academy of Sciences* 8:77-125, 1878. Br572C An8141 v.157.

3142. Packard, Alpheus S. Notes on the Labrador Eskimo and their former range southward. *American Naturalist* 19(5-6): 471-481, 553-560, 1885. Br572C An8141 v.13.

3143. Packard, Alpheus S. Notes on the physical geography of Labrador. pp. 403-422, n.d. Br572C An8141 v.23.

3144. Packard, Alpheus S. Over the Mexican plateau in a diligence. pp. 215-250, n.d. Br572C An8141 v.157.

3145. Packard, R. L. The Copper Age in America. *American Antiquarian*, 1893. 24 p. Br572C An8141 v.124.

3146. Pajeken, Clemens A. *Reise-Erinnerungen und Ubenfeuer aus der Neuen Welt.* F. G. Henfe's Verlag, Bremen, 1861. 168 p. Br572C An8141 v.61.

3147. Palacios, Enrique. *Memoria leida en la junta general que celebró la Sociedad Económica de Amigos del Pais, el 26 de diciembre de 1861.* Imprenta de Luna, Guatemala, 1861. 23 p. Br572C An8141 v.69.

3148. Palma, Miguel T. *Constitución federal de los estados unidos mexicanos, con sus adiciones y reformas traducida al idioma azteca o mexicano, por Miguel T. Palma.* Imprenta del Hospicio, Puebla, 1888. 58 p. Br342.72 M57.

3149. Palma, Miguel T. *Gramática de la lengua azteca ó mejicana; escrita con arreglo al programa oficial para que sirva de texto en las escuelas normales del estado, por Miguel Trinidad Palma.* Imprenta M. Corona, Puebla, 1886. 126 p. Br498.22 AzP 18.

3150. Palmer, Edward. Australian tribes. *Journal of the Anthropological Institute of Great Britain and Ireland* 13(3): 276-334, 1884. Br572C An8141 v.67.

3151. Palmer, Edward. Cave dwellings in Utah. *Annual Reports of the Trustees of the Peabody Museum of American Archaeology and Ethnology* 2(2): 269-272, 1878. Br913.07 H265. Palmer (1831-1911) served as a contract surgeon at Army posts in Colorado, Kansas, and Arizona between 1862 and 1867, and as medical officer at the Kiowa-Comanche Agency in Oklahoma in 1868. Later he devoted himself to collecting biological and other material in Mexico and the western United States.

3152. Palmer, Edward. Mexican caves with human remains. *American Naturalist* 16:306-311, 1882. Br572C An8141 v.13.

3153. Panceri, Paolo. *La mummia peruviana del Museo Nazionale di Napoli.* Stameria della Regia Università, Napoli, 1868. 8p. Br572C An8141 v.97.

3154. Pander, Eugen. *Das Pantheon des Tschangtscha Hutuktu, Ein Beitrag zur Iconographie des Lamaismus,* Albert Grünwedel, ed. Veröffentlichungen der Museum für Völkerkunde 1(2-3). W. Spemann, Berlin, 1890. 116 p. Br281.3 P19.

Miguel T. Palma (from Frederick Starr, Recent Mexican Study of the Native Languages of Mexico. *Chicago: University of Chicago Press, 1900. p. 18). [3]*

3155. Pandosy, Marie C. *Grammar and Dictionary of the Yakama Language, Translated by George Gibbs and J. G. Shea.* Shea's Library of American Linguistics, 6. Cramoisy Press, New York, 1862. 59 p. Br497C Sh3; Br497C Sh3a. "The author of this grammar resided for several years among [the Yakima] as a missionary, and thus became perfectly familiar with their language. The original manuscript, written in French, was lost in the conflagration by which the mission establishment was destroyed" (Field 1873:298-299).

3156. Pansch, Adolf. Anthropologie. *Zweite deutsche Nordpolfahrt* 2:144-156, 1873. Br572C An8141 v.19.

3157. Papers relating to Count de Frontenac's expedition against the Onondaga's, XI, 1696. Br572C An8141 v.62.

3158. Papers relating to De Courcelles and De Tracy's expeditions against the Mohawk Indians, III, 1665-1666. Br572C An8141 v.62.

3159. Papers relating to M. [Lefebre] de La Barre's expedition to Hungry Bay, Jefferson County, V, 1684. Br572C An8141 v.62.

3160. Papers relating to M. de Dononville's expedition to the Genesee country and Niagara, VII, 1687. 277 p. Br572C An8141 v.62.

3161. Papers relating to the invasion of New York and the burning of Schnectady, IX, 1690. Br572C An8141 v.62.

3162. Papers relating to the Iroquois and other Indian tribes, I, 1666-1763. Br572C An8141 v.62.

3163. Pardo de Tavero, Trinidad H. *Contribución para el estudio de los antiguos alfabetos filipinos.* Hermanos, Losana, 1884. Br499.216 PP 213.

3164. Paredes, Ignacio de. *Analisis gramatical de algunos textos mexicanos, de las obras...por Agustin de la Rosa*. Rodíguez, Guadalajara, 1871 Br498.22 AzP 21.

3165. Paredes, Ignacio de. Doctrina breve sacada del catecismo mexicano, c.1750. Br498.22 AzSa 53.

3166. Paredes, Ignacio de. *Promptuario manual mexicano; que á la verdad podrá ser utilissimo á los parrochos para la enseñanza; á los necessitados indios para su instrucción; y á los que aprenden la lengua para la expedición*. Imprenta de la Bibliotheca Mexicana, México, 1759. 380 p. Br498.22 AzP 21.2.

3167. Pareja, F. *Arte de la lengua timuquana, compuesto en 1614 y publicado conforme al ejemplar original unico por Lucien Adam y E. H. J. Vinson*. Bibliothèque Linguistique Américaine, 11. Maisonneuve, Paris, 1886. Br497C Am3.

3168. Parker, Samuel. *Journal of An Exploring Tour Beyond the Rocky Mountains, Under the Direction of the A. B. C. F. M., Containing a Description of the Geography, Geology, Climate, Productions of the Country, and the Numbers, Manners, and Customs of the Natives; With a Map of Oregon Territory, by Rev. Samuel Parker, A. M.* 5th ed. J. C. Derby and Company, Auburn, NY; M. H. Newman and Company, New York, 1846. 422 p. Br917.8 P22b. "The author's personal experience among the nomads of the Plains, the root-diggers of the mountains, and the fish eaters of the western slope, is given with sufficient detail to attract our interest...the author indeed anticipates the requirements of his day, and furnishes the philologist with a vocabulary of four Indian tongues" (Field 1873:301).

3169. Parry, Francis. The sacred symbols and numbers of aboriginal America in ancient and modern times. *Bulletin of the American Geographical Society* 2, 1894. 45 p. Br572C An8141 v.136.

3170. Parsons, Usher. *Indian Names of Places in Rhode-Island*. Knowles, Anthony, and Company, Providence, 1861. 32 p. Br572C An8141 v.81.

3171. Pasión de jueves santo en lengua chapaneca, a 18 de marzo 1818; Pasión de juebes santo quesi yospaque tzesi iscohina is año de 1818. 4 leaves. Br498C B457. Manuscript.

3172. Pasión de Nro. Señor Jesuchristo en la lengua zoque, n.d. Br898.22 AzP267. Manuscript.

3173. Pasión de Nro. Señor Jesucristo, en lengua zoque; os evangelios del Domingo de Ramos, jueves santo y viernes santo, como los cantan los indios de Tuxtla. Tuxtla Gutiérrez, 1870. 55 p. Br498.35 ZP264. Manuscript, transcribed by Karl H. Berendt.

3174. Pasión en lengua chapaneca; canciones de los indios de Suchiapa. Tuxtla Gutiérrez, 1870. 93 p. Br498.21 CP264. Manuscript; volume contains the rules or ordenanzas in Chiapanec for three fraternities (cofradías) devoted to the adoration respectively of Jesus of Nazareth, the Holy Cross, and the Virgin of the Rosary; including "Las ordenanzas de la cofradía de la Santa Cruz," 1780; "Las ordenanzas de la cofradía de Jesus Nazareno," 1781; and "Las ordenanzas de la cofradía de la Nra. Sra. de Rosario," 1723.

3175. Pasión; fragmento en lengua zoque. 3 leaves. Br498.35 ZP263. Manuscript.

3176. Paul H. B. B. *Estournelles de Constant, Les congrégations religiouses chez les Arabes et la conquète de l'Afrique du Nord*. Bibliothèque Ethnographique, 8.

Maisonneuve et Ch. Leclerc, Paris, 1887. 72 p. Br572C R737.

3177. Pauli, Carl. *Eine Vorgreichische Inschrift von Lemnos.* Leipzig, 1886. 81 p. Br572C An8141 v.56.

3178. Payne, F. F. Eskimo of Hudson's Strait. *Proceedings of the Canadian Institute* 6:213-230, 1889. Br572C An8141 v.23.

3179. Payró, Roberto J. *La Australia Argentina; excursión periodistica a las costas patagónicas, Tierra del Fuego é Isla de los Estados; con una carta-prólogo del general Bartolmé Mitre.* Imprenta de "La Nación", Buenos Aires, 1898. 448 p. Br918.2 P296.

3180. Peabody Museum of American Archaeology and Ethnology, Harvard University. *Reports.* v.1-20 (1868-1886). Br913.07 H265.

3181. Peal, S. E. Comparison of numerals in 41 dialects and languages. Assam, 1895. 2 p. Br409.2 P315.

3182. Peal, S. E. On the "morong" as possibly a relic of pre-marriage communism. *Journal of the Anthropological Institute of Great Britain and Ireland* 22:244-261, 1893. Br572C An8141 v.143. Ex-libris Horatio Hale, with marginal notes.

3183. Peal, S. E. The communal barracks of primitive races. *Journal of the Asiatic Society of Brazil* 61(3): 246-269, 1892. Br572C An8141 v.128; Br572C An8141 v.141.

3184. Peale, Franklin. Communication: Pottery on the Delaware, n.d. 6 p. Br572C An8141 v.38.

3185. Peale, Titian R. Men ignorant of fire. *American Naturalist* 18(2): 229-232, 1884. Br572C An8141 v.13.

3186. Pech, Nakuk. *Chrestomathie maya d'après la Chronique de Chac-Xulub-Chen, par Nakuk Pech; extrait de la "Library of Aboriginal American Littérature" de M. le Dr. D.-G. Brinton; texte avec traduction interlinéaire, analyse grammaticale et vocabulare maya-français, publié par le comte H. de Charencey.* C. Klincksieck, Paris, 1891. 301 p. Br498.21 MP332.

3187. Peck, Edmund J. *Portions of the Book of Common Prayer; Together With Hymns, Addresses, etc. for the Use of the Eskimo of Hudson's Bay.* Society for Promoting Christian Knowledge, London, 1881. 90 p. Br497.25 MC47. Church of England Book of Common Prayer translated into Eskimo.

3188. Peck, Edmund J. *Portions of the Holy Scripture for the Use of the Esquimaux on the Northern and Eastern Shores of Hudson's Bay.* Printed for the Society for Promoting Christian Knowledge, London, 1878. 93 p. Br497.25 MB45. Selections from the Bible translated into Eskimo.

3189. Pector, Désiré. *Aperçu des principales communications relatives à la linguistique faites au Congres International des Americanistes.* J. Maisonneuve, Libraire-Éditeur, Paris, 1890. 16 p. Br572C An8141 v.84.

3190. Pector, Désiré. *Considérations sur quelques noms indigènes de localités de l'isthme Centre-Américain.* Ernest Leroux, Paris, 1892. 23 p. Br572C An8141 v.119.

3191. Pector, Désiré. Essai de localisation des inhabitants précolombiens de l'Amérique Centrale. *Internationales Archiv für Ethnographie* 3:31-33, 1890. Br572C An8141 v.91.

3192. Pector, Désiré. Ethnographie de l'archipel Magellanique. *Internationales Archiv für Ethnographie* 5:215-221, 1892. Br572C An8141 v.105. "An excellent summary of the Yahgan cultural data" (Cooper 1917:118).

3193. Pector, Désiré. Étude économique sur la république de Nicaragua. *Bulletin de la Société Neuchateloise de Géographie et par Pauteur* 7:5-167, 1893. Br572C An8141 v.119.

3194. Pector, Désiré. Exposé sommaire des voyages et travaux géographiques au Nicaragua, 1891. 8 p. Br572C An8141 v.7; Br572C An 8141 v.119.

3195. Pector, Désiré. *Exposé sommaire des voyages et travaux géographiques au Nicaragua dans le cours du XIXe siècle.* Bibliothèque des Annales Économiques, Société d'Éditions Scientifiques, Paris, 1891. 160 p. Br572C An8141 v.119.

3196. Pector, Désiré. José Triana: membre libre de la Société Américaine de France: notice historique. *Archives de la Société Américaine de France* 1:63-68, 1892. Br572C8141v. 83; Br572C An8141 v.119.

3197. Pector, Désiré. La nuova città America de. Il R. Prinzapolka nel Nicaragua. *Cosmos di Guido Cora* 10(5-6): 187-188, 1889-1891. Br572C An8141 v.98.

3198. Pector, Desiré. *Notice sur le Salvador.* Imprimerie Typographique J. Kugelman, Paris, 1889. 139 p. Br572C An8141 v.7.

3199. Pector, Desiré. *Notice sur les collections ethnographiques et archéologiques de Nicaragua...á l'Exposition Universette de 1889.* Leroux, Paris, 1890. 8 p. Br572C An8141 v.40.

3200. Pector, Desiré. *Questions anthropologiques et ethnographiques traitées au Congres International des Americanistes.* Paris, 1890. 16 p. Br572C An8141 v.7.

3201. Pector, Désiré. *Sur le nom Amérique.* Ernest Leroux, Paris, 1892. 8 p. Br572C An8141 v.119.

3202. Peet, Stephen D. The Delaware Indians in Ohio. *American Antiquarian* 2(2): 132-144, 1878. Br572C An8141 v.32. Stephen Dennison Peet (1831-1914), a Congregational clergyman and archaeologist, was the son of Rev. Stephen Peet, a founder of Beloit College and the Chicago Theological Seminary. After becoming pastor of the Congregational church at Ashtabula, Ohio, in 1873, Peet established himself as an authority on local archaeology. His greatest contribution was the founding and editing of the *American Antiquarian*, which remains an invaluable index of the concerns that defined American anthropology in its early years.

3203. Peet, Stephen D. The Mound Builders; their works and relics. Office of the American Antiquarian, Chicago, 1892. 376 p. Br571.91 P34.5.

3204. Peet, Stephen D. The religious beliefs and traditions of the aborigines of North America. *The Victoria Institute,* pp. 1-15, 1887. Br572C An8141 v.60.

3205. Pelleschi, Juan. *Los Indios Matacos y su lengua.* Imprenta La Buenos Aires, Buenos Aires, 1897. 248 p. Br498.972 P 36. Includes Vocabularios, español-mataco y mataco-español, frases y relaciones (pp. 171-246).

3206. Pelleschi, Juan. *Otto mesi nel Gran Ciacco; viaggio lungo il fiume Vermiglio di Giovanni Pelleschi.* Firenze, 1881. 428 p. Br918.2 P363.

3207. Peñafiel, Antonio. *Arte decorativo mexicano*. México, 1898. 1 v. color plates. Br913.72 P37.2.

3208. Peñafiel, Antonio. *Explication de l'Edifice Mexicain à l'Exposition Internationale de Paris*. Barcelona, 1889. 72 p. Br572C An8141 v.28.

3209. Peñafiel, Antonio. *Fábulas de esopo en idioma mexicano*. Oficina Tipografica de la Secretaria de Fomento, Mexico, 1895. 37 p. Br572C An8141 v.141.

3210. Peñafiel, Antonio. *Manuscrito americano numero 4 de la Biblioteca Real de Berlin, copiado en febrero de 1890 por el doctor Antonio Peñafiel*. Oficina Tipográfica de la Secretaría de Fomento, México, 1897. 74 p. Br898.22 AzB453P. Consists of "Títulos de tierras pertenecientes al Pueblo de Santa Isabel Tola, in Spanish and Nahuatl.

3211. Peñafiel, Antonio. *Nombres geográficos de México; catálogo alfabético de los nombres de lugar pertenecientes al idioma "nahuatl"; estudio jeroglífico de la Matrícula de los tributos del Códice Mendocino por el Dr. Antonio Peñafiel…dibujos de las "Antigüedades mexicanas" de Lord Kingsborough por el Sr. Domingo Carral y grabados por el Sr. Antonio H. Galaviz*. Oficina Tipográfica de la Secretaría de Fomento, México, 1885. 260 p. Br498.22 AzP 37. Capítulo III: "Nociones de Ortografía mexicana, por el Sr. Lic. D. Eufemio Mendoza," from Mendoza's Apuntes para un catálogo razonado de las palabras mexicanas introducidas al castellano (1872).

3212. Penhallow, Samuel. *The History of the Wars of New-England With the Eastern Indians; Or a Narrative of Their Continued Perfidy and Cruelty, From the 10th of August, 1703, To the Peace Renewed 13th of July, 1713; And from the 25th of July, 1722, to their Submission 15th December, Which was Ratified August 5th,*

Antonio Peñafiel (from Frederick Starr, Recent Mexican Study of the Native Languages of Mexico. *Chicago: University of Chicago Press, 1900. p. 10).*

1726. Re-printed from the Boston edition of 1726…for W. Dodge, by J. Harpel, Cincinnati, 1859. 138, 36 p. Br974 P37.

3213. Penka, Karl. *Die Kupferzeit in Europa*. Karl Fromme, Wien, n.d. 13 p. Br572C An8141 v.127.

3214. Peralta, Manuel M. de, and Anastasio Alfaro. *Ethnología Centro-Americana; catálogo razonado de los objectos arqueológicos de la República de Costa-Rica en la Exposición Histórico-Americana de Madrid, 1892*. Manuel Ginés Hernández, Madrid, 1893. 112 p. Br572C An8141 v.122; Br913.7286 P41.

3215. Peralta, Manuel M. de. *Costa-Rica, Nicaragua y Panamá en el siglo XVI; su historia y sus límites según los documentos del Archivo de Indias de Sevilla, del de Simancas, etc.; recogidos y publicados con notas y aclaraciones históricas y geográficas, por D. Manuel M. de Peralta*. M. Murillo, Madrid; Paris, J. I. Ferrer, Paris, 1883. 832 p. Br972.8 P41.

3216. Pérez de Ribas, Andrés. *Historia de los triumphos de nuestra santa fee entre gentes las mas barbaras, y fieras del Nuevo Orbe; conseguidos por los soldados de la milicia de la Compañia de Iesus en las missiones de la prouincia de Nueua-Espana.…escrita por el padre Andres Pérez de Ribas*. Por Alo[n]so de Paredes, ju[n]to a los estudios de la Co[m]pañia, Madrid, 1645. 763 p. Br980.6 P413.

3217. Pérez de Velasco, Andres M. *El ayudante de cura instruido en el porte a que le obliga su dignidad, en los deberes a que le estrecha su empleo, y en la fructuosa practica de su ministerio*. Impresso en el Colegio Real de San Ignacio de la Puebla, Puebla, 1766. 106 p. Br262 F413.

3218. Pérez, Felipe. *Jeografia fisica i politica de los Estados Unidos de Colombia, escrita de orden del gobierno jeneral, por Felipe Pérez*. Imprenta de la Nación, Bogotá, 1862-1863. 2 v. Br918.6 P41. Contents include: 1. "La jeografía del Distrito federal i las de los estados de Panamá i el Cauca"; 2. "Las jeografías de los estados del Tolima, Cundinamarca, Boyacá, Santander, Bolívar i el Magdalena."

3219. Pérez, Francisco. *Catecismo de la doctrina cristiana en lengua otomí*. Imprenta de la testamentaría de Valdés, á cargo de José María Gallegos, México, 1834. 17 p. Br498.23 OP 413.

3220. Pérez, Jerónimo. *Memorias para la historia de la revolución de Nicaragua y de la guerra nacional contra los filibusteros, 1854 a 1857; por Jerónimo Pérez*. Imprenta del Gobierno, Managua, 1865-1873. 2 v. Br972.85 P41.

3221. Pérez, Juan Pío. Apuntes del diccionario de la lengua maya, compuestos con vista de varios catalogos antiquos de sus voces y aumentado con oran suma de las de uso comun y otras que se han extractado de manuscritos antiquos, por un yucateco aficionado a la lengua, 1855. 468 p. Br498.21 MP 413.2. Manuscript. Juan Pío Pérez (1798–1859) was the first modern Yucatec Maya scholar. He was selected as the Yucatec interpreter to the Secretary of State at Merida. The duties of this office gave him access to much material written in Yucatec. Pérez realized the importance of preserving material on Yucatec that was rapidly disappearing. He made a collection of original documents in Yucatec and copies of manuscripts which he did not possess. This collection was copied in part by Karl H. Berendt and these copies are the foundation of the Berendt collection at the University of Pennsylvania Museum Library (Tozzer 1921:143-144).

3222. Pérez, Juan Pío. Apuntes para un diccionario de la lengua maya; compuestos con vista de varios catalogos antiguos de sus voces y aumentado con gran suma de las de uso comun y otras que se han estractado de manuscritos antiguos, 1870. 26 p. Br498.21 MP 413.5. Manuscript, transcribed by Karl H. Berendt, Mérida, 1870.

3223. Pérez, Juan Pío. Apuntes para una gramática maya por D. Juan Pío Pérez; copia de los fragmentos en poder de D. Pedro Regil. Mérida, 1868. Br498.21 MP413.4. Manuscript; notes on a Yucatec grammar based on the notes of Juan Pío Pérez.

3224. Pérez, Juan Pío. *Diccionario de la lengua maya*. Imprenta Literaria de Juan F. Molina Solís, Mérida de Yucatán, 1866-1877. 437 p. Br498.21 MP413.3. "This monument of a life-long labor did not appear until some years after the author's death (March 6, 1859). The printing was begun in 1866, interrupted in 1867 by the civil war, during which the manuscript copy came near destruction, and finally completed in 1877. Although Pío Pérez was considered a thorough Maya scholar, errors are not infrequent in his dictionary owing to faulty orthography or typography. Berendt points out *eche* for *ecbe*, *bich* for *abich*, etc., but on the whole his corrections are few. Pérez left his manuscript incomplete, ceasing at the word *ulchabal*. The remainder was prepared by Don Crescencio Carrillo down to *xen*, and from that word to the end, Dr. Berendt. In fullness Pérez's dictionary is much inferior to the *Diccionario de Motul*. Thus, under the letter *A* Pérez gives 586 words and the Motul 2,059, and about this proportion is maintained throughout" (Brinton 1900).

3225. Pérez, Juan Pío. Recetarios de indios en lengua maya: índices de plantas medicinales y de enfermedades coordinados por D. Juan Pío Pérez; con estractos de los recetarios, notas y añadiduras, por C. Hermann Berendt, M.D. Mérida, 1870. 79 p. Br498.21 MP413. Manuscript based on the medical parts of the Books of Chilam Balam; includes many traditional remedies for illnesses and ailments such as colic, worms, stomachaches, snakebites, burns, childbirth complications, gangrene, and depression.

3226. Perier, Joanny A. N. Des races dites Berbères et de leur ethnogénie. *Mémoires de la Société d'Anthropologie de Paris* 1:1-52, 1870. Br572C An8141 v.9.

3227. Perkins, George H. Archaeological researches in the Champlain Valley. *Memoirs of the International Congress of Anthropology*, pp. 84-91, 1894. Br572C An8141 v.136.

3228. Perkins, George H. The stone ax in Vermont: 1. Celts. *American Naturalist* 19(12): 1143-1149, 1885. Br572C An8141 v.13.

3229. Perkins, George H. The stone ax in Vermont: 2. Notched and grooved axes. *American Naturalist* 20(4): 333, 1886. Br572C An8141 v.13.

3230. Perkins, James H. *Annals of the West; Embracing a Concise Account of Principal Events, Which Have Occurred in the Western States and Territories, From the Discovery of the Mississippi Valley to the Year Eighteen Hundred and Fifty*. 2d ed. St. Louis, J. R. Albach, 1850. 25 p. Br978 P413.

3231. Perrot, Nicola. *Mémoire sur les moeurs, coustumes et relligion* [sic] *des sauvages de l'Amérique Septentrionale, par Nicolas Perrot; publié pour la première fois par le R. P. J. Tailhan*. A. Franck, Leipzig, Paris, 1864. 341 p. Br970.1 P424.

Oscar Peschel (from Justin Winsor, Aboriginal America. *Cambridge, MA: Houghton, Mifflin, 1889. p. 391).*

3232. Perthes, Justus. *Atlas antiquus; pocket-atlas of the ancient world, by Alb. Van Kampen.* Justus Perthes, Gotha, 1893. 60 p., 24 col. double maps. Br911.3 P432.

3233. Peschel, Oscar, *Völkerkunde.* Duncker und Humblot, Leipzig, 1874. 570 p. Br572 P435.

3234. Peters, John P. Christ's treatment of the Old Testament. *Journal of Biblical Literature,* pp. 87-105, n.d. Br572C An8141 v.157.

3235. Peters, John P. Notes on the Old Testament. *Journal of Biblical Literature,* pp. 106-117, n.d. Br572C An8141 v.157.

3236. Peters, John P. Some recent results of the University of Pennsylvania excavations at Nippur, especially of the Temple Hill. *Journal of Archaeology* 10:13-46, 1895. Br572C An8141 v.141.

3237. Peters, John P. The seat of the earliest civilization in Babylonia, and the date of its beginning. *Proceedings of the American Oriental Society* 17:163-171, 1896. Br572C An8141 v.157.

3238. Peters, John P. University of Pennsylvania excavations at Nippur: The Nippur Arch. *Journal of Archaeology* 10:352-368, 1895. Br572C An8141 v.141.

3239. Petersen, H. Gravpladsen fra den aeldre jernalder paa Nordrup mark ved ringsted. *Nordiske Fortidsminder* 1:1-14, 1890. Br572C An8141 v.91.

3240. Petersen, H. Polyandre de l'ancien Age de Fer a Nordrup en Selande. *Nordiske Fortidsminder* 1:15-18, 1890. Br572C An8141 v.91.

3241. Petitot, Emile F. *Accord des mythologies dans la cosmogonie des danites arctiques.* Émile Bouillon, Paris, 1890. 493 p. Br398.22 DP443. Petitot joined the Oblates of Mary Immaculate in 1860 and was sent to the missions of the Canadian North in 1862. He lived at Fort Good Hope, Northwest Territories, and traveled extensively among many tribes, especially the Kutchin and Hare. During his stay in the North Petitot became an authority on Indian languages.

3242. Petitot, Emile F. *Chants indigènes du Canada nord-oueste*. *Revue des Traditions Populaires*. 4(11): 590–591, 1889. Br572C An8141 v.49; Br572C An8141 v.84.

3243. Petitot, Emile F. *Dictionnaire de la langue dènè-dindjié dialectes Montagnais or Chippewyan, peaux de lievre et Loucheux renfermant en outre un grand nombre de termes propres à sept autres dialectes de la meme langue; precede d'une monographie des Dènè-Dindjié, d'une grammaire et de tableaux synoptiques des conjugasions; par le R. P. E. Petitot.* Ernest Leroux, Paris; A. L. Bancroft and Company, San Francisco, 1876. 367 p. Br497.11 P44.

3244. Petitot, Emile F. *La station néolithqiue de Mareuil-Lès-Meaux (Seine-et-Marne)*. Imprimerie Marguerith-Dupré, 1895. 30 p. Br572C An8141 v.143.

3245. Petitot, Emile F. *Monographie des Dènè-Dindjié*. Ernest Leroux, Paris, 1876. 109 p. Br497.12 DP 44.

3246. Petitot, Emile F. *Origines et migrations des peuples de la Gaule jusqu'à l'avènement des Francs, ar Émile Petitot*. J. Maisonneuve, Paris, 1894 716 p. Br572.944 P44.

3247. Petitot, Emile F. *Traditions indiennes du Canada nord-ouest*. Maisonneuve Frères et C. Leclerc, Paris, 1886. 521 p. Br398.21 P443; Br398.21 P443a.

3248. Petitot, Emile F. *Vocabulaire français-esquimau. Dialecte des Tchiglit des bouches du Mackenzie et de l'Anderson. Précédé d'une monographie de cette tribu et de notes grammaticales.* Ernest Leroux, Paris, 1876. 76 p. Br497.25 AP44.

3249. Petroff, Ivan. The limit of the Innuit tribes on the Alaskan coast. *American Naturalist* 16:567–575, 1882. Br572C An8141 v.13; Br572C An8141 v.32.

3250. Pfizmaier, August. *Aufklärungen über die Sprache der Koloschen*. Gerold, Wien, 1885. 68. Br572C An8141 v.43.

3251. Pfizmaier, August. *Darlegungen Grönländer Verbalformen*. Gerold, Wien, 1884. 82 p. Br572C An8141 v.43.

3252. Pfizmaier, August. *Der Prophet Jesaias Grönlandisch*. Gerold, Wien, 1886. 78 p. Br572C An8141 v.43.

3253. Pfizmaier, August. *Die Abarten der Grönländischen Sprache*. Gerold, Wien, 1884. 82 p. Br572C An8141 v.43.

3254. Pfizmaier, August. *Die Sprache der Aleuten und Fuchsinseln*. Gerold, Wien, 1884. r572C An8141 v.43.

3255. Pfizmaier, August. *Kennzewichnungen des kalalekischen Sprachstammes*. Gerold, Wien, 1885. 82 p. Br572C An8141 v.43.

3256. Pfleiderer, J. G. *Die Genesis des Mythus der Indogermanischen Völker*. Cavalry, Berlin. 1873. Br572C An8141 v.56.

3257. Philippi, Federico. Reise nach der provinz Tarapaca. pp. 135–163, 1884. Br572C An8141 v.98.

3258. Philippi, Rudolfo A. *Una cabeza humana adorado como dios entre los Jivaros.* Imprenta Nacional, Quito, 1872. Br572C An8141 v.37.

3259. Philips, George M. *Historic Letters from the Collection of the West Chester State*

Normal School. J. B. Lippincott Company, Philadelphia, 1898. Br572C An8141 v.157.

3260. Phillips, Henry. An account of two maps of America published respectively in the years 1550 and 1555. *Proceedings of the American Philosophical Society*, 1880. 3 p. Br572C An8141 v.165.

3261. Phillips, Henry. *An Historical Sketch of the Paper Money Issued by Pennsylvania.* A. C. Kline, Philadelphia1, 1862. Br572C An8141 v.58.

3262. Phillips, Henry. First contribution to the study of folk-lore of Philadelphia and its vicinity. *Proceedings of the American Philosophical Society* 25:159-170, 1888. Br572C An8141 v.88.

3263. Phillips, Henry. Notes upon the Codex Ramirez with a translation of the same. *Proceedings of the American Philosophical Society* 21:616-651, 1884. Br572C An8141 v.28; Br572C An8141 v.39.

3264. Phillips, Henry. On a supposed ruin inscription at Yarmouth, Nova Scotia. *Proceedings of the American Philosophical Society* 21:491-492, 1884. Br572C An8141 v.39.

3265. Pichardo y Tapia, Esteban. *Diccionario provincial, casi-razonado de vozes cubanas.* 3d ed. Imprenta la Antilla, Habana, 186. 281 p. Br467 P583.

3266. Pickering, John. *An Essay on a Uniform Orthography for the Indian Languages of North America.* Hilliard and Metcalf, Cambridge, 1820. 42 p. Br497 P585.2; Br572C An8141 v.96. Originally published as "On the adoption of a uniform orthography for the Indian languages of North America" (*Memoirs of the American Academy of Arts and Sciences* 4(2): 9-360, 1818).

3267. Pickett, Thomas E. *The Testimony of the Mounds Considered With Special Reference to the Pre-Historic Inhabitants of Kentucky and the Adjoining States.* Maysville, Kentucky, 1875. 45 p. Br572C An8141 v.35.

3268. Pierre, R. P. *Viaggio d'esplorazione fra le tribu selvaggie dell'Equatore nell'America del Sud.* San Giuseppe, Milano, 1890. 254 p. Br918.62 P615.

3269. Pierson, A., and J. H. Trumbull, eds. *Some Help for the Indians: A Catechism in the Language of the Quiripi Indians.* Collections of the Connecticut Historical Society, 3. M. H. Mallory and Company, Hartford, 1873. 67 p. Br572C An8141 v.80.

3270. Piétrement, Charles A. *Le Crane de Remagen, le Kertag les Chevux de Rekhmara et el livre Le Cheval, de M. Mégnin.* Asselin et Houzeau, Paris, 1896. 31 p. Br572C An8141 v.157.

3271. Piétrement, Charles A. *Rapport sur un travail de M. Pader intitulé Notes sur une troisième phalange de Cheval provenant de la Grotte de la Salpétrière, Commune de Saint-Laurent-le-Minier, Canton de Sumène (Gard).* Asselin et Houzeau, 1898. 14 p. Br572C An8141 v.157.

3272. Piétrement, Charles A. *Sur les mots solipede et solipédisation.* Typographie et Lith. Maulde, Doumenc et Ce., Paris, n.d. 8 p. Br572C An8141 v.99.

3273. Piette, Edouard, and Joseph de la Porterie. Études d'ethnographie préhistorique, 4: fouilles a Brassempouy en 1896. *L'Anthropologie* 8:165-173, 1897. Br572C An8141 v.99.

3274. Piette, Edouard. *L'Époque éburnéenne et les races humaines de la période Glyptique.* Imprimerie Charles Poette, Saint-Quentin, 1894. 27 p. Br572C An8141 v.132.

3275. Piette, Édouard. Les galets coloriés du Mas d'Azil; 25 panches en chronolithographie gravées par M. Pilloy. *Revue l'Anthropologie* 7(4), 1896. 25 leaves. Br572.05 An8.

3276. Pigorini, Luigi. Di alcuni oggetti ethnologici dell'Ecuador. *Memorie della Classe di Scienze Morali, Storiche e Filologiche, Reale Accademia dei Lincei* 6:3–12, 1881. Roma. Br572C An8141 v.95. Luigi Pigorini (1842-1925) was one of the pioneers of Italian prehistory and ethnographic museology.

3277. Pilling, James C. *Bibliography of the Algonquian Languages*. Bulletin of the Bureau of Ethnology, Smithsonian Institution, 13. Washington, DC, 1891. 614 p. Br497.11B P64. In 1879, John Wesley Powell engaged James Constantine Pilling (1846-1895) for the United States Geographical and Geological Survey of the Rocky Mountain Regions. In 1879 Pilling was appointed chief clerk of the Bureau of American Ethnology. Pilling's *Proof Sheets of a Bibliography* was intended to stimulate interest in Pilling's bibliographic project and to promote cooperation from scholars of American Indian linguistics. Pilling is credited with the early development of the Bureau of American Ethnology library.

3278. Pilling, James C. *Bibliography of the Athapascan Languages*. Bulletin of the Bureau of Ethnology, Smithsonian Institution, 14. Washington, DC, 1892. 125 p. Br497.11 P64.

3279. Pilling, James C. *Bibliography of the Chinookan Languages (Including the Chinook Jargon)*. Bulletin of the Bureau of Ethnology, Smithsonian Institution, 15, Washington, DC, 1893. 81 p. Br497.19B P64.

3280. Pilling, James C. *Bibliography of the Eskimo Language*. Bulletin of the Bureau of Ethnology, Smithsonian Institution, 1. Washington, DC, 1887. 116 p. Br497.25B P64.

3281. Pilling, James C. *Bibliography of the Iroquoian Languages*. Bulletin of the Bureau of Ethnology, Smithsonian Institution, 6. Washington, DC, 1888. 208 p. Br497.27B P64.

3282. Pilling, James C. *Bibliography of the Muskohegan Languages*. Bulletin of the Bureau of Ethnology, Smithsonian Institution, 9. Washington, DC, 1889. 114 p. Br497.25B P64.

3283. Pilling, James C. *Bibliography of the Salishan Languages*. Bulletin of the Bureau of Ethnology, Smithsonian Institution, 16. Washington, DC, 1893. 86 p. Br497.25B P64; Br497.46B P64.

3284. Pilling, James C. *Bibliography of the Siouan Languages*. Bulletin of the Bureau of Ethnology, Smithsonian Institution, 5. Washington, DC, 1887. 87 p. Br497.25B P64; Br497.5B P64.

3285. Pilling, James C. *Bibliography of the Wakashan Languages*. Bulletin of the Smithsonian Institution. Bureau of Ethnology, 19. Washington, DC, 1894. 70 p. Br497.59B P64; Br572C An8141 v.137.

3286. Pilling, James C. *Proof-Sheets of a Bibliography of the Languages of the North American Indians*. Miscellaneous Publication of the Bureau of Ethnology, Smithsonian Institution, 2. Washington, DC, 1885. 1,135 p. Br497B P649.

3287. Pilling, James C. The writings of padre Andres de Olmos in the languages of Mexico. *American Anthropologist* 8(1): 43–60, 1895, 18 p. Br572C An8141 v.137.

3288. Pimentel, Francisco, conde de Heras. *Cuadro descriptivo y comparativo de las lenguas indígenas de México.* Imprenta de Andrade y Escalante, México, 1862-1865. 2 v. Br498 P647.

3289. Pimentel, Francisco, conde de Heras. *Cuadro descriptivo y comparativo de las lenguas indígenas de México, o tratado filologia mexicana.* 2d ed. Tipografia de Isidro Epstein, México, 1874. 426 p. Br498 P647a.

3290. Pimentel, Francisco, conde de Heras. *Memoria sobre las causas que han originado la situación actual de la raza indigena de México, y medios de remediarla, por don Francisco Pimentel.* Imprenta de Andrade y Escalante, México, 1864. 241 p. Br972 P647.

3291. Pinart, Alphonse L. *Aperçu sur l'Île d'Aruba; ses habitants, ses antiquités, ses pétroglyphes.* Paris, 1890. 8 p. Br572C An8141 v.106. Manuscript. Alphonse Pinart (1852-1911) conducted ethnographic and linguistic studies and made museum collections among the Aleut, Koniag Eskimo, and Tlingit in 1871 and 1872. In 1875-876 he spent several months in Arizona and British Columbia, and in 1877-1878 he conducted archaeological studies in the Santa Barbara region of California. From 1882 to 1885 he made expeditions to Panama and Central America. He was a prolific writer and much of his work is important because of its early date and high quality.

3292. Pinart, Alphonse L. *Catalogue des collections rapportées de l'Amérique Russe (aujourd'hui territoire d'Alaska)…exposées dans l'une des galeries du Museum d'Histoire Naturelle de Paris, Section d'Anthropologie.* Imprimerie de J. Claye, Paris, 1872. 30 p. Br572C An8141 v.30.

3293. Pinart, Alphonse L. Chiriqui: Bocas del Toro. *Bulletin de la Société de Géographie* 7(6): 433-452, 1885. 20 p. Br572C An8141 v.30.

3294. Pinart, Alphonse L. *Déformations dentaires artificielles…chez les Indiens de l'Isthme,* 1890. 8 p. Br572C An8141 v.106. Manuscript.

3295. Pinart, Alphonse L. Documentos sobre Panama, Chiriqui, Veraguas, Darien. Br572C An8141 v.106. Reproduction of manuscripts collected by Pinart.

3296. Pinart, Alphonse L. Eskimaux et Koloches: idées religieuses et traditions des Kaniagmioutes. *Revue d'Anthropologie* 2:673-680, 1873. Br572C An8141 v.30.

3297. Pinart, Alphonse L. Exploration de l'Ile de Paques. *Bulletin de la Société de Géographie,* 1878. 23 p. Br572C An8141 v.30.

3298. Pinart, Alphonse L. *La caverne d'Aknañh Île d'Ounga.* Ernest Leroux, Éditeur, Paris, 1875. 11 p. Br572C An8141 v.90.

3299. Pinart, Alphonse L. Les Aléoutes et leur origines et leurs légendes. *Actes de la Société d'Ethnographie de Paris* 3:87-92, 1872. Br572C An8141 v.30.

3300. Pinart, Alphonse L. Limite des civilisations dans l'Isthme Américain; petroglyphes et notes anthropologiques. Paris, 1890. 8 p. Br572C An8141 v.106. Facsimile of a Pinart manuscript.

3301. Pinart, Alphonse L. Note sur les pétroglyphes et antiquités des Grandes et Petites Antilles. Paris, 1890. 16 p. Br572C An8141 v.106. Manuscript; published in *Annual Report of the Bureau of Ethnology, Smithsonian Institution* 10:136-140, 1893.

3302. Pinart, Alphonse L. Notes sur les Koloches. *Bulletin de la Société d'Anthropologie de Paris* 7, 1872. 23 p. Br572C An8141 v.30.

3303. Pinart, Alphonse L. *Noticias de los indios del departamento de Veragua, y vocabularios de las lenguas guaymi, norteño, sabanero y dorasque.* Bancroft, San Francisco, 1882. 73 p. Br498.16 CP65.

3304. Pinart, Alphonse L. Recent literature: Bonaparte's Suriname. *American Naturalist* 19:868-869, 1885. Br572C An 8141 v. 13;.Br572C An8141 v.82.

3305. Pinart, Alphonse L. Sur les Atnahs. *Revue de Philologie et d'Ethnographie* 1:120-127, 1875. Br572C An8141 v.119.

3306. Pinart, Alphonse L. *Vocabulario castellano guaymie, dialectos move-valiente norteño y guaymie-penonomeño.* Leroux, Paris, 1892. 79 p. Br498.16 CP652a.

3307. Pinart, Alphonse L. Vocabulario castellano-cuna, compuesto por el Sr. Dr. Alfonso L. Pinart, Panama, 1882-1884. 20 leaves. Br572C An8141 v.106. Manuscript.

3308. Pinart, Alphonse L. *Vocabulario castellano-cuna.* Petite Bibliothèque Américaine, 1. Ernest Leroux, Paris, 1890. 63 p. Br498.16 CP652.

3309. Pinart, Alphonse L. *Vocabulario castellano-dorasque, dialectos chumulu, gualaca y changuina.* Leroux, Paris, 1890. 42 p. Br498.16 CP652a.

3310. Pinart, Alphonse L. Voyage dans l'Arizona. *Bulletin de la Société de Géographie,* 1877. 16 p. Br572C An8141 v.30.

3311. Pineda, Emeterio. *Descripción geografica del departamento de Chiapas y Soconusco.* I. Cumplido, México, 1845. 150 p. Br917.2 P653.

3312. Pineda, Vicente. *Historia de las sublevaciones indígenas habidas en el Estado de Chiapas; gramática de la lengua tzel-tal que habla la generalidad de los habitantes de los pueblos que quedan al oriente y al noreste del estado; y diccionario de la misma, por el lic. Vicente Pineda.* Tipografía del Gobierno, Chiapas, 1888. 340 p. Br498.21 TzP 653.

3313. Pittier, Henri, and C. Gagini. *Ensayo lexicografico sobre la lengua de Térraba.* Tipografía Nacional, San José, 1892. 86 p. Br572C An8141 v.129.

3314. Pittier, Henri, and Friedrich Müller. *Die Sprache der Bribri-Indianer in Costa Rica.* Akademie der Wissenschaften, Vienna. Philosohisch-Historische Clase. Sitzungsberichte, Bd. 138. In Commission bei C. Gerold's Sohn, Wien, 1898. 149 p. Br498.13 TBP684.

3315. Pittier, Henri. *Primera contribución para el estudio de las razas indígenas de Costa Rica.* Tipografía Nacional, San José, 1897. 15 p. Br913.7286 P68.

3316. Pittier, Henri. Viaje de' exploración al valle del Río Grande de Térraba. *Anales del Instituto Fisico-Geográfico Nacional* 3:3-138, 1890. Br572C An8141 v.129.

3317. Pláticas de la historia sagrada en lengua cacchi, con un fragmento de un tratado por Fr. Domingo de Vico, 1629. 18 leaves. Br498.21 KP698. Manuscript.

3318. Pláticas de la historia sagrada en lengua cacchii del siglo XVII mo. 126 leaves. Br498.21 KP698a. "Manuscript, original, several of the leaves nearly destroyed and the whole much stained" (Brinton 1900); introduction signed "Dr. C. Hermann Berendt, Cobán, abril 1875."

3319. Platicas piadosas en lengua mexicana vulgar de Guatemala, n.d. 59-71 leaves.

Br498.22 AzP 698. Manuscript; from the library of Charles E. Brasseur de Bourbourg.

3320. Pláticas sobre los mandamientos de la ley de Dios en el idioma kekchí, n.d. 8 p. Br498.212 KC684. Manuscript; transcription by Karl H. Berendt, 1855, forms only a part of the "Primer mandamiento of Platicas sobre los mandamientos del decálogo en lengua kekchí," which manuscript Berendt had begun to copy.

3321. Pláticas sobre los mandamientos del decálogo en lengua kekchí, traducidos por un indio de Cobán de orden del padre cura; del archivo de la parroquia de Cahabón, 1856. 184 leaves. Br498.21 KP699. Original manuscript containing eleven sermons written by the cura of Cobán, Alta Verapaz, between 1853 and 1856.

3322. Platt, Luciano. *Nociones prácticas y esperimentos nuevos sobre el trabajo del añil.* Imprenta de La Democracia, San Salvador, 1872. 57 p. Br572C An8141 v.69.

3323. Platzmann, Julius. *Abschrift eines im Privatbesitz des Herrn von Guelich dei findlichern Handschriftlichen Guaraní fragmentes im Autrage...für Herrn Karl Hemming amgefertist durch Emanuel Forchammer.* Leipzig, 1878. 156 p. Br498.75 GP697.

3324. Platzmann, Julius. *Algunas obras raras sobre la lengua cumanagota, publicadas de nuevo por Julio Platzmann.* B. G. Teubner, Leipzig, 1888. 5 v. Br498.78 CP69. Contents include: 1. "Arte, Bocabulario, Doctrina christiana y Catecismo de la lengua de Cumana, compuestos por el R.P. Fr. Francisco de Tauste"; 2. "Principios y reglas de la lengua cummanagota, compuestos por el R.P. Fr. Manuel de Yangues con un Diccionario"; 3. "Arte y Tesoro de la lengua cumanagota por Fr. Matias Ruiz Blanco"; 4. "Confessonario mas breve en lengua cumanagota por Fr. Diego de Tapia."

3325. Platzmann, Julius. *Amerikanisch-asiatische Etymologien via Behringstrasse 'From the East to the West.'* Druck von B. G. Trübner, Leipzig, 1871. 112 p. Br498.03 P698.

3326. Platzmann, Julius. *Glosser der feuerländischen Sprache von Julius Platzmann.* B. G. Trübner, Leipzig, 1882. 22 p. Br498.978 P 69. Based upon Thomas Bridge's translation of St. Luke's Gospel into the Yahgan dialect (London, 1881).

3327. Platzmann, Julius. *Irokesen, entnommen der veröffentlichungen des Abbé Cuoq.* Gedruckt bei E. Polz, Leipzig, 1879. 8 p. Br572C An8141 v.71.

3328. Platzmann, Julius. *Verzeichnis der Seitherigen Publikationen.* B. G. Teubner, Leipzig, n.d. Br572C An8141 v.60.

3329. Platzmann, Julius. *Verzeichniss einer Auswahl amerikanischer Grammatiken, Wörterbücher, Katechismen.* K. F. Köhler, Leipzig, 1876. 38 p. Br497B P69.

3330. Platzmann, Julius. *Wesshalb ich neudrucke der alten amerikanischen grammatiker veranlasst habe, von Julius Platzmann.* Druck von B. G. Trübner, Leipzig, 1893. 136 p. Br497 P687.

3331. Playfair, R. Lambert. *A Bibliography of Algeria; From the Expedition of Charles V in 1541 to 1887.* J. Murray, London, 1888. Br965B P69.

3332. Playfair, R. Lambert. *Bibliography of Tripoli and the Cyrenaica.* Supplementary Papers of the Royal Geographical Society 2(4): 557–614, 1889. Br961.2B P69.

3333. Pleyte, C. M. *Systematische Beschrijving eener Ethnographische Verzomeling Bi-*

jeengebracht ter Noordkust van Ceram. E. J. Brill, Leiden, 1894, 18 p. Br572C An8141 v.135.

3334. Pleyte, W. *Zur Geschichte der Hieroglyphenschrift; nach dem Holländischen von Carl Abel.* Verlag von Wilhelm Friedrich, Leipzig, 1890. 48 p. Br572C An8141 v.46.

3335. Podhorsky, Josef M. O puvodu americkeho lidstva. Braze, Grégra, 1889. 17 p. Br572.97 P753.

3336. Pohlman, Julius. A study in heads. *Buffalo Medical Journal,* August, 1895. 4 p. Br572C An8141 v.141.

3337. Pohlman, Julius. Duration of life of the nervous American. *Medical News,* 1893. 8 p. Br572C An8141 v.128; Br572C An8141 v.129.

3338. Pohlman, Julius. *On the Origin of the Eastern End of Lake Erie.* Bigelow Brothers, Buffalo, 1884. 3 p. Br572C An8141 v.41.

3339. Polak, J. E. R. *A Grammar and a Vocabulary of the Ipuriná Language.* Kegan Paul, Trench, Trübner, London, 1894. 111 p. Br572C An8141 v.135.

3340. Polland, G. *The Pamunkey Indians of Virginia.* Government Printing Office, Washington, DC, 1894. 19 p. Br572C An8141 v.136.

3341. Pond, Gideon H. Dakota superstitions. *Collections of the Minnesota Historical Society* 2(3): 32-62, 1867. Br572C An8141 v.27.

3342. Pope, John. *A Tour Through the Southern and Western Territories of the United States of North-America; The Spanish Dominions on the River Mississippi, and the Floridas; The Countries of the Creek Nations; And Many Uninhabited Parts.* Printed by John Dixon, for the author and his three children. Alexander D. Pope, Lucinda C. Pope, and Anne Pope, Richmond, 1792. 105 p. Br917.3 P81.

3343. Porter, Thomas C. Indian hieroglyphics on the Susquehanna, 1865. 3 p. Br572C An8141 v.38.

3344. Portilla, Anselmo de la. *Información recibida en México y Puebla, el año de 1565, a solicitud del gobernador y cabildo de naturales de Tlaxcala, sobre los servicios que prestaron los Tlaxcaltecas á Hernán Cortés en la conquista de México, siendo los testigos algunos de los mismos conquistadores.* Escalante, México, 1875. 204 p. Br972.4 P83.

3345. Posada, Ramon M. Miscelanea en lengua yndia-kiche, n.d. 263 p. Br498.21KiP 842. Manuscript.

3346. Post, Albert H. Ethnological jurisprudence; translated from the manuscript of Dr. Albert Hermann Post by Thomas J. McCormack. *The Monist* 2(1): 31-40, 1891. Br572C An8141 v.8.

3347. Post, Albert H. *Grundriss der ethnologischen Jurisprudenz.* Schulze'sche Hof-Buchhandlung, A. Schwartz, Oldenburg, Leipzig, 1894–1895. 2 v. Br572 P843.

3348. Post, V. H. Ethnologische Gedanken. *Globus* 59(19), n.d 4 p. Br572C An8141 v.107.

3349. Potier, Pierre. Elementa grammaticae huronicae & de litteris, ca. 1750. 173 p. Br497.27 WP848. Manuscript; includes a grammar of Huron, a census dated 1745, a list of Huron groups, and English and French settlements with their names in Huron and French.

3350. Potter, W. B. Archaeological remains in southeastern Missouri. In *Contributions to the Archaeology of Missouri, by the Archaeological Section of the St. Louis Academy of Science.* v. 1, pp. 5-20. George A. Bates, Naturalist's Bureau, Salem, 1880. Br572C An8141 v.90.

3351. Powell, John W. *Address.* Gibson Bros, Washington, DC, 1884. 20 p. Br572C An8141 v.29. Despite periodic fieldwork among the Shoshone, Ute, and Paiute of the Great Basin and Grand Canyon regions, John Wesley Powell's (1834-1902) influence in anthropology lay in his strong unilinear evolutionism and his founding of the Smithsonian Institution's Bureau of American Ethnology, which he directed from 1879 to 1902. The Bureau sponsored the survey of North American Indian mounds by Cyrus Thomas, the collection of Native American vocabularies, the 1891 linguistic map of North America, and the fieldwork of Frank Hamilton Cushing, Matilda Coxe Stevenson, James Mooney, Victor and Cosmos Mindeleff, William Henry Holmes, and others.

3352. Powell, John W. Human evolution. *Transactions of the Anthropological Society of Washington* 2:176-208, 1883. Br572C An8141 v.29.

3353. Powell, John W. *Introduction to the Study of Indian Languages; With Words, Phrases, and Sentences to be Collected.* Government Printing Office, Washington, DC, 1877. 104 p. Br497P87.

3354. Powell, John W. *Introduction to the Study of Indian Languages; With Words, Phrases, and Sentences to be Collected.* 2d ed. Government Printing Office, Washington, DC, 1880. 228 p. Br497 P87a.

3355. Powell, John W. *James Constantine Pilling (1846-1895).* n.d. 13 p. Br572C An8141 v.141.

3356. Powell, John W. Mythologic philosophy. *Popular Science Monthly* 15:765-808, 1879. Br572C An8141 v.29.

3357. Powell, John W. *On Primitive Institutions.* Dando Printing and Publishing, Philadelphia, 1896. 21 p. Br572C An8141 v.157.

3358. Powell, John W. Outlines of sociology; presidential address to the Anthropological Society of Washington, DC, February 2, 1882. *Transactions of the Anthropological Society of Washington*, pp. 106-129, 1882. Br572C An8141 v.29.

3359. Powell, John W. Outlines of the philosophy of the North American Indians; read before the American Geographical Society at Chickering Hall, December, 1876. New York, 1877. 19 p. Br572C An8141 v.29.

3360. Powell, John W. Relation of primitive peoples to environment, illustrated by American examples. *Annual Report of the United States National Museum, Smithsonian Institution, for 1895*, pp. 625-637, 1896. Br572C An8141 v.157.

3361. Powell, John W. *The Philosophic Bearings of Darwinism: An Address Delivered Before the Biological Society of Washington at the Darwin Memorial Meeting, May 12, 1882.* Judd and Detweiler, 1882. 13 p. Br572C An8141 v.29.

3362. Powell, John W. Wyandotte government: a short study of tribal society. *Annual Report of the Bureau of Ethnology, Smithsonian Institution, for 1879*, pp. 59-69, 1880. Br572C An8141 v.29.

3363. Powell, W. D. *Black Christ of Toluca; or Romanism As It Is In Mexico.* Maryland

John W. Powell (from Justin Winsor, Aboriginal America. *Cambridge, MA: Houghton, Mifflin, 1889. p. 411).*

Baptist Mission Rooms, Baltimore, 1829. 16 p. Br262 P872.

3364. Powers, Stephen. *Tribes of California: Comparative Vocabularies of Northern California Indian Tribes.* Smithsonian Institution, Contributions to American Ethnology, 3. Government Printing Office, Washington, DC, 1877. 635 p. Br557.3 Un319. Powers (1840-1904), a newspaper journalist and author, was commissioned in 1875 to make a collection of Indian material culture on the eastern slope of the Sierras and in California for the Centennial Exposition of 1876. His *Tribes of California* is a basic work on California ethnography and was the first attempt to treat the indigenous cultures systematically.

3365. Poyet, C. F. Notices géographiques...des différentes loaclitiés du Mexique, 1863. 40 p. Br572C An8141 v.34.

3366. *Prähistorische Blätter.* v. 9(1-6)-10(1-6), 1897-1898. München. Br913.05 P88.

3367. Prato, Slanislao. *Le novelle del mambriano del cieco da Ferrara esposte ed illustrado da Giuseppe Rua.* Alfred Dörffel, Leipzig, 1889. 13 p. Br572C An8141 v.120.

3368. Prato, Stanislao. *Le dodici parole della verità; novellina-cantilena popolare considerata nelle varie redazioni italiane e straniere.* Tipografia del Giornale di Sicilia, Palermo, 1892. 68 p. Br572C An8141 v.120.

3369. Prato, Stanislao. *Quelques contes littéraires dans la tradition populaire.* Maisonneuve et Ch. Leclerc, Émile Lechevalier, Paris, 1889. 16 p. Br572C An8141 v.120.

3370. Prato, Stanislao. *Une particularité du livre de Tobie et la tradition populaire.* Aux Bureau de La Tradition, Paris, 1889. 14 p. Br572C An8141 v.120.

3371. Presbytery of Buffalo. *Second Report to the Presbytery of Buffalo of a Committee Appointed to Investigate Charges Made Against the Indians of Western New York*. Presbytery of Buffalo, Buffalo, 1890. 22 p. Br572C An8141 v.34.

3372. *Prêtre missionaire de la Nouvelle-Grenade; notice sur plusieurs langues indiennes de la Nouvelle-Grenade, aujourd'hui États-Unis de la Colombie, Amérique du Sud*. Paris, 1899. 8 p. Br572C An8141 v.60.

3373. Priest, Josiah. *American Antiquities and Discoveries in the West; Being an Exhibition of the Evidence That An Ancient Population of Partially Civilized Nations Differing Entirely From Those of the Present Indians Peopled America Many Centuries Before Its Discovery by Columbus, and Inquiries Into Their Origin, With a Copious Description of Many of Their Stupendous Works Now in Ruins, With Conjectures Concerning What May Have Become of Them*. 4th ed. Hoffman and White, Albany, NY, 1838. 400 p. Br913.7 P934a.

3374. *Primer calendario civil, histórico y religioso del Fenix*. Campeche, 1851. Br313.726 P735. Bound with *Calendario…arreglado al meridiano de Mérida* (1852-1853, 1858, 1867-1872, 1876-1877).

3375. Prince, J. Dyneley. Notes on the language of the eastern Algonkin tribes. *Journal of Philology* 9(3), 1888. 9 p. Br572C An8141 v.157.

3376. Prince, J. Dyneley. Some Passamaquoddy documents. *Annals of the New York Academy of Sciences* 11:369-377. New York. Br497.11 AP93.

3377. Prince, J. Dyneley. The Pssamaquoddy wampum records. *Proceedings of the American Philosophical Society* 36(156): 479-495, 1897. Br572C An8141 v.99.

3378. *Proceso instruido á los ex-ministros de estado, señores D. Luis G. Cuevas, D. Manuel Diez de Bonilla, D. Manuel Piña y Cuevas y D. Teofilo Marín, y ex-gobernador del Distrito D. Miguel María Azcárate; acusados de usurpación del poder público por las funciones que desempeñaron en la República entre los años de 1858 y 1860; artículo de incompetencia*. Imprenta de J.M. Lara, México, 1861. 233, 220 p. Br917.2 R144. Contents include: "Introducción"; "Exposición al Tribunal Superior del Distrito Federal, por M[anuel] Piña y Cuevas"; "Informé de J[osé] F[ernando] Ramírez, defensor de M[anuel] Diez de Bonilla"; "Informé de J[ose] M[aria] Cuevas, defensor de L[uis] G[onzaga] Cuevas"; "Informé de M[anuel de] Castañeda y Nájera, defensor de M[iguel] M[aría] Azcárate"; "Informé de E[ulalio] M[aría] Ortega, defensor de M[anuel] Piña y Cuevas, y T[eófilo] Marín"; "Auto de vista pronunciado por la Primera sala del Tribunal Superior, confirmando el del juez del Distrito. Observaciones"; "Auto denegatorio de la súplica. Observaciones"; "Exposición del L[uis] G[onzaga] Cuevas al Tribunal Superior del Distrito Federal."

3379. *Professor Aguchekikos on Totemism*. Edward Bumpus, London, 1886. 15 p. Br572C An8141 v.88.

3380. Proudfit, S.V. A collection of stone implements from the District of Columbia. *Proceedings of the United States National Museum, Smithsonian Institution* 13:187-194, n.d. Br572C An8141 v.12.

3381. Pruner-Bey, M. Discussion sur les Américaines. In *De Pathologie et de clinique medicales*, pp. 417-432, 1883. Paris. Br572C An8141 v.10.

3382. Pruner-Bey, M. Rapport sur l'ouvrage de M. Brasseur de Bourbourg: Grammaire de la langue quiché et vocabulaire; Drame quiché Rabinal Achi; Musique du Guatemala, Paris, 1862. pp. 8-16, 1863. Br572C An8141 v.48.

3383. Purry, Jean P. *Memorial Presented to His Grace, My lord the Duke of Newcastle, Upon the Present Condition of Carolina, and the Means of its Amelioration, by Jean Pierre Purry.* Privately printed, Augusta, 1880. 24 p. Br572C An8141 v.64.

3384. Putman, J. J. *Bida di besoe kriestoe, nos di bienoe adorabel sabador I libradoor.* Martinus, St. Rosa, Curaçao, 1852. 42 p. Br498.78 BP 98.

3385. Putnam, Charles E. Elephant pipes and inscribed tablets in the Museum of the Academy of Natural Sciences, Davenport, Iowa. *Proceedings of the Davenport Academy of Natural Sciences* 4:255-347, 1886. Br572C An8141 v.20; Br572C An8141 v.117.

3386. Putnam, Charles E. *Vindication of Authenticity of the Elephant Pipes and Incised Tablets in the Davenport Academy of Natural Science, From the Accusations of the Bureau of Ethnology, of the Smithsonian Institution.* Davenport, IA, 1885. Br572C An8141 v.39.

3387. Putnam, Frederick W. Archaeological explorations in Tennessee. *Annual Reports of the Trustees of the Peabody Museum of American Archaeology and Ethnology* 2(2): 305-360, 1878. Br913.07 H265. Putnam (1839-1915) was a major institution-builder in early American anthropology. He studied zoology with Louis Agassiz and Asa Gray at Harvard and, after the death of Jeffries Wyman in 1874, was appointed director of the Peabody Museum of American Archaeology and Ethnology at Harvard. He was a founding member of the Archaeological Institute of America and from 1891 to 1894 serves as Chief of the Department of Ethnology of the World's Columbian Exposition in Chicago. From 1894 to 1903 he was curator of anthropology at the American Museum of Natural History and, in 1903, he founded the Department of Anthropology at the University of California, Berkeley.

3388. Putnam, Frederick W. Archaeological researches in Kentucky and Indiana, 1874. *Proceedings of the Boston Society of Natural History* 17:314-332, 1875. Br572C An8141 v.39.

3389. Putnam, Frederick W. Conventionalism in ancient American art. *Bulletin of the Essex Institute* 18:155-167, 1886. Br572C An8141 v.20.

3390. Putnam, Frederick W. Explorations in Ohio; the Marriott Mound, No. 1, and its contents. *Annual Reports of the Trustees of the Peabody Museum of American Archaeology and Ethnology* 3(5-6): 449-466, 1886. Br913.07 H265.

3391. Putnam, Frederick W. Mounds at Merom and Hutsonville on the Wabash. *Proceedings of the Boston Society of Natural History* 15:28-35, 1872. Br572C An8141 v.39.

3392. Putnam, Frederick W. Notes on the copper objects from North and South America contained in the collections of the Peabody Museum. *Annual Reports of the Trustees of the Peabody Museum of American Archaeology and Ethnology* 3(2): 83-148, 1882. Br913.07 H265.

3393. Putnam, Frederick W. Remarks upon chipped stone implements. *Bulletin of the Essex Institute* 15:137–142, 1883. Br572C An8141 v.41.

3394. Putnam, Frederick W. Report of the Peabody Museum of American Archaeology and Ethnology. Cambridge, MA, 1892. 13 p. Br572C An8141 v.124.

3395. Putnam, Frederick W. Report of the Peabody Museum of American Archaeology and Ethnology. Cambridge, MA, 1893. 10 p. Br572C An8141 v.127.

3396. Putnam, Frederick W. The first notice of the Pine Grove or Forest River shellheap. *Bulletin of the Essex Institute* 15:86–92, 1883. Br572C An8141 v.41.

3397. Putnam, Frederick W. The manufacture of soapstone pots by the Indians of New England. *Annual Reports of the Trustees of the Peabody Museum of American Archaeology and Ethnology* 2(2): 273–276, 1878. Br913.07 H265.

3398. Putnam, Frederick W. The Peabody Museum of American Archaeology and Ethnology. *Proceedings of the American Antiquarian Society*, 1889. 11 p. Br572C An8141 v.110.

3399. Putnam, Frederick W. The Peabody Museum of American Archaeology and Ethnology in Cambridge. *Proceedings of the American Antiquarian Society*, 1890. 13 p. Br572C An8141 v.17; Br572C An8141 v.110.

3400. Putnam, Frederick W. The Peabody Museum of American Archaeology and Ethnology, 1895. 9 p. Br572C An8141 v.157.

3401. Putnam, Frederick W. The Peabody Museum of American Archaeology and Ethnology, 1896. 11 p. Br572C An8141 v.157.

3402. Putnam, Frederick W. The Peabody Museum's explorations in Ohio. *American Naturalist* 20(11): 1018–1027, 1886. Br572C An8141 v.13.

3403. Putnam, Frederick W. The way bone fish-hooks were made in the Little Miami Valley. *Annual Reports of the Trustees of the Peabody Museum of American Archaeology and Ethnology* 3(7): 581–586, 1887. Br913.07 H265.

3404. Putnam, Frederick W. *Thirty-First Report of the Peabody Museum of American Archaeology and Ethnology, Harvard University, 1896-1897.* Cambridge, MA, 1898. 16 p. Br572C An8141 v.99.

3405. Putnam, Frederick W. *World's Columbian Exposition, Chicago, USA, 1893: Plan and Classification.* World's Columbian Exposition, Chicago, 1892. 27 p. Br572C An8141 v.88.

3406. Putnam, Frederick W., and C. C. Willoughby. Symbolism in ancient American art. *Proceedings of the American Association for the Advancement of Science* 44:302–322, 1896. Br572C An8141 v.157.

3407. Quandt, Christlieb. *Nachricht von Suriname und seinen Einwohnern; sonderlich den Arawacken, Waraün und Karaiben, von den nüzlichsten Gewächsen und thieren des Landes, des Geschäften der dortigen Missionarien der Brüderunität und der Sprache der Arawacken. Nebst einer Charte und zwey kupfern.* Gedruckt bey J. G. Burghart, Görlitz, 1807. 316 p. Br913.8 Q23.

3408. Quaritch, Bernard. *General Catalogue of America, And Circumnavigation of the Globe; Including Also Voyages of Discovery in the Atlantic and Pacific Oceans, And in the Polar Regions.* Quaritch, London, 1879. Br970B Q2.2. From pp. 1144-1270 of part III of his *Bibliotheca Geographica-Linguistica.*

3409. Quatrefages de Bréau, Armand de. *Histoire générale des races humaines; introduction à l'étude des races humaines.* A. Hennuyer, Paris, 1899. 618 p. Br572 Q2.2. In 1855 Quatrefages (1810-1892) was named to the chair of anthropology at the Muséum d'Histoire Naturelle in Paris. He approached various problems posed by the study of man from the perspective of a naturalist, and fought the theory of the primate origin of man and the ideas of Charles Darwin.

3410. Quelch, J. J. *Carib remains from Pln. Mon Repos.* Argosy, Demerara, 1894. 7 p. Br572C An8141 v.143.

3411. Quesada, Vicente G. Estudios históricos. *Revista de Buenos Aires*, 1864. 103 p. Br572C An8141 v.33.

3412. Questionnaire de sociologie et d'ethnographie. *Bulletin de la Société d'Anthropologie*, 1883. 24 p. Br572C An8141 v.26.

3413. *Questions on the Apostles' Creed, With Other Simple Instruction, for the Warau Indians at the Missions in Guiana.* W. M. Watts, for the Society for Promoting Christian Knowledge, London, 1890. 16 p. Br498.77 AC 47; Br498.77 ArQ 34.

3414. *Questions on the Apostles' Creed, With Other Simple Instruction, for the Arawak Indians at the Missions in Guiana; With A Card for Distribution Among the Indians.* W. M. Watts, London, 1860. 16 p. Br498.77 ArQ 34.

3415. *Questions on the Apostles' Creed, With Other Simple Instruction, for the Accowoio Indians, Containing the Lord's Prayer and the Apostle's Creed*, n.d. 2 p. Br498.77 ArQ 34.

3416. *Questions on the Apostles' Creed, With Other Simple Instruction, for the Caribi Indians at the Missions in Guiana.* William M. Watts, Crown Court, Temple Bar, London, 1880. Br498.77 ArQ 34; Br572C An8141 v.84. Includes Lord's Prayer, Apostles' Creed, Ten Commandments, etc., in the Carib dialects of Upper Pomeroon and Isororo.

3417. Quetelet, Adolphe. Sur les indiens O-jib-be-wa's et les proportions de leur corps. *Bulletins des Académie Royale de Belgique* 13(2), 1860. 11 p. Br572C An8141 v.34. Quetelet (1796-1874), a mathematician and astronomer, was founder of the Observatory of Belgium and played an important role in the development of the sciences in Belgium. He sought to establish social laws comparable to physical laws. His major contribution was his application of probability to the interpretation of data for phenomena that were not susceptible to experimental verification.

3418. Quick, Edgar R. Stone mounds on the Whitewater. *Bulletin of the Society of Natural History* 1:3-5, 1885. Br572C An8141 v.20.

3419. Quintana, Augustín de. Confessonario en lengua mixe; con una construcción de las oraciones de la doctrina christiana y un compendio de voces mixes para ensenarse a pronunciar la dicha lengua; escrito todo por el R. P. Augustín de Quintana, cura que fué de la doctrina de San Juan Bautista de Xvquila, año de 1733. 202 p. Br498.35 MQ45a. Transcript by Karl H. Berendt of *Confes-*

*sonario en lengua mixe; con una construcción de las oraciones de la doc-
trina christiana, y un compendio de voces mixes, para enseñarse a pronunciar la dicha lengua; escrito todo por el P. Fr. Augustín de Quintana de
la Orden de Predicadores, cura q. fué de la doctrina de S. Juan Bautista de
Xuquila; dedicalo al Glorioso Apostol de la Europa, S. Vicente Ferrer* (En la
Puebla: Por la Viuda de Miguel de Ortega, año de 1733); Spanish and Mixe
arranged in parallel columns.

3420. Quintana, Augustin de. Las oraciones de la doctrina christiana, compuestas del
analisis que el ellos trae el confessionario en lengua mixe. 1733. Br498.35 MQ
45.2. Manuscript, transcribed by Karl H. Berendt, 1871.

3421. Quiroga, Adán. *Calchaquí; ilustraciones de Fernán Gonzalez.* Imprenta Española,
Tucumán, 1897. 492 p. Br980.3 CQ45.

3422. Quiroz Yolcecel, B. *La enseñanza nahuatl.* Oficina Tipo. de la Secretaría de Fomento, 1889, 18 p. Br572C An8141 v.92.

3423. Radloff, Leopold, and Anton Schiefner. *Wörterbuch der Kinai-Sprache; Herausgegeben von A. Schiefner.* Mémoires de l'Académie Impériale des Sciences de St.
Pétersbourg, VII sér., t. 21(8). Académie Impériale des Sciences, St. Pétersbourg,
1874. 33 p. Br497.12 KR113.

3424. Rafinesque, Constantine S. *The Ancient Monuments of North and South America.* 2d ed. Printed for the author, Philadelphia, 1838. 28 p. Br913 R123. Constantine
Samuel Rafinesque-Schmaltz (1783-1840) first recognized the Maya inscriptions
of Palenque and the Codex Dresden as the same writing system, the first to real-
ize the values of the bars and dots in the Maya numerical system, and suggested
that the language represented by this script is still spoken.

3425. Rafn, Karl C. View of the ancient geography of the Arctic regions of America.
Transactions of the American Ethnological Society 2:209-214, 1848. Br572C
An8141 v.40.

3426. Rahon, Joseph. Recherches sur les ossements humains anciens et préhistoriques
en vue de la reconstitution de la taille; époques Quaternaire, Néolithique, Protohis-
torique et Moyen Age. *Mémoires de la Société d'Anthropologie de Paris*
4:403-458, 1893. Br572C An8141 v.121.

3427. Raimondi, Antonio. On the Indian tribes of the Great District of Loreto, in northern Peru. *Anthropological Review* 1:33-48, 1863. Br572C An8141 v.33.

3428. Ramírez, Antonio de Guadalupe. *Breve compendio de todo lo que debe saber, y
entender el christiano para poder lograr, ver, conocer, y gozar de Dios nuestro
señor en el cielo eternamente.* Imprenta Nueva Madrileña de los Herederos del
Lic. J. de Jauregui, México, 1785. 9 p. 80 p. Br498.23 OR 143. A brief catechism preceded by an explanation of the Otomi alphabet and pronunciation.

3429. Ramírez, José F. *Bibliotheca Mexicana, or a Catalogue of the Library of Rare
Books and Important Manuscripts Relating to Mexico and Other Parts of Span-
ish America; Formed by the Late José Fernando Ramirez...Comprising Fine
Specimens of the Presses of the Early Mexican Typographers, Juan Cromberger,
Juan Pablos, Antonio Espinosa, Pedro Ocharte, Pedro Balli, Antonio Ricardo,*

Karl C. Rafn (from Justin Winsor, Aboriginal America. *Cambridge, MA: Houghton, Mifflin, 1889. p. 90).*

Melchior Ocharte; a Large Number of Works, Both Printed and MS., on the Mexican Indian Languages and Dialects; the Civil and Ecclesiastical History of Mexico and Its Provinces; Collections of Laws and Ordinances Relating to the Indies; Valuable Unpublished Manuscripts Relating to the Jesuit Missions in Texas, California, China, Peru, Chile, Brasil, Etc. G. Norman and Son, London, 1880. 165 p. Br972B R14.

3430. *Ramona Mission and the Mission Indians.* The Women's National Indian Association, 1889, 18 p. Br572C An8141 v.10.

3431. Rand, Silas T. *A First Reading Book in the Micmac Language; Comprising the Micmac Numerals, and the Names of the Different Kinds of Beasts, Birds, Fishes, Trees, &c. of the Maritime Provinces of Canada. Also, Some of the Indian Names of Places, and Many Familiar Words and Phrases, Translated Literally into English.* Nova Scotia Printing Company, Halifax, Nova Scotia, 1875. 108p. Br497.11 McR15.2. Bound with: *Pela kesagunoodumum kawa, tan tula uksakumamenoo westowoolkw' Sasoogoole Clistawit; ootenink; Megumawcesimk* (Megumagea Ledakun weekugemkawa Moweome, Cebooktook (Halifax, Nova Scotia), 1871. 126 p.).

3432. Rand, Silas T. *A Short Statement of Facts Relating to the History, Manners, Customs, Language and Literature of the Micmac Tribe of Indians in Nova-Scotia and P.E. Island; Being the Substance of Two Lectures Delivered in Halifax, in November, 1849, At the Public Meetings Held for the Purpose of Instituting a Mis-*

sion to That Tribe. J. Bowes, Halifax, Nova Scotia, 1850. 40p. Br497.11 McR 15. Bound with: *Cisulc uceluswocn agenudasic* (Halifax, 1850. 16 p.); *History of Poor Sarah; A Pious Indian Woman* (Halifax, 1850. 12 p.); *Micmac Mission* (Hantsport, 1892. 22 p.). Written by Rand, a missionary, for the purposes of raising money for the Mission. Chapter 3 contains grammatic forms and specimens of the Micmac language.

3433. Rand, Silas T. *A Specimen of the Micmac Dictionary; Being Prepared at the Expense of the Dominion Government of Canada.* Hantsport, Nova Scotia, 1885. 8 p. Br572C An8141 v.60.

3434. Rand, Silas T. *Dictionary of the Language of the Micmac Indians, Who Reside in Nova Scotia, New Brunswick, Prince Edward Island, Cape Breton and Newfoundland.* Nova Scotia Printing Company, Halifax, Nova Scotia, 1888. 286 p. Br497.11 McR15.3.

3435. Rand, Silas T. *Legends of the Micmac Indians; Extracts From the Micmac Prayer Book, With Interlinear Translation into English.* Longmans, Green, New York, London, 1894. 452 p. Br497.11 McR15.4.

3436. Rand, Silas T. *Nine Indian Legendary Tales, Written Down in Micmac As Dictated by Native Indians; With an Interlinear Translation. Hautiput,* 1887. 104, 121 p. Br897.11 McR153.

3437. Rand, Silas T. *Pela kesagunoodumumkaw ̄tan tula uksakumamenoo westowoolkw Sasoogoole Clistawit ootenink. Megumoweesimk.* Megumagealedakunweekugemkawa moweome, Chebooktook [Halifax, Nova Scotia], 1871. 126 p. Br497.11 McB 47.1. Gospel of St. Matthew translated into Micmac.

3438. Rand, Silas T. *Tan teladakadidjik apostalewidjik; the akts ov de aposelz.* Printed for the Britiç and Foren Beibel Soseieti, bei Eizak Pitman, Bath, 1863. 140 p. Br497.11 McB 47.6. Acts of the Apostles translated into Micmac.

3439. Rand, Silas T. *The Ten Commandments, the Lord's Prayer, etc.; In the Maliseet Language.* Printed for the Micmac Missionary Society, Halifax, Nova Scotia; Printed by Isaac Pitman, Phonetic Institution, Bath, 1863. 22 p. Br497.11 MlR15. Biblical selections translated into Malecite.

3440. Randall, Caleb D. *The Fourth International Prison Congress, St. Petersburg, Russia.* United States Bureau of Education Circulars of Information, 2. Government Printing Office, Washington, DC, 1891. 253 p. Br365 In84.

3441. Rasles, Sébastian. *A Dictionary of the Abnaki Language, in North America; By Father Sebastian Rasles; Published From the Original Manuscript of the Author; With an Introductory Memoir and Notes by John Pickering, A. A. S.* Charles Folsom, Cambridge, MA, 1833. Br497.11 AR18.

3442. Räss, Andreas, and Nikolaus von Weis. *Berichte über die Missionen von Luisiana.* Mainz, 1821. 73 p. Br572C An8141 v.34.

3443. Ratzel, Friedrich, and K. Lamprecht. Ethnographie und Geschichtswissenschaft in Amerika. *Deutschen Zeitschrift für Geschichtswissenschaft,* pp. 65-74, 1897-1898. Br572C An8141 v.157. Ratzel (1844-1904) is considered one of the most important of 19th century geographers.

3444. Ratzel, Friedrich. *Der Staat und sein Boden: geographisch Betrachtet*. Abhandlungen der Philologisch-Historischen Classe der Königl. Schsischen Gesellschaft der Wissenschaften, 17(4). S. Hirzel, Leipzig, 1896. 127 p. Br572C An8141 v.160.

3445. Ratzel, Friedrich. *The History of Mankind, by Professor Friedrich Ratzel; Translated From the Second German Edition by A. J. Butler, M. A.; With Introduction by E. B. Tylor; With Coloured Plates, Maps, and Illustrations*. Macmillan and Company, Ltd., London; The Macmillan Company, New York, 1896-98. 3 v. Br572 R18.

3446. Ratzel, Friedrich. Über die geographische Lage, eine politisch-geographische Betrachtung. pp. 257-261, n.d. Br911.3 R18.

3447. Ratzel, Friedrich. *Völkerkunde*. Bibliographisches Institut, Leipzig, 1885-1890. 3 v. Br572 R18.2.

3448. Rau, Charles. A deposit of agricultural flint implements found in southern Illinois. *Annual Report of the United States National Museum, Smithsonian Institution, for 1868*, pp. 401-407, 1869. Br572C An8141 v.42; Br913.7 R19.3. Charles Rau (1826-1887) immigrated to the United States from Germany in 1848 and carried out archaeological excavations in Missouri and Illinois. He was acknowledged as one of the leading archaeologists of the United States during his lifetime. In 1875 Rau prepared the Smithsonian Institution-Bureau of Indian Affairs exhibit for the Centennial Exposition in Philadelphia and, in 1881, he was appointed curator in the Department of Archaeology of the United States National Museum, the first permanent anthropology curatorship at the Smithsonian Institution.

3449. Rau, Charles. Aboriginal stone drilling. *American Naturalist* 15(7): 536-542, 1881. Br572C An8141 v.13; Br572C An8141 v.42; Br572C An8141 v.59.

3450. Rau, Charles. Agricultural implements of the North American stone period. In *Articles on Anthropological Subjects, Contributed to the Annual Reports of the Smithsonian Institution from 1863 to 1877 by Charles Rau*. Smithsonian Institution, Washington, DC, 1882. Br913.7 R19.3.

3451. Rau, Charles. An account of the aboriginal inhabitants of the California peninsula. In *Articles on Anthropological Subjects, Contributed to the Annual Reports of the Smithsonian Institution from 1863 to 1877 by Charles Rau*, pp. 352-399. Smithsonian Institution, Washington, DC, 1882. Br572C An8141 v.42; Br913.7 R19.3.

3452. Rau, Charles. Ancient aboriginal trade in North America. *Annual Report of the United States National Museum, Smithsonian Institution, for 1872*, pp. 348-394, 1873. Br572C An8141 v.38.; Br572C An8141 v.42.

3453. Rau, Charles. *Articles on Anthropological Subjects, Contributed to the Annual Reports of the Smithsonian Institution from 1863 to 1877 by Charles Rau*. Smithsonian Institution, Washington, DC, 1882. 169 p. Br913.7 R19.3.

3454. Rau, Charles. Artificial shell-deposits in New Jersey. *Annual Report of the United States National Museum, Smithsonian Institution*, pp. 370-374, 1860-1861. Br572C An8141 v.42; Br913.7 R19.3.

3455. Rau, Charles. Circular relative to contributions of aboriginal antiquities to the United States National Museum. *Proceedings of the United States National Museum, Smithsonian Institution* 6: 479-483, 1884. Br572C An8141 v.59.

3456. Rau, Charles. Die durchbohrten Geräthe der Steinperiode. *Archiv für Anthropologie* 3(2): 187-196, 1868. Br571.16 R193.2.

3457. Rau, Charles. Die Jadeitgegenstände des National-Museums zu Washington. pp. 157-163, 1881. Br572C An8141 v.97.

3458. Rau, Charles. Die Tauschverhältnisse der Eingebornen Nordamerika's. *Archiv für Anthropologie* 5(1): 1-43, 1870. Br572C An8141 v.97.

3459. Rau, Charles. Die Thongefässe der nordamerikanischen Indianer. *Archiv für Anthropologie* 3(1): 19-30, 1868. Br572C An8141 v.97.

3460. Rau, Charles. Drilling in stone without metal. *Annual Report of the United States National Museum, Smithsonian Institution, for 1868*, pp. 392-400, 1869. 7 p. Br572C An8141 v.42; Br913.7 R19.3.

3461. Rau, Charles. *Early Man in Europe*. Harper and Brothers, New York, 1876. 162 p. Br572.94 R19.

3462. Rau, Charles. Indian netsinkers and hammerstones. *American Naturalist* 7, 1878. 4 p. Br572C An8141 v.42.

3463. Rau, Charles. Indian pottery. *Annual Report of the United States National Museum, Smithsonian Institution, for 1866*, pp. 343-355, 1872. Br572C An8141 v.42; Br913.7 R19.3.

3464. Rau, Charles. Indian stone graves. *American Naturalist* 17:130-135, 1883. Br572C An8141 v.13; Br572C An8141 v.59.

3465. Rau, Charles. Indianische Netzsenker und Hammersteine. *Archiv für Anthropologie* 5(3): 261-266, 1870. Br572C An8141 v.97.

3466. Rau, Charles. *La stèle de Palenqué du Musée National des États-Unis a Washington*. Imprimerie Pitrat Ainé, Lyon, 1884. 103 p. Br572C An8141 v.102.

3467. Rau, Charles. List of anthropological publications, 1859-1882. *Proceedings of the United States National Museum, Smithsonian Institution* 4:455-458, 1881. Br572C An8141 v.42.

3468. Rau, Charles. Memoir of C. F. P. von Martius. In *Articles on Anthropological Subjects, Contributed to the Annual Reports of the Smithsonian Institution from 1863 to 1877 by Charles Rau*, pp. 169-178. Smithsonian Institution, Washington, DC, 1882. Br572C An8141 v.42; Br913.7 R19.3.

3469. Rau, Charles. Nordamerikamische Steinwerkzeuge. *Annual Report of the United States National Museum, Smithsonian Institution*, 1872. 17 p. Br572C An8141 v.42.

3470. Rau, Charles. North American stone implements. *Annual Report of the United States National Museum, Smithsonian Institution, for 1872*, pp. 395-408, 1873. Br572C An8141 v.38; Br572C An8141 v.42; Br913.7 R19.3.

3471. Rau, Charles. Observations on a gold ornament from a mound in Florida. *Annual Report of the United States National Museum, Smithsonian Report, for 1877*, pp. 298-302, 1878. Br572C An8141 v.42; Br913.7 R19.3.

3472. Rau, Charles. *Observations on Cup-Shaped and Other Lapidarian Sculptures in the Old World and in America*. Smithsonian Institution, Contributions to American Ethnology, 5(1). Government Printing Office, Washington, DC, 1881.

112 p. Br557.3 Un319; Br571.73 R193.

3473. Rau, Charles. *Prehistoric Fishing in Europe and North America.* Smithsonian Institution, Contributions to Knowledge, 25. Washington, DC, 1884. 342 p. Br913.7 R19.2. Includes extracts from various writings of the 16th, 17th, 18th, and 19th centuries, in which reference is made to aboriginal fishing in North America.

3474. Rau, Charles. Steinere Ackerbaugeräthe der Nordamerikanischen Indianer. *Archiv für Anthropologie* 4:1-9, 1870. Br913.7 R19.

3475. Rau, Charles. *The Archaeological Collection of the United States National Museum, in Charge of the Smithsonian Institution, Washington, D.C.* Smithsonian Institution, Contributions to Knowledge, 22(4). Washington, DC, 1876. 104 p. Br572C An8141 v.90; Br572C An8141 v.100.

3476. Rau, Charles. *The Palenque Tablet in the Unites States National Museum.* Smithsonian Institution, Contributions to Knowledge, 22(5). Washington, DC, 1879. 81 p. Br572C An8141 v.94.

3477. Rau, Charles. The stock-in-trade of an aboriginal lapidary [Mississippi]. *Annual Report of the United States National Museum, Smithsonian Institution, for 1877,* pp. 291-298, 1878. Br572C An8141 v.42; Br913.7 R19.3.

3478. Rau, Charles. Über künstliche Muschelbetten in Amerika. *Archic für Anthropologie* 2(3): 321-326, 1867. Br572C An8141 v.97.

3479. Rau, Charles. Von Martius on some points of South American ethnology. *Journal of the Anthropological Institute of New York* 1:43-46, 1871-1872. Br572C An8141 v.42.

3480. Ray, S. H., and A. C. Haddon. A study of the languages of the Torres Straits, with vocabularies and grammatical notes. *Proceedings of the Royal Irish Academy* 2(4): 463-616, 1893. Dublin. Br572C An8141 v.127.

3481. Raynaud, Georges, Le livre d'Or et le trésor indien, traduit de l'espagnol. *L'Alliance Scientifique,* Georges Carr, ed., pp. 61-86. Paris, 1891. Br572C An8141 v.9.

3482. Rea, Alonso de la. *Cronica de la orden de N. Serafico P. S. Francisco, provincia de San Pedro y San Pablo de Mechoacan en la Nueva España; compuesta por el P. lector de teologia Fr. Alonso de la Rea da la misma provincia...dedicada á N. P. Fr. Cristóbal Vaz, ministro provincial de ella. años de 1639. Con privilegio. En México por la viuda de Bernardo Calderon. Año de 1643.* Imprenta de J. R. Barbedillo, México, 1882. 488 p. Br243.2 R22.

3483. Read, Charles H. On an ancient Mexican head-piece, coated with mosaic. *Archaeologia* 54:383-398, 1895. Br572C An8141 v.144.

3484. Read, Charles H. On antiquities from Huasco (Guasco), Chile. *Journal of the Anthropological Institute of Great Britain and Ireland,* August, pp. 57-62, 1889. Br572C An8141 v.20.

3485. Read, Daniel B. The Hurons. *Transactions of the Canadian Institute* 1:86-95, 1890. Br572C An8141 v.10.

3486. Read, M. C., and C. Whittlesey. *Antiquities of Ohio; Report of the Committee of the State Archaeological Society,* pp. 81-141. Ohio State Board of Centennial Managers, Cleveland, 1877. Br913 R22.6.

3487. Reade, John. Language and conquest: a retrospect and a forecast. *Transactions of the Royal Society of Canada* 1:17-33, 1882. Br572C An8141 v.102.

3488. Reade, John. The literary faculty of the native races of America. *Transactions of the Royal Society of Canada* 2(2): 17-30, 1884. Br572C An8141 v.97.

3489. Reade, John. The making of Canada. *Transactions of the Royal Society of Canada* 2:1-15, 1884. 15 p. Br572C An8141 v.104.

3490. *Récit de François Kaondinoketc, chef des Nipissingues (tribu derace Algonqume) écrit per luimême en 1848; traduit en français et accompagné de notes par M. N.O.* [J.A. Cuoq]. Imprimerie Jules Moureau, Saint-Quentin, 1848. 8p. Br572C An8141 v.51. Nipissing and French texts in double columns.

3491. Reclus Élie. *Primitive Folk; Studies in Comparative Ethnology.* W. Scott, London, 1891. 339 p. Br572 R245. Translation of the author's *Les primitifs*, 1885.

3492. Reeland, Adrianus. *Hadriani Relandi dissertationum miscellanearum pars prima [- tertia et ultima].* Ex Officina G. Broedelet, Trajecti ad Rhenum, 1706-1708. Br490.7 R25.

3493. Reeve, William D., and William C. Bompas. *The Gospel of St. Mark, Translated into the Slave Language for Indians of North-West America, In the Syllabic Character.* Society for Promoting Christian Knowledge, London, 1886. 136 p. Br497.12 SlB47.2R.

3494. Regazzoni, Innocenzo. *L'uomo preistórico nella provincia di Como.* Hoepli, Milan, 1878. 136 p. Br573 R26.

3495. Régil y Peón, Alonso de, ed. *Poetas yucatecos y tabasqueños; colección de sus mejores producciones.* Imprenta de la Sociedad Tipografica, Merida, 1861. 252 p. Br572C An8141 v.63.

3496. *Registro yucateco; periódico literario; redactado por una Sociedad de Amigos.* Imprenta de Castillo y Cía, Mérida, v. 1-4, 1845-1849. Br868.1 R26.

3497. Reglas más comunes del Arte del idioma zapoteca del Valle; con una lista de los nombres más usuales, el confesionario y las oraciones principales de la doctrina cristiana en la misma lengua. San Martin Tilcaxete, 1793; copiado en Mérida, 1871. 148 p. Br498.34 ZR 264. Transcript of an original manuscript in the John Carter Brown Library, Providence, titled "Quaderno de idioma zapoteco del Valle, que contiene algunas reglas más comunes del Arte, un vocabulario algo copioso y otras cosas que verá el Christiano Lector; se ha escrito procurando toda lo posible imitar la pronunciación natural de los Indios; sacado lo más de los autores antiguos que escrivieron de este idioma; sea todo a mayor honra y gloria de Dios Ntro. Sr. Alivio de los Ministros y utilidad de las almas, Sn. Martín Tilcaxete y junio 22 de 1793; includes "Arte" (leaves 1-12), "Vocabulario" (leaves 13-266), "Lista de los nombres, etc." (leaves 285-286), "Confessionario" (leaves 273-285), "Protestación de la fee" (leaves 285-286), and "Interrogatorio" (leaves 287-288).

3498. Regnaud, Pau. *Origine et philosphie du language.* 10th ed. Paris, Fischbacher, Paris, 1889. 443 p. Br409.1 R26.

3499. Reibmayr, Albert. *Inzucht und Vermischung beim Menschen.* F. Deuticke, Leipzig und Wien, 1897. 268 p. Br572 R272.

3500. Reichelt, G. The literary works of the foreign missionaries of the Moravian Church, by the Rev. G. Th. Reichelt, of Herrnhut, Saxony; translated and annotated by Bishop Edmond de Schweinitz. *Transactions of the Moravian Historical Society*, n.d. 21 p. Br572C An8141 v.141.

3501. Reid, G.A. *Temperance Question from a Biological Standpoint*. Medical Magazine Company, London, 1898. 26 p. Br148 R27.

3502. Reinach, Salomon. L'Art plastique en Gaule et le Druidisme. *Revue Celtique* 13, 1892. 13 p. Br572C An8141 v.83.

3503. Reinach, Salomon. L'Etain celtique. *L'Anthropologie* 3:275-281, 1892. Br572C An8141 v.83.

3504. Reinisch, Simon L. Vocabulario desta lengua zaelohpaeap. pp. 260-349, 1896. Br572C An8141 v.157.

3505. Reiss, Wilhelm. Ein Besuch bei den Jivaros Indianern. *Verhandlungen der Gesellschaft für Erdkunde zu Berlin*, 1880. Br572C An8141 v.10.

3506. Reiss, Wilhelm. Funde aus der Steinzeit Ägyptens. *Verhandlungen der Berliner Anthropologischen Gesellschaft für Anthropologie, Ethnologie und Urgeschichte*, pp. 700-712, 1889. Br572C An8141 v.9.

3507. Reiss, Wilhelm. Sinken die Anden? *Verhandlungen der Gesellschaft für Erdkunde zu Berlin* 1, 1880. 12 p. Br572C An8141 v.7.

3508. Reiss, Wilhelm. Spielzeug und Zierrath aus Ägypten. *Verhandlungen der Berliner Anthropologischen Gesellschaft für Anthropologie, Ethnologie und Urgeschichte*, pp. 700-712, 1889. Br572C An8141 v.10.

3509. Rejón, Manuel G. Apuntes históricos, 1850. 12 p. Br572C An8141 v.71.

3510. *Rélations des Jésuites; contenant ce qui s'est passé de plus remarquable dans les missions des pères de la Compagnie de Jésus dans la Nouvelle-France; ouvrage publié sous les auspices du Gouvernement Canadien.* A. Côté, Québec, 1858. 3 v. Br970.6 J498.2. Contents include: 1. Embrassant les années 1611, 1626 et la période 1632 à 1641; 2. Embrassant les années 1642 à 1655; 3. Embrassant les années de 1656 à 1672, et une table analytique des matières contenues dans tout l'ouvrage. "This is the most extraordinary and valuable collection of material relating to the history and life of the Indians ever made. It is composed of the narratives of a class of men who, two centuries before what we…term civilization, had prostrated the forests and exterminated their free occupants, explored the vast territories covered by them, recorded the peculiarities of their natives, and in many instances bestowed the blessings of Christianity among them. These relations, for many years looked upon through the haze of sectarian distrust, were lightly esteemed by the students of American history, but the more their character and statements were investigated, the more important and valuable they appear. They have become the sources from which we must draw almost all the historic material of New York and Canada, during the first century and a half of their exploration by Europeans" (Field 1873:326).

3511. *Religion und Theologie; Lose Blätter der Zeit von einem Lehrling im Dienste der Anthropologie III*. Verlag von Wiegandt und Hempel, Berlin, 1783. 60 p. Br572C An8141 v.121.

3512. Remedi, Joaquin. *Los indios matacos y su lengua, con vocabularios ordenandos por Samuel A. Lafone y Quevedo.* Imprenta Roma, Buenos Aires, 1896. 34 p. Br498.972 MR 28.

3513. Rensselaer, J. King van. Playing cards from Japan. *Proceedings of the United States National Museum, Smithsonian Institution* 13(836): 381-383, n.d. Br572C An8141 v.9.

3514. Renvilk, John Baptiste, trans. *Woonspie itakibna ebakeun okaga, Precept Upon Precept; Translated into the Dakota Language.* Hurd, New York, 1864. 228 p. Br497.5 DSR29. Volume is edited by S. R. Riggs.

3515. *Repertorio Salvadoreño: publicación mensual de la Academia de Ciencias y Bellas Letras de San Salvador* 6(4), 1892. Br572C An8141 v.122.

3516. Requena, Pedro. *Breve informé sobre la agricultura, industria y comercio de Tabasco.* Imprenta del Gobierno, San Juan Bautista, 1847. 56 p. Br917.26 R297.

3517. Restivo, Paulo. *Brevis linguae guaraní grammatica hispanice, a Paul Restivoi…in Paraquaria anno 1718 y composita et Breve noticia de la lengua guaraní.* G. Kohlhammer, Stuttgardiae, 1890. 81 p. Br498.75 GR 851.

3518. Restrepo Tirado, Ernesto. *Ensayo etnographico y arqueologico de la provincia de Los Quimbayas en el Nuevo Reino de Granada.* Imprenta de la Luz, Bogota, 1892. 62 p. Br572C An8141 v.114.

3519. Restrepo Tirado, Ernesto. *Estudios sobre los aborigenes de Colombia; primera parte.* Imprenta de la Luz, Bogota, 1892, 181 p. Br572C An8141 v.114; Br980.4 CR313.

3520. Restrepo, Vicente. *Critica de los trabajos arqueologicos del Dr. José Domingo Duquesne.* Imprenta de "La Nation," Bogota, 1892. 45 p. Br572C An8141 v.114.

3521. Restrepo, Vicente. *Los chibchas antes de la conquista española.* Imprenta de la Luz, Bogota, 1895. 239 p. Br572C An8141 v.160.

3522. Restrepo, Vicente. *Viajes de Lionel Wafer al istmo del Darién.* Imprenta de Silvestre y Compañía, Bogota, 1888. 129 p. Br572C An8141 v.114.

3523. *Revista de Mérida; periodico de literatura y variedades.* Imprenta del Esitor, Mérida. v. 1-2, 1869-1870. Br868.1 R32.

3524. Révoil, B. H. *Les Aztecs.* Publié par Georges Barba, Libraire-Éditeur, Paris, 1855. 48 p. Br572C An8141 v.101.

3525. *Revue Américaine.* Paris. v.1, 1866. Br917.05 R325.

3526. *Revue Américaine; recueil exclusivement consacré aux récherches archéologiques, historiques, philologiques, ethnographiques et littéraires sur le nouveau-monde.* Libraire de la Société d'Ethnographie, Paris, 1865. 404 p. Br913.7 R325.

3527. *Revue Mensuelle de l'Ecole d'Anthropologie de Paris.* January, February, May, 1891 Br572C An8141 v.8.

3528. Rey, Philippe-Marius. *Étude anthropologique sur les Botocudos; thèse pour le doctorat en médecine, faculté de médecine de Paris.* Paris, 1880. 81 p. Br572C An8141 v.33. "Contains…the description and measurements of a skull collected at Punta Arenas. It was presented by M. Lejanne as Patagonian but according to Dr. Francisco Moreno it is Fuegian" (Copper 1917:122).

3529. Reyes, Antonio de los. *Arte en lengua mixteca; compuesta por el padre fray Antonio de los Reyes; publiè par le comte H. de Charencey.* Typographie E. Renaut-de Broise, Alençon, 1889. 96 p. Br498.34 MR 333.

3530. Reyes, Gaspar de los. *Gramática de las lemguas* [sic] *zapoteca-serrana y zapoteca del valle; por Gaspar de los Reyes.* Imprenta del Estado, a cargo de Ignacio Candiani, Oaxaca, 1891. 105 p. Br498.34 R 333.

3531. Reynolds, Sheldon. Local shell-beds. *Proceedings of the Wyoming Historical and Geographical Society* 2(1): 68-75, 1885. Br572C An8141 v.39.

3532. Reynoso, Diego de. *Arte y vocabulario en lengva mame dirigido; publié. par le comte de Charencey.* C. Chadenat, Paris, 1897. 157 p. Br498.21 MaR 33.

3533. Reynoso, Diego de. Extractos del Arte y vocabulario en lengua mame. México, 1644. 9 p. Br498.21 MaR33.9. Extract with some 150 words in Mam by Karl H. Berendt from *Arte, y vocabulario en lengua mame; dirigido a nuestro reuerendissimo padre maestro F. Marcos Salmerón, calificador del supremo consejo de la inquisición, general de todo el Orden de N. Señora de la Merced, señor de la varonía de Algar* (En México: Por Francisco Robledo, Impresor del Secreto del S. Oficio, 1644).

3534. Rhode Island Historical Society. *Publications.* New series. v. 2, no. 1, 1894. Br572C An8141 v.123.

3535. Rialle, G. de. *De l'anthropologie; étude d'ethnologie comparée.* Ernest Leroux, Éditeur, Paris, 1875. 31 p. Br572C An8141 v.88.

3536. Ribbe, F.C. *L'ordre d'obliteration des sutures du crane dans les races humanines; Fakulte de medecine de Paris, these pour le doctorat.* O. Berthier, Paris, 1885. 164 p. Br572C An8141 v.8.

3537. Riccardi, P. Studi intorno ad alcuni crani arauccinos e pampas appartenenti al Museo Nazionale d'Antropologia e di Etnologia in France. *Memorie deella Classe di Scienze Morali, Storiche e Filologiche, Reale Accademia dei Lincei* 4:139-161, 1879. Roma. Br572C An8141 v.95.

3538. Rico Frontaura, Plácido. *Explicación de una parte de la doctrina cristiana, ó instrucciones dogmatico-morales en que se vierte toda la doctrina del catecismo romano; se amplian los diferentes puntos que el mismo catecismo remite á los párrocos para su extencion; y se tratan de nuevo otros importantes.* J. D. Espinosa, Mérida de Yucatán, 1847. 389 p. Br498.21 MaF 92. Apostle's Creed translated into Yucatec by Joaquín Ruz.

3539. Ridley, William. *Am da malshk ga na damsh St. Matthew Ligi; The Gospel According to St. Matthew, Translated into Zimshian.* Society for Promoting Christian Knowledge, London, 1885. 59 p. Br497.18 TB47.1. Gospel according to St. Matthew translated into Tsimshian.

3540. Riggs, Alfred L. *Wicoie wowapi kin; The Word Book.* Published for the Dakota Mission, American Tract Society, New York, 1881. 24 p. Br497.5 DSR44. Primer in Santee Sioux. Alfred Longley Riggs (1837-1916) was the eldest son of Stephen R. Riggs. In 1870 he joined the Congregationalist mission at Santee Agency in Nebraska. He began the Santee Normal Training School, which became one of the foremost Indian boarding schools. Riggs edited the Dakota newspaper *Iapi Oaye* and its English counterpart, *The Word Carrier*, which were printed on the school press.

3541. Riggs, Stephen R. *A Dakota-English Dictionary, Edited by J. O. Dorsey*. Smithsonian Institution, Contributions to American Ethnology, 7. Government Printing Office, Washington, DC, 1890. 665 p. Br557.3 Un319. Stephen Return Riggs (1812–1883) and his wife Mary Ann joined the Congregationalist mission to the Sioux Indians of Minnesota, sponsored by the American Board of Commissioners. In 1837 they established themselves among the Wahpeton Sioux and began studying the Sioux language and preparing translations of scriptures. After the Santee uprising, Riggs served in 1862 as chaplain for the military expedition against them, and in 1863 he acted as interpreter. In 1865 Riggs moved to Beloit, Wisconsin, and organized a mission and school among the Santee prisoners at Davenport.

3542. Riggs, Stephen R. *An English and Dakota Vocabulary; Extracted From His "Grammar and Dictionary of the Dakota Language," by M. A. C. Riggs*. R. Craighead, New York, 1852. 120 p. Br497.5 DR44.2.

3543. Riggs, Stephen R. *Dakota Grammar, Texts and Ethnology, Edited by J. O. Dorsey*. Smithsonian Institution, Contributions to American Ethnology, 9. Government Printing Office, Washington, DC, 1893. 239 p. Br557.3 Un319.

3544. Riggs, Stephen R. *Grammar and Dictionary of the Dakota Language*. Smithsonian Institution, Contributions to Knowledge, 4. Washington, DC; G. P. Putnam, New York, 1852. 338 p. Br497.5 DR44.

3545. *Rijks Ethnographischen Museum Catalogue, ser. 839*. Rijks Ethnographischen Museum, Leiden, n.d. 25 p. Br913.06 L534.

3546. Rincón, Antonio del. *Arte mexicana; compvesta por el padre Antonio del Rincon de la Compañia de Iesus; dirigido al illustrissimo y reuerendissimo S. don Diego*

H. Johannes Rink (from Justin Winsor, Aboriginal America. *Cambridge, MA: Houghton, Mifflin, 1889. p. 106*).

Romano obispo de Tlaxcallan,...en México en casa de Pedro, Balli. 1595; se reimprimé en 1885 bajo el cuidado del Dr.Antonio Peñafiel. Oficina Tipografica de la Secretaría de Fomento, México, 1885. 94 p. Br498.22 AzR 47.

3547. Rink, H. Johannes, and Franz Boas. Eskimo tales and songs. *Journal of American Folk-Lore* 2(5): 123-132, 1889. Br572C An8141 v.23; Br572C An8141 v.52. Rink, born in Copenhagen in 1819, spent much of the period from 1853 to 1872 in Greenland. He was considered the best authority on the Eskimos at the end of the 19th century.

3548. Rink, H. Johannes. Bemærkninger til G. Holms Samling af Sagn og Fortaellinger fra Angmagsalik. In *Sagn af Fortaellinger fra Angmagsalik samlede af G. Holm*, pp. 101-111. B. Lunos Kgl. Hol-Bogtrykkeri, Kjobenhavn, 1888. Br572C An8141 v.11. Eskimo folklore.

3549. Rink, H. Johannes. Den østgrønlandske Dialekt efter de af den danske Østkyst Expedition meddelte Bemaekninger til kleinschmidts grønlandske Ordbog. *Meddelelser om Grønland* 10, 1887. 28 p. Br572C An8141 v.48.

3550. Rink, H. Johannes. Dialectes de la langue Esquimaude. *Proceedings of the International Congress of Americanists* (5 session, Copenhagen, 1883), pp. 328-337, 1884. Br572C An8141 v.52.

3551. Rink, H. Johannes. Om resultaterne af de nyeste etnografiscke Undersogelser i Amerika. *Geografisk Tidskrift* 9, 1892. 8 p. Br572C An8141 v.107.

3552. Rink, H. Johannes. *Tales and Traditions of the Eskimo, With a Sketch of Their Habits, Religion, Language and Other Peculiarities, by Dr.henry Rink, Knight of Dannebrog, Director of the Royal Greenland Board of Trade, and Formerly Royal Inspector of South Greenland.* W. Blackwood and Sons, Edinburgh, London, 1875. 472 p. Br398.22. ER473.ER. Translation from Danish of *Eskimoiske eventyr og sagn* (Copenhagen, 1866).

3553. Rink, H. Johannes. The Eskimo dialects. *Journal of the Anthropological Institute of Great Britain and Ireland* 15(2): 239-245, 1885. Br572C An8141 v.52.

3554. Rink, H. Johannes. The recent Danish explorations in Greenland and their significance as to Arctic science in general. *Proceedings of the American Philosophical Society* 22:280-296, 1885. Br572C An8141 v.32.

3555. Rio, Antonio del. *Beschreibung einer alten Stadt, die in Guatimala (Neuspanien), unfern Palenque entdeckt worden ist.* G. Reimer, Berlin, 1832. 123, 88 p. Br913.7281 R476.GM.

3556. Rio, Antonio del. *Description of the Ruins of An Ancient City Discovered Near Palenque, in the Kingdom of Guatemala.* H. Berthoud, and Suttaby, Evance and Fox, London, 1822. 128 p. Br913.7281 R476.EB.

3557. Ripalda, Gerónimo de. *Catecismo de la doctrina cristiana...traducida al idioma mejicano, por Miguel Trinidad Palma.* Imprenta de M. Corona, Puebla, 1886. 114 p. Br498.22 AzR 482. Catechism in Nahuatl.

3558. Ripalda, Gerónimo de. *Catecismo y exposición breve de la doctrina cristiana*, pp. 159-207. Imprimerie Renaut-DeBroise, Alençon, 1847. Br572C An8141 v.129.

3559. Ripalda, Gerónimo de. *Catecismo y exposición breve de la doctrina cristiana, publié par...Hyacinthe, comte de Charencey; traducida al idioma yucateco con...Joaquin Ruz.* Imprimerie Renaut de Broise, Alençon, 1892. 51 p. Br498.21 MR 48a; Br498.21 MR 48b.

3560. Ripalda, Gerónimo de. *Catecismo y exposición breve de la doctrina cristiana; por el padre maestro Gerónimo de Ripalda; traducida al idioma yucateco con unos afectos para socorrer á los moribundos por el M. R. P. Fr. Joaquin Ruz.* J. D. Espinosa, Mérida, 1847. 88p. Br498.21 MR 48.

3561. Ripalda, Gerónimo de. *Christianoyotl mexicanemachtiloni, in itech onactica, ihuan ontzauctica in imelahualoca, ihuan in icaquitztica in izquitlamantli nepapan teotlatolli, ihuan teotemachtilli; in cemix quich in teotlaneltocani, in christiano tlacatl ca huei inahuatl, huei imamal, inic cacicamatiz, qui chicahuacaneltocaz, ihuan quitequipanoz, inic momaquixtiz, auh yehuatlin temachtilli oquimachto patecpanili, caxtillancopa in toteopixcatatzin yehuatzin.* Bibliotheca Mexicana, Mexico, 1758. 32, 170 p. Br498.22 AzR 482.2.

3562. Ripalda, Gerónimo de. Doctrina cristiana según el P. Ripalda en idioma zoque, n.d. 52 leaves. Br498.35 ZD653. Manuscript; bound with: Doctrina christiana en lengua zoque, 1736. 53 leaves.

3563. Ripley, William Z. *A Selected Bibliography of the Anthropology and Ethnology of Europe.* D. Appleton, New York, 1899. 160 p. Br572.94B R484.

3564. Ripley, William Z. Acclimatization. *Popular Science Monthly* 49:662-675, 779-793, 1896. Br572C An8141 v.141; Br572C An8141 v.157.

3565. Ripley, William Z. Deniker's classification of the races of Europe. *Journal of the Royal Anthropological Institute of Great Britain and Ireland,* pp. 166-173, 1898. Br572.94 D415yR.

3566. Ripley, William Z. Ethnic influences in vital statistics. *American Statistical Association,* March, pp. 18-40, 1896. Br572C An8141 v.141.

3567. Ripley, William Z. Notes et documents pour la construction d'ine carte de l'indice céphalique en Europe. *L'Anthropologie* 7:513-525, n.d. Br572C An8141 v.157.

3568. Rittich, Aleksandr F. *Die Ethnographie Russland's.* Justus Perthes, Gotha, 1878. 43 p. Br572C An8141 v.95.

3569. Rittich, Aleksandr F. *Travaux ethnographiques en Russie.* Kharkoff, 1879. 36 p. Br572C An8141 v.58.

3570. Riva Palacio, Vicente. *México a través de los siglos; historia general y completa del desenvolvimiento social, político, religioso, militar, artístico, científico y literario de México desde la antígüedad más remota hasta la época actual.* Espasa, Barcelona, 1888-1889. 5 v. Br972 R52.

3571. Rivas, Manual A. *Manual enciclopedico de ciencias, agricultura y artes, extractado de las mejores obras I ilustrado con articulos del pais.* Rivas, Mérida, 1866. 289 p. Br630 R522.

3572. Rivera, Gregorio. *Silabario de la lengua mexicana, por el presbitero D. Gregorio Rivera.* En la oficina de D. Mariano Ontiveros, Calle del Espíritu Santo, México, 1818. 29 p. Br498.22 AzR 522.

3573. Rivero y Ustariz, Mariano Eduardo de, and Johann Jakob von Tschudi.

Antigüedades peruanas. Imprenta Imperial de la Corte y del Estado, Vienna, 1851. 328 p. Br913.85 R52.2. "This work was the result of...research by two learned gentlemen, Dr. Tschudi, a German long resident in Peru, and Dr. Riviero, a native of that country. Their contribution to ethnological and philological science has been esteemed by the learned world among the most valuable...of those relating to South America" (Field 1873:332).

3574. Rivero, Juan. *Historia de las misiones de los llanos de Casanare y los rios Orinoco y Meta; escrita el ano de 1736 por el padre Juan Rivero.* Imprenta de Silvestre y Companía, Bogotá, 1883. 443 p. Br986 R523.

3575. Rivière, Émile. *Découverte d'un squelette humain de l'époque paléolithique; dans les cavernes des Baoussé-Roussé, dites grottes de Menton.* 2d ed. J.-B. Baillière, Paris, 1873. 64 p. Br571.1 R52.

3576. Robelo, C. A. *Vocabulario comparativo castellano y nahuatl.* 2d ed. Miranda, Cuernavaca, 1889. 114 p. Br498.22 R 544.

3577. Roberts, Orlando W. *Narrative of Voyages and Excursions on the East Coast and in the Interior of Central America; Describing a Journey up the River San Juan, and Passage Across the Lake of Nicaragua to the City of Leon; Pointing Out the Advantages of a Direct Commerical Intercourse with the Natives; by Orlando W. Roberts, Many Years a Resident Trader; With Notes and Observations by Edward Irving.* Printed for Constable and Company, Edinburgh; Hurst, Chance and Company, London, 1827. 302 p. Br917.28 R547.

3578. Robertson, Ann E. W. *Cokv vpastel Pal kelesvlke ohtotvte; The Epistle of Paul The Apostle to the Galatians; Translated From the Original Greek into the Muskokee*

Cecilio A. Robelo (from Frederick Starr, Recent Mexican Study of the Native Languages of Mexico. Chicago: University of Chicago Press, 1900. p. 11). [3]

Language. American Bible Society, New York, 1885. 16 p. Br497.39 CrB47.8. Epistle of St. Paul translated into Creek.

3579. Robertson, William S. *Nakcokv es kerretv enhvtecskv; Muskokee or Creek First Reader*. 2d ed. Mission House, New York, 1867. 48 p. Br497.39 CrR54. A child's picture-book, with the names of the objects and animals in Muskogee, with their descriptions in the same language" (Field 1873:333).

3580. Rocafuerte, Vicente. *Memoria politico-instructiva, enviada desde Filadelfia en agosto de 1821, a los gefes independientes del Anahuac, llamado por los españoles Nueva-España*. G. and R. White, New York, 1821. 126 p. Br972 R582.

3581. Rocha, Juan Eligio de la. Apuntamientos de la lengua mangue, por D. Juan Eligio de la Rocha. Masaya, 1842. 11 p. Br498.12 MR583. Manuscript; transcript made in 1874 at Granada, Nicaragua, by Karl H. Berendt; includes a "Vocabulario," arranged Spanish-Mangue (pp. 5–7) and "Frases de la conversación" (1 leaf).

3582. Rochefort, César de. *Histoire naturelle et morale des iles Antilles de l'Amérique. 2 ed. rev. et augm. de plusieurs descriptions, et de quelques éclaircissemens, qu'on desiroit en la precedente*. A. Leers, Roterdam, 1665. 583 p. Br972.9 P754. This important work on the islands of the Caribbean, with interesting information on Florida, Georgia, and the Eskimos, was originally published in French in 1658, its main purpose being the encouragement of Huguenot emigration to America. Its greatest copntribution was the contemporary information on the Caribbean islands, especially the French and British colonies developing as sugar plantations.

3583. Rockstroh, Edwin. Los indigenas de la America Central y sus idiomas. pp. 1–16, n.d. Br572C An8141 v.115.

3584. Rodrigues, J. Barbosa. Idolo amazonico achado no rio Amazonas. *Journal do Commercio*, pp. 438–444, 1875. Br572C An8141 v.103.

3585. Rodrigues, J. Barbosa. *Muirakitan*. Typographia a Vapor do-Cruzeiro, Rio de Janeiro, 1882. 16 p. Br572C An8141 v.71.

3586. Rodrigues, J. Barbosa. *Poranduba amazonense; ou, Kochiymauara porandub*. G. Leuzinger & Filhos, Rio de Janeiro, 1890. 334 p. Br498.75 AmB 23.

3587. Rodrigues, J. Barbosa. *Rio Jauapery pacificação dos Crichanás*. Imprensa Nacional, Rio de Janeiro, 1885. 274 p. Br498.78 CrB 233. Includes Vocabulario [Portuguez-Crichaná-Ipurucotó-Macuchy.]

3588. Rodrigues, J. Barbosa. *Vocabulario indigena comparado para mostrar a aduteração da lingua*. G. Leuzinger & Filhos, Rio de Janeiro, 1892. 83 p. Br572C An8141 v.107.

3589. Rodway, J. *Hand-Book of British Guiana*. Press of Rockwell and Churchill, Boston, 1893. 93 p. Br572C An8141 v.130.

3590. Roehrig, F. L. O. The language of the Dakota or Sioux Indians. *Annual Report of the United States National Museum, Smithsonian Institution, for 1871*, pp. 434–450, 1873. Br572C An8141 v.52; Br572C An8141 v.81.

3591. Rojas, Arístides. *Estudios indigenas. Contribuciones a la historia antigua de Venezuela*. Impremta [sic] Nacional, Caracas, 1878. 217 p. Br498.6 R 634. Contents include: "Los jeroglíficos venezolanos"; "Orígenes venezolanos"; "La península de los Carácas"; "La bella frase en las lenguas americanas"; "La sílaba gua ó hua, como interjección, sustantivo, artículo, verbo, adjetivo, advervio, radical, afijo y partícula en las lenguas americanas"; "Las radicales del agua en las lenguas americanas"; "De algunos vocablos de geografía general, en las provincias caribes de Venezuela"; "Literatura de las lenguas indigenas de Venezuela"; "La Oración Dominical en lenguas venezolanas."

3592. Roldan, Bartholomé. Cathecismo en lengua chuchona y castellana, 1867. 32 p. Br572C An8141 v.55.

3593. Roldan, Bartholome. *Cathecismo en lengua chuchona y castellana; por el muy reverendo padre fray Bartholome Roldan; publié par M. de Charencey.* E. Renaut-de Broise, Alençon, 1887. 32 p. Br498.34 ChR 64; Br498.34 ChR 64a; Br572C An8141 v.48. Contains also Doctrina cristiana and Preguntas tocante a la doctrina.

3594. Romer, Floris F. The prehistoric antiquities of Hungary. In *Articles on Anthropological Subjects, Contributed to the Annual Reports of the Smithsonian Institution from 1863 to 1877 by Charles Rau.* Smithsonian Institution, Washington, DC, 1882. Br913.7 R19.3.

3595. Rosa, Agustin de la. *Estudio de la filosofia y riqueza de la lengua mexicana para uso de los alumnos del seminario de Guadalajara por el Presb. Agustin de la Rosa.* Imprenta de N. Parga, Guadalajara, 1877. 84 p. Br498.22 AzR 712.

3596. Rosa, Daniele. Le nov Latin: internationale scientific lingua super natural bases. *Bolletino dei Musei di Zoologia ed Anatomia Comparata* 5, 1890. 10 p. Br572C An8141 v.21.

3597. Rosa, Daniele. Terricolas ex Birminia et ex austral America. *Bolletino dei Musei di Zoologia ed Anatomia Comparata* 5, 1890. 3 p. Br572C An8141 v.21.

Agustin de la Rosa (from Frederick Starr, Recent Mexican Study of the Native Languages of Mexico. *Chicago: University of Chicago Press, 1900. p. 12).*

Léon Louis Lucien Prunol de Rosny (from Justin Winsor, Aboriginal America. *Cambridge, MA: Houghton, Mifflin, 1889. p. 202).*

3598. Roskoff, Gustav. *Das Religionswesen der rohesten Naturvölker.* F. A. Brockhaus Leipzig, 1880. 179 p. Br390 R736.

3599. Rosny, J.-H. *Les origines.* L. Borel, Paris, 1895. 258 p. Br573.2 R735.

3600. Rosny, Léon Louis Lucien Prunol de. *Archives paléographiques de l'Orient et de l'Amérique, publiées avec de notices historiques et philologiques, par Léon de Rosny; tome premier.* Mainsonneuve, Paris, 1869-1871. 240 p. Br411 R736. "A quarterly publication designed for the collection of alphabets of all known languages, of inscriptions and medals, with facsimiles of Oriental maniscripts in black and colored" (Field 1873:336); contains *Codex Telleriano-Remensis* on plates 24-96. Leon Louis Lucien Prunol de Rosny (1837-1914) was a distinguished Orientalist, with a bibliography encompassing works on Chinese, Japanese, Korean, Thai, and Vietnamese, as well as more general works on language and writing systems.

3601. Rosny, Léon Louis Lucien Prunol de. *Bibliothèque ethnographique.* Maisonneuve et Ch. Leclerc, Paris, 1885-1887. 8 v. Br572C R737.

3602. Rosny, Léon Louis Lucien Prunol de. *Ensayo sobre la interpretación de la escritura hierática de la América Central.* Imprenta de M. Tello, Madrid, 1881. 113 p. Br498 R735SR.

3603. Rosny, Léon Louis Lucien Prunol de. *Essai sur le déchiffrement de l'écriture hiératique de l'Amérique Centrale.* Maisonneuve et Cie., Paris, 1876. 60 p. Br498 R73. In this essay Rosny correctly identified the Maya glyphs for world directions, and was the first to identify phonetic elements in the day and months signs given by Landa and the codices.

3604. Rosny, Léon Louis Lucien Prunol de. *Japonskiego jezyka*, 1874. Br572C An8141 v.55.

3605. Rosny, Léon Louis Lucien Prunol de. *L'interpretation des anciens textes mayas par Leon de Rosny, professeur de l'enseignement superieur, membre de la Société Américaine de France; suivie d'un apercu de la grammaire maya d'un choix de textes originaux avec traduction et d'un vocabulaire*. Gustave Bossange, Paris, 1875. 70 p. Br498.21 MR745. Includes an overview of Mayan grammar (pp. 13-34), selected texts with translations (pp. 35-46) and a Maya-French vocabulary (pp. 47-70).

3606. Rosny, Léon Louis Lucien Prunol de. *La morale du Bouddhisme*. Georges Carré, Paris, 1891. 24 p. Br572C An8141 v.9.

3607. Rosny, Léon Louis Lucien Prunol de. *Le peuple siamois ou Thai*. Bibliothèque Ethnographique, 3. Maisonneuve et Ch. Leclerc, Paris, 1885. 120 p. Br572C R737.

3608. Rosny, Léon Louis Lucien Prunol de. *Les Coréens; aperçu ethnographique et historique*. Bibliothèque Ethnographique, 6. Maisonneuve et Ch. Leclerc, Paris, 1886. 91 p. Br572C R737.

3609. Rosny, Léon Louis Lucien Prunol de. *Les documents écrits de l'antiquité américaine, compte rendu d'une Mission Scientifique en Espagne et en Portugal, par Léon de Rosny accompagné d'une carte aztèque en chromolithographie et de dix planches héliogravées sur les photographies de l'auteur*. Maisonneuve et Cie., Paris, 1882. 48 p. Br572C An8141 v.95; Br572C An8141 v.97; Br913.7 R73.

3610. Rosny, Léon Louis Lucien Prunol de. *Les romains d'Orient, aperçu de l'ethnographie de Roumane*. Bibliothèque Ethnographique, 4. Maisonneuve et Ch. Leclerc, Paris, 1885. 140 p. Br572C R737.

3611. Rosny, Léon Louis Lucien Prunol de. *Premières notions d'ethnographie générale*. Bibliothèque Ethnographique, 1. Maisonneuve et Ch. Leclerc, Paris, 1885. 116 p. Br572C R737.

3612. Rosny, Lucien Joseph de. Les Antilles: étude d'ethnographie et d'archéologie américaines. *Mémoires de la Société d'Ethnographie* 6(95): 3-152, 1886. Br572C An8141 v.95.

3613. Ross, William P. *Early Creek History, Speech of Hon. W. P. Ross, at the Tullahasse Manual Labor Boarding School, July 1878*. Printed at the Office of the Indian Journal, 1878. Br572C An8141 v.52.

3614. Rosse, Irving C. Sexual hypochondriasis and perversion of the genesic instinct. *Journal of Nervous and Mental Disease*, November, pp. 3-19, 1892. Br572C An8141 v.116.

3615. Rosse, Irving C. The neuroses from a demographic point of view. *Journal of Nervous and Mental Disease* 18, 1891. 14 p. Br572C An8141 v.121.

3616. Rota, Pedro. Arte y vocabulario de la lengua achaqua, n.d. 61 leaves. Br498.77 AcR 472. Manuscript.

3617. Roth, H. Ling, Marion E. Butler, James B. Walker, and J. G. Garson. *The Aborigines of Tasmania*. 2d ed. F. King and Sons, Halifax, England, 1899. 228 p Br572.9946 R74.

3618. Roth, H. Ling. Notes on Benin art. *Reliquary and Illustrated Archaeologist*, July, 1896. 13 p. Br572C An8141 v.163.

3619. Roth, H. Ling. *Toreutie Art from Benin*. London, 1898. 13 p. Br913.665 R743.

3620. Roth, Rudolph. Der Bock und das Messer. pp. 371-372, n.d. Br572C An8141 v.46.

3621. Roth, S., and J. Kollmann. Über den Schädel von Pontimelo. *Verhandlungen der Naturforschenden Gesellschaft du Basel* 10(1), 1892. 36 p. Br572C An8141 v.129.

3622. Roth, Walter E. *Ethnological Studies Among the North-West-Central Queensland Aborigines*. E. Gregory, Government Printer, Brisbane, 1897. 199 p. Br572.9 R743.

3623. Rotzell, W. E. Some vestigial structures in man. *Hahnemannian Monthly*, June, 1895. 5 p. Br572C An8141 v.141.

3624. Roustan, H. *Le république de l'Uruguay á l'Exposition Universelle de Paris de 1889*.Tipografía a vapor de El Siglo, Montevideo, 1889. 109 p. Br572C An8141 v.98.

3625. Rovirosa, José N. *Ensayo histórico sobre el Río Grijalva; ó Examen crítico de las obras antiguas y modernas que tratan de los descubrimientos de Juan de Grijalva y de los primeros establecimientos de los conquistadores españoles en Tabasco, por José N. Rovirosa*. Oficina tipografica de la Secretaría de Fomento, México, 1897. 63 p. Br572C An8141 v.157; Br972 R76.

3626. Rovirosa, José N. *Nombres geográficos del estado de Tabasco: estudio etimológico*. Oficina Tipografica de la Secretaría de Fomento, México, 1888. 36 p. Br498 R766; Br572C An8141 v.144.

3627. Royal Society of London. *International Catalogue of Scientific Literature: Report of the Committee of the Royal Society of London, With Schedules of Classification*. Royal Society of London, London, 1898. n.p. Br572C An8141 v.164.

3628. Rudimentos gramaticales u oserbaciones en ydioma tzotzil de Cinacantlan, n.d. 28 p. Br498.21 TR 834. Manuscript.

3629. *Rudo ensayo; tantative de una prevencional descripción geographica de la Provincia de Sonora, sus terminos y confines; o mejor, colección de materiales para hacerla quien lo supiere mejor*. San Augustine de La Florida; Albany, NY, 1863. 208 p. Br917.21 R83.

3630. Ruge, S. Was kostete die Endeckung Amerika's? *Globus* 63(11), n.d. 3 p. Br572C An8141 v.107.

3631. Ruinas de la fortaleza de Cuelap. *Boletín de la Sociedad Geográfica de Lima* 2(4-6): 147-153, 1892. Br572C An8141 v.109.

3632. Ruiz Blanco, Matías. *Conversión en Piritú (Colombia) de Indios Cumanagotos y Palenques, con la práctica que se observa en la enseñanza de los naturales en lengua cumanagota*. V. Suarez, Madrid, 1892. 228 p. Br243.2 R853a. Contents include: M. Ruiz Blanco, "Práctica que hay en la enseñanza de los indios y un directivo para que los religiosos puedan comodamente instruirlos en las cosas esenciales de la religión cristiana en lengua cumanagota y castellana"; F. Alvarez de Villanueva, "Relación histórica de todas las misiones de los PP. franciscanos en las Indias."

3633. Ruiz de Montoya, Antonio. *Arte de la lengua guaraní, ó mas bien tupí*. Faesy y Frick, Vienna, 1876. 400 p. Br498.75 GR 85.

3634. Ruiz de Montoya, Antonio. *Gramatica y dicionarios; arte, vocabulario y tesoro de la lengua tupí o guaraní.* Faesy y Frick, Viena, 1876. Br498.75 GR 85.4a. Includes: "Arte de la lengua guarani, ó mas bien tupí"; "Vocabulario y tesoro de la lengua guaraní, ó mas bien tupi"; "Vocabulario español-guaraní, ó tupi"; "Tesoro guaraní, ó tupí-español."

3635. Ruiz de Montoya, Antonio. *Lexicon hispano-guaranicum; vocabulario de la lengua guaraní, inscriptum a...Paulo Restivo...redimpressum necnon praefatione notisque instructum opera et studus C. F. Seybold.* G. Kohlhammer, Stuttgardiae, 1893. 545 p. Br498.75 GR 851.2.

3636. Ruiz de Montoya, Antonio. *Linguae guaraní grammatica, hispanice. in aedibus a...Paul Restivo...redimpressum necnon praefatione notisque instructum opera et studus C. F. Seybold.* Guilielmi Kohlhammer, Stuttgardiæ, 1892. 330 p. Br498.75 GR 85.5.

3637. Ruiz de Montoya, Antonio. *Manuscripto guaraní...sobre a primitiva catechese dos indios das missões...vertido para guarani por outro padre Jesuita, e agora publicado com a traducção portugueza, notas, e um esboço grammatical da Abánee pelo B. C. de Almeida Nogueira.* Leuzinger, Rio de Janeiro, 1879. 366 p. Br498.75 GR 85.3.

3638. Ruiz de Montoya, Antonio. *Vocabulario das palavras guaranís usadas pelo traductor da conquista espiritual.* Typ. Nacional, Rio de Janeiro, 1879. 603 p. Br498.75 GR 85.2.

3639. Rumpelt, Friedrich H. B. *Die Deutschen Zahlwörter.* Oxford, 1893. 48 p. Br572C An8141 v.116.

3640. Russell, Frank. Human remains from the Trenton Gravels. *American Naturalist* 33:143–153, 1899. Br573.7 R913.

3641. Russell, Israel C. Mountaineering in Alaska. *Bulletin of the American Geographical Society* 28(3): 217–228, 1896. Br572C An8141 v.147.

3642. Ruttenber, Edward M. *History of the Indian Tribes of Hudson's River; Their Origin, Manners and Customs; Tribal and Sub-Tribal Organizations; Wars, Treaties, etc.* J. Munsell, Albany, NY, 1872. 415p. Br970.4 NeR935.

3643. Ruz, José Joaquín Francisco Carrillo de. A Yucatecan grammar; by the R. J. Ruz, of Mérida, abridged for the instruction of the native Indians from the compendium of Diego Narciso Herranz y Quiros; translated from the Maya or Yucatecan language, by John Kingdon, Baptist missionary, Belize, Honduras. Printed at the Baptist Mission Press, 1847, Belize. 121 p. Br498.21 MR944.4EK. "Copy and annotations by Dr. C.H. Berendt. New York, 1865." Jose Joaquin Francisco Carrillo de Ruz (1785–1855), a Franciscan, was the first modern author of works on Yucatec Maya.

3644. Ruz, José Joaquín Francisco Carrillo de. *Análisis del idioma yucateco al castellano, por el R.P. Fray Joaquín Ruz.* Impreso por Maríano Guzmán, Mérida de Yucatán, 1851. 16 p. Br498.21 MR944.3. Literal translation of two articles of the Roman catechism into Yucatec.

3645. Ruz, José Joaquín Francisco Carrillo de. *Cartilla ó silabario de lengua maya, para la enseñanza de los niños indígenas, por el padre Fr. Joaquín Ruz.* Por Rafael

Pedrera, Mérida de Yucatán, 1845. 16 p. Br498.21 MR 944.2.

3646. Ruz, José Joaquín Francisco Carrillo de. *Catecismo histórico ó compendio de la istoria sagrada, y de la doctrina cristiana; con preguntas, y respuestas, y lecciones seguidas, por el Abad Fleuri; y traducidas del castellano al idioma yucateco, con un breve exortó para el entrego del santo cristo a los enfermos, por el P.P.Fr.Joaquín Ruz de la Orden de San Francisco; para instrucción de los naturales.* En la Oficina a Cargo de Domingo Cantón, Mérida de Yucatán, 1822, 186 p. Br498.21 MF639. A translation into Yucatec of the *Catecisme historique* by Claude Fleury (Paris, 1690. 2 v.) in an abbreviated form.

3647. Ruz, José Joaquín Francisco Carrillo de. *Catecismo y exposición breve de la doctrina cristiana, por el padre maestro Gerónimo de Ripalda de la Compañía de Jesús; traducido al idioma yucateco con unos afectos para socorrer a los moribundos por el M. R. P.Fr.Joaquín Ruz.* Impreso por José D. Espinosa, Mérida de Yucatán, 1847. 88 p. Br498.21 MB456a.

3648. Ruz, José Joaquín Francisco Carrillo de. *Colección de sermones para los domingos de todo el año, y cuaresma, tomados de varios autores, y traducidos libremente al idioma yucateco, por el Padre Fray Joaquín Ruz.* Imprenta de José D. Espinosa, Mérida, 1846-1850. 4 v. 145, 268, 254, 228 p. Br498.21 MR 944a. Contents include: 1. "Contiene las dominicas desde Adviento hasta Quincuagésima" (Imprenta de José Espinosa, Mérida, 1846); 2. "Contiene desde ceniza, viernes de cuaresma y dominicas hasta Pentecostes" (Impreso por Nazario Novelo, Mérida, 1849); 3. "Contiene desde pentecostes hasta la dominica vigesima cuarta" (Impreso por Nazario Novelo, Mérida, 1850); and 4. "Contiene las festividades principales del Señor, de Nuestra Señora, de algunos santos, y cuatro pláticas de Animas, sobre el dogma" (Impreso por Nazario Novelo, Mérida, 1850).

3649. Ruz, José Joaquín Francisco Carrillo de. El devoto instruido en el santo sacrificio de la misa, por el P. Luiz Lanzzi, de la Compañía de Jesús; traducción libre al idioma yucateco, con unos afectos. Impreso por José Antonio Pino, Mérida de Yucatán, 1835. 41 p. Br498.21 ML299. Manuscript; transcript by Karl H. Berendt "copiado del ejemplar en la librería de la Sociedad Historica en Nueva York, Diciembre de 1873."

3650. Ruz, José Joaquín Francisco Carrillo de. *Explicación de una parte de la doctrina cristiana, o instrucciones dogmatico-morales en que se vierte toda la doctrina del catecismo romano; se amplian los diferentes puntos que el mismo catecismo remite a los parrocos para su extención; y se tratan de nuevo otros importantes; por el R. P. M. Fr. Placido Rico Frontaura, ex-abad de los monasterios de celorio y ona y maestro general de la religión de San Benito; traducido al idioma yucateco por el R. P. Fr. Joaquín Ruz.* Oficina de J. D. Espinosa, Mérida de Yucatán, 1847. 389 p. Br498.21 MgF92.

3651. Ruz, José Joaquín Francisco Carrillo de. *Gramática yucateca por el P. Fr. Joaquín Ruz, formada para la instrucción de los indígenas, sobre el compendio de D. Diego Narciso Herranz y Quiros.* Por Rafael Pedrera, Mérida de Yucatán, 1844. 119 p. Br498.21 MR 944.4; Br61 M17. This is almost a verbal translation into Maya of the *Compendio mayor de gramática castellana para uso de los niños que concurren a las escuelas* by Herranz, first published at Madrid in 1834.

3652. Ruz, José Joaquín Francisco Carrillo de. *Manual romana toledano, y yucateco para la administración de los santos sacramentos, por el R. P. Fr. Joaquín Ruz.* En la Oficina de José D. Espinosa, Mérida de Yucatán, 1846. 191 p. Br498.21 MR662. Contents include "Admonición del bautismo en lengua yucateca" (8v-9v); "Admonición del sacramento de la penitencia [Maya]" (pp. 29-31); "Admonición [before communion] en lengua yucateca" (pp. 41-43); "Admonición [before extreme unction] en lengua maya" (pp. 56-67); "Amonestación para contraer matrimonio en lengua yucateca" (p. 97); "El orden de celebrar el matrimonio en lengua yucateca" (pp. 97-98); "Admonición para el matrimonio en lengua yucateca" (pp. 98-100); the remainder of the work is in Spanish.

3653. Ruz, José Joaquín Francisco Carrillo de. *Via sacra del divino amante corazón de Jesús, puesta por las cruces del calvario, por el presbitero José de Herrera Villavicencio; traducida al idioma yucateco por el R. P. Fr. Joaquín Ruz.* Impreso por Nazario Novelo, Mérida de Yucatán, 1849. 34 p. Br498.21 MR662.

3654. Sachse, J. F. Horologium Achaz. *Proceedings of the American Philosophical Society* 34(17), 1895. 14 p. Br572C An8141 v.13.

3655. Sacred stones of the vicinity of Newark, Licking County, Ohio. *Occident*, pp. 65-76, 107-114, 1886. Br572C An8141 v.38.

3656. Sagard, Gabriel. *Dictionnaire de la langue huronne; necessaire a cevx qui n'ont l'intelligence d'icelle, et ont a traiter avec les sauvages du pays, par Fr. Gabriel Sagard, recollet de S. François, de la province de S. Denys.* Chez Denys Moreau, Paris, 1632. 132 p. Br497.27 Wsa14. "Father Sagard, a member of the Recollects in Paris, was directed by a congregation of his order to accompany Father Nicholas in a mission to the savages of New France…he proceeded at once to the scene of his mission among the Hurons, one hundred and fifty leagues west of Quebec. Here he remained but a few months, when it was determined to send him to Quebec for supplies. His fortitude was not equal to the emergency, and worn down with the privations and sufferings of a missionary's life, he allowed himself to be persuaded by his brethren that it was not his vocation. He…returned to his convent in Paris, where he wrote the work we have considered" (Field 1873:342); French and Huron are arranged in double columns.

3657. Sâgean, Mathieu. *Extrait de la relation des avantures et voyage de Mathieu Sâgean.* À la Presse Cramoisy de J. M. Shea, Nouvelle York, 1863. 32 p. Br917 S1.

3658. Sahagún, Bernardino de. *Histoire générale des choses de la Nouvelle-Espagne, traduite et annotée par D. Jourdanet et par Remí Simeon.* G. Masson, Paris, 1880. 898 p. Br972 Sa14.2. Translation of *Historia general de las cosas de Nueva España.*

3659. Sahagún, Bernardino de. *Historia de la conquista de Mexico, escrita por el R. P. Fr. Bernardino Sahagún.* Carlos M. de Bustamente, ed. Imprenta de Galvan a cargo de Mariano Arévalo, Mexico, 1829. 69 p. Br572C An8141 v.64.

Bernardino de Sahagún (from Justin Winsor, Aboriginal America. Cambridge, MA: Houghton, Mifflin, 1889. p. 156).

3660. Sahagún, Bernardino de. Historia de México, 1889. 91 p. Br972 Sa14. Manuscript, copied from an original in the Medicean Library in Florence for Daniel G. Brinton, May 1889.

3661. Saint-Crico, M. Fragment de la relation inédite du voyage du Pérou au Brésil par les fleuves Ucayali et Amazone. *Bulletin de la Société de Géographie* 5:297-352, 1853. Br572C An8141 v.157.

3662. Sallusti, Guiseppe. *Storia delle missioni apostoliche dello stato del Chile; colla descrizione del viaggio dal Vecchio al Nuovo mondo fatto dall'autore.* Presso G. Mauri, Roma, 1827. 4 v. Br918 Sa34.

3663. Salmon, Philippe. Age de la Pierre: division palethnologique en six époques. *Bulletin de la Société Dauphinoise d'Ethnologie et d'Anthropologie*, 1894. 3 p. Br572C An8141 v.132.

3664. Salmon, Philippe. *Age de la pierre; habitations néolithiques, le campignien, fouille d'un fond de cabane au Campigny, commune de Blangy-sur-Bresle, Seine-inférievre.* Alcan, Paris, 1898. 44 p. Br571.2 Sa3.

3665. Salmon, Philippe. Dénombrement et types des cranes néolithqiues de la Gaule. *Revue Mensuelle de l'Ecole d'Anthropologie de Paris*, 1895. 76 p. Br572C An8141 v.142.

3666. Salmon, Philippe. *L'anthropologie au Congrès de Saint-Étienne, 26 session de l'Association Française pour l'Avancement des Sciences, 6-12 aout 1897.* Ancienne Librarie Germer Baillière et Cte., Paris, 1898. 10 p. Br572C An8141 v.163.

3667. Salmon, Philippe. L'Atlantide et le Renne. *Revue Mensuelle de l'École d'Anthropologie de Paris*, 1897. 8 p. Br572C An8141 v.157.

3668. Salvin, Osbert. Views of the Mayan ruins at Copán in Honduras, 1862-1863.

Br913.7283 Sa38. Two photographic prints; albumen; 21.5 x 16.5 cm. or smaller, on mounts 51 x 41 cm. Each photograph shows a standing stone stela with elaborate sculptural relief. One depicts a standing figure; the other has an additional carved fragment lying near its base. Photographs are unsigned.

3669. San Buenaventura, Gabriel de. Arte de la lengva maya, 1684. 41 leaves. Br498.21 MSa 53a. Manuscript; transcription by Karl H. Berendt of *Arte de la lengva maya, compuesto por el R. P. Fr. Gabriel de San Buenaventura a Predicador, y definidor habitual de la Provincia de San Joséph de Yucatán del Orden de N. P. S. Francisco* (Por la Viuda de Bernardo Calderón, En México, 1684).

3670. San Buenaventura, Gabriel de. *Arte de la lengva maya, compuesto por el R. P. Fr. Gabriel de San Buenaventura a Predicador, y definidor habitual de la Provincia de San Joséph de Yucatán del Orden de N. P. S. Francisco.* Por la Viuda de Bernardo Calderón, México, 1684. 163 p. Br498.21 MSa 53.

3671. San Roman, Francisco J. La lengua cunza de los naturales de Atacama. *Revista de la Dirección de Obras Públicas*, 1890. 20 p. Br572C An8141 v.47.

3672. Sanborn, John W. *Hymnal in the Seneca Language; Also Ten Psalms of David, Together With a Choice Collection of English Hymns With Tunes and an Index.* Oyo-ga-weh [Batavia], NY, 1892. 30 p. Br497.27 Ssa52. Hymnal and Psalms of David translated into Seneca.

3673. Sanborn, John W. *Legends, Customs and Social Life of the Seneca Indians, of Western New York.* Horton and Deming, Gowanda, NY, 1878. 76 p. Br398.22 Ssa52.

3674. Sánchez de León, José. Apuntamientos de la historia de Guatemala, n.d. 148 p. Br972.81 Sa53. Contains also: Thomas de Arano, "Relación de los estragos y ruinas que ha padecido la ciudad de Santiago de Guatemala," 1876; Agustin Cano, "Informe dado al Rey, sobre la entrada que por la parte de la Verapaz se hizo al Petén, el año de 1695," n.d.

3675. Sánchez, José M. Apuntes en lengua zapoteca, con añadiduras. Tuxtla, 1870. 31 leaves. Br498.34 Sa 53. Partial manuscript, with memoranda and additions by Karl H. Berendt.

3676. Sánchez, José M. Fragmento de unas exhortaciones para la observancia de los mandamientos del decalago, en lengua zoque, por D. José María Sánchez, cura de Ocosocantla, 1864. 3 leaves. Br498. Original manuscript by the cura of Ocosocantla.

3677. Sánchez, José M. *Gramática de la lengua zoque; formada por el presbítero Br. D. José M. Sánchez para que sirva de texto en el Colegio tridentino de la diócesis de Chiapas.* Imprenta de la "Sociedad católica" á cargo de M. Armendariz, Chiapa, 1877. 56 p. Br498.97 Zsa 53.

3678. Sánchez, José M. Vocabulario comparativo de las lenguas zoque de Tuxtla, zotzil de San Bartolomé de los Llanos, chaneabal de Comitán, por D. José M.a Sánchez, cura de Ocosocantla; con una exhoración para la confesión en lengua zoque y castellano. 25 p. Br498.21. Comparative vocabulary including 710 words in Zoque, 490 in Tzotzil, and 261 in Tojolabal.

3679. Sandoval, Rafael. *Arte de la lengua mexicana, por el Br. en sagrada teologia D. Rafael Sandoval.* En la oficína de D. Manuel Antonio Valdés, México, 1810. 62 p. Br498.22 AzSa 53.

3680. Sanger, Edward B. Notes on the aborigines of Cooper's Creek, Australia. *American Naturalist* 17:1220-1224, 1883. Br572C An8141 v.13.

3681. Sans, Rafael. *Memoria histórica del Colegio de misiones de San José de La Paz.* Imprenta de La Paz, La Paz, 1887. 239 p. Br243.2 F84S.

3682. *Santo Evangelio de nuestro Señor Jesu-Cristo según San Marcos; are ua uuhil tioxilah Evangelio rech canimahaual Jesu-Cristo quereka San Marcos.* Government Press, Guatemala, 1898. 80 p. Br498.21 KiB 47.2. Translation of the Gospel of St. Mark into Quiché Maya.

3683. Santo Tomas, Domingo de. *Arte de la lengua quichua; edición facsimilar.* B. G. Teubner, Leipzig, 1891. 96 p. Br498.7 KD 713.

3684. Sapper, Karl T. Beiträge zur Ethnographie der Republik Guatemala. *Petermanns Geographische Mitteilungen,* 1893. 14 p. Br572C An8141 v.107.

3685. Sapper, Karl T. Bemerkungen über raümliche Vertheilung und morphologischen Eigenthümlichkeiten der Vulcane Guatemalas. *Zeitschrift der Deutsche Geologische Gesellschaft,* pp. 54-62, 1893. Br572C An8141 v.128.

3686. Sapper, Karl T. *Das Nördliche Mittel-Amerika nebst einem Ausflug nach dem Hochland von Anachuac; Reisen und Studien aus den Jahren 1888-1895.* F. Vieweg, Braunschweig, 1897. 436 p. Br917.28 Sa63.2.

3687. Sapper, Karl T. *Die Ruinen von Mixco, Guatemala.* P. W. M. Trap, Leiden, 1898. Br913.728 Sa68.

3688. Sapper, Karl T. Grundzüge der physikalischen Geographie von Guatemala. *Petermanns Mitteilungen* 14(113), 1894. 59 p. Br572C An8141 v.145.

3689. Sapper, Karl T. Mittelamericanische Caraiben. *Internationales Archiv für Ethnographie* 10:53-68, 1897. Br572C An8141 v.161.

3690. Sapper, Karl T. Über Alterthümer vom Río Ulúa in der Republik Honduras. *Verhandlungen der Berliner Anthropologischen Gesellschaft für Anthropologie, Ethnologie und Urgeschichte,* pp. 133-137, 1898. Br572C An8141 v.163.

3691. Sapper, Karl T. Über Erderschütterungen in der Alta Verapaz (Guatemala). *Zeitschrift der Deutsche Geologische Gesellschaft,* pp. 832-838, 1894. Br572C An8141 v.142.

3692. Sargent, Withrop. A letter from Colonel Winthrop Sargent to Dr. Benjamin Smith, Boston, accompanying drawings and some account of certain articles, which were taken out of an ancient tumulus, or grave, in the western country. pp. 177-216, 1794. Br572C An8141 v.97. Letters are dated 1794-1795.

3693. Sartain, John. On the ancient art of painting in Encaustic. *Journal of the Franklin Institute,* September, 1885. 12 p. Br572C An8141 v.82.

3694. Satoh, A. The wooden statue of Baron II Kamon-no-kami Naosuké, pioneer diplomat of Japan. *Annual Report of the United States National Museum, Smithsonian Institution, for 1894,* pp. 619-622, 1896. Br572C An8141 v.157.

3695. Savi López, Maria. Miti e leggende degli indigeni americani. *Natura ed Arte* 4(3), 1894. 12 p. Br572C An8141 v.113.

3696. Saville, Marshall H. A primitive Maya musical instrument. *American Anthropologist* 10, 1897. 1 p. Br572C An8141 v.158.

3697. Saville, Marshall H. An ancient figure of terra cotta from the Valley of Mexico. *Bulletin of the American Museum of Natural History* 9:221-224, 1897. Br572C An8141 v.157.

3698. Saville, Marshall H. Exploration of Zapotecan tombs in southern Mexico. *American Anthropologist* 1(4): 350-362, 1899. Br913.727 Sa9.

3699. Saville, Marshall H. Musical bow in ancient Mexico. *American Anthropologist* 11:280-284, 1898. Br913.72 Sa913.2.

3700. Saville, Marshall H. The Temple of Tepoztlan, Mexico. *Bulletin of the American Museum of Natural History* 8:221-226, 1896. Br572C An8141 v.158.

3701. Sayce, A. H. The primitive home of the Aryans. *Annual Report of the United States National Museum, Smithsonian Institution, for 1890,* pp. 475-487, 1891. Br572C An8141 v.121.

3702. Schaaffhausen, Geheimrath. Das alter der Menschemrassen. *Naturwissenschaftliche Wochenschrift* 6(7): 63-70, 1891. Br572.3 Sch1.

3703. Schaaffhausen, Hermann. Alte und Neue Mammuths Funde. pp. 61-70, n.d. Br572C An8141 v.82.

3704. Schaaffhausen, Hermann. *Anthropologische Studien.* A. Marcus, Bonn, 1885. 677 p. Br572 Sch1.

3705. Schaaffhausen, Hermann. Damoney-Neger. pp. 100-110, n.d. Br572C An8141 v.82.

3706. Schaaffhausen, Hermann. Die alten Völker Europas. pp. 65-72, n.d. Br572C An8141 v.9.

3707. Schaaffhausen, Hermann. Die Kelten. In *Festschrift zum Fünfzigjahrenigen Jubiläum des Vereins von Alterthumsfreuden im Rheinlande,* pp. 276-283. Adolph Marcus, Bonn, 1892. Br572C An8141 v.98; Br572C An8141 v.109.

3708. Schaaffhausen, Hermann. Sogenannten Azteken in Coln. *Sitzungsberichten der Niederhein,* pp. 97-102, 1891. 2 p. Br572C An8141 v.82.

3709. Schasler, Maximilian F. A. *Die Elemente der philosophischen Sprachwissenschaft Wilhelm von Humboldt's, aus seinem Werke, über die Verschiedenheit des menschlichen Sprachbauer und ihren Einfluss aud die geistige Entwicklung des menschenhgeschichts in systematischer Entwicklung dargestellt und kritisch Erläutert.* Guttentag, Berlin, 1847. 221 p. Br409 Sch1.

3710. Schattenberg, H. Der Schimmelreiter im Braunschweigischen. *Beiträge zur Anthropologie Braunschweigs* 21:155-163, 1898. Br572C An8141 v.164.

3711. Schellhas, Paul. Alte Thongefässe aus Guatemala. *Internationales Archiv für Ethnographie* 8:123-124, 1895. Br572C An8141 v.144. Schellhas (1859-1945) studied law and served in the Prussian civil service as a judge. His free time was dedicated mainly to Maya research. Schellhas identified name glyphs for Maya deities and mythical animals, and made a systematic inventory and description of the nearly thirty deities represented in the prehispanic Maya pictorial codices.

3712. Schellhas, Paul. Die Göttergestalten der Maya-Handschriften. *Zeitschrift für Ethnologie,* pp. 103-121, 1892. Br572C An8141 v.83.

3713. Schellhas, Paul. *Die Maya-Handschrift der Königlichen Bibliothek zu Dresden.* Berlin, 1886. 77 p. Br572C An8141 v.4.

3714. Schellhas, Paul. *Ein mythologisches Kulturbild aus dem alten Amerika; die Göttergestalten der mayahandschriften.* Verlag von Richard Bertling, Dresden, 18997. 34 p. Br572C An8141 v.158.

3715. Schellhas, Paul. Maya-Hieroglyphen. *Verhandlungen der Berliner Anthropologischen Gesellschaft für Anthropologie, Ethnologie und Urgeschichte* 15:17-19, 1887. Br572C An8141 v.83.

3716. Schellhas, Paul. Neue Ausgrabungen des Hrn. Dieseldorff in Chajcar, Guatemala. *Verhandlungen der Berliner Anthropologischen Gesellschaft für Anthropologie, Ethnologie und Urgeschichte* 27:320-322, 1895. Br572C An8141 v.142.

3717. Schellhas, Paul. Vergleichende Studien auf dem Felde der Maya-Alterthümer. *Internationales Archiv für Ethnographie* 3:209-231, 1890. Br572C An8141 v.102.

3718. Scherzer, Karl, Ritter von. *Aus dem Natur- und Völkerleben im tropischen Amerika.* G. Wigand, Leipzig, 1864. 380 p. Br917.28 Sch27.

3719. Scherzer, Karl, Ritter von. Die Indianer von Santa Catalina Istlávacan, 1856. 15 p. Br572C An8141 v.81.

3720. Scherzer, Karl, Ritter von. *Ein Besuch bei den Ruinen von Quiriguá im Staat Guatemala in Central-Amerika.* Sitzungs. Berichte der Philogische und Historische Abhandlungen der Königlichen Akademie der Wissenschaften zu Berlin, 16. Berlin, 1855. 15 p. Br572C An8141 v.38.

3721. Scherzer, Karl, Ritter von. Sprachen der Indianer Central-Amerikas; während seinen mehrjährigen Reisen in der verschiedenen Staaten Mittel-Amerika's aufgezeichnet und zusammengestellt. Vienna, 1855. 11 p. Br572C An8141 v.81. Includes a comparative vocabulary of Tlaxcallan, Quiché, Pokomchi, Popoluca, and the languages of Costa Rica.

3722. Schiefner, Franz A. Leopold Radloff's Wörterbuch der Kinai-Sprache. *Mémoires de l'Académie Impériale des Sciences de St. Pétersbourg* 21(8), 1874. 33 p. Br572C An8141 v.92.

3723. Schiffmann, A. *Una idea sobre la jeologia de Nicaragua.* Managua, 1873. 159 p. Br917.285 Sch33.

3724. Schirmacher, Kaethe. *Féminisme aux États-Unis, en France, dans la Grande-Bretagne, en Suéde, et én Russie.* Armand Colin, Paris, 1898. 73 p. Br396 Sch37.

3725. Schlegel, Gustave. A Canton flower-boat. *Internationales Archiv für Ethnographie* v. 7, 1894. 9 p. Br915.12 Sch6.

3726. Schlegel, Gustave. *Die chinesische Inschrift auf dem Uigurischen Denkmal in Kara Balgassun: Übersetzt und Erläutert.* Imprimerie de la Socété de Littérature Finnoise, 1896. 141 p. Br572C An8141 v.158.

3727. Schlegel, Gustave. La femme chinoise. *Actes du Congrès International des Orientalistes (10 session, Genève, 1894),* pp. 115-139. E. J. Brill, Leide, 1896. Br572C An8141 v.158.

3728. Schlegel, Gustave. Lang-ga-siu or Lang-ga-su and Sih-lan Shan Ceylan. pp. 15-24, n.d. Br572C An8141 v.163.

3729. Schlegel, Gustave. Problemes géographiques; les peuples étrangers chez les historiens Chinois. XVIII. San Sien Chan. *T'oung-Pao* 6(1), 1895. 66 p. Br572C An8141 v.132.

3730. Schlegel, Gustave. Problemes géographiques; les peuples étrangers chez les historiens Chinois. XIII. Ni-Li Kouo; XIV. Pei-Ming Kouo; XV. Youh-I Kouo; XVI. Han-Ming Kouo. *T'oung-Pao* 5(3), 1894. 57 p. Br572C An8141 v.132.

3731. Schlegel, Gustave. Problèmes géographiques; les peuples étrangers chez les historiens chinois: XIX. Lieou-Kieou-Kovo. *T'oung-Pao* 6(2), 1895. 51 p. Br572C An8141 v.142.

3732. Schlegel, Gustave. Problèmes géographiques; les peuples étrangers chez les historiens chinois: XX. Niu-Jin-Kouo. *T'oung-Pao* 6(3), 1895. 11 p. Br572C An8141 v.142.

3733. Schlegel, Gustave. Problèmes géographiques; les peuples étrangers chez les historiens chinois. *T'oung-Pao* 3(5): 3–23, 1892. Br572C An8141 v.109.

3734. Schlegel, Gustave. *Problèmes géographiques; les peuples étrangers chez les historiens chinois: IV. Siao-jin kouo; V. Ta-han kouo; VI. Ta-jin kouo ou Tchang-jin kouo; VII. Kiun-tsze kouo; VIII. Peh-min kouo.* E. J. Brill, Leiden, 1893. 42 p. Br572C An8141 v.120.

3735. Schlegel, Gustave. *Problèmes géographiques; les peuples étrangers chez les historiens chinois: IX. Ts'ing-k'ieou kouo; X. Heh-tchi kouo; XI. Hiouen-kou Kouo; XII. Lo-min kouo ou Kiao-min kouo.* E. J. Brill, Leiden, 1893. 15 p. Br572C An8141 v.123.

3736. Schlegel, Gustave. The Nicobar and Andaman Islands, n.d. 24 p. Br572C An8141 v.163.

3737. Schleyer, Johann Martin. *Mittlere Grammatik der Universalsprache Volapük.* 8th ed. Verlag von Schleyer's Weltsprache-Zentralbüro, Konstanz in Baden, 1887. 144 p. Br409.09 Sch3.

3738. Schlosser, Max. Über die Deutung des milchebisses der Säugethiere, n.d. 37 p. Br599 Sch31.

3739. Schmeltz, Johann D. E. *Das Schwirrholz: Versuch einer Monographie.* L. Friederichsen, Hamburg, 1896. 36 p. Br572C An8141 v.158.

3740. Schmeltz, Johann D. E. *Ethnographische Musea in Midden-Europ, verslag einer Studiereis 19 mei–31 juli 1895.* Brill, Leiden, 1896. 109 p. Br572 Sch521.

3741. Schmeltz, Johann D. E. Rijks Ethnographisch Museum te Leiden, 1895. 40 p. Br572C An8141 v.158.

3742. Schmeltz, Johann D. E. *Schnecken und Muscheln im Leben der Völker Indonesiens und Oceaniens.* E. J. Brill, Leiden, 1894. 43 p. Br572C An8141 v.141.

3743. Schmidt, Emil. *Anthropologische methoden. Anleitung zum Beobachten und Sammeln für Laboratorium und Reise.* Veit und Comp., Leipzig, 1888. 336 p. Br572 Sch52.

3744. Schmidt, Emil. *Ceylon.* Schall und Grund, Berlin, 1897. 323 p. Br915.48 Sch52.

3745. Schmidt, Emil. Die Animalai Gebirge. *Globus* 60(1–2), 1890. 8 p. Br572C An8141 v.91.

3746. Schmidt, Emil. Die Anthropologische Indiens. *Globus* 61(2–3), 1891. 11 p. Br572C An8141 v.91.

3747. Schmidt, Emil. Physische Anthropologie…im Jahre 1891 [bibliography]. *Jahresberichte der Anatomie und Physiologie* 20:523–580, 1891. Br572C An8141 v.121.

3748. Schmidt, Emil. Physische Anthropologie. *Jahresberichte der Anatomie und Physiologie*, pp. 780–852, 1896. Br572C An8141 v.163.

3749. Schmidt, Emil. Török Craniometrie. *Referate*, pp. 280–285, n.d. Br572C An8141 v.91.

3750. Schmidt, Emil. *Vorgeschichte Nordamerikas im gebiet der Vereingten Staaten*. F. Vieweg und Sohn, Braunschweig, 1894. 216 p. Br913.73 Sch5.

3751. Schneider, H. C. *Beiträge zur Geschichte der Deutschen in Amerika*. Leipzig, 1883. 72 p. Br572C An8141 v.65.

3752. Schneider, Wilhelm. *Die Naturvölker. Missverständnisse, Missdeutungen, und Misshandlungen*. Schöningh, Paderborn, 1885–1886. Br572 Sch56.

3753. Schoolcraft, Henry R. *Algic Researches Comprising Inquiries Respecting the Mental Characteristics of the North American Indians; First Series; Indian Tales and Legends*. Harper, New York, 1839. 2 v. Br398.21 Sch65. Henry Rowe Schoolcraft (1793-1864) began as nineteen-year career in the Federal Indian service in 1822 when he was appointed the first Indian agent at Sault Ste. Marie, Michigan. With the aid of his Ojibwa-Irish wife, Schoolcraft began a pioneer study of Ojibwa language and oral literature. In his *Algic Researches*, Schoolcraft (1793-1864) argued that the legends revealed an indigenous mentality that was decidedly Oriental and, he believed, impervious to change. He was one of the founding members of the American Ethnological Society and an important resource on Great Lake Indian ethnology.

3754. Schoolcraft, Henry R. *Index to Schoolcraft's Indian Tribes of the United States, Compiled by Frances S. Nichols*. Bulletin of the Bureau of Ethnology, Smithsonian Institution, 152, 1954. 257 p. Br970.4 USch65 Index.

3755. Schoolcraft, Henry R. *Information Respecting the History, Condition and Prospects of the Indian Tribes of the United States; Collected and Prepared Under the Direction of the Bureau of Indian Affairs, per Act of Congress of March 3d, 1847; Illustrated by E. Eastman; Published by Authority of Congress*. Lippincott, Grambo, Philadelphia, 1853–1856. 5 v. Br970.4 USch 65 1853.

3756. Schoolcraft, Henry R. *Notes on the Iroquois; or, Contributions to American History, Antiquities, and General Ethnology*. E. H. Pease and Company, Alabny, NY, 1847. 498 p. Br970.3 IrSch65. "This is the most valuable of Mr. Schoolcraft's works, having been executed after personal examination in an official capacity of all the tribes inhabiting New York...an appendix...is filled with letters from persons resident or familiar with the various Indian tribes, conveying minute and doubtless truthful information regarding them" (Field 1873:351).

3757. Schoolcraft, Henry R. *Oneóta, or, the Red Race of America; Their History, Traditions, Customs, Poetry, Picture-Writing, etc.; in Extracts from Notes, Journals, and Other Unpublished Writing*. Burgess, Stringer, New York, 1844. 64 p. Br970.1 Sch6.3.

3758. Schrader, Otto. *Sprachvergleichung und Urgeschichte; Linguitisch-historische Beiträge zur Erforschung des indogermanischen Altertums*. H. Costenoble, Jena, 1883. 490 p. Br410 Sch6.

3759. Schuch, J. Über zwei peruanische Mumien aus der Küste von Atacama im Hochlande Bolivias. *Korrespondenzblatt des Zoologisch, Mineralogischen*

Vereines in Regensburg 9:129-144, 1850. Br572C An8141 v.71.

3760. Schuchardt, H. E. Modifications phonetique. *Literaturblatt für Germaische und Romanische Philologie* 9:1-6, 1892. Br572C An8141 v.102.

3761. Schuchardt, H. E. Romano-Magyarisches. *Zeitschrift für Romanische Philologie*, pp. 88-123, n.d. Br572C An8141 v.6.

3762. Schuchardt, H. E. *Weltsprache und Weltsprachen an Gustav Meyer.* Verlag von Karl J. Trübner, Strassburg, 1894. 53 p. Br572C An8141 v.127.

3763. Schuchardt, Hugo E. Das Datum der Pilgerfahrt nach Canterbury. *Englische Studien* 12:469-474, n.d. Br572C An8141 v.26.

3764. Schuchardt, Hugo E. *Kreolische Studien.* Sitzungsberichte der Kais. Akademie der Wissenschaften in Wien, Philosophisch-Historische Classe, Band 122. F. Tempsky, Wien, 1889. 256 p. Br572C An8141 v.46.

3765. Schulenburg, Albrecht C., graf von der. *Die Sprache der Zimshian-Indianer in Nordwest America.* R. Sattler, Braunschweig, 1894. 372 p. Br497.18 TSch 8.

3766. Schultz, Woldemar. *Natur- und Culturstudien über Südamerika und seine Bewohner, mit besonderer Berücksichtigung der Colonisationsfrage; von Woldemar Schultz. (Nachgelassenes werk, hrsg. vom Vereine für Erdkunde in Dresden).* G. Schönfeld, Dresden, 1868. 137 p. Br572.98 Sch8.

3767. Schultze, Augustus. *A Brief Grammar and Vocabulary of the Eskimo Language of North-West Alaska.* Society for Propagating the Gospel Among the Heathen, Bethlehem Press, 1889. 21 p. Br572C An8141 v.51.

3768. Schumacher, Hermann A. Die Thule Indianer des Staats Panama (Columbia). Bogota, 1872. 9 leaves. Br498.2. Manuscript by the German Minister-Resident in Bogota; probably taken from Schumacher's *Sudamerikanische Studien Drei Lebens- und Culturbilder, Mutis.* Caldas. Codazzi. 1760-1860 (E.S. Mittler, Berlin, 1884).

3769. Schumacher, Paul. The method of manufacture of several articles by the former Indians of southern California. *Annual Reports of the Trustees of the Peabody Museum of American Archaeology and Ethnology* 2(2): 258-268, 1878. Br913.07 H265.

3770. Schumacher, Paul. The method of manufacturing pottery and baskets among the Indians of southern California. *Annual Reports of the Trustees of the Peabody Museum of American Archaeology and Ethnology* 2(3): 523-535, 1880. Br913.07 H265.

3771. Schurtz, Heinrich. *Katechismus der Völkerkunde.* J. J. Weber, Leipzig, 1893. 370 p. Br572 Sch85.

3772. Schütz-Holzhausen, Damien. *Der Amazonas; Wanderbilder aus Peru, Bolivia und Nord Brasilien.* Herder, Freiburg, 1883. 243 p. Br918 Sch74.

3773. Schwartz, Friedrich L. W. *Der Ursprung der Mythologie, dargelegt an griechischer und deutscher Sage.* W. Hertz, Berlin, 1860. 299 p. Br280 Sch91.

3774. Scott, Charles P. G. The devil and his imps: an etymological inquisition. *Transactions of the American Philological Association* 26:79-146, 1895. Br572C An8141 v.158.

3775. Searcy, J. T. Insanity in the South. *American Academy of Medicine*, 1896. 6 p. Br572C An8141 v.158.

3776. Searcy, J. T. *Self-Adjustability.* Tuscaloosa, 1895. 54 p. Br572C An8141 v.141.

3777. Secretaria de Fomento (Mexico). *Indice alfabetico de la obra de Francisco*

Jiménez titulada; cuatro libros de la naturaleza y virtudes de las plantas y animales de uso medicinal en la Nueva España. México, 1900. 22 p. Br615.32 H425.

3778. Seler, Eduard. Alterthümer aus Guatemala. *Ethnologisches Notizblatt* 1(2): 20-26, 1895. Br572C An8141 v.141. Seler (1849-1922) was the founder of Mesoamerican iconographic research. He was the first to demonstrate from prehispanic art and codices that there was fundamental unity to Mexican and Maya thought and religion. He also made major contributions to the study of deity and animal figures in the Maya codices, and was a collector of archaeological and botanical specimens for the Berlin Museum.

3779. Seler, Eduard. *Altmexikanische Studien: 1. Ein Kapitel aus den in aztekischer Sprache geschriebenen ungedruckten Materialien zu dem Geschichtswerk des p. Sahagún. (Ms. der Biblioteca del Palacio zu Madrid.).* W. Spemann, Berlin, 1890. Br572C An8141 v.101; Br913.72 Se47.4. Extract from *Veröffentlichungen aus dem Königlichen Museum für Völkerkunde,* Bd. 1, no. 4, pp. 117-188, 1890; includes: Die Sogenannten Sacralen Gefässe der Zapoteken (pp. 182-188).

3780. Seler, Eduard. Altmexikanischen Schmuck und militärische Ragabzeichen. *Zeitschrift für Ethnologie* 23:114-144, 1891. Br572C An8141 v.12.

3781. Seler, Eduard. Archäologische Reise in Mexico. *Verhandlungen der Gesellschaft für Erdkunde zu Berlin* 2, 1889. 21 p. Br572C An8141 v.83.

3782. Seler, Eduard. Das Gefäss von Chamá. *Zeitschrift für Ethnologie* 36:307-320, 1895. Br572C An8141 v.141.

3783. Seler, Eduard. Das Konjugationssystem der Maya-Sprachen. Berlin, 1887. 52 p. Br572C An8141 v.84. Inaugural dissertation, Leipzig, 1887.

3784. Seler, Eduard. Den altmexikanischen Federschmuck des Wiener Hofmuseums und über mexikanische Rangabezichen im Allgemeinen. *Zeitschrift für Ethnologie* 10:63-85, 1889. Br572C An8141 v.83.

3785. Seler, Eduard. Der Charakter der aztekischen und der Maya-Handschriften. *Zeitschrift für Ethnologie* 10:407-416, 1888. Br572C An8141 v.4.

3786. Seler, Eduard. Der Codex Borgia und die Verwandten aztekischen Bilderschriften. *Zeitschrift für Ethnologie* 19:105-114, 1887. Br572C An8141 v.83.

3787. Seler, Eduard. Der Fledermaus-Gott der Maya-Stämme. *Zeitschrift für Ethnologie* 26:577-585, 1894. Br572C An8141 v.141.

3788. Seler, Eduard. Die Bedeutung des Mayakalenders für die historische Chronologie. *Globus* 68(3): 37-41, 1895. Br572C An8141 v.144.

3789. Seler, Eduard. Die Lichbringer bei den Indianerstämmen der Nordwestküste. *Globus* 61(13-16): 1-16, 1891. Br572C An8141 v.102; Br572C An8141 v.103.

3790. Seler, Eduard. *Die mexikanischen Bilderhandschriften Alexander von Humboldt's in der Königlichen Bibliothek zu Berlin.* Berlin, 1893. 136 p. Br572C An8141 v.109; Br572C An8141 v.113.

3791. Seler, Eduard. Die Quimbaya und ihre Nachbarn. *Globus* 64(15): 242-248, 1915. Br572C An8141 v.160.

3792. Seler, Eduard. Die Ruinen von Xochicalco. *Zeitschrift für Ethnologie* 20:94-111,

1888. Br572C An8141 v.83.

3793. Seler, Eduard. Eine Liste der mexikanischen Monatfeste. *Zeitschrift für Ethnologie* 19:172-176, 1887. Br572C An8141 v.88.

3794. Seler, Eduard. Geräthe und Ornamente der Pueblo-Indianer. *Zeitschrift für Ethnologie* 19:599-603, 1887. Br572C An8141 v.83.

3795. Seler, Eduard. Maya-Handschriften und Maya-Götter. *Zeitschrift für Ethnologie* 18:416-420, 1886. Br572C An8141 v.4.

3796. Seler, Eduard. Merito und Mittelamerika aus der amerikanisch-historischen Austellung in Madrid. *Globus* 63(15), 1914. 5 p. Br572C An8141 v.107.

3797. Seler, Eduard. Namen der in der Dresdener Handschrift abgebildeten Maya-Götter. *Zeitschrift für Ethnologie* 19:224-241, 1887. Br572C An8141 v.110.

3798. Seler, Eduard. *Reisebriefe aus Mexiko*. Ferd. Dümmlers Verlagsbuchhandlung, Berlin, 1889. 267 p. Br917.2 Se43.

3799. Seler, Eduard. Über den Ursprung der altmexikanischen Kulturen. *Prüssischen Jahrbücher* 79(3): 488-502, 1895. Br572C An8141 v.136.

3800. Seler, Eduard. *Wandmalereien von Mitla; eine mexikanische Bilderschrift in Fresko, nach eigenen an Ort und stelle aufgenommenen Zeichnungen*. A. Asher, Berlin, 1895. 58 p. Br913.727 Se47.

3801. Seler, Eduard. Wo lag Aztlan, die Heimat der Azteken?. *Globus* 65(20): 317-324, 1894. 8 p. Br572C An8141 v.160.

3802. Seler, Eduard. Zur mexikanischen Chronologie, mit besonderer Berücksichtgung des Zapotekischen Kalenders. *Zeitschrift für Ethnologie* 13:89-193, 1891. 133 p. Br572C An8141 v.12.

3803. Sellers, George E. Aboriginal pottery of the Salt-Springs, Illinois. *Popular Science Monthly* 11:573-586, 1877. Br572C An8141 v.19.

3804. *Seminole Tragedy; A Narrative of the Life and Sufferings of Mrs. Jane Johns, Who was Wounded and Scalped by Seminole Indians in East Florida in 1836.* Jacksonville, 1875. 15 p. Br923.9 J623S.

3805. Sergi, Giuseppe. *Africa; antropologia della stirpe camitica (Spedie eurafricana)*. Bocca, Torino, 1897. 426 p. Br572.9 Se67.

3806. Sergi, Giuseppe. Al Congresso Internazionale di Medicina a Mosca, sezione di anatomia e di antropologia. *Societa Romana di Antropologia* 5(1): 1-5, 1898. Br572C An8141 v.158; Br573.7 Se65.4.

3807. Sergi, Giuseppe. *Arii e Italici; attorno all'Italia preistorica, con figure dimonstrative*. Fratelli Bocca, Torino, 1898. 228 p. Br572.891 Se67.

3808. Sergi, Giuseppe. *Catalogo sistematico delle varietà umane della Russia*. R. Stabilimiento Prosperini, Padova, 1893. 19 p. Br572C An8141 v.122.

3809. Sergi, Giuseppe. Crani antichi di Sicilia e Creta. *Atti della Società Romana di Antropologia* 2(2): 287-291, 1895. Br572C An8141 v.142.

3810. Sergi, Giuseppe. *Crani Preistorici della Sicilia*. Tip. dello Stabilimento Rocco Carabba, Lanciano, 1899. 11 p. Br573.7 Se65.

3811. Sergi, Giuseppe. Crani siculi neolitici. *Bolletino di Paletnologia Italiano* 17:157-172, 1891. Br572C An8141 v.17.

3812. Sergi, Giuseppe. *Di alcune varieta umane della Sardegna.* Tipografía Innocenzo Artero, Roma, 1892. 17 p. Br572C An8141 v.122.

3813. Sergi, Giuseppe. Die Menschen-Varietäten in Melanesian. *Archiv für Anthropologie* 22(3): 339-383, 1893. 64 p. Br572C An8141 v.107.

3814. Sergi, Giuseppe. *Etruschi e Pelasgi.* Tipografía della Camera dei Deputati, Roma, 1893. 15 p. Br572C An8141 v.122.

3815. Sergi, Giuseppe. *I dati antropologici in sociologia.* Tessitori, Scansano, 1898. 11 p. Br572 Se67.

3816. Sergi, Giuseppe. Intorno ai pigmei d'Europa. *Atti della Societa Romana di Antropologia* 2:288-291, 1895. Br572C An8141 v.142.

3817. Sergi, Giuseppe. *Le influenze celtiche e gl'Italici: un problema antropologico.* Tipografía dell'Unione Cooperativa Editrice, Roma, 1895. 15 p. Br572C An8141 v.142.

3818. Sergi, Giuseppe. *Le varietà umane; principi e metodo di classificazione.* Premiato Stabilimiento Tipo-Litografico P. Bruno, Torino, 1893. 60 p. Br572C An8141 v.122.

3819. Sergi, Giuseppe. *Origine e diffusione della Stirpe Mediterranea: induzioni antropologische.* Società Editrice Dante Alighieri, Roma, 1895. 144 p. Br572C An8141 v.142.

3820. Sergi, Giuseppe. Pensare senza coscienza. Florence. *Rivista Moderna* 2(1), 1899, 18 p. Br188.3 Se67.

3821. Sergi, Giuseppe. *Relazione del Congresso di Antropologia e di Archeologia prehistorica di Mosca.* Tipografía di S. Landi, Firenze, 1893. 82 p. Br572C An8141 v.122.

3822. Sergi, Giuseppe. Sopra due crani di tombe dette Barbariche. *Atti della Societa Romana di Antropologia* 2:284-285, 1895. Br572C An8141 v.142.

3823. Sergi, Giuseppe. Studi di antropologia laziale. *Bulletino della R. Accademie Medica di Roma* 21:3-60, 1895. Br572C An8141 v.135.

3824. Sergi, Giuseppe. Sulla nuova teoria delle emozioni. *Rivisti di Sociologia,* pp. 23-38, 1896. Br572C An8141 v.142.

3825. Sergi, Giuseppe. *The Varieties of the Human Species; Principles and Method of Classification.* Smithsonian Institution, Miscellaneous Collections, 38, 1898. 61 p. Br572C An8141 v.135; Br572.2 Se 67.

3826. Sergi, Giuseppe. Über den sogenannten Reihengräbertypus. *Centralblatt für Anthropologie, Ethnologie und Urgeschichte,* 1898. 8 p. Br572C An8141 v.158.

3827. Sermon para el dia de San Juan en lengua kekchí. Cobán, n.d. 3 leaves. Br498.21 KC684. Manuscript, transcribed by Karl H. Berendt, 1875; "copiado de un manuscrito en cuarto del archivo de la parroquia de Cobán, transcrito por Juan de Morales."

3828. Sermoncerio la lengua nahuatl, n.d. 373 leaves. Br498.22 AzSa67. Manuscript.

3829. Sermones en lengua maya, copiados de un manuscrito anciano; ejemplos, discursos y vidas de santos, 1750. 144 p. Br498.21 ML545. A compilation of anonymous sermons in Maya from Sotutá, Mexico, probably from around 1750, concerning the lives of various Catholic saints. The first sermon, entitled "Libro de matrimonio de predicaciones de parientes," is a discourse on marriage. Other sermons present the lives and significance of Saints Julian, Bárbara, Nicolás, Bartolomé, Ana, María Magdalena, Andrés and Tomás. Also included are a sermon explaining the Assumption of the Virgin, and a sermon for All Saints Day.

3830. Sermones en lengua maya; copiados de un manuscrito anciano en quarto de 196 pajas en poder del presbitero don Crescencio Carrillo, Mérida, 1870. Br498.21. Transcription by Karl H. Berendt of a late 18th-century manuscript in the library of the Rev. Crescencio Carrillo, Mérida.

3831. Serra, Angel. *Manual de administrar los santos sacramentos à los españoles, y naturales de esta provinica de Michuacan, conforme à la reforma de Paulo V. y Vrbana VIII.* Maria de Benavides I. de Ribera, Ciudad de México, 1697. 12 p. 129 leaves. Br498.27 Tse 67.

3832. Serrurier, Lindor. *De wajang poerwa, eene ethnologische studie.* E. J. Brill, Leiden, 1896. 352 p. Br572.992 Se6.

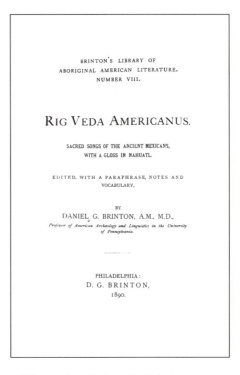

BRINTON'S LIBRARY OF
ABORIGINAL AMERICAN LITERATURE.
NUMBER VIII.

RIG VEDA AMERICANUS.

SACRED SONGS OF THE ANCIENT MEXICANS,
WITH A GLOSS IN NAHUATL.

EDITED, WITH A PARAPHRASE, NOTES AND
VOCABULARY,

BY
DANIEL G. BRINTON, A.M., M.D.,
Professor of American Archæology and Linguistics in the University of Pennsylvania.

PHILADELPHIA:
D. G. BRINTON,
1890.

Title page from Brinton's Rig Veda Americanus *(1890).*

3833. Sessions, F. Folk-lore topics, 2. Dowsing or divining rod. *Gloucester Journal,* 1894. 9 p. Br572C An8141 v.130.Br572C An8141 v.130.

3834. Sessions, F. Folk-lore topics, 3. A lucky stone. *Gloucester Journal,* 1894. 8 p. Br572C An8141 v.130.Br572C An8141 v.130.

3835. Sessions, F. Folk-lore topics, 4. Beating the bounds. *Gloucester Journal,* 1894. 8 p. Br572C An8141 v.130.

3836. Sessions, F. Folk-lore topics, 5. The younger son. *Gloucester Journal,* 1894. 8 p. Br572C An8141 v.130.

3837. Sewall, Rufus K. *Sketches of St. Augustine; With a View of Its History and Advantages as a Resort for Invalids.* G. P. Putnam, New York, 1848. 69 p. Br917.39 Se82.

3838. *Shahguhnahshe ahnuhmeahwene muzzeneegun. Ojebwag anwawaud azheuhnekenootahbeegahdag.* Diocesan Press, Toronto, 1846. 467 p. Br497.11 CC475. Church of England Book of Common Prayer, translated by Frederick A. O'Meara into Chippewa. Pilling (1885, no. 2833) gives authorship as James D. O'Meara.

3839. Shaler, N. S. Report on the age of the Delaware gravel beds containing chipped pebbles. *Annual Reports of the Trustees of the Peabody Museum of American Archaeology and Ethnology* 2(1): 44–47, 1877. Br913.07 H265.

3840. Shaler, S. On the language of the Berbers. *Transactions of the American Philosophical Society* 2(3): 438–465, 1823. Br572C An8141 v.102.

3841. Shea, John G. *Dictionnaire françois-onontagué; édité d'apres un manuscrit du 17e siècle, par Jean-Marie Shea.* Shea's Library of American Linguistics, 1. Cramoisy Press, New York, 1859. 103 p. Br497C Sh3; Br497C Sh3a. English title on p. 1.2 recto reads *A French Onondaga Dictionary, From a Manuscript of the Seventeenth Century, by John Gilmary Shea, Member of the New York, Massachusetts, Maryland, Michigan Historical and New England Historical and Genealogical Societies.* "The original manuscript of this work is still preserved in the Mazarin Library at Paris, and is supposed to date from the close of the seventeenth century. It is undoubtedly the work of one of the Jesuit fathers, whose missions commenced at Onondaga in 1655" (Field 1873:356).

3842. Shea, John G. *Illinois and Miami Vocabulary and Lord's Prayer.* New York, 1891. 9 p. Br572C An8141 v.48.

3843. *Shea's Library of American Linguistics.* Cramoisy Press, New York, 1859–1864. 12 v. Br497C Sh3; Br497C Sh3a.

3844. *Shea's Library of American Linguistics.* Series 2. Cramoisy Press, New York, 1873–1874. 2 v. Br497C Sh3.

3845. Sheafer, Peter W. *Historical Map of Pennsylvania; Showing the Indian Names of Streams and Villages, and Paths of Travel, the Sites of Old Forts and Battlefields, the Successive Purchases from the Indians, and the Names and Dates of Counties and County Towns, with Tales of Forts and Proprietary Manors.* Historical Society of Pennsylvania, Philadelphia, 1875. 26 p. Br912.748 Sh3.

3846. Shepherd, Henry A. *Antiquities of the State of Ohio.* J. C. Yorston and Company, Cincinatti, 1887. 139 p. Br913.771 Sh346.

3847. Sherborn, C. Davies, St. George Mivart, and Agnes Crane. [Obituary: Sir Richard] Owen. *Natural Science* 2(11), 1893. 30 p. Br572C An8141 v.121.

3848. Short, John T. *The North Americans of Antiquity; Their Origin, Migration, and Type of Civilization Considered.* 2d ed. Harper and Brothers, New York, 1880. 544 p. Br970.1 Sh8a.

3849. Shufeldt, Robert W. A maid of Wolpai. *Proceedings of the United States National Museum, Smithsonian Institution* 15:29–31, 1892. Br572C An8141 v.86.

3850. Shufeldt, Robert W. Indian types of beauty. *The American Field* 36(23–25): 3–24, 1891. Br572C An8141 v.110.

3851. Shufeldt, Robert W. Physiognomy of Indians. *Nature's Realm* 2(5): 161–179, 1891. Br572C An8141 v.89.

3852. Shufeldt, Robert W. Some observations on the Havesu-Pai Indians. *Proceedings of the United States National Museum, Smithsonian Institution* 14:387–390, 1891. Br572C An8141 v.10.

3853. Shufeldt, Robert W. The evolution of house building among the Navajo Indians. *Proceedings of the United States National Museum, Smithsonian Institution* 15:279–282, 1892. Br572C An8141 v.86.

3854. Shultz, Theodore. *The Acts of the Apostles, Translated Into the Arrawack Tongue,*

By the Rev. Theodore Shultz, In Eighteen Hundred and Two. American Bible Society, New York, 1850. 119 p. Br498.77 ArB 47.6. Acts of the Apostles translated into Arawak.

3855. Siemiradzki, Josef von. Beiträge zur Ethnographie der Südamerikanischen Indianer. *Mitteilungen der Anthropologischen Gesellschaft in Wien* 28:127-170, 1898. Br498.77 ArB 775; Br572C An8141 v.93; Br972.98 Si14. "Contains…suggestions regarding the kinship and cultural relations of…South American aborigines" (Cooper 1917:127).

3856. Sievers, Carl G. Über ein normännisches Schiffsgrab bei Ronneburg und die Ausgrabung des Rinnehügels am Burtneek-See (Livland). *Verhandlungen der Berliner Gesellschaft für Anthropologie, Ethnologie und Urgeschichte*, pp. 14-25, 1875. Br572C An8141 v.162.

3857. Sigüenza y Góngora, Carlos de. *Piedad heroica de D. Fernando Cortes, marques del Valle*. Talleres de la Librería Religiosa, México, 1898. 46 p. Br572C An8141 v.154; Br572C An8141 v.166.

3858. Silva Guimarães, João Joaquim da. *Diccionario da lingua geral dos indios do Brasil; reimpresso e augmentado com diversos vocabularios*. Typ. de C. de Lellis Masson & C., Bahia, 1854. 36 p. Br498.75 Gsi 37.2.

3859. Silva Guimarães, João Joaquim da. *Grammatica da lingua geral dos indios do Brasil. Reimpressa pela primeira vez neste continente depois de tão longo tempo de sua publicação em Lisboa*. M. F. Sepulveda, Bahia, 1851. 105, 31 p. Br498.75 Gsi 37.

3860. Siméon, Rémi. *Dictionnaire de la langue nahuatl ou mexicaine, rédige d'après les documents imprimés et manuscrits les plus authentiques et précédé d'une introduction, par Rémi Siméon*. Imprimerie nationale, Paris, 1885. 710 p. Br498.22 AzSi 43.

3861. Siméon, Rémi. *Estudios gramaticales del idioma nahuatl; escritos en francés por Remí Siméon, y traducidos, con notas y adiciones, por el Lic. Cecilio A. Robelo*. Edición del Museo Nacional de México. Imprenta del Museo Nacional, México, 1902. 64 p. Br498.22 AzSi 43.2.SR.

3862. Siméon, Rémi. *Les Annales Mexicaines de Chimalpahin*. Ernest Laroux, Paris, 1884. 16 p. Br572C An8141 v.60.

3863. Simonin, M. Sur les races de l'Amérique du Nord. pp. 445-456, 1869. Br572C An8141 v.10.

3864. Siret, Henri, and Louis Siret. Les premiers ages du métal dans le sud-est de l'Espagne. *Revue des Questions Scientifique*, 1888. 110 p. Br572C An8141 v.24; Br572C An8141 v.83.

3865. Sitgreaves, Lorenzo. *Report of an Expedition Down the Zuni and Colorado Rivers, by Captain L. Sitgreaves, Corps Topographical Engineers; Accompanied by Maps, Sketches, and Illustrations*. R. Armstrong, Public Printer Washington, DC, 1853. 198 p. BrF788 U57 1854. Contents include: Report of Capt. Sitgreaves; Tables of distances, geographical positions, and meterological observations; Report on the natural history of the country, by S. W. Woodhouse; Mammals, by S. W.

Woodhouse; Birds, by S.W. Woodhouse; Reptiles, by Edward Hallowell; Fishes, by S. F. Baird and Charles Girard; Botany, by John Torrey; Medical report, by S. W. Woodhouse. Ten of the illustrations represent the Mohave, Zuni, and other groups of the Colorado plateau.

3866. Sitjar, Boenaventure. *Vocabulario de la lengua de los naturales de la mision de San Antonio, Alta California; Compuesto por el Rev. Padre Fray Buenaventura Sitjar, del Orden Serafico de N. P. San Francisco.* Shea's Library of American Linguistics, 7. Cramoisy Press, New York, 1861. 53 p. Br497C Sh3; Br497C Sh3a. "Father Sitjar and Pierras were the first to attempt the conversion of this tribe [Mutsun] which occupied a mountainous range, twenty-five leagues southwest of Monterrey, in California. Although it was one so numerous that more than twenty dialects were spoken by its branches, it was reduced to less than fifty individuals in 1860. The manuscript consists of four hundred and forty-four pages, and together with the grammar, were obtained by Mr. A. S. Taylor, who deposited them in the Smithsonian Institute" (Field 1873:361).

3867. Smet, Pierre J. de. *New Indian Sketches.* D. and J. Sadlier, New York, 1865. 175 p. Br970.1 Sm35. Includes "Vocabulary of the Skalzi, or Koetenay, tribe" (pp. 118–125). De Smet (1801–1873) left Belgium to join the American Jesuits in 1821 and was ordained in 1827. When the Jesuits were assigned the evangelization of the trans-Mississippi tribes, he worked among the Potawatomi between 1837 and 1839, and later with more than 100 tribes, including the Blackfeet, Coeur d'Alene, Crow, Flathead, and Sioux. He later founded a network of Jesuit missions from the Rockies to the Pacific Ocean.

3868. Smet, Pierre J. de. *Western Missions and Missionaries; A Series of Letters.* J. B. Kirker, late E. Dunigan, New York, 1863. 532 p. Br970.626 Sm35.

3869. Smith, Albert A. The Halliwell-Phillipps Collection. pp. 3–5. Pennsylvania Library Club, Occasional Papers, 2. Philadelphia, 1895. Br572C An8141 v.145.

3870. Smith, Buckingham. *A Grammatical Sketch of the Heve language, Translated From an Unpublished Spanish Manuscript.* Shea's Library of American Linguistics, 3. Cramoisy Press, New York, 1861. 26 p. Br497C Sh3; Br497C Sh3a.

3871. Smith, Buckingham. *Arte de la lengua névome, que se dice Pima, propia de Sonora; con la doctrina christiana y confesionario añadidos.* Shea's Library of American Linguistics, 5. Cramoisy Press, New York, 1862. 97, 32 p. Br497C Sh3; Br497C Sh3a. Appended is *Doctrina chrsitiana y confesionariuo en lengua nevome, ó la Pima, propia de Sonora* (San Agustin de la Florida, 1862. 32 p.).

3872. Smith, Buckingham. *Colección de varios documentos para la historia de la Florida y tierras adyacentes.* Trübner y compañía, Londres, 1857. 208 p. Br975.9D Sm53.

3873. Smith, Edmond R. *The Araucanians; Or, Notes of a Tour Among the Indian Tribes of Southern Chile, by Edmond Reuel Smith.* Harper and Brothers, New York, 1855. 355 p. Br980.3 ArSm53.

3874. Smith, Harlan I. Archaeological investigations on the North Pacific Coast of America. *Science* 9(224): 535-539, 1899. New York. Br913.711 Sm53.2.

3875. Smith, Harlan I. *Archaeology of Lytton, British Columbia.* Memoirs of the American Museum of Natural History, v. 2, Anthropology I: The Jesup North Pacific Expedition. pp. 129-161, 1899. New York. Br913.711 Sm53a.

3876. Smith, Harlan I. Caches of the Saginaw Valley, Michigan. *Proceedings of the American Association for the Advancement of Science* 62:1-4, 1894. Br572C An8141 v.136.

3877. Smith, Harlan I. Certain shamanistic ceremonies among the Ojibwas. *American Antiquarian* 18:282-284, 1896. 3 p. Br572C An8141 v.158.

3878. Smith, Harlan I. Notes on Eskimo traditions. *Journal of American Folk-Lore* 17:209-216, 1894. Br572C An8141 v.137.

3879. Smith, Harlan I. Notes on the data of Michigan archaeology. *American Antiquarian* 18:144-153, 1896. 9 p. Br572C An8141 v.158.

3880. Smith, Harlan I. The archaeology of the Saginaw Valley, as illustrated at the World's Columbian Exposition. *American Antiquarian* 16(2): 106-109, n.d. Br572C An8141 v.136.

3881. Smith, Harlan I. The development of Michigan archaeology. *Inländer* 6(8), 1896. 4 p. Br572C An8141 v.158.

3882. Smith, Harlan I. Work in anthropology, for the year 1892, at the University of Michigan. *University Record*, pp. 98-100, 1894. Br572C An8141 v.127.

3883. Smith, John. *Capt. John Smith, of Willoughby by Alford, Lincolnshire; President of Virginia, and Admiral of New England; Works, 1608-1631; Edited by Edward Arber.* The English Scholar's Library, 16. Birmingham, 1884. 984 p. Br828C Ar1.2.

3884. Smith, Spencer. Origin of the Big Mounds of St. Louis. Read before the St. Louis Academy of Science, 1869. 7 p. Br572C An8141 v.38.

3885. Smith, Worthington G. *Man, The Primeval Savage; His Haunts and Relics From the Hill-Tops of Bedfordshire to Blackwall.* E. Stanford, London, 1894. 349 p. Br571 Sm55.

3886. Smith, Worthington G. On a Paleolithic floor at north-east London. *Journal of the Anthropological Institute of Great Britain and Ireland* 13(3): 357-384, 1884. Br572C An8141 v.67.

3887. Smithsonian Institution. *List of Foreign Correspondents of the Smithsonian Museum*, 1878. Br61 Sm5.92a.

3888. Smithsonian Institution. *Price List of Publications*, 1885. Br61 Sm5.11.

3889. Smucker, Isaac. *Centennial History of Licking County, Ohio.* Newark, OH, 1876. 80 p. Br572C An8141 v.65.

3890. Smucker, Isaac. Moundbuilder's works near Newark, Ohio. *American Antiquarian* 3(4): 251-270, 1881. Br572C An8141 v.72.

3891. Smyth, Albert H. *The Halliwell-Phillipps Collection.* Pennsylvania Library Club Occasional Papers, 2. Burk and McFetridge, Philadelphia, 1895. 5 p. Br572C An8141 v.145.

3892. Snyder, J. F. A primitive urn burial. *Annual Report of the United States National Museum, Smithsonian Institution, for 1890*, pp. 609-613, 1891. Br572C An8141 v.136.

3893. Sobrón, Félix C. *Los idiomas de la América Latina; estudios biografico-bibliográficos, por D. Félix C. y Sobron, médico cirujano é individuo der varias sociedades científicas.* Imprenta á cargo de V. Saiz, Madrid, 1875. 137 p. Br498.6 So 12.

3894. Sociedad Económica de Amigos de Guatemala. *Miscelanea*, n.d. Br917.281 G932. Contents include:"Memoria sobre el cultivo del café en Escuintla por Enrique Palacios," 1862; 2. A. B. Jáuregui,"Apuntamientos biográficos sobre el señor doctor J. M. Padilla," n.d.; 3. "Colección de memorias trabajos. Paz, Guatemala," v.1 (1-4, 1866); 4. José Guadalupe Romero, "Noticia de las personas que han escrito ó publicado algunas obras sobre idiomas que se hablan en la republica," 1861; 5. "Catalogo de las obras impresas y manuscritas [en el Museo Nacional]...por Juan Gavarrete," 1875; 6. "Catalogo general [de the biblioteca de la Academia Guatemalteca]...por A. B. Jáuregui," 1873; 7. A. Spina, "Estadistica del departamento de Sonsonate," n.d.; 8. Jerónimo Pérez, "Biografia de don Manuel Antonio de la Cerda, primer jefe del estado de Nicaragua," 1872.

3895. Sociedad Mexicana de Geografía y Estadística de la Republica Mexicana. *Boletín especial para el cuadragesimo noveno aniversario de la fundación de la sociedad.* Mexico, 1900. 156 p. Br917.2 M5738.

3896. Società Romana di Antropologia (Rome). *Statuto della Società Romana di Antropologia.* Presso la Sede della Società, Roma, 1893. 14 p. Br572C An8141 v.122.

3897. Société Américaine de France (Paris). *Annuaire du Comité d'archéologie américaine, publié sous la direction de la commission de rédaction par les secrétaires.* Au Bureau du Comité, Chez Maisonneuve, Paris, 1863-1867 2 v. Br913.7 So12.

3898. Société Américaine de France (Paris). *Archives de la Société Américaine de France.* Aux Bureaux de la Société Américaine, Paris, 1875-1888. 4 v. Br913.7 So13.

3899. Société Archéologique (Moscow). Collection of manuscripts, plans, designs, and drawings to transactions, of the first archaeological society, 1871. 2 p., 55 plates. Br913.06 M854.6.

3900. Société d'Anthropologie de Paris. *Règlement et personnel*, 1894. Br572C An8141 v.136.

3901. Société d'Ethnographie (Paris). *Actes* 7(29-31, 33, 34), 1873. Br572.06 P215.

3902. Société d'Ethnographie (Paris). *Annuaire* 1, 1876. Br572.06 P215.

3903. Société d'Ethnographie (Paris). *Bulletin* 21, 1877; 55, 57, 1884; 1, 3-8, 10, 1887; 13, 16, 18, 19, 22, 1888. Br572.06 P215.

3904. Société d'Ethnographie (Paris). *Comptes rendus des séances*, 1862, 1872, 1875, 1882. Br572.06 P215.

3905. Société d'Ethnographie (Paris). *Mémoires* 2(1,3), 1872. Br572.06 P215.2.

3906. Société d'Ethnographie (Paris). *Mémoires* 12(3), 1873. Br572.06 P215.

3907. Société Philologique (Paris). *Actes* 14, 16-18, 23, 25-27. Br406 So13.

3908. Société Philologique (Paris). *Boletin de séances* 2, 1898 Br406 So131.

3909. Society of Friends. Executive Committee of the Yearly Meetings. *The Case of the Seneca Indians in the State of New York. Illustrated by Facts.* Printed...By direction of the Joint Committee on Indian Affairs, of the four Yearly Meetings of Friends of Genesee, New York, Philadelphia, and Baltimore. Merrihew and Thompson,

Printers, Philadelphia, 1840. 256 p. Br970.3 SF91.

3910. Society of Friends. London Yearly Meeting. Meeting for Sufferings. Aborigines' Committee. *Some Account of the Conduct of the Religious Society of Friends Towards the Indian Tribes in the Settlement of the Colonies of East and West Jersey and Pennsylvania; With a Brief Narrative of Their Labours for the Civilization and Christian Instruction of the Indians, From the Time of Their Settlement in America, to the Year 1843*. E. Marsh, London, 1844. 247 p. Br970.4 NF914.

3911. Solis y Ribadeneira, Antonio de. *Historia de la conquista de México*. Brussels, 1704. Br972 So4.1.

3912. Solotaroff, H. On the origin of the family. *American Anthropologist* 11:229-242, 1898. Br572C An8141 v.163.

3913. Sommier, Stephen. *Siriéni Ostiacchi e Samoiedi dell'Ob*. Firenze, 1887. Br572C An8141 v.82.

3914. Sonnenstern, Maximilian von. *Descripción de cada uno de los departamentos del Estado del Salvador; relativamente á su topografía, suelo, minerales, agua y temperatura*. Nueva York, 1858. 35 p. Br917.284 So52.

3915. Sonnenstern, Maximilian von. *Mapa general de la republica de Guatemala*. Publicado por orden del gobierno, Guatemala Br912.7281 So52.

3916. Sosa, Francisco. *Ensayo biográfico de Don Crescencio Carrillo*. Imprenta de Nabor Chavez, Mexico, 1873. Br572C An8141 v.74.

3917. Sosa, Francisco. *Manual de biografia yucateca, por Francisco de P. Sosa*. Imprenta de J. D. Espinosa e hijos, Mérida, 1866. 228 p. Br920.7 So7.

3918. Soto, Hernando de. *Letter of Hernando de Sato, and Memoir of Hernando de Escalante Fontaneda; Translated from the Spanish, by Buckingham Smith*. Washington, DC, 1854. 67 p. Br917.59 So78.ES. Translated transcripts of documents in the archives at Simancas, attested by Muñoz and preserved in the James Lenox library. Contents include: Letter from Hernando de Soto, in Florida, to the Justice and Board of Magistrates in Santiago de Cuba. July 9, 1539; Memoir of Hernando de Escalante Fontaneda, respecting Florida; written in Spain, about the year 1575; notes by the translator; Espiritu Santo Bay [a comparative statement of authorities relating to De Soto].

3919. Soto, Marco A. *Proyecto de una institución de Crédito Nacional Hipotecario, presentado á la Comisión de Agricultura de la Sociedad Económica de Guatemala*. Imprenta de La Paz, Guatemala, 1870. 26 p. Br572C An8141 v.69.

3920. South Kensington Museum. *Reproductions of Carved Ivories; A Priced Inventory of the Casts in Fictile Ivory in the South Kensington Museum, Manufactured by Elkington and Co., Limited*. Hanby, London, 1890. 70 p. Br736 So8.

3921. Souza Andrade, Joaquim de. Memorabilia. pp. 109-188, 1876. Br572C An8141 v.72.

3922. Spalding, Henry H. *Matthewnim taaiskt; The Gospel According to Matthew, Translated into the Nez Perces Language, by Rev. H. H. Spalding*. American Bible Society, New York, 1871. 130 p. Br497.48 CB47. In 1836 the American Board of Commissioners for Foreign Missions assigned Spalding (1803-1874) and his wife, Eliza, to the

Oregon Territory. They located among the Nez Perce at Lapwai, Idaho, and based their mission program on agriculture. In 1840 he printed an instructional pamphlet in the Nez Perce language, the first item to be printed in the Pacific Northwest.

3923. Spencer, Herbert. *Descriptive Sociology; or, Groups of Sociological Facts.* Williams and Norgate, London, 1874. 63 leaves. Br303 Sp34. Spencer's (1820-1903) main contribution to science was to formulate the concept of evolution in a comprehensive and systematic way and apply it to a broad range of phenomena, especially to human societies.

3924. Spivak, C. D. Kephir. *New York Medical Journal,* January 18, 1896, 18 p. Br572C An8141 v.143.

3925. Spivak, C. D. *Menstruation; A Brief Summary of the Theories of the Ancients, With Special Reference to the Views Held by the Talmudists.* Philadelphia, 1890. 12 p. Br572C An8141 v.143. Prize thesis at Jefferson Medical College in 1890.

3926. Squier, Ephraim G. *A List of Books, Pamphlets, and More Important Contributions to Periodicals, etc.* New York, 1876. 6 p. Br572C An8141 v.77. Squier (1821-1888) began his archaeological explorations in the Ohio Valley mounds, and later excavated New York mounds. He also excavated sites in Central and South America while in the diplomatic service.

3927. Squier, Ephraim G. A monograph of the ancient monuments of the state of Kentucky. *American Journal of Science and Arts* 8(22): 1-14, 1849. Br572C An8141 v.76.

3928. Squier, Ephraim G. A visit to the Guajiquero Indians. *Harper's New Monthly Magazine* 19(113): 602-619, 1859. Br572C An8141 v.75.

3929. Squier, Ephraim G. *Aboriginal Monuments of the State of New York; Comprising the Results of Original Surveys and Explorations; With an Illustrative Appendix.* Smithsonian Institution, Contributions to Knowledge, 2(9). Washington, DC, 1849. 84, 188 leaves. Br913.747 Sq43.

3930. Squier, Ephraim G. Alleged discovery of the arch among the aboriginal remains of New Mexico. *Proceedings of the Lyceum of Natural History in New York,* pp. 91-94, 1871. Br572C An8141 v.77.

3931. Squier, Ephraim G. American ethnology; being a summary of some of the results which have followed the investigation of this subject. *American Review* 3(4): 1-14, 1849. Br572C An8141 v.76.

3932. Squier, Ephraim G. Among the Andes of Peru and Bolivia. *Harper's New Monthly Magazine* 37(215-219): 545-566, 681-700, 16-33, 145-165, 307-332, 1868. Br572C An8141 v.75.

3933. Squier, Ephraim G. Ancient monuments in the United States. *Harper's New Monthly Magazine* 20(120): 737-753; 21(121): 20-36; 21(122): 165-178, 1860. Br572C An8141 v.77.

3934. Squier, Ephraim G. Ancient Peru, its people and its monuments. *Harper's New Monthly Magazine* 7(37): 7-38, 1853. Br572C An8141 v.76.

3935. Squier, Ephraim G. Antiquities from the Guano or Huanu Islands of Peru. *Journal of the Anthropological Institute of New York* 1:47-56, 1871-1872. Br572C An8141 v.77.

3936. Squier, Ephraim G. *Antiquities of the State of New York; Being the Results of Extensive Original Surveys and Explorations, With a Supplement on the Antiquities of the West; Illustrated by Fourteen Quarto Plates and Eighty Engravings on Wood*. George H. Derby and Company, Buffalo, 1851. 343 p. Br913.747 Sq43.2. Originally published in the Smithsonian Institution Contributions to Knowledge, 2, as *Aborginal Monuments of the State of New York. Supplement: The Ancient Monuments of the Mississippi Valley*, by E. G. Squier and E. H. Davis.

3937. Squier, Ephraim G. *Catalogue of the Library of E. G. Squier; Edited by Joseph Sabin, to be Sold by Auction, on Monday, April 24, 1876, and Following Days, by Bangs, Merwin, and Company*. C. C. Shelley, New York, 1876. 277 p. Br27.173 Sq43.

3938. Squier, Ephraim G. *Coal Mines of the Rio Lempa, San Salvador*. Chiswick Press, London, 1856. 16 p. Br572C An8141 v.72.

3939. Squier, Ephraim G. *Compendio de la historia política de Centro-America*. Paris, 1856. 114 p. Br572C An8141 v.74.

3940. Squier, Ephraim G. Gold hunting in California in the sixteenth century. *American Review: A Whig Journal Devoted to Politics and Literature* 49(13): 84–88, 1849. Br572C An8141 v.76.

3941. Squier, Ephraim G. Historical and mythological traditions of the Algonquins; with a translation of the "Walum-Olum," or bark record of the Linni-Lenape. *American Review: A Whig Journal Devoted to Politics and Literature* 3(2): 3–23, 1849. Br572C An8141 v.76.

3942. Squier, Ephraim G. Honduras and Guatemala, 1854. 14 p. Br572C An8141 v.58.

3943. Squier, Ephraim G. *Honduras; Descriptive, Historical, and Statistical*. Trübner and Company, London, 1870. 278 p. Br917.283 Sq4.

3944. Squier, Ephraim G. Hunting a pass: a sketch of tropical adventure. *The Atlantic Monthly: A Magazine of Literature, Art, and Politics* 5(30): 447–457, 6(33): 44–58, 1860. Br572C An8141 v.75.

3945. Squier, Ephraim G. Lenca vocabularies from the villages of Guajiquero, Opatoro, Intibucat, and Similatón (Honduras), collected by E. Geo. Squier. 11 p. Br498.19 LSq43. Manuscript; working notes bound with Squier's "A visit to the Guajiquiro Indians" (*Harper's New Monthly Magazine* 19(113): 602–619, 1859).

3946. Squier, Ephraim G. Manabozho and the Great Serpent. *American Review: A Whig Journal Devoted to Politics and Literature* 2(4): 392–398, 1848. Br572C An8141 v.76.

3947. Squier, Ephraim G. *Monograph of Authors Who Have Written on the Languages of Central America, and Collected Vocabularies or Composed Works in the Native Dialects of That Country*. Trübner and Company, London, 1861. 70 p. Br489B Sq44.

3948. Squier, Ephraim G. More about the gold discoveries of the Isthmus. *Harper's Weekly*, August 20, 1859. 4 p. Br572C An8141 v.77.

3949. Squier, Ephraim G. Ne-she-kay-be-nais, or the "Lone Bird": an Ojibway legend. *American Review: A Whig Journal Devoted to Politics and Literature* 3(45): 255–259, 1848. Br572C An8141 v.76.

3950. Squier, Ephraim G. New Mexico and California; the ancient monuments, and the aboriginal, semi-civilized nations of New Mexico and California; with an abstract of the early Spanish explorations and conquests in those regions, particularly those now falling within the territory of the United States. *American Review: A Whig Journal Devoted to Politics and Literature* 5(47): 503-528, 1848. Br572C An8141 v.76.

3951. Squier, Ephraim G. Nicaragua, an exploration from ocean to ocean. *Harper's New Monthly Magazine* 11(65-66): 577-590, 744-763, 1855. Br572C An8141 v.75.

3952. Squier, Ephraim G. *Nicaragua, Its People, Scenery, Monuments, and the Proposed Interoceanic Canal, With Numerous Original Maps and Illustrations, By E. G. Squier, Late Charge d'Affairs of the United States to the Republics of Central America.* Longman, Brown, Green and Longmans, London, 1852. 2 v. Br917.285 Sq4.

3953. Squier, Ephraim G. *Nicaragua, Its People, Scenery, Monuments, and the Proposed Interoceanic Canal, With Numerous Original Maps and Illustrations, By E. G. Squier, Formerly Charge d'Affairs of the United States to the Republics of Central America.* D. Appleton and Co., New York, 1856. 2 v. Br917.285 Sq4a. "Mr. Squier's explorations form a fitting sequel to those of Mr. Stephens, extending as they did over an adjacent territory, equally rich in the relics of the indigenous and civilized race of aborigines which once peopled it. Almost every article of their manufacture, which was not readily perishable, is represented in the excellent engravings. Their idols, temples, columns, sculptures, utensils, and architecture are most copiously illustrated, and clearly described. A division of the second volume, entitled 'Aborigines of Nicaragua,' pp. 303 to 362, treats of the Indians now resident in that portion of the peninsula" (Field 1873:377).

3954. Squier, Ephraim G. *Notes on Central America; Particularly the States of Honduras and San Salvador; Their Geography, Topography, Climate, Population, Resources, Productions, etc., etc., and the Proposed Honduras Inter-Oceanic Railway.* Harper and Brothers, New York, 1855. 393 p. Br917.28 Sq4.1.

3955. Squier, Ephraim G. Notes sur les états de Honduras et de San Salvador, dans l'Amérque Centrale. *Bulletin de la Société de Géographie*, 1855. 36 p. Br572C An8141 v.165.

3956. Squier, Ephraim G. Observations on a collection of chalchihuitls from Central America. *Annals of the Lyceum of Natural History of New York* 9(8): 246-265, 1869. Br572C An8141 v.38; Br572C An8141 v.77.

3957. Squier, Ephraim G. *Observations on the Aboriginal Monuments of the Mississippi Valley; The Character of the Ancient Earth-Works, and the Structure, Contents, and Purposes of the Mounds, With Notices of the Minor Remains of Ancient Art.* Bartlett and Welford, New York, 1847. 79 p. Br572C An8141 v.70; Br572C An8141 v.76.

3958. Squier, Ephraim G. Observations on the chalchiuitl of Mexico and Central America. *Annals of the Lyceum of Natural History of New York*, 1869. 22 p. Br572C An8141 v.165.

3959. Squier, Ephraim G. *Observations on the Geography and Archaeology of Peru.* Trübner and Company, London, 1870. 27 p. Br572C An8141 v.77; Br572C An8141 v.165.

3960. Squier, Ephraim G. Observations on the memoir on the European colonization of America, in ante-historic times, by Dr. C. A. Adolph Zestermann, of Leipsic; with critical observations thereon, by E. G. Squier, Esq. *Proceedings of the American Ethnological Society*, pp. 20-32, 1851. Br572C An8141 v.76. Zestermann attempts to demonstrate a connection between the peoples who built the mounds of the Ohio Valley with the early peoples of northwestern Europe. He places the immigration of Europeans at least 1,200 years before Christ.

3961. Squier, Ephraim G. Observations on the uses of the Mounds of the West, with an attempt at their classification. *American Journal of Science and Arts* 3(8): 237-248, 1847. Br572C An8141 v.76.

3962. Squier, Ephraim G. On the discoidal stones of the Indian Mounds. *American Journal of Science and Arts* 2(5): 216-218, 1846. Br572C An8141 v.76.

3963. Squier, Ephraim G. *Peru; Incidents of Travel and Exploration in the Land of the Incas, by E. George Squier*. Macmillan and Company, London, 1877. 599 p. Br918.5 Sq4.

3964. Squier, Ephraim G. *Quelques remarques sur la géographie et les monuments du Pérou*. Imprimerie de E. Martinet, Paris, 1868. 28 p. Br572C An8141 v.77.

3965. Squier, Ephraim G. Ruins of Tenampua, Honduras, Central America. *Proceedings of the Historical Society of New York*, 1853. 8 p. Br572C An8141 v.76.

3966. Squier, Ephraim G. San Juan de Nicaragua. *Harper's New Monthly Magazine* 10(54): 50-61, 1854. Br572C An8141 v.75.

3967. Squier, Ephraim G. Santa Rosa of Lima. *Harper's New Monthly Magazine* 34(199): 88-94, 1866. Br572C An8141 v.75.

3968. Squier, Ephraim G. Some critical observations on the "Literature of American Aboriginal Languages." *New York Daily Tribune*, January, 1859. 3 p. Br572C An8141 v.77.

3969. Squier, Ephraim G. Some new discoveries respecting the dates on the great calendar stone of the ancient Mexicans, with observations on the Mexican cycle of fifty-two years. *American Journal of Science and Arts* 7(20): 153-157, 1849. Br572C An8141 v.76.

3970. Squier, Ephraim G. The great South American earthquakes of 1868. *Harper's New Monthly Magazine* 38(227): 603-623, 1869. Br572C An8141 v.75.

3971. Squier, Ephraim G. The monumental evidence of the discovery of America by the Northmen critically examined. *Ethnological Journal* 1:315-326, 1848. Br572C An8141 v.76.

3972. Squier, Ephraim G. The primeval monuments of Peru, compared to those in other parts of the world. *American Naturalist* 4:1-17, 1870. Br572C An8141 v.38; Br572C An8141 v.77.

3973. Squier, Ephraim G. *The States of Central America; Their Geography, Topography, Climate, Population, Resources, Productions, Commerce, Political Organization, Aborigines, etc., etc., Comprising Chapters on Honduras, San Salvador, Nicaragua, Costa Rica, Guatemala, Belize, the Bay Islands, the Mosquito Shore, and the Honduras Inter-Oceanic Railway; by E. G. Squier, Formerly Charge d'Affairs of the United States to the Republics of Central America, With Numerous*

Original Maps and Illustrations. Harper and Brothers, New York, 1858. 782 p. Br917.28 Sq4.

3974. Squier, Ephraim G. Tongues from the tombs, or, the stories that graves tell: 1. The mounds of the United States. *Frank Leslie's Illustrated Newspaper*, 1869. 5 p. Br572C An8141 v.77.

3975. Squier, Ephraim G. Tongues from the tombs, or, the stories that graves tell: 2. A plain man's tomb in Peru. *Frank Leslie's Illustrated Newspaper*, 1869. 5 p. Br572C An8141 v.77.

3976. Squier, Ephraim G. Tongues from the tombs, or, the stories that graves tell: 3. Agricultural laborers and the princes of Chimu. *Frank Leslie's Illustrated Newspaper*, 1869. 6 p. Br572C An8141 v.77.

3977. Squier, Ephraim G. Tongues from the tombs, or, the stories that graves tell: 4. Grand Chimu and New Granada. *Frank Leslie's Illustrated Newspaper*, 1869. 6 p. Br572C An8141 v.77.

3978. Squier, Ephraim G. Tongues from the tombs, or, the stories that graves tell: 5. Central America. *Frank Leslie's Illustrated Newspaper*, 1869. 7 p. Br572C An8141 v.77.

3979. Squier, Ephraim G. Tongues from the tombs, or, the stories that graves tell: 6. Central America and Yucatan. *Frank Leslie's Illustrated Newspaper*, 1869. 7 p. Br572C An8141 v.77.

3980. Squier, Ephraim G. Tongues from the tombs, or, the stories that graves tell: 7. Mexico. *Frank Leslie's Illustrated Newspaper*, 1869. 7 p. Br572C An8141 v.77.

3981. Squier, Ephraim G. Tongues from the tombs, or, the stories that graves tell: 8. The Egyptians. *Frank Leslie's Illustrated Newspaper*, 1869. 5 p. Br572C An8141 v.77.

3982. Squier, Ephraim G. Unexplored regions of Central America. *Putnam's Monthly Magazine of Literature, Science, Art, and National Interests* 9:549-561, 1868. Br572C An8141 v.75.

3983. Squier, Ephraim G. The volcanos of Central America. *Harper's New Monthly Magazine* 19(114): 739-762, 1859. Br572C An8141 v.75.

3984. *St. Matthew, Mark, Luke, John nanni gospelka. Apostel nanni storka ba sin. Moskito bila.* G. Winter, Stolpenra, Germany, 1889. 454 p. Br498.44 B 47.5. Translation of the Gospels into the Mosquito language.

3985. Starr, Frederick. A shell gorget from Mexico. *Proceedings of the Davenport Academy of Natural Sciences* 6:173-178, 1896. Br572C An8141 v.158. Frederick Starr's (1858-1933) professional career focused on anthropology and museology. Between 1884 and 1888 Starr taught anthropology at Coe College in Iowa and undertook important work in Iowa archaeology. Starr was later appointed to the Department of Sociology and Anthropology at the University of Chicago, a post he held for thirty-one years.

3986. Starr, Frederick. A shell inscription from Tula, Mexico. *Proceedings of the Davenport Academy of Natural Sciences* 7:8-10, 1898. Br572C An8141 v.163.

3987. Starr, Frederick. A study of a census of the pueblo of Cochiti, New Mexico. *Proceedings of the Davenport Academy of Natural Sciences* 7:33-44, 1897. Br572C An8141 v.158. Br572C An8141 v.158.

3988. Starr, Frederick. *Aztec Place-Names, Their Meaning and Mode of Composition, Translated from the Spanish of Padre Agustin de la Rosa and Dr. Antonio Peñafiel*. University of Chicago Press, Chicago, 1895. 12 p. Br572C An8141 v.158.

3989. Starr, Frederick. Bibliography of Iowa antiquities. *Proceedings of the Davenport Academy of Natural Sciences* 6:1-24, 1892. Br572C An8141 v.119.

3990. Starr, Frederick. Comparative Religion Notes: Notes on current anthropological literature. *Biblical World*, pp. 45-53, 1895. Br572C An8141 v.134; Br572C An8141 v.142.

3991. Starr, Frederick. Folk-lore of stone tools. *Journal of American Folk-Lore* 4(12): 27-28, 1891. Br572C An8141 v.119.

3992. Starr, Frederick. *Native Races of North America: Syllabus of a Course of Six Lecture-Studies in Anthropology*. University of Chicago, Chicago, 1893. 12 p. Br572C An8141 v.119.

3993. Starr, Frederick. Notched bones from Mexico. *Proceedings of the Davenport Academy of Natural Sciences* 7:1-7, 1898. Br572C An8141 v.163.

3994. Starr, Frederick. Note on color-hearing. *American Journal of Psychology* 5(3), n.d. 3 p. Br572C An8141 v.119.

3995. Starr, Frederick. *Notes on Mexican Archaeology*. University of Chicago Press, Chicago, 1894. 16 p. Br572C An8141 v.134.

3996. Starr, Frederick. Page of child-lore. *Journal of American Folk-Lore*, pp. 55-56, n.d. Br572C An8141 v.119.

3997. Starr, Frederick. Popular celebrations in Mexico. *Journal of American Folk-Lore* 9(34): 161-169, 1896. Br572C An8141 v.158.

3998. Starr, Frederick. Report on a recent trip to Guatemala and southern Mexico. *University Record, University of Chicago*, pp. 148-150, n.d. Br572C An8141 v.158.

3999. Starr, Frederick. *Some First Steps in Human Progress: Syllabus of a Course of Six Lecture-Studies in Anthropology*. University of Chicago, Chicago, 1892. 15 p. Br572C An8141 v.119.

4000. Starr, Frederick. Some Pennsylvania German lore. *Journal of American Folk-Lore* 4(15): 321-326, 1891. Br572C An8141 v.119.

4001. Starr, Frederick. Stone images from Tarascan territory, Mexico. *American Anthropologist* 10(1): 45-47, 1897. Br572C An8141 v.158.

4002. Starr, Frederick. Study of the criminal in Mexico. *American Journal of Sociology*, pp. 13-17, n.d. Br572C An8141 v.158.

4003. Starr, Frederick. *The Aztecs of Ancient Mexico: Syllabus of a Course of Six Lecture-Studies in Anthropology*. University of Chicago Press, Chicago, 1897. 15 p. Br572C An8141 v.158.

4004. Starr, Frederick. *The Little Pottery Objects of Lake Chapala, Mexico*. University of Chicago Press, Chicago, 1897. 27 p. Br572C An8141 v.158.

4005. Starr, Frederick. *The Mapa de Cuauhtlantzinco or Códice Campos*. Department of Anthropology, University of Chicago, Bulletin 3, 1898. Chicago. 38 p. Br572C An8141 v.163.

4006. Starr, Frederick. *Work in Anthropology at the University of Chicago*. Press of Edward Borcherdt, Davenport, IA, 1897. 8 p. Br572C An8141 v.158.

4007. Stearns, Robert E. C. On certain aboriginal implements from Napa County, California. *American Naturalist* 15(12):203-209, 1881. Br572C An8141 v.13.

4008. Steenstrup, J. Japetus S. Det store solvfund ved Gundestrup (i Aarsherred, 1891): Orienterende Betragtninger over de tretten Solvpladers talrige Relief-Fremstillinger. *Mémoires de l'Académe Royale des Sciences et del Lettres de Danemark* 2:134-150, 1893. Br572C An8141 v.142.

4009. Steenstrup, J. Japetus S. Det store solvfund ved Gundestrup (i Jylland, 1891). *Mémoires de l'Académe Royale des Sciences et del Lettres de Danemark* 3(4): 319-434, 1895. Br572C An8141 v.145.

4010. Steenstrup, J. Japetus S. Yaklungta-bracteaterne, archaeologernes nordiske Gruppe af Guld bracteater. *Mémoires de l'Académe Royale des Sciences et del Lettres de Danemark* 3(4): 311-448, 1893. Br572C An8141 v.145.

PUBLICATIONS OF THE UNIVERSITY OF PENNSYLVANIA

SERIES IN

Philology Literature and Archæology

VOL. III No. 2

A PRIMER OF

MAYAN HIEROGLYPHICS

BY

DANIEL G. BRINTON, A.M., M.D., LL.D., SC.D.

PROFESSOR OF AMERICAN ARCHÆOLOGY AND LINGUISTICS IN THE UNIVERSITY OF PENNSYLVANIA,
PRESIDENT OF THE AMERICAN ASSOCIATION FOR THE ADVANCE-
MENT OF SCIENCE, ETC., ETC.

" Hieroglyphics old,
Which sages and keen-eyed astrologers,
Then living on the earth, with labouring thought,
Won from the gaze of many centuries."
—KEATS

GINN & COMPANY   MAX NIEMEYER
Agents for United States, Canada, and England   Agent for the Continent of Europe
7-13 Tremont Place, Boston, U.S.A.   Halle, a S., Germany

Title page from Brinton's A Primer of Maya Hieroglyphics (1894).

4011. Steffen, Max. *Die Landwirtschaft bei den Alt- Amerikanischen Kulturvölkern.* Verlag von Duncker und Humblot, Leipzig, 1883. 139 p. 80. Br913.7 St36.

4012. Steinen, Karl von den. *Die Bakaïrí-Sprache. Wörterverzeichnis, Sätze, Sagen, Grammatik; mit Beiträgen zu einer lautlehre der karaïbischen Grundsprache; von Karl von den Steinen.* K. F. Koehler's Antiquarium, Leipzig, 1892. 403 p. Br498.78 BSt 33. Steinen (1855-1929) organized two ethnographical expeditions into the interior of Brazil resulting in landmark studies in early ethnographic and linguistic exploration of the unknown regions of the Upper Xingu and Mato Grosso. His revision of the classification of Carib, Ge, and Tupi languages is a major contribution to South American Indian linguistics. His ethnographic and linguistic data on the Bakairí tribe are the only scholarly works on that tribe prior to its assimilation into Brazilian folk culture.

4013. Steinen, Karl von den. *Durch Central-Brasilien; Expedition zur Erforschung des Schingú im Jahre 1884.* F.A. Brockhaus, Leipzig, 1886. 372 p. Br918.1 St34.2.

4014. Steinen, Karl von den. Prä*historische Zeichen und Ornamente*. D. Reimer, Berlin, 1896. 42 p. Br572C An8141 v.159.

4015. Steinen, Karl von den. *Unter den naturvölkern Zentral-Brasiliens. Reiseschilderung und Ergebnisse der zweiten Schingú-Expedition, 1887-1888.* D. Reimer (Hoefer und Vohsen), Berlin, 1894. 570 p. Br918.1 St34. The report of the author's first expedition was published, Leipzig, 1886, as *Durch Central-Brasilien. Expedition zur erforschung des Schingú im Jahre 1884.*

4016. Steinen, Max von den. Reise nach den Marquesas Inseln. *Verhandlungen der Gesellschaft für Erdkunde zu Berlin*, pp. 489-513, 1898. Br919.62 St37.

4017. Steiner, P. *Die Sprache von Pan-Amerika und die universal-Sprache.* Heuser, Neuwied, n.d. 16 p. Br409.9 St41.

4018. Steiner, P. *Elementargrammatik nebst Übungstucken zur Gemein oder Weltpradje.* Berlin, 1885. 80 p. Br572C An8141 v.73.

4019. Steiner, P. *Kurz Gefasstes Deutsch Pohlingua Wörterbuch mit Regeln der Wortbildung und Wortbeigung.* Berlin, 1887. 88 p. Br572C An8141 v.73.

4020. Steiner, P. *Sommaire de la langue universelle pasilingua.* Haun, Darmstadt, 1889. 34 p. Br572C An8141 v.21.

4021. Steiner, P. *Übungen zur Pasilingua nebst grammatischen Bemerkungen auch zum selbstunterrich.* Heuser, Berlin, 1888. 103 p. Br409.9 St411.

4022. Steinmetz, Sebald R. Anthropologie als universiteitsvak. *De Nederlandsche Spectator* 41, 1892. 7 p. Br572C An8141 v.129; Br572C An8141 v.135. Steinmetz (1862-1940) attempted to reconstruct evolutionary sequences of particular institutions, and made contributions to the study of penal law.

4023. Steinmetz, Sebald R. Continuität oder Sohn und Strafe im Jenseits der Wilden. *Archiv für Anthropologie* 24(12): 577-608, 1896-1897. Br572C An8141 v.160.

4024. Steinmetz, Sebald R. De "Fosterage" of Opvoeding in Vreemde families. *Tijdschrift van het Koninklijt Nederlandsch Aardrijkskundig Genootschap.* E. J. Brill, Leiden, 1893. 92 p. Br572C An8141 v.130.

4025. Steinmetz, Sebald R. *Die neueren Forschungen zur Geschichte der menschlichen Familie, von S. R. Steinmetz.* G. Reimer, Berlin, 1899. Br392.3 St34. Extract from *Zeitschrift für Socialwissenschaft*, pp. 685-695, 1899.

4026. Steinmetz, Sebald R. Die organische Socialphilosophie. *Zeitschrift für Socialwissenschaft* 1(3): 197-200, 1898. Br572C An8141 v.163.

4027. Steinmetz, Sebald R. Dr. G. A. Wilken. *Overdruk vit het Rechtsgeleerd Magazijn*, pp. 567-570, 1891. Br572C An8141 v.88.

4028. Steinmetz, Sebald R. Endokannibalismus. *Mitteilungen der Anthropologischen Gesellschaft in Wien* 26:1-60, 1896. Br572C An8141 v.160.

4029. Steinmetz, Sebald R. *Ethnologische Jurisprudentie; Indische Gids, 1890.* E. J. Brill, Leiden, 1890. 24 p. Br572C An8141 v.88.

4030. Steinmetz, Sebald R. *Ethnologische Studien zur ersten Entwicklung der Strafe; nebst einer psychologischen Abhandlung über Grausamkeit und Rachsucht, von S. R. Steinmetz.* S. C. Van Doesburgh, Leiden, 1894. 2 v. Br174.2 St33; Br174.2 St33a. The second volume first appeared in 1892 as his doctoral dissertation.

4031. Steinmetz, Sebald R. Gli antichi scongiuri giuridici contro I debitori, n.d. 32 p. Br572C An8141 v.163.

4032. Steinmetz, Sebald R. Vooruitgang in folklore en ethnologie. *De Gids* 5, 1893. 32 p. Br572C An8141 v.121.

4033. Steinthal, Heymann. *Charakteristik der hauptsächlichsten Typen des Sprachbaues; von Dr. H. Steinthal, Privatdocenten für allgemeine Sprachwissenschaft an der Universität zu Berlin; zweite Bearbeitung seiner Classification der Sprachen*. Ferd. Dümmlers Verlagsbuchhandlung, Berlin, 1860. 355 p. Br409 St4.

4034. Steinthal, Heymann. *Der Ursprung der Sprache im Zusammenhange mit den letzten Fragen alles Wissens. Eine Darstellung, Kritik und Fortentwicklung der vorzüglichsten Ansichten, von H. Steinthal*. Ferd. Dümmlers Verlagsbuchhandlung, Berlin, 1888. 380 p. Br409.1 St4c.

4035. Steinthal, Heymann. *Die Sprachwissenschaft Wilh. v. Humboldt's und die Hegel'sche Philosophie*. Berlin, 1848. 172 p. Br572C An8141 v.54.

4036. Steinthal, Heymann. *Grammatik, Logik, und Psychologie, ihre Principien und ihr Verhältniss zu einander*. Ferd. Dümmlers Verlagsbuchhandlung, Berlin, 1855. 392 p. Br409.01 St3.

4037. Steinthal, Heymann. Über die sprachwissenschaftliche Richtung der Ethnologie. *Verhandlungen der Berliner Gesellschaft für Anthropologie, Ethnologie und Urgeschichte*, pp. 8-15, 1872. Br572C An8141 v.162.

4038. Stellers, Georg W. *Beschreibung von dem Lande Kamtschatka*. J. G. Fleischer, Frankfurt am Main, 1774. 296 p. Br915.7 St36.

4039. Stephen, A. M. Legend of the Snake Order of the Moquis as told by outsiders. *Journal of American Folk-Lore* 1(2): 109-114, 1888. Br572C An8141 v.51.

4040. Stephens, John L. *Incidents of Travel in Central America, Chiapas, and Yucatan*. Harper, New York, 1841. 2 v. Br917.28 St4. Stephens (1805-1852) gained early fame for his travel accounts of Europe and the Middle East in the 1820s and early 1830s. Between 1839 and 1842 he and English architect Frederick Catherwood (1799-1854) made two overland journeys through Central America and southeastern Mexico. The results of these expeditions, published in 1841 and 1843, revealed the extent and nature of the ruined cities of the ancient Maya. For most scholars it represents a beginning of the scientific study of Maya archaeology. "It is difficult to believe that two individuals were capable of such an astonishing amount of labor, as evidenced in these volumes. The wonderful structures of the race of Indians which once inhabited the peninsula of Central America are here described by pen and pencil, with great clearness and minuteness. The temples, sculptures, idols, utensils, buildings, and architecture, of that active, intelligent, and almost mythical people, are illustrated by more than seventy large engravings, from drawings by Mr. Catherwood. Mr. Stephens did not neglect their modern representatives, as his book is filled with incidents of his associations with them" (Field 1873:380-381).

4041. Stephens, John L. *Incidents of Travel in Yucatán*. J. Murray, London, 1843. 2 v. Br917.26 St41a. "In October, 1841, one year after the termination of his first explorations, the author set out upon the one, the incidents of which are here narrated. So far from exhausting the antiquities of the peninsula in his first two volumes, these add to our astonishment by portraying the gigantic ruins of still more imposing structures, erected by the vanished race of peninsular aborigines" (Field 1873:380).

4042. Stephens, John L. Ruins of Copán and Quiriguá, with notes and additions by Karl Hermann Berendt, n.d. Br913.72 St44. From pp. 85-160 from Stephen's *Incidents of Travel in Central America, Chiapas, and Yucatan* (1841); bound with: J[sic]. Catherwood, Notes on Quiriguá, n.d.; John Baily, Sketches from Quiriguá, n.d.

4043. Stephens, John L. Some words of the Chorti language of Zacapa, 1839. 1 leaf. Br498.21 CrSt 47. Manuscript, transcribed by Karl H. Berendt.

4044. Stevens, Edward T. *Guide to the Blackmore Museum, Salisbury*. Bell and Daldy, London, n.d. 160 p. Br572C An8141 v.17.

4045. Stevens, Henry. *Bibliotheca Historica, or A Catalogue of 5,000 Volumes of Books and Manuscripts Relating Chiefly to the History and Literature of North and South America, Among Which is Included the Larger Proportion of the Extraordinary Library of...Henry Stevens, Senior*. Houghton, Boston, 1870. 234 p. Br970B St47.

4046. Stevenson, James. Ceremonial of Hasjelti Dialjis and mythical sand painting of the Navajo Indians. *Annual Report of the Bureau of Ethnology, Smithsonian Institution*, pp. 229-284, 1891. Br970.3 NaSt45.

4047. Stevenson, Matilda C. The Sia. *Annual Report of the Bureau of Ethnology, Smithsonian Institution,* pp. 3-157, 1894. Br970.3 KSt46. Stevenson (1849-1915) accompanied her husband, James Stevenson, on the United States Geological Survey of the Territories and began to study some of the Indian groups they encountered. She continued this work among the Zuni after her husband joined John Wesley Powell's Bureau of American Ethnology. With the death of her husband, Stevenson was employed by the Bureau of American Ethnology and engaged in the study of the Hopi and the Tewa.

4048. Stevenson, Matilda C. Zuni ancestral gods and masks. *American Anthropologist* 11(1): 33-40, 1898. Br572C An8141 v.159.

4049. Stickney, Gardner P. The use of maize by Wisconsin Indians. *Milwaukee Parkman Club Publications* 13:63-87, 1897. Br572C An8141 v.159.

4050. Stieler, Adolf. *Hand Atlas über alle Theile der Erde und über das Weltgebäude*. J. Perthes, Gotha, 1873. 11 p. Br912 St5.

4051. Stoll, Otto. Die Ethnologie der Indianstämme von Guatemala. *Internationales Archiv für Ethnographie*, v. 1, supplement, 1889. 112 p. Br572C An8141 v.105.

4052. Stoll, Otto. *Die Maya-Sprachen der Pokom-Gruppe*. A. Hölder, Wien, Leipzig, 1888-1896. 2 v. Br498.21 St 65. Contents include: v. 1. Die Sprache der Pokonchí-Indianer, v. 2. Die Sprache der K'e'kchi-Indianer. Nebst einem Anhang; Die Uspanteca.

4053. Stoll, Otto. *Die Sprache der Ixil-Indianer; Ein Beitrag zur ethnologie und linguistik der Maya-Völker. Nebst einem Anhang; Wortverzeichnisse aus dem nordwestlichen Guatemala*. F. A. Brockhaus, Leipzig, 1887. 156 p. Br498.21 Ist 65.

4054. Stoll, Otto. *Guatemala Reisen und Schilderungen aus den Jahren 1878-1883*. F. A. Brockhaus, Leipzig, 188. 518 p. Br917.281 St64.

4055. Stoll, Otto. *Suggestion und Hypnotismus in der Völkerpsychologie*. K. F. Koehler's Antiquarium, Leipzig, 1894. 523 p. Br177 St65.

4056. Stoll, Otto. Supplementary remarks to the grammar of the Cakchiquel language of Guatemala, edited by Daniel G. Brinton, 1885. 13 p. Br497 B77.5.

4057. Stoll, Otto. *Zur Ethnographie der Republik Guatemala*. Orell Füssli, Zürich, 1884. 175 p. Br498 St63.

4058. Stolp, K. *Indianische Zeichen aus der Cordillere Chile's; Vortrag gehalten im Deutschen Wissenschaftlichen Verein zu Santiago am 22 August 1888*, pp. 35-37, 1888. Br572C An8141 v.127.

4059. Strack, H. L. *Der Blutaberglaube in der Menschheit, Blutmorde und Blutritus*. C. H. Beck, München, 1892. 155 p. Br572C An8141 v.126.

4060. Strebel, Hermann. *Alt-Mexico archäologische Beiträge zur Kulturgeschichte seiner Bewohner*. L. Voss, Hamburg, Leipzig, 1885-1889. 2 v. Br913.72 St82.

4061. Strobel, Pellegrino. *Dell eta della Pietra Levigata rinvenuti nella provincia di San Luis nella Republica Argentina*. Parma, 1867. 13 p. Br572C An8141 v.37.

4062. Strobel, Pellegrino. *Materiali di paletnologia comparata raccolti in Sudamerica*. Parma, 1868. 16 p. Br572C An8141 v.37.

4063. Strobel, Pellegrino. Paraderos preistorici in Patagonia con Tavola. *Societá Italiana di Scienze Naturali* 19(2), 1867. 6 p. Br572C An8141 v.37.

4064. Strobel, Pellegrino. Solidungulo biungulato. *Societá Italiana di Scienze Naturali* 8, 1866. 5 p. Br572C An8141 v.14.

4065. Stroud, Bert B. The mammalian cerebellum, part 1: The development of the cerebellum in man and the cat. *Journal of Comparative Neurology* 5: 71-118, 1895. Br591.48 St8.

4066. Stübel, Alphons, and Wilhelm Reiss. *Indianer-typen aus Ecuador and Colombia. 28 Lichtdruck-bilder. Den mitgliedern des VII*. Druck von H. S. Hermann, Berlin, 1888. 2 p., 28 plates in portfolio. Br980.4 EST931.

4067. Stübel, Alphons. Über altperuanische Gewebemuster und ihnen Analoge Ornamente der altklassischen Kunst. In *Festschrift zur Jubelfeier des 25 Jahrigen bestehens des Vereins für Erdkunde zu Dresden*, 1888. 22 p. Br572C An8141 v.59.

4068. Studley, Cordelia A. Notes upon human remains from caves in Coahuila. *Annual Reports of the Trustees of the Peabody Museum of American Archaeology and Ethnology* 3(3-4): 233-259, 1884. Br913.07 H265.

4069. Sturtevant, E. Lewis. Indian corn and the Indian. *American Naturalist* 19(3): 225-234, 1885. Br572C An8141 v.13.

4070. Sturtevant, E. Lewis. Indian corn. *Annual Report of the New York State Agricultural Society* 38, 1878. 31 p. Br572C An8141 v.27.

4071. Sullivan, Jeremiah. Hopitu calendar, n.d. Br913.73 Su53. Manuscript.

4072. Swan, James G. *Indians of Cape Flattery, at the Entrance to the Strait of Fuca, Washington Territory*. Smithsonian Institution, Contributions to Knowledge, 16(5), 1870. Washington, DC. Br913.768 J713. Swan (1818-1900), born in Massachusetts, journeyed to California in 1850 and settled as an oysterman on Willapa Bay, Washington, in 1852. He compiled notes and sketches of the Indians. In 1854 he served the territory's Indian Commission in treaty negotiations with the Chehalis, Chinook, Cowlitz, and Quinault. From 1862 to 1866 Swan was Indian agent to the Makah at Neah Bay. On several major expeditions in the 1870s and 1880s he traveled to southeast Alaska to collect artifacts.

4073. *Syllabarium for the Chipewyan Language.* Society for Promoting Christian Knowledge, London, 1882. Br497.11 Osy 5.

4074. Takayanagi, T. *Japanese Women.* A. C. McClurg and Company, Chicago, 1893. 159 p. Br572C An8141 v.130.

4075. Tamajuncosa, Antonio. *Descripción de las misiones, al cargo del Colegio de Nuestra Señora de los Angeles de la villa de Tarija.* Buenos Aires, 1836. 50 p. Br572C An8141 v.90.

4076. Tanner, John, and Edwin James. *A Narrative of the Captivity and Adventures of John Tanner, (United States Interpreter at the Saut de Ste. Marie), During Thirty Years Residence Among the Indians in the Interior of North America.* G. and C. and H. Carvili, New York, 1830. 426 p. Br970.1 T152. "Tanner was abducted from his home near the mouth of the Miami River when he was a boy. He was taken to a Saukee settlement near Detroit where he lived as an Indian for nearly thirty years. Reassimilation into white society was unsuccessful" (Sieber Library 1999:2:309).

4077. Tapia Zenteno, Carlos de. *Arte novissima de lengua mexicana, que dictò D. Carlos de Tapia Zenteno.* Por la viuda de D. Joseph Bernardo de Hogal, México, 1753. 22, 58 p. Br498.22 AzT 163.

4078. Tapia Zenteno, Carlos de. Diccionario huasteco-español estractado de la Noticia de la lengua huasteca con catecismo y doctrina christiana y con un copioso diccionario, por Carlos de Tapia Zenteno; por C. H. Berendt, M.D. Nueva York, 1867. 288 p. Br498.21 HT 16.2. Transcript by Berendt of *Noticia de la lengua huasteca, que en beneficio de sus nacionales, de orden del Ilmo. Sr. Arzopispo de esta Santa Iglesia Metropolitana, y a sus expensas, da Carlos de Tapia Zenteno, cura que fué de la iglesia parrochial de Tampamolón, juez eclesiastico de la villa de los Valles, comissario del santo oficio de la inquisición, cathedrático de prima de lengua mexicana en esta real universidad, y el primero en el real, y pontificio colegio seminario, examinador synodal de este arzobispado y capellán mayor del monasterio de Santa Inés; con cathecismo, y doctrina christiana para su instrucción, según lo que ordena el santo concilio mexicano, enchiridion sacramental para su administración, con todo lo que parece necessario hablar en ella los neoministros, y copioso diccionario para facilitar su inteligencia* (En la imprenta de la Bibliotheca Mexicana, en el Puente del Espiritu Santo, México, año de 1767. 128 p.); includes: "Diccionario castellano-huasteco" (pp. 48–88), "Doctrina christiana fielmente traducida de la que escribo el R. P. Bartholomé Castaño de la Compañía de Jesús" (pp. 96–128). Text of Tapia Zenteno's "Noticia de la lengua huasteca," transcribed by an unidentified secretary, and forwarded, with cover letter dated November 2, 1857, to the Minister of Development, Bernardo Flores, in México City, by the governor of Veracruz, Manuel Zamora. Zamora's cover letter explains that the manuscript was sent to him by the jefe politico of Tampico who, in turn, had received it from a justice of the peace in Ozuluama. Tapia Zenteno's work on the Huastec language, first published in México in 1767, contains explanations and examples of parts of speech and verb tenses, as well as a Huastec dictionary. Also translated into Huastec are a catechism (including the Lord's Prayer, the Apostles' Creed, Ten Commandments, and the deadly sins); and a series of doctrinal questions, written by the Jesuit Bartolomé Castaño.

4079. Tapia Zenteno, Carlos de. *Noticia de la lengua huasteca, con cathecismo y doctrina christiana.* Bibliotheca Mexicana, México, 1767. 128 p. Br498.21 HT16.

4080. Tarayre, E. Guillemin. *Exploration minéralogique des régions mexicaines suivie de notes archéologiques ethnographiques.* Imprimerie Imperiale, Paris, 1869. 304 p. Br557.2 G94. "Rapport adressé à son excellence M. Duruy, ministre de l'instruction publique." "Extrait du tome III des *Archives de la Commission Scientifique du Mexique.*"

4081. Taylor, Alexander S. *Bibliographia Californica; or Notes and Materials to Aid in Forming a More Perfect Bibliography of Those Countries Anciently Called California, and Lying Within the Limits of the Gulf of Cortez to the Arctic Seas, and West of the Rocky Mountains to the Pacific Ocean.* Sacramento Daily Union, San Francisco, 1863. Br979.4B T215. Alexander Taylor (1817–1876) traveled extensively in India and Southeast Asia, and went to California in 1848 during the Gold Rush. He served a clerk of the United States District Court in Monterey, and developed an interest in California history and bibliography of the Spanish-Mexican period, 1542–1846.

4082. Taylor, Isaac. *The Origin of the Aryans; An Account of the Prehistoric Ethnology and Civilization of Europe.* Humboldt, New York, 1890. 198 p. Br572.891 T214.

4083. Taylor, Isaac. The prehistoric races of Italy. *Annual Report of the United States National Museum, Smithsonian Institution, for 1890,* pp. 489–498, 1891. Br572C An8141 v.121.

4084. Techo (Du Toiet), Nicolás del. *Historia provinciæ Paraquariæ Societatis Jesu. Authore P. Nicolao del Techo.* Ex officina typog. J. M. Hovii, Leodii, 1673. 390 p. Br989 T22.

4085. Teit, James. A rock painting of the Thompson River Indians, British Columbia. F. Boas, ed. *Bulletin of the American Museum of Natural History* 8(12): 227–230, 1896. Br572C An8141 v.159. James Alexander Teit (1864-1922) emigrated to Canada from the Shetland Islands and settled at Spencer's Bridge, British Columbia, near a village of Thompson Indians. In 1895 he met Franz Boas, whom he aided as a field collaborator until 1920, contributing data on the ethnography and mythology of Plateau tribes.

4086. Tellechea, Miguel. *Compendio gramatical para la inteligencia del idióma tarahumar; oraciones, doctrina cristiana, pláticas, y otras cosas necesarias para la recta administration de los santos sacramentos en el mismo idióma.* Imprenta de la Federación en Palacio, México, 1826. 162 p. Br498.22 TT23; Br498.22 TT23a.

4087. Tello, Antonio. *Libro segundo de la Cronica miscelanea, en que se trata de la conquista espiritual y temporal de la Santa provincia de Xalisco en el Nuevo reino de la Galicia y Nueva Vizcaya y descubrimiento del Nuevo México.* Imprenta de "La República literaria," de C. L. de Guevara y ca., Guadalajara, 1891. 886 p. Br972.3 T234.

4088. Tempsky, Gustav Ferdinand von. *Mitla; A Narrative of Incidents and Personal Adventures on a Journey in Mexico, Guatemala, and Salvador in the Years 1853 to 1855; With Observations on the Modes of Life in Those Countries.* Longman, Brown, Green, Longmans, and Roberts, London, 1858. 436 p. Br917.2 T245. "This description of the antiquities of Mitla, and of the savage and unconquered tribes of Indians inhabiting Central America, possesses much to elicit our interest. Yet he is accused by the authors of other works on Central America, with supplying by invention what his investigation failed to discover" (Field 1873:409).

4089. ten Kate, H. F. C. *Reizen en onderzoekingen in Noord-Amerika.* E. J. Brill, Leiden, 1885. 464 p. Br970.1 K154. An account of a journey through the southwestern part of the United States and western Mexico. Ten Kate (1858-1931) is known for his archaeological, physical anthropological, and ethnological studies of American Indians, Indonesian peoples and Japanese, as well as contributions to applied anthropology. He was a member of the Hemenway Southwestern Archaeological Expedition under Frank Hamilton Cushing in the American Southwest (1887-1888).

4090. Tepano Jaussen, Florentin E. *L'ile de Paques: historique, écriture et répertoire des signes des tablettes ou bois d'hibiscus intelligents.* Ernest Leroux, Paris, 1893. 32 p. Br572C An8141 v.123.

4091. *Tercero catecismo, y exposición de la doctrina christiana por sermones para que los curas y otros ministros prediquer, e enseñer á los indios y a las demas personas.* Oficina de la calle de San Jacinto, San Jacinto, 1773. 515 p. Br498.7 KT272.

4092. Ternaux-Compans, Henri. Essai sur la théologonie mexicain. In *Nouvelles Annales des Voyages, de la Géographie et de l'Histoire.* Gide Fils, Paris, 1840. 52 p. Br572C An8141 v.65.

4093. Ternaux-Compans, Henri. *Recueil de pièces relatives à la conquête du Mexique.* A. Bertrand, Paris, 1838. 472 p. Br972 T274. Contents include: De l'ordre de succession observé par les Indiens relativement à leurs terres et de léurs territoires communaux; Des cérémonies observées autrefois par les Indiens lorsqu'ils faisaient un tecle; S. Ramírez de Fuenleal, Lettre…à Sa Majesté Charles V…México, 3 novembre, 1532; A. de Mendoza, conde de Tendilla, Rapport…sur les sept villes et les iles du Cuchant de 1539 à 1543; Adressé à Juan de Aguilar, pur être transmis à Sa Majesté; Relation de ce qui, d'après la volonté de Dieu, est arrivé le samedi 10 du mois de septembre 1541, à deux heures après le coucher du soleil, dans la ville de Santiago de Guatimala; J. de Zarate, Lettre…à Philippe II [à México le 30 de mai 1544]; L. de Bienvenida, Lettre…à Philippe II. [de Yucatan, le 10 de février 1548]; A. de

Mendoza, conde de Tendilla, Avis…sur les prestations personnelles et les tamemes, 1550; Mémoire des services rendus par le gouverneur Don Francisco de Ibarra pendant la conquête et la colonisation qu'il a faites dans les provinces de Copala; extrait des enquêtes…1574; Fray T. Motolinia, Lettre des chapelains frère Toribio et frère Diégo d'Olarte, à Don Luis de Velasco [27 d'août 1554]; Requête de plusieurs chefs indiens d'Atitlan à Philippe II [1 de février 1571]; L. Cabrera de Cordóba, Extrait de l'Histoire de Philippe II. Madrid, 1619; Envois d'or et d'argent, faits par les gouverneurs et vice-rois du Mexique; Liste général des flottes et azogues qui sont entrés dans le port de la Vera-Cruz depuis la conquête jusqu'à l'année 1760; J. Diaz, Itinéraire du voyage de la flotte du roi catholique à l'ile de Yucatán dans l'Inde; fait en l'an 1518, sous les ordres du capitaine général Juan de Grijalva; Relation abrégée sur la Nouvelle-Espagne, et sur le grande ville de Temixtitan México, écrite par un gentilhomme de la suite de Fernand Cortès; Pedro de Alvarado, Lettres…à Fernand Cortès; D. de Godoy, Relation…adressée à Fernand Cortès; Pierre de Gand, Lettre…[de México] 27 juin 1529; Francesco, da Bologna, Lettre…écrite de la ville de México…au révérend père Clément de Monélia. "All the pieces are illustrative of the conquest of the Aztecs, and are copies of the original relations of the conquerors themselves; but some are more particularly descriptive of the characteristics of the various tribes of the conquered people" (Field 1873:389).

4094. Terry, James. *Sculptured Anthropoid Ape Heads, Found In or Near the Valley of the John Day River, A Tributary of the Columbia River, Oregon.* New York, 1891. 15 p. Br572C An8141 v.101.

4095. *Testamentitak tamædsa; Nalegapta Piulijipta Jêsusib Kristusib apostelingitalo piniarningit ajokertusingillo.* Printed for the British and Foreign Bible Society in London, for the use of the Moravian Mission in Labrador. G. Winterib nênilauktangit, Stolpen, 1876–1878. 282, 225 p. Br497.25 LB47. New Testament translated into Labrador Eskimo.

4096. Testimonio de la real provission executoria expedida por el rey y supremo Consejo de Yndias a favor de D. J. C. Savedra en representación de su muger…Moctesuma, hija que fue del Emperador de este título, n.d. 99 leaves. Br970.4 MM578. Manuscript.

4097. *Textes en langue tarasque publiés.* H. Charencey, ed. Typographie de C. Peeters, Louvian, 1900. 6 p. Br498.27 Tse 67.2. Texts, in Spanish and Tarascan, are taken from Ángel Serra's liturgical compilation *Manual de administrar los santos sacramentos* (México, 1697).

4098. Teza, Emilio. *Catechismo dei missionari cattolici in lingua algonchina; pubblicato per cura di E. Teza.* Tipografia Nistri, Pisa, 1872. 81 p. Br497.11 T31. "Catéchisme algonquin, traduit mot pour mot en latin et phrase pour phrase en français."

4099. Teza, Emilio. Intorno agli studi, del Thavenet sulla lingua algonchina. *Annali delle Universitá Toscane* 18, 1880. 22 p. Br572C An8141 v.92.

4100. Teza, Emilio. *Saggi inediti di lingue americane, appunti bibliografici di E. Teza.* Dalla tipografia Nistri, Pisa, 1868. 91 p. Br497 T318.2; Br572C An8141 v.92.

4101. Thatcher, Benjamin B. *Indian Biography; or, An Historical Account of Those Indi-*

viduals Who Have Been Distinguished Among the North American Natives as Orators, Warriors, Statesmen, and Other Remarkable Characters. J. and J. Harper, New York, 1860. 2 v. Br970.2 T326.

4102. *Theilung der Erde und die Theilung Samoa's; eine Momentaufnahme in augenblicklicher Sachlage.* Dietrich Reimer, Berlin, 1899. 78 p. Br572 B1.

4103. Thiel, Bernardo A. *Apuntes lexicograficos de las lenguas y dialectos de los indios de Costa-Rica; reunidos y alfabéticamente dispuestos por Bernardo Augusto Thiel, obispo de Costa Rica.* Imprenta Nacional, San José, Costa-Rica, 1882. 177 p. Br498 T34. Contents include:"Lengua y dialectos de los Talamancas ó Biceitas, Bribri, Cabécar, Estrella, Chirripó, Tucurrique y Orosí"; "Lenguas de Térraba y Boruca"; "Lengua de los Guatusos."

4104. Thiel, Bernhard A., and H. Polakowsky. Vocabularium der Sprachen der Boruca-, Terraba-, und Guatuso-Indianer in Costa-Rica. *Archiv für Anthropologie* 16:592–627, 1886. Br572C An8141 v.92.

4105. Thieullen, Adrien. *Les véritables instruments usuels de l'âge de la pierre.* Imprimerie Larousse, Paris, 1897. 70 p. Br571.1 T342.3.

4106. Thieullen, Adrien. *Lettre à M. Chauvet, président de la Société Historique et Anthropologique de la Charente pour faire suite aux Véritables instruments usuels de l'âge de la pierre.* Imprimerie Larousse, Paris, 1898. 22 p. Br571.1 T342.

4107. Thieullen, Adrien. Silex anti-classiques présentés à la Société Normande d'Études Préhistoriques. *Bulletin de la Société d'Anthropologique de Paris* 10:297–303, 1899. Br571.15.

4108. Thomas, Cyrus, and James Douglas. Certain river mounds of Duval County, Florida; Two Sand Mounds on Murphy Island, Florida; certain sand mounds of the Ocklawaha River, Florida, by Clarence B. Moore, Philadelphia, 1895 [review]. *American Anthropologist* 9:101–105, 1896. Br572C An8141 v.142. Cyrus Thomas (1825-1910) held many positions, such as deputy county clerk, postmaster, minister, and lawyer, before he settled upon anthropology. In 1858 helped found the Illinois Natural History Society and, later, Southern Illinois Normal College. While working for the Bureau of American Ethnology from 1881-1910, Thomas published on Mesoamerican writing systems, and conducted extensive field surveys and mound excavations. His most lasting contribution was his demolition of the racist theory that the earthworks of the eastern United States were the work of a non-Indian race of Moundbuilders.

4109. Thomas, Cyrus. *A Study of the Manuscript Troano, With an Introduction by Daniel G. Brinton.* Smithsonian Institution, Contributions to American Ethnology, 5(3). Government Printing Office, Washington, DC, 1882. 237 p. Br557.3 Un319; Br898.21 MT742.yT. Extracts and translations from the "Relación de cosas de Yucatán" of Diego de Landa on pp. 209-234.

4110. Thomas, Cyrus. An attempt to reconcile the differences between authorities in reference to the Maya calendar and certain dates; also to determine the age of the Manuscript Troano. *American Naturalist* 15(7): 767-772, 1881. Br572C An8141 v.13.

4111. Thomas, Cyrus. Are the Maya hieroglyphics phonetic? *American Anthropologist* 6:241–270, 1893. Br572C An8141 v.120; Br572C An8141 v.134.

4112. Thomas, Cyrus. *Biologia Centrali-Americana, Archaeology, Appendix: The Archaic Maya Inscriptions,* by J. T. Goodman [review]. *American Anthropologist* 9:123-126, 1898. Br572C An8141 v.163; Br913.726 T365.3.

4113. Thomas, Cyrus. Burial mounds of the northern sections of the United States. *Annual Report of the Bureau of Ethnology, Smithsonian Institution, for 1884-1885,* pp. 3-119, 1888. Br571.92 T36.

4114. Thomas, Cyrus. *Catalogue of Prehistoric Works.* Bureau of Ethnology, Smithsonian Institution, Washington, DC, 1891. 246 p. Br572C An8141 v.14; Br572C An8141 v.19.

4115. Thomas, Cyrus. Day symbols of the Maya year. *Annual Report of the Bureau of Ethnology, Smithsonian Institution, for 1894-1895,* pp. 199-265, 1897. Br913.726 T365.2.

4116. Thomas, Cyrus. Discoveries in the Mexican and Maya codices. *American Antiquarian* 8(2): 69-76, 1886. Br572C An8141 v.44.

4117. Thomas, Cyrus. Grave mounds in North Carolina and East Tennessee. *American Naturalist* 18(2): 232-240, 1884. Br572C An8141 v.13; Br572C An8141 v.59.

4118. Thomas, Cyrus. *Introduction to the Study of North American Archaeology.* The Robert Clarke Company, Cincinnati, 1898. 391 p. Br913.7 T36.2; Br913.73 T364.yN. Thomas argues that Native Americans and their ancestors built the mounds he was excavating and were, therefore, not a lost race.

4119. Thomas, Cyrus. Notes on certain Maya and Mexican manuscripts. *Annual Report of the Bureau of Ethnology, Smithsonian Institution, for 1881-1882,* pp. 3-65, 1885. Br572C An8141 v.92; Br898.21 MyT36.

4120. Thomas, Cyrus. On certain stone images. *American Anthropologist* 10:376-377, 1897. Br572C An8141 v.159.

4121. Thomas, Cyrus. Report on the mound explorations of the Bureau of Ethnology. *Annual Report of the Bureau of Ethnology, Smithsonian Institution, for 1890-1891,* pp. 3-742, 1894. Br913.73 T364.2.

4122. Thomas, Cyrus. Stone images from mounds and ancient graves. *American Anthropologist* 11(4): 404-408, 1896. Br572C An8141 v.159.

4123. Thomas, Cyrus. Story of a mound or the Shawnees of pre-Columbian times. *American Anthropologist* 4(2-3): 237-273, 1891. Br572C An8141 v.14.

4124. Thomas, Cyrus. *The Circular, Square and Octagonal Earthworks of Ohio.* Bureau of Ethnology, Smithsonian Institution, Washington, DC, 1889. 35 p. Br572C An8141 v.14; Br572C An8141 v.19.

4125. Thomas, Cyrus. The Manuscript Troano. *American Naturalist* 15(7): 625-641, 1881. Br572C An8141 v.13; Br572C An8141 v.44.

4126. Thomas, Cyrus. *The Maya Year.* Bureau of Ethnology, Smithsonian Institution, Bulletin 18, Washington, DC, 1894. 64 p. Br572C An8141 v.134; Br913.726 T365.

4127. Thomas, Cyrus. *The Native Calendar of Central America and Mexico,* by Daniel G. Brinton [review]. *American Anthropologist* 7:122-124, 1894. Br572C An8141 v.123.

4128. Thomas, Cyrus. *The Problem of the Ohio Mounds.* Bureau of American Ethnology, Smithsonian Institution, Washington, DC, 1889. 54 p. Br572C An8141 v.14; Br572C An8141 v.19.

4129. Thomas, Cyrus. The vigesimal system of enumeration. *American Anthropologist* 9:409-410, 1896. Br572C An8141 v.159.

4130. Thomas, Cyrus. Who were the Moundbuilders? *American Antiquarian* 9:65-74, 1885. Br572C An8141 v.39.

4131. Thomas, Cyrus. *Work in Mound Exploration of the Bureau of Ethnology*. Bureau of Ethnology, Smnithsonian Institution, Washington, DC, 1887. 34 p. Br572C An8141 v.14; Br572C An8141 v.19.

4132. Thompson, Alton H. Ethnology of teeth, 1899. 13 p. Br617.7 T37.

4133. Thompson, Alton H. The ethnology of the face. *The Dental Cosmos*, pp. 11-16, 1892. Br572C An8141 v.88.

4134. Thompson, Alton H. The origin and evolution of the face. *The Dental Cosmos*, pp. 633-638, 683-763, 1890. Br572C An8141 v.88.

4135. Thompson, Alton H. The origin and evolution of the human face, and the descent of facial expression, n.d. 20 p. Br572C An8141 v.121.

4136. Thompson, Edward H. *Cave of Loltun, Yucatan: Report of Explorations by the Museum, 1888-1889 and 1890-1891*. Memoirs of the Peabody Museum of American Archaeology and Ethnology, Harvard University, v. 1(2), 1897. 24 p. Cambridge, MA. Br572C An8141 v.161.

4137. Thompson, Edward H. Ruins of Xkichmook, Yucatan. *Anthropological Series, Field Columbian Museum* 2(3): 211-229, 1898. Br572C An8141 v.163.

4138. Thompson, Edward H. *The Chultunes of Labna, Yucatan: Report of Explorations by the Museum, 1888-1889 and 1890-1891*. Memoirs of the Peabody Museum of American Archaeology and Ethnology, Harvard University, v. 1(3), 1897. 20 p. Cambridge, MA. Br572C An8141 v.161.

4139. Thompson, Edward M. *Handbook of Greek and Latin Palæography*. D. Appleton, New York, 1893. 343 p. Br417 T36.

4140. Thorburn, John. Counting and time reckoning. *Transactions of the Canadian Institute* 5:311-323, 1896-1897. Br572C An8141 v.163.

4141. Thouar, Arthur. *Explorations dans l'Amérique du Sud; I. A la recherche de la mission Crevaux. II. Dans le delta du Pilcomayo. III. De Buenos Aires à Sucre. IV. Dans le Chaco Boréal*. Hachette et Cie., Paris, 1891. 421 p. Br918 T398. "L'idiome des Tobas du haut Pilcomayo" (pp. 419-421).

4142. Thruston, Gates P. Ancient society in Tennessee; the Mound Builders were Indians. *Magazine of American History* 19:374-400, 1888. Br572C An8141 v.59.

4143. Thruston, Gates P. *The Antiquities of Tennessee and the Adjacent States and the State of Aboriginal Society in the Scale of Civilization Represented by Them*. R. Clarke and Company, Cincinnati, 1890. 369 p. Br913.768 T427.

4144. Thruston, Gates P. *The Antiquities of Tennessee and the Adjacent States and the State of Aboriginal Society in the Scale of Civilization Represented by Them; A Series of Historical and Ethnological Studies*. 2nd ed. R. Clarke Company, Cincinnati, 1897. 369 p. Br913.768 T427a.

4145. Tibbles, Thomas H. *The Ponca Chiefs; An Indian's Attempt to Appeal From the Tomahawk to the Courts; A Full History of the Robbery of the Ponca Tribe of In-*

dians, With All the Papers Filed and Evidence Taken in the Standing Bear Habeas Corpus Case, and Full Text of Judge Dundy's Celebrated Decision, With Some Suggestions Towards a Solution of the Indian Question, by Zylyff With an Introduction by Inshtatheamba (Bright Eyes) and Dedication by Wendell Phillips. Lockwood, Brooks and Company, Boston, 1880. 146 p. Br970.5 Z94.

4146. Tiele, Cornelis P. *History of the Egyptian Religion*. Houghton Mifflin, Boston, 1882. 230 p. Br271 T44.

4147. *Tillæg til Aarbøger for nordisk oldkyndighed og historie*. Kjöbenhavn, 1888. Br571.05 T46.

4148. Tim, John W. *Readings from the Holy Scriptures in the Language of the Blackfoot Indians*. Society for Promoting Christian Knowledge, London, 1890. 47 p. Br497.11 SiT 48.2.

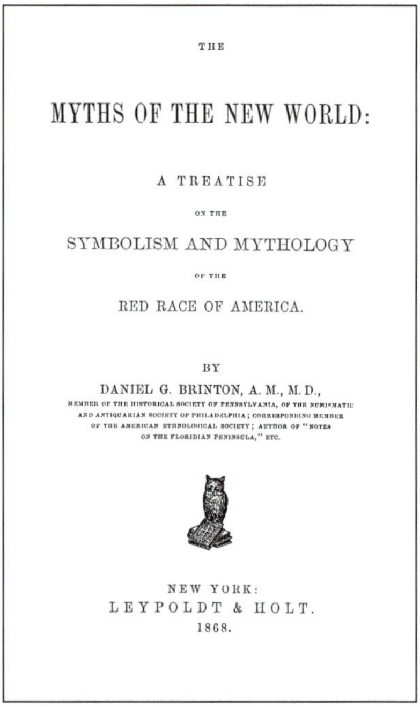
THE

MYTHS OF THE NEW WORLD:

A TREATISE

ON THE

SYMBOLISM AND MYTHOLOGY

OF THE

RED RACE OF AMERICA.

BY

DANIEL G. BRINTON, A. M., M. D.,

MEMBER OF THE HISTORICAL SOCIETY OF PENNSYLVANIA, OF THE NUMISMATIC AND ANTIQUARIAN SOCIETY OF PHILADELPHIA; CORRESPONDING MEMBER OF THE AMERICAN ETHNOLOGICAL SOCIETY; AUTHOR OF "NOTES ON THE FLORIDIAN PENINSULA," ETC.

NEW YORK:

LEYPOLDT & HOLT.

1868.

Title page from Brinton's The Myths of the New World *(1896).*

4149. Timberlake, Henry. *The Memoirs of Lieut. Henry Timberlake (Who Accompanied the Three Cherokee Indians to England in the Year 1762); Containing Whatever he Observed Remarkable, or Worthy of Public Notice, During his Travels to and From that Nation; Wherein the Country, Government, Genius, and Customs of the Inhabitants, are Authentically Described; Also the Principal Occurrences During Their Residence in London*. Printed for the author, London, 1765. 160 p. Br970.5 T48. "Timberlake's *Memoirs* record his advcentures among the Overhill Cherokee and other travels in Tennessee, Georgia, the Carolinas, and Virginia after the French and Indian War. In 1762, Timberlake escorted the Cherokee chief Outacity and two of his warriors to London, where they created a sensation" (*Frank T. Siebert Library* 1999:1:204).

4150. Tims, John W. *Grammar and Dictionary of the Blackfoot Language in the Dominion of Canada For the Use of Missionaries, School Teachers and Others*. Society for Promoting Christian Knowledge, London, 1875. 191 p. Br497.11 SiT 48.

4151. Tims, John W. *The Gospel According to St. Matthew; Translated Into the Language of the Blackfoot Indians by the Rev. J. W. Tims*. British and Foreign Bible Society, London, 1890. 109 p. Br497.11 SiB 47.1.

4152. *Titulo de los señores de Totonicapan, escrito en lengua quiché, el año de 1554;*

y traducido al la [sic] *castellana el año de 1834, por...Dionisio José Chonay; traduit de l'espagnol por Hyacinthe de Charencey.* Broise, Alençon, 1855. Br572C An8141 v.11; Br572C An8141 v.55; Br498.21 KiQ15; Br498.21 KiQ15a.

4153. Título de los señores de Totonicapan. *Titre généalogique des seigneurs de Totonicapan.* E. Renaut-de Broise, imprimeur, Alençon, 1885. 69 p. Br498.21 KiQ 15. Extract from the *Bulletin des Actes de la Sociéte Philologique.* Spanish and French on opposite pages. The former is the copy made by Brasseur de Bourbourg of the original Spanish translation of padre Chonay, with title: "Título de los señores de Totonicapan, escrito en lengua quiché, el año de 1554, y traducido al la (sic) castellana el año de 1834 por el padre Dionisio- José Chonay, indigena, cura de Sacapulas."

4154. *Títulos de la casa de Ixcuín-Neharb* [sic], *señora del territorio de Otzoyá.* Sociedad Económica, Guatemala, 1876. 13 p. Br929.7 T538.

4155. Todd, James E. Boulder mosaics in Dakota. *American Naturalist* 20(1), 1886. 4 p. Br572C An8141 v.13.

4156. Tolmie, W. Fraser. *Comparative Vocabularies of the Indian Tribes of British Columbia, with a Map llustrating Distribution.* Dawson Brothers, Montreal, 1884. 131 p. Br497 T58.

4157. Tooker, William W. Discovery of Chaonis Temoatan of 1586. *American Antiquarian* 17(1): 3-15, 1895. Br572C An8141 v.142.

4158. Tooker, William W. Indian geographic names, and why we should study them; illustrated by some Rhode Island examples; abstract of a paper read before the Rhode Island Historical Society, March 25, 1897. pp. 203-215, n.d. Br572C An8141 v.163.

4159. Tooker, William W. *Indian Place-Names in East-Hampton Town, With their Probable Significations.* East-Hampton Town Records v. 4. J. Hunt, Sag Harbor, 1889. 10 p. Br572C An8141 v.51.

4160. Tooker, William W. *John Eliot's First Indian Teacher and Interpreter, Cockenoe-de-Long Island and the Story of His Career From the Early Records.* F. P. Harper, New York, 1896. 60 p. Br270.2 C64.yT.

4161. Tooker, William W. On the meaning of the name Anacostia. *American Anthropologist* 7(4): 389-393, 1894. Br572C An8141 v.136.

4162. Tooker, William W. Roger Williams vindicated; or, an answer to "A Keyhole for Roger Williams' key." *Publications of the Rhode Island Historical Society* 2(1): 61-67, 1894. Br572C An8141 v.123.

4163. Tooker, William W. Some Indian fishing stations upon Long Island. *Brooklyn Daily Eagle Almanac,* pp. 54-57, 1895. Br572C An8141 v.136.

4164. Tooker, William W. The Algonquian appellatives of the Siouan tribes of Virginia. *American Anthropologist* 8:376-392, 1895. Br572C An8141 v.142.

4165. Tooker, William W. The Algonquin terms *patawomeke* and *massawomeke. American Anthropologist* 6:174-185, 1894. Br572C An8141 v.127.

4166. Tooker, William W. *The Indian Place-Names on Long Island and Islands Adjacent, With Their Probable Significations.* G. P. Putnam's Sons, New York, London, 1911. 314 p. Br497.11 T612.

4167. Tooker, William W. The problem of the Rechahecrian Indians of Virginia. *Ameri-*

can Anthropologist 9:261-270, 1898. Br572C An8141 v.163.

4168. Tooker, William W. The significance of John Eliot's Natick. *American Anthropologist* 10:281-287, 1897. Br572C An8141 v.159.

4169. Tooker, William W. The signification of the name Montauk. *Brooklyn Daily Eagle Almanac*, 1896. 1 p. Br572C An8141 v.142.

4170. Topinard, Paul. Crane trépané sur le vivant et aprés la mort. *Bulletin de la Société d'Anthropologie*, 1887. 24 p. Br572C An8141 v.31.

4171. Topinard, Paul. De l'evolution des molaires et prémolaires chez les primates et en particular chez l'homme. *L'Anthropologie* 3(6): 641-710, 1892. Br572C An8141 v.109; Br572C An8141 v.123.

4172. Topinard, Paul. De la race en anthropologie. In *Congrès International d'Archéologique Prehistorique et d'Anthropologie* (11 session), pp. 161-170, 1892. Br572C An8141 v.109.

4173. Topinard, Paul. *Eléments d'anthropologie générale.* Vigot Frères, Paris, 1885. 1157 p. Br572 T624.

4174. Topinard, Paul. L'anthropologie aux États-Unis. *L'Anthropologie* 4:301-351, 1893. Br572C An8141 v.109; Br572C An8141 v.132.

4175. Topinard, Paul. *La société, l'ecole, le laboratoire et le Musée Broca.* Chamerot, Paris, 1890. 40 p. Br572C An8141 v.31.

4176. Topinard, Paul. La transformation du crâne humain. *L'Anthropologie* 2:649-675, 1891. Br572C An8141 v.8.

4177. Topinard, Paul. Les dernieres étapes de la généalogie de l'homme. *Revue d'Anthropologie*, pp. 298-332, 1888. Br572C An8141 v.8.

4178. Topinard, Paul. *L'homme dans la nature.* F. Alcan, Paris, 1891. 352 p. Br573 T624.

4179. Topinard, Paul. Présentation de quatre boshimans vivants. *Bulletin de la Société d'Anthropologie de Paris* 8:73-83, 1886. Br572C An8141 v.26.

4180. Torell, Otto. On the causes of the glacial phenomena in the northeastern portion of North America. *Bihang till K. Svenska Vet. Akad. Handlingar* 5(1), 1877. 8 p. Br572C An8141 v.24.

4181. Torell, Otto. *Sur les traces les plus anciennes de l'existence de l'homme en Suéde.* Sveriges Geologiska Undersökning, Stockholm, 1876. 16 p. Br572C An8141 v.24.

4182. Török, Aurel. Über den yézoer Ainoschädel aus der ostasiatischen Reise des Herrn Grafen Béla Széchenyi und über den Sachaliner Ainoschädel. *Archiv für Anthropologie* 23:249-345, 1894. Br572C An8141 v.145.

4183. Török, Aurel. Über die neue paläethnologische Eintheilung der Steinzeit. *Correspondenz-Blatt der Deutschen Anthropologischen Gesellschaft* 3, 1895. 4 p. Br572C An8141 v.145.

4184. Torquemada, Juan de. *Primera [segunda, tercera] parte de los veinte i vn libros rituales i monarchia indiana con el origen y guerras, de los Indios Occidentales, de sus poblaçones descubrimiento, conquista, conuersion y otras cosas marauillosas de la mesma tierra disibuydos en tres tomos.* En la oficina y a costa de Nicholas Rodríguez Franco, Madrid, 1723. 3 v. Br970.1 T636. "Juan de Torquemada…studied in Mexico where he took the habit of St. Francis, and became the Provincial of the order for that country. He wrote his *Indian Monarchy* after having collected everything which he could find that related to the history of the country, and the customs, manners, laws, etc., of its original inhabitants. This work forms a collection, indispensable to all who desire to know much of the ancient history of Mexico, and its inhabitants, as well as to all those writers who expect to borrow their material from the stores of others. The edition of 1723 is the most complete" (Field 1873:394).

4185. Torres, Francisco G. Calendario azteca para el año 1886 v acatl. Ochoa, Zapotlan, n.d. 39 p. Br498.22 AzT 177. Contains: Ignacio de Paredes, "Doctrina breve sacada de catecismo mexicana," n.d.; Macario Torres, "Estudios gramaticales sobre el nahuatl…publicados por Eusebio Ortega," n.d.; "Vocabulario de las lenguas castellana y mexicana," n.d.

4186. Torresano, Estevan. Arte de lengua cakchiquel, etc., incluiendo un parallelo de las lenguas kiche, cakchiquel y tzutuhil, año de 1754, 180 p. Br498.21 CF667T. Torresano's grammar, based on Flores' *Arte de la lengua metropolitana del reyno cakchiquel* of 1753, also includes a section on counting in Cakchiquel (leaves 98-116). Leaves 117-135 contain a "Parallelo," a comparison of some of the grammar points of Cakchiquel, Quiché, and Tzutujil, and a vocabulary list in four columns comparing common words in the three languages, with translations in Spanish. The final section, entitled "Ortographía para la buena pronunciación de estas tres lenguas" (leaves 134-143), discusses the letters which these languages have in common with Spanish and those letters omitted, as well as the Parra letters used to represent the six sounds unique to these three languages.

4187. Tounens, Orllie-Antoine. *Sa captivité au Chili*. Librarie de Thevelin, 1863. 174 p. Br572C An8141 v.16.

4188. Tovar, Juan de. *Historia de los yndios mexicanos*. Jacobus Rogers impressit, Typis Medio-Montanis, 1860. 12 p. Br970.4 MT642. A fragment, privately printed by Sir Thomas Phillipps at his press, Middle Hill, Worcester.

4189. Tower, C. *Report of the Board of Managers of the Department of Archaeology and Palaeontology of the University of Pennsylvania, 1893*. Philadelphia, 1894. 29 p. Br572C An8141 v.127.

4190. *Transactions of the New York Academy of Anthropology*, October 1888-May 1890. 75 p. Br572C An8141 v.8.

4191. *Treaty Between the United States and the Choctaws and Chickasaw*, 1866. 56 p. Br572C An8141 v.50; Br572C An8141 v.58.

4192. Treutler, Paul. *Fünfzehn Jahre in Süd-Amerika an den Ufern des stillen Oceans*. Richard Lesser, Leipzig, 1882. 3 v. in 1. Br918 T728.

4193. Treutler, Paul. *La provincia de Valdivia i los Araucanos*. Imprenta Chilena, Santiago de Chile, 1861 244 p. Br498.977 T 728. A more extensive work of the author appeared in Germany with title, *Fünfzehn Jahre in Süd-America* (Leipzig, 1882). Mapuche Indians.

4194. Trioen, L. F. B. *Indagaciones sobre las antigüedades mexicanas; pruebas de la civilización adelantada de los mexicanos en el XV siglo, sacadas de los principales autores y citadas en apoyo.* Impreso por I. Cumplido, México, 1841. 35 p. Br913.72 T735.

4195. *Trois lettres sur la découverte du Yucatán et les merveilles de ce pays; escrites par des compagnons de l'expedition sous Jean de Grijalva, mai 1518; imprimées sur vieux papier d'aprés le ms; original d'une version allemande de 1529, et en traduction allemande et française moderne.* Imprimerie de Jean Euschede et Fils, Harlem, 1871. Br972.6 T743.

4196. Trouessart, E. Les primates tertiaires et l'homme fossile Sud-Américain. *L'Anthropologie* (3): 257-274, 1892. Br572C An8141 v.83.

4197. Troyer, Carlos. *Two Zuñi Songs, Transcribed and Harmonized by Carlos Troyer.* Sherman, Clay and Company, San Francisco, 1893. 5 p. Br497.67 T756. Two musical scores for voice and piano; contents include I. Zuñian lullaby; an incantation upon a sleeping infant (Mahi wáha niema naha. English and Zuni), and II. Zuñian lover's wooing (Shanetandamey, shanelulu. English and Zuni).

4198. Trumbull, H. Clay. *The Threshold Covenant, Or, The Beginning of Religious Rites.* 2nd ed. Charles Scribner, New York, 1896. 336 p. Br291 T77a.

4199. Trumbull, J. Hammond. *Indian Names of Places, etc., In and On the Borders of Connecticut; With Interpretations of Some of Them.* Press of the Case, Lockwood and Brainard Company, Hartford, 1881. 93 p. Br497.11 T77.

4200. Trumbull, J. Hammond. On numerals in American Indian languages and the Indian mode of counting. *Transactions of the American Philological Association for 1874,* pp. 41-76, 1875. Hartford. Br572C An8141 v.50; Br572C An8141 v.55.

4201. Trumbull, J. Hammond. On some alleged specimens of Indian onomatopoeia. *Transactions of the Connecticut Academy of Arts and Sciences* 2:177-185, 1870. Br572C An8141 v.80.

4202. Trumbull, J. Hammond. On some mistaken notions of Algonkin grammar. *Transactions of the American Philological Association for 1869-1870,* pp. 105-123, 1871. Hartford. Br572C An8141 v.51. "Among other heresies which Mr. Trumbull exterminates is that bewildering one of which Mr. Duponceau was the apostle, that the (Massachusett) Natick language could be demonstrated from [John] Eliot's Bible, to possess an infinitive mood…another error in the opposite direction…that verbs had no expression unless associated with both actor and subject, is completely refuted" (Field 1873:398).

4203. Trumbull, J. Hammond. On the Algonkin name "manit" (or "manitou"), sometimes translated as "Great Spirit", and "God." *Old and New* 1(3): 337-342, 1870. Br572C An8141 v.80.

4204. Trumbull, J. Hammond. On the best method of studying the American languages. *Transactions of the American Philological Association for 1869-1870,* pp. 55-79, 1871. Hartford. Br572C An8141 v.51. The polysyllabic, or synthetic, structure of the words of all Indian languages is most clearly exhibited and demonstrated in this essay" (Field 1873:398).

4205. Trumbull, J. Hammond. *The Composition of Indian Geographical Names, Illus-*

trated From the Algonkin Languages. Collections of the Connecticut Historical Society, 5(2). Press of Case, Lockwood and Brainard, Hartford, 1870. Br572C An8141 v.80.

4206. Tschudi, Johann Jakob von. *Beiträge zur Kenntniss des alten Perú.* In Commission bei F. Tempsky, Wien, 1891. 220 p. Br572C An8141 v.91.

4207. Tschudi, Johann Jakob von. Das Lama. *Berliner Gesellschaft für Anthropologie, Ethnologie, und Urgeschichte* 4(13): 93-109, 1885. Br572C An8141 v.4.

4208. Tschudi, Johann Jakob von. Die Calchaquis. *Verhandlungen der Berliner Anthropologischen Gesellschaft für Anthropologie, Ethnologie und Urgeschichte* 4(2): 184-186, 1885. Br572C An8141 v.4.

4209. Tschudi, Johann Jakob von. Die Geographischen Namen in Perú. *Zeitschrift für Wissenschaft,* pp. 1-7, n.d. Br572C An8141 v.4.

4210. Tschudi, Johann Jakob von. *Organismus der Khet ua-Sprache.* F. A. Brockhaus, Leipzig, 1884. 534 p. Br498.7 T 788.

4211. Tschudi, Johann Jakob von. *Reisen durch Südamerika.* F. A. Brockhaus, Leipzig, 1866-1869. 5 v. Br918 T787.

4212. Tunis, W. R. B. Professor Aguchekikos on totemism, 1886. 15 p. Br572C An8141 v.83.

4213. Tylor, Edward B. *Anthropology; An Introduction to the Study of Man and Civilization.* D. Appleton, New York, 1881. 347 p. Br572 T97.1b. Sir Edward Burnett Tylor (1832-1917) was the evolutionary anthropologist who is best remembered for his formulation of the 'doctrine of survivals' and the 'theory of animism.' Considered by many to be the founder of modern anthropology, he was influential in the gradual acceptance of anthropology as a scientific discipline. In 1896 he became Oxford Universities first professor of anthropology.

4214. Tylor, Edward B. Old Scandinavian civilization among the modern Esquimaux. *Journal of the Anthropological Institute of Great Britain and Ireland* 13(3): 348-356, 1884. Br572C An8141 v.67. Tylor argues that the Greenlanders still preserve some of Norse customs as a result of some lost Scandinavian survivors being assimilated into Greenland culture.

4215. Tylor, Edward B. On American lot-games as evidence of Asiatic intercourse before the time of Columbus. *Internationales Archiv für Ethnographie* 9:55-67, 1896. Br572C An8141 v.161.

4216. Tylor, Edward B. On the game of patolli in ancient Mexico and its probably Asiatic origin. *Journal of the Anthropological Institute of Great Britain and Ireland* 8(2): 116-132, 1878. Br572C An8141 v.59.

4217. Tylor, Edward B. On the Tasmanians as representatives of Palaeolithic man. *Journal of the Anthropological Institute* 23(2): 141-152, 1893. Br572C An8141 v.127.

4218. Tylor, Edward B. Totem-post from the Haida village of Masset; Two British Columbian house-posts with totemic carvings; Remarks on totemism. *Journal of the Anthropological Institute,* pp. 133-148, 1898. Br913.711 T974.

4219. Tylor, Edward B., *et al. Fourth report on the Northwestern tribes of Canada.* Spottiswoode and Company, London, 1888. Br572C An8141 v.112.

4220. Tylor, Edward B., *et al. Fifth Report of the Committee on the Northwestern Tribes of the Dominion of Canada.* Spottiswoode and Company, London, 1889. Br572C An8141 v.112.

4221. Tylor, Edward B., *et al. Sixth Report on the Northwestern Tribes of Canada.* Spottiswoode and Company, London, 1890. Br572C An8141 v.112.

4222. Tylor, Edward B., G. M. Dawson, R. G. Haliburton, and H. Hale. *On the North-Western Tribes of Canada; Tenth Report of the Committee [of the British Association for the Advancement of Science].* Spottiswoode, 1895. London. 71 p. Br572C An8141 v.143.

4223. Tyson, Philip T. *Report of the Secretary of War, Communicating Information in Relation to the Geology and Topography of California.* Washington, DC, 1850. Br5328.73 31.1SD.

4224. *Uganu buiditi kaysi St. Mark; the Gospel According to St. Mark in Carib. Uganu buiditi kaysi St. Mark lidan garifuna.* British and Foreign Bible Society, London, 1901. 66 p. Br498.78 B 47.2. Gospel of St. Mark translated into Carib.

4225. Uhle, Max. A modern kipu from Cutusuma, Bolivia. *Bulletin of the Museum of Science and Art, University of Pennsylvania* 1(2): 51–63, 1897. Br572C An8141 v.159. Max Uhle (1856–1944), studied philology at Göttingen and Leipzig, was one of a group of archaeologists who, at the end of the 19th and beginning of the 20th centuries, commenced a systematic investigation of the prehispanic cultures of South America. He was the first to develop a general framework of the historical and chronological cultural sequences in the Andean region. Between 1897 and 1899 he directed excavations at Pachacamac for the University of Pennsylvania.

4226. Uhle, Max. A snuffing tube from Tiahuanaco. *Bulletin of the Museum of Science and Art, University of Pennsylvania* 1(4): 159–177, 1898. Br572C An8141 v.163.

4227. Uhle, Max. *Kultur und Industrie südamerikanischer Völker; nach den im Besitze des Museums für Völkerkunde zu Leipzig befindlichen Sammlungen von A. Stübel, W. Reiss und P. Koppel.* A. Asher, Berlin, 1889–1890. 2 v. Br572.98 Uh63.

4228. Uhle, Max. Zwei prähistorische Elephanendarstellungen aus Amerika. *Verhandlungen der Berliner Anthropologischen Gesellschaft für Anthropologie, Ethnologie und Urgeschichte,* pp. 322–328, 1886. Br572C An8141 v.4.

4229. Ujfalvy, Karoly Jeno. *Les Aryens au nord et au sud de l'Hindou-Kouch.* Masson, Paris, 1896. 488 p. Br572.891 Uj39.

4230. Ule, Otto E. V. *Die Erde und die Erscheinungen ihrer Oberfläche in ihrer Beziehung zur Geschichte derselben und zum Leben ihrer Bewohner. Eine physische Erdbeschreibung nach E. Reclus.* Druck von Bär und Hermann, Leipzig, 1873. Br572C An8141 v.65.

4231. Ulloa, Antonio de, Admiral. *Noticias Americanas; entretenimientos phisicoshistóricos sobre la América Meridional, y la Septentrianal* [sic] *Oriental. Comparación general de los territorios, climas, y produciones, etc.* Madrid, 1772. Br918 U144.

4232. United States. Board on Geographical Names. *Bulletin* 1, Smithsonian Institution, Washington, DC, 1890. 13 p. Br572C An8141 v.7.

4233. United States. Bureau of Indian Affairs. *Report of the Commissioner of Indian Af-*

fairs. Government Printing Office, Washington, DC. Br353.3 I1. Includes reports for 1851, 1855-1858, 1860, 1860, 1862, 1864-1866, 1868-1875, 1876, 1877, and 1883.

4234. United States. Bureau of Indian Affairs. *Treaties Between the United States of America and the Several Indian Tribes from 1778 to 1837, With a Copious Table of Contents*. Langtree, Washington, DC, 1837. 699 p. Br970.5 Un31.1.

4235. United States. Congress. 38 Session, 1864-1865. *Joint Special Committee to Inquire into the Condition of the Indian Tribes; Report of the Joint Special Committee, Appointed Under Joint Resolution of March 3, 1865; With an Appendix*. Washington, DC, 1867. 10 p. 38 Session. Report. Br970.6 Un35.

4236. United States. Congress. Indian Affairs Commission. *Report of the Special Commission Appointed to Investigate the Affairs of the Red Cloud Indian Agency, July 1875, Together With the Testimony and Accompanying Documents*. Washington, DC, 1875. 852 p. Br970.5 Un37.

4237. United States. Department of the Interior. Geographical and Geological Survey of the Rocky Mountain Region. *Contributions to North American Ethnology*. Government Printing Office, Washington, DC, 1877-1893. 8 v. Br557.3 Un319.

4238. United States. Geographical Surveys, West of the 100th Meridian. *Reports... 1889*. Washington, DC, 1889. Br557.3 Un32.2.

4239. United States. Geographical Surveys, West of the 100th Meridian. *Reports... 1879*. Washington, DC, 1879. Br912.73 Un34.

4240. United States. Navy Department. *Reports of Explorations and Surveys, to Ascertain the Practibility of a Ship-Canal Between the Atlantic and Pacific Ocean by the Way of the Isthmus of Tehuantepec by R. W. Shufeldt*. Washington, DC, 1872. 151 p. Br626.9 Un35.

4241. United States. Revenue Cutter Service. *Cruise of the Revenue Steamer Corwin in Alaska and the N.W. Arctic Ocean in 1881. Notes and Memoranda; Medical and Anthropological; Botanical; Ornithological*. Washington, DC, 1883. 120 p. Br919.8 Un33b. Contents include I. C. Rosse, "Medical and anthropological notes on Alaska"; J. Muir, "Botanical notes on Alaska"; E. W. Nelson, "The birds of Bering Sea and the Arctic Ocean"; T. H. Bean, "List of fishes known to occur in the Arctic Ocean, north of Bering Strait."

4242. United States. War Department. *Reports of Explorations and Surveys, to Ascertain the Most Practicable and Economical Route for a Railroad From the Mississippi River to the Pacific Ocean; Made Under the Direction of the Secretary of War, in 1853-6*. A. O. P. Nicholson, Printer, Washington, DC, 1855-1860. 12 v. Br508.73 Un7a. Volumes 1-11 were issued in the Congressional series of United States public documents. The reports of the Pacific railroad surveys were prepared under the direct supervision of the Engineer department. The volumes dealing with the soil, climate, geology, botany and zoology of the regions surveyed were edited and revised by Professors Henry and Baird, of the Smithsonian Institution. Contents include: 1. Introduction. Route near the 47th and 49th parallels; 2. Routes near 38th and 39th, 41st, and 32d parallels. Lander's report; 3-4. Route near the 35th and 32d parallels; 5. Routes in California to connect with those near the 35th and 32d parallels; 6. Routes in Oregon and California; 7. Route in California to connect with those near the 35th and 32d parallels; route between the Rio Grande and Pimas villages; 8. Mammals of the several routes; 9. Birds of the several routes; 10. Reptiles and fishes of the several routes; zoological reports on routes near 38th and 39th, 41st, 35th and 32d parallels; on routes in California to connect with those near the 35th and 32d parallels; reptiles of routes in California and Oregon; 12. Material used and methods employed in compiling the general map; topographical maps, etc.; 12. Route near the 47th and 49th parallels (concluded).

4243. United States. War Department. Office of Indian Affairs. *Report of the Commissioner of Indian Affairs to the Secretary of the Interior*. Government Printing Office, Washington, DC, 1891. 210 p. Br572C An8141 v.112.

4244. United States. War Department. Office of Indian Affairs. *Report on the Commission Appointed to Negotiate with the Ute Indians in Colorado Territory*. Washington, DC, 1873. 48 p. Br572C An8141 v.32.

4245. Université de Brussels. Institut Géographique. Cours préparatoires donnés à la Faculté des Sciences, n.d. 4 p. Br572C An8141 v.163.

4246. University of Pennsylvania. Department of Archaeology and Palaeontology. *Report of the Board of Managers of the Department of Archaeology and Palaeontology of the University of Pennsylvania*. Philadelphia, 1893. 35 p. Br572C An8141 v.136; Br572C An8141 v.124.

4247. University of Pennsylvania. Department of Archaeology and Palaeontology. *Report of the Department of Archaeology and Palaeontology, University of Pennsylvania*. Philadelphia, 1894. 10 p. Br572C An8141 v.134.

4248. University of Pennsylvania. Department of Archaeology and Palaeontology. *Resolutions Submitted by the Trustees of the University to the University Archaeological Association*, 1891. 7 p. Br572C An8141 v.129.

4249. University of Pennsylvania. Museum of American Archaeology. *Annual Report of the Curator of the Museum of American Archaeology; Presented to the President and Council of the University of Pennsylvania Archaeological Association*, 1890. Br572C An8141 v.17.

4250. Uricoechea, Ezequiel. *Bibliothèque Linguistique Américaine*. Maisonneuve, Paris. 24 v. Br497C Am3.

4251. Uricoechea, Ezequiel. *Gramática, vocabulario, catecismo i confesionario de la lengua Chibcha; según antiguos manuscritos anónimos e inéditos, aumentados i corejidos*. Bibliothèque Linguistique Américaine, 1. J. Maisonneuve, Paris, 1871. 252 p. Br497C Am3; Br498.64 CUr 33.

4252. Uricoechea, Ezequiel. *Memoria sobre las antigüedades neo-granadinas*. F. Schneider i Cía., Berlin, 1854. 76 p. Br913.86 Ur32. "The social and private life, the rites and ceremonies, the commerce, and…the usages and customs, are the indices by which we mark the state of civilization. These characteristics of the Chibchas and Armas Indian nations, inhabiting New Granada, form the entire material of this work. The plates are representations of their idols, weapons, utensils, and craniology" (Field 1873:402).

4253. *Urquell: Eine Monatschrift für Volkskunde*. E. J. Brill, Leiden. v. 1(1897)–v. 2(1898). Br398 Ur65.

4254. Uvarov, Aleksiei Sergieevich, graf. *Étude sur les peuples primitifs de la Russie Les Mériens*. Imprimerie de l'Académie impériale des sciences, Saint-Petersbourg, 1875. 308 p. Br913.47 Uv17.FM.

4255. Vaïsse y Echeverría, E. F., and Aníbal Reyes, Glosario de la lengua atacamea, 1896. Br498.977 L545.

4256. Valadés, Diego. *Rhetorica christiana ad concionandi et orandi vsum accommodata, vtriusq[ue] facultatis exemplis suo loco insertis; quae quidem ex Indorum maximè deprompta sunt historiis; vnde praeter doctrinam, sum[m]a quoque delectatio comparabitur*. Apud Petrumiacobum Petrutium, Perusiae, 1579. 378 p. Br238 B232.

4257. Valdés, José F. *Vida de la gloriosísima madre de la Madre de Dios, y abuela de Jesuchristo Señora Santa Ana; dada á luz á expensas de un humilde cordialísimo devoto suyo*. Por los Herederos de Don Felipe de Zúñiga y Ontiveros, México, 1794. 208 p. Br262.13 V233.

4258. Váldez, Sebastián. Vocabulario de la lengua pocomam de Mita, por D. Sebastián Váldez, cura de Jutiapa, 1868; copiado del original en poder de D. Juan Gavarrete en Guatemala, febrero de 1875. 7 p. Br498.21 PoV 233. Manuscript.

4259. Valdivia, Luis de. *Arte, vocabulario y confesionario de la lengua de Chile, compuestos por Luiz de Valdivia; pub. de nuevo por Julio Platzmann. Edición facsimilar*. B. G. Teubner, Leipzig, 1887. 265 p. Br498.977 AV233.

4260. Valdivia, Luis de. *Doctrina cristiana y catecismo; con un Confesionario, Arte y Vocabulario breves en lengua allentiac*. Imprenta de E. Rasco, Sevilla, 1894. 78, 91 p. Br498.977 GV 23. The reprints of the *Doctrina cristiana, Confessionario, Arte y gramática* and *Vocabulario* include facsimiles of original title pages, dated 1607.

4261. Valentini, Philipp J. J. Analysis of the pictorial text inscribed on two Palenque tables I. *Proceedings of the American Antiquarian Society* 9:423–450, 1894. Br572C An8141 v.142.

4262. Valentini, Philipp J. J. Analysis of the pictorial text inscribed on two Palenque tables II. *Proceedings of the American Antiquarian Society* 9(3): 429–450, 1895. 21 p. Br572C An8141 v.142.

4263. Valentini, Philipp J. J. Das Geschichliche in den mythischen Städten "Tulan". *Zeitschrift für Ethnologie*, pp. 44–55, 1886. Br572C An8141 v.159.

4264. Valentini, Philipp J. J. The Humboldt celt and the Layden plate. *Proceedings of the American Antiquarian Society*, April, 1881. 24 p. Br572C An8141 v.19.

4265. Valentini, Philipp J. J. The katunes of Maya history. *Proceedings of the American Antiquarian Society* 74:71–117, 1880. Br572C An8141 v.50.

4266. Valentini, Philipp J. J. The Landa alphabet; a Spanish fabrication. *Proceedings of the American Antiquarian Society* 75:59–91, 1880. Br572C An8141 v.50. Valentini argues that the Yucatec Maya alphabet in Diego de Landa's *Relación* is a Spanish fabrication. This essay is an early attack on the phonetic basis of Maya inscriptions.

4267. Valentini, Philipp. J. J. *Mexican Paper: an Article of Tribute, Its Manufacture, Vari-*

eties, Employment, and Uses. Press of Charles Hamilton, Worcester, 1881. 26 p. Br572C An8141 v.165.

4268. Valentini, Phillip J. J. The Olmecas and the Tultecas: a study in early Mexican ethnology and history. *Proceedings of the American Antiquarian Society* 2:193-230, 1883. Br572C An8141 v.23.

4269. Valentini, Phillip J. J. Vocabulario de la lengua de las vicéitas, en Costa Rica, por Ph. Valentini, Costa de Limón, 1866. 39 leaves. Br498.13 GGV414. Manuscript, transcription by K. Hermann Berendt; leaf 34 is titled "Vocabularios de lengua indígena de la parte sureña de la provincia de Costarica, colectadas por F.V."

4270. Valle Cabral, Alfredo. *Bibliographia da lingua tupí ou guaraní tambem chamada lingua geral do Brazil.* Typographia Nacional, Rio de Janeiro, 1880. 78 p. Br498.75 GC 114. Extract from v. 8 of *Annaes de Bibliotheca Nacional do Rio de Janeiro.*

4271. Vance, L. J. Folk-lore study in America. *Popular Science Monthly* 63(42): 586-598, 1893. Br572C An8141 v.119.

4272. Vandever, William. The Aryan race and language. *Pacific Science Monthly* 1(4): 41-48, 1885. Br572C An8141 v.59.

4273. Vargas Machuca, Bernardo de. *Milicia y descripción de las Indias, escrita por el capitán D. Bernardo de Vargas Machuca.* V. Suarez, Madrid, 1892. 242 p. Br972.9 V424.

4274. Varnhagen, Francisco Adolfo de, visconde de Porto Seguro. *La verdadera Guanahani de Colon.* Imprenta Nacional, Calle de la Maneda, Santiago, 1864. 14 p. Br572C An8141 v.165.

4275. Varnhagen, Francisco Adolfo de, visconde de Porto Seguro. *L'origine touranienne des américains tupís-caribes et des anciens Égyptiens, montrée principalement par la philologie comparée; et notice d'une émigration en Amérique effectuée à travers l'Atlantique plusieurs siècles avant notre ère.* I. et R. de Faesy et Frick, Vienne, 1876. 154 p. Br498.75 V43a.

4276. Vasel, A. Volkstümliche Schnitzereien an Gerätschaften im Lande Braunschweig. *Beiträge zur Anthropologie Braunschweigs* 21:135-154, 1898. Br572C An8141 v.164.

4277. Vázquez Gaztelu, Antonio. *Arte de lengua mexicana; compuesto por Antonio Vasquez Gastelu; corregido segun su original por Antonio de Olmedo y Torre.* Imprenta de Diego Fernández de León, Puebla, México, 1716. 54 leaves, 1716 Br498.22 AzV 447.

4278. Vedel, Emil. *Efterskrift til Bornholms oldtidsminder og oldsager.* G. E. C. Gad, Kjøbenhavn, 1897. 166 p. Br913.489 V51.

4279. Vedia, Enrique de, ed. *Historiadores primitivos de Indias.* Biblioteca de autores españoles desde la formación del lenguaje hasta nuestros dias, 22, 26. M. Rivadeneyra, Madrid, 1852-1853. 2 v. Br868C Ar4.

4280. Vega, Garcilaso de la. *Primera parte de los Commentarios reales, que tratan, de el origen de los Incas, reies, qve fveron del Perù, de sv idolatria, leies, y govierno, en pas, y en guerra; de svs vidas, y conquistas; y de podo lo que fue aquel imperio, y su republica, antes que los españoles pasaran, à èl; escritos por el*

Inca Garcilaso de la Vega…segvnda impresion, enmendada; y añadida la vida de Inti Cusi Titu Iupanqui, penultimo Inca. En la Oficina Real, y à costa de Nicolas Rodriguez Franco, Madrid, 1723. 351, 33 p. Br985 L33.2.

4281. Veith, Von. Arbalo und Aliso. In *Festschrift zum Fünfzigjährigen Jubiläum des Vereins von Alterthumsfreunden im Rheinlande*, pp. 107-128. Gedruckt auf Kosten des Vereins, Bonn, 1891. Br572C An8141 v.98.

4282. Velásquez de Cárdenas y León, Carlos C. *Breve practica, y regimen del confessonario de indios, en mexicano y castellano; para instrucción del confessor principiante, habilitación, y examen del penitente, que dispone para los seminaristas el Br. D. Carlos Celedonio Velasquez de Cardenas, y Leon.* Imprenta de la Bibliotheca mexicana, México, 1761. 54 p. Br498.22 AzV 54.

4283. Venek, G. F. Pravek palestiny, 1893. Br492 V286.

4284. Veness, William T. *Ten Years of Mission Life in British Guiana; Being a Memoir of the Rev. Thomas Youd, by the Rev. W. T. Veness.* Society for Promoting Christian Knowledge, London, 1875. 136 p. Br918.8 V55.

4285. Venezuela. Dirección General de Estadística y Censos Nacionales. *Anuario estadístico de Venezuela*, 1889. Caracas. Br318.7 V559.

4286. Verneau, René. *Las pintaderas de Gran Canaria.* Imprenta de Fortanet, Madrid, 1883. 21 p. Br572C An8141 v.82.

4287. Vetancurt, Agustín de. *Arte de lengva mexicana, dispuesto por orden y mandato de N. Rmo. P. Fr. Francisco Treviño. Dedicado al bienaventurado San Antonio de Padua por el P. Fr. Augustin de Vetancurt.* Por Francisco Rodriguez Lupercio, México, 1673. 49 p. Br498.22 AzV 64.

4288. Vetancurt, Agustín de. *Menologio franciscano de los varones mas señalados, que con sus vidas, perfección religiosa, ciencia, predicación evangelica, en su viday, y muerte ilustraron la provincia de el Santo Evangelio de México.* Mexico, 1871. 485 p. Br972 V64.2.

4289. Vetancurt, Agustín de. *Teatro mexicano, descripción breve de los sucesos ejemplares…históricos, politicos, militares y religiosos del nuevo mundo occidental de las Indias.* Imprenta de I. Escalante, México, 1870-1871. 4 v. Br972 V64.

4290. Vetromile, Eugene. *Aborigines of Acadia.* Biddleford, ME, 1862. 16 p. Br497.11 McV647. Manuscript. Vetromile, a Jesuit missionary, served in Maine among the Penobscot and Micmac.

4291. Vetromile, Eugene. *The Abnakis and Their History; or, Historical Notices on the Aborigines of Acadia.* James B. Kirker, New York, 1866. 171 p. Br970.3 AbV645.

4292. Via sacra en lengua ccakcchi, copiado de un m[anuscrito] en poder de Domingo Coy, indio de Cobán. Cobán, abril, 1875. 30 p. Br498.21 KC684. Manuscript; transcript by Berendt of "Via sacra en lengua ccakchi, año de 1861."

4293. Via sacra en lengua ccakchi, año de 1861. 24 leaves. Br498.21 KC838.2. Manuscript; transcription by Domingo Coy of an early manuscript; bound with J. Domingo Coy, "Ortografía en lengua kekchí, 1870."

4294. Viana, Francisco, Lucas Gallego, and Guillén Cadena. Relación de la provincia i tierra de la Vera Paz i de las cosas contenidas en ella…desde el año de 1544 hasta este de 1574. 19 p. Br572C An8141 v.106. Manuscript copy by Karl H. Berendt, October 1872, of copy in the library of E. G. Squier made by Buckingham Smith, March 1859, of an original manuscript in v. 39 of the Muñoz Collection in the Royal Academy of History was originally transcribed by Buckingham Smith.

4295. Vico, Domingo de. Sermon y platica des Mathias apostol, n.d. leaves 188–203. Br498.21 TzV 665. Manuscript.

4296. Vico, Domingo de. Theologia indorum, scripta in lingua tzutuhila, 1553. 29 leaves. Br498.21 TzV 665. Manuscript; original is in the Bibliothèque Nationale in Paris.

4297. Vierkandt, Alfred. *Naturvölker und Kulturvölker ein Beitrag zur Socialpsychologie.* Duncker und Humboldt, Leipzig, 1896. 497 p. Br572 V67.

4298. Vigil, José M. Cantares mexicanos. *Revista Nacional de Letras y Ciencias* 1:361–370, 1889. Br572C An8141 v.49.

4299. Vigil, José M. *Discurso que en la session extraordinaria, celebra el 31 de Diciembre de 1889 con asistencia del señor presidente de la Republica por la Sociedad de Geografía y Estadística.* Oficina Tipografica de la Secretaria de Fomento, Mexico, 1890. 16 p. Br572C An8141 v.49.

4300. Vignoli, Tito. *Myth and Science; An Essay.* D. Appleton and Company, New York, 1882. 330 p. Br270 V68.

4301. Villacañas, Benito de. Arte y vocabulario de la lengua kachiquel; copiado en Nueva York, 1871. 346 p. Br498.21 CV 714. Manuscript; trancription by Berendt of "Arte y vocabulario en lengua cakchiquel, por el P. Fray Benito de Villacañas, Ornis. Pre-ry.; hecho despues de aver tratado cuarenta años con los indios de esta lengua sin interrupción con ejemplo y zelo de las animas muy singular cuyo fruto y premio goza en las jardines de la gloria" (1692; inserted is a brief life of Villacañas and a list of his works taken from an unpublished work of don Juan Gavarrete, titled "Apuntes para los anales del antiguo reino de Guatemala."

4302. Villacorta, Rafael. Doctrina cristiana en lengua castellana, quekchi y pocomchí, coordinada por Rafael Villacorta, Santo Domingo Cobán, 1875. 7 leaves. Br498.21. Original manuscript comprising an interlinear translation of the doctrina into Kekchí and Pokomchí; includes "Oración dominical," "La salutación angelica," "El simbolo," "El Decalogo," and "Las obras de misericordia."

4303. Villagutierre Soto-Mayor, Juan de. *Historia de la conquista de la provincia de el Itza, redvcción, y progressos de la de el Lacandon, y otros naciones de Indios barbaros, de la mediación de el reyno de Gvatimala, a las provincias de Yvcatan, en la America Septentrional. Primera parte Escrivela Don Jvan de Villagvtierre Soto-Mayor.* Imprenta de L.A. de Bedmar, y Narvaez, Madrid, 1701. 32 p., 660, 34 p. Br970.4 CeV712. "Villagutierre's relation of the wars by which the Spaniards conquered the Indians of Yucatan and Guatemala, has from its extreme rarity remained almost unknown. Like most of the Spanish histories of affairs in America, it is more largely devoted to the spiritual than the military conquest of the Indians; yet it is a valuable repertory of facts relating to the savages of the peninsula" (Field 1873:407).

4304. Villamus, V. Voyage dans l'Amerique du Sud: Quito. pp. 416-437, n.d. Br572C An8141 v.7.

4305. Villavicencio, Diego Jaime Ricardo. *Luz, y methodo, de confesar idolatras, y destierro de idolatrias, debajo del tratado sigviente. Tratado de avisos, y puntos importantes, de la abominable seta de la idolatria; para examinar por ellos al penitente en el fuero interior de la conciencia, y exterior judicial. Sacados no de los libros; sino de la experiencia en las aberiguaciones con los rabbies de ella.* Imprenta de D. Fernández de Leon, Puebla de los Angeles, 1692. 136 p. Br262.143 V714.

4306. Viñaza, Cipriano Muñoz y Manzano, conde de la. *Bibliografía española de lenguas indígenas de América.* Sucesores de Rivadeneyra, Madrid, 1892. 427 p. Br498B V73.

4307. Vinson, Julien. *L'ècriture arabe appliquée aux langues Dravidiennes.* Imprimerie Nationale, Paris, 1895. 11 p. Br572C An8141 v.142.

4308. Vinson, Julien. La langue taensa, 1886. 23 p. Br572C An8141 v.47.

4309. Virchow, Rudolf L. K. Anlage und Variation. *Königlich Prüssischen Akademie der Wissenschaften zu Berlin* 23:515-531, 1896. Br572C An8141 v.159.

4310. Virchow, Rudolf L. K. Ausgrabungen auf der Insel Wollin. *Berliner Gesellschaft für Anthropologie, Ethnologie und Urgeschichte* 13:17-26, 1872. Br572C An8141 v.165.

4311. Virchow, Rudolf L. K. Brasilianischen Indianerschädel. *Verhandlungen der Berliner Gesellschaft für Anthropologie, Ethnologie und Urgeschichte,* pp. 17-39, 1875. Br572C An8141 v.162.

4312. Virchow, Rudolf L. K. *Crania ethnica Americana; Sammlung auserlesener amerikanischer Schädeltypen.* Asher, Berlin, 1892. 33 p. Br573.7 V817.

4313. Virchow, Rudolf L. K. Die Bevölkerung der Philippinen. *Königlich Prüssischen Akademie der Wissenschaften zu Berlin* 16:279-289, 1897. Br572C An8141 v.159.

4314. Virchow, Rudolf L. K. Die Continuität des Lebens als Grundlage der modernen biologischen Anschauung. *Archiv für Pathologische Anatomie und Physiologie und für Klinische Medicin* 150:4-15, 1897. Br572C An8141 v.159.

4315. Virchow, Rudolf L. K. Die Stellung der Lepra under den Infectionskrankheiten und die pathologisch-anatomische Erfahrung. Lepra-Conferenz, 1897. 7 p. Br572C An8141 v.159.

4316. Virchow, Rudolf L. K. Die Verbreitung des blonden und des brünetten Typus in Mitteleuropa. pp. 39-47, n.d. Br572C An8141 v.4.

4317. Virchow, Rudolf L. K. Ein Gräberfeld bei Zaborowo (Prov. Posen). *Berliner Gesellschaft für Anthropologie, Ethnologie und Urgeschichte* 13:6-14, 1872. Br572C An8141 v.165.

4318. Virchow, Rudolf L. K. Festrede des Ehren-Präsidenten. *Verhandlungen der Berliner Anthropologischen Gesellschaft für Anthropologie, Ethnologie und Urgeschichte* 17:17-21, 1894. Br572C An8141 v.136.

4319. Virchow, Rudolf L. K. Schädel aus Süd-America, insbesondere aus Argentinien und Bolivien. *Verhandlungen der Berliner Anthropologischen Gesellschaft für*

Anthropologie, Ethnologie und Urgeschichte 21:386-408, 1894. Br572C
An8141 v.137.

4320. Virchow, Rudolf L. K. Über bewohnte Höhlen der Vorzeit, namentlich die Einhornshöhle im Harz. *Verhandlungen der Berliner Gesellschaft für Anthropologie, Ethnologie und Urgeschichte*, pp. 13-30, 1872. Br572C An8141 v.162.

4321. Virchow, Rudolf L. K. Über den Hermaphroditismus beim Menschen. *Verhandlungen der Berliner Gesellschaft für Anthropologie, Ethnologie und Urgeschichte*, pp. 7-13, 1872. Br572C An8141 v.162.

4322. Virchow, Rudolf L. K. *Über die culturgeschichtliche Stellung des Kaukasus, unter besonderer Berücksichtigung der ornamentirten Bronzegürtel aus transkaukasischen Gräbern.* G. Reimer, Berlin, 1895. 66 p. Br571.3 V81.

4323. Virchow, Rudolf L. K. Über die Urbevölkerung Belgiens. *Verhandlungen der Berliner Gesellschaft für Anthropologie, Ethnologie und Urgeschichte*, pp. 8-15, 1872. Br572C An8141 v.162.

4324. Virchow, Rudolf L. K. Über Gräberfelder und Burgwälle der Nieder-Lausitz und des überoderischen Gebietes. *Verhandlungen der Berliner Gesellschaft für Anthropologie, Ethnologie und Urgeschichte*, pp. 4-16, 1872. Br572C An8141 v.162.

4325. Virchow, Rudolf L. K. Über griechische Schädel aus alter und neuer Zeit und über einen Schädel von Menidi, der für den des Sophokles gehalten ist. *Sitzungsberichte der Königlich Prüssischen Akademie der Wissenschaften zu Berlin* 34:677-700, 1893. Br572C An8141 v.121.

4326. Virchow, Rudolf L. K. Über italienische Cranologie und Ethnologie. *Berliner Gesellschaft für Anthropologie, Ethnologie und Urgeschichte* 12:10-20, 1871. Br572C An8141 v.165.

4327. Virchow, Rudolf L. K. Über Schädel von Neu-Guinea. *Verhandlungen der Berliner Gesellschaft für Anthropologie, Ethnologie und Urgeschichte*, pp. 7-15, 1873. Br572C An8141 v.162.

4328. Virchow, Rudolf L. K. Über verschiedene deutsche Alterthümersammlungen, sowie neue Ausgrabungen bei Priment, Zaborowo und Wollstein. *Verhandlungen der Berliner Gesellschaft für Anthropologie, Ethnologie und Urgeschichte*, pp. 6-23, 1875. Br572C An8141 v.162.

4329. Virchow, Rudolf L. K. Untersuchung des Neanderthal-Schädels. *Verhandlungen der Berliner Gesellschaft für Anthropologie, Ethnologie und Urgeschichte*, pp. 4-12, 1872. Br572C An8141 v.162.

4330. Virchow, Rudolf L. K. Vergleichung finnischer und esthnischer Schädel mit alten Gräberschädeln des nordostlichen Deutschlands. *Verhandlungen der Berliner Gesellschaft für Anthropologie, Ethnologie und Urgeschichte*, pp. 6-18, 1872. Br572C An8141 v.162.

4331. Virchow, Rudolf L. K. Verwaltungs-Bericht für das verflossene Gesellschafts-Jahr. *Verhandlungen der Berliner Gesellschaft für Anthropologie, Ethnologie und Urgeschichte*, 1875. 8 p. Br572C An8141 v.162.

4332. Vissier, Paul. *Histoire de la tribu des Osages, peuplade sauvage de l'Amerique Septentrionale dans l'état du Missouri, l'un des États-Unis d'Amérique.* Chez

Charles Bechet Libraire, Paris, 1827. 92 p. Br572C An8141 v.61. "Vissier was inspired by the visit to Paris of a 'prince,' two 'princesses,' and four 'warriors' from the Osage people" (Siebert Library 1999:2:201).

4333. Vivien de Saint-Martin, Louis. *Le nord de l'Afrique dans l'antiquité grecquë et romaine, étude historique et géographique...accompagné de quatre cartes, par M. Vivien de Saint-Martin.* Imprimerie impériale, Paris, 1863. 519 p. Br961 Sa24.

4334. *Vocabulario castellano-zapoteco, pub. por la Junta Columbina de México, con motivo de la celebración del cuarto centenartio de descubrimiento de America.* Oficina Tipografica de la Secretaria de Fomento, México, 1893. 222 p. Br498.34 ZV 852. Edited from a manuscript of the 18th century entitled "Diccionario sapoteco deel balle," at one time the property of the library of the Dominican Order in Oaxaca, later presented to Porfirio Diaz.

4335. Vocabulario de la lengua zoque, año de 1733; copiado de un manuscrito en posesión del licenciado don José Maríano Rodríguez, Tuxtla, por C. Hermann Berendt, M.D., Tuxtla Gutiérrez, 1870. 255 leaves. Br498.35 ZV 853. Manuscript; "El original de esta vocabulario es un volumen en cuarto, encuadernado en cuero. Tiene 176 fojas faltándole una o más al fin. Esta escrita en dos columnas, una para al castellano, la otra para al Zoque."

4336. Vocabulario del idioma zapoteca del valle, 1793. Br498.34 ZV 853. Manuscript copy by Karl H. Berendt.

4337. *Vocabulario para aprender con perfección el quecchi.* Tipografía Municipal, Cobán, 1890. 86 p. Br498.21 KV85.

4338. Vocabularios de la lengua xinca de Sinacantan por D. Juan Gavarrete (1868) y de Yupiltepeque y Jalapa por D. Sebastián Váldez, cura de Intiapa (1868); copiado de los originales en poder de don Juan Gavarrete, en Guatemala, febrero de 1875. 15 leaves. Br498.32 XJG 242. Manuscript; vocabulary arranged in four columns, Spanish and the three indigenous dialects (pp. 4-15); "Los presentes vocabularios forman parte de la colección que esta reuniendo don Juan Gavarrete para un cuadro comparativo de las lenguas aborígenes de Guatemala" (Berendt Introduction).

4339. Vogel, Hermann W. Über die Bewohner der Nicobaren. *Verhandlungen der Berliner Gesellschaft für Anthropologie, Ethnologie und Urgeschichte,* pp. 4-14, 1875. Br572C An8141 v.162.

4340. Voges, Thomas. Bronzen aus dem nördlichen Teile des landes Braunschweig und den angrenzenden Gebieten. *Beiträge zur Anthropologie Braunschweigs* 21:69-89, 1898. Br572C An8141 v.164.

4341. Vogt, Casimir. *Gete-dibadjimowin tchi bwa ondadisid Jesus Christ gaie Jesus o bimadisiwin gaie o nibowin.* B. Herder, St. Louis, Missouri, 1885. 140 p. Br497.11 OV86. Bible history, entirely in the Chippewa language. A mixed-blood Indian from Red Cliff Reservation named John Gordon [or Gafron?] assisted in the preparation of the work.

4342. Vollers, Karl. Aus der viceköniglichen Bibliothek in Kairo. pp. 373-378, 1889. Br572C An8141 v.46.

4343. Von Torma, S. *Ein Beitrag zur Gestaltungs- und Entwicklungsgeschichte der Religionem; Ethnographische Analogien.* Hermann Costenoble, Jena, 1894. 76 p. Br572C An8141 v.131.

4344. Von Wlislocki, H. *Aus dem inneren Leben der Zigeuner.* Verlag von Emil Felber, Berlin, 1892. Br572C An8141 v.126.

4345. Vossion, Louis P. *Grammaire franco-birmane d'après A. Judson; augmentée d'un grand nombre d'exemples inédits, d'un appendice relatif aux livres sacrés et à la littérature des birmans, et de la prononciation en français de tous les mots birmans qui paraissent dans le texte.* 2d éd. Imprimerie Nationale, Ernest Leroux, Paris, 1889. 111 p. Br495.2 J927.

4346. Vossion, Louis P. *Khartoum et le Soudan d'Egypt.* Challamel Aîné, Paris, 1890. 22 p. Br572C An8141 v.5.

4347. Vossion, Louis P. Nat worship among the Burmese. *Journal of American Folk-Lore* 4:107-114, 1891. Br572C An8141 v.9.

4348. Voyle, Joseph. Characteristic rays, 1896. 8 p. Br572C An8141 v.142.

4349. Waitz, Theodor. *Anthropologie der Naturvölker.* F. Fleischer, Leipzig, 1859-1872. 6 v. Br572 W135. Contents include: 1. Über die Einheit des Menschengeschlechtes und den Naturzustand des Menschen, 1859; 2. Die Negervölker und ihre Verwandten. Ethnographisch und culturhistorisch dargestellt, 1860; 3-4. Die Amerikaner. Ethnographisch und culturhistorisch dargestellt, 1862-1864; 5-6. Die Völker der Südsee. 1. Abth. Die Malaien, 1865. 2. Abth. Die Mikronesier undnordwestlichen Polynesier. Ethnographisch und culturhistorisch dargestellt von Dr. Georg Gerland, 1870. 3. Abth. Die Polynesier, Melanesier, Australier und Tasmanier. Ethnographisch und culturhistorisch dargestellt von Dr. Georg Gerland, 1872.

4350. Waitz, Theodor. *Die Indianer Nordamerica's; Eine Studie.* F. Fleischer, Leipzig, 1865, 180 p. Br970.1 W137.

4351. Wake, Charles S. English and Malagasy vocabulary. *Modern Language Notes* 6(7): 6-26, 1891. Br572C An8141 v.91.

4352. Wake, Charles S. *Memoirs of the International Congress of Anthropology.* Chicago, 1894. 375 p. Br572.06 In84.

4353. Wake, Charles S. The distribution of American totems. *American Antiquarian* 11(6): 359-368, 1889. Br572C An8141 v.20.

4354. Wake, Charles S. The Papuas and the Polynesians. *Journal of the Anthropological Institute of Great Britain and Ireland* 8:144-179, 1878-1879. Br572C An8141 v.26.

4355. Wake, Charles S. The primitive human horde. *Journal of the Anthropological Institute of Great Britain and Ireland* 17:276-282, 1887-1888. Br572C An8141 v.26.

4356. Walker, Elkanah, and Cushing Ellis. *Etshiit thlu sitskai thlu siais thlu Sitskaisitlinish.* A. H. Clark Company, Glendale, California, 1842. 16 p. Br497.46 SpW15.

4357. Walker, Mrs. James E. *Biscayne Bay: A Complete Manual of Information.* Weed, Parsons, and Company, Albany, NY, 1876, 18 p. Br572C An8141 v.18.

4358. Wallam olum...the painted engraved traditions of the Linnilinapi...with the original glyphs or signs for each verse of the poems or songs translated word for word

Theodor Waitz (from Justin Winsor, Aboriginal America. Cambridge, MA: Houghton, Mifflin, 1889. p. 378).

by C. S. Rafineque, 1833. 49 leaves. Br497.11 DW154. Manuscript; part 1 contains three original traditional poems; part 2 contains historical chronicles or annals in two chronicles.

4359. Walsh, Robert M. A mission to Costa Rica. *Lippincott's Magazine of Popular Literature and Science,* pp. 511-518, 1872. Br572C An8141 v.44.

4360. Wampum, J. B., and H. C. Hogg. *Morning and Evening Prayer, The Administration of the Sacraments, and Certain Other Rites and Ceremonies of the Church of England; Together with Hymns; Translated into Munsee by J. B. Wampum, Assisted by H. C. Hogg.* Society for Promoting Christian Knowledge, London, 187?. 349 p. Br497.11 MuW 18. Translation of the Book of Common Prayer, Church of England, into Munsee.

4361. Ward, Duren J. H. An outline of anthropology, n.d. 8 p. Br572C An8141 v.88.

4362. Ward, H.A. Lettre de M. Henry A. Ward sur les musées argentins. *Revista del Museo de La Plata* 1, 1890. 11 p. Br572C An8141 v.98.

4363. Ward, James W. Sculptured rocks, Belmont County, Ohio. *Journal of the Anthropological Institute of New York* 1:57-66, 1871-1872. Br572C An8141 v.59.

4364. Ward, Lester F. Ethical aspects of social science. *International Journal of Ethics,* pp. 441-456, n.d. Br572C An8141 v.159.

4365. Ward, Lester F. Principles of sociology. *Annals of the American Academy of Political and Social Science* 3(1): 1-31, 1896. Br572C An8141 v.159.

4366. Ward, Lester F. Relation of sociology to anthropology. *American Anthropologist* 8:241-256, 1895. Br572C An8141 v.142.

4367. Ward, Lester F. Review: Organisme et société, par René Worms; La Pathologie sociale, par Paul de Lilienfeld. *American Journal of Sociology*, pp. 258-265, n.d. Br572C An8141 v.159.

4368. Ward, Lester F. Sociology and anthropology: IV. Contributions to social philosophy. *American Journal of Sociology* 1(4): 426-433, 1896. Br572C An8141 v.142; Br572C An8141 v.163.

4369. Ward, Lester F. Sociology and psychology: V. Contributions to social philosophy; also a review of Dr. Patten's *Theory of Social Forces. American Journal of Sociology* 1(5): 618-639, 1896. Br572C An8141 v.142.

4370. Ward, Lester F. Status of the mind problem. *Anthropological Society of Washington, Special Papers* 1:603-620, 1894. Br572C An8141 v.131.

4371. Ward, Lester F. The data of sociology: VI. Contributions to social philosophy. *American Journal of Sociology*, pp. 738-752, n.d. Br572C An8141 v.159.

4372. Warren, G. K. *Explorations in the Dakota Country, in the Year 1855, by Lieut. G. K. Warren, Topographic Engineer of the Sioux Expedition.* A. O. P. Nicholson, Senate Printer, Washington, DC, 1856. 79 p. Br328.7326.2 Sd. "On pp. 15 to 19 is a category of the Indian tribes occupying the territory explored, with the number of lodges, inmates, and warriors" (Field 1873:414).

4373. Warren, William W. History of the Ojibways; based upon traditions and oral statements, by William W. Warren. *Minnesota Historical Society Collections* 5:21-394, 1885. Br970.3 OjW253.

4374. Washington, John. *Eskimaux and English Vocabulary, For the Use of the Arctic Expeditions.* J. Murray, London, 1850. 160 p. Br497.25 W27.

4375. Waterbury, Jared B. *Cesvs oh vyares; I Will Go to Jesus, by J. B. Waterbury; Translated Into Creek by Thomas Perryman and A. E. W. Robertson.* American Tract Society, New York, 1871. 23 p. Br497.39 CrW29.

4376. Watkins, Edwin. *A Dictionary of the Cree Language; As Spoken by the Indians of the Hudson's Bay Company's Territories, Compiled by E. A. Watkins.* Society for Promoting Christian Knowledge, London, 1865. 460 p. Br497.11 CrW32. "Watkins was a missionary on Hudson's Bay and at Red River" (Siebert Library 1999:1:66).

4377. Watt, Thomas. Agricultural societies in British Guiana. *Temehri: the Journal of the Royal Agricultural; and Commercial Society* 5:255-273, 1886. Br572C An8141 v.68.

4378. Weaver, George A. Simon Kentor. *Proceedings of the Central Ohio Scientific Association* 1(1): 88-95, 1878. Br572C An8141 v.59.

4379. Webb, DeWitt. The shell heaps of the east coast of Florida. *Proceedings of the United States National Museum, Smithsonian Institution* 16(966): 695-698, 1893. Br572C An8141 v.125.

4380. Weeden, William B. Indian money as a factor in New England civilization. Baltimore, 1884. 51 p. Br572C An8141 v.39.

4381. Weerth, C. *Die Entwicklung der Menschen-Rassen; Durch Einwirkungen der*

Mussenwelt. Meyer'sche Hof-Buchhandlung, Lemgo, 1842. 350 p. Br572 W413.

4382. Weissbach, Franz H. Neue Beiträge zur Kunde der Susischen Inschriften. *Abhandlungen der Philologisch-Historischen Classe der Königlichen Sächsischen Gesellschaft der Wissenschaften* 7:731-777, 1894. Leipzig. Br572C An8141 v.144.

4383. Weissbach. Franz H. Das Grab des Cyrus und die Inschriften von Murghab. pp. 653-665, n.d. Br572C An8141 v.142.

4384. Welling, J. C. The law of torture: a study in the evolution of law. Judd and Detweiler, Washington, DC, 1892. 23 p. Br572C An8141 v.88.

4385. Wells, Roger, and John W. Kelly. *English-Eskimo and Eskimo-English Vocabularies; Compiled by Ensign Roger Wells, Jr....and Interpreter John W. Kelly; Preceded by Ethnographical Memoranda Concerning the Arctic Eskimos in Alaska and Siberia*. United States Bureau of Education, Circular of Information, no. 2, 1890. 72 p. Br572C An8141 v.52.

4386. Wells, William V. *Walker's Expedition to Nicaragua;A History of the Central American War; and the Sonora and Kinney Expeditions, Including all1the Recent Diplomatic Correspondence, Together with a New and Accurate Map of Central America, and a Memoir and Portrait of General William Walker*. Stringer and Townsend, New York, 1856. 316 p. Br972.85 W15W.

4387. Werren, J. E. Report of a sculptured rock from Marblehead, Ohio. *Proceedings of the Central Ohio Scientific Association* 1(1): 66-69, 1878. Br572C An8141 v.59.

4388. Werren, J. E. Report of the survey of ancient earthworks near Osborne, Ohio. *Proceedings of the Central Ohio Scientific Association* 1(1): 52-62, 1878. Br572C An8141 v.59.

4389. West, G. M. Anthropometrische Untersuchungen über die Schulkinder in Worcester, Mass., Amerika. *Archiv für Anthropologie* 22:13-48, 1892. Br572C An8141 v.109.

4390. Westcott, W. Wynn. *Numbers; Their Occult Power and Mystic Virtue, Being a Résumé of the Views of the Kabbalists, Pythagoreans, Adepts of India, Chaldean Magi, and Mediaeval Magicians.* Theosophical Publishing Society, London, 1890. 52 p. Br290 W523.

4391. Weule, Karl. *Der afrikanische Pfeil; eine anthropogeographische Studie*. O. Schmidt, Leipzig, 1899. 64 p. Br572.96 W54.

4392. Weule, Karl. Die Eidechse als Ornament in Afrika. *Bastian Festschrift*, pp. 166-194. Verlag von Dietrich Reimer (Ernst Vohsen), Berlin, 1896. Br572C An8141 v.159.

4393. What is being said of Hubert H. Bancroft and his literary work, 1883. 13 p. Br572C An8141 v.58.

4394. Whipple, Amiel W. *Diegueño and Yuma Grammars*. Report to the Secretary of War, February 1851. 28 p. Br572C An8141 v.51.

4395. Whipple, Amiel W., Thomas Ewbank, and William W. Turner. Report upon the Indian tribes. *In Explorations and Surveys for a Railroad Route from the Mississippi River to the Pacific Ocean; War Department; Route Near the Thirty-Fifth Parallel*. Bevereley Tucker, Washington, DC, 1855. 127 p. Br572C An8141 v.93.

4396. White, R. B. Notes on the aboriginal races of the north-western provinces of South

America. *Journal of the Anthropological Institute of Great Britain and Ireland* 13(2): 239-258, 1884. Br572C An8141 v.33; Br572C An8141 v.67.

4397. Whitney, William D. *Max Müller and The Science of Language: A Criticism.* D. Appleton and Company, New York, 1892. Br572C An8141 v.87.

4398. Whitney, William D. *The Life and Growth of Language; An Outline of Linguistic Science.* D. Appleton, New York, 1876. 326 p. Br409 W61.7a.

4399. Whitney, William D. The value of linguistic science to ethnology. *New Englander,* January, pp. 30-52, 1867. Br572C An8141 v.31.

4400. Whitney, William F. Notes on the anomalies, injuries and diseases of the bones of the native races of North America. *Annual Reports of the Trustees of the Peabody Museum of American Archaeology and Ethnology* 3(5-6): 433-448, 1886. Br913.07 H265.

4401. Whittlesey, Charles. Abstract of a verbal discourse upon the mounds and the Mound Builders of Ohio. Read before Fire Lands Historical Society, Ohio, March 15, 1865. 5 p. Br572C An8141 v.38.

4402. Whittlesey, Charles. Ancient earth forts of the Cuyahoga Valley, Ohio. *Transactions of the Western Reserve and Northern Ohio Historical Society* 5, 1871. 40 p. Br572C An8141 v.38.

4403. Whittlesey, Charles. *Ancient Mining on the Shores of Lake Superior.* Smithsonian Institution Contributions to Knowledge, 155. Washington, DC, 1863. 29 p. Br572C An8141 v.90; Br913.77 W618.

4404. Whittlesey, Charles. Metrical standard of the Mound Builders; deduced by the method of even divisors. *Science* 2(32): 365, 1883. Br572C An8141 v.59.

4405. Whittlesey, Charles. On the weapons and military character of the race of the Mounds. *Memoirs of the Boston Society of Natural History* 1(4): 473-481, 1867. Br572C An8141 v.93.

4406. Whittlesey, Charles. The cross and crucifix: their various forms. *Kansas City Review* 6(6): 357, 1882. Br572C An8141 v.59.

4407. Wickersham, James. Is it Mt. Tacoma or Rainier? What do history and tradition say? *Proceedings of the Tacoma Academy of Science,* 1893. 16 p. Br572C An8141 v.128.

4408. Wickersham, James. *Major Powell's Inquiry, "Whence Came the American Indians?" An Answer, A Study in Comparative Ethnology.* Allen and Lamborn, Tacoma, WA, 1899. 28 p. Br970.1 W63.

4409. Wickersham, James. *The Constitution of China; A Study in Primitive Law.* Wilson and Blankenship, Olympia, Washington, 1898. 19 p. Br342.51 W63.

4410. Wied, Maximilian Alexander Philip, prinz von. *Reise in das innere Nord-Amerika in den Jahren 1832 bis 1834; von Maximilian prinz zu Wied.* J. Hölscher, Coblenz, 1839-41. 2 v. Br497 W633. "Karl Bodmer was a little-known Swiss painter when he was engaged by Prince Maximilian to record his travels among the Plains Indians from 1832 to 1834, a time when the Plains and the Rockies were still virtually unknown. With the rest of their company, the royal ethnologist and his artist journeyed from St. Louis up the Missouri River on the American Fur Company steamboat *Yellowstone,* stopping at a series of forts built by the Fur Company and meeting their first

Indians at Bellevue. The travelers continued on another steamboat, *Assiniboine*, to Fort Union, where they met the Crees and Assiniboines. The expeditrion spent its first winter at Fort Clark, where the Mandans in particular excited Bodmer's attention, although he was also to draw the Minitari and Crow peoples. The explorers continued by keelboat to Fort Mackenzie, which proved to be the westernmost point of their journey. After living among and studying the Blackfeet for several weeks, Maximilian decided that it was too dangerous to continue, so the travelers turned southward, reaching St. Louis in May 1834" (*Frank T. Siebert Library* 1999:2:213).

4411. Wied, Maximilian Alexander Philip, prinz von. Spracheproblem der in diesem Reisebericht erwahnten Urvölker von Brasilien. pp. 302–330, n.d. Br572C An8141 v.93.

4412. Wied, Maximilian Alexander Philip, prinz von. Spracheproblem der Urvölker von Brasilien, n.d. Br572C An8141 v.93.

4413. Wiedersheim, Robert Ernst E. *The Structure of Man; An Index to His Past History*. Macmillan and Company, London and New York, 1895. 227 p. Br573 W634.

4414. Wiener, Charles. *Essai sur les institutions politiques, religieuses, economiques et sociales de l'empire des Incas*. Librarie Maisonneuve et Cie., Paris, 1874. 101 p. Br572C An8141 v.96.

4415. Wiener, Charles. *Pérou et Bolivie. Récit de voyage suivi d'études archéologiques et ethnographiques et de notes sur l'écriture et les langues des populations indiennes*. Hachette, Paris, 1880. 796 p. Br572.985 W63. Includes "Vocabulaire quichua-aymara avec traduction espagnole et française" (p. 781–788) and "Vocabulaire campa avec traduction espagnole et française" (p. 789–791).

4416. Wilder, Burt G. Harrison Allen, 1841–1897. *Proceedings of the Annual Meeting of American Anatomists*, 1897. 16 p. Br572C An8141 v.163.

4417. Wilder, Burt G. Neural terms: international and national. *Journal of Comparative Neurology* 6:217–352, 1896. Cincinnati. Br590.1 W64.

4418. Wilder, Burt G. Some misapprehensions as to the simplified nomenclature of anatomy. *Proceedings of the Association of American Anatomists*, 11 session, pp. 15–39, 1898. New York. Br611.01 W645.

4419. William George's Sons. *The New World Book List*. W. George's Sons, Bristol, England, 1890. 146 p. Br970B G29.

4420. Williams, Frederick W. Chinese and mediaeval gilds. *Yale Review*, pp. 200–233, 1892. Br572C An8141 v.116.

4421. Williams, J. J. *El istmo de Tehuantepec; resultado del reconocimiento que para la construcción de un ferro-carril de comunicación entre los oceanos Atlantico y Pacifico*. Imprenta de Vicente García Torres, Mexico, 1852. 327 p. Br572C An8141 v.25.

4422. Williams, Loring S. *Religious Tracts in the Choctaw Language*. 2d revised edition. Printed for the American Board of Commissioners for Foreign Missions, by Crocker and Brewster, Boston, 1835. 39 p. Br497.39 ChW67.

4423. Williams, Roger. *A Key Into the Language of America, Or, An Help to the Language of the Natives In That Part of America, Called New-England; Together, With Briefe Observations of the Customs, Manners and Worships, &c. of the Aforesaid Natives, in Peace and Warre, in Life and Death*. Gregory Dexter, London, 1643. 197 p.

Br497.11 W67. "Roger Williams interspersed indigenous vocabulary with a wealth of ethnographic information. His thirty-two chapters cover such topics as eating and entertainment, fish and fishing, nakedness and clothing, marriage, and paintings. Most sections include poetic commentary by the author confirming his respect for the Indians of Rhode Island...The book appeared in print while Williams was in London, circumventing the Massachusetts Bay authorities and organizing the charter for the Providence Plantations in Narragansett Bay" (*Frank T. Siebert Library* 1999:1:324).

4424. Williams, Talcott. Historical survivals in Morocco. *Papers of the American Historical Association*, pp. 15–34, 1890. Br572C An8141 v.9.

4425. Williams, Talcott. The spoken Arabic of north Morocco. *Beiträge zur Assyriologie und Semitischen Sprachwissenschaft* 3:561–587, 587a–587f, 1898. Leipzig. Br492.573 W67.

4426. Williams, Talcott. The surroundings and site of Raleigh's colony. *Annual Report of the American Historical Association for 1895*, pp. 45–61, 1896. Br973.1 W675.

4427. Williams, Talcott. Was primitive man a modern savage? *Annual Report of the United States National Museum, Smithsonian Institution, for 1896*, pp. 541–548, 1898. Br572 W67.

4428. Williamson, John P. *Oowa wowapi; Dakota iapi en.* Printed for the American Board by the American Tract Society, New York, 1876. 80 p. Br497.5 DW67.2; Br497.5 DW67.2a. "Williamson, the son of Dr. Thomas Williamson, was a missionary among the Dakota at Lower Agency, Minnesota, from 1860 until the Sioux Uprising of 1862, and afterwards on the Missouri River" (*Frank T. Siebert Library* 1999:2:351).

4429. Williamson, John P., and Alfred L. Riggs. *Dakota odowan; Dakota Hymns.* Printed by the American Tract Society, New York, 1879. 133 p. Br497.5 DW67. "Fifth revision and enlargement of our Dakota hymn book" (p. 3).

4430. Williamson, Thomas S., and Stephen R. Riggs. *Dakota wowapi wakan kin; the Holy Bible, In the Language of the Dakotas.* American Bible Society, New York, 1880, 1,695 p. Br497.5D B45. New Testament translated into Dakota. "Dr. Thomas S. Williamson, 'the father of the Dakota mission,' received his medical training at Yale and started his missionarey work at Fort Snelling [present-day Minnesota]. He remains among the Indians until the Sioux Outbreak of 1862" (*Frank T. Siebert Library* 1999:2:352).

4431. Willoughby, Charles C. Prehistoric burial places in Maine. *Archaeological and Ethnological Papers of the Peabody Museum, Harvard University*, 1(6): 385–436, 1898. Br572C An8141 v.163.

4432. Wilson, Daniel. *Anthropology... With an Appendix on Archaeology, by E. B. Tylor.* J. Fitzgerald, New York, 1885. 55 p. Br572C An8141 v.120.

4433. Wilson, Daniel. Palaeolithic dexterity. *Transactions of the Royal Society of Canada* 7(2): 119–133, 1885. Br572C An8141 v.97.

4434. Wilson, Daniel. The artistic faculty in aboriginal races. *Transactions of the Royal Society of Canada* 6(2): 67–117, 1885. Br572C An8141 v.97.

4435. Wilson, Daniel. The Huron race and its head-form. *Canadian Journal* 74:112–134, 1871. Br572C An8141 v.10.

Daniel Wilson (from Justin Winsor, Aboriginal America. *Cambridge, MA: Houghton, Mifflin, 1889. p. 375).*

4436. Wilson, Daniel. *The Right Hand Left-Handedness.* Macmillan, London, 1891. 215, 55 p. Br591.47 W695.

4437. Wilson, Daniel. The Vinland of the Northmen. *Transactions of the Royal Society of Canada* 2:109-125, 1890. Br572C An8141 v.101.

4438. Wilson, Daniel. Trade and commerce in the Stone Age. *Transactions of the Royal Society of Canada* 8(2): 59-87, 1889. Br572C An8141 v.97.

4439. Wilson, Samuel. Prehistoric art. *Annual Report of the United States National Museum, Smithsonian Institution, for 1896,* pp. 325-664, 1898. Br571.7 W691.

4440. Wilson, Thomas. A study of prehistoric anthropology; handbook for beginners. *Annual Report of the United States National Museum, Smithsonian Institution, for 1887-1888,* pp. 597-671. Br572C An8141 v.12.

4441. Wilson, Thomas. Anthropology at the Paris Exposition in 1889. *Annual Report of the United States National Museum, Smithsonian Institution, for 1890,* pp. 641-680, 1892. Br572C An8141 v.86.

4442. Wilson, Thomas. Criminal anthropology. *Annual Report of the United States National Museum, Smithsonian Institution, for 1890,* pp. 617-686, 1891. Br572C An8141 v.86.

4443. Wilson, Thomas. Description of exhibit made by the Department of Prehistoric Anthropology in the National Museum at the Ohio Valley and Central States Exposition in Cincinnati, Ohio, 1888. *Proceedings of the United States National Museum, Smithsonian Institution* 11, 1888. 31 p. Washington, DC. Br572C An8141 v.59.

4444. Wilson, Thomas. *Le Phénomérne glaciaire.* Ernest Leroux, Paris, 1891. Br572C An8141 v.7.

4445. Wilson, Thomas. Les instruments de peirre dure en Amérique. *Compte Rendu de la Congrès International d'Anthropologie et d'Archéologie Préhistoriques (11 session, Paris, 1888),* pp. 508-516, 1891. Paris. Br572C An8141 v.86.

4446. Wilson,Thomas. Man and the Mylodon: their possible contemporaneous existence in the Mississippi Valley. *American Naturalist* 26:629-631, 1892. Br572C An8141 v.137.

4447. Wilson,Thomas. Minute stone implements from India. *Annual Report of the United States National Museum, Smithsonian Institution, for 1892,* pp. 455-460, 1894. Br572C An8141 v.132.

4448. Wilson,Thomas. *Proposed classification of the Section of Anthropology and Prehistoric Archaeology at the Chicago Exposition.* Washington, DC, 1890. Br572C An8141 v.12.

4449. Wilson,Thomas. Results of an inquiry as to the existence of man in North America during the Paleolithic period of the Stone Age. *Annual Report of the United States National Museum, Smithsonian Institution, for 1888,* pp. 677-702, 1890. Br572C An8141 v.12.

4450. Wilson,Thomas. Swastika. *Annual Report of the United States National Museum, Smithsonian Institution, for 1894,* pp. 757-1011, 1896. Br571.7 W69.

4451. Wilson,Thomas. The golden paera of Rennes. *Annual Report of the United States National Museum, Smithsonian Institution, for 1894,* pp. 609-617, 1896. Br572C An8141 v.159.

4452. Wilson,Thomas. The Palaeolithic period in the District of Columbia. *Proceedings of the United States National Museum, Smithsonian Institution* 12:371-376, 1889. Br572C An8141 v.41.

4453. Winkler, Heinrich. *Das Uralattaische und Seine Gruppen.* Ferd. Dümmlers Verlagsbuchhandlung, Berlin, 1885. 24 p. Br572C An8141 v.115.

4454. Winkler, Heinrich. *Die Sprache der zweiten Columne der dreisprachigen Inschriften und das Altaische.* Druck von Grass, Barth u. Comp., Breslau, 1896. 65 p. Br572C An8141 v.160.

4455. Winkler, Heinrich. *Germanische casussyntax.* Ferd. Dümmlers Verlagsbuchhandlung, Berlin, 1896. v. 1 only. Br431.3 W723. Contains: v. 1. Der Dativ, instrumental Örtliche und halbörtliche Verhältnisse.

4456. Winkler, Heinrich. *Japaner und Altaier.* Ferd. Dümmlers Verlagsbuchhandlung, Berlin, 1894. Br572C An8141 v.132.

4457. Winkler, Heinrich. Sprachliche Formung und Formlosigkeit. pp. 257-270. Breslau, 1867-1872. Br572C An8141 v.49.

4458. Winkler, Heinrich. *Uraltaische Völker und Sprachen.* Ferd. Dümmlers Verlagsbuchhandlung, Berlin, 1884. 480 p. Br494.3 W727.

4459. Winkler, Heinrich. *Zur indogermanischen Syntax.* Druck von Grab, Barth, Breslau, n.d. 21 p. Br572C An8141 v.145.

4460. Winkler, Heinrich. *Zur Sprachgeschichte, Nomen, Verb und Satz, Antikritik.* Ferd. Dümmlers Verlagsbuchhandlung, Berlin, 1887. 306 p. Br409.4 W72.

4461. Winship, George P. A list of works useful to the student of the Coronado expedition by George Parker Winship. *Annual Report of the Bureau of Ethnology, Smithsonian Institution, for 1893-1894,* pp. 559-613, 1896.

4462. Winship, George P. List of titles of documents relating to America contained in volumes I-LX of the Colección de documentos ineditos para la historia de España. *Bulletin of the Public Library of the City of Boston*, 1894. 14 p. Br572C An8141 v.136.

4463. Winship, George P. The journey of Coronado, 1540-1542, from the city of Mexico to the Grand Canyon of the Colorado and the buffalo plains of Texas, Kansas, and Nebraska, as told by himself and his followers; translated and edited with an introduction, by George Parker Winship. *Annual Report of the Bureau of Ethnology, Smithsonian Institution, for 1893-1894*, pp. 329-613, 1896. Br973.1 V44.

4464. Winship, George P. Why Coronado went to New Mexico in 1540. *Annual Report of the American Historical Association for 1894*, pp. 83-92, 1896. Br572C An8141 v.159.

4465. Winsor, Justin. *The Literature of Witchcraft in New England*. Charles Hamilton, Worcester, MA, 1896. 25 p. Br572C An8141 v.159. Winsor (1831-1897) was named director of the Boston Public Library in 1866 and, over the next nine years, he expanded the library, made it more useful to the public, and began the national professionalizing of librarians. He helped establish the American Library Association (1876) and served as its first president (1876-1885). In 1887 he was appointed Librarian of Harvard College. As an historian, Winsor considered history as both literary and scientific, and provided a transition between the amateurish historians of the late 19th century and the professional ones emerging at the beginning of the 20th century.

4466. Winsor, Justin. *The New England Indians: A Bibliographical Survey, 1630-1700*. John Wilson and Son, University Press, Cambridge, MA, 1895. 35 p. Br572C An8141 v.159.

4467. Wislizenus, Frederick A. *Memoir of a Tour to Northern Mexico Connected with Col. Doniphan's Expedition, in 1846 and 1847; With a Scientific Appendix and Three Maps*. Tippin and Streeper, Washington, DC, 1848. 141 p. Br917.2 W754. Includes: J.W. Abert, Report and map of the examination of New Mexico, 1848; J. D. Webster, Report of a survey of the Gulf Coast at the mouth of the Río Grande, 1850; M. S. Smith and E. S. F. Hardcastle, Survey of the valley of Mexico, 1849; J. D. Webster, Survey of the Gulf Coast at the mouth of the Rio Grande, 1850; J. H. Simpson, Report and map of the route from Fort Smith, Arkansas, to Santa Fé, New Mexico, 1850; G.A. McCall, Reports in relation to New Mexico, 1851; A. W. Whipple, Extract from a journal of an expedition from San Diego, California, to the Rio Colorado, 1851; David Fergusson, Report on the country, its resources, and the route between Tucson and Lobos Bay, 1863.

4468. *Wissenschaftliche Mitteilungen aus Bosnien und der Hercegovina...redigirt von Moriz Hoernes*. Gerold, Wien, 1894. v. 2. Br913.4395 Sa72. Contents include: Archaeologie und Geschichte; Völkskunde; Naturwissenschaft.

4469. Wolf, Theodor. *Viajes científicos por la república del Ecuador, verificados y publicados por órden del supremo gobierno de la misma república*. Imprenta del Comercio, Guayaquil, 1879. 3 v. in 1. Br918.62 W832. Includes: 1. Relación de un viaje geognóstico por la provincia de Loja, 1879; 2. Relación de un viaje geognóstico por la provincia del Azuay, 1879; 3. Memoria sobre la geografía y geología de la provincia de Esmeráldas, 1879.

4470. Woman's Anthropological Society. *Proceedings of the One Hundredth Meeting.* Gibson Brothers, Printers and Bookbinders, Washington, DC, 1893. 31 p. Br572C An8141 v.125.

4471. Worcester, George W. The life history of Stentor Coerulens, or Blue Stentor. *Proceedings of Central Ohio Scientific Association,* pp. 97–106. Saxton and Brand, Urbana, Ohio, 1884. Br572C An8141 v.58.

4472. World's Columbian Exposition (Chicago, 1893). Department of Publicity and Promotion. *Official Catalogue of Exhibits: Anthropological Building, Midway Plaisance and Isolated Exhibits, Part XII.* W. B. Conkey Company, Chicago, 1893. Br572C An8141 v.128.

4473. World's Columbian Exposition (Chicago, 1893). Jamaica. Honorary Commissioner. *World's Fair; Jamaica at Chicago; An Account Descriptive of the Colony of Jamaica, With Historical and Other Appendices.* Pell, New York, 1893. 95 p. Br606 C1893JM.

4474. Worsaae, Jens J. A. Des ages de pierre et de bronze dans l'ancien et le Nouveau Monde; comparisons archeologico-ethnographiques; traduit du danois par E. Beauvois. *Mémoires des Antiquaires du Nord,* pp. 132–244, 1881. Br572C An8141 v.24.

4475. Wrenshall, L. H. A study of aboriginal relics from the stone graves of Tennessee. *Transactions of the Maryland Academy of Sciences,* pp. 229–240, 1895. Br572C An8141 v.142.

4476. Wright, Alfred. *The Books of Joshua, Judges, and Ruth, Translated into the Choctaw Language; Choshua, nan Apesa Vhleha holisso, micha Lulh holisso, aiena kvt toshowvt Chahta anumpa toba hoke.* American Bible Society, New York, 1852. 151 p. Br497.39 ChB46.9.

4477. Wright, Alfred, and C. Byington. *Chahta uba isht taloa holisso; Choctaw Hymn Book.* 6th ed. T. R. Marvin, Boston, 1858. 252 p. Br497.39 ChW94. "Byington left Stockbridge, Massachusetts, in 1819 for the Choctaw Nation in Mississippi, and was a missionary among the Choctaw for nearly fifty years. He was joined in 1820 by Alfred Wright" (*Frank T. Siebert Library* 1999:2:331).

4478. Wright, Allen. *Chahta leksikon; A Choctaw in English Definition; For the Choctaw Academies and Schools.* Printed by the Presbyterian Publishing Company, St. Louis, 1880. 311 p. Br497.39 ChW93. Allen Wright was a native Choctaw who graduated from Union College in Schenectady, New York, and Union Theological Seminary. He was later elected principal chief.

4479. Wright, Asher. *Go'wana gwa'ih sat'hah yon de' yas dah'gwah; A Spelling Book in the Seneca Language, With English Definitions.* Mission Press, Buffalo Creek Reservation, 1842. 112 p. Br497.27 SW93. "The first book published on the Seneca Mission Press at Buffalo-Creek Reservation. Although called a spelling book, the work is actually a grammar and dictionary of the Seneca language" (*Frank T. Siebert Library* 1900:331). In 1831 the American Board of Commissioners for Foreign Missions sent Wright (1803–1875) as a missionary to the Senecas at Buffalo Creek Reservation. He devised the first adequate orthography for Seneca, and persuaded his sponsors to equip him with a press.

In 1841 he set up the Mission Press, which produced the first books printed in Buffalo.

4480. Wright, Asher. *Ho iwi yòsdos hah neh Cha gao hee dus, gee ih ni ga?a dos ha gee, neh nando wahgaah heni adi wanoh daah; The Four Gospels in the Seneca Language.* American Bible Society, New York, 1878. 445 p. Br497.27 SB47.5.

4481. Wright, George F. Detailed report of inventigations along the boundary of the glaciated area in Ohio and Indiana; lecture given before the Western Reserve Historical Society in Case Hall, Cleveland, Ohio, November 27, 1882. pp. 34-86, 1882. Br572C An8141 v.37.

4482. Wright, George F. Evidences of glacial man in Ohio. *Popular Science Monthly* 43:29-39, 1893. Br572C An8141 v.124.

4483. Wright, George F. *Man and the Glacial Period.* Appleton, New York, 1892. 385 p. Br573.3 W93.

4484. Wright, George F. The glacial boundary in Ohio, Indiana, and Kentucky. *Transactions of the Western Reserve Historical Society* 2(60): 193-228, 1888. Br572C An8141 v.41.

4485. Wright, George F. Unity of the glacial epoch. *American Journal of Science* 64:351-373, 1892. Br572C An8141 v.124.

4486. Wright, Harrison. Archaeological report on the Athens Locality, Pennsylvania. *Proceedings of the Wyoming Historical and Geographical Society* 2(1): 55-75, 1885. Br572C An8141 v.39.

4487. Wyman, Jeffries. *An Account of Some of the Kjœkkenmœddings, or Shellheaps, in Maine and Massachusetts.* Essex Institute Press, Salem, MA, 1867. 26 p. Br913.93 W982. Jeffries Wyman (1814-1874), trained as a physician, acquired a

Jeffries Wyman (from Justin Winsor, Aboriginal America. *Cambridge, MA: Houghton, Mifflin, 1889. p. 392).*

reputation as an excellent comparative anatomist during the 1840s. He began the extensive Museum of Comparative Anatomy at Harvard University and, in 1866 was appointed the first curator of the Peabody Museum of American Archaeology and Ethnology. Wyman wrote on craniology and the archaeology of shell mounds, and through major purchases built the collections.

4488. Wyman, Jeffries. An account of the fresh-water shell-heaps on the St. Johns River, East Florida. *American Naturalist* 2(8-9), 1868. 27 p. Br572C An8141 v.38.

4489. Wzokolain, Peter P. *Kagakimzouiasis ueji up'banakiah adali kimo'gik aliuit-zo'ki za plasua.* Imprimé par Fréchette et Cie, Québec, 1832. 44 p. Br497.11 AW99. This translation of the *Catéchisme du Diocèse de Quebec* is attributed to Wzokhilain on the authority of J. Hammond Trumbull. It is quite certain, however, that the version is of a much older date. "Wzokhilain had been a Protestant but converted to the Catholic faith in 1832 in order to marry the daughter of Chief Simon Obomnsawin of St. François, who was himself a fervent Catholic. In order to affirm the sincerity of his conversion, Wzokhilain produced this Abenaki translation of the Catholic catechism, which was published with the printed endorsement of the Bishop of Quebec. For unknown reasons, Wzokhilain renounced his Catholic faith and returned to the Protestant fold in 1835" (*Frank T. Siebert Library* 1999:1:58).

4490. Ximenez, Francisco. Bocabulario de la lengua cakchiquel, n.d. 35, 52 leaves. Br498.21 CX45. Manuscript.

4491. Ximenez, Francisco. *Las historias del origen de los Indios de esta provincia de Guatemala; traducidas de la lengua quiché al castellano para mas comodidad de los ministros del S. Evangelio; por el R. P. F. Francisco Ximenez, cura doctrinero por el Real Patronato del pueblo de S. Thomas Chuila; exactamente según el texto español del manuscrito original que se halla en la biblioteca de la Universidad de Guatemala, publicado por la primera vez, y aumentado con una introducción y anotaciones por Karl Scherzer.* Trübner, Londres, 1857. 215 p. Br498.22 KiX45. "The work of Father Ximenez on the origin of the American Indians was published by Dr. Scherzer from a copy of the original MS which he found in the library of the University of Guatemala" (Field 1873:429).

4492. *Yacuic iyec tenonotzaltzin in Jesu-Christo, que nami oquimo ihcuilhuili in San Lucas.* Imprenta evangelica, México, 1889. 139 p. Br498.23 OB 47. New Testament Gospel of St. Luke translated into Otomi.

4493. Yale University. Class of 1858. *Third Biographical Record of the Class of Fifty-Eight, Yale College, 1858-1883.* New York, 1883. Br378.73 Y13 U.2.

4494. Yarrow, Harry C. A further contribution to the study of the mortuary customs of the North American Indians. *Annual Report of the Bureau of Ethnology, Smithsonian Institution, for 1879-1880,* pp. 91-203, 1881. Br970.6 Y27.2.

4495. Yarrow, Harry C. *Introduction to the Study of Mortuary Customs Among the North American Indians.* Bureau of Ethnology, Smithsonian Institution, Washington, DC, 1880. 114 p. Br572C An8141 v.93.

4496. Young, John H. Incidents connected with the early history of Champaign County.

Proceedings of the Ohio Scientific Association, pp. 77–87. Saxton and Brand, Urbana, Ohio, 1878. Br572C An8141 v.59.

4497. Zaccicoxol, o baile de Cortes, en kiche y castellano. Cobán, 1875. 69 leaves. Br898.21 KZ13. Manuscript; "This is a modern drama, written by a native, in Kiche and Spanish, the plot based on the conquest of Mexico. It is one of the few correct specimens of the native drama which have been preserved, and although not possessing the claim of antiquity, presents the general style and manner of treatment adopted in the primitive scenic representations" (Brinton 1900).

4498. Zárate, Agustin de. *Histoire de la découverte et de la conquête du Perou.* Par la Compagnie des Libraires, Paris, 1774. 2 v. Br985 Za17.FC. Translation by S. de Broë of *Historia del descubrimiento y conquista de la provincia del Peru* (Antwerp, 1555) "whose early narrative of the Spanish conquest fully confirms the terrible story of [Bartolome de] Las Casas. The prints are principally descriptive of the horrible cruelties perpetrated by the Spanish monsters on the Indians" (Field 1873:430).

4499. Zeisberger, David. *A Collection of Hymns, for the Use of the Delaware Christian Indians, of the Missions of the United Brethren, in North America. 2 ed., Revised and Abridged by A. Luckenbach.* Printed by J. and W. Held, Bethlehem, 1847. 305 p. Br497.11 DM79. A collection of hymns in the Delaware language, translated from German and English hymn-books of the Moravian Church, by David Zeisberger. "The Moravian missionary David Zeisberger (1721–1808) lived among the Indians of North America for more than sixty years, establishing churches and teaching English and Christian doctrine…Zeisberger was persecuted [on the eve of the American Revolution] because of patriots who assumed that Native Americans were potential allies of the British, but later he continued his work and finally settled in Goshen, Ohio" (*Frank T. Siebert Library* 1999:1:314).

4500. Zeisberger, David. *Essay of an Onondaga Grammar; or, A Short Introduction to Learn the Onondaga or Maqua Tongue.* Lippincott, Philadelphia, 1888. 45 p. Br497.27 OnZ35.2; Br572C An8141 v.49. Translated from the German manuscript of the author by Bishop John Ettwein.

4501. Zeisberger, David. Grammar of the language of the Lenni Lenape or Delaware Indians. *Transactions of the American Philosophical Society* 3(2): 65–250, 1827, 188 p. Br497.11 DZ35a. "The manuscript of this jewel of philological research was written by the linguistics scholar Pierre Étienne Du Ponceau, who had emigrated to America in 1777 and settled in Philadelphia. David Zeisberger, Moravian missionary to the Delaware Indians, translated the text and added his 34-page introduction concerning historical philology. He included an oblique defense of the Delaware: 'all languages have a regular organization, and none can be called *barbarous* in the sense which presumption has affixed that word'." Translated from the German manuscript of Rev. David Zeisberger for the American Philosophical Society by Peter Duponceau.

4502. Zeisberger, David. *Rlathemwakunek wtclawswakun nrvlalkwf krthwvalkwf Nhesus Klyst; cntu jijwanukifwuntunasw cntu linexsif tclextwnrw mplcnhes.*

Nhime tcli wehwmat. Tali Kejetwn, Jawanouf; J. Meeker, Printer, Shawanoe Baptist Mission, 1837. 221 p. Br497.5 OtL62. Translation of the New Testament Gospels into Delaware.

4503. Zeisberger, David. *The History of Our Lord and Saviour Jesus Christ, Comprehending All That the Four Evangelists Have Recorded Concerning Him; All Their Relations Being Brought Together In One Narration, So That No Circumstances is Omitted, But That Inestimable History is Continued In One Series, In The Very Words of Scripture.* Printed by Daniel Fanshaw, New York, 1821. 222 p. Br497.11 DL62. Translation of the New Testament Gospels into Delaware.

4504. Zeisberger, David. *Vocabularies by Zeisberger, From the Collection of Manuscripts Presented by Judge Lane to Harvard University, nos. 1 and 2.* J. Wilson and Son, University Press, Cambridge MA 1887. 20 p. Br497.11 DZ35.2; Br572C An8141 v.96. Vocabulary no. 1 consists of three parallel columns: German, Maqua-Onondaga and Delaware; no. 2, of four parallel columns: English, Maqua, Delaware and Mahican.

4505. Zeisberger, David. *Zeisberger's Indian Dictionary; English, German, Iroquois, the Onondaga and Algonquin, the Delaware; Printed From the Original Manuscript in Harvard College Library.* J. Wilson, Cambridge, MA, 1887. 236 p. Br497.27 OnZ35.

4506. *Zeitschrift für Völkerpsychologie und Sprachwissenschaft.* Ferd. Dümmlers Verlagsbuchhandlung, Berlin. v. 1(1860)–v. 2(1889). Br305 Z3125.

4507. Zeltner, M.A. de. *Note sur les sepultures indiennes du Departement de Chiriqui, Etat du Panama.* Imprimerie de T. M. Cash, Panama, 1866. 12 p. Br572C An8141 v.18; Br572C An8141 v.165.

4508. Zerda, L. *El Dorado: estudio histórico, etnográfico y arqueológico de los Chibchas, habitantes de la antigua Cundinamarca, y algunas otras tribus.* Imprenta de Silvestre y Compañía, Bogota, 1883. Br572C An8141 v.105.

4509. Zestermann, C. A. A. Colonization of America in ante-historic times. *New York Semi-Weekly Tribune,* May 3, 1851. 12 p. Br572C An8141 v.165.

4510. Zestermann, C. A.A. Memoir on the European colonization of America, in ante-historic times. *Proceedings of the American Ethnological Society,* 1851. 32 p. Br572C An8141 v.76.

4511. *Zimshian Version of Portions of the Book of Common Prayer.* Society for Promoting Christian Knowledge, London, n.d. 35 p. Br497.18 TC47. Church of England Book of Common Prayer translated into Tsimshian.

4512. Zmigrodzki, Michal von. *Die Mutter bei den Völkern des arischen Stammes; eine anthropologisch-historische Skizze als Beitrag zur Lösung der Frauenfrage.* T. Ackermann, München, 1886. 444 p. Br396 Z74.

4513. Zmigrodzki, Michal von. Zur Geschichte der Svastika. *Archiv fü Anthropologie* 19:173–181, 1890. Br572C An8141 v.103.

4514. Zoja, G. Di un teschio boliviano microcefalo. *Archivo per l'Anthropologia e la Etnologia* 4(2): 205–217, 1874. Br572C An8141 v.165.

Index

All numbers refer to catalog entries except for those in italics, which are page numbers in the Introduction.

Abbeville, France 2770
Abbott Collection. *See* collections
Abdiheba 2196
Abel, C. 3334
Abenaki. *See* Abnaki
Abert, J. W. 1421, 4467
Abipón 52, 1301, 2327, 2331
Abnaki 796, 2184, 2672, 3060, 3441, 4291, 4489
Academia Guatemalteca 3894
Academia Venezolana 839
Academy of Natural Sciences of Philadelphia *3, 22,* 2741
Acadia, ME 4290, 4291
Acadia. *See* Micmac
Acanceh, Mexico 391
Acasaguastlán, Guatemala 788
Acawai 2242, 3415
Acawoio. *See* Acawai
acclimatization 3564
Accowoio. *See* Acawai
acculturation 2710
Achagua 3616
Achaqua. *See* Achagua
Achelis, T. 167
Acolhuacan, Mexico 2020
Acopia 2584
Adam, L. 765, 1162, 1191, 2362, 2556, 3167
Adelman, Jean Shaw *16*
Adepts of India 4390
adornments 1348
adze 1715
Africa 143, 443, 942, 1061, 1199, 1609, 1705, 2424, 2522, 2905, 3805, 4391, 4392; Central, 1727, 2936, 2939; East, 2529, 3048, 3176; North 427, 428, 1014, 1464, 1856, 4333
African Americans 906

Agramer National Museum. *See* museums
agriculture 38, 1614, 1941, 2719, 3450, 3516, 4377; agricultural implements 3450
Aguchekikos, Prof. (pseud.) 3379, 4212
Aguilar, J. de 4093
Aguilar, J. H. 2826
Aguilera, H. de 2470
Ahpozotziles 610
Aimará. *See* Aymara
Aino 1094, 2026, 2887, 4182
Ajusco, Mexico 1371
Akka. *See* Makak
alabaster 2120
Alacaluf 1472, 2505, 2508, 2605, 2611
Alacalufan. *See* Alacaluf
Alagüilac 712
Alakaluf. *See* Alacaluf
Alasapas 1642
Alaska 294, 295, 476, 485, 530, 1227, 1231, 1232, 2063, 2185, 2186, 2566, 2970, 3249, 3292, 3641, 3767, 4241, 4385
albinos 2909
Alcazar, Spain 1118
Alcedo, A. de 434
Aleoutes. *See* Aleut
Aletsch Glacier 547
Aleut 2169, 2937, 3254, 3299
Aleutian Islands 1225, 1227, 1232, 1789, 2125
Alfaro, A. 3214
Algeria 185, 1463, 1629, 2105, 3331
Algic. *See* Algonkin
Algonkin 750, 849, 963, 968, 1003, 1387, 1389, 1207, 1952, 2383, 2384, 2487, 2548, 2649-2651, 2934, 2937, 3277, 3375, 3642, 3753, 3941, 4098, 4099, 4164, 4165, 4202, 4203, 4205, 4423, 4466, 4498

Algonquian. *See* Abnaki, Algonkin, Chippewa, Delaware, Gros Ventre, Mahican, Malicite, Miami, Micmac, Mississauga, Mohegan, Montagnais, Montauk, Munsee, Nanticoke, Narragansett, Naskapi, Natick, Nipissing, Ojibwa, Passamaquoddy, Penobscot, Shawnee, Siksika, Wampanoag

Alhambra, Spain 1118, 2738

Alikhulip. *See* Alacaluf

Alikuluf. *See* Alacaluf

Aliso 4281

All Saints Day 3829

Allemtíak 2821, 4260

Allen, H. 655, 3077, 4416

Allentíac. *See* Allemtíak

Almeida Nogueira, B. C. de 3637

alphabet. *See* syllabary

Alta Verapaz 62, 65, 3321, 3691. *See also* Guatemala

Altaic 266, 4454, 4456

altars 1503, 1515, 1516, 1523, 2056

Alukulup. *See* Alacaluf

Alvarado, L. 388

Alvarado, P. de 397, 4093

Alvarez de Villanueva, F. 3632

Amador de los Ríos, J. 1477

Amazon River 144, 172, 290, 1399, 1610, 1925, 2806, 3113, 3584, 3586, 3661, 3772

Ambras Castle, Austria 1955

Ambraser Collection. *See* collections

American Antiquarian Society 100-103

American Association for the Advancement of Science 578, 743, 1231, 1851, 2189, 2565, 2569, 2721

American Bible Society 104

American Dialect Society 221

American Ethnological Society 105, 106, 1628

American Folklore Society 107, 108

American Geographical Society 406, 2100, 2102, 3359

American Historical Association 109-111

American Museum of Natural History. *See* museums

American Numismatic and Archaeological Society 114

American Oriental Society 115

American Philological Association 116-117, 2347

American Philosophical Society *11,* 118, 510, 691, 759, 774, 775, 1770, 1952, 2856, 3034, 4501

American Psychological Association 930

Americas 157, 237

amulets and charms 442, 447, 1553, 1948

Anacostia, Washington, DC 4161

Anahuac, Mexico 609, 713, 1771, 3580

Anales de Cuauhtitlan 121

anatomy 497, 1268, 2119, 2592, 2611, 3806, 4418

ancestors 4048. *See also* physical anthropology

Ancón, Peru 376, 785, 1330

Ancona, E. 2479

Andagueda 737

Andaman Islands 3736

Andaquí 66

Anderson River 3248

Andes 247, 3507, 3932

Angmagsalik. *See* Angmagsalingmiut

Angmagslingmiut 2062, 3548. *See also* Eskimo, Greenland

Angola 1041

Añil 216, 2835, 3322

Animas River, NM 2870

animism 2160, 4213. *See also* religion

Annals of Chimalpahin 3862

Annals of the Cakchiquels. See Memorial de Sololá

Antarctic 580, 2508

Antequera, Mexico 298

Anthony, A. S. 771

Anthropological Institute of Great Britain and Ireland 160, 593-595, 2218

Anthropological Institute of New York 1690, 2219

Anthropological Society of Washington 162-164, 572, 2663, 2694, 3358

anthropology *x, 1, 2, 6,* 972, 1093, 1100, 1463, 2115, 2637, 2699, 2721, 2987, 3024, 3156, 3563, 3704, 3806, 3992, 3999, 4173, 4213, 4361, 4432; and craniometry 2369; and ethnography 2151, 2590, 2922, 3200; and ethnology 640, 1729, 3535; and linguistics 1842; and political science 684, 685, 2352; and science 641, 743, 2571, 2639; and sociology 3815, 4366, 4368; history 1331, 1554, 2124, 4006, 4174, 4441; methods 2652, 2901, 3743; teaching 689, 2610, 4022

anthropometry 460, 501, 503, 1386, 1554,

1561, 1729, 4389. *See also* physical anthropology

anthropophagy 1281, 1783, 1945, 2777, 4028

antiquities, destruction of 1638

Antis. *See* Campas

Antuño, E. de 1309

Apache 572, 573, 1141, 1673, 2036, 2843

Apalachee 399. *See also* Florida

Aparaï 1158, 1162

Apollo 534

Apostles' Creed 1307, 3413-3416, 4078. *See also* Christian doctrine

Appomatox Formation 2723

Arabic 4307, 4425

Arabs 1118, 3176, 3177

Araguayo 1160

Aranzadi, T. de 2124

Arano, T. de 3674

Araote. *See* Warrau

Araucanians 1239, 1391, 1471, 1472, 1935, 2224, 2400, 2402-2404, 2508, 2572, 2740, 2821, 3537, 3873, 4193, 4255. *See also* Auca

Araukan. *See* Araucanian

Aravaco. *See* Arawak

Arawak 37, 748, 1184, 2937, 3407, 3414, 3854, 4274

Arawakan. *See* Achagua, Arawak, Arrouage, Baniwa, Baure, Campa, Carib, Chiquito, Garífuna, Guana, Piapoco

Arbalo 4281

Archaeological Institute of America 176, 177

archaeology *1,* 4, 130, 140, 142, 156, 168, 232, 233, 282, 285, 287, 305, 306, 346, 452, 558, 581, 600, 643, 657, 668, 680, 729, 733, 734, 1065, 1201, 1243, 1244, 1250, 1258, 1264, 1535, 1797, 1798, 1837, 1902, 1904, 1951, 1962, 2252, 2253, 2374, 2507-2513, 2703, 2709, 2712, 2736, 2763, 2853, 2861, 2862, 2901, 2946, 2992-2994, 3015, 3027, 3056, 3071, 3079, 3081, 3239, 3274, 3385, 3386, 3393, 3449, 3455, 3462-3465, 3520, 3525, 3526, 3597, 3663, 3899, 4008-4010, 4090, 4105, 4106, 4120, 4340, 4432, 4440, 4448, 4474; Abbeville 2770; Africa 143, 443, 2905, 4391; Africa, North 4333; Alaska 530, 1227, 1232, 3292; Aleutian islands 1227, 1232, 1245; Algeria 1629; Ancon 376, 1325, 1330; Animas River, NM 2870; Argentina 96-98; Arizona 281, 286, 1808, 2043, 2813; Arkansas 977; Armenia 2865; Aruba 3291; Ash Cave 153; Asia 443, 2905; Asia, West 727; Australasia 2010; Babylonia 3118; Balzi Rossi Cave 1085; Belgium 2984, 2990; Belmont County, OH 4363; Berks County, PA 803; Biblical 56; Bolivia 364, 1120, 4225, 4226, 4415; Bone Hole, PA 2759; Borneo 1966; Bosnia 4468; Brassempouy 3273; Brazil 603, 1274, 1485; British Columbia 3875; Calaveras 218; California 879, 1276, 2058, 3950, 4007; Canada 585-592, 947, 4085; Caribbean 702, 2070, 2163, 2634, 3410, 3612; Catamara 2860; Catherina Archipelago 1227; Caucasus 974; Centla 397; Central America 397, 406, 513, 3300, 3978, 3979, 3982, 3983, 4040; Chacota Bay 449; Chajcar, Guatemala 3716; Chamá 1292, 1293; Champlain Valley 3227; Charente, France 3000; Chelles 2770; Chequest Creek 1224; Chesapeake River 2074; Chiapas 397, 4040; Chichén Itzá 1037, 2745; Chile 3484; Chipolém 1295; Chiriquí 1608, 2076, 2791; Cobán 1291 Colombia 1773; Colorado 280, 3080; Copan 1754-1756, 2670, 2796, 3668; Copán 4042; Costa Rica 76, 181, 1533, 3214; Crécy 2913, 2914; Crump Burial Cave 818; Cuenca 2004; Culbin sands 445; Delaware Valley 167, 2777; Delaware 2217, 3184; Duval County, FL 4108; Egypt 513, 1558, 1559, 3506, 3508, 3981; Elginshire 445; Europe 1155, 1256, 1596, 1597, 2774, 2905, 2506, 2962, 3002, 3022, 3023, 3213, 3473, 3856, 4082; Florida 167, 694, 695, 1361, 1363, 1835, 2283, 2764, 3471, 4108, 4379, 4488, 4500-4503; Forest River 3396; France 513, 1088, 1096, 2903, 2904, 3246; Georgia 2205-2207, 2211, 2212; Germany 1902, 1931, 1959, 3038, 3040, 3064; Great Britain 1454; Greece 513; Guadaloupe 1899, 2634, 3001; Guatemala 167, 327, 513, 1290-1296, 1675, 1822, 2669-2671, 3555, 3556, 3716, 3778; Guatemala 4112; Hartman's

Cave 2775; Havre 2915; Honduras 1754-1756, 2670, 3690; Hungary 3005, 3594; Hutsonville, OH 3391; Ibverleny 442; Illinois 2058, 2680, 3448, 3803; Indiana 792, 3388; Iowa 3989; Ireland 1454; Irwin's Cave, PA 2759; Isle of Man 444; Italy 848, 1557, 3055, 3494, 3807, 4083; Izamal 1037; Japan 2023, 2025, 2027, 2227, 2897; John Day River, OR 4094; Kentucky 878, 3267, 3388, 3927; Kirk Andreas 444; Labná 4138; Lake Dwellers 3022; Lake of the Woods 2358; Lake Titicaca 1130; Lehigh 2766, 2773; Lengyel, Hungary 3005; Little Miami Valley 3403; Loltún 4136; Long Island 637; Louisiana 683; Lytton British Columbia 3875; Maine 4431; Maine 4487; Marajó 1274; Marbelhead, OH 4387; Mareuil-Lès-Meaux 3244; Massachusetts 4487; Mehrum 1616; Merom, OH 3391; Mesa Verde 3080; Mexico 1, 211-213, 253, 271, 292, 352, 450, 513, 1036-1040, 1042, 1181, 1434, 1465, 1638, 1775, 1776, 1801, 1879, 1884, 2029, 2406, 2675, 2744, 2745, 3070, 3099, 3625, 3696, 3698, 3700, 3779, 3781, 3799, 3800, 3980, 3986, 3993, 3995, 4001, 4004, 4040, 4060, 4080, 4112, 4194, 4261, 4362, 4264; Michigan 1735, 1736, 3876, 3879-3881; Michoacan 4001, 4004; Minnesota 222, 2079; Mississippi Valley 885, 1108, 2552, 3004, 3957; Missouri 783, 1455, 2006, 3350; Mitla 1037, 2675, 3800; Mixco Viejo 3687; Monaco 3037; Montgaudier cave 3000; Moundbuilders 3017, 3203, 3267, 3373, 3424, 3848, 3933, 3936, 3961, 3962, 4122-4124, 4128, 4131, 4388; Murphy Island, FL 4108; Muskinggum, OH 2855; Namur 2984, 2990; Napa County, CA 4007; New Jersey 3454; New Mexico 2043, 2870, 3930, 3950; New York 348, 1905, 3929, 3936; Newark, OH 3655; Newfoundland 947; Nicaragua 167, 605, 703, 1631, 3199, 3952, 3953; Nippur 3236-3238; North America 3, 6, 279, 1805, 1947, 3003, 3006, 3009, 3016, 3021, 3145, 3458-3460, 3469, 3470, 3473, 3692, 3874, 4118, 4155, 4161, 4449; North Carolina 4117; Nova Scotia 3264; Ochlawaha River 4108; Ohio Valley 2552; Ohio 152, 708, 1063, 1594, 1595, 2078, 2597, 2854, 2855, 3202, 3390, 3391, 3402, 3486, 3655, 3846, 4124, 4128, 4363, 4387, 4388; Omitlán 3070; Oregon 4094; Osborne, OH 4388; Palenque 613, 1037, 1569, 1573, 3466, 3476, 4361, 4362; Panama 1608; Patagonia 4063; Pecos River 247; Pennsylvania 167, 1815, 1836, 2759, 2778, 4486; Pérgueux 1470; Peru 202, 308, 364, 449, 787, 917, 1145, 1324, 1325, 1330, 1335, 1761, 1762, 1898, 2075, 2170, 2202, 2320, 2664, 2961, 3573, 3935, 3959, 3964, 3972, 3975-3977, 4067, 4206, 4415; Pine Grove 3396; Pittsburgh 1224; Polynesia 2010; Port Kennedy, PA 2759, 2778; Portugal 901; Potomac River 2074, 2632; Prescott, AZ 1808; Pucara 2345; Quimbaya 3518, 3791; Quiriguá 397, 2796, 4042; Rehoboth. DE 2217; Rome 513; Russia 2865; Saginaw valley 3876, 3880; Salt Springs, IL 3803; San Isidro 341, 344; San Lucia Cotzumalhuapa 1822; Santa Barbara, CA 582; Santo Domingo Pueblo 1505; Sardinia 3110; Scioto, OH 2855; Scugog Island 958; Seine-et-Marne 2913, 3244; South America 364, 513, 4062, 4252; Spain 901, 2738, 3864; St. Acheul 2770; St. Johns River, FL 4488; St. Vincent 702; Stroudsburg, PA 2775; Susquehanna River 3343; Switzerland 1955-1957, 1961; Tabasco 397; Tennessee 881, 1377, 2213, 2214, 3387, 4142-4144, 4417, 4475; Teotihuacan 1879, 2011, 3099; Tepoztlán 3711; Thenny 568; Tiahuanaco 2819; Trenton Gravels 2, 7-10, 2068, 2758, 2772, 2788, 3640; Tula 3986; Ulster, NY 167; Ulúa River 3690; United States 1589, 1934, 3028, 3053, 3750, 3974; United States, East 2760, 2761, 3397; United States, Northeast 710, 880, 1944; United States, Southwest 1497, 1500, 1505, 1507, 1517, 2070; Usumacinta River 397; Utah 281, 3151; Uxmal 1037; Venezuela 1436, 2581; Verapaz 397l; Verde Valley AZ 2813; Vermont 3227-3229; Virginia 883, 1592, 1593; Warren County, OH 2852; Washington, DC 2238, 3380, 4452;

Watungasta 2346; Whitesides County, IL 2056; Whitewater River 3418; Winslow, AZ 1509, 1510; Wisconsin 919, 2350; Xicalango 397; Xkichmook 4137; Yucatan 150, 397, 2559, 2560, 2762, 3979, 4040, 4041, 4136–4138; Zachila 2614

architecture 156, 1487, 1489, 1490, 2596, 2758, 3853, 3930, 3953, 4040; naval architecture 516

archives 1213, 1286, 3013, 3215, 3600, 3918

Archivo de Indias 3215

Arctic 461, 2988, 3241, 3408, 3425, 3554

Arctic Ocean 4081, 4241

Arequipa, Peru 2584

Argentina 95–98, 407, 2331, 2332, 2339, 2345, 2346, 2860, 2861, 3114, 3135, 3136, 3179, 3411, 4075, 4141, 4319, 4362. See also Chanar-Yaco

argillite 2, 167

Arias, C. 2479

Arias Davila, P. 1308

Arikara 2872

Arizona 281, 572, 577, 1318, 1508–1511, 1803, 1808, 2033, 2043, 2049, 2107, 2664, 2813, 2815, 3310, 4467

Arkansas 563, 977, 1421, 2681, 4467

Armenia 2865

Armentia, N. 1394

Arorai. See Gilbert Islands

Arrouague. See Arawak

art 84, 280, 499, 524, 669, 1219, 1278, 1475, 1491, 1781, 1825, 1966–1970, 2042, 2051, 2069, 2786, 2992, 3207, 3389, 3406, 3502, 3618, 3619, 3693, 4434, 4439

Arte. See grammar

Aruba Island 1665, 3291

Aryans 1847, 2268, 3118, 3701, 4082, 4229, 4272

Ash Cave, OH 153

Ashiwi. See Zuni

Asia 254, 443, 975, 1061, 1429, 1609, 1720, 2424, 2899, 2905, 2949; East 198, 994, 2281, 2298, 2323, 2891, 3913; West 727, 2002

Assab 1730

Assam 167, 3181

Association Française pour l'Avancement des Sciences 3666

Assyria 2193

Assyriology 2472

Astrato 387

astrology 2673

astronomy 1, 1864, 2407

Atacama, Chile 3671, 3759

Ataguitan. See Atacama

Athapascan 104, 828, 2937, 3241, 3278. See also Apache, Dene, Euskarienne, Navaho, Pueblo Indians, Takulli, Tinne, Tonto, Tsattine, Tukkuthkutchin, Yuma

Athapaskan. See Athapascan

Athens locality, PA 4486

Athens, Greece 2494

Atlanta, GA 56, 558

atlases. See cartography

atlatl. See spear throwers

Atnah 3305

Aubin, A. M. E. 1382, 1680, 1763, 2579

Aubin Collection. See collections

Aubry, M. Y. E. de 2479

Auca 2310, 2399. See also Araucanians

Aucan. See Araucanian

Aucanian. See Araucanian

Augustinians. See religious orders

Australasia 1716, 2010

Australia 844, 3622, 3680, 4349. See also Australian Aborigines

Australian Aborigines 844, 1339, 2009, 3150, 3622, 3680

Austria 2253, 3083

Avila, J. 2835

Awatobi 1493, 1508. See also Hopi

axes 1721, 3228, 3229

Aymara 407, 430, 913, 914, 1472, 1565, 2807, 4415

Azcarate, M. M. 3378

Aztec 234, 240, 250–252, 432, 609, 814, 832, 1004, 1042, 1064, 1180, 1281–1284, 1571, 1681, 1869, 1892, 2019, 2021, 2406, 3057, 3058, 3524, 3708, 3779, 3780, 3786, 3787, 3792, 3801, 3969, 3988, 4003, 4096, 4185, 4188. See also Nahuatl

Aztlán, Mexico 3057, 3801

Azuay province, Ecuador 1748, 4469

Babylonia 2014, 2190, 3118, 3236–3238

Bacalar, Belize 391

bacillus 197

Bacon, Mr. 2398

Baden 1931, 1959. See also Germany

Baduvi 1718
Baffinland 469, 490, 491
Baily, J. 4042
Baird, S. F. 3865
Bakairi 2653, 4012
Baldwin, C.C. 2698
Ballas 1558
ballgame 2849
Balli, P. 3429
Baltimore, C.C. 2619
Balzi Rossi, Italy 1085
Bancroft, H. H. 233, 244, 606, 4393
Bandelier, A. F. 205, 1497, 2030
Bang, W. 1277
Baniva. *See* Baniwa
Baniwa 2301
Baoussé-Roussé 3575
Baptist Indian Mission 2681
Baptists 3643. *See also* missionaries
Barbachano, M. 1309
Barbados 1424
Barbariche 3822
Barcena, A. 2331, 2335
Barrientos, L. 67
barrow archaeology 3014
Barton, G. A. 3118
Basel, Switzerland 2231, 2974
basketry 2621, 3770
Basque 786, 982, 986, 989, 1000, 1006, 1025, 1095, 1097, 1619
Basse-Bretagne, Algeria 1629
Bastian, A. *11, 12,* 24
bat deity 1294, 3793
Battista Memmi, G. 1482
Batungasta 2324
Baubo 1831
Bauré 2556
Bavaria 2369, 3039, 3040. *See also* Germany
Bay Islands, Honduras 388, 3973
Bay of Honduras 1982, 1983
Bayano 384, 387
beads 281, 1835
Bean, T. H. 4241
Beauchamp, W. M. 167
Beauvois, E. 4474
Beaver Indians. *See* Tsattine
beaver traps 2963
Bedfordshire, England 3885
Beebe, Major 167
Belén, Argentina 2806

Belgium 3083, 4323
Belize 387, 388, 1550-1552, 1979, 1983, 1984, 2243, 3643, 3973. *See also* Central America
Bella Coola 495
Bellenger, J. M. 2557
Belmont County, OH 4363
Belmonte y Bermudez, L. de 2022
Bengal 167
Beni province, Bolivia 1950
Bénin 2525, 3010, 3618, 3619
Benneville Keim, G. de 700
Benton Township, OH 153
Benzoni, G. 388
Beothuk 2692
Berbers 422, 634, 1620, 1709, 2476, 2978, 3118, 3226, 3840, 4390
Berendt, K. H. *x, 5, 7, 14,* 62, 65, 92, 167, 193, 198, 372, 841, 842, 1080, 1081, 1110, 1056, 1110, 1119, 1301, 304-1307, 1176, 1285-1287, 1302, 1303, 1315, 1323, 1477, 1614, 1819, 1982, 2386, 2427, 2434, 2436, 2438, 2468, 2485, 2616, 2750, 2826, 2827, 3222, 3224, 3225, 3033, 3058, 3074, 3173, 3419, 3320, 3321, 3533, 3649, 3643, 3676, 3669, 3827, 4042, 4043, 4078, 4269, 4292, 4294, 4301, 4325, 4326, 4328; collecting trips *7, 9, 10, 11*
Berendt Linguistic Collection *11, 12, 13,* 397, 648
Bering Sea 4241
Bering Strait 198, 1245, 2275
Berks County, PA 803
Berlin Leprosy Conference 199
Berliner Gesellschaft für Anthropologie, Ethnologie und Urgeschichte 418
Betancur, Antonio Melian de 157
Bethlehem, PA 771
Betoya 665
Bible 37, 104, 433, 1389; NT, 276, 538, 1739, 2097, 2182, 2249, 2644, 2645, 2691, 3051, 3188, 3439, 3922, 4341; NT, 4095, 4430, 4480; NT, Acts of the Apostles 806, 2507, 3438, 3854; NT, Epistle of St. Paul 3578; NT, Gospels 4495, 4496; NT, John 543, 789, 1267, 1757, 1759, 1979, 2501, 2142, 3984; NT, Luke 544, 789, 807, 1591, 1759, 2008, 2243, 2427, 3326, 3984, 4492; NT, Mark 180, 1648, 1649, 1759, 2143, 2428, 3493,

3682, 3984, 4224; NT, Matthew 1552, 1758, 1759, 1907, 1981, 2095, 2138, 2144, 2242, 2501, 2653, 3437, 3539, 3922, 3984, 4151, 4295; OT, 1587, 1740, 2094, 2644, 3234, 3235; NT, Psalms 3672; OT, Deuteronomy 835, 2685; OT, Ecclesiastes 2873, 3118; OT, Exodus 835, 2948; OT, Genesis 835, 976, 1461, 2242, 3108; OT, Job 2873; OT, Judges 4476; OT, Leviticus 835; OT, Numbers 835, 2685; OT, Pentateuch 2687; OT, Prophets 2690; OT, Proverbs 337, 2873; OT, Psalms 2141, 2873, 3118; OT, Ruth 4476; OT, Song of Solomon 2873; OT, Song of Songs 2873

bibliography 132, 157, 302, 383, 393, 398, 416, 434–436, 450, 525, 561, 606, 627, 631, 632, 646, 648, 678, 739, 776, 858, 874, 915, 916, 947, 970, 1070, 1123, 1164, 1193, 1225, 1275, 1324, 1342, 1391, 1459, 1531, 1636, 1637, 1763, 1786, 1911, 1913, 2363, 2411, 2419, 2437, 2549, 2031, 2032, 2240, 2789, 2821, 2971, 3067, 3069, 3277–3286, 3329, 3332, 3408, 3429, 3467, 3563, 3601, 3627, 3747, 3893, 3926, 3946, 3989, 3990, 4045, 4081, 4100, 4270, 4306, 4419, 4462, 4466

Biblioteca del General Mitre. *See* libraries
Bibliothèque Imperiale. *See* libraries
Bibliothèque Nationale. *See* libraries
Biceita. *See* Viceita
Biche aus Roches cave, Belgium 2990
Bien-Hoa 1875
Bienvenida, Lorenzo de 1308
Big Bone Cave, TN 2781
Big Sioux River 2451. *See also* Iowa, South Dakota
Bilbao, Guatemala *11*
Billings, J. S. 2654
Biloxi 1354
biography 1364, 3076, 3917, 4101
Biological Society of Washington 3361
biology *1*, 1266, 3501
birds 3865, 4241, 4242
Birket-el-Kerun 2003
Biscayne Bay, FL 4357
Bismarck archipelago, Papua New Guinea 1711
Black Carib. *See* Garifuna

Black Christ 3363
Black, G. F. 128
Blackfoot. *See* Siksika
Blackmore Museum. *See* museums
Blackwall 3885
Blanco. *See* Bribri
Blanco. *See* Viceita
Blang-sur-Bresle, France 3664
Blossuom, L. 2351
Blue Stentor. *See* Stentor Coerulens
Blue language 528, 529
Boanes, Argentina 2331
Boas, F. 2065, 3547, 4085
boats 2553, 3725
Boban Collection 2576
Boca del Toro, Costa Rica 388, 3293
Boggiani, G. 2331
Bohemia 3064
Boissy Island, New Guinea 1716
Bolivar, Columbia 3218
Bolivia 196, 364, 407, 872, 1565, 1721, 1950, 2030, 3102, 3681, 3759, 3772, 3932, 4225, 4226, 4319, 4415, 4507
Bollaert, W. 387
Bologna, Italy 2917
Bompas, W. C. 2250, 2251, 3493
Bonacca. *See* Bay Islands
Bonaparte, R. 1443, 3304
Bone Hole. *See* Irwin's Cave
bone 6, 2664, 2872, 3403
Book of Common Prayer, Chippewa 2087, 2082, 2096, 2140, 2146, 2248, 2251, 3838; Dakota 817; Eskimo 3187; Iroquois 1242; Kwakiutl 1860; Munsee 2884, 4360; Santee 2017; Tukkuthkutchin 2684, 2688. *See also* Christian doctrine
Book of the Dead 1420, 2481
Book of the Younger Nations 1849
book trade. *See* publishing
Boose, J. R. 1186
Boré. *See* Pororoca
Borneo 1966
Boruca 384, 388, 412, 4103, 4104
Bosnia 4468
Boston, MA 2103
botany 1182, 2276, 3865. *See also* ethnobotany
Botocudo 1404, 3528
Boturini Benaducci, L. 1064, 1680
Boule, M. 1674

bow and arrow 2627, 2800, 2889, 2966.
    See also projectile points
Bowditch, C. P. *13*
bow-pullers 736, 2895. *See also* bow and
    arrow
Boyacá, Colombia 3218
Brainerd, J. 1396
Bransford, J. F. 387
Brassempouy, France 3273
Brasseur de Bourbourg, C. E. *5,* 68, 174,
    191, 391, 398, 407, 1056, 2342, 2750,
    3382, 4153
Braunschweig, Germany 4340
Brazil 21, 123, 124, 407, 523, 602, 603,
    821, 837, 871, 934, 1153, 1169, 1272,
    1274, 1280, 1392, 1399-1401,
    1404-1406, 1451, 1485, 1598, 1777,
    1787, 1791, 1792, 1923, 1987, 2426,
    2540, 2570, 2617, 2618, 2928, 2973,
    3429, 3588, 3661, 3858, 3859, 4312,
    4411, 4412; Central 2801, 4013, 4014;
    North 3772
Bremer Geographischen Gesellschaft 2275
Brer Rabbit 2586. *See also* folklore
Brettes, J. de 2561
Bribri 388, 2937, 3306, 3314, 4103
Bridge, T. 3326
Brignier, J. 2327
Brinton, D. G. *3,* 167, 383, 798, 833, 834,
    863, 1770, 2674, 2748, 3118, 3186, 3660,
    4056, 4109, 4127; and Karl Berendt *11,
    14*; bequest of library *5;* career as
    physician *3;* education *3;* military
    service *3;* obituaries of *31, n. 1;*
    research interests *5, 13*
Bristol, RI 2812
British Association for the Advancement of
    Science 596, 1255
British Columbia 478, 504, 506, 924, 948,
    1246, 1248, 1249, 1252, 1750, 1845,
    1890, 2012, 2288, 2547, 2566, 4085, 4156
British Guiana. *See* Guayana
British Museum. *See* museums
Broca, P. 1554
Broë, S. de 4498
Bromowicz, F. 3033
Bronze Age 1962, 2946, 2947, 3038, 4474
bronze 1454, 4322. *See also* metals
Brooklyn Institute 1488
Brosse, G. de la 1896
Brown, J. C. *7,* 298, 1056

Browning, R. 647, 656, 662, 760, 2393
Browning Society 662, 760
Brühl, G. 167
Brunca. *See* Boruca
Bruno, G. 1241
Bucks County, PA 2785
Bucks County Historical Society 2769,
    2785
Buddhism 313, 322, 1223, 1599, 2233,
    2938, 3154, 3606
Buenos Aires, Argentina 2373, 4141
Buffalo Lake, WI 2465
Bunyan, J. 816
Bureau of Ethnology *2, 12,* 1983, 2477,
    2031, 2032, 2701, 3386, 4121, 4131
Bureau of Indian Affairs 3755, 4233, 4234
Bureau of the Corps of Topographical
    Engineers 3062
burials 292, 2278, 2279, 3464, 3892, 4310,
    4431; urn burials 3892
Burma 4347
Burmese 4345
Burtneek Sea 3856
Bushmen 4179
Butler, A. J. 3445
Butler, M. E. 3617
Butler County, OH 2552
Byington, C. 4477

Cabécar 4103
Cabot, J. 1914, 2100
Cabrera de Cordóba, L. 4093
Cacama 2331, 2334
Cacaopera 2755
Caché 92, 412, 388
caches 3876
Caddoan. *See* Arikara, Pawnee, Pausanes,
    Wichita
Cadena, G. 4294
Caduveos 525, 2331. *See also* Mbayá
Cágaba 936
Cahabón, Guatemala 62, 63, 3321
Cahita 831. *See also* Mayo, Yaqui
Cahuilla 583. *See also* California
Cairo, Egypt 4342
Cakchiquel 388, 391, 398, 399, 608, 610,
    747, 841, 1560, 1770, 1819, 2748-2750,
    4056, 4186, 4301, 4490. *See also* Maya
Calaveras, CA 218
Calbuco volcano, Chile 2401
Calchaquí, Argentina 96, 3421, 4208

Caledonia Bay, Panama 387

calendrics 1, 240, 332, 380, 399, 403, 688, 759, 841, 842, 1042, 1569, 1579, 1584, 1650, 2223, 2406, 2562, 2668, 3094, 3374, 3782, 3792, 3802, 3969, 4071, 4110, 4115, 4126, 4127, 4129, 4185. *See also* Tonalamatl

California State Mining Bureau 131

California 131, 224, 304, 460, 879, 1044, 1189, 1190, 1276, 1421, 1607, 1652, 1653, 1989, 2048, 2049, 2051, 2058, 2364, 2509, 2641, 2848, 3364, 3429, 3451, 3769, 3770, 3866, 3940, 3950, 4007, 4081, 4223, 4242, 4467

Calvun, J. 2402, 2403

Camacan. *See* Coroado

Cambridge University 1367, 1370, 1825, 2668

Cambridge University, Anatomical Museum. *See* museums

Campa 4415

Campas 2362

Campeche, Mexico 1309, 2827. *See also* Mexico

Campigny, France 3664

Canada 493, 507, 538-544, 778, 781, 782, 947, 1251-1253, 1300, 1412, 1467, 1840, 1865, 2359, 2508, 2602, 2647, 3067, 3489, 4150; Maritime Provinces 3431; Northwest 3242, 3247, 4219-4222. *See also* New France

Canadian Institute 585-588, 590-592, 852-861, 2240, 3485

Canary Islands 1748, 4286

candles 2768

cannibalism. *See* anthropophagy

Cano, A. 3674

canoes 2208

Canseco, A. 1993

Canterbury, England 3763

Canton, China 3725

Cape Bathhurst, Canada 2106

Cape Breton 3434. *See also* Micmac, Nova Scotia

Cape Flaherty, WA 4072

Cape Horn 2151

Cape May, NJ 167

captivity narratives 4076

Cará 3122

Caracas, Venezuela 3591

Carajan. *See* Carayá

Carayá 310, 1406

cardinal directions 1020, 1027

Carib 51, 398, 619-622, 1981, 2239, 2285, 3407, 3410, 3416, 3591, 4012, 4224, 4275

Cariban. *See* Acawai, Apalaí, Bakairi, Carib, Kalingo, Karina, Ouayana, Piritú

Caribbean 702, 2070, 2161, 2163, 2285, 2634, 3067, 3301, 3582, 3612, 3301, 4274

Carlos V 1149, 1150

Carnas, A. 1303

Carolina. *See* North Carolina, South Carolina

Carr, G. 3481

Carrajal, F. 1081

Carral, D. 3211

Carranza, A. J. 291

Carranza, D. 2483

Carrier. *See* Takulli

Carrillo, E. 1286

Carrillo, F. 2479

Carrillo y Ancona, C. 391, 1310, 2479, 3224, 3916

Carson, NV 2986

Carson footprints 2054

Carthage, Tunisia 194, 2194

Cartier, J. 1209, 1360

cartography 230, 397-399, 438, 554, 672, 1601, 1686, 1889, 1894, 1913, 1956, 2257, 2577, 3067, 3232, 3260, 3915, 4050, 4242

Casa Grande, AZ 1497, 2815

Casanare River, Colombia 3574

Casanowics, M. 56

Casiquiare Valley, Venezuela 2806

Castañeda y Najera, M. de 3378

Castaño, B. 4078

Castanoan. *See* Mutsún

Caste War 391, 398, 1310

Casteñeda, E. I. de 1308

Castro, J. M. 1309

cat 4065

Catalan 2114

Catamarca, Argentina 2860

Catawba 960

catechism 1057, 4091; Algonkin 4098; Cágaba 936; Carrier 2877, 2878; Chinook 924; Chippewa 275, Chiriguano 1146; Chuchona 980, 3592, 3593; Cumana 3324; Goajira

935; Guarani 3637; Huastec 4078, 4079; Kalispel 920; Laguna 2753; Lillooet 924; Moxa 2580; Munsee 4260; Nahuatl 923, 3557, 3558, 4185; Okanagan 924; Oneida 1242; Otomi 3219, 3329, 3428; Quiripi 3269; Sheshel 924; Squamish 924; Slayamen 924; Snohomish 567, Stalo 924; Tacaná 921; Tarascan 922; Totonac 1316; Yucatec 1550, 1555, 3559, 3560, 3644, 3646, 3647; Zoque 191
Catherina Archipelago, AK 1227
Catherine II 1484
Catherwood, F. 4042
Catlin, G. 926
Catlin Collection. *See* collections
Catlinite 282
Catlotq. *See* Comox
Cauca 3218
Caucasia 973, 974, 4322
Cavalletti, Italy 1086
caves 581, 1085, 2445, 2738, 2760-2762, 2770, 2777, 2782, 2913, 3151, 3152, 3298, 3575, 4068, 4136
Cayuga 1320. *See also* Iroquois
Ccakcchi. *See* Kekchí
Cebécar. *See* Cabécar
Cegiha 1343, 1347, 1355. *See also* Kansa, Omaha, Osage, Ponca
Celebes 1700
Celts 354, 3503, 3707, 3817
Cenozoic 1136
census 937
Centla, Mexico *11*, 397, 749
Central America 167, 184, 243, 246, 377, 388, 397, 401, 402, 409, 414, 513, 515, 525, 609, 627, 671, 675, 682, 683, 688, 759, 1039, 1061, 1423, 1484, 1493, 1562, 1631, 1636, 1821, 1822, 1829, 1868, 1999, 2363, 2669-2671, 2747, 2782, 2840, 2858, 2899, 3113, 3115, 3190, 3191, 3214, 3231, 3424, 3577, 3583, 3602, 3603, 3686, 3689, 3718, 3720, 3721, 3939, 3947, 3948, 3954, 3956, 3958, 3973, 3978, 3979, 3982, 3983, 4040-4043, 4127. *See also* Belize, Costa Rica, Honduras, Nicaragua, Panama
Central American War 4386
cephalic index 3567. *See also* physical anthropology
ceramics. *See* pottery

Cerda, M.A. de la 3894
ceremonies 167, 1061, 1504, 1511, 1520, 1522, 1528, 1540, 1545; birth 1497; death 1346; Elk Mystery 1540; fire 1519; Flute 2108; Four Winds 1544; Hasjelti Dialjis 4046; initiation 1527; rain 1420; shamanistic 3877; Snake 1525, 2035; summer 1499; solar 288, 391, 1546; Sun Dance 1546; White Buffalo 1548
Cerezo, B. 2836
Cerro Golgota 1303
Cesareo Fernandez Duro (ship) 3137
Ceylon 3744
Chac Xulub Chen 757
Chaco, Argentina 672, 737, 2053, 3114
Chacota Bay, Peru 449
Chacxulubchen. *See* Chixulub
Chahta. *See* Choctaw
Chajcar, Guatemala 3716
Chajul, Guatemala 1307
Chaldeans 4390
Chamá, Guatemala 1292, 1293, 1570, 3782
Chamacoco 517, 522, 1721
Champaign County, OH 4496
Champlain, S. de 971, 1177, 1360, 2647
Champlain Valley, NY 3227
Chamula, Mexico 910
Chana. *See* Yaro
Chanar-Yaco 2326, 2329. *See also* Argentina
Chanases 2331
Chaneabal. *See* Tojolabal
Changuena 3309
Changuina. *See* Changuena
Chaonis Temoatan 4157
Charencey, H. de 3186, 3529, 3593, 4152
Charente, France 1088, 3000, 4106
Charles, C. 438
Charles V 194, 3331, 4093
Charleston, SC 458
charms. *See* amulets and charms
Chavero, A. 845, 1382
Chayopin 1642. *See also* Texas
Chelles 2770
Chemakum 483
Chemax, Mexico 391
Chequest Creek, PA 1224
Cherokee 104, 307, 1043, 1317, 1588, 2182, 2280, 2734, 2843-2846, 2849-2850, 2879, 2937, 4149, 4164

Chesapeake River 2074
Chester County, PA *3*
Cheval, France 74, 75, 3270, 3271
Chiantla, Guatemala 1119
Chiapa de la Real Corona, Mexico 3130
Chiapa de Mota, Mexico 90
Chiapanec 46, 67, 68, 380, 388, 407, 1303, 2468
Chiapas, Mexico 397, 398, 407, 608, 616, 707, 906, 937, 1033, 1110, 1154, 1215, 1303, 1457, 2067, 2826, 3171, 3174, 3311, 3312, 3677, 4040. *See also* Mexico
Chibcha, 44, 387, 1768, 3521, 4251, 4501
Chibchan. *See* Bayano, Betoya, Boruca, Bribri, Cabécar, Caché, Cagaba, Chibcha, Chiripo, Choco, Coiba, Cueva, Cuna, Darien, Dorasque, Goajira, Guatuso, Guaymi, Muisca, Orosí, Paez, Paya, Sabanero, San Blas, Sumo, Talamanca, Terraba, Tucurrique, Tule, Valiente, Viceita, Zambo
Chicago Exposition. *See* expositions
Chichén Itzá, Mexico 1037, 2745, 3085
Chichimec 398, 1163, 2020
Chickasaw 4191
Chicxulub 757
Chihuahua, Mexico, 304. *See also* Mexico
Chilam Balam 645, 3225; Chumayel 391, 757, 1047; Ixil 391; Mani 391, 757; Oxkutzcab 391; Tizimin 391, 757, 1047
children 473
Chile 407, 1471, 1935, 2312, 2402, 2600, 2740, 3429, 3484, 3662, 3873, 4059, 4187, 4259
Chilidugi 1935
Chilidugu. *See* Chilidugi
Chim, D. 3078
Chimakum. *See* Chemakum
Chimalapa, Mexico 407, 1614
Chimalpahin Quauhtlehuanitzin, S.A.M. 158, 3862
Chimalpopoca, F. 121
Chimbote, Peru 1326
Chimmesyan. *See* Tsimshian
chimpanzee 618
Chimu 2807, 3976, 3977. *See* Yunga
Chin Shi Sei 209
China 209, 1195, 1277, 1737, 2601, 2998, 3047, 3429, 3727-3735, 4399, 4420
Chinantec 298, 407, 701

Chinantecan. *See* Chinantec
Chinese 530, 1013, 1195-1197, 1200, 1202, 3118, 3726
Chinook 463, 464, 484, 500, 924, 1670, 1671, 1739, 1740, 2225, 2226, 3279
Chinookan. *See* Chinook
chipmunks 944
Chipolem, Guatemala 1295
Chippewa 43, 104, 272, 276, 365, 366, 453, 978, 1087, 1138, 2016, 2050, 2052, 2087, 2088, 2090, 2091, 2093-2097, 2122, 2138, 2139-2148, 2215, 2216, 2244, 2246-2249, 2251, 2318, 2319, 2355, 2487, 2544-2546, 2548, 2644-2646, 2690, 2841, 3243, 3417, 3838, 3877, 3949, 4073, 4373, 4376, 4073
Chippeway. *See* Chippewa
Chiquita 39
Chiquitos. *See* Towarnodentiel
Chiriguana. *See* Chiriguano
Chiriguano 1146
Chiripo. *See* Cabécar
Chiriqui, Panama 387, 398, 1608, 2076, 2791, 3293, 3295, 4500
Chirripo. *See* Cabécar
chisels 1721
Chixulub 391
Chocó 384, 387, 769
Choctaw 104, 307, 686, 833, 834, 835, 1833, 2937, 3051, 4191, 4422, 4476, 4477, 4478
Cholchol, Guatemala 2402
Cholenec, P. 1052
Cholo. *See* Chocó
Choltí 2856, 2857
Chon. *See* Tehuelche
Chonay, D. J. 4152, 4153
Chono 1472, 2740
Chontal 399, 413, 454, 3073
Choptank River, MD 2777
Chorotega 388, 389, 397
Chortí 2746, 2857, 4043
Christfried, J. 1932
Christian doctrine 36, 3217, 4091, 4256, 4257, 4489; Acawai 2242, 3415; Alasapas 1642; Algonkin 4098; Allemtíak 4260; Altaic 266; Arawak 3414, 3854; Athapascan 104; Blackfoot 4148, 4151; Cakchiquel 1819, 4301; Carib 3416, 4224; Cherokee 104;

Chiapanec 67, 1303, 3171, 3174; Chibcha 4251; Chilidugi 1471; Chinantec 298; Chinook 924; Chippewa 104, 365, 453, 2087-2090, 2092, 2094-2097, 2138-2148, 2244-2249, 2251, 2355, 2544-2546, 2644-2646, 2690, 2841, 3838, 4341; Chiriguano 1146; Choctaw 104, 835, 3051, 4422, 4476, 4477; Choltí 2856; Chuchona 3592, 3593; Cora 3871; Creek 104, 2502, 2503, 4375; Cumanagoto 3324; Cuna 2483; Dakota 104, 2136, 3514, 4428; Delaware 104, 1587, 2478, 2507, 4499, 4502, 4503; Eskimo 104, 1750, 3187, 3188, 3384, 4095; Ettchaottine 538-544, 3493; Guaraní 1395, 3637; Huastec 4078, 4079; Inuktitut 2873; Iroquois 3108; Ixil 1307; Kalispel 920; Kekchí 1174, 1306, 2028, 2470, 2818, 3320, 3321, 4302; Laguna 2753; Lillooet 924; Malecite 104, 3439; Micmac 3437, 3438; Miskito 3984, Mixe 1111, 3419, 3420; Mohawk 104, 1206; Monsoni 2091; Montagnais 188, 2366-2368; Mosetena 1998; Munsee 4360; Nahuatl 215, 267, 268, 439, 440, 923, 1057, 2361, 2408, 2574, 3165, 3166, 3319, 3557, 3558, 3561, 4185; Natick 1409, 1410; Nez Perce 104, 3922; Nipissing 2649-2651; Okanagan 924; Onondaga 167; Orejónes 1642; Otomí 2491, 3043, 3219, 3428, 4492; Pacóas 1642; Pajalate 1642; Pausanes 1642; Pokomchí 65, 1305, 4302; Quechua 623, 3112; Quiché 3111, 3682, 4295; Quiripí 3269; Santee 1411; Seneca 104, 4480; Sheshel 924, 925; Shuswap 924, 925; Slayamen 924; Snohomish 567; Squamish 924, 925; Stalo 924; Tacaná 921; Tarahumara 4086; Tarascan 922, 4097; Thompson 3100; Tilijayas 1642; Timucua 2979; Totonac 1316; Tsattine 1647-1649, 2250; Tsimshian 3539, 4511; Tukkuthkutchin 2683, 2684-2689; Tzeltal 2826; Tzutuhil 4296; Warau 3413; Winnebago 2679; Yucatec 34, 104, 373, 374, 391, 903, 1081, 1315, 1550-1552, 1555, 1627, 1807, 1997, 2243, 2349, 3221-3225, 3538, 3559, 3560, 3644, 3646-3653; Zapotec 1476, 2434, 2616, 3497; Zoque 191, 1304, 3172, 3173, 3175, 3562. See also Apostles Creed, Bible, Book of Common Prayer, confessionary, devotionary, hymnal, Lord's Prayer

chronology 2703, 2907, 2914, 3015, 3782
Chuba, M. 1311
Chuchona 980, 3592, 3593
Chukchi 1228
Chulituqui 2584
Chulupí 2331. See Vilela
Chumash 582
Chumeto. See Chumtéya
Chumtéya 1662, 1663
Chumulu 3309. See also Dorasque
churches 2413, 2469
Cibola 2038
Cichiti 1482
Cinacantlán. See Zinacantan
Cincinnati 1063, 4443
Cincinnati Society of Natural History 2220
Cincinnati Tablet 1063
Cintla. See Centla
Cirenaica. See Cyrenaica
Cirerol, M. 1309
Cisneros, J. A. D. 2479
Cisulc uceluswocn agenudasic 3432
citizenship. See political anthropology
Ciudad Real, A. 1956
Ciudad Real, Mexico 174
Clallam 1672. See also Salish
clan. See social organziation
class system 2121
Claymont, DE 1183
cliff dwellers 3080
climate 1251, 1490, 3168, 3973
Clinton, D. 1909
cloisonnée 345
Co, B. 1305
Coahuila, Mexico 2510, 4068
Coahuiltecan. See Karankawa, Pacaos, Pakawa, Tonkawa
coal mines 3938
Cobán, Guatemala 397, 1080, 1110, 1174, 1175, 1176, 1291, 1305, 1306, 2028, 2470, 2818, 3321, 3827, 4302, 4497, 4292, 4293
Cochiti, NM 3987
Cockenoe-de-Long Island 4160
Codex Campos. See codices, Campos
Codex Cortesianus. See codices, Madrid

Codex Troano. *See* codices, Madrid
codices 211-213, 1498, 1572, 1574, 1576,
1578-1583, 1763, 1828, 2575, 2576,
3096, 3263, 3712-3714, 3786, 3787,
3789, 3795, 3800, 4005, 4116, 4119;
Becker 1071; Borgia 3787; Boturini
1072; Campos 4005; Dresden 1075,
1572, 1576, 1581-1583, 1828, 3713,
3797; Fernández Leal 1076; Florentine
3658-3660; Ixtlilxochitl 1382; Madrid
611, 693, 998, 999, 1022, 1073, 1074,
1513, 4109, 4110, 4125; Mendocino
3211; Mexicano 439, 440; Paris 2575;
Perez 391; Ramírez 2021, 3263; Rios
1077; Telleriano-Remensis 1077;
Vaticanus 1077
Coeslin, Germany 3071
coffee 3894
Cofradia de Jesus Nazareno 3174
Cofradia de la Nuestra Senora de Rosario
2468, 3174
Cofradia de la Santa Cruz 3174
Coiba 387. *See also* Cueva
Colden, C. 1909
Colegio Catolica de Mérida 2479
Colini, G.A. 525
collections: Abbott 12; Ambraser 2029;
Aubin 2579; Catlin 662; Emmons 476;
Guesende 2634; Halliwell-Phillipps
3891; Hemenway 2654; Latimer 2635;
Mitchell 919; Muñoz 4294; Nave 3037;
Newbold 3052; Pinedo 1878; Ray
2638; Sarg 397; Tyskiewicz 1237;
Uhde 1869
College of Physicians of Philadelphia
2677
Collitz, H. 3118
Cologne, Germany 3708
Colombia 201, 1773, 3012, 3218, 3519,
3520, 3768, 3632, 4066
colonialism 33, 2981
Colorado 280, 3080, 3128, 3865
Colorado River, NV 1652, 2183, 4463,
4467
colors 1651, 1810; color cognition 3994;
color symbolism 1030
Columbia River, OR 4094
Columbia University 929
Columbian Historical Exposition at
Madrid. *See* expositions
Columbus, Christopher 54, 609, 632, 811,

1105, 1212-1214, 1795, 1912, 4274
Comalis 1897
Comanche 2585
Combe, W. 2548
Comitán, Mexico 3678
commerce 2431, 3452, 3516, 4438
Commission Scientifique du Mexique. *See*
expeditions
Como, Italy 3494
Comox 480. *See also* Salish
Comte, A. 2
Conchilla Valley, CA 583
Confessionary, Allemtíak 4260; Chibcha
1768, 4251; Chilidugi 1471; Choltí
2856; Cora 3871; Cumanagota 3324;
Kekchí 2470; Mixe 3419, 3420;
Nahuatl 90, 1107, 4282; Natick 1409;
Pokomchí 1110, 2470; Tojolabal 983;
Yucatec 1081; Zapotec 2616, 3497.
See also Christian doctrine
congresses 3131; Hispanic American
Pedagogical Congress 2167; Internal
Prision Congress 3440; International
Congress of Americanists 236, 238, 239,
667, 684, 685, 753, 1800, 1928, 1971,
2173-2178, 3189, 3200, 4352; Inter-
national Congress of Anthropology, Prehistoric Archaeology, and Zoology
1113, 2179, 2180, 2922, 3821; Inter-
national Congress of Ethnographic
Sciences 1112; International Congress
of Orientalists 2181, 2377; International Geological Congress 2711;
Latin American Scientific Congress
1114, 2369
Connecticut 458, 1259, 4199
consanguinity 2868, 2871. *See also* kinship
conscience. *See* psychology
Conservatorio Yucateca 2479
Cook, J. 918
Cook, P. S. 1421
Cooper's Creek, Australia 3680
Copán, Honduras 193, 1754, 1755, 1867,
2628, 2670, 2796, 3668, 4042
Copanaguastla, Mexico 174
Cope, E. D. 1123, 2777
copper 11, 1218, 1326, 2446, 2448, 2628,
3145, 3392. *See also* metals
Copper Age 3213
Coptic 2960

Cora 831
Cora, G. 2080
Cordoba, Spain 1118
corn. *See* maize
Coroado 1987, 1988
Coronado Expedition. *See* expeditions
Coronado, F. V. de 1265, 4463, 4464
Corozal, Belize 1550-1552
Correze 1088
Cortés, H. *11*, 398, 1148-1152, 2416,
    2490, 3344, 3857, 4093
Corumbá 523
Corwin (ship) 4241
cosmology 27, 1032, 2280, 2745, 2845,
    3241
Costa Rica 76, 78, 181, 384, 388, 412, 438,
    658, 1308, 1456, 1479, 1483, 1486, 1533,
    1601-1609, 1617, 1618, 2839, 3214,
    3215, 3313-3316, 3973, 4103, 4104,
    4269, 4359. *See also* Central America
Cosumni Indians 2848. *See also* California
Cotheal, A. I. 388
Coto. *See* Boruca, Orejón
Cotton States International Exposition. *See*
    expositions
Cotzal, Guatemala 1307
Courcelle, Mr. de 3158
courtship 1833. *See also* marriage
Coy, D. 4292, 4293
Coyaghtun 1471
crania. *See* skeletal remains
cranial deformation 2601. *See also* defor-
    mation
cranial sutures 3536
craniometry. *See* skeletal remains
Crécy, France 2913
Crédito Nacional Hipotecario de
    Guatemala 3919
Cree. *See* Chippewa
Creek 104, 307, 652, 686, 810, 1538, 1659,
    1664, 1936, 2040, 2501, 2502, 2503,
    2808, 3342, 3578, 3579, 3613, 4375
cremation 1793, 1794. *See also* mortuary
    customs
Creoles 3764
Crete 940, 3809
Creuse, France 1088
Crichaná 3587
criminology 2236, 2537, 2538, 2893,
    3993, 4002
Cromberger, J. 3429

Crónica Chac-Xulub-Chen 3186
Crónica de la Campana 398
Crónica Mexicana 91
Crump Burial Cave, AL 818
Crux Chen 391
crystal 442
Cuautla, Mexico 2486
Cuba 386, 1585, 2577, 2858, 3084, 3265
Cudena, P. 2973
Cuelpa 3631
Cuera 387
Cueva 384, 397
Cuevas, J. M. 3378
Cuevas, L. G. 3378
Cuisick, D. 349
Culbin Sands, England 445
Culin, S. 3118
Cullen, E. 387
cultural ecology 2631, 3360
Cumaná, Venezuela 933
Cumanagota. *See* Cumanagoto
Cumanagoto 3324, 3632
Cumberland Sound, Canada 467
Cuna 384, 387, 2483, 3307, 3308
Cunacuna. *See* Cuna
Cundinamarca, Colombia 3218, 4501
Cunza 3671
Cuoq, J. A. 1052, 3327
cups 3472
cup-stones 2447
currency 1193, 1708, 1852, 3261, 4380
Curupira 1926
Cusco. *See* Cuzco
Cushing, F. H. 167, 339
Cushiquilica 1051
Cusi-Kcuylor 3072
Cutusuma, Bolivia 4225
Cuyahoga Valley, OH 4392
Cuzco, Peru 2584, 2807
Cyrenaica, Libya 557, 3332
Cyrus 4383

d'Albaigne, A. 1874
d'Albaigne, F. 1874
d'Olarte, D. de 4093
d'Orbigny, A. D. 407, 2331
Dahomey 3705
Dakota 44, 104, 119, 599, 816, 817, 899,
    1345, 1353, 1390, 1411, 1540, 1541,
    1544, 1548, 1621, 1817, 1818, 2136,
    2443, 2444, 2562, 2937, 3044, 3284,

3341, 3514, 3541-3544, 3590, 4428, 4429, 4430
Dall, W. H. 1232
Dalrymple, E. A. 2619
Daly, Chief Justice 2100
Danakil 1730
dance dramas 1529; Cortes 397, 4497; Caxlan Queh 397; Güegüence 226, 752; Uaxteca 397; Moros y Cristianos 397; Snake 577, 1493, 1494; Tablet 577; Zaccicoxol 4497. *See also* drama
Dards 2378
Darien, Panama 384, 387, 2076, 2483, 3295, 3522
Darnell, R. *31*
Darwin, C. *1, 2*
Darwin Memorial Meeting 3361
Darwinism 3361
Davenport, IA 3385, 3386
Davenport Academy of Sciences 2066
Dawkins, B. 3030
Dawkins, W. B. 2774
Dayak 1622, 1702, 1966
De Tracy, Mr. 3158
deformation 205. *See also* cranial deformation
deities 682, 750, 1575, 1811, 2611, 3712, 3714, 3795, 3797; ancestor deities, 4048; God D, 1513. *See also* religion
Delafield, J. 1072
Delaware 5, 11, 104, 754, 771, 1182, 1183, 1267, 1452, 1587, 2217, 2478, 2507, 2534
Delaware Indians 3202, 3941, 4358, 4499, 4494, 4495, 4497, 4498
Delaware River Valley 7-10, 167, 2777, 3184, 3839
Delgado, E. 66
Delgado, N. 903
delusions. *See* psychology
Demerara, Guyana 1425
Demeter 1831
demography 2568, 2643, 3012, 3022, 3023, 3615, 3973, 3987, 4285. *See also* vital statistics
Demotic 2954. *See also* Egyptian
Dene. *See* Na-Dene
Deniker, J. 2151, 3565
Denmark 3083, 4008-4010, 4278
dentition 1128, 1332, 1333, 3126, 3127, 4132, 4171. *See also* physical anthropology

Derby, I. C. 3081
dermatology 2927. *See also* phyical anthropology
descent 2868, 2869. *See also* kinship
Desjardins, E. 1275
Deutschen Wissenschaftlichen Verein zu Santiago, Chile 4059
devotionary 1550-1552. *See also* Christian doctrine
Dhammapada 2938
Dhegiha. *See* Cegiha
Diaz Gebuta Queh, F. 2748-2750
Diaz, J. 4093
Diaz, P. 4324
dice. *See* games and gaming
dictionary. *See* vocabulary
Diede, C. 2130
Diegueño 4394
Dieseldorff, E. P. 3716
Diez de Bonilla, M. 3378
Digger Indians 1673
Dindjie. *See* Na-Dene
Diria. *See* Mangue
discovery. *See* European exploration
disease 87, 500, 1866. *See also* scarlet fever, syphilis
distillation 570
District of Columbia. *See* Washington, DC
divination 574
divining rod. *See* dowsing
Dixon's Entrance, British Columbia 1327
Djelma 1718
Djemschid 993
dodecahedron 2886
dogs 3036
dolls 1415, 1502
domestic architecture. *See* architecture
Domínguez y Argaiz, F.E. 1081
Dominican Republic 1505
Dominicans. *See* religious orders
dominoes. *See* games and gaming
Donaldson, T. 928
Doniphan Expedition. *See* expeditions
Dononville, Mr. de 3159
Dorasque 1600, 3303, 3309
Dorchester County, MD 2777
Dorobgne, France 1088
Dorsey, J. O. 3543
Douglas, J. 4108
Douin, Mr. 563
Dousman, G. G. 2351

dowsing 3835
drama 69, 226, 673, 674, 752, 2479, 2593, 2595, 2807, 2823, 3072, 3103, 3104, 3382. *See also* dance dramas
Dravidian languages 4307
drills and drilling 2727, 3449, 3460
Dropmore 3013
Druids 3502
Duck Creek, WI 1242
Dupaix, G. 271
Duponceau, P. 4494
Duquesne, J. D. 3520
Durham 2779
Durham Cave, PA 2777
Durieu, P. 924, 1739, 1740
Durocher, F. 1052
Dutch New Guinea. *See* Netherlands New Guinea
Duval County, FL 4108
dwarfs 206, 1857, 1858, 3816. *See also* pygmies
Dwason, G. M. 4222
dwellings 504, 2099, 2867, 3183, 4218
Dymock, England 1920

earthquakes 3970
East Hampton, NY 4159
East Indian archipelago. *See* East Indies
East Indies 2798, 2835
Easter Island 1121, 3297, 4090
Eastman, E. 3755
Easton, M. W. 3118
Ebers, G. 2949
Echarati 2584
Eckart, A. 2973
economics 3193
Ecuador 1748, 3276, 4066, 4469
Edinburgh, Scotland 2553
education 448, 1058, 2429, 2940
Edwards, A. 388
effigy mounds 2441, 2449-2451. *See also* Mound Builders
effigy pottery 1264, 1294. *See also* pottery
Egypt 167, 513, 711, 1558, 1873, 1942, 2481, 2528, 2949, 2955-2960, 3506, 3508, 3981, 4146, 4275, 4346
Egyptian 13-19, 2954. *See also* Demotic
El Amarna, Egypt 2197
El Salvador 388, 1634, 1635, 3198, 3515, 3914, 3938, 3954, 3955, 3973, 4088. *See also* Central America
electricity 1646
Elginshire, England 445
Eliot, J. 1389, 4160, 4168
Elk Mystery. *See* ceremonies
Emerillon 1162
Emmons Collection. *See* collections
Emory, W. H. 1422
emotions. *See* psychology
Encarnación Avila, M. 391
encaustic 3693
Enchanted Mesa, NM 2037
Encomienda 906
endocannibalism. *See* anthropophagy
England 3886
English 2388, 2500, 2604, 2829; Australian 2388; Pidgin 2388; South African 2388; West Indian 2388
Enriquez, J. A. 434
Enriquez, M. 2834
environment 2107, 2623, 3360
Eocene 1130
epigraphy. *See* inscriptions, writing systems
Erman, Prof. 14
Ernantez Arana Xahila, F. 2748-2750
Escalante Fontaneda, H. de 3918
Escuintla, Guatemala 192, 3894
Eskimo 295, 361, 459, 467, 469, 474, 475, 485, 490, 491, 579, 805, 1226, 1231, 1232, 1398, 1427, 1684, 1759, 1986, 2045, 2059, 2060, 2106, 2111, 2113, 2487, 2508, 2548, 2640, 2883, 2937, 2965-2970, 3178, 3248, 3280, 3296, 3547, 3548, 3550, 3552, 3553, 4374, 4385; Alaska 3767; Central 470, 496; Greenland 104, 1461, 2254, 3251-3254, 3549, 3554; Hudson's Bay 3187, 3188; Labrador 2254, 3142, 3384, 4095; Point Barrow 2965, 2968; Western 2969, 3878, 4214
Eskimo-Aleut. *See* Aleut, Eskimo, Inuktitut
Eskimoan. *See* Aleut, Eskimo
Esmeraldas province, Ecuador 4469
Espinosa, A. 3429
Estala, P. 387
Estrada de Salvago, J. 1308
Estrada y Zenca, J. 2479
Estrella Indians 1604, 4103
Etchemin. *See* Malecite
ethics 29, 4364

Ethiopia 560, 3026
ethnicity 3566
ethnobotany 219, 399, 575, 794, 884, 946,
1170, 1171, 1322, 1323, 1468, 1495,
18191838, 1915-1917, 2411, 2110,
2158, 2659, 3225, 3777. *See also* botany
ethnocide 1059
ethnography 145-147, 225, 455, 456, 728,
597, 1084, 1447, 1495, 1655, 1657, 1806,
1824, 1826, 1854, 1863, 1900, 1972,
1973, 2039, 2151, 2353, 2681, 2798,
2867, 2932, 2980, 3185, 3200, 3273,
3412, 3525, 3526, 3545, 3601, 3611,
3850, 4011, 4343; Abnaki 2184, 2672,
3060, 4291; Africa 942, 2522; Africa,
East 2529; Africa, North 1464; Alaska
1231, 2063, 2186, 3292; Algeria 2105;
Algonkin 750, 3753, 3757; Amazon
3584; Apache 572, 1141; Araucanians
2508, 2740, 3873; Arawak 748; Argentina 2929; Arikara 2872; Arizona
1511, 1803, 2049; Asia 975, 1720; Asia,
West 727; Atnah 3305; Auca 2401;
Australia 844, 3150, 3622; Aymara
1565; Baffinland 491; Bella Coola 495;
Beothuk 2692; Berbers 422, 1709,
3226; Biloxi 1354; Bismarck Archipelago 1711; Boissy Island 1716;
Bolivia 872, 4415; Bosnia 4468; Botocudo 3528; Brazil 871, 1400, 1451,
1485, 1777, 2426, 2617, 2618, 2928;
British Guiana 622, 2157, 2159, 2160,
3589; Cacaopera 2755; Caduveos
517, 521, 525; Cahuilla 583; Cakchiquel 398; California 1044, 2048, 2049,
2051, 2364, 2509, 3364, 3451, 3769,
3770; Canada 493, 778-782, 852-861,
1840, 1845, 1865, 2359, 4219-4222;
Cape Bathurst 2106; Cape Flattery
4072; Carib 2285; Caribbean 2161,
3612; Cayuga 1320; Central America
401, 402, 513, 3583; Ceram 3333;
Chamacoco 517, 522, 1721; Chemakum 483; Cherokee 307, 1043, 1317,
1588; China 3726; Chinook 463, 464,
484; Chippewa 1138, 2052; Chiriqui
398; Choctaw 307, 1833; Chukchi
1228; Coeur d'Alene 3867; Colombia
3518, 3519; Comalis 1897; Comox
480; Costa Rica 1617, 1618,
3214-3316; Cosumni 2848; Creek

307, 1659, 2040; Crow 3867; Cuba
1585; Cuna 1618; Dakota 119, 599,
899, 1345, 1352, 1356, 1357, 1390, 1357,
1539, 1541, 1546, 1548, 2562, 2722,
3044, 3542, 3867; Danakil 1730; Dards
2378; Dayak 1702; Delaware 4501;
Ecuador 3276; Eskimo 431, 459, 467,
469, 470, 474-476, 485, 496, 805, 1684,
2061, 2106, 2111, 2965-2970, 3142,
3178, 3547, 3549, 3551, 3552, 4385;
Europe 3563; Flathead 3867; France
908; Fraser River 505; Galla 1722;
Garífuna 398; Ghiliaks 1269; Great
Britain 1446, 1919, 2357; Greenland
2061; Guaicurí 520; Guatemala 513,
3684, 3719, 4051, 4057; Guayaquí
2372; Guaycurú 525; Haida; Hano
Pueblo 1523; Havasupai 3852; Hidatsa
2655, 2656; Hindustan 1725; Hopi
1512, 1518, 2110; Housatonic Valley
3116; Hudson's Bay 2228, 3642;
Huichol 2513; Hunza 2380; Huron
1062, 3362; Illinois 1888; India 324,
325, 1954; Indonesia 3742; Iowa
1615; Iroquois 1360, 1839, 2321, 2583,
3162, 3756; Jivaro 3505; Juniata 1816;
Kafirs 2378; Kansas 1346; Kekchí
397; Klamath 1667, 1668; Korea
3608; Kwakiutl 462, 468, 494, 1247;
Labrador 2015; Lacandon 397, 2405;
Lapps 553; Lenca 3928; Lifou 1270;
Loyalty Islands 1272; Lucayan 790;
Makak 1727; Mandan 2667; Mangue
695; Matto Grosso 517, 2928; Matty
Island 2533; Mbayá 525; Melanesia
1708, 1710; Mexico 513, 1626, 1868,
2931, 3120, 4080, 4088, 4093, 4299;
Micmac 297, 3432, 3443; Miconinovi
1515; Minas Geraes 821; Miskito
1474; Missouri Valley 1939; Mixe
1614; Modoc 2739; Mohave 82;
Mohawk 1320; Mohegan 1259;
Mohave 1141; Montagnais 2015;
Moqui Pubelo 577, 1318, 1499; Nahua
432; Nanaimo 486; Naskapi 2015;
Natchez 429; Naugatuck Valley 3116;
Navaho 481, 2657-2661, 2663, 2665,
3853; Nevada 2049; New Britain
1704; New England 1941, 1945; New
Guinea 1703, 1706, 1711, 1716, 2519;
New Holland 2523; New Ireland

1715; New Jersey 3046; Nez Perce 1418; Nicaragua 3199; Nicobar island 1717, 1719; Nootka Sound 2201; North America 420, 927, 928, 2344, 2567, 2643, 2662, 3168, 3863, 4350, 4395; Northwest Coast 794, 1381, 1628; Oceania 323, 3742; Omaha 1347, 1348, 1349, 1542, 1545, 1547; Oneida 1320; Onondaga 1320; Oraibi 1516; Oregon 479, 2757; Orinoco River 1809; Osage 1341, 1351; Panama 3295, 3522; Papua New Guinea 1954; Paraguay 518, 519, 2372; Passamaquoddy 297, 1501, 3376, 3377; Pawnee 2900; Pequot 1259; Peru 1324, 3427, 4415; Pima 1803; Pokom 4053; Ponca 1347; Popoluca 398; Pororóca 604; Powhatan 3340; Pueblo Indians 1318; Quechua 1325; Queen Charlotte's Island 2051; Querandí 3135, 3136; Quetaré 658; Quiché 398; Red River Settlement 1467; Río Napo 1313; Romania 3610; Roraima 2158; Russia 3568, 3569, 4254; Salish 492; Santo Domingo Pueblo 577; Seneca 1320, 2792, 3673; Shetimasha 1674; Shuswap 478, 1249; Sia 1494; Siberia 1726; Sierra Madre 2512; Siksika 1846; Siletz 1344; South America 513, 3123, 3268, 3479, 3855, 4396; Takulli 2875; Tasmania 3617; Teton 1353; Texas 554; Thailand 3607; Tibet 1473; Tierra del Fuego 2150, 2504; Timucua 694; Tlingit 167, 1327; Toda 2599; Totonac 398; Trobriand Islands 1827; Tsimshian 471; Tunisia 424; Tupí 1169; Tusayan 1493, 1494, 1496, 1502-1504, 1514, 1517, 1519, 1520, 1524-1527; Tuscarora 1320, 1816, 2203; Tzotzil 397; United States 1319, 1853; United States, Southwest 248, 1497, 2433; Walpi 1521, 1522; Washington 479; Wisconsin 4049; Yahgan 3192; Yaqui 3061; Yuit 1228; Yukon 1248; Yuma 1141; Zapotec 1614; Zoque 398, 1614; Zuni 578, 1497, 1499, 2811
ethnohistory 1637, 1639, 1996, 2221, 2342, 2412, 2415, 2482, 2489, 2588, 2754, 2839, 3790, 3872, 4096, 4109, 4184, 4188, 4279, 4491. *See also* history

Ethnologisches Notizblatt 1448-1450
ethnology 127, 134-136, 167, 455, 531, 555, 593-596, 617, 692, 744, 799, 877, 1078, 1089, 1090, 1099, 1179, 1321, 1426, 1497, 1685, 1687, 1688, 1760, 1782, 1784, 1823, 2041, 2042, 2082, 2116, 2119, 2234, 2239, 2241, 2263-2265, 2277, 2475, 2521, 2630, 2737, 2866, 2885, 2997, 2999, 3032, 3118, 3233, 3347, 3348, 3357, 3381, 3409, 3444, 3445, 3447, 3491, 3535, 3599, 3745, 3746, 3752, 3771, 3819, 3823, 3832, 3912, 3923, 3931, 4023-4026, 4029-4031, 4230, 4253, 4276, 4349, 4355, 4367, 4381, 4399, 4413, 4427; and anthropology 640, 1729; and ethics 29; and folklore 1745, 4032; and history 660; and linguistics 1492, 2116, 4398, 4399; and mythology 330; and physical anthropology 4326; and political science 3346, 4029; and psychology 330, 4297; and religion 2235, 3598; and sociology 1489, 1490, 3923, 4297; history 26, 28, 31, 311, 312, 314, 315, 318-321, 326; methods 30, 214, 328; 331. *See also* anthropology
Etritrea 560
Etruria 848
Etruscans 167, 556, 659, 661, 705, 1606, 2000, 2273, 2274, 2425, 2945, 3055, 3063, 3814
Ettchaottine 538-544, 1758, 2245, 2251, 3493
Ettwein, J. 4493
etymology 167, 713, 717, 945, 991, 1001, 1358, 1432, 1435, 2044, 2103, 2237, 2340, 2613, 2960, 3046, 3170, 3190, 3201, 3211, 3325, 3626, 3774, 3845, 3988, 4158, 4159, 4161, 4199. *See also* linguistics; toponyms
Eudeve 3870
Euphrates River 793
Europe 724, 1098, 1155, 1256, 2042, 2266, 2268, 2774, 2788, 2905, 2949, 2962, 3002, 3022, 3023, 3213, 3461, 3473, 3563, 3565, 3567, 3706, 3816; Central 3740; East 3064; Northern 516
European exploration 33, 351, 353-363, 398, 563, 580, 815, 870, 904, 915, 971, 978, 1144, 1159-1162, 1164, 1178,

1186, 1188, 1213, 1258, 1279, 1477, 1483, 1567, 1610, 1821, 1911–1914, 1940, 1977, 2127, 2561, 2806, 2808, 2972, 2988, 3062, 3067, 3146, 3194, 3195, 3268, 3342, 3408, 3522, 3661, 3865, 3950, 3960, 4013, 4141, 4231, 4274. *See also* expeditions

Euskarienne 1001

Evans, J. 2215

evil spirit. *See* Curupira

evolution *1*, 1124–1127, 1131, 1135, 1240, 1266, 1469, 1630, 1825, 2154–2156, 2360, 2375, 2573, 2893, 2902, 2994, 3125, 3352

Ewbank, T. 4395

exogamy 2737. *See also* kinship

expeditions, Commission Scientifique du Mexique 2342; Coronado Expedition 4461; Doniphan Expedition 4467; Exploring Expedition to the Rocky Mountains 1607; Geographical and Geological Survey of the Rocky Mountain Region 4237; Geographical Survey West of the 100th Meridian 4238, 4239; Hemenway Southwestern Archaeological Expedition 249, 339, 1499; Jesup Expedition 3875; Kinney Expedition 4386, Northwestern Archaeological Survey 2452; Mission Scientifique au Caucase 2865; Office of Explorations and Surveys 2183; Pepper-Heart Expedition 1220; Roraima Expedition 2158; Sioux Expedition 4372; Sonora Expedition 4386; United States Exploring Expedition 1854

Exploring Expedition to the Rocky Mountains. *See* expeditions

Exposición Centro Americana de Guatemala. *See* expositions

Exposición Histórico-Americana. *See* expositions

Exposition Internationale de Paris. *See* expositions

expositions, Chicago Exposition 4448; Columbian Historical Exposition at Madrid, 733, 2109, 2763, 3091; Cotton States International Exposition 56; Exposición Centro Americana de Guatemala 1456; Exposición Histórico-Americana 1458, 3214; Exposition Internationale de Paris 3199, 3208;

Ohio Centennial 3101; Ohio Valley and Central States Exposition 4443; Paris Exposition of 1889 4441; Universal Exposition of Paris 3624; World Columbian Exposition of 1893 3405, 3880, 4472, 4473; World's Fair Congress of Anthropology 2077

Eyiguayegi. *See* Guaicurú

faith healing 1172

Falkner, T. 407

Fan t'an 1200

fans 819

fauna 3128, 3129

feathers and featherworking 1271, 1512, 3091, 3785

Fellechner, A. M. 388

feminism 3724

Fergusson, D. 4467

Fernández de Quros, P. 2022

Fessan, Libya 557

festivals 3997

fetishism 312, 1215, 1221

fetus 1368

Field Columbian Museum. *See* museums

figurines 1465, 3099, 3697. *See also* pottery

filibusters 3220

Finland 553, 3083, 4330

fire 2111–2113

Fischer, A. *11*

fishing 3473, 3865, 4241; fish-hooks 3403; fishing stations 4163

Five Nations. *See* Iroquois

Flatey Book 1537

Flathead. *See* Kalispel

Fletcher, R. 1979

Fleury, Claude 3646

Flinders, P. W. M. 711

flint 4, 568, 1819, 1904, 1942, 2120, 2768, 2905, 3448, 4107. *See also* lithics

Flores, B. 4078

Florida 38, 85, 167, 307, 694, 695, 1220, 1311, 1361, 1363, 1393, 1645, 1764, 1835, 2283, 2354, 2764, 3342, 3471, 3582, 3804, 3837, 3872, 3833–3836, 3918, 4108, 4379, 4488

flutes 1521

folk medicine 2047

folklore 167, 657, 663, 681, 964, 970, 1173, 1745, 1921, 2356, 2554, 3491,

3996, 4032; Abnaki 3060; Aleut 3299; Algonkin 2384, 3753; Araucanian 2403; Australasia 1716; Brazil 1787; Canada 3241, 3242, 3247; Chippewa 2016, 2050, 3949; Creek 1664; Dakota 1353; Delaware 3941; Eskimo 474, 475, 2259, 2883, 2965, 3547, 3548, 3552, 3878; Europe 724; Guatemala 289; Hitchiti 1664; Ireland 2847; Italy 3367-3370; Kwakiutl 494; Mauritius 227; Mexico 735, 2586, 3090, 3092, 3093, 3209, 3801; Micmac 2383, 3435, 3436; Mississaga 943; Moqui Pueblo 4039; North America 472, 944, 945, 953-957, 1799, 2493, 3695, 4271; Osage 1351; Passamaquoddy 1501, 2383; Pennsylvania Germans 2046, 4000; Pennsylvania 732; Penobscot 2383; Peru 1788; Philadelphia 3262; Scotland 1778; Tsets'aut 508; Tsimshian 509; Venezuela 1437, 1438; Yucatan 664. *See also* Brer Rabbit, mythology, oral history
Folklore Society 1564
food quest 2625, 2626
Forbes, D. 407
Forchammer, E. 3323
forensic anthropology 4442. *See also* physical anthropology
Forest River shellheap, MA 3396
Förstemann, E. 1075
Fort Ancient, OH 2852
Fort Leavenworth, KS 1421
Fort Ransom, ND 2447
Fort Smith, AR 4467
Fort Snelling, MN 1390
fortifications 3631. *See also* warfare
Fortnightly Club for the Study of Anthropology 1586
fossil man 1256, 1365, 1366, 1374, 1596, 1744, 2119, 2374, 2598, 2606, 2608, 2892, 3461. *See also* physical anthropology
Fou-Sang 1142
Fox 2695
Fox River 1675. *See also* Illinois, Wisconsin
France 342, 513, 908, 1088, 1091, 1874, 2903, 2982, 3246, 3724
Franciscans. *See* religious orders
Franklin, B. 1909
Frantzius, A. von 1635

Fraser River, Canada 505
Free Masonry 2423
French 1412, 1590. *See also* Romance languages
Fröbel, J. 388
Frontenac, L. de B. 3157
Fuertes, E. A. 407
fur trade 1187, 2548
Furman, G. 1273
Furnhelm, J. 1232

Gabb, W. M. 387
Gabilis 437
Gabon 1876
Gage, T. 409
Galaviz, A. H. 3211
Galindo, J. 388
Galla 1722
Gallatin, A. *4,* 1379
Gallego, L. 4294
Galloway, Scotland 1778
Galvez, M. 2856
Gambia 1070
gambling. *See* games and gaming
games and gaming 1192, 1197-1200, 2052, 2162, 2658, 4215, 4216
García Icazbalceta, J. 391, 2021
García Montero, J. M. 2479
Gard province, France 3271
Garífuna 388, 398, 413, 1981, 1982. *See also* Carib
Garin, A. M. 2355
Garson, J. G. 3617
Gates, W. E. *13, 14*
Gauchos, 1054
Gaul 513, 3246, 3502, 3665
Gavarrete, J. 841, 1119, 3894, 4258, 4301, 4338
gems 513
Genesee region, NY 1905, 3159
Geneva Oriental Congress 1679
Genf 2267
Genin, A. 1763
Gennaken. *See* Puelche
Geographical and Geological Survey of the Rocky Mountain Region. *See* expeditions
Geographical Club of Philadelphia 1682, 1683
Geographical Survey West of the 100th Meridian. *See* expeditions

geography *2,* 1083, 1749, 1802, 1975, 1976, 2129, 2130, 2271, 2702, 2809, 2810, 2814, 2948, 3443-3447; Africa 4391; Argentina 2492; Brazil 1405, 2540; California 4223; Canada 1253, 3425; Central America 1562, 3973; Chiapas 3311; China 3729-3735; Colombia 3218; Costa Rica 1601, 1602; Dakota 1817; El Salvador 3914; Guatemala 398, 1675-1677, 2221, 3688; India 3118; Labrador 3143; Mexico 406, 2931, 3120, 3311, 3365, 3629; Middle East 1818; Nicaragua 2437, 3194, 3195; North America 3168; Paraguay 520, Peru 3959, 3964; Sonora 3629; South America 1790; Tsimshian 1336; Yucatan 398, 896; medical 1791

geology *1,* 513, 1136, 1245, 1253, 1254, 1372, 1614, 1734, 1774, 2064, 2504, 2696, 2702, 2715-2719, 2723, 2724, 2993, 3168, 3685, 3688, 3723, 4223

George Catlin Indian Gallery 928

Georgia Historical Society 2211

Georgia 307, 2205-2207, 2209, 2211, 2212

Gerba 425

Gerland, G. 4349

German 2390, 2500, 2829, 3639, 4455

Germany 802, 1902, 1931, 2082, 2276, 2370, 2539, 3083, 3751, 4330

Ghiliaks 1269

Gibbs, G. 1232, 3155

Giglioli, E. H. 1313

Gila River, AZ 1421

Gilbert Islands 1104

Gilii, F. S. 2973

Gilman, B. I. 1497

Gimeno Echeverría, F. 2827

Girard, C. 3865

glaciation 232, 1250, 1251, 1359, 1595, 2078, 2698, 2705, 2707, 2708, 2713, 2983, 2993, 2994, 4188, 4444, 4481-4485. *See also* Aletsch Glacier

Gladston, W. S. 2348

Glazier, Capt. 2007

Gloucestershire, England 1920

gnat worship 4347. *See also* religion

Goajira 935

Goajire. *See* Goajira

Gobeo de Vitoria, P. 441

God D. *See* deities

Gody, D. de 4093

goiter 206

gold 1604, 2076, 2283, 3133, 3471, 3481, 3940, 3948. *See also* metals

Golgota. *See* Cerro Golgata

González, F. 3421

González, L. 191

Goodman, J. T. 2668, 4112

Gordon, J. 4341

gorgets 3985

Gorilla savagei 1368

Goths 345

government. *See* political anthropology

Governor's Island, NY 369

Goyaz. *See* Carayá

Graham Island, British Columbia 2547

Graham, A. 194

grammar 71, 123, 124, 220, 1995, 2500, 3164, 4018, 4036; Abipón 52; Achagua 3616; Algonkin 4202; Allemtíak 4260; Arawak 1884; Bakaïrí 4012; Bauré 2556; Cágaba 936; Cakchiquel 1560, 1819, 4056, 4186, 4301; Campas 2362; Carib 51, 620; Chiapanec 46, 67, 68, 380; Chibcha 1768, 4251; Cree 43, 274, 2093, 2122, 2139, 3243; Chiquita 39; Choltí 2856; Chorotega 389; Cora 3871; Creek 652, 810; Cumangoto 3324; 3329, 3330; Dakota 1621, 3542, 3544; Dayak 1622; Diegueño 4494; Eskimo 579, 1986; Eudeve 3870; Garífuna 1983; Goajira 935; Guaicurí 52; Guaraní 3633-3638; Haida 1907; Hidatsa 2655, 2656; Huastec 70, 1011; Huron 3349; Ipuriná 3339; Ixil 1307; Jâgare 45; Kekchi 193, 2470; Kimbundú 1041; Kiriri 50, 1623, 2570; Kwakiutl 1859; Lule 2332, 2543; Mam 3532, 3533; Mandan 1937; Mangue 389, 3581; Mbayá 52; Micmac 2557; Miskito 388, 1980; Mixe 3419; Mixtec 3529; Mocoví 52; Moxa 2580; Mutsún 189, 190; Nahuatl 182, 183, 192, 215, 875, 876, 1048, 2832, 3105, 3106, 3149, 3546, 3861, 4077, 4185, 4277, 4282, 4287; Nez-Perce 2916; Otomí 813, 3049, 3050, 3428; Páez 911; Piapoco 1184; Pokomchí 2470; Puelche 278; Quechua 125, 909, 1746, 1747, 2593, 3683; Quiché 72, 158, 608, 3382, 4186; Roucouyenne 1184; Selocae 2756; Siksika 2348, 4150; Subtibia 389;

Taensa 742, 764, 765, 1927; Tarahumara 4086; Tarascan 309, 1733, 2336, 3035; Timucua 3167; Tlingit 3248; Toba 52, 2331; Tonocoté 2543; Torres Straits 3480; Tupí 53; Tzoneca 278; Tzotzil 3628; Tzutuhil 4186; Yakima 3155; Yucatec 399, 404, 372, 607, 995, 996, 3186, 3223, 3605, 3651, 3669, 3670; Yuma 4494; Zapotec 1143, 1767, 3497, 3530; Zoque 191. *See also* linguistics
Gran Chaco 3206, 4141
Gran Pará. *See* Pará
Granada, Nicaragua 388, 3581
Granada, Spain 1118, 2738, 3977
Grand Canyon 3351, 4463
Grand Morin, France 1374
gravitation 151
Great Britain 1446, 1454, 3014, 3724
Great Lakes 2237
Great Plains 1250
Great Platte River, NE 1607
Greater Antilles. *See* Caribbean
Greece 317, 513, 1832, 2423, 3177, 4333
Greek 795, 864, 2942, 2954, 4139, 4325
Green Bay, WI 1675
Green Lake County, WI 919
Green Springs County, OH 231
Greenland 358, 1140, 2061, 2099, 2188, 2883, 2970, 3251-3253, 3549, 3554
Greenup County, KY 2465
Griffin, C. *15*
Grijalva, J. de 3625, 4093, 4195
Grijalva River, Mexico 3625
Gros Ventre 2656
Grypotherium domesticum 1932
Guadalajara, Mexico 829, 3122, 3595
Guadeloupe 1899, 2634, 3001
Guaicurí 520, 525
Guaicurú. *See* Abipon, Caduveo, Guaicurí, Mbaya, Mocovi, Toba
Guajiquero, Honduras 1992, 3945. *See also* Lenca
Guajiquiro. *See* Lenca
Gualaca. *See* Dorasque
Guaná 526
Guanahani 4274. *See also* Caribbean
Guani Islands, Peru 3935
Guaraná 88, 407, 1395, 2337, 2964
Guaraní 88, 407, 1395, 2337, 3323, 3517, 3633-3638, 4084, 4270
Guarau. *See* Warrau

Guasco. *See* Huasco
Guatelateco. *See* Cakchiquel
Guatemala 167, 216, 327, 392, 397, 398, 513, 606, 608, 612, 616, 714, 840, 1215, 1290-1295, 1307, 1308, 1376, 1408, 1612, 1625, 1640, 1675-1677, 1770, 1819, 1822, 2221, 2387, 2671, 2748-2750, 2796, 2840, 2840, 2857, 3041, 3130, 3147, 3319, 3382, 3674, 3684-3689, 3691, 3711, 3720, 3778, 3915, 3942, 3973, 3998, 4051, 4054, 4056, 4057, 4088, 4258, 4303, 4328, 4491. *See also* Alta Verapaz, Petén, Central America
Guatemala City 3042, 4093
Guatemala de Concepción de Villa Nueva. *See* Guatemala City
Guatuso 387, 408, 412, 4103, 4104
Guay, C. 167
Guayaná 172, 622, 933, 1139, 1184, 2157-2160, 3589, 4284, 4377
Guayaquí 2372
Guaycururú 525, 2328
Guaymí 412, 1600, 3303, 3306; Northern 388, 412
Guaynía River, Venezuela 2806
Güegüence. *See* dance dramas
Guenoa 2331
Guerandí 2331
Guerra, J. M. 2479
Guesende Collection. *See* collections
Guetar. *See* Talamanca
Guiana, 748, 1144, 3413-3416. *See also* Guayaná, Surinam
Guichicore, Mexico 1614
Guichiovian, Mexico 407. *See also* Mixe
guilds 2084, 2085, 4420
Gulf. *See* Natchez
Gulf Coast 4467
Gulf of Cortes 4081
Gulf of Mexico 2718
Gundestrup, Denmark 4008, 4009
Guyana 1184. *See* Guayaná
Guzmán, A. de 174
Guzmán, P. de 7
Gypsies 820

Haddon, A. C. 3480
Haebler, K. 1976
Haida 510, 1327, 1906, 1907, 2566, 4218
hair 4316

Hakonsson, J. 1537
Haldemann, S. S. 677
Hale, H. 949, 1104, 1628, 3182, 4222
Haliburton, R.G. 4222
Halliwell-Phillipps Collection. *See* collections
Hallowell, E. 3865
Halloy, d'Omalius d' 1380
Hallstatt 3039
hallucinogens 2735. *See also* snuffing tubes
Haly, Mr. 388
hammerstones 3462, 3465
Hammond, C.A. 1666
Hano 1523
Harlez, C. de 20
Harrison, A. 388
Harrisse, H. 1275
Hartland, E. S. 780
Hartman's Cave, PA 2775
Harvard University 2, 1331, 4497. *See also* museums
Harz region, Germany 4320
Hastings, T. 1106
Haupt, P. 3118
Havana, Cuba 187, 2239
Havasupai 3852
Havre 2915
Hawaii 83, 1198
Haynes, H.W. 2101
Haywood, Judge 1909
headdress 3097
Hebrew 600
Hegel, Mr. 4035
Hellas 535
Helmstedt, Germany 1765
Hemenway Collection. *See* collections
Hemenway Southwestern Archaeological Expedition. *See* expeditions
Hemming, Karl 3323
Henderson, A. *8,* 387, 1591, 2427
Henderson, G. 388
Henry, G. 2215
heredity 1630, 3125
hermaphroditism 4321
Hernandez Spina, V. 2223
Herodot 3048
Herranz y Quirosa, D. N. 3643, 3651
Herrera, A. L. 2421
Herrera Villavicencio, J. de 3653
Hertha (ship) 1178

Herve, G. 2115
Herzogovina 4468
Hess, W. 2008
Hesse, C. L. C. 388
Heve. *See* Eudeve
Hidatsa 2655, 2656
hieroglyphic writing 167, 628, 722, 2342, 2420, 2668. *See also* inscriptions, writing systems
Higginson, T.W. 2101
Hilprecht, H. V. 3118
Hindu 2084, 2085, 2347
Hindu Kush 2376, 4229
Hindustan, India 1725
Hippel, M. von 1309
Historical and Philosophical Society of Ohio 1566
history *2,* 245, 246, 598, 609, 660, 895, 3068, 3509, 3525, 3526, 3570, 3613. *See also* ethnohistory
Hitchiti 1664. *See also* Creek
Hittites 848, 2200
Hocking County, OH 153
Hodgson, W. B. 1936
Hoernes, M. 4468
Hokaltecan. *See* Subtiaba
Hokan. *See* Chumash, Digueño, Havasupai, Mohave, Salinan
Holland. *See* Netherlands
Holm, G. 3548
Holmul, Guatemala 391
Honduras 388, 398, 413, 1149, 1308, 1634, 1635, 1754–1756, 2670, 2746, 2796, 3668, 3690, 3942, 3943, 3954, 3955, 3973. *See also* Central America
Honduras Inter-Oceanic Railway 3954, 3973
Hoosier Mineralogist and Archaeologist 2083
Hopedale 1759. *See also* Eskimo
Hopi 1493, 1494, 1496, 1497, 1500–1504, 1506–1508, 1512, 1514, 1517–1520, 1524–1529, 2108, 2110, 4071
Hopitu. *See* Hopi
Hopkins, E.W. 3118
Horn, G.H. 3077
Housatonic River Valley, CT 3116
houses. *See* architecture
Hovelacque, A. 1900
Huacals 2791
huacas. *See* shrines

Huaco 205
Huani Islands. *See* Guani islands
Huarpean. *See* Allemtíak
Huasco, Chile 3484
Huastec 70, 385, 391, 399, 1011, 1024, 4078, 4079
Huatuso. *See* Guatuso
Huave 407, 1613
Huavean. *See* Huave
Hudson River 3642
Hudson's Bay Company 2229, 4376
Hudson's Bay, Canada 978, 1467, 2228, 2355, 3178, 3188
Huehuetlahtolli 269
Huerfano Lake, CO 3128
Huichay, Peru 2320
Huichol 2513
Hulliché. *See* Araucanian
Humboldt, A. von 3790
Humboldt, W. von 61, 721, 1299, 3709, 4035
Humboldt celt 4264
Hungary 3005, 3594
Hungry Bay 3159
Hunkpapa 1548. *See also* Dakota
Hunter, J. 2148
Hunza 2378, 2380
Huron 882, 1062, 1891, 2137, 2321, 3349, 3362, 3485, 3656, 3657, 4435
Hutsonville 3391
Huxley, T. H. 3124
Huzvares 261
hydrology 1792
hygiene 1646
hymnal, Choctaw 4477; Cree 1087, 2088, 2148, 2215, 2246, 2248, 2545–2546; Creek 1538; Dakota 4429; Delaware 4499; Ettchaottine 2245; Laguna 2752; Munsee 1855, 2884; Oto 2790; Seneca 3672; Shuswap 1750; Takudh 2683, 2686. *See also* Christian doctrine
hypnotism. *See* psychology

Ibarra, F. de 4093
Iceland 1428, 2099
iconography 1498, 3154, 4396
Idaho 1536
idols and idolatry 5, 144, 1215, 3584, 4305. *See also* religion
Ilex cassine 1838

Illinois 2056, 2450, 2680, 3448, 3803
Illinois Indians 1888, 3842
immunity 207
Inca 125, 241, 407, 785, 909, 1055, 1203, 1480, 1746, 1747, 1898, 2316, 2320, 2593, 2595, 2664, 3104, 4280, 4414
India 317, 324, 325, 537, 838, 959, 1005, 1279, 1954, 2084–2086, 3118, 4447; South 2599
Indian Affairs Commission 4236
Indian House (rockshelter) 2777
Indian Rights Association 2164
Indiana 792, 3388, 4484
Indo-European 13, 16, 17, 19
Indo-Germanic 18, 258, 1103, 3256, 3758, 4459
Indonesia 3742, 4089
infanticide 2599
inheritance 1127. *See also* social organization
Innok. *See* Eskimo
Innuit. *See* Eskimo
inoculation 207
insanity 808, 3775
inscriptions 1606, 1811–1813, 1892, 1920, 2358, 2199, 3177, 3385, 3386, 3726, 3986, 4261, 4262, 4266, 4382, 4383. *See also* epigraphy, writing systems
Institut Royal de France 1379
Instituto Campechano 2479
Instituto Medico Nacional de Mexico 2171, 2411
intelligence 2991
International Catalogue of Scientific Literature 2172
Interoceanic Canal, Nicaragua 2437
Intibuca, Honduras 3945. *See also* Lenca
Inuit 295, 296, 1232, 1427, 1759, 2937, 3249
Inuktitut 2873
invention 2633
Inverleny 442
Iowa 1615, 2449, 2451, 2462, 2708, 2713, 3385, 3386, 3989
Ipurina 3339
Ipurucotó 3587
Iran 2081
Ireland 353, 359, 1454, 1766, 2847
Irish 1766
Iron Age 974, 2624, 2946, 3240
Iroquoian. *See* Cayuga, Cherokee, Huron,

Iroquois, Mohawk, Oneida, Onondaga, Seneca, Tuscarora
Iroquois 348, 349, 804, 882, 1079, 1116, 1117, 1204, 1206–1208, 1210, 1222, 1233, 1242, 1273, 1320, 1360, 1839, 1849, 1851, 1909, 2203, 2321, 2487, 2583, 2792, 2843, 2866, 2868, 2937, 3108, 3162, 3281, 3371, 3642, 3756, 4498
irrigation 2033
Irving, E. 3577
Irwin's Cave, KY 2759
Islam 820, 2379, 2381
Isle of Man 444
Isororo River, Guayana 3416
Israelites 2565
Itaboca, Brazil 1158
Itacayuno, Brazil 1159
Italian 1261, 2500. *See also* Romance languages
Italy 1557, 3807, 3817, 4083, 4326
Itapetininga 1792
Itzá 4303
ivory 513, 3920
Ixil 1307, 4053. *See also* Maya
Iximaya 2747
Iximché, Guatemala 609
Ixtahuacán, Guatemala 388
Izalco, El Salvador 388
Izamal, Mexico 391, 1037, 2482

Jacobs, J. 1087
Jacobs, P. 1087
jade 513, 1246, 3956, 3958. *See also* jadeite, nephrite
jadeite 1535, 2255, 3457. *See also* jade, nephrite
Jagare 45
Jahva 717
Jalapa, Guatemala 4328
Jalisco, Mexico 4087
Jamaica 4473
James River Valley, VA 1593
Japan 210, 809, 1475, 2023–2027, 2227, 2535, 2897, 3513, 3604, 3694, 4074
Japanese 120, 208, 2536, 3118, 4456
jasper 2766, 2767, 2773
Jastrow, Marcus 3118
Jastrow, Morris 751, 772, 3118
Jauaperí River, Brazil 3587
Jáuregui, A. B. 3894
Java 1949, 2598

Jefferson County, NY 3159
Jesuit relations 3510. *See also* religious orders
Jesuits. *See* religious orders
Jesup Expedition. *See* expeditions
Jews 820, 2550, 3499
Jicaque 388, 413, 2746
Jilotepec, Guatemala 788
Jiménez, F. 3777
Jiménez, M. 1143
Jivaro 3258, 3505
John Carter Brown Library. *See* libraries
John Day River, OR 4094
Johns Hopkins University 1414, 2587
Johns, J. 3804
Jones, P. 1087
Jourdanet, D. 1281, 3658
Judah 2197
Judson, A. 4345
Jujuy, Argentina 95
Juniata Indians 1816. *See also* Pennsylvania
jurisprudence. *See* political anthropology
Jurjura, Algeria 2476
Jutiapa, Guatemala 4258

Kabal 2783
Kabbalists. *See* Berbers
Kachiquel. *See* Cakchiquel
Kalalit 3255
Kalina. *See* Carib
Kalingo 2937. *See also* Carib
Kalispel 920, 1015, 1741. *See also* Salish
Kalmouck 1453
Kambyses 2474
Kamchatka region, Siberia 4038
Kamloops Wawa 925, 2225, 2226
Kaniagmioutes. *See* Kaniagmiut
Kaniagmiut 3296. *See also* Eskimo
Kansa 1346
Kansas 195, 1607, 4463
Kaom-no-kami-naosuké 3694
Kaondinoketc, F. 3490
Kapsu, New Ireland 1715
Karadza. *See* Caraya
Karankawa 1666. *See also* Texas
Karaya. *See* Caraya
Karina 2937. *See also* Carib
Karinyes. *See* Carib
Kariri. *See* Kiriri
Kassitesv 2013

katchinas 1524
Katun 757, 4265. *See also* calendrics, Maya
Kawia. *See* Cahuilla
Kekchí 193, 397, 1080, 1174–1176, 1302, 1306, 2028, 2470, 2818, 3111, 3317, 3318, 3320, 3321, 3827, 4052, 4292, 4293, 4302, 4327. *See also* Maya
Kelam-I-Pir 2381
Kennebec River, ME 338
Kent, England 597
Kent County, Ontario 2478
Kentor, S. 4378
Kentucky 878, 2465, 2467, 3267, 3388, 3927, 4484
Kephir 3924
Kerandi. *See* Querandi
Keres 2725
Keresan. *See* Laguna
Keshua. *See* Quechua
Khartoum, Sudan 4346
Khetsua 4210
Khoumire 426
Kiche. *See* Quiché
Kilimanjaro, Tanzania 12
Kimbundú 1041
Kinai 3423, 3722
King Philip 2812
Kingdon, J. 1591, 3643
Kingsborough, Lord 2745, 3211
Kinney Expedition. *See* expeditions
kinship 1514. *See also* consanguinity, descent, exogamy
Kipp, J. 2348
Kipú. *See* Quipú
Kiriri 50, 1623, 2570
Kirk Andreas, Isle of Man 444
Kitona'qa. *See* Kutanai
Kitunahin. *See* Kutenai
Kizh. *See* Netela
Klamath 1171, 1651, 1667, 1668
Knisteneaux. *See* Cree
knives 2636, 2640
Koch, Dr. 2123
Koggaba. *See* Cágaba
Kohler, J. 1976
Köktürk 263, 265
Koloche. *See* Tlingit
Koluschan. *See* Tlingit
Kongeligt Nordiske Oldskrift Selskab 2269, 2270

Königliche Museum. *See* museums
Königlichen Bibliothek zu Berlin. *See* libraries
Königlichen Bibliothek zu Dresden. *See* libraries
Kootenay. *See* Kutenai
Koppel, P. 4227
Korea 1178, 2890, 3600, 3608
Krakatau Island 550, 2149
Krause, A. 2275
Krauss, F. 3083
Kunnu. *See* Puelche
Kunza. *See* Atacama
Kutenai 948, 950, 969, 3867
Kwakiutl 462, 469, 494, 504, 511, 1247, 1337, 1340, 1859, 1860, 2012

La Barre, Mr. de 3160
La Grasserie, R. G. de 2399, 2404
La Paz, Bolivia 3681
La Plata River, Argentina 97, 2373, 2394, 2492, 2929, 3113
La Porterie, J. de 3273
La Rabida monastery 1214
La Sagittaria. *See* Tahiti
La Salle, R. 228
Labna, Mexico 4138
Labrador 579, 1427, 1759, 2015, 2254, 3142, 3143, 3384, 4095
Lacandon 397, 1038, 2405, 2856, 4303
Ladrone Islands. *See* Mariana Islands
Lafone y Quevedo, S.A. 291, 3512
Laguna 2725, 2752, 2753
Lake Chapala, Mexico 4004
Lake Erie 3338
Lake Leman, Switzerland 1660
Lake Nicaragua, Nicaragua 3577
Lake of the Woods, MN 2358
Lake Ontario 2487
Lake Superior 2261, 4403
lake-dwellings 2962
Lamaism. *See* Buddhism
Lampa 2584
Lamprecht, K. 3443
lamps 2768
land tenure 251
Land, A. 795
Landa, D. de 653, 4109, 4266
lanterns 2768
Lanzinni, L. 3649
lapis lazuli 2014

Lapland, Finland 1443
Laponie. *See* Lapland
Lapps 553, 2838
Las Casas, B. de 906, 1477, 2415
Latimer Collection. *See* collections
Latin 81, 1166, 3596, 4139
Latin America 601
latrines 2891
Lavalle, P. 1309
Law, P. H. 698
laws. *See* political anthropology
Le Jeune, J. 2225, 2226
Le Jeune, P. M. 924, 925, 1880
League of the Iroquois 2869
Lebanon 2376
Lebkowitz, Mr. 388
Leclerc, C. 2556
Lee County, VA 883
left-handedness 669
legends. *See* folklore, mythology
Lehigh Hills, PA 2766, 2773
Lehmann-Nitsche, R. 1932
Leicest Literary and Philosophical Society 2927
Leiden. *See* Leyden
Leiste, C. 837, 2973
Lemnos 3177
Lenape. *See* Delaware
Lenape Stone 2784
Lenca 413, 1992, 2746, 3928, 3945
Lengyel, Hungary 3005
Lenni Lenape. *See* Delaware Indians
Lenox Library. *See* libraries
Lenz, R. 301, 2224
León, N. 1993, 2336
León, Nicaragua 3577
leprosy 195, 199, 201, 203, 210, 2371, 4315
Lesser Antilles. *See* Caribbean
Leveque, L. 1104
Lévy, P. 388
Lewis, J., and A. H. H. Lewis *16*
Leyden 3741
Leyden plate 4264
libraries 4342; Biblioteca del General Mitre 2332; Bibliothèque Imperiale 2575; Bibliothèque Nationale 157, 1382, 2020, 4296; John Carter Brown 1477, 3497; Königlichen Bibliothek zu Berlin 3789; Königlichen Bibliothek zu Dresden 3713; Lenox Library 3918; Medicean Library 3660; Real Biblioteca

434; Royal Library of Berlin 3210; Library of the University of Pennsylvania Museum *14-17*
Library of Aboriginal American Literature 755
Libreria Meridiana de Canton 2789
Libya 661, 705
Licking County, OH 3655, 3889
Liebrecht, F. 3083
Lifou 1270
Lilienfeld, P. de 4367
Lillooet 924. *See also* British Columbia
Lima, Peru 3967
Limón, Costa Rica 388, 4269
lineal measures 671
linguistics 40-42, 55, 61, 94, 123, 124, 132, 138, 254, 301, 302, 3330-335, 367, 368, 377, 383, 394, 400-402, 414, 435, 436, 456, 465, 487, 533, 536, 584, 602, 606, 627-629, 631, 633, 636, 646, 649, 657, 666, 670, 672, 704, 706, 721, 722, 725, 738, 739, 745, 776, 830, 872, 893, 934, 945, 952, 959, 965-967, 979, 987, 988, 991, 997, 999, 1014, 1016-1018, 1025, 1027-1030, 1060, 1077, 1102, 1165-1168, 1209, 1210, 1232, 1238, 1260, 1358, 1379, 1392, 1401, 1404, 1416, 1435, 1440, 1441, 1444, 1460, 1460, 1481, 1484, 1531, 1574-1584, 1598, 1600, 1609, 1617, 1618, 1632, 1636, 1651, 1652, 1653, 1656, 1658, 1660, 1670, 1693, 1799, 1842, 1848, 1851, 1939, 1950, 1991, 1999, 2005, 2103, 2117, 2118, 2131-2134, 2237, 2281, 2287-2295, 2297-2299, 2302-2309, 2313, 2322, 2325, 2338, 2380, 2394, 2411, 2412, 2496-2500, 2509, 2511, 2542, 2558, 2563, 2564, 2569, 2617, 2756, 2936, 2939-2943, 2950-2953, 2959, 3075, 3086, 3120, 3132, 3139, 3163, 3170, 3177, 3188, 3218, 3266, 3286, 3288, 3289, 3329, 3330, 3334, 3343, 3353, 3354, 3364, 3480, 3583, 3588, 3591, 3603, 3605, 3709, 3721, 3726, 3760-3762, 3772, 3783, 3785, 3786, 3789, 3790, 3795, 3797, 3843, 3844, 3866, 3893, 3894, 3947, 4017-4021, 4033-4037, 4051, 4091, 4100, 4109-4111, 4115, 4116, 4119, 4125-4127, 4129, 4156, 4158-4162, 4166, 4168, 4169,

4199-4201, 4204, 4209, 4250, 4261, 4262, 4264, 4266, 4306, 4398, 4411, 4412, 4423, 4457, 4460; Abipón 52, 2327; Abnaki 3441, 4489; Acawai 2242, 3415; Achagua 3616; Akua 1402; Alacaluf 1472; Alaguilac 712; Alasapas 1642; Aleut 2169, 2937; Algonkin 850, 963, 1003, 1207, 1387, 1952, 2649-2651, 2934, 2937, 3277, 3375, 4098, 4099, 4164, 4165, 4202, 4203, 4205, 4498; Allemtíak 2821, 4260; Altaic 266, 4454; Andagueda 737; Apache 1673; Apalachee 399, 1311; Aparai 1162; Arabic 4306, 4425; Araucanian 1238, 1391, 1471, 1472, 2400, 2403-2405, 2402, 2403, 2821, 4255, 4259; Arawak 37, 748, 2239, 2937, 3414, 3854; Arrouage 1184; Athapascan 827, 2937, 3278; Auca, 2310, 2399, 2404; Aymara 407, 430, 913, 914, 1472, 4415; Bakaïri 2653, 4012; Baniva 2301; Basque 786, 982, 986, 989, 1006, 1025, 1620; Bauré 2556; Bayano 384, 387; Bella Coola 495; Berber 634, 1620, 3118, 3840; Betoya 665; Blackfoot 2348, 4148, 4150, 4151; Boane 2331; Bolak 528, 529; Boruca 384, 388, 412, 4103, 4104; Bribri 2937, 3314, 4103; Burmese 4345; Cabécar 4103; Cágaba 936; Cacama 2331, 2334; Caché 92, 388, 412; Caduveo 525; Cakchiquel 388, 398, 399, 608, 610, 747, 841, 984, 1560, 1661, 1770, 1819, 1820, 2748-2750, 4056, 4186, 4490, 4301; Campa 2362, 4415; Carayá 310, 1403; Carib 51, 388, 398, 619-621, 1980-1983, 2239, 3416, 4224; Catawba 960; Cegiha 1343, 1347, 1355; Chaco 737; Chamacoco 523; Chanase 2331; Chemakum 483; Cherokee 104, 1043, 2182, 2734, 2843, 2846, 2879, 2937; Chiapanec 46, 67, 68, 380, 407, 1303, 2468, 3171, 3174; Chibcha 44, 387, 1768, 4251; Chilidugu 1935; Chinantec 298, 407, 701; Chinese 260; Chinook 463, 464, 484, 924, 1690, 1691, 1739, 1740, 2225, 2226, 3279; Chippewa 43, 272-275, 366, 2090, 2246-2249, 2251, 2319, 2690, 3243, 3838, 4073, 4341; Chiquita 39; Chiriguano 1146; Chirripó 4103; Chocó 384, 387, 769; Choctaw 104,

833-835, 2937, 3051, 4422, 4476-4478; Choltí 2856, 2857; Chono 1472; Chontal 399, 413, 454, 3073; Chorotega 388, 389; Chortí 2746, 2857, 4043; Chuchona 980, 3592, 3593; Chulupí 2331; Chumtéya 1662, 1662; Chunupu 2331; Cichiti 1482; Clallam 1692; Coiba 387; Coptic 2960; Cora 3122, 3871; Cree 43, 104, 2089, 2091-2094, 2097, 2097, 2122, 2139-2148, 2244, 2318, 2355, 2544-2546, 2644-2646, 2841; Creek 104, 652, 810, 1538, 1659, 2501-2503, 3578, 3579, 3282, 4375; Crichana 3587; Cudena 837; Cuera 387; Cueva 384; Cumanagoto 3324, 3632; Cuna 384, 387, 1618, 2483, 3307, 3308; Cunza 3671; Dakota 44, 104, 119, 816, 817, 1621, 1817, 1818, 2136, 2562, 2937, 3514, 3542-3544, 3590, 4428-4430; Darien 387; Dayak 1622; Delaware 104, 754, 771, 1267, 1452, 1587, 2478, 2507, 2534, 4358, 4499, 4494-4498; Demotic 2954; Digger Indians 1673; Digueño 4394; Dorasque 3309; Dravidian 4307; Egyptian 13-19; Emerillon 1162; English 2829; Eskimo 295, 467, 474, 475, 1398, 1427, 1986, 2873, 2883, 2937, 3187, 3188, 3248, 3254, 3280, 3550, 3553, 3767, 4374, 4385; Eskimo, Alaska 295, 3254; Eskimo, Baffinland 491; Eskimo, Greenland 104, 1461, 3250-3255, 3549; Eskimo, Labrador 1759, 2254, 2679, 3142, 3384, 4095; Estrella 4103; Etchareottine 538-544, 1758, 2245, 3493; Eudeve 3870; Euskarienne 1001; French 1002; Garifuna 388, 398, 413; German 1619, 4455; Goajira 935; Greek 2954; Gros Ventre 2656; Guaicurú 52, 520, 525; Guajiquiro 1992; Guaná 526; Guaraní 407, 1395, 2337, 3517, 3633-3638, 3858, 3859, 4270; Guatuso 408, 412, 4103, 4104; Guaymí 412, 3306; Guenoa 2331; Guerandí 2331, 3135; Haida 510, 1907; Hidatsa 2655, 2656; Huastec 70, 385, 399, 1011, 1024, 4078, 4079; Huave 407, 1613; Huron 1062, 3349, 3656; Huzvar 261; Indo-European 13, 16, 19; Indo-Germanic 17-19, 1103, 4459; Iroquois 1052, 1053, 1208, 1242, 2843,

2937, 3108, 3281, 4498; Iruriná 3339; Italian 1261, 1262; Ixil 1307, 4053; Jagare 45; Japanese 3118; Jicaque 388, 413, 2746; Kalalek 3255; Kalingo 2937; Kalispel 1015, 1741, 1920; Karankawa 1666; Karina 2937; Kekchí 193, 1080, 1174-1176, 1302, 1306, 2028, 2470, 2818, 3318, 3320, 3321, 3827, 4052, 4292, 4293, 4302, 4337, 4497; Kimbundu 1041; Kinai 3423, 3722; Kiriri 50, 1623, 2570; Klamath 1171, 1667, 1668; Kökturkish 263, 265; Kutenai 948, 950, 969; Kwakiutl 494, 511, 1859, 1860; Laguna 2725, 2753; Latin 81; Lenca 413, 1992, 2746, 3945; Lillooet 924; Lule 2332, 2543; Lummi 1692; Mahican 4497; Malagasy 4351; Maliseet 104, 3439; Mam 399, 1024, 1119, 3504, 3532, 3533; Mangue 226, 389, 696, 2486, 3581; Mapuche 2403; Mataco 2331, 3114, 3205, 3512; Matagalpa 675, 756; Mataguayo 3114; Matlatzinga 2937; Maya 1073-1075; Mazatec 371; Mbayá 52, 525, 2328; Micmac 297, 2557, 3431-3438; Minuane 2331; Miskito 49, 388, 413, 433, 767, 1442, 2937; Mississaga 961, 962; Mixe 379, 407, 1111, 1614, 2312, 2820, 3419, 3420; Mixtec 2937, 3529; Mocoví 52, 2333; Mohawk 104, 1206, 1849, 2008; Montagnais 188, 1383, 1384, 2366-2368, 2647, 3243; Moreno 2746; Mosetena 1998; Moxa 2580; Muisca 387; Munsee 1855, 2087, 2088, 2884, 4360; Mutsún 189, 190, 1187, 1190, 2937; Na-Dene 2880, 2881, 2882, 2876, 3243; Nahuatl 44, 90, 91, 121, 169, 182, 183, 192, 215, 226, 267-269, 399, 439, 440, 639, 713, 735, 740, 798, 814, 829, 832, 836, 869, 875, 876, 902, 923, 1048, 1050, 1057, 1071, 1072, 1076, 1107, 1163, 1413, 1468, 1479, 1633, 1763, 1993, 2020, 2021, 2361, 2408, 2574-2576, 2831-2834, 2937, 3033, 3057, 3058, 3164, 3165, 3209-3211, 3319, 3422, 3546, 3557, 3558, 3561, 3572, 3576, 3105, 3106, 3287, 3679, 3828, 3860-3862, 3988, 4077, 4185, 4277, 4282, 4287; Nanticoke 630, 768; Natchez 399, 709; Natick 1157, 1389, 1409, 1410; Navaho 2659; Nez Perce 104, 3922; Nipissing 1204, 2651, 3490; Ntlakyapamuk 3100; Ojibwa 104, 276, 277, 365, 453, 1087, 2016, 2095, 2096, 2138, 2215, 2216; Okanagan 924; Omaha 1347, 1938; Onondaga 1848, 3841, 4493, 4497, 4498; Orejón 1642; Orosí 4103; Oto 2791; Otomí 399, 813, 1021, 2491, 2937, 3034, 3043, 3049, 3050, 3219, 3428, 4492; Ouayana 1162; Oyampí 1162; Pacoas 1642; Páez 911; Paiute 2044; Pajalat 1642; Pakawa 1642; Pampa 1472; Pano 2296; Papiamento 1665; Pasilingua 4019-4021; Passamaquoddy 79, 297, 1501, 3376, 3377; Pausanes 1642; Pawnee 1938; Paya 2746; Persian 264; Piapoco 1184; Pipil 388; Pirinda 1021; Piritú 3632; Pokomam 409, 788, 4258; Pokomchí 62-65, 388, 399, 1110, 1287, 1305, 2470, 4052, 4302; Ponca 1347; Popoluca 398, 410, 840, 3073; Pueblo Indians 1673; Puelche 278; Puquina 691, 2311; Quechua 36, 44, 125, 407, 623, 909, 913, 992, 1472, 1480, 1746, 1747, 2593-2595, 2823, 3103, 3104, 3112, 3683, 4210, 4415; Quiché 44, 72, 158, 180, 289, 388, 398, 399, 608, 612, 682, 842, 984, 1020, 1026, 1560, 2223, 3345, 3382, 3682, 4152-4154, 4186, 4491; Quiripí 3268; Roucouyenne 1162; Sabanero 384, 387; Sahaptin 2937; Salish 924, 2044, 2055, 2937; Salishan 492; Santee 1411, 2017, 3540; Sechel 924, 925; Sechuana 905; Seneca 104, 2792, 3672, 4479, 4480; Shoshoni 2044; Shuswap 925, 1750; Siouan 1352, 3284; Slayamen 924; Snohomish 567; Souletine 1019; Spanish 71, 220, 405, 1742, 2586, 2587, 3265; Squamish 924, 925; Stalo 924, 925; Subtiaba 389; Sumo 2746; Tacana 921; Taensa 47, 48, 742, 764, 765, 1927, 1985, 4308; Tahkaht 2256; Takudh 2683, 2691; Takulli 2874, 2877, 2878; Talamanca 388, 412, 4103; Tapachulane 1011; Tarahumara 831, 4086; Tarascan 309, 922, 1031, 1733, 2286, 2336, 2417, 2937, 3035, 3831; Tarawa 1104; Tasmanian 1023; Tehuelche 278, 1472, 2976; Tekinica 1472; Térraba 3313, 4103, 4104; Thompson 924, 925;

Tilijayas 1642; Timucua 789, 1311, 1671, 1672, 2300, 2314, 2979, 3167; Tinne 104, 538-544; Tlingit 510, 2937, 3250; Toba 52, 290, 2331, 2335; Tojolabal 378, 707, 952, 983; Tonkawa 1673; Tonocoté 2543; Tonto 1673; Totonac 398, 1316, 2937; Tsattine 1647-1649, 2250; Tsimshian 509, 510, 3539, 3765, 4504; Tucurrique 4103; Tuda 2599; Tukkuthkutchin 2684-2689; Tule 384, 387; Tupí 53, 73, 1169, 1280, 1624, 1925, 4270; Tutelo 1852; Tzeltal 174, 175, 2826, 3312; Tzotzil 910, 952, 1033, 3628; Tzutuhil 399, 608, 984, 1560, 4186, 4296; Ulva 388, 413, 2483, 3074; Ural-Altaic 257-258, 262, 4453, 4458; Uspantec 4052; Ute 284, 1673; Valiente 388, 412; Vicéita 92, 384, 388, 412, 4103, 4269; Volapuk 774; Wakashan 3285; Walla Walla 1288; Warrau 3413; Winnebago 1543, 1938, 2679; Xinca 714, 4338; Yahgan 626, 806, 807, 1757, 3326; Yakama 3155; Yaro 2331; Yucatec 34, 44, 104, 219, 372-374, 382, 390, 391, 395, 398, 399, 403, 404, 407, 607, 611, 614, 615, 645, 653, 693, 746, 757, 759, 903, 912, 990, 995, 996, 1045-1047, 1056, 1081, 1082, 1285, 1286, 1309, 1315, 1323, 1550-1552, 1555, 1591, 1627, 1644, 1807, 1979, 1984, 1997, 2243, 2342, 2349, 2427, 2428, 2479, 2615, 2674, 2827, 2937, 3078, 3186, 3221-3225, 3538, 3559, 3560, 3605, 3643-3653, 3669, 3670, 3829, 3830; Yuma 4394; Yunga 886; Yuracare 1191, 1143, 1476, 1614; Zambo 2746; Zapotec 407, 1767, 2434-2436, 2616, 2937, 3497, 3530, 3675, 4334, 4336; Zoque 191, 381, 398, 407, 411, 1304, 1614, 2312, 2820, 3172, 3173, 3175, 3562, 3676-3678, 4335; Zuni 4197. See also etymology, grammar, philology, phonology, syllabary, toponyms
Lipe. See Atacama
Literary and Historical Society of Quebec 2385
literature 559, 670, 1799, 2152, 2153, 2395, 2400, 2511, 2604, 3118, 3367-3370, 3496, 3523, 3591

Literature of American Aboriginal Languages 3968
lithics 6, 8-10, 287, 443, 1721, 1774, 1875, 1924, 2074, 2163, 2204, 2227, 2727, 2730, 2731, 2763, 2772, 2803, 2853, 2872, 2902, 2905, 3019, 3228, 3229, 3380, 3393, 3449, 3450, 3460, 3469, 3470, 3472, 3477, 3839, 3962, 3991, 4007, 4445, 4447. See also flint, obsidian
Little Falls, MN 2459
Little Miami Valley, OH 3403
Livorno, Italy 2589
lizard 1716
llama 4207
Llergo, S. L. de 1309
Lobos Bay, CA 4467
Loja province, Ecuador 4469
Loltún, Mexico 4136
London, England 3886
Long Island, NY 637, 4163, 4166, 4169
López Ayala, J. 1074
Lord's Prayer 388, 3842, 4489. See also Christian doctrine
Loreto, Peru 3427
Lorraine, France 1096
Los Angeles County, CA 2048
lotophagi. See lotus-eaters
lotus-eaters 423
Loubat, Duc de 562
Louis IX 194
Louisades Islands 625
Louisiana 683, 1354, 1669, 2585, 3442
love 651, 662
Lower Frazer. See Stalo
Loyalty Islands 1270
Lubbock, J. 2
Lucayo 790. See also Caribbean
Luckenbach, A. 4499
Lule 2332, 2543
Lule-Vilela. See Lule
Lull, E. P. 387
Lummi 1672. See also Salish
Lusatia 4324
Luschan, F. von 167
Lyman, B. S. 3118
Lytton, British Colombia 3875

Macalester Museum. See museums
Machoni, A. 2332
Mackenzie River, Canada 538-544, 1467, 2245, 3248

Macuchy 3587
Mad River, OH 2925
Madagascar 1367, 1885
Madog 2439
Madrid 344, 3091
Magdalena, Colombia 3218
Magellan Strait 2673, 3192
magic 2673, 4390
Magyar 3761
Mahedia. *See* Tunisia
Mahican 4497, 4504
Maine 338, 2777, 2926, 4290, 4431, 4487
maize 1916, 4049, 4069, 4070
Makak 1402, 1727
Malagasy 4351
Malaya 1886, 4349
Malaysia 1532
Malecite 104, 297, 3439
Maler, T. 150
Maliseet. *See* Malecite
Mam 399, 1024, 1119, 3504, 3532, 3533.
   See also Maya
Mamabozho 3946
mammals 78, 3865
mammoths 3703, 4228
mancala 1199
Manché 867. *See also* Maya
Manchu 260
Mandan 1937, 2667, 4410
Mandragora 2530
Mangue 226, 388, 389, 696, 2485, 3581
Manitoba, Canada 817
Manzaneros 2403
Maori 1328
Mapa de Cuauhtlantzinco 4005
maple tree 963
Mappe de Tepechpan 2578, 2579
Mappe Tlotzin 2020
maps. *See* cartography
Mapuche 1391, 2403, 4192, 4193
Maqua. *See* Onondaga
Marajó Island, Brazil 1274
Marañon River, Peru 837, 2806
Marblehead, OH 4387
Marchesi Island. *See* Marquesas Islands
Marcy, R. B. 2585
Mareuil les Meaux 3244
Maria Candelaria 673, 674
Mariana Islands 1186
Maribia 389
Marietta, OH 2886

Marin, T. 3378
Marjelen, Switzerland 547
Markham, C. R. 407
Markland 358, 359
Marne River 3056, 3244
Marpicokawin, E. 1411
Marquesas Islands 1712, 4016
Marquette, J. 228
Marquette County, WI 919
marriage 1833, 2987, 2994, 3100, 3182.
   See also polyandry, social organization
Marriott Mound, OH 3390
Martin, J. E. A. 2976
Martínez de Arredondo, F. 1309
Martius, C. F. P. von 3468, 3479
Marx, K. *2*
Maryland 2777
Maryland Historical Society 2619
Masaya, Nicaragua 226, 3073, 3581
Mashacali. *See* Coroado
Mashpee 171
Masjwke. *See* Creek
masks 139, 1326, 1723, 1890
Mason, E. 338
Massachusett. *See* Natick
Massachusetts 171, 338, 943, 1373, 4389,
   4487
Massawomeke 4165
Massei, I. 2331,
Masset, British Columbia 4218
Mataco 2331, 3114, 3205, 3512. *See also*
   Vejos
Mataco-Maca. *See* Chulupi, Chunupu,
   Mataco, Mataguayo, Tonocote
Matagalpa, Nicaragua 675, 756, 3073
Mataguayo 3114. *See also* Mataco
material culture 1219, 1429, 2623, 2728,
   2729, 2787, 2853, 2929
mathematics 2968. *See also* numerals
Matlatzinga 2937
matrimony. *See* marriage
Matto Grosso, Brazil 1399, 2928, 4012
Matty Island, Canada 2533
Maui 25
Mauritius 227, 548
Maximillian 391, 1309
Maya 44, 391, 392, 394, 395, 397, 399, 400,
   403, 406, 628, 680, 693, 722, 757, 866,
   867, 990, 995–997, 1037, 1040, 1045,
   1046, 1290–1294, 1407, 1408, 1498,
   1513, 1569, 1570, 1572–1584,

1754-1756, 1811-1813, 1828, 1867,
2067, 2315, 2342, 2349, 2405, 2420,
2422, 2424, 2479, 2559, 2560, 2575,
2668-2671, 2674, 2783, 2830, 2856,
2937, 3186, 3312, 3466, 3476, 3555,
3556, 3602, 3603, 3605, 3668, 3696,
3711-3717, 3719, 3721, 3782-3784,
3786, 3793, 3795-3797, 4052, 4053,
4110-4112, 4115, 4116, 4119,
4136-4138, 4125, 4126, 4195, 4261,
4262, 4264, 4265, 4294, 4303, 4490; dictionaries *7, 8*
Mayan. *See* Cakchiquel, Chol, Chontal,
Chortí, Huastec, Itzá, Ixil, Kekchí,
Lacandon, Mam, Manché, Maya,
Pokomam, Pokomchí, Quiché, Tojolabal,
Tzeltal, Tzotzil, Tzutuhil, Uspantec,
Yucatec
Maynas, Peru 2973
Mayo 3061
Mazatec 371, 701
Mbayá 52, 525, 2328. *See also* Caduveos
McCall, G. A. 4467
McClellan, G. B. 2585
McCormack, T. J. 3346
McGee, W. J. 2961
medals 1193
Medicean Library. *See* libraries
medicine 1830, 2171, 2410, 2837, 2844,
2850
Mediterranean Sea 3819
megaliths 1464, 2903, 2904. *See also*
sculpture
Mehrum, Germany 1616
Mejborg, R. 3083
Melanesia 625, 1708, 1710, 3813, 4349
Melgar, J. M. 2616
Memorial de Sololá 610, 747, 1661,
2748-2750
Mendan, Sr. 2020
Mendez, S. 1309
Mendoza, A. de 4093
Mendoza, E. 3211
Mendoza, G. 121
Menelik II 3026
Mengarelli, R. 1086
Mengarini, G. 1741
Menidi 4325
menstruation 3925
Menton cave, France 3575
Mercedarians. *See* religious orders

Mercer, H. C. 167
Mérida, Mexico 372, 391, 1285, 1309,
1439, 2479, 2789
Merom, IL 3391
Mesa Pintada. *See* Painted Mesa
Mesa Verde, CO 3080
mescal 1837
Mescaleros 1642. *See also* Apache
Mesozoic 1136
Messina, Italy 865
Mestorf, J. 3083
metals 140, 148, 2535, 3864. *See also*
bronze, copper, gold
meteorology 1607
Metz, F. 2599
Mexica. *See* Aztec
Mexican War 2480
Mexicana. *See* Nahuatl
Mexicano. *See* Nahuatl
Mexico 1, 121, 211-214, 253, 271, 332,
352, 377, 396, 398, 414, 450, 513, 564,
606, 607, 609, 613, 671, 688, 735, 759,
906, 907, 939, 981, 1004, 1018, 1039,
1064, 1181, 1281-1284, 1371, 1434,
1458, 1468, 1626, 1631, 1636, 1638,
1639, 1760, 1763, 1771, 1775, 1785,
1801, 1868, 1884, 1915, 1916, 1955,
2018-2022, 2029, 2067, 2071, 2265,
2407, 2411, 2412, 2419, 2468, 2486,
2512, 2515, 2576, 2578, 2579, 2586,
2596, 2641, 2669, 2675, 2744, 2745,
2754, 2793-2795, 2816, 2930, 2931,
3047, 3070, 3084, 3090-3099, 3120,
3121, 3144, 3148, 3152, 3207, 3211,
3216, 3287-3290, 3344, 3363, 3365,
3429, 3431-3438, 3483, 3570, 3571,
3686, 3697, 3698, 3699, 3700, 3781,
3792, 3798, 3799, 3800, 3802, 3911,
3958, 3969, 3980, 3985, 3992, 3995,
3997, 4002, 4003, 4004, 4005, 4060,
4080, 4088, 4092, 4093, 4116, 4119,
4127, 4184, 4188, 4194, 4195, 4267,
4288, 4289, 4298, 4305, 4463; North
575, 829, 4467; South 3998; West
4089. *See also* Campeche, Chiapas,
Chihuahua, Jalisco, Michoacan, Nayarit,
Oaxaca, Querétaro, Sonora, Tamaulipas,
Yucatan
Mexico City 292, 2406, 2587. *See also*
Tenochtitlan
Meyer, A. B. 1246

Meyer, G. 18, 3762
Mezquit 1933
Mgale 1605
Miami Indians 3842
Michigan 1735, 3876, 3879, 3880, 3881
Michoacan, Mexico 350, 609, 1143, 1733, 2410, 2514, 2612, 3482, 3830. *See also* Mexico
Micmac 167, 297, 2383, 2557, 3431-3438
Miconinovi 1515
microcephalia 3059, 4507
Micronesia 625, 4349
Middle Ages 354, 2474, 2673, 2743, 3426, 4420
migration 198, 1004, 1345, 1841, 1974, 2137, 2330, 2625, 2626, 2899
Mijangos, S. 1110
Mikmaque. *See* Micmac
Milpa Alta, Mexico 215
Milton, J. 2396
Minas Gerais, Brazil 821
mineralogy 513, 977, 1603, 1604, 1773, 2120, 2446
mining 2766, 2773, 4393
Minnesota 222, 1861, 2079, 2459, 2461, 2462
Minnesota River 2453
Minnetaree. *See* Hidatsa
Minuané. *See* Guenoas
Miocene 568
miscegenation 3499
Miskito 49, 387, 388, 413, 433, 767, 1442, 1474, 1980, 2937, 3984
Mission Indians 460, 3430
Mission Río de San Antonio 1642
Mission Río Grande 1642
Mission San Antonio de Padua 3866
Mission San Antonio Indians. *See* Salinan Indians
Mission San Juan Bautista 189, 190, 1189, 1190
Mission Scientifique au Caucase. *See* expeditions
missionaries 294, 1300, 2495, 2583, 2647, 2973, 2974, 3868. *See also* religious orders
missions 1147, 2231, 2495, 3010, 3113, 3442, 3574, 3657, 3662, 3681, 3868, 4075, 4084
Mississauga 943, 951, 957, 962. *See also* Chippewa

Mississippi 3477
Mississippi River Valley 38, 885, 1108, 1833, 2007, 2066, 2338, 2344, 2455, 2552, 3004, 3062, 3230, 3342, 3957, 4242, 4395, 4446
Missouri 783, 1421, 1455, 2006, 2123, 2656, 3350
Missouri Historical Society 2006
Missouri River Valley 1607, 1939, 2866
Misumalpan. *See* Cacaopera, Matagalpa, Miskito, Sumo, Ulva
Mita, Guatemala 4258
Mitchell Collection. *See* collections
Mitla, Mexico 271, 421, 1037, 2675, 3800, 4088
Mitre, B. 2593, 3179
Mixco, Guatemala 3687
Mixe 379, 407, 1111, 1614, 2312, 2820, 3419, 3420
Mixe-Zoquean. *See* Mixe, Popoluca, Zoque
Mixtec 2937, 3529
Mixtecan. *See* Mixtec
Mochica. *See* Yunga
Mocoví 52, 2332. *See also* Guaicuru
Modern Language Association of America 2824, 2825
Modoc 2739. *See also* Oregon
Mohave 82, 1141
Mohawk 104, 1053, 1206, 1320, 1849, 2008, 3158. *See also* Iroquois
Mohegan 2487
Mojave. *See* Mohave
Molinero del Cerro, C. 2836
Moluché. *See* Araucanians
Monaco 3037
Mondolingue. *See* world language
Monélia, C. de 4093
money. *See* currency
Mongolia 1277
Monongahela River, PA 1257
Monsoni 2091. *See also* Cree
Montagnais 188, 1052, 1383, 1384, 2015, 2366-2368, 2647, 3243
Montauk 4169
Montejo, F. de 398, 1308
Montesdeoca, F. 438
Montgaudier Cave, France 3000
Montgomery County, PA 2759
Montreal, Canada 2548
Moore, C. B. 4108
Moose Indians. *See* Monsoni

Moqui Pueblo 577, 1318, 1499, 4039. *See also* Hopi
Morales, J. de 193, 1080, 3827
Moravian Church 3500, 4499
Moravians 2478, 4499. *See also* Delaware, Mahican, Munsee
Moraviantown, Canada 2478
Morelos, J .M. 2414
Moreno 2746
Morgan, L. H. *2, 4,* 1918
Moris 2003
Morocco 4424, 4425
Morong 3182
Morris, J. C. 773
mortuary customs 279, 4495, 4496
Morvan 2115
mosaics 3483
Mosca. *See* Muisca
Moscow, Russia 3806
Mosetena 1998
Mosetenan. *See* Mosetena
Moshonaland. *See* Zimbabwe
Moskito. *See* Miskito
Mosquito. *See* Miskito
Mosquito Coast, Nicaragua 388, 767, 3689, 3973
Motolinia, T. 4093
Mound Builders 152, 761, 792, 885, 1108, 1568, 1736, 1978, 2214, 2441, 2446, 2455-2457, 2461, 2464, 2466, 2467, 2551-2552, 2597, 2680, 2852, 2853, 3017, 3053, 3203, 3267, 3390, 3391, 3424, 3884, 3890, 3927, 3929, 3934, 3936, 3957, 3961, 3962, 3974, 4108, 4113, 4114, 4117, 4121-4124, 4128, 4130, 4131, 4142-4144, 4388, 4391, 4392, 4394, 4395
Mount Atlas, Africa 1857, 1858
Mount Hope Bay, RI 2812
Mount Rainier, WA 4397
Mount Tacoma, WA 4397
mountaineering 3641
Mové 3306. *See also* Northern Guaymí
Moxa 2580
Moxos 2556, 3113
Muhammadanism. *See* Islam
Mühlenbach, Germany 3071
Muir, J. 4241
Muirakitan 3585
Muisca 387. *See also* Chibchan
Muller, Dr. 388

Müller, F. 795, 915, 916
Müller, M. 4397
Müller, W. M. 3118
mummies 1145, 1798, 2273, 2274, 3153, 3759
Muncey. *See* Munsee
Muneraty, J. 1893
Muñoz, J. B. 434, 1634, 3918
Muñoz Collection. *See* collections
Munsee 1855, 2884, 4360
murals 3800
Murghab, Afghanistan 4383
Murillo, T. 2856
murmex 690
Murphy, H. C. 5
Murphy Island, FL 4108
Muscogulges. *See* Creek
Musée Broca. *See* museums
Musée d'Ethnographie. *See* museums
Musée de La Plata. *See* museums
Musée du Trocadero. *See* museums
Museo Nacional del Río de Janeiro. *See* museums
Museo Nazionale di Napoli. *See* museums
Museum d'Histoire Naturelle de Paris. *See* museums
Museum des Missionshauses zu Basel. *See* museums
Museum für Völkerkunde. *See* museums
Museum für Völkerkunde zu Leipzig. *See* museums
Museum of American Archaeology. *See* museums
Museum of Human Anatomy, Cambridge University. *See* museums
Museum of the Academy of Natural Sciences. *See* museums
museums 128, 186, 446, 450, 514, 1201, 1447, 1751-1753, 1871, 1872, 1887, 2373, 2448, 2864, 3081, 3292, 3740, 4044, 4362; Agramer National Museum 2273; American Museum of Natural History 1362; Anatomical Museum, Cambridge University 1367, 1370; Blackmore Museum 4044; British Museum 3057; Field Columbian Museum 1530; Königliche Museum *11,* 1447; Macalester Museum of History and Archaeology 2448; Musée Broca 4175; Musée d'Ethnographie 1883; Musée de La Plata 2864; Musée

du Trocadero 1892; Museo Nacional de Mexico 2482; Museo Nacional del Río de Janeiro 1924; Museo Nazionale di Napoli 3153; Museum d'Histoire Naturelle de Paris 3292; Museum des Missionshauses zu Basel 2231, 2974; Museum für Völkerkunde 1447; Museum of American Archaeology 2975; Museum of the Academy of Natural Sciences, Iowa 3385, 3386; Nordiska Museet, Stockholm 3081-3083; Ontario Archaeological Museum 591; Peabody Museum of American Archaeology and Ethnology *ix, 11, 13, 32, 38,* 883, 1754-1756, 3180, 3392, 3394, 3395, 3398-3402, 3404, 4136, 4138; Rijks Ethnographischen Museum 3741, 3545; South Kensington Museum 3920; United States Army Medical Museum 2654

music 229, 283, 687, 1106, 1180, 1737, 2108, 2232, 2658, 2666, 3382, 3696, 4197, 4298

musical bow 2622, 3699

Muskhogean 3282. *See also* Apalachee, Chickasaw, Choctaw, Creek, Natchez, Taensa

Muskinggum River Valley, OH 2855

Muskokee. *See* Creek

Muskwaki. *See* Fox

mutilation 2409

Mutsúm. *See* Mutsún

Mutsún 189, 190, 1189, 1190, 2937. *See also* California

Muysca. *See* Muisca

Mylodon 4446

mythology 25, 32, 141, 330, 419, 480, 502, 534, 612, 622, 635, 657, 682, 686, 756, 758, 795, 862, 964, 981, 1009, 1010, 1061, 1173, 1217, 1342, 1343, 1689, 1743, 1832, 1921, 1926, 2024, 2190, 2203, 2260, 2343, 2384, 2407, 2493, 2657, 2875, 2883, 3118, 3241, 3256, 3299, 3317, 3318, 3356, 3695, 3714, 3773, 3801, 3941, 4300; migration mythology 1659. *See also* folklore

Na'nniboju 943

Naaman's Creek, DE 1183

Na-Dene 2012, 2874, 2876, 2880-2882, 3243, 3245. *See also* Apache, Navaho, Takulli, Tlingit, Tsattine

Nadouesis. *See* Sioux

Nagada, Egypt 1558

Nagualism 681, 863. *See also* religion

Nagyr 2378

Nahuatl 44, 90, 94, 169, 182, 183, 192, 215, 226, 267-271, 391, 399, 439, 440, 639, 713, 735, 740, 752, 798, 814, 828, 832, 869, 875, 876, 902, 923, 1048-1050, 1057, 1107, 1413, 1633, 1681, 2361, 2408, 2574, 2831-2834, 2937, 3033, 3057, 3058, 3105, 3106, 3148, 3149, 3164-3166, 3209-3211, 3263, 3287, 3319, 3422, 3524, 3546, 3557-3561, 3572, 3576, 3595, 3679, 3828, 3860, 3861, 3988, 4077, 4185, 4277, 4282, 4287. *See also* Aztec

Nain, Canada 1759

Namollo. *See* Yuit

Namotivá 2485

Namur, France 2984, 2990

Nanaimo 486

Nancy, France 1096

Nanticoke 630, 768

Napa County, CA 4007

Napp, A. *11*

Narbrough (ship) 1144

Narraganset 3170

Nascapee. *See* Naskapi

Naskapi 2015

Nasquapee. *See* Naskapi

Nass River, Canada 1890

Natchez 399, 429, 683, 709

Natick 1157, 1389, 1409, 1410

National Anthropological Archives *12*

national character 2536

National Geographic Society 2128

National Union Catalog *ix, 18*

nationhood 684, 685

natural history 3582

Naugatuck River Valley, CT 3116

Nauta 2584, 2806

Navaho 481, 2036, 2657-2661, 2663, 2665, 3853, 4046

naval architecture. *See* architecture

Navarro, J. M. 434

Nave Collection. *See* collections

Navigators Islands. *See* Samoa

Nayarit 1870. *See also* Mexico

Neanderthal 428, 1596, 3124, 4329. *See also* fossil man

Nebaj, Guatemala 1307
Nebraska 1115, 4463
negritos. *See* nigritos
negroes 1887
negroids 1720
Neklakapamuk. *See* Shuswap
Nelson, E. W. 4241
Neocene 2706
Neolithic 1597, 3244, 3426, 3664, 3811
nephrite 1246, 1431, 1534, 1535, 2797.
    See also jade, jadeite
Nepos, C. 941
Netela 828
Netherlands 548, 549, 551, 552, 1779,
    3083
Netherlands New Guinea 2516
netsinkers 3462, 3465
neurology 4417
neurosis. *See* psychology
Neutral Indians 1177
Nevada 1652, 2049, 2697, 2986
Nevome. *See* Cora
New Britain 1704
New Brunswick, Canada 1632, 3434
New Caledonia 1707
New Century Club 662, 760
New England 297, 880, 1941, 1944, 1945,
    3212, 3397, 4380, 4465, 4466
New France 1913, 2385, 2602, 3510. *See
    also* Canada
New Granada 33, 66, 3086, 3518, 3372,
    4252
New Guinea. *See* Papua New Guinea
New Hebrides 2022
New Holland, Australia 2523
New Ireland 1715
New Jersey 1312, 3046, 3454, 3640, 3910
New London, CT 458
New Mexico 304, 577, 578, 830, 1130,
    1215, 1318, 1421, 1656, 2043, 2725,
    2811, 2870, 3930, 3950, 3987, 4087,
    4464, 4467
New Netherlands 1273
New South Wales, Australia 2009
New Spain 91, 1017, 1382, 1993, 3216,
    3482, 3580, 3658-3660, 4093. *See also*
    Mexico
New Vizcaya 4087
New York 348, 971, 1079, 1273, 2792,
    3161, 3227, 3371, 3929, 3936, 4159,
    4166

New York Academy of Archaeology 4190
New York Academy of Sciences 532
New York Colored Orphan Asylum 2125
New York Historical Society 3649
New York Juvenile Asylum 2125
New York Liberal Club 1241
New Zealand 1186
Newark, DE 3655
Newark, OH 89, 2597, 3890
Newbold Collection. *See* collections
Newfoundland, Canada 947, 3434
Nez Perce 104, 1418, 2916, 2937, 3922
Niagara Falls. *See* Niagara River
Niagara River 1731, 1732, 3159
Nicaragua 167, 226, 388, 389, 397, 405,
    413, 605, 696, 703, 752, 756, 1308, 1413,
    1631, 2437, 2438, 3073, 3193-3195,
    3197, 3199, 3215, 3220, 3723, 3894,
    3951-3953, 3973, 4386. *See also* Central
    America
Nichols, F.S. 3754
Nicobar Islands 1717, 1719, 3726, 4329
Nicosia, Cyprus 1263
Nicosiana. *See* Nicosia
Niede-Lausitz. *See* Lusatia
nigritos 330, 1728, 2799
nihilism 2938
Nineteenth Century Club 633
Nipissing 1204, 2651, 3490
Nippur Arch 3238
Nippur, Iraq 3118, 3236, 3238
Noaname. *See* Chocó
Noluche. *See* Araucanians
Nootka Sound, Canada 2201
Nootka 2012
Norambègue 355
Nordiska Museet, Stockholm. *See* museums
Normans. *See* Norsemen
Norsemen 129, 166, 357, 1832,
    2099-2104, 3856, 3971, 4437
Norteño 3303, 3306. *See also* Northern
    Guaymí, Terraba
North America 232, 233, 420, 1734, 3002,
    3750, 4045, 4350, 4410; Northeast
    4180; Northwest Coast 465, 482, 499,
    502, 507, 794, 1300, 1336, 2262, 2275,
    2281, 2771, 3765, 3788, 3874, 3875
North Carolina 38, 307, 1317, 3383, 4117
North Dakota 2447, 2464, 4155, 4372
North Simcoe, Canada 2137
Northwest Coast. *See* North America

Northwestern Archaeological Survey. *See* expeditions

Norumbega, ME 2100-2102, 2104

notched bones 3992

Nova Scotia, Canada 3264, 3432, 3434

Ntlakapmah. *See* Thompson

Ntlakyapamuk. *See* Thompson

Nuestra Señora de Belem, Guatemala 2469

Nuestra Señora de Izamal. *See* Izamal

Nuestra Señora de los Dolores, Guatemala 2856

Nueva Andalucia, Venezuela 933

Nueva Barcelona, Venezuela 933

Nueva Espana. *See* New Spain

Nueva Galicia 4087

Nueva Granada, Colombia 33, 66, 3518, 3977, 4252

Nuevo Reino de León, Mexico 843

Nuix, J. 3087

numerals 391, 716, 1109, 3169, 3181, 3431, 4200, 4390. *See also* mathematics

Numismatic and Antiquarian Society of Philadelphia 2217

numismatics 2414

Nuñez Cabeza de Vaca, A. 3089

O'Meara, Dr. 1087

Oaxaca 298, 421, 454, 887, 888, 1678, 2067, 2434-2436, 2613, 4324. *See also* Mexico

Oberbayern, Germany 3038

obsidian 1722, 2697. *See also* lithics

Oceania 316, 323, 551, 1532, 2012, 2523, 3742, 4349

oceanography 2704

Ocharte, M. 3429

Ocharte, P. 3429

Ochogauia, Miguel de 904

Ocklawaha River, FL 4108

Ocosocantla, Mexico 1304, 3676, 3678

Office of Explorations and Surveys. *See* expeditions

Office of Indian Affairs 4243, 4244

Ogalala Sioux. *See* Oglala

Oglala 1540, 1546. *See also* Dakota

Ohio Centennial. *See* expositions

Ohio River Valley 1909, 2552, 2855

Ohio Valley and Central States Exposition. *See* expositions

Ohio 89, 152, 153, 230, 231, 708, 1065, 1566, 1593, 1595, 2078, 2442, 2552,

2597, 2852, 2853, 2886, 2925, 3202, 3390, 3402, 3486, 3655, 3846, 3889, 3890, 4124, 4128, 4363, 4387, 4388, 4391, 4392, 4481, 4482, 4484, 4496

Ojibwa. *See* Chippewa

Ojibway. *See* Chippewa

Okanagan 924

Okkak 1759

Old Settlers. *See* Cherokee

Oliver Cromwell (ship) 458

Oliver, A. W. 1666

Ollanta 2594, 2595, 2807, 2823, 3072, 3103, 3104

Ollendorf system 836, 1169

Olmec 398, 4268

Olmedo y Torre, A. de 4277

Olmos, Andres de 3287

Oluta 410

Omaha 1347, 1348, 1349, 1542, 1545, 1547, 1938

Omitlán, Mexico 3070

Omori 2896, 2898

Oneida 1242, 1320. *See also* Iroquois

Oneota 3757

Onondaga 167, 1320, 1849, 3157, 3841, 4493, 4498, 4497. *See also* Iroquois

Ontario Archaeological Museum. *See* museums

Ontario, Canada 592, 1187, 2478

Opata 304, 831, 2937

Opatoro, Honduras 3945. *See also* Lenca

Ophelia 2392

Oraibi 1515. *See also* Hopi

oral history 4373. *See also* folklore

Orange Bay 2150

orangutan 1268

Ore, G. de 2311

Oregon Territory. *See* Oregon

Oregon 479, 1171, 1344, 1607, 1670, 1671, 1674, 2757, 3168, 4094, 4242

Orejónes 1642

Oriental Club of Philadelphia 751, 3118

oriental studies 57-59, 2377

Orinoco River 172, 904, 933, 1440, 1441, 1809, 2401, 2581, 2806, 2973, 3574

Orizaba, Mexico 1775

Orosí Indians 4103

Orozco y Berra, M. 398

Ortega, E. M. 3378

orthography 68, 3050, 3266, 4293

Osage 1341, 1351, 4332

Osborn, G. 2216
Osborne, OH 4388
osteology 2057, 2605, 4400. *See also* skeletal remains
Otchipwe. *See* Chippewa
Oto 2790
Otoe. *See* Oto
Oto-Manguean. *See* Chiapanec, Chinantec, Chorotega, Mangue, Matlatzinga, Mazatec, Mixtec, Otomí, Zapotec
Otomí 391, 399, 813, 1021, 2491, 2937, 3034, 3043, 3049–3050, 3219, 3428, 4492
otter traps 2963
Ouayana 1162
Ounga Island 3298
Our Forest Children 3134
Oviedo y Valdés, Gonzalo F. de 391, 397
Owen, Richard 3847
Oyampí 1162
Oyana. *See* Ouayana

Pablos, J. 3429
Pacaos. *See* Pakawa
Paccay, J.S. 1302
Pachitea River, Peru 1610
Pacific Ocean 3408
Pacóas 1642
Pacuaches. *See* Pakawa
Padilla, I. de 1315
Padilla, J. M. 3894
Páez 911
Pahlavi-Gathas 256
Pah-Ute. *See* Paiute
Paine, N. 101
Painted Mesa, NV 1673
Paiute 2044
Pajalate 1642. *See also* Texas
Pajalates. *See* Pajalate
Pak kop piu 1200
Pakawa 1642. *See also* Texas
Palacios, E. 3894
Palaeolithic 341, 344, 452, 668, 1942, 1946, 2709, 2774, 2838, 2915
Palatinate, Germany 3039
Palcazu River, Peru 1610
Palenque Indians 3632
Palenque, Mexico 10, 271, 397, 613, 1037, 997, 999, 1569, 1573, 2315, 3466, 3476, 3555, 3556, 4261, 4262
paleography 3600, 4139

Paleo-Indian 3839
Paleolithic 3575, 3663, 3886, 4105, 4106, 4183, 4217, 4433, 4438, 4449, 4452, 4474
paleontology 513, 976, 1225, 1674, 2694, 2781
paleopathology 2777. *See also* physical anthropology, skeletal remains
Paleozoic 1861
Palestine 4283
Palín, Guatemala 388, 409
Palmer, Mr. 2121
Pamaque 1642. *See also* Texas
Pamir region, Southwest Asia 2376
Pampa 278, 1472, 3537. *See also* Araucanians, Puelche
Pampopas. *See* Pamposas
Pamposas 1642. *See also* Texas
Pamunkey. *See* Powhatan
Panama 387, 1608, 2791, 3133, 3215, 3218, 3294, 3295, 3300, 3307, 3308, 3768, 4500. *See also* Central America
Pano 2296
Panuco River, Mexico 3084
Papantla, Mexico 1316
paper 4267
Papiamento 1665
Papua New Guinea 330, 546, 549, 552, 625, 1333, 1703, 1706, 1711, 1716, 1954, 2073, 2519, 4327, 4354
Papua. *See* Papua New Guinea
papyrus 2958
Paques Island. *See* Easter Island
Pará 837, 2806
Paraguay 518, 519, 1301, 1395, 2331, 2372, 2964, 3517, 4084
Paranapanema River, Brazil 1792
Paredes, I. de 876, 4185
Paris Exposition of 1889. *See* expositions
Parkman, F. 2101
Parrastah 3074
Parthenon 2494
Pasilingua 4019–4021
Passamaquoddy 79, 1501, 2383, 3376, 3377
Patagonia 407, 431, 580, 1472, 1932, 2505, 2603, 2863, 2976, 3179, 4063
Patawomeke 4165
Path of Virtue. *See* Dhammapada
pathology 195
patolli. *See* games and gaming
Patten, Dr. 4369

Patzcuaro, Mexico 2413
Pausanes 1642. *See also* Texas
Pawnee 1375, 1938, 2900
Paya. *See* Pech
Peabody Museum of American Archaeo-
logy and Ethnology. *See* museums
pearls 1229
Peary, R. E. 1140
Pech 2746
Pech, N. 757
Pecos River, NM 247
Pehuenche. *See* Araucanians
Pela kesagunoodumum kawa 3431
Pelasgi 3814
Pelleschi, G. 291, 2331
Pembrokeshire, Wales 2357
Peñafiel, A. 309, 1076, 3546, 3988
Pennsylvania 732, 1836, 1953, 2258, 2759,
2775, 2778, 3845, 3910, 4486
Pennsylvania Germans 2046, 2047, 2780,
2786, 4000
Pennsylvania Library Club 3869
Penobscot 2383
Penonomeño 3306
Penutian. *See* Klamath, Modoc, Nez Perce,
Tsimshian, Walla Walla, Yakima
Pepper-Heart Expedition. *See* expeditions
Pequod. *See* Pequot
Pequot 170, 171, 1259. *See also* Algonkin
Peralta, M. A. 3078
Pérez, J. P., 391, 394, 1045, 1046, 1285,
1286, 1323
Pérez, J. 3894
Pergamon, Greece 2002
Pergamos. *See* Pergamon
Perigueux, France 1470
Perryman, T. 4375
Persian 264
Peru 196, 202, 308, 364, 407, 449, 691,
785, 787, 886, 917, 992, 1012, 1055,
1145, 1324-1326, 1330, 1332, 1335,
1394, 1565, 1723, 1761, 1762, 1788,
1898, 2030, 2075, 2170, 2202, 2524,
2541, 2580, 2594, 2807, 2817, 2961,
3123, 3089, 3153, 3427, 3429, 3507,
3573, 3661, 3759, 3772, 3932, 3935,
3959, 3963, 3964, 3972, 3975, 4067,
4206, 4280, 4415, 4498
Petén, Guatemala 390, 391, 866, 867,
1466. *See also* Guatemala
Petich's Old Mexican Collection 1465

Petit, N. M. 1877
petroglyphs 397, 603, 702, 708, 1436,
1496, 1673, 1923, 2358, 2443, 2444,
2453, 2460, 2812, 2903, 3018, 3264,
3291, 3300, 3301, 3343, 4085, 4155. *See
also* pictographs
phallicism 133, 809
Pheidas 2494
Philadelphia Conference of Baptist
Ministers 457
Philadelphia, PA *14,* 2440, 3262, 3580
Philip II 4093
Philippines 270, 456, 1186, 2187, 2363,
2799, 3163, 4313
Phillips, H. 773-775, 2021
Phillips, W. 4145
philology *1,* 1673, 1689, 1854, 1939,
1950, 2353, 2655. *See also* linguistics
philosophy 155, 1211, 1241, 3356, 3359,
3361, 3498, 4036, 4369, 4371
Phoenicians 1092, 1901, 2191
phonetics. *See* phonology
phonology 1843, 2587, 3760. *See also* linguistics
physical anthropology 167, 488, 489, 497,
501, 1068, 1216, 1388, 1563, 2611,
3272, 3417, 3567, 3813, 3818, 3825,
3851, 3747, 3748, 4133-4135,
4177-4179, 4309, 4314-4329, 4400,
4436. *See also* anatomy, anthropometry,
cephalic index, dentition, dermatology,
forensic anthropology, fossil man, paleopathology, physiology, skeletal
remains, trephination
physiology 1067, 1134, 1908, 2591, 2592,
2776. *See also* physical anthropology
Piapoco 1184
Piazzese 1263
Pickering, J. 3441
pictographs 167, 2045, 2565. *See also* petroglyphs
Picunche. *See* Araucanians
Pilcomayo River, Argentina 4141
Pilgrim's Progress 186
Pilling, J. C. 1389, 3355
Pilloy, M. 3275
Pima 1803, 3871, 4242
Pina y Cuevas, M. 3378
Pinart, A. L. *5,* 1992, 2483
Pine Grove shellheap, MA 3396
Pinedo Collection. *See* collections

Pinzon, J. 398
Pío Pérez, J. *See* Pérez, J.P.
Pipe Dance 1547
pipes 285, 1714, 3020, 3385, 3386
Pipil 388
Pirinda 1021
Piritú 3632
Pithecanthropus erectus 1365, 2590, 2606, 2608. *See also* fossil man
Pittsburgh, PA 1224
Pizarro, F. 2720
plaster casts 1123
Platzmann, J. 2833, 4259
playing cards 3513. *See also* games and gaming
Pleiaden 141
Pleistocene 2697, 2706
Pliocene 1276
Pocomchí. *See* Pokomchí
poetry 639, 726, 760, 798, 1082, 1168, 1681, 3495
Point Barrow, Alaska 2968
Pointe-a-Pirte, Guadeloupe 2634. *See also* Guadeloupe
Pokom. *See* Pokomchí, Pokomam
Pokomam 788, 4052, 4258. *See also* Maya
Pokomchí 62–65, 388, 399, 409, 1110, 1287, 1305, 2470, 4052, 4302. *See also* Maya
Polakowsky, H. 4104
polar exploration. *See* European exploration and Arctic
Polari, G. 167
political anthropology 252, 576, 2352, 3362, 3054, 3973, 4029, 4384, 4399
polyandry 2599, 3240. *See also* marriage
Polynesia 625, 2010, 4349, 4354
polysynthesis 2005
Pomeroon River, British Guiana 3416
Ponca 1347, 4145
Ponce, J. 2835
Pontiac's War 1615
Pontimelo 3621
Poor Sarah 3432
Poou, F. 1080
Pope Leo XIII 900
Pope, G. U. 2599
Popocatepetl (volcano), Mexico 3140
Popol Vub 397, 612, 4491
Popoluca 398, 410, 840, 3073

population. *See* demography
Pororoca 604
Port Clarence, AK 485
Port Kennedy, PA 2759, 2778
Porter, W. T. 473
Porto Rico. *See* Puerto Rico
Portsmouth, OH 1978
Portugal 901
Portuguese 1478
Porzia 2392
Posen province, Poland 4317
Potomac River 1593, 2074, 2632, 2717
pottery 6, 237, 286, 348, 1181, 1224, 1264, 1291–1294, 1455, 1570, 1675, 1882, 2066, 2070, 2695, 2783, 2894, 3003, 3080, 3099, 3184, 3463, 3697, 3770, 3779, 3783, 3803, 4004. *See also* effigy pottery, figurines, shoe vessels
Powell, J. E. 4398
Powhatan 3340
Pownal, T. 1909
Prähistorishe Blätter 3366
Prato, Stanislas 874
prehistory. *See* archaeology
Prescott, AZ 1808
primates 1366–1369, 4196
Priment, Germany 4328
Prince Edward Island, Nova Scotia 3432, 3434
Prince of Wales Archipelago, Alaska 2566
printing. *See* publishing
Prinzapolka River, Nicaragua 3197
privateers 458
Progreso, Mexico 466, 1309
projectile points 2803, 3045. *See also* bow and arrow, lithics
protohistory 3426
Prussia 1278
psychology 330, 331, 415, 929–932, 1590, 1780, 2352, 2360, 2735, 3138, 3615, 3776, 3820, 3824, 3994, 4036, 4055, 4370, 4499; emotions 3815
publishing 1910, 1912, 2714
Pucara 2345
Puebla, Mexico 3344
Pueblo Indians 286, 1318, 2034, 2035, 3794
Puelche 278
Puelchean. *See* Pampa, Puelche
Pueltse. *See* Puelche
Puerta, J. de 1308

Puerto Rico 2635
Pukina. *See* Puquina
pulmonary consumption 2678
Punctun. *See* Putún
Punic Wars 194
Puquina 691, 2311
Puri. *See* Coroado
Purús River 1399, 1406
Putún 391. *See also* Maya, Nahuatl
Puydt, L. de 387
pygmies 1856, 2266, 3059. *See also*
    dwarfs
Pyrennes 1858
Pythagoreans 4390

Qabbalah. *See* Berbers
quarries 1943, 2065, 2120, 2728, 2767,
    2788
quartz 2459
Quaternary 2902, 3426
Quechua 44, 125, 407, 623, 909, 913, 914,
    1325, 1472, 1480, 1746, 1747, 2594,
    2807, 2823, 3072, 3103, 3104, 3112,
    3683, 4415
Queen Charlotte Island, British Columbia
    2051, 2547, 2566
Queensland, Australia 3622
Queipo de Llano, F. de B. 2202
Querandí 3135, 3136
Querétaro, Mexico 1642. *See also* Mexico
Quetare 658
Quetzalcoatl 993
Quiché 44, 72, 157, 180, 289, 388, 398, 608,
    612, 682, 842, 984, 1020, 1026, 1560,
    2423, 3111, 3345, 3382, 3681, 4152–4154,
    4186, 4491, 4497. *See also* Maya
Quimbaya, Colombia 3518, 3790
Quintana, A. de 1111
Quipú 4225
Quiriguá, Guatemala 397, 2796, 3720, 4042
Quiripí 3268
Quiroga y Lossada, Diego de 1311
Quito, Peru, 4304
quivers 2627. *See also* bow and arrow

Rabinal Achi 608, 3382
Rabinal, Guatemala 608, 610, 3111
race 207, 223, 477, 715, 730, 1069, 1563,
    1844, 1885, 1886, 1903, 2609, 3107,
    3488, 3565, 3702, 3818, 4172, 4381
Rada, J. de D. de la 1974

Radloff, L. 3722
Rafinesque, C. S. 754, 4358
Ragazzi 1725, 2590
railroads 4242
Raleigh, W. 1144, 4426
Ramírez de Fuenleal, S. 2021, 4093
Ramírez de Utrilla, A. 157
Ramírez, J. F. 121, 1371, 3378
Rammannirari 2199
Ramona Mission, CA 3430
Ramos, D. de 3173
Ranke, J. 1976
Ranqueles. *See* Araucanians
Rapa Nui. *See* Easter Island
Raramurí. *See* Tarahumara
Ratzel, R. 1976
Ray Collection. *See* collections
Raynal, Mr. 3087
Rayon, J. S. 1611
Real, A. C 7
Real Biblioteca. *See* libraries
Rechahecrian Indians 4167
Reclus, E. 4230
recreation 796
Red Cliff Reservation, WI 4341
Red Cloud Indian Agency, WY 4236
Red Jacket 1117
Red River, LA 2585
Red River, MN 2456,
Red Rock, AZ 1508
Reeve, W. D. 543, 544
regeneration 1235
Regil y Paon, P. de 1323, 3223
Rehoboth, DE 2217
Reid, H., 2048
reindeer 2185
Reiss, W. 4227
Rejon, A. G. 1310
Relación de Tecuanapan 398
Relaciones geográficos 2817
religion 290, 313, 399, 456, 457, 470, 569,
    635, 731, 763, 777, 864, 1202, 1473,
    1539, 1556, 1599, 2086, 2195, 2230,
    2235, 2282, 2323, 2337, 2347, 2376,
    2550, 2661, 2665, 2666, 2938, 2944,
    3154, 3169, 3176, 3204, 3296, 3341,
    3511, 3552, 3598, 3712, 3793, 3877,
    3990, 4092, 4146, 4198, 4343, 4414;
    religious conversion 3632. *See also* ani-
    mism, deities, idols and idolatry,
    Nagualism, soul, totemism, witchcraft

religious orders, Augustinians 1315;
Dominicans 174, 1110, 1287, 1477,
1625, 2434-2436, 2616, 4324; Francis-
cans 157, 215, 267, 350, 372, 398, 841,
921, 1111, 1147, 1285, 2827, 3482, 3632,
3646, 3656, 3669, 3670, 3866, 4288;
Jesuits 224, 875, 876, 920, 1315, 2432,
2580, 2602, 2964, 2973, 3216, 3429,
3510, 3546, 3647, 3649, 4078, 4084;
Mercedarians 1283, 3533. See also
Jesuit relations, missionaries
Remagen 74, 3270
Remon, A. 1283
Renan, E. 1205
Rennes, France 3667, 4451
Repertorio Salvadoreño 3515
reptiles 3865, 4242
Restivo, P. 3635, 3636
Revista de Mérida 3523
Revue Americaine 3525, 3526
*Revue Mensuelle de l'Ecole d'Anthropolo-
gie de Paris* 3527
Rhode Island Historical Society 3534,
4158
Rhode Island 2812, 3170, 4158
Ribero, D. 1889
Ricardo, A. 3429
Rico Frontaura, P. 3650
Rig Veda 3118
Riggs, A. L. 4429, 4430
Riggs, M. A. C. 3543
Rijks Ethnographischen Museum. See
museums
Rink, H. 2062, 2967
Río Apuré, Venezuela 904
Río de Janeiro, Brazil 2806
Río Grande do Sul, Brazil 1987
Río Grande, TX 573, 575, 1372, 4242,
4467
Rio Grande, Costa Rica 3316
Rio Lempa, El Salvador 3938
Río Meta, Colombia 2806, 2865, 3574
Río Napo, Ecuador 1313
Río Negro 2976. See also Guaynia River
Riou, P. I. 2584
Ripalda, G. de 3647
ritual. See ceremonies
Roatan, Honduras. See Bay Islands
Robelo, C. A. 3861
Robertson, A. E. W. 4375
Robertson, Mr. 3087

Robertson, W. S. 2501
Rocha, D. J. E. de la 71
rock shelter 1836
Rockford tablet 2842
Rocky Mountains 1251, 1536, 1607, 3168
Rodríguez de Castro, J. 434
Rodríguez de la Gala, L. 2479
Rodríguez, J. M. 4325
Romance languages 1414. See also
French, Italian, Spanish
Romania 1297, 3610
Romano, D. 3546
Romans 1772, 4333
Rome 513, 522, 2341
Romero, J. G. 3894
Ronneburg, Germany 3856
roofing tiles 2894
Roraima Expedition. See expeditions
Rosa, A. de la 3988
Rosamond (ship) 978
Rosny, L. L. O. de 1073
Ross County, OH 1595
Rosse, I. C. 4241
Roth, H. L. 1186
Roth, S. 1932
Roucouyenne 1184
Roxas, F. de 1311
Royal Library of Berlin. See libraries
Royal Society of Canada 1254
Royal Society of London 3627
Rua, G. 3367
Ruíz Blanco, M. 3324
Ruíz, J. 193
Runa Simi. See Quechua
Rupert's Land, Canada 817, 2138-2148,
2248, 2646
Ruschenberger, W. S. W. 3076
Russia 293, 2865, 3568, 3569, 3724, 3808,
4254
Russian America. See Alaska
Russian 2169
Ruz, J. 1555, 1591, 2349, 2427, 3559-3561

Sabanero 384, 387, 1600, 3303
Sabin, J. 3937
Sacatepequez, Guatemala 1819
Sacluc. See San Lucas Saclac de El Chol
Sacluk. See San Lucas Saclac de El Chol
sacrifice 1783, 1850
Saginaw Valley, Michigan 3876, 3880
Sagoyewatha 1117

Sahagún, B. de 1004, 3779
Sahaptin. *See* Nez Perce
Saint Acheul, France 2770
Saint Augustine, FL 3837
Saint Johns River, FL 85, 2184, 4488
Saint Joseph-Kankakee portage, IN 228
Saint Laurent le Minier, France 3271
Saint Lawrence River 1209, 1360, 2487, 2548
Saint Louis, MO 473, 926, 3884
Saint Mary's Parish, LA 1669
Saint Paul's Mission, British Columbia 1750
Saint Regis. *See* Mohawk
Saint Vincent 702, 797. *See also* Caribbean
saints; Santa Ana 3829; San Andres 3829; San Bartolome 3829; San Julian 3829; Santa Maria Magdalena 3829; San Nicolas 3829; Santo Tomas 3829
Sakalin Island 4182
Salinan Indians 3866
Salisbury, England 4044
Salish 492, 924, 925, 1337, 2012, 2044, 2055, 2937, 3283
Salishan. *See* Bella Coola, Clallam, Kalispel, Lillooet, Lummi, Ntlakyapamuk, Okanagan, Salish, Shuswap, Snohomish, Squamish, Twana
Salmeron, M. 3533
Salpetriere Cave, France 75, 3271
Salt Springs, IL 3803
Salvador. *See* El Salvador
Sambo. *See* Miskito
Samoa 316, 2518, 4102
Samoids 3913
San Agustín Acasaguastlán, Guatemala 3033
San Bartolomé de Los Llanos, Guatemala 3678
San Blas. *See* Cuna
San Blas, Panama 384, 387, 388
San Cristóbal Acasaguastlán, Guatemala 3033
San Cristobal Cahcoh, Guatemala 1287
San Diego, CA 1421, 4467
San Dionisio de la Mar, Mexico 1613
San Francisco Panajachel, Guatemala 158
San Isidro, Spain 341, 344
San Jorge, Uruguay 1054
San José de la Paz, Bolivia 3681
San Joseph, M. de 1311

San Juan Bautista de Xuquila, Mexico 1111, 3419
San Juan Bautista, Mexico 411
San Juan Chamelco, Guatemala 193
San Juan de Dios hospital, Yucatan 1309
San Juan River, Nicaragua 3577
San Juan, Nicaragua 3966
San Lucas Saclac de el Chol *10, 11,* 390, 2856
San Luis, Argentina 4061
San Martin Tilcaxete, Mexico 3497
San Matheo, F. de 1311
San Miguel Ecatepec, Mexico 454
San Miguel Milpas Duenas, Guatemala 3041
San Pedro de Yolos, Mexico 298
San Pedro do Río Grande, Brazil 1153
Sánchez de Aguilar, P. 398
Sánchez Solis, F. 121
Sánchez, J. M. 1304
sand painting 2657, 4046
Sanders, J. 2087, 2138
Sandusky County, OH 231
Sanfratellano, Italy 1263
Santa Bárbara Indians. *See* Chumash
Santa Bárbara, CA 1653
Santa Catalina Ixtahuacán, Guatemala 2223, 3719
Santa Catarina, Nicaragua 2485
Santa Cruz Island, Ecuador 2022
Santa Cruz Pachacuti Yamqui, J. de 2202
Santa Fe, NM 577, 1421, 4467
Santa Inés monastery, Mexico 4078
Santa Isabel Tola, Mexico 3210
Santa Lucia Cotzumalhuapa, Guatemala 1822
Santa Maria de Belem do Para, Brazil 2584
Santa Maria de Jesus Pache, Guatemala 1819
Santa Maria Tactic, Guatemala 65
Santa María, Guatemala 388
Santa Rosa de Lima. *See* Lima
Santander, Colombia 3218
Santee 1411, 1544, 2017, 3540. *See also* Sioux
Santiago de Cuba 3918
Santiago de Guatemala 4093
Santiago Tlatelolco, Mexico 1882
Santillan, F. de 2202
Santo Domingo Cobán. *See* Cobán
Santo Domingo Pueblo 577

Santo Domingo. *See* Dominican Republic
Santo Tomas Loviguisca, Mexico 3074
São Paulo, Brazil 1792
Sarayacu 2584
Sardinia 397, 3059, 3109, 3110, 3812
Sarg Collection. *See* collections
Saulteux. *See* Chippewa
Saussure, H. de 1071
Saut de Ste. Marie, Michigan 4076
Sauteaux. *See* Chippewa
Savannah River 2208
Savedra, D. J. C. 4097
Savoy River, France 2906
Sawkin, J. G. 2675
Sayce, A. H. 1856
Sayenqueragtha 1116. *See also* Seneca
Sayil, Yucatan 3085
scalp-lock 1545
Scandinavia 129, 357, 4214
scarlet fever 208. *See also* disease
scatalogical ritual 574
Scherzer, K. 388, 409, 4491
Schiefner, A. 3423
Schingú River. *See* Xingú River
Schnectady, NY 3161
Schwatka, F. 167
Schweinitz, E. de 3500
Scioto River Valley, OH 2855
Scotland 128, 442–447, 1778, 2385
sculpture 327, 342, 444, 1295, 1408, 1430,
    1533, 1869, 1890, 1901, 1989, 2098,
    2732, 2796, 2903, 3472, 4001, 4120,
    4122, 4363, 4387, 4500. *See also* stone
    yokes
Scythians 1866
seals 2191
Sechel. *See* Sheshel
Sechuana. *See* Sotho
Seeman, B. 387
Seine River, France 3244, 3664
Seine-et-Marne, France 2913
Seler, E. 1215
Selocae 2756
Seminole 3804
Semites 19, 306, 751, 772
Sendschiri 2517
Seneca County, OH 231
Seneca Indians 104, 1116, 1117, 1320,
    2792, 3672, 3673, 3909, 4479, 4480. *See
    also* Iroquois
Senegal 1070

Sequoyah 1588
sermonary 62, 63, 64, 90, 169, 267, 1641,
    2470, 2841, 3648, 3827, 3828, 3829,
    3831, 4091, 4295. *See also* Christian
    doctrine
serpent worship. *See* ceremonies
Serra, A. 4097
Sevilla, Spain 1118
sex 1122, 1129, 1132, 1133, 2236; sexual
    characteristics 1417; sexual hypo-
    chrondriasis 3614
Seybold, C. F. 3635, 3636
Shahaptian. *See* Walla Walla
Shakespeare, W. 2397, 2398
shamanism 2665, 2886, 3877. *See also*
    ceremonies
Shastan. *See* Klamath
Shawanee. *See* Shawnee
Shawnee 2487, 4123
Shea, J. G. 3155
Sheffield School 1738
shell heaps. *See* shell middens
shell middens 167, 1232, 1363, 2777,
    2896, 2898, 2926, 3531, 3454, 4379,
    4487, 4488. *See also* shell
shell 1506, 2069, 3396, 3985, 3986. *See
    also* shell middens
Sheshel 924, 925
Shetimasha 1669
shields 3095
Shimshian. *See* Tsimshian
Shinto 2024
Shoa 1722
shoe vessels 397. *See also* pottery
Shofar 60
Shoshonean. *See* Paiute, Shoshoni, Ute
Shoshoni 2044
shrines 2326, 2329
Shufeldt, R. W. 4240
Shuswap 478, 924, 925, 1249, 3100, 4085.
    See also Salish
Shuswapntlakyapamuk. *See* Shuswap
Sia 1494, 4047
Siah Posh 1701
Siam. *See* Thailand
Siberia 1228, 1726, 2969, 4038, 4385
Sicily 556, 2920, 3809, 3810
Siemiradzki, J. von 748
Sierra, J. 1309, 2479
Sierra Madre 2512
sign language 167, 1060, 2563, 2564,

2569. *See also* linguistics
Sigüenza y Gongora, C. 2418
Siksika 1846, 2348, 4148, 4150, 4151
Sikyachi 1508. *See also* Hopi
Sikyatki. *See* Sikyachi
Siletz Reservation, OR 1344
silver 442, 2283, 2467, 2660
Simeon, R. 3105, 3106, 3658
Similaton, Honduras 3945. *See also* Lenca
Simpson, J. H. 4467
Sinkeuel 1644
Siouan 1345, 1350, 1352, 1356, 1357,
    1539, 2722, 2851. *See also* Biloxi,
    Catawba, Cegiha, Dakota, Gros Ventre,
    Hidatsa, Iowa, Kansas, Omaha, Osage,
    Oto, Ponca, Santee, Tutelo, Winnebago
Sioux Expedition. *See* expeditions
Sioux. *See* Dakota
Siret, L. 3864
sisal 1309
Siva worship 1061
Skalzi. *See* Kutenai
skeletal remains 74, 75, 83, 85, 86, 131,
    167, 187, 417, 421, 466, 766, 784,
    822-826, 879-881, 1012, 1086, 1092,
    1096, 1234, 1328-1330, 1332-1334,
    1337-1340, 1367, 1385, 1386, 1393,
    1433, 1439, 1553, 1608, 1704, 1705,
    1723, 1735, 1736, 1775, 1776, 1931,
    1988, 2053, 2057, 2073, 2126, 2267,
    2369, 2373, 2514, 2516, 2517,
    2524-2527, 2531, 2532, 2603, 2654,
    2664, 2741, 2771, 2777, 2778, 2805,
    2917-2921, 3152, 3258, 3270, 3271,
    3294, 3336, 3426, 3535, 3536, 3575,
    3621, 3665, 3749, 3808-3812, 3822,
    3856, 4068, 4170-4173, 4176, 4182,
    4311, 4312, 4319-4329, 4435. *See also*
    paleopathology, physical anthropology
Skittagetan. *See* Haida
Skokomish. *See* Twana
Skrälings 361. *See also* Eskimo
Skugog Island, Canada 958, 961
skulls. *See* skeletal remains
Skwamish. *See* Squamish
Slafter, E. F. 2101
Slave Indians. *See* Ettchaottine
slavery 1865, 1978, 2430
Slavonia 2272
Slavs 1289, 3065, 3066
Slayamen 924

Smith, B. 3089, 3692, 4294
Smithsonian Institution 7, 8, 11, 12, 58,
    59, 407, 915, 928, 1554, 1156,
    1751-1753, 2233, 2477, 2635, 2636,
    2642, 2966, 3386, 3453, 3455, 3457,
    3466, 3476, 3475, 4443; members
    3887; publications 3888
Snanaimuq. *See* Nanaimo
Snohomish 567. *See also* Salish
snuffing tubes 4226. *See also* hallucino-
    gens
Snyder, Monroe B. 774, 775
soapstone 1943, 2728, 3397
social organization 252, 572, 573, 1203,
    1230, 1356, 1357, 2034, 2663, 2868,
    2871, 2994, 2995. *See also* courtship,
    inheritance, marriage
social philosophy. *See* philosophy
social sciences 4364
Sociedad Científica Argentina 1114
Sociedad Económica de Amigos de Guate-
    mala 2751, 3147, 3496, 3894, 3919
Sociedad Geografica de Lima 527
Sociedad Mexicana de Geografía y
    Estadística 3895, 4299
Società Geográfica di Río de Janeiro 1795
Società Geografica Italiana 522, 525
Società Romana di Antropologia 3896
Société Americaine de France 3196, 3605,
    3897, 3898
Société Archeologique, Moscow 3899
Société d'Anthropologie de Paris 784,
    3900, 3901-3906
Société de l'Histoire de France 2985
Société Historique et Anthropologie de la
    Charente 4106
Société Normande d'Études Préhistoriques
    4107
Société Philologique de Paris 3907-3908
Society for Scientific Research 1185
Society of Friends 3909-3910
sociology 1266, 1676-1678, 1900, 3358,
    3412, 3815, 4365, 4366, 4368
Soconusco, Mexico 1029, 3311
solar worship. *See* ceremonies
Solis Rosales, D. J. V. 3078
Sololá, Guatemala 610, 2748-2750
Solorsano, M. L. 910
Solutré, France 2911
Somme Gravels, France 2788
songs 463

Sonora Expedition. *See* expeditions
Sonora Indians. *See* Opata
Sonora, Mexico 3629, 3871. *See also*
　Mexico
Sonsonate, El Salvador 3894
Sotho 905
Soto, Hernando de 1645, 2209
Sotutá, Yucatan 391, 3829
Soucheux. *See* Tukudh
soul 500. *See also* religion
Souletine 1019
South Africa 303, 850
South America 364, 407, 513, 739, 1734,
　1790, 1821, 1822, 1999, 2128, 2584, 2806,
　2817, 2819, 2859, 2973, 3102, 3114–3216,
　3230, 3268, 3392, 3424, 3479, 3766, 3855,
　3970, 4045, 4062, 4141, 4192, 4196, 4211,
　4227, 4304, 4319; Northwest, 4396
South Carolina 38, 307, 458, 3383
South Dakota 2463, 2464, 4155, 4372
South Kensington Museum. *See* museums
Spain 576, 901, 1611, 1856, 2124, 3215
Spanish conquest 398, 609, 749, 939,
　1055, 1148, 1149, 1281–1284, 1466,
　1483, 1643, 1977, 2490, 2071, 3121,
　3137, 3344, 3521, 3625, 3658–3660,
　3911, 4279, 4498
Spanish. *See also* Romance languages
Spanish 1742, 2587, 3265
spear thrower 3098
Spear, J. C. 1614
speech 2558
Spelin 334, 335
spelling reform 738. *See also* orthography
Spencer, H. *2*
Spina, A. 3894
Spy Cave, France 2984
Squamish 924, 925. *See also* Salish
Squier, E. G. 157, 388, 3937, 4294
squirrel 944
Stalo 924, 925
standards 3097
Standing Bear 4145
Stanton, E. M. 1536
Starr, F. 167, 1856
statistics 173, 1445, 1462, 2612,
　2793–2795, 2816, 2931. *See also* vital
　statistics
stature. *See* physiology
steel 2768
Stentor Coerulens 4471

Stephen, A. M. 1527, 1528
Stephens, J. L. 2857
Stevenson, S. Y. 3118
stirpiculture 2693
Stlatliemoch. *See* Lillooet
Stockholm, Sweden 3081
stone. *See* lithics
stone hammer 2733
stone yokes 1434. *See also* sculpture
stove plates 2779, 2780
Strait of Fuca, WA 4072
Stroudsburg, PA 2775
Stuart's Lake, Canada 2878
Stübel, A. 4227
Suárez y Navarro, Juan 1309
Subtiaba 389
Suchiapa, Mexico 2468, 3174
Suchitán, Mexico 1614
Sucre, Argentina 4141
Sudan 1070, 4346
Suffolk, England 1814
Sumene, Germany 3271
Sumo 2746
Sumu. *See* Sumo
Sun Dance. *See* ceremonies
sun worship. *See* ceremonies
superstition. *See* religion
surgery 2370
Surinam 3304, 3407
surnames 403
Susquehanna River 1815, 3343
Swan, James G. 2566
swastika 741, 4450, 4506
Sweden 2838, 3081, 3724, 4181
Swedish 2534
Switzerland 1956–1966, 2267, 2609
swords 2535. *See also* warfare
Sydney, Australia 2009
syllabary 377, 2187; Berber 634, 3118;
　Cherokee 2734, 2846, 2879; Chippewa
　4073; Na-Dene 2880, 2882; Nahuatl
　3572; Philippines 3163; Tarascan
　2417; Tukudh 2689; Winnebago 1543;
　Yucatec 399, 746, 3645. *See also* lin-
　guistics
symbolism 758, 987, 988, 994, 998, 2745,
　3169, 3406. *See also* iconography
syphilis 196, 198, 200, 204, 205, 209, 800,
　801. *See also* disease
Syria 1948
Széchenyi, B. 4182

Tabasco, Mexico 397, 410, 1082, 1457, 3495, 3516, 3625, 3626. *See also* Mexico
Tabatinga, Brazil 2584
Tablet Dance. *See* dance
Tacamé 1642
Tacaná 921
Tactic, Guatemala 62, 1110, 1305
Taensa 47, 48, 742, 764, 765, 1927, 1985, 4308
Tahiti 2022
Tahkaht 2256
Taino 4274
Takana. *See* Tacana
Takudh 2683-2691
Takulli 2874, 2875, 2877, 2878. *See also* Athapascan
Talamanca 388, 412, 4103. *See also* Boruca, Bribri, Cabécar
Talbot, Mr. 1177
Tamahú, Guatemala 62
Tamaulipas, Mexico 2510, 3084. *See also* Mexico
Tampamolón, Mexico 4078
Tampico, Mexico 4078
Tanis 2958
Taos, NM 2811
Tapachulane. *See* Huastec
Tapajoz 1160
Tapia Zenteno, C. de 385
Tapia, D. de 3324
Tapijulapa, Mexico 411
Taquinvitz, Mexico 1820
Tarahumara 831, 4087
Tarapaca 3257
Tarascan 309, 350, 922, 1031, 1733, 2286, 2336, 2409, 2410, 2417, 2514, 2937, 3035, 4001, 4097
Tarawa 1104
Tarija, Bolivia 1147, 4075
Tasmania 1023, 1186, 3617, 4217, 4349
tattoos 2518, 2566
Tauste, F. de 3324
Tavolini, F. 2332
Tecoh, Yucatan 391
Tecpán Atitlán. *See* Sololá
Tecpatlán, Mexico 191
Tecumseh 1062
teeth. *See* dentition
Tehuantepec, Mexico 398, 399, 407, 616, 1614, 4240, 4421. *See also* Mexico

Tehueiches. *See* Tehuelche
Tehuelche 1472
Teit, James 478
Tekakwitha, Catherine 1052, 1053
Tekinica 1472
Temia 1094
Temistitán. *See* Temixtitán
Temixtitán, Guatemala 1148, 1152, 4093
temperance 3501
Temple Hill, Iraq 3236
ten Kate, H. F. C. 1497
Tenampua, Honduras 3965
Tenerife, Canary Islands 2527
Teni. *See* Athapascan
Tennessee 881, 1377, 2213, 2214, 2222, 2781, 3387, 4117, 4142-4144, 4475
Tenni. *See* Athapascan
Tenochtitlán 2406, 3057. *See also* Mexico City
Teocalli 1801
Teotihuacán, Mexico 1879, 2011, 3099
Tepechpan 2578, 2579
Tepehua 831
Tepoztlán, Mexico 3700
Térraba 3313, 3316, 4103, 4104
Teton 1353. *See also* Dakota
Texas 304, 554, 1666, 2510, 3429, 4463
Texcoco, Mexico 565, 1163, 2020
textiles 918, 2072, 2075
Thailand 3607
Thebes, Egypt 1559, 2951
theology 3511
Thompson River Indians. *See* Shuswap
Thornbury, PA 3
thought-connectives. *See* psychology
Thring, E. 2391
throwing sticks 2641, 2642, 2970
Thule Indians 3768. *See also* Eskimo
Tiahuanaco, Bolivia 364, 2819, 4226
Tibet 1473
Ticul, Mexico 1285, 1286
Tierra Austral del EsPiritú Santo. *See* New Hebrides
Tierra del Fuego, Argentina 93, 431, 580, 666, 2150, 2504, 2505, 2582, 2611, 3121, 3137, 3179, 3326
Tihosuco, Mexico 391
Tilijayas 1642
Timucua 789, 1311, 1671, 1672, 2300, 2314, 2979, 3167
Timucuan. *See* Timucua

Timuqua. *See* Timucua
Tinne. *See* Athapascan
Tirol, Austria 1955
Tisingal, Costa Rica 1604
Titicaca basin, Bolivia 1120
Título Acanceh 391
Título Ixcuin-Nijaib 4154
Título Totonicapán 4152, 4153
Tixcacalcupul, Mexico 2827
Tizimín, Mexico 391
Tlalpilli 332. *See also* calendrics
Tlaxcala, Mexico 845, 902, 3344, 3546
Tlingit 167, 510, 1327, 2275, 2937, 2933,
    3248, 3250, 3296, 3302
Toba 52, 291, 2331, 2335
tobacco 282, 1435, 3020
Tocantins River, Brazil 1160
Toda. *See* Tuda
Tojolabal 378, 707, 952, 983, 3678
Tolima 3218
Tollan. *See* Tula
Toltec 398, 609, 770, 938, 1296, 1465,
    1771, 3986, 4268
Toluca, Mexico 3363
Tomebamba, Peru 242
Tomo-chi-chi 2210
Tonalamatl 1571. *See also* calendrics
Tonapa 2323
Toner Medal 2238
Tonkawa 1673
Tonkawan. *See* Pajalat, Tonkawa
Tonocoté 2543
Tonto 1673
Topinard, Mr. 1137
toponyms 167, 391, 403, 584, 814, 832,
    1632, 3170, 3190, 3211, 3626, 3988,
    4199, 4205, 4209. *See also* etymology,
    linguistics
torches 2768
Török 3749
Torres Straits, Australia 3480
Torres, M. 4185
Torrey, J. 1607, 3865
torture 4384
totem poles 4218
totemism 1526, 1542, 3379, 4212, 4218,
    4353. *See also* religion
Totonac 398, 1316, 1775, 1776, 2937
Totonacan. *See* Tepehua, Totonac
toys 2887
Tozzer, A. M. *13*

Trans-Caucasus. *See* Caucasus
transportation 2629
trees 137, 1541
Trempeleau 2458, 2460
Trenton Gravels, NJ 2, 3, 6–10, 710, 2068,
    2758, 2772, 2788, 3640
trephination 787, 1553, 2515, 2527, 2961.
    See also physical anthropology
Treviño, F. 4287
Triana, A. de 2856
Triana, J. 3196
Trinidad Bay 2484
Tripoli, Libya 557, 3332
Trobriand Islands 1827
troglodytes 1881
Tropelius, J. 3083
Trübner, N. 2511
Trujillo, Peru 886
Trumbull, J. H. 3268, 4489
Truxillo, Honduras 388
Tsattine 164, 1647–1649, 2250. *See also*
    Athapascan
Tschangtscha Hutuktu 3154
Tschudi, J. J. von 3103, 3573
Tsets'aut 508
Tsimshian 471, 509, 510, 1336, 3539,
    3765, 4504
Tsitsumovi 1673
Tsoneca. *See* Tzoneca
tuberculosis 210
Tucson, AZ 4467
Tucurrike 4103
Tucurrique. *See* Tucurrike
Tuda 2599
Tukkuthkutchin 2684, 2689
Tukudh. *See* Tukkuthkutchin
Tula, Mexico 1007, 3986, 4263
Tulan. *See* Tula
Tule 384, 387, 812. *See also* San Blas
Tullahasse Manual Labor Boarding School,
    OK 3613
Tulteca. *See* Toltec
Tunisia 194, 422–428, 1092, 1709, 1718,
    1901, 2471
Tunkiní 2584
Tupa Reservation 2638
Tupí 53, 73, 88, 1169, 1272, 1280, 1624,
    1925, 3633–3638, 1925, 3858, 3859,
    4270, 4275
Tupí-Guaraní. *See* Auca, Chiriguano,
    Guaraní, Tupí

Turner, W. W. 2511, 2585, 4395
Tusayan. *See* Hopi
Tuscarora 1816, 1320, 2203
Tutelo 1853
Tuxpán, Mexico 1462
Tuxtla Gutíerrez, Mexico 1303, 3173, 4325
Twahka 388
Twaka. *See* Twahka
Twana 1397
Two Sand Mounds, FL 4108
Tylor, E. B. *2*, 3445, 4432
Tyrol. *See* Tirol
Tyskiewicz Collection. *See* collections
Tzeltal 174, 175, 1650, 1820, 2826, 3312. *See also* Maya
Tzoneca 278, 2976
Tzotzil 397, 910, 952, 1033, 3628, 3678. *See also* Maya
Tzutuhil 399, 608, 1560, 4186, 4296. *See also* Maya

Uarauno. *See* Warrau
Uarow. *See* Warrau
Ucayalí River, Peru 1610, 2806, 3661
Ufford, W. Q. von 3083
Uhde Collection. *See* collections
Ulba. *See* Ulva
Ulipe. *See* Atacama
Ulster County, NY 167
Ultima Esperanza, Chile 1932
Ulu 2640
Ulúa River, Honduras 1756, 3690
Ulva 388, 413, 2438, 3074
Uncpapa Sioux. *See* Hunkpapa
United Church of England and Ireland 2646
United Kingdom 779, 780, 1919. *See also* England, Scotland, Wales
United States 3724, 3750, 3934, 4174; East, 2777; North 4113; Northeast 2760, 2761; South 3342, 3775; Southwest 248, 249, 2433, 4089; West 3342
United States and Mexican Boundary Commission 304, 1422
United States Army Medical Museum. *See* museums
United States Board on Geographical Names 4232
United States Department of the Interior, Indian Affairs Commission. *See* Indian Affairs Commission
United States Exploring Expedition. *See* expeditions
United States Geological Survey 2700
United States National Museum. *See* Smithsonian Institution
United States Revenue Cutter Service 4241
United States War Department Geographical and Geological Survey of the Rocky Mountain Region. *See* expeditions
United States War Department Geographical Survey West of the 100th Meridian. *See* expeditions
United States War Department Office of Indian Affairs. *See* Office of Indian Affairs 4243, 4244
Universal Exposition of Paris. *See* expositions
Universidad de Chile 2400
Université de Brussels, Institut Géographie 4245
University College, London 1558, 1559
University of Chicago 4006
University of Michigan 3882
University of Pennsylvania *2, 3-4, 5, 14, 16,* 632, 711, 932, 1193, 1194, 1201, 2764, 3236-3238; Department of Archaeology and Paleontology *16,* 2782, 4189, 4246-4249
Upper Guinea, Africa 2531
Ural-Altaic 257, 258, 262, 4453, 4458
urbanism 3011
Uricoechea, E. 935
urine 569, 578
Uru. *See* Puquina
Urubamba River, Peru 1610
Uruguay 407, 1054, 3624
Uspantec 4052
Usumacinta River 300, 397
Utah 281, 1102, 1673, 3151
Ute 284
Utica, Tunisia 194
Uto-Aztecan. *See* Alaguilac, Cahuilla, Comache, Cora, Eudeve, Hopi, Huichol, Mayo, Nahuatl, Opata, Pima, Pipil, Shoshoni, Tarahumara, Tepehuan, Ute, Yaqui
Uvpune 736
Uxmal, Mexico 1037, 2479, 3085

Valdes, J. P. 1627

Váldez, S. 4328
Valdivia, Chile 4193
Valdivia, L. de 2821
Valente, C. 1272
Valentini, P. 388
Valiente. *See* Bribri, Guaymí, Northern
Valladolid, Mexico 391
Valley of Mexico 2067
Vancouver Island, Canada 480, 1247, 2229, 2256
Vandervelde, E. 1266
Varela y Ulloa, P. 3087
Vasantasena 537
Vásquez de Coronado, J. 1308
Vatican 1213
Vaz, C. 3482
Vedas 537
Vejos 2331. *See also* Mataco
Vela, J. C. 892, 1807
Velasco, L. de 4093
Venados 1642
Venezuela 172, 1139, 1430, 1431, 1432, 1433, 1436, 1437, 1679, 2581, 3137, 3591, 4285
Veracruz, Mexico 2616, 4093
Veraguas, Panama 1600, 3303, 3295
Verapaz, Guatemala 397, 866, 1080, 1290-1294, 2470, 2616, 3674, 4294
Verde Valley, AZ 2813
Verein für Erdkunde in Dresden 3766
Vergara y Vergara, J. M. 66
Vermont 3228, 3229
Verrazzano, G. da 2972
Vespucci, Amerigo 1567
vestigial structures 3623
Vetromile, E. 4489
Viceita 92, 384, 412, 4103, 4269. *See also* Bribrí
Vico, D. de 3316
Viegl, F. X. 2973
Vienne River, France 1088
Vilches, J. 2434
Vilela. *See* Chulupí
Villa, A. F. 3035
Ville Lorillard. *See* Yaxchilán
Vindonissa 1930
Vinland 2099, 4437
Vinson, E. H. J. 1900, 3167
Virchow, R. 310, 1856
Virginia 38, 883, 1592, 3340, 4164, 4167
vital statistics 3566. *See also* demography, statistics

Vizeita. *See* Viceita
vocabulary 2500, 3329, 3364, 3866, 4156; Abipón 2331, 3441; Achagua 3616; Aleut 2169; Algonkin 1207, 1952; Allemtíak 4260; Arawak 1184; Arorai 1104; Aymara 430, 4415;Bayano 384, 387; Blackfoot 2348, 4150;Boruca 384, 388, 412; Caché 388, 412; Caduveo 525; Cágaba 936; Cakchiquel 1820, 4301, 4490; Campas 2362, 4415; Carib 388, 619, 621; Chiapanec 46; Chibcha 387, 1768, 4251; Chilidugi 1471; Chippewa 272, 273, 978, 4376; Chiquita 39; Chiriqui 387; Chocó 384, 387, 769; Choltí 2857; Chontal 413, 3073; Chorotega 399; Chortí 2746; Comanche 2585; Cora 3122; Crichaná 3587; Cueva 384, 387; Cumana 3324; Cuna 384, 387, 388; Dakota 3541, 3543, 3544; Darien 387; Delaware 771, 1452; Dorasque 3303, 3309; Eskimo 1427, 3248, 4374, 4385; French 1167; Garifuna 413, 1982; Goajira 935; Guaná 526; Guaraní 3634-3638; Guatuso 408, 412; Guaycururú 525; Guaymi 412, 3303, 3306; Haida 510; Hidatsa 2655, 2656; Huastec 70, 385, 4078; Huave 1613; Huron 3656; Illinois 3842; Ipuriná 3339; Ipurucotó 3587; Ixil 1307; Jicaque 388, 413, 2746; Kalispel 1741; Kekchí 1306, 4337; Kinai 3423; Kwakiutl 511; Lenca 413, 2746; Lule 2543; Macuchy 3587; Malagasy 4351; Mam 1119, 3532, 3533; Mangue 399, 3581; Maribia 399; Mataco 3205, 3512; Mbayá 525; Miami 3842; Micmac 297, 3433, 3434; Miskito 49, 388, 413, 767, 1442; Mixe 1111; Moreno 2746; Moxa 2580; Muisca 387; Mutsum 1189, 1190; Nahuatl 182, 183, 226, 439, 440, 639, 735, 1049, 1050, 2831, 2833, 2834, 3576, 3860, 4185; Nanticoke 768; Natick 1157; Nipissing 3490; Norteño 3303; Onondaga 3841; Otomí 2491, 3050; Páez 911; Passamaquoddy 297; Piapoco 1184; Pokomam 409, 788; Popoluca 410, 840, 3073; Puelche 278; Quechua 909, 4415; Roucouyenne

1184; Sabanero 384, 387, 3303; Salish 2055; Spanish 1742, 3265; Suere 388; Sumo 2746; Taensa 47, 48, 742, 764, 765, 1927; Talamanca 412; Tarascan 2336; Timucua 1672; Tlingit 510; Toba 291, 2335; Tojolabal 378; Torres Straits 3480; Tsimshian 510; Tule 384, 387; Tupí 1280; Twaha 388; Tzeltal 174, 175, 3312; Tzoneca 278; Tzotzil 1033; Ulva 388, 413, 2438; Viceita 384, 388, 412; Walla Walla 1288; Wichita 2585; Xinca 4338; Yucatec 389, 391, 398, 607, 614, 615, 903, 2342, 2615, 2674, 3186, 3221, 3222, 3224; Yuracare 1191; Zälohpäap 3504; Zambo 2746; Zapotec 2617, 3497, 4334, 4336; Zoque 411, 4335. *See also* linguistics
Volapük 774, 2499, 3727
volcanos 3685, 3983
Volney, Comte de 1379
Voss, A. 310
Votan 1007, 1010
Voto. *See* Talamanca
voyageurs 228, 1187
Vreemde 4024

Wabanaki. *See* Abenaki
Wabash River, IL 3391
Wabi 407
Wafer, L. 387, 3522
Wagner, W. 1225
Waicurian. *See* Cora
Waicuru. *See* Guaicurú
Waithman, W. S. 699
Wakashan 3285. *See also* Kwakiutl, Nootka, Wakashan
Wake, C.S. 1061
Walam Olum 754, 3941, 4358
Waldeck, F. 391, 613
Walker, J. B. 3617
Walker, W. 1087, 1115, 4386
Walla Walla 1288
Walpi 1521, 1522. *See also* Hopi
Wampanoag 2812
wampum 1891, 2168, 3377, 4380
Wapanica, S. 141
Waraw. *See* Warrau
Waraweti. *See* Warrau
warfare 250, 1341, 1346, 2627, 3780, 4395. *See also* fortifications, swords

Warrau 3407, 3413
Warrauan. *See* Warrau
Warren County, OH 2852
Washington 479, 1397, 1674, 4072
Washington, DC 1298, 2238, 3380, 4452
Washington, G. 2977
Washington Territory. *See* Washington
Watertown Historical Society, MA 2104
Watungasta, Argentina 2346
Wawan 1547
weaponry. *See* warfare
Webster, J. D. 4467
Weis, N. von 3442
Welch, H. 231
Welsh 1258
Wesleyan Methodist Missionary Society 2216
West Chester, PA *3*
West Chester State Normal School, PA 3259
West Indies. *See* Caribbean
Whipple, A. W. 4467
White, Andrew 2619
White Buffalo Festival. *See* ceremonies
Whitesides County, IL 2056
Whitewater River 3418
Whittlesey, C. 3486
Wichita 2585
Wilken, G.A. 4027
Wilkes, C. 1853
Wilkes, J.A. 2008
Williams, R. 1419, 4162
Willoughby, C. C. 3406
Wind River 3128
Winema 2739
Winnebago 1341, 1543, 1938, 2679
Winslett, D. 2503
Winslow, AZ 1509
Winsor, J. 2101
winter solstice 1522, 1523
Wisconsin 919, 1242, 1675, 2350, 2351, 2458, 2460, 2466, 4049
witchcraft 574, 4465. *See also* religion
Witotoan. *See* Orejon
Wollin Island, Germany 4310
Wollstein 4328
Wolpai. *See* Wolpi
Wolpi 3849
women 882, 970, 1417, 2677, 3727, 4074
Women's Anthropological Society of Washington 3117, 4470

woodcarving 1827
Woodhouse, S. W. 3865
Woolwa. *See* Ulva
Worcester, MA 4389
World Columbian Exposition of 1893. *See* expositions
world language 2497, 2498, 2500
World's Fair Congress of Anthropology. *See* expositions
Worms, R. 4367
Wortman, J. L. 2654
Wright, G. F. 232, 1066
writing systems 1, 89, 399, 1236, 1277, 2193, 2792, 2959, 2935, 2941, 2950, 2952-2954, 3334, 3602, 3603, 3715, 3717, 4111. *See also* epigraphy, inscriptions
Wyandott. *See* Huron
Wyandotte Cave, IN 2120, 2767
Wyman, J. 3141

Xalisco. *See* Jalisco
Xalpán 1316
Xibalba 1034
Xicalango, Mexico 397, 398
Ximénez, F. 608, 1993
Xinca 714, 4328
Xingu River, Brazil 1162, 4013, 4012, 4014
Xkickmook, Mexico 4137
Xochicalco, Mexico 3791
Xtepén, Mexico 391

Yagan. *See* Yahgan
Yahgan 45, 626, 666, 806, 807, 1757, 2611, 3192, 3326
Yahganan. *See* Yahgan
Yakima 3155
Yale University 3, 1738, 4493
Yamacraws 2210
Yamana. *See* Yahgan
Yangues, M. de 3324
Yaqui 3061
Yarmouth 3264
Yaxchilán, Mexico 1038, 2668
Yezo 2026, 2027
Ymos-yima 1035
York River, ME 2777
Youd, T. 4284
Young, T. 388
Yucatan 173, 217, 299, 397, 398, 403, 466, 609, 645, 654, 664, 746, 889-898, 912, 1082, 1040, 1308, 1309, 1310, 1322, 1323, 1445, 1466, 1285, 1286, 1315, 1862, 2067, 2342, 2422, 2479, 2482, 2489, 2559, 2560, 2762, 2782, 2783, 2830, 2858, 3085, 3495, 3496, 3523, 3571, 3917, 3979, 4040, 4041, 4136-4138, 4195. *See also* Mexico
Yucatec 34, 44, 104, 126, 150, 219, 372, 373, 374, 382, 390, 391, 399, 403, 404, 407, 607, 611, 614, 615, 645, 653, 757, 897, 903, 1045-1047, 1056, 1081, 1081, 1550-1552, 1555, 1591, 1627, 1644, 1650, 1807, 1979, 1984, 1997, 2243, 2342, 2349, 2386, 2422, 2423, 2427, 2428, 2479, 2479, 2615, 2827, 2830, 3078, 3186, 3221-3225, 3538, 3559, 3560, 3643-3653, 3669, 3670, 3829, 4109. *See also* Maya
Yucca augustifolia 2802
Yud-hey 2198
Yukon Territory 1248, 1940
Yule. *See* Tule
Yuma 1141, 4394
Yunca. *See* Yunga
Yunga 886
Yupiltepeque, Guatemala 4328
Yuracare 1191
Yuracarean. *See* Yuracare
Yurujure. *See* Yuracare
Yurukare. *See* Yurucare
Yuruyure. *See* Yurucare

Zabalburn, F. de 1611
Zaborowo, Poland 4317, 4328
Zacapa, Guatemala 2857, 4043
Zaccicoxol. *See* dance dramas
Zachila, Mexico 2614
Zambo 2746
Zapotec 370, 379, 407, 1143, 1476, 1614, 1767, 2434-2436, 2616, 2675, 2937, 3497, 3530, 3675, 3698, 3779, 3802, 4324, 4326
Zapotecan. *See* Zapotec
Zaragoza, J. 2022
Zarate, J. de 4093
Zemes 1505. *See also* sculpture
Zeno 362, 1796
Zent River, Costa Rica 388
Zestermann, C. C. A. 3960
Zigeuner 4344
Zimbabwe 303, 3007

Zinacantán, Mexico 3628
Zohar 2978
zoology 451, 1922, 2620
Zoque 191, 379, 381, 398, 407, 411, 1304,
    1614, 2312, 2820, 3172, 3173, 3175,
    3562, 3676-3678, 3678, 4325

Zuni 578, 1215, 1217, 1221, 1497, 1499,
    4047, 4048, 4197
Zuni River, NM 3865
Zunian. *See* Zuni
Zuñiga, D. de 1287
Zurich, Switzerland 1956